A Documentary History

of

UNITARIAN UNIVERSALISM

FROM THE BEGINNING TO 1899

Edited by Dan McKanan

EDITORIAL COMMITTEE
Mark W. Harris
Peter Hughes
Nicole C. Kirk
Emily Mace
Natalie Malter
Mark D. Morrison-Reed
Susan Ritchie

Skinner House Books
BOSTON

Copyright © 2017 by the Unitarian Universalist Association. All rights reserved. Published by Skinner House Books, an imprint of the Unitarian Universalist Association, a liberal religious organization with more than 1,000 congregations in the U.S. and Canada, 24 Farnsworth St., Boston, MA 02210–1409.

www.skinnerhouse.org

Printed in the United States

Cover design by Suzanne Morgan
Text design by Jeff Miller

print ISBN: 978-1-55896-789-2
eBook ISBN: 978-1-55896-790-8

6 5 4 3 2 1
19 18 17

Library of Congress Cataloging-in-Publication Data is available

We gratefully acknowledge permission to reprint the following:

Francis David, "The Edict of Torda" in John Erdö, *Transylvanian Unitarian Church* (Chico, CA: Center for Free Religion, 1990). Translated from Hungarian by Dr. Judit Gellérd. Used with permission of Judit Gellérd.
THE COLLECTED WORKS OF RALPH WALDO EMERSON, VOLUME I: NATURE, ADDRESSES AND LECTURES, Introduction and Notes by Robert E. Spiller, text established by Alfred R. Ferguson, Albert R. Ferguson, General Editor, Cambridge, Mass.: The Belknap Press of Harvard University Press, Copyright © 1971 by the President and Fellows of Harvard College.
THE COLLECTED WORKS OF RALPH WALDO EMERSON, VOLUME II: ESSAYS—FIRST SERIES, Introduction and Notes by Joseph Slater, text established by Alfred R. Ferguson and Jean Ferguson Carr, Albert R. Ferguson, General Editor, Cambridge, Mass.: The Belknap Press of Harvard University Press, Copyright © 1979 by the President and Fellows of Harvard College.
All sermon material by Ralph Waldo Emerson copyright © 1992 by Ralph Waldo Emerson Memorial Asociation. Introduction and all scholarly apparatus copyright © 1992 by the Curators of the University of Missouri. University of Missouri Press, Columbia, Missouri 65201.
Creeds and Platforms of Congregationalism by Walker, Williston. Reproduced with permission of Pilgrim Press in the format Republish in a book via Copyright Clearance Center.
Reform papers by *Thoreau, Henry David*. Reproduced with permission of *Princeton University Press* in the format Book via Copyright Clearance Center.
Drude Krog Janson, *A Saloonkeeper's Daughter*, trans. Gerald Thorson, edited, with an introduction by Orm Øverland (Baltimore: Johns Hopkins, 2002). Used with permission of Longfellow Institute.
Constitution and By-Laws of the First Icelandic Unitarian Church of Winnipeg and sermon delivered at Gimli by Magnús Skaptason, in V. Emil Gudmundson, *The Icelandic Unitarian Connection: Beginnings of Icelandic Unitarianism in North America, 1885–1900* (Winnipeg, Manitoba: Wheatfield Press, 1984). Permission granted by Marti Gudmondson.
"Obedience to the Heavenly Vision" by Mary A. Safford, Iowa Unitarian Association Collection, State Historical Society of Iowa, Iowa City, Iowa.

Contents

Introduction to the Collection

Primary sources are the building blocks of history. By reading sermons, letters, journal entries, meeting minutes, hymns, and other written sources from the past—as well as by examining buildings, paintings, and other physical objects—we get a glimpse of how historical events appeared to the people who created and experienced them. Sermons preached in rural Iowa in 1900 or in Harlem in 1925, for example, illumine the diverse ways in which ordinary people were introduced to liberal faith in those contexts, just as the founding documents of the Universalist Convention (1790), the American Unitarian Association (1825), and the Unitarian Universalist Association (1961) represent three different visions of how people of liberal faith should sustain their shared work. The selections included in this volume represent only a tiny slice of the sources available for the study of Unitarian Universalist history, but it is—to the best of our ability—a representative slice. Within this volume, you can explore Unitarian Universalist theology, polity, worship, religious education, missionary outreach, and social witness from multiple generations. You can also hear the voices of leaders and followers, institution builders and rebels, scholars and activists.

We have chosen to arrange the sources in strictly chronological order, rather than organizing them by theme or genre. Our hope is that this will help readers understand the context for each selection and that the juxtaposition of Unitarian and Universalist texts, or of hymns and theological treatises, will spark new insights about how different traditions and genres may have influenced one another, or failed to do so. Early nineteenth-century Unitarians and Universalists could work just steps from one another without ever becoming acquainted, as was the case for William Ellery Channing and Hosea Ballou. Readers should not feel obliged to read the selections in the order we have presented them; for those who prefer a more thematic ordering, we have included an index of sources by genre and topic.

Relatively few of the sources included in this collection appear in their entirety. We have excerpted sources in order to present a variety of voices within two volumes and to highlight the ideas and phrases that have exerted the most historical influence. Readers should not assume that the beginning and end of the texts presented here correspond to the beginning and end of the original sources; in many cases, the selection we offer has been taken from the middle. Within each selection, we have used ellipses to indicate deletions of a paragraph or less, and three asterisks to mark longer deletions. Many of the sources—though not all—are publicly available in their entirety through online resources, and readers who become interested in a specific text should use these resources to read it in its entirety.

We anticipate that most readers will use this volume alongside a narrative history of Unitarian Universalism. Several of these are listed in the bibliography, along with several of the primary source collections that preceded this one. Readers who are just discovering Unitarian Universalist history should be aware that there is no consensus about how to tell the story. Some scholars stress the ancient roots of "unitarian" and "universalist" ideas, claiming such early Christians as Arius and Origen as part of our common heritage; others accent the distinctively American character of the denominations founded in the United States in the decades just after the Revolution. Likewise, some place primary emphasis on the ideas and leaders that were dominant in each historical epoch, while others prefer to stress the visionaries who may have been neglected in their own time but cherished by subsequent generations. This volume is doubtless shaped by the biases of its editors, but our conscious intent has been to avoid taking sides in such historiographical debates and to provide readers with the resources needed to begin reaching their own conclusions.

History changes with each generation. This collection differs from its predecessors not only by including sources from the years 1960 to 2015, and not only because it includes Unitarian and Universalist sources alongside one another, but also because it reflects the commitments and curiosities of Unitarian Universalists, and of historians, over the past two generations. Recognizing that Unitarian Universalism has always been shaped by both lay and ordained persons of diverse ethnicities and genders, we have sought a balanced mix of voices throughout the collection, even as we recognize that ordained white men have held a preponderance of institutional power until recently. In this collection, we feature exemplars and "saints" who form part of our living heritage, but we have also included many voices that Unitarian Universalists have forgotten, or have tried to forget. In addition, we offer a sampling of documents from Unitarian, Universalist, and related traditions outside the United States, while keeping a primary focus on the Unitarian Universalist Association and its predecessors.

The majority of individuals appearing in this volume were members of Unitarian, Universalist, or Unitarian Universalist congregations, but some were not. Our tradition has always cherished rebellious responses to inherited institutions. As a result, the living heritage of Unitarian Universalism includes such figures as Margaret Fuller and Abner Kneeland, both of whom repudiated Unitarian or Universalist churches on the basis of values that would be embraced by those same churches generations later. It also includes such precursors as Michael Servetus and George de Benneville, both of whom articulated liberal religious beliefs long before the creation of liberal denominations. Nevertheless, ideas and values rarely survive without institutional support, so we have been careful to balance individual voices with documents that reflect the policies and practices of institutions.

Each selection contains a brief scholarly introduction, and most include recommendations for further reading. Some of the authors featured here are the subjects of book-length biographies, and most also appear in the online *Dictionary of Unitarian & Universalist Biography*, which is an indispensable resource for historians of Unitarian Universalism. Several of the volumes listed in the bibliography also provide biographical information on the persons featured in this collection.

Introduction to Volume One

This volume covers Unitarian and Universalist history from its beginnings to the year 1899. The turn of the twentieth century has no unique significance for the history of Unitarianism and Universalism, but it does represent an approximate chronological midpoint of the two traditions' organizational history in the United States. Institutional Universalism is typically dated to the 1779 establishment of an independent congregation in Gloucester, Massachusetts, or to the first national Convention of Universalists in 1790, while official Unitarianism is linked to King's Chapel's adoption of a new prayer book in 1785 and to the establishment of the American Unitarian Association in 1825. Prior to the twentieth century, clear majorities of both Unitarians and Universalists understood themselves as Protestant Christians, while during the twentieth century the numbers of post-Christians and non-Christians in both traditions swelled dramatically. Theological disagreements threatened the unity of both denominations in the nineteenth century, but by the turn of the century they were so deeply committed to noncreedalism that even the rise of religious humanism did not lead to significant schism. But these changes involved gradual evolution rather than abrupt turns that can be linked to a single date. Thus we encourage readers to treat the two volumes as a single collection, divided more for convenience than to make a historical point.

This volume tells a story that begins long before 1779. The first two selections, in fact, come from the early centuries of Christian history. Origen and Arius are often remembered as the theological progenitors of universalism—the belief that all human beings will be saved by the Christian God—and unitarianism—the claim that the Christian God is a unity rather than a Trinity, and thus that Jesus Christ was less than fully divine. (A lower case "u" is typically used when these terms designate theological positions, while upper case is reserved for references to organized congregations and denominations.) Not all historians would agree that Origen and Arius belong in a collection like this, since no continuous chain of institutions or even influences binds them to the Unitarians and Universalists of the modern period. On the other hand, many Unitarians and Universalists have claimed them as part of their living heritage. Readers should form their own judgments about the coherence between the ideas expressed in these selections and those found later in the collection. In at least one respect, though, Origen and Arius anticipated later developments: During his own lifetime Origen was universally regarded as an orthodox Christian, while Arius was condemned as a heretic. For the next millennium and a half, likewise, universalist views were often quietly held by Christians who comfortably participated in the mainstream church, while unitarians faced intense opposition and were thus more likely to form rival church bodies.

The Protestant Reformation opened up new space for the creation of rival churches, and the next several selections represent the emergence of a small Unitarian tradition in Europe in the sixteenth and seventeenth centuries. Michael Servetus was executed for his public critique of orthodox Trinitarianism, and his admirers Celio Secondo Curione, Matteo Gribaldi, Sebastian Castellio, Laelius Socinus, Faustus Socinus, and Francis David laid the foundations for anti-Trinitarian movements in Poland and Transylvania. The latter, which survives to this day, was the first to formally claim *Unitarian* as its name.

The Puritanism of seventeenth-century Britain was rooted in a different wing of the Protestant Reformation, the Reformed movement of Ulrich Zwingli and John Calvin. Though this movement was in many ways diametrically opposed to both unitarianism and universalism, nineteenth-century Unitarians and Universalists were more likely to trace their roots to Puritanism than directly to the traditions of Poland and Transylvania. One Puritan idea that remains central to Unitarian Universalism today is that of congregational polity, which regards each local congregation as a church in the fullest sense, bound together by free covenant of its members and not dependent on the external authority of bishops. Congregational polity is represented here by the writings of Robert Browne, the Salem Covenant, and the Cambridge Platform, though it should be noted that in the British Isles some Unitarian congregations emerged from the rival Presbyterian branch of Puritanism. John Biddle's *Twelve Arguments* represents the perspective of one of the few early Puritans who embraced Transylvanian-style unitarianism. The seventeenth century also saw some of the earliest articulations of universalist sentiment in English, here represented by the writings of Gerrard Winstanley and Jane Leade.

The Enlightenment, with its emphasis on reason, tolerance, and critical study of ancient texts, transformed many Puritans (and a few Anglicans) into Unitarians in Great Britain, its American colonies, and the new American nation. The process was gradual. Enlightenment principles led to the espousal of religious tolerance and to a more optimistic view of human nature long before they inspired many people to reject the Trinity. Enlightenment-tinged Puritanism also led educated church leaders to criticize what they regarded as emotional and irrational elements in the religious revivals that swept North America beginning in the 1730s. John Locke, Charles Chauncy, Jonathan Mayhew, and Ebenezer Gay typify the rational Christianity of the eighteenth century. At the same time, a few Enlightenment thinkers (represented here by Ethan Allen and Thomas Jefferson) set themselves in opposition to Christian revelation, preaching instead a deistic religion rooted entirely in reason. Though such views became widespread within Unitarianism and Universalism in the second half of the nineteenth century, the founders of both denominations regarded deism as anathema and presented liberal Christianity as a middle path between deism and orthodoxy.

In part because Enlightenment values became so comfortably ensconced within Puritanism (especially in eastern Massachusetts), Universalists in the United States began organizing themselves into a denomination well before the Unitarians, even though they had few organizational antecedents in Europe. The founding generation of Universalists—represented in this collection by James Relly, George de Benneville, Elhanan Winchester, Judith Sargent Murray, John Murray, Caleb Rich, and Hosea Ballou—were theologically diverse. Some came to believe, after intense visionary experiences, that all humanity would be saved; others were convinced by careful biblical study or the reading of deist authors. Some were Trinitarian and some were unitarian. Some celebrated the traditional Christian sacraments while others rejected all outward ceremonies. Many held fast to the Puritan doctrine of human depravity, regarding salvation as a free gift imposed by a sovereign God on unworthy humans. Unlike the Unitarians, most first-generation Universalists had previously been part of revivalist traditions. They organized congregations in 1779 in Gloucester and in 1781 in Philadelphia, where a national convention took place in 1790. In many ways, the enduring denomination of the nineteenth century evolved from the New England Convention of Universalists, which began gathering in 1793. This was the group that crafted the Winchester Profession of 1803, the unifying statement of Universalist belief throughout the nineteenth century.

The beginnings of organized Unitarianism in Great Britain coincided roughly with that of Universalism in the United States. A former Anglican priest, Theophilus Lindsey, organized the Essex Street Chapel in 1774 as the first avowedly Unitarian congregation in England. It inspired a growing network of congregations throughout Great Britain, most with Puritan rather than Anglican antecedents, and also inspired King's Chapel in Boston to purge Trinitarian references from its liturgy in the wake of the American Revolution. The theological leader of British Unitarianism was Joseph Priestley, who also made his mark in the United States after his immigration to Pennsylvania in 1794.

Though Priestley planted several congregations in Pennsylvania, the numerically dominant faction of American Unitarianism emerged from the "Unitarian controversy" that roiled the churches of Massachusetts after the appointment of Henry Ware as Hollis Professor at Harvard. Because Ware's sentiments were identifiably (if quietly) anti-Trinitarian, this appointment provoked more orthodox Puritans to establish Andover Seminary as a rival school for ministerial preparation. Harvard-affiliated liberals, who held a range of anti-Trinitarian views, responded by gradually accepting the Unitarian label, by organizing Harvard Divinity School as a distinct (and non-sectarian) unit within Harvard, and finally by organizing the American Unitarian Association in 1825.

In this collection, first-generation Universalists and Unitarians are represented by denominational documents; by the sermons and theological writings of major leaders such as Universalist Hosea Ballou and Unitarian William Ellery Channing; by biographical, autobiographical, and fictional texts; and by catechisms and devotional writings, including those by such relatively obscure authors as Universalist Lucy Barns and Unitarian Dorcas Cleveland.

In part because of the justice-seeking commitments of contemporary Unitarian Universalists, we have chosen to give social reform texts considerable space in this anthology. Both revivalist fervor and Enlightenment reason inspired early Universalists and Unitarians to work toward transforming society, and many became leaders in broad-based movements for social reform. The first published exponents of women's rights in English, Judith Sargent Murray and Mary Wollstonecraft, were respectively an American Universalist and a British Unitarian. Unitarian leader William Ellery Channing began preaching against war during the War of 1812, which was widely unpopular in New England. Joseph Tuckerman's ministry-at-large in Boston launched Unitarian concern for urban poverty, while Orestes Brownson espoused a sweeping critique of capitalism. In the 1830s, Unitarian Lydia Maria Child and Universalist Adin Ballou began prodding their respective denominations toward the abolitionist movement, and in the 1840s Adin Ballou and Unitarian George Ripley founded utopian socialist communities. In the wake of the 1848 women's rights convention at Seneca Falls, both denominations ordained female ministers, among them Antoinette Brown (who transferred her fellowship to the Unitarians after being ordained by a freestanding congregation), Olympia Brown, and Phebe Hanaford. Most of these ministers pursued careers as women's rights lecturers as well as congregational pastors, and in this work they were joined by laywomen Lucy Stone, Mary Livermore, and Julia Ward Howe. Yet no social reform cause was uniformly embraced by the denominational power structures. Some of the social reformers featured here were closely aligned with denominational leaders, but others were largely alienated from what they regarded as reactionary ecclesiastical structures.

Both Unitarians and Universalists experienced divisive theological controversies almost as soon as they became established as denominations. The first great struggle among Universalists pitted restorationists, who believed that most human beings would experience a period of purification between death and final salvation, against ultra-universalists, who held that all would go to heaven immediately after death. This debate began in 1817, with Hosea Ballou as the great champion of the ultras and Edward Turner and Adin Ballou as significant leaders of the restorationists. In the 1820s, several prominent Universalist ministers defected to the freethinking movement inspired by Robert Owen and Frances Wright. The denomination held together through the circuit-riding evangelism of men like Nathaniel Stacy and Stephen Smith, as well as the journalistic efforts of Thomas Whittemore. But the most wrenching division came in the 1850s, as huge numbers of Universalists were drawn to the spiritualist movement, which offered not only a practice of communicating with the spirits of the dead but also a fount of revelation independent from Christian scripture.

The defining controversy within Unitarianism is better known, because it gave birth to the most influential philosophical and literary movement of nineteenth-century America. Ralph Waldo Emerson first articulated the complex of ideas known as Transcendentalism in his 1835 book, *Nature,* and the full-blown controversy began with Emerson's 1838 "Divinity School Address," which proposed a religion of intuitive connection to the divine in opposition to "historical Christianity." Emerson's associates Theodore Parker, James Freeman Clarke, Frederic Henry Hedge, and (in England) James Martineau carved out space for Transcendentalism within the Unitarian denomination, while Margaret Fuller, George Ripley, Henry David Thoreau, and Elizabeth Palmer Peabody carried the impulse into utopian socialism, women's rights, civil disobedience, concern for the environment, and child-centered education. Andrews Norton and Henry Ware, Jr., on the other hand, defended their vision of Christian Unitarianism against what they regarded as a dangerous innovation.

Almost from the beginning, some Unitarians and Universalists were interested in building bridges to people of non-Christian faiths, especially those who shared the liberal religious values of freedom, reason, and tolerance. Hannah Adams's *Dictionary* anticipated later contributions to interfaith understanding by Lydia Maria Child, Thomas Wentworth Higginson, and Jenkin Lloyd Jones. Beginning in the 1820s, some Unitarians allied themselves with the Hindu reform movement known as the Brahmo Samaj.

The Civil War was a watershed for both denominations. The end of slavery validated the decades-long efforts of Unitarian and Universalist abolitionists and inspired women's rights advocates to redouble their own. The war also created an arena for organizing at the national level. Unitarian Henry Whitney Bellows and Universalist Mary Livermore were among the most important organizers of the Sanitary Commission, which placed volunteers in medical service to the Union troops. This organizational impulse led both Unitarians and Universalists to create more robust denominational structures in the decade after the war, allowing for more systemic planting of congregations beyond New England. It also exposed the ongoing division between liberal Christians and religious liberals who wished to operate beyond the bounds of normative Christianity. Among the Unitarians, Broad Church leaders such as Frederic Henry Hedge, Thomas Starr King, and above all Henry Whitney Bellows strove to hold the Christians and the Transcendentalists in a single church body. But this wasn't good enough for radicals Francis Ellingwood Abbot and William James Potter, who created a rival Free Religious Association in protest of what they regarded as Unitarian creedalism. The Western Unitarian Conference, which mostly represented Unitarians in what is now the Midwest, was more accepting of post-Christian sentiments than were Unitarian leaders in Boston—provoking conflict between the relatively conservative Jabez Sunderland and the "Unity Men" William Channing Gannett and Jenkin Lloyd Jones. These divisions were echoed in other parts of the European world, with Montreal's John Cordner representing a fairly traditional Christian Unitarianism while the Englishman Francis William Newman explained why he could no longer call himself a Christian. The conflict on the Universalist side was quieter, in part because the denomination had affirmed a strong commitment to the authority of Christian revelation in its response to spiritualism in the 1850s, though Christian spiritualists remained an important part of Universalism well into the twentieth century.

In the final decade of the nineteenth century, both Unitarianism and Universalism affirmed their non-creedal identities more emphatically—the Unitarians at the Saratoga Conference of 1895 and the Universalists in Boston in 1899. At the time, both denominations were still composed predominantly of professed Christians. Congregations were still concentrated in New England and in communities of transplanted New Englanders—though an Icelandic Unitarian movement was emerging in Manitoba, Minnesota, and the Dakotas; a remarkable network of women ministers dominated Iowa Unitarianism; and the Universalist "grasshopper missionary," Quillen Shinn, was planting dozens of congregations in his native South. These pockets of energetic expansion only barely offset numerical decline elsewhere. With members numbering less than a quarter of one percent of the United States population, Unitarians and Universalists still aspired to be the religion of the future, but with little plausibility. Nevertheless, their strong organizational structure and committed non-creedalism positioned them for a coming century of theological transformation and energetic activism for social change.

ORIGEN

On First Principles

ca. 225

Ancient Christian writers and modern historians alike recognize Origen (ca. 185–253) as the most important Christian intellectual and biblical scholar prior to the Council of Nicaea. He produced close to one thousand written works, including letters, homilies, scriptural commentaries, apologetic works, and On First Principles, *one of the earliest Christian systematic theologies. In this work, Origen outlines the teaching of the apostles and then develops what he sees as the implications of this teaching into a coherent theological system. Above all, Origen was concerned with defending the justice of God in the face of apparently undeserved human suffering on earth. Origen's solution entailed the preexistence of all rational souls, all created equally but endowed with free will, the use of which might lead these rational beings gradually to fall away from God even before their incarnation, resulting in a variegation of souls: some angelic, some human—both good and wicked—and some demonic (see first excerpt below). The wicked would be subjected to sufferings after death proportional in duration and intensity to their degree of fallenness; these punishments were not retributive but a way of cleansing the wicked to enable them to return to their stainless original state (see second excerpt). Origen thus acknowledged universal human capacities for good and evil, but denied good and evil innate human natures. The results of his speculations were not uncontroversial even within his lifetime, but they were first attacked as heretical only about a century after his death. The logic of his system demands the subordination of the Son and Holy Spirit to the Father, the reincarnation of souls, a spiritual resurrection body, and the possibility of even the devil's salvation. The third excerpt below describes the final reconciliation of all rational beings in spiritual bodies. Here, when he discusses death, he sometimes means the necrotic processes, while sometimes he is referring to the one that has power over death—namely, the devil. Serious opposition to Origen's works began in the context of the Arian controversy and continued until the mid-sixth century, when he was declared a heretic. His works were destroyed in the Greek East, although a fraction survived in the West in Latin translation, including* On First Principles. *Further Reading: Joseph Wilson Trigg,* Origen: The Bible and Philosophy in the Third-Century Church *(Atlanta: John Knox Press, 1983).*

—David Jorgensen

1

II.9.2

But since these rational beings, which as we said above were made in the beginning, were made when before they did not exist, by this very fact that they did not exist and then began to exist they are of necessity subject to change and alteration. For whatever may have been the goodness that existed in their being, it existed in them not by nature, but as a result of their Creator's beneficence. What they are, therefore, is something neither their own nor eternal, but given by God. For it did not always exist, and everything that is given can also be withdrawn and taken away. But the cause of the withdrawal will lie in this, that the movements of their minds are not rightly and worthily directed. For the Creator granted to the minds created by him the power of free and voluntary movement, in order that the good that was in them might become their own, since it was preserved by their own free will; but sloth and weariness of taking trouble to preserve the good, coupled with disregard and neglect of better things, began the process of withdrawal from the good. . . . And so each mind, neglecting the good either more or less in proportion to its own movements, was drawn to the opposite of good, which undoubtedly is evil. From this source, it appears, the Creator of all things obtained certain seeds and causes of variety and diversity, in order that, according to the diversity of minds, that is, of rational beings (which diversity they must be supposed to have produced from the causes we have stated above) he might create a world that was various and diverse.

II.10.4, 6

If then this is the character of the body which rises from the dead, let us now see what is the meaning of the threatened "eternal fire" (e.g. Mt 25:41). Now we find in the prophet Isaiah that the fire by which each man is punished is described as belonging to himself. For it says, "Walk in the light of your fire and in the flame which you have kindled for yourselves" (Is 50:11). These words seem to indicate that every sinner kindles for himself the flame of his own fire, and is not plunged into a fire which has been previously kindled by someone else or which existed before him. Of this fire the food and material are our sins, which are called by the apostle Paul wood and hay and stubble (1 Cor 3:12–15). And I think that just as in the body an abundance of eatables or food that disagrees with us either by its quality or its quantity gives rise to fevers differing in kind and duration according to the degree in which the combination of noxious elements supplies material and fuel for them—the quality of which material, made up of the diverse noxious elements, being the cause which renders the attack sharper or more protracted—so when the soul has gathered within itself a multitude of evil deeds and an abundance of sins, at the requisite time the whole mass of evil boils up into punishment and is kindled into penalties; at which time also the mind or conscience, bringing to memory through divine power all things the signs and forms of which it had impressed upon itself at the moment of sinning, will see exposed before its eyes a kind of history of its evil deeds, of every foul and disgraceful act and all unholy conduct. Then the conscience is harassed and pricked by its own stings, and becomes an accuser and witness against itself.

This, I think, was what the apostle Paul felt when he said, "Their thoughts one with another accusing or else excusing them, in the day when God shall judge the secrets of men, according to my gospel, by Jesus Christ" (Rom 2:15–16). From which we understand that in the very essence of the soul certain torments are produced from the harmful desires themselves that lead to sin.

*　*　*

There are many other matters, too, which are hidden from us, and are known only to him who is the physician of our souls. For if in regard to bodily health we occasionally find it necessary to take some very unpleasant and bitter medicine as a cure for the ills we have brought on through eating and drinking, and sometimes, if the character of the ill demands it, we need the severe treatment of the knife and a painful operation, yes, and should the disease have extended beyond the reach even of these remedies, in the last resort the ill is burnt out by fire, how much more should we realize that God our physician, in his desire to wash away the ills of our souls, which they have brought on themselves through a variety of sins and crimes, makes use of penal remedies of a similar sort, even to the infliction of a punishment of fire on those who have lost their soul's health.

Allusions to this are found also in the holy scriptures. For instance, in Deuteronomy the divine word threatens that sinners are to be punished with "fevers and cold and pallor," and tortured with "feebleness of eyes and insanity and paralysis and blindness and weakness of the reins" (cf. Dt 28:22, 28, 29). And so if anyone will gather at his leisure from the whole of scripture all the references to sufferings which in threats against sinners are called by the names of bodily sicknesses, he will find that through them allusion is being made to either the ills or the punishments of souls.

III.6.5–6

It is on this account, moreover, that the last enemy, who is called death, is said to be destroyed (1 Cor 15:26); in order, namely, that there may be no longer any sadness when there is no death nor diversity when there is no enemy. For the destruction of the last enemy must be understood in this way, not that its substance which was made by God shall perish, but that the hostile purpose and will which proceeded not from God but from itself will come to an end. It will be destroyed, therefore, not in the sense of ceasing to exist, but of being no longer an enemy and no longer death. For to the Almighty nothing is impossible (Jb 42:2), nor is anything beyond the reach of cure by its Maker; for it was on this account that he made all things, that they might exist, and those things which were made in order to exist cannot cease to exist. . . .

3

Our flesh indeed is considered by the uneducated and by unbelievers to perish so completely after death that nothing whatever of its substance is left. We, however, who believe in its resurrection, know that death only causes a change in it and that its substance certainly persists and is restored to life again at a definite time by the will of its Creator and once more undergoes a transformation. . . .

Into this condition, therefore, we must suppose that the entire substance of this body of ours will develop at the time when all things are restored and become one and when "God shall be all in all" (1 Cor 15:28). We must not think, however, that it will happen all of a sudden, but gradually and by degrees, during the lapse of infinite and immeasurable ages, seeing that the improvement and correction will be realized slowly and separately in each individual person. Some will take the lead and hasten with swifter speed to the highest goal, others will follow them at a close interval, while others will be left far behind; and so the process will go on through the innumerable ranks of those who are making progress and becoming reconciled to God from their state of enmity, until it reaches even to the last enemy, who is called death (1 Cor 15:26), in order that he, too, may be destroyed and remain an enemy no longer. When therefore all rational souls have been restored to a condition like this, then also the nature of this body of ours will develop into the glory of a "spiritual body" (1 Cor 15:44).

SOURCE: Origen, *On First Principles*, trans. G. W. Butterworth (Notre Dame, IN: Ave Maria Press, 2013), 162–63, 177–80, 326–28.

"Thalia"

ca. 325–360

Arius (ca. 250–336 CE) was a popular priest in Alexandria, Egypt. He is primarily remembered for his role in the Council of Nicaea (325 CE), called by Emperor Constantine to resolve the question of Jesus Christ's divinity. While the church was largely untroubled by the diversity of understandings on the topic, Constantine felt a more homogenized Christianity would better serve the needs of empire. At Nicaea, Arius argued that the divinity of the Son was less than that of the Father because only God had existed for all eternity (God having created the logos that was incarnate in Jesus). The contrasting point of view, primarily developed by Athanasius, held that the Son and the Father were of the same essence/substance (homoousious). The Council ruled against Arius and excommunicated him. While there is no direct link between Arius and the much later development of Unitarianism, Nicaea represents the church's first insistence on a creedal assertion of the full divinity of Christ, creating the basis for the persecution of later anti-Trinitarians. Because Arius's works were ordered destroyed, his only extant texts are fragments quoted in the works of opponents. Such is the case with the "Thalia," a text attributed to Arius that has been reconstructed primarily through the later writings of Athanasius, which date approximately to 356–60 CE. The "Thalia," often translated as banquet, *is an example of Arius's talent for popularizing his theological ideas in verse. Further Reading: Rowan Williams,* Arius: Heresy and Tradition *(Grand Rapids, MI: W. B. Eerdmans, 2002).*

—Susan Ritchie

In accordance with the faith of the elect of God, God's sage servants,
holy and orthodox, who had received God's holy Spirit,
I learned these things from various participants in wisdom,
skillful, taught by God in every way and wise.
In their steps came I, stepping with the same opinions,
the notorious, the one who suffered much for God's glory;
having learned from God I myself know wisdom and knowledge.

God then himself is in essence ineffable to all.
He alone has neither equal nor like, none comparable in glory;
We call him Unbegotten because of the one in nature begotten;

We raise hymns to him as Unbegun because of him who has beginning.
We adore him as eternal because of the one born in time.

The Unbegun appointed the Son to be Beginning of things begotten,
and bore him as his own Son, in this case giving birth.
He has nothing proper to God in his essential property,
for neither is he equal nor yet cosubstantial with him.

Wise is God, since he himself is Wisdom's teacher.
There is proof enough that God is invisible to all,
and to those through the Son and to the Son himself the same (God) is invisible.
I will say exactly how the Invisible is seen by the Son:
By the power by which (a) God can see, and in proper measures,
the Son sustains the vision of the Father as is right.

Or rather there is a Trinity with glories not alike;
Their existences are unmixable with each other;
One is more glorious than another by an infinity of glories.

The Father is essentially foreign to the Son because he exists unbegun.
Understand then that the Unity was, but the Duality was not, before he existed.
So straight away when there is no Son, the Father is God.
Thus the Son who was not, but existed at the paternal will,
is only-begotten God, and he is distinct from everything else.
Wisdom existed as wisdom by the will of a wise God.

He is conceived by so many million concepts,
as spirit . . . , power, wisdom, glory of God, truth and image and word.
Understand that he is conceived also as effulgence and light.
One equal to the Son the Supreme is able to beget,
but more excellent, superior, or greater he cannot.
How old and how great the Son is by God's will—
since when, and from what point, even since then he existed from God.
For being a mighty God he hymns the Supreme in part.

To sum up, God exists ineffable to the Son,
for he is to himself what he is, that is, unutterable,
so that none of the things said . . .
will the Son know how to express comprehensively;
for it is impossible for him to explore the father who exists by himself.
For the Son himself does not know his own essence;
for being Son he truly came to be at his Father's will.
What logic then permits the one who is from a Father

6

to know by comprehension the one who begot him?
For clearly for what has a beginning to encompass
by thought or apprehension the one who is unbegun, is impossible.

SOURCE: Arius, "Thalia," in *A New Eusebius: Documents illustrating the history of the Church to AD 337*, rev. ed., ed. J. Stevenson (Cambridge: Cambridge University Press, 1987), 330–32.

MICHAEL SERVETUS

On the Errors of the Trinity

1531

*Michael Servetus (ca. 1506–1553) left his native Spain in 1530 in the entou-
rage of the Emperor Charles V. He took with him a manuscript work he had
written in response to the religious situation in Spain, including the problem
of the conversion of the Muslims. After leaving his position with the imperial
confessor, he published his work* On the Errors of the Trinity *in Germany in
1531. Reaction was so negative that he changed his name to Michel de Ville-
neuve and went to the University of Paris to study medicine. While working
as a physician in the 1540s, he wrote* The Restoration of Christianity, *an
expansion of* Errors *that incorporated his new interests in Neoplatonism and
Anabaptism. In his discussion of the working of the Holy Spirit, he was the
first European to describe the transit of the blood through the lungs. Publication of* Restoration *in 1553 led to his imprisonment by the Inquisition and,
after his escape, his trial and execution by burning at the stake in Calvin's
Geneva. Servetus's anti-Trinitarianism, which included the idea that Jesus
was God, incorporates features of several divergent ancient heresies, including both Arianism and Sabellianism. Further Reading: Roland H. Bainton,*
Hunted Heretic: The Life and Death of Michael Servetus, 1511–1553, *ed.
Peter Hughes (Providence, RI: Blackstone Editions, 2005).*

—Peter Hughes

In investigating the holy mysteries of the divine Triad, I have decided to begin with
the man Jesus Christ; since I see so many embarking on speculation about the Word,
without a foundation in Christ, paying little or no attention to the human being and
consigning the true Christ wholly to oblivion. I intend to remind them who *that*
Christ is. . . . Since the masculine demonstrative pronouns, "this" or "that," indicate
that he was a man, or what theologians call "a human nature," I submit the following
three propositions: (1) this man is Jesus Christ; (2) this man is the Son of God; and
(3) this man is God.

Christ the Man

In the first place, who would deny that this man was called Jesus? That was the name
given to the child, at the angel's command, on the day of his circumcision, just as
your name, for instance, is John, and his, Peter (Luke 1 and 2). Jesus, as Tertullian
says, is a masculine proper name, while Christ is a title. The Jews all admitted that

he was Jesus, but when Pilate was asking them about *Jesus who is called Christ*, they denied that he was the Christ. And they *put out of the synagogue* those who *confessed him to be the Christ*. The apostles frequently argued with them about whether Jesus was the Christ. But there was never any doubt or question that he was Jesus, nor did anyone ever deny this.

Consider the intent of Paul's words, with what zeal he *testified to the Jews that Jesus was the Christ* (Acts 18), and *with* what *spiritual fervor Apollos of Alexandria*, in the same chapter, *confuted the Jews in public, showing by the scriptures that* the man *Jesus was the Messiah*. What Jesus do you think those "acts" are about? You don't believe, do you, that Paul and Apollos were thinking of a hypostasis?

Therefore I have to concede that he is the Christ as well as Jesus, since I admit that he was anointed by God. For he is *your holy servant, whom you have anointed* (Acts 4). He is the *holy of holies*, whose anointing was predicted in Daniel 9. And in Acts 10 Peter said, "*You know*"—as if it were something easy to understand, for what was said about Jesus was common knowledge—"*how God anointed Jesus of Nazareth with the Holy Spirit and with power, for God was with him*, and *he is the one ordained by God to be judge of the living and the dead.*" "*Let all the house of Israel know assuredly*," Peter says in Acts 2, "*that God has made this Jesus, whom you crucified, both Lord and Christ*"—that is, the anointed one. Nonetheless, some use the pronouns in these scripture passages—"him," "he," and "this"—to indicate another being, even though John says that *whoever denies that Jesus* is God's anointed is a *liar*, while whoever accepts *that Jesus is the Christ is born of God* (1 John 2 and 5).

Likewise Tertullian says that the word "Christ" is a noun pertaining to a human nature. And in Books 3 and 4 of *Against Marcion*, having carefully investigated the term "Christ," he mentions nothing about that being which some consider to be Christ. Who, he asks, is the Son of man, if not an actual man, born of a human being, "flesh born from flesh"? For the Hebrew expression "son of man," like "son of Adam," means nothing other than a man. The word Christ conveys the same meaning, for "to be anointed" can only refer to a human nature. If, therefore, as Tertullian says, "to be anointed is an experience of the body," who can deny that it was a man who was anointed?

Furthermore, the apostle Peter expresses the true meaning of the word anointed in the first book of Clement's *Recognitions*: "Because kings were commonly called Christs, therefore Jesus, on account of the superior nature of his anointing, above all others, is called Christ the King." For "just as God made an angel first among angels, a beast first among beasts, and a star first among stars, so too did he make Christ first among men." Likewise, the authority of the holy scriptures very clearly teaches us that it was a man who was called Christ, since even an earthly king can be called Christ (1 Samuel 12 and 22, and Isaiah 45). . . .

Now if Christ were not a man how can you speak of our brotherhood with Christ? Who is the one who is exalted *above his fellows*? What kind of comparison between Christ and Moses is the Apostle making in Hebrews, when he says that Christ is *worthy of greater glory than Moses*, since *Moses was faithful as a servant, but Christ truly as a son?* Why, in Hebrews 1 and 2, is the Apostle so insistent in declaring that Christ was exalted above even the angels? For to prove that this "second nature of God" is more exalted than the angels would be a very frivolous exercise. Nor can Paul's deliberately chosen words be forced to serve that interpretation. For the Apostle is quoting the words of the Prophet David, who marveled at the greatness of Christ's glory because, although he was a man, *all things were made subject to him* (Psalm 8).

Again, in John 20, Jesus *performed miracles in order that* we might *believe that Jesus is the Christ, the Son of God.* Note what he considers important about Jesus: that we believe that this Jesus, who was the only begotten Son of God the Father, was the anointed one. How could that unknown second being be recognized by the miracles that Jesus performed, unless this being is recognized to be the one whom they saw performing the miracles, as Nicodemus does in John 3? For these publicly performed miracles do not argue in favor of the philosophers' esoteric speculations. . . . In John 6, because of the miracles he performed, Peter concludes, "*We have come to know that you are the Christ, the Son of the living God.*"

Christ, the Son of God

These conclusions reached by those who witnessed Christ's miracles also clearly confirm the truth of my second proposition: that this man, whom I call the Christ, is the Son of God. For based on the miracles that he performed, they concluded that he was the Son of God. And once it has been proven that he is Jesus Christ, it logically follows that anyone who denies that he is the Son denies Jesus Christ. For scripture proclaims nothing else but that Jesus Christ is the Son of God.

Besides, he is specifically identified as the Son in many scriptural passages, and thus, in relation to him, God is called the Father—truly the Father, I say, because Jesus was begotten by God, who assumed the role of a human father. For Jesus was not in fact born of the seed of Joseph, as Carpocrates, Cerinthus, and Photinus falsely and impiously claimed. Instead, in place of human seed, the almighty power of the Word of God overshadowed Mary, and the Holy Spirit acted within her. Luke Chapter 1 continues: *And therefore the child to be born will be holy, and will be called the Son of God.* Consider carefully the word "therefore." Note the logical conclusion. And note the reason why the man Jesus ought to be called the Son of God.

Finally, the prophet Daniel reveals to us the nature of the sonship in the man Jesus Christ, calling him *a stone uncut by human hands.* This same kind of sonship is also presented in Matthew 1, where it is said that Mary was made *pregnant by the Holy Spirit*, and *what was conceived in her came from the Holy Spirit.* Pray tell me, who is that child who was begotten and conceived in her, who comes from the Holy

Spirit? From this Matthew concludes, following the prophecy in Isaiah, that *the son whom she will bear* will be the savior *Emmanuel.* . . .

How a Human Being Can Be God

With pure hearts we acknowledge the true Christ, who is completely filled with divinity. . . . God is able to share *the fullness of deity* with a human being, and to give him *a name which is above every name.* If, indeed, we grant that Moses was *made a god to Pharaoh*, then, in a far more powerful and superior way, Christ became the God, Lord, and Teacher of Thomas and of us all. Because God was in him in a unique way, and because through him we have access to a merciful God, he is expressly *called Emmanuel, that is, God with us.* What is more, in Isaiah 9 he himself is called by the Hebrew word *El* (God).

Furthermore, if God has given us the privilege *that we should be called the sons of God* (1 John 3), with Christ this privilege will be even greater, so that not only is he called the Son of God, but he is called—and is—our God as well. For *worthy is the lamb who was slain* to receive divinity, that is, *to receive power, riches, wisdom, strength, honor, glory, and blessing* (Revelation 5). And there is in him another far more manifold *fullness of deity*, as well as his other *unsearchable riches.* . . . These are all attributes that God shares with the man Jesus Christ. . . .

Now, there are three divine dispositions, but not by some distinction of beings in God. Rather, that God might bring about our salvation, there are various aspects of deity. For the same divinity that is in the Father is communicated to the Son, Jesus Christ, and to our spirit, which is *the temple of the living God.* Both the Son and our sanctified spirit "share in the substance of the Father, and are members of the deity, pledges of his love, and instruments of his will," although the appearance of deity differs in each of them. This is why they are said to be "distinct persons," that is, the multiform aspects of deity, having different likenesses and appearances. . . .

The Holy Spirit

Philosophers have invented a third absolute being, really and truly distinct from the other two, which they call the third person, or the Holy Spirit. In this way they have devised an imaginary trinity—three beings in one nature. In reality, however, under the guise of, and using words denoting unity, three beings, three gods, or one god in three parts are being foisted upon us. . . . For such philosophers see no difficulty in saying that there are three beings—taking these words in their absolute sense—which are absolutely, simply, truly, and in reality different or distinct from each other, so that one of them can be born from a second, and yet another blown forth from the first two, while all three of them are enclosed in one enormous jar. . . . I will call them the first being, the second being, and the third being. For in the scriptures I cannot find any better name for them. . . .

11

Granting the existence of these three beings, whom it is their custom to call "persons," by arguing from lesser to greater, these philosophers absolutely admit that there are several beings, several entities, several essences, several substances, and several *ousias*. As a result, since they take the word "God" in an absolute sense, they will have several gods. But if this is the case, why are the tritheists, who say that there are three gods, subject to reproach? For the philosophers themselves also labor to construct three gods, or one god in three parts. These three gods of theirs form one composite *ousia* (substance). And even though some of them refuse to use words such as "composite," they nevertheless use the word "constitute," and say that God is constituted out of three beings. Clearly, then, we Christians are all tritheists, and we have a tripartite God. We have thus all become atheists, that is, a people without God. For as soon as we try to think about God, our thoughts are diverted to three images, so that no conception of unity is able to endure in our minds. But what does being without God mean, other than not being able to think about God? As a confused jumble of three beings is constantly looming before our minds and hampering our understanding, it drives us to madness whenever we try to think about God. . . .

Scripture speaks about the Holy Spirit in another way, unknown to the philosophers. . . . For scripture deals with this subject in a mysterious and nearly incomprehensible way, especially for those who are not accustomed to the unusual manner in which it speaks about the Holy Spirit. For by "holy spirit" Scripture sometimes means God himself, sometimes an angel, sometimes the spirit of a man, sometimes a kind of inspiration, or the breath of the divinity on the mind, a mental impulse, or respiration; although a distinction between breath and Spirit is sometimes observed. And some would have "the holy spirit" understood as nothing but correct human understanding and reasoning. The Hebrew word "spirit" means simply a breathing or blowing, which among them is used without distinction to mean either wind or spirit, whereas among the Greeks, "breath" is used for any kind of spirit or mental impulse whatsoever. It presents no difficulty that this spirit is called holy, for all stirrings of the mind, when they concern the religion of Christ, are called holy, and are sacred to God. For *no one can say that Jesus is the Lord, except by the Holy Spirit*. . . .

The scriptures often mention the existence of God the Father, and the Son, and people seeing and worshipping them, but they do not mention the Holy Spirit except when discussing an action. . . . This is worth noting. For, in Scripture, it appears that "Holy Spirit" designates not a separate being, but is the activity of God, that is to say, a certain kind of energy or the inspiration of the power of God. . . .

The Real Basis of Divine Unity

It remains to discuss several scriptural texts, on the basis of which the modern theologians think their three beings can be proven philosophically. For instance: *There are three who bear witness in heaven, the Father, the Word, and the Holy Spirit, and these three are one* (1 John 5). But first, in order to provide a more satisfactory response, I will address two other passages of scripture, which the *moderni* [philosophers of the modern school] also use in proving their case: *I and the Father are one* (John 10) and *The Father is in me and I am in the Father* (John 14). Augustine makes use of the first text to counter Arius, saying, "because John says 'one,'" and, against Sabellius, "because John says 'we are.'" Thus, from the very same text Augustine concludes that there are two beings when countering Sabellius, while, against Arius, he concludes that they have one nature.

I think, however, that these words possess a simpler meaning, for it is Christ who is speaking and it is he who says "we are" because he is both God and man. And, as Tertullian says in *Against Praxeas*, Christ said "'one' in the neuter gender, and not 'one' in the masculine gender." For "the masculine word 'one' appears to mean something singular in number," as if it were denoting the singularity of one and the same being. But "'one' in the neuter form as used by John pertains not to singularity, but to unanimity" or concord, "so that the two, God and Christ, are thought of as existing in one divine power." And this is what the early Church Fathers correctly called "one substance," because there is only one divine power which was bestowed on the Son by the Father.

Nevertheless the later Church Fathers have unfortunately made a mockery of the word *homoousia* (same substance)—just as they have with "hypostasis" and "persons"—claiming that the word "substance" means "a nature." This is not only contrary to the proper meaning of the word "substance" but also runs counter to all of the passages of scripture in which the word is found. For in John, and in the last chapter of Matthew, and everywhere that Christ speaks about the power given to him by the Father, the word *"substance"* is used, which to the Greeks does not mean "nature" but abilities, works, prosperity, wealth, and power, all of which Christ has in abundant measure. And he and the Father share one power, one accord, and one will. The meaning of the Latin word *"one,"* like the Greek word for "one," embraces unanimity of purpose, similarity, and sharing the same wisdom. But to understand the word "one" in scripture as meaning "one nature" is metaphysical rather than Christian. Indeed, except when philosophizing about Scripture, the Greeks have never understood the word "one" as meaning "one nature." If then you ask, why the Greek Church Fathers understand the word in this way, consider the answer that Basil the Great provides in Book 4 of *Against Eunomius*. Here he does not argue according to the proper meaning of the Greek word "one" but instead resorts to syllogistic reasoning in order to philosophize.

Accordingly, we ought to accept an interpretation of the Greek word "one" either based on its proper meaning or guided by other passages of scripture. In the scriptures, however, you will never find the word "one" being used to convey the metaphysical unity of nature. Quite the opposite, as is clear from the words of Christ himself, who, in John 17, reveals himself as a faithful teacher. For he prays to the Father on behalf of the Apostles, *"that they may all be one, as you, Father, are in me and I in you, that they also may be one in us,"* and *"that they may be one, even as we are one."* Frequently repeating the word "one," he prays that his disciples may be one. Does it then follow that we, who are one in a way similar to them, constitute one nature? We are certainly one, in that we are all in concord, *preserving the unity of the Spirit in the bond of peace.* See also Jeremiah 32: *I will give them one heart, and one way.*

Also, in Acts 4, we read that *the multitude of those who believed were of one heart and of one soul.* And in Book 8 of *Against Celsus*, Origen expressly says that the passage, *"I and the Father are one,"* should be understood according to the interpretation of this passage from Acts. He says that the Father and the Son are one, for, although it is clear that "they are two beings in substance, they are one in agreement, harmony, and oneness of will." . . .

Christian Theology Gone Astray

Yet the cruelest thing is that this tradition of the Trinity has provided the Muslims with God only knows how many opportunities for laughter. The Jews, too, shudder at the thought of believing in these figments of our imaginations, and mock our stupidity along with the Trinity. Also, it is because of the blasphemies inherent in the doctrine of the Trinity that the Jews do not believe that this man Jesus is the Messiah who was promised to them in the Law. Not only the Muslims and the Jews but even the beasts of the field would laugh at us if they could ever comprehend our bizarre ideas. For *all the Lord's works praise* the One God.

Listen, as well, to what Muhammad has to say. For greater trust is to be placed in one truth spoken by an enemy, than in a hundred of our own lies. For he says in his Qur'an that Christ was the greatest of the prophets, the spirit of God, the power of God, the breath of God, the very soul of God, and the Word born of a perpetual virgin by the breath of God—and that it is because of the malice of the Jews toward Christ that they are in their current state of wretchedness and misfortune. He says, moreover, that the Apostles and Evangelists as well as the first Christians were the very best of men, who wrote the truth and believed neither in the doctrine of the Trinity nor in the idea of three Persons in the Divine Being, and that it was men from later times who added these things.

Thus this raging pestilence was superimposed on the scriptural account, and *new gods* were added, *who have come but recently, gods whom our forefathers never worshipped.* And this philosophical plague was inflicted on us by the Greeks, for it is they, above all others, who are most devoted to philosophy. And we, hanging upon every word they speak, have been turned into philosophers as well.

Perhaps some will consider it a sin if I propose that the philosophers could possibly have gone astray. But to prove this, I need only show that they have never understood the passages of scripture which they have brought forward as proof-texts of their doctrine of the Trinity. If they could only compare the clarity that existed in apostolic times with their own confused obscurity, they would realize how deservedly Paul called the *church of God the support and pillar of the truth*. Paul's words mean nothing other than that what is said in the Gospel is true. And this is the message of the Gospel: that Jesus Christ is the Son of God. For . . . the most solid support and foundation of the truth—the foundation upon which the church is built—is the belief that Jesus Christ is the Son of God. And it is because of this foundation that Paul calls the church *the pillar of the truth*. Therefore, it cannot be said that our church lacks a foundation. Indeed, this respect for the solid truth is called *the rock, the pillar,* and *the church of God*. For a church can still be a church when it has ceased to be the Church of God, and Peter might still be present in it though the rock on which the church is built no longer remains. Matters such as these might seem too trivial to be worth mentioning, except that there are those with *teeth of iron*, who are content if they can only sink their teeth into and tear away a single passage of scripture. But I would prefer that they pay just as careful attention to other passages of scripture. . . .

Pay attention to what follows and you will then understand the stipulation that Christ attached to his promise: *"Preach the gospel, and teach them to observe all I have commanded you, and behold, I am with you."* Where, I ask you, are those who preach Christ now? Where are those who keep his commandments? Especially the injunction to believe that he is the Son of God, so that Christ can be truly with them. Later, I will demonstrate to you that you do not know what this gospel is which Christ directed his disciples to preach. Indeed, I will prove to you that you are not actually Christian.

You believe that the Church is a mathematical body, holding the spirit of God imprisoned, bound by the hair, even though none of you know either Christ or his spirit. Jesus said, "As often as you are *gathered in my name I am there*." But how can those who do not know Christ be gathered in the name of Christ? And how shall the Holy Spirit be in that congregation, if they are all full of the spirit of fornication and theft? Beware, therefore, lest by merely repeating the words, "The church cannot err," you stand in the way of a true knowledge of Christ, and are defending the error of being ignorant of him.

May the Lord give you understanding, so that you may devote yourself to the simplicity which is to be found in the scriptures. If you seek Christ *with all your heart and soul*, he will unfailingly bestow his grace upon you.

SOURCE: Michael Servetus, *De Trinitatis erroribus* (1531). Previously unpublished translation by Lynn Hughes, Peter Hughes, and Peter Zerner.

On the Great Extent of
God's Blessed Kingdom

1554

In his youth Celio Secondo Curione (1503–1569) led a colorful and danger-filled life as a fugitive in Italy, more than once making a hair-raising escape from the Inquisition. Once settled in Switzerland, he was more circumspect. As professor of eloquence at Basel, he presented himself as an orthodox Protestant while secretly abetting the activities of Matteo Gribaldi and Sebastian Castellio in their protests against the trial and execution of Michael Servetus. Curione had his closest brush with trouble after he published his nearly universalist On the Great Extent of God's Blessed Kingdom, *which he dedicated to King Sigismund II of Poland. Further Reading: Jules Bonnet,* La famille de Curione; Recit du seizieme siècle *(Basel, 1878); Robert Wallace,* Antitrinitarian Biography, *vol. 2 (London: E. T. Whitfield, 1850).*

—Peter Hughes

Those who have been living in recently discovered lands, or amongst the Troglodytes, have not received true teaching about our Lord, nor have they been raised in the faith. For all these, through so many generations, to have been destined for destruction, is not consistent with divine goodness and the fairest administration of justice. . . . This is the law of our king, and his very just ruling: to the extent that, having heard the Gospel, a person believes, he is saved. And he who, having heard the Gospel, does not believe, is condemned. From this it follows that he who has not yet heard the Gospel is not by the Gospel to be condemned. Those who are condemned are condemned because they have rejected natural law and the witness and judgment of their own conscience. . . .

God could, and today still can, teach certain persons, endowed with spiritual aptitude, about Christ. Even in the most remote nations he can stir up people by his spirit and send them out to teach others. He himself can also enlighten his people within, that they may know about him. For his divine goodness never left anyone without knowledge of him.

SOURCE: Celio Secondo Curione, *De amplitudine beati regni Dei* (1554). Previously unpublished translation by Peter Hughes and Peter Zerner.

Apology for Michael Servetus

1554

Matteo Gribaldi (ca. 1505–1564), a distinguished law professor at univer-
sities in France, Italy, and Germany, had an estate only a few miles from
Geneva. He promoted the ideas of Servetus among his students in Padua.
He tried unsuccessfully to get an audience with Calvin during Servetus's trial.
Afterward, he wrote an Apology for Michael Servetus *(under the pseudo-*
nym Alphonsus Lyncurius Tarraconensis) and circulated among his Polish
students a manuscript work of his own composition, A Revelation of Jesus
Christ, the Son of God, *which he credited to Servetus. Gribaldi, who never*
long remained silent about his unorthodox opinions, was forced to flee from
his posts in Padua and Tübingen and narrowly avoided execution in Bern.
Further Reading: Matteo Gribaldi, Declaratio: Michael Servetus's Revelation of Jesus Christ the Son of God and Other Antitrinitarian Works, *ed.*
Peter Hughes and Peter Zerner, trans. Peter Zerner with Peter Hughes and
Lynn Gordon Hughes (Providence, RI: Blackstone Editions, 2010); Frederic
C. Church, The Italian Reformers, 1534–1564 *(New York: Columbia Univer-*
sity Press, 1932).

—Peter Hughes

Look at what you have done, you evangelicals! You have basely and disgracefully
slandered and horribly and savagely killed this harmless man, this *stranger and*
sojourner who trusted in your evangelical profession and Christian charity. Although
he trusted you, did not stir up any trouble or sedition, and caused you no harm, you
have accused him of crime, detained him by treachery, tossed him into prison, pros-
ecuted him, and finally, totally casting aside all humanity and mercy, burned him
alive on a blazing pyre. What a noble crime, whose memory ought never to be
obliterated!

Is this your Christian charity, your evangelical profession, about which you
strove so hard to persuade the entire world? . . . Even if he had conceived an idea
about the word "Trinity" which diverged from the view generally held by the
learned—which you also accept and approve—and an interpretation or revelation
of the Word, which he hoped to be ready and able to defend using scripture and
reason, should he therefore have been condemned by such sudden and precipitate
judgment, and monstrously and disgracefully delivered to horrible punishment in

the flames, especially in a free and evangelical city? When the council of the fathers and leading citizens was convoked, should they not have maturely deliberated over this difficult and serious matter, putting aside all human emotion (or, to put it in a more vulgar way, hurt feelings)? In the extinction of this one frail soul, you yourselves were the accusers, recorders, judges, and executioners. Pray tell me, what advocate or defender did you appoint for him when he was in prison? What freedom did you grant him to speak and make his arguments, without fear of punishment? . . .

As if he, who was continuously held in prison, could have pleaded his case freely before untrustworthy judges who were bent on prosecuting him with the most deadly hatred and who wrote the record of the trial as it pleased them. There was no one to intercede on the prisoner's behalf or to help him compose a written defense. This unfortunate man was supported by no friendly defender or legal advocate, with whose aid he might have explained his state of mind and his arguments. . . .

But if we consider the laws of justice in a calmer state of mind, how much injustice, how much barbarity, soon appears! For no one who does not have evil intent is punished with death. But how can anyone be convicted of having evil intent, who has an opinion that he considers true and evangelical, based on scripture and reason, and which he is prepared to defend and even to die for? I believe that there is no one of such dull intelligence, so feeble in understanding, or so lacking in common sense, that he would choose to defend what he knew to be false, when it was obviously not in his interest to do so.

SOURCE: Matteo Gribaldi, *Apologia pro Michaele Serveto* (1554), from *Declaratio: Michael Servetus's Revelation of Jesus Christ the Son of God and Other Antitrinitarian Works*, ed. Peter Hughes and Peter Zerner, trans. Peter Zerner with Peter Hughes and Lynn Gordon Hughes (Providence, RI: Blackstone Editions, 2010), 169–99.

LAELIUS SOCINUS (LELIO SOZZINI)

A Brief Exposition of the First Chapter of John

ca. 1561

Lelio Sozzini (1525–1562), a.k.a. Laelius Socinus, the uncle of Faustus Soci-
nus, traveled widely in his short life, visiting Poland twice. While a student in
Padua he was associated with unitarian anabaptists in nearby Vicenza. After
making a public protest at the Council of Trent, he fled to Switzerland. Like
his friend Celio Curione, but unlike another friend, Matteo Gribaldi, he was
careful in his public utterances not to offend his more orthodox Protestant
friends, such as Heinrich Bullinger, Philipp Melanchthon, and John Calvin.
When he was suspected of co-authoring Sebastian Castellio's protest against
Servetus's execution, Concerning Heretics, *Bullinger had him prepare a con-*
fession of faith to demonstrate his orthodoxy. In this carefully worded credo,
he included a statement promoting freedom of inquiry: "I shall never allow
myself to be deprived of that sacred liberty to ask questions." In his A Brief
Exposition of the First Chapter of John, *published after his death, Sozzini*
portrayed a Christ who was entirely and only a human being. Further Read-
ing: George Huntston Williams, Studies in the Radical Reformation (1517–
1618) *(Philadelphia: American Society of Church History, 1958); Earl Morse*
Wilbur, A History of Unitarianism: Socinianism and Its Antecedents *(Bos-*
ton: Beacon Press, 1945). See also the entry on Gribaldi.

—Peter Hughes

In the Beginning Was the Word. . . . Many believe that the noun "Word" indicates an
eternal Son, through whom God carried out all things under the old covenant and
spoke with the Patriarchs. But many passages of scripture refute these fabrications of
men, especially Chapter 13 of Acts, where it is stated that one God the Father brought
about everything done or promised in the Old Testament, and that he also brought
forth his son from the seed of David. . . . We, indeed, say that the Word is Christ the
visible man, born of Mary, who taught men the Father's will. And thus because he
was the articulator of his father's commandments, he acquired the name "Word." All
these passages of scripture which speak of the Word, do not have in mind an eternal Christ before Mary, or something twice-born, but him about whom we are now
speaking, the man. In 1 John 1 the Word is described as visible, touchable, and audible. John understood by this Christ the man. . . . Clearly the Word is he who spoke

through his teaching, not some eternal being, who is never described in Scripture as having taught anything. . . .

John teaches that the Word was with God but adds "in the beginning," that is the beginning of his ministry and service . . . For in that beginning Christ began to be the Word to us, both a teacher and a prophet, proclaiming his father's commandments. . . . Theologians have amazingly misread this brief passage from the prologue of John in their attempt to prove the idea that Christ is the creator of all things in heaven and on earth. They are mistaken in the following ways: 1. They have imagined that Christ is one God with the Father, co-eternal and co-equal with him. Hence they have also fabricated the idea that the creator and Christ are one. 2. They do not understand that the word "creation" in scripture is often to be taken as also expressing re-creation, renewal, reconciliation, recapitulation or restoration. . . .

Moses accurately describes creation and no one gives a better day-by-day account of the creation of all things (for this duty was given by God to him alone). He even enumerates all of the living things: the beasts, the insects, the vegetation, and everything after its kind. Can you tell me where the Son of God appears in the story of creation? Can it be that Moses did not think him worth mentioning? . . .

Therefore, just as the Old Testament attributes that previous creation to the one and only God the creator, the Father of all things, so too the New Testament attributes that subsequent creation, or renewal or recovery of all things in heaven and on earth, to Christ, who has been made the mediator of the new covenant.

SOURCE: Lelio Sozzini, *Brevis explicatio in primum Johannis caput.* Previously unpublished translation by Peter Hughes and Peter Zerner.

"The Edict of Torda"

1568

The Edict of Torda (also The Patent of Toleration) was issued in 1568 by the Transylvanian King John Sigismund Zápolya shortly after his conversion to Unitarianism. Authored by Sigismund's court preacher Francis David (1510–1579), it also shows the influence of other prominent Unitarians such as Giorgio Biandrata (1515–1588). Historians have praised the edict as an outstanding early example of religious toleration in that it grants freedom of practice to four churches (Lutheran, Calvinist, Catholic, and Unitarian) rather than to a single religion of state. Sigismund's edict followed those issued in 1557 and 1565 by his mother, Isabella, a noted humanist in the liberal tradition of Erasmus, acting as regent for her underage son. The 1557 edict originated mainly as a plea to Catholics and Lutherans to refrain from violence in their dealings with each other, while the 1568 edict also bears a close relationship to previous edicts and practices of toleration originating with the officials of the Islamic Ottoman Empire. The Ottomans held ultimate suzerainty over Transylvania at the time of the edict and for much of the sixteenth and seventeenth centuries. Further Reading: Susan Ritchie, Children of the Same God: The Historical Relationship Between Unitarianism, Judaism, and Islam *(Boston: Skinner House, 2014).*

— Susan Ritchie

Preachers everywhere are to preach the gospel according to their understanding of it; if the parish willingly receives it, well: but if not, let there be no compulsion on it to do so, since that would not ease any man's soul; but let each parish keep a minister whose teaching is acceptable to it. Let no superintendent or anyone else act violently or abusively to a preacher. No one may threaten another on account of his teaching with imprisonment or deprivation of office. For faith is a gift of God; it comes from listening, and listening is through God's word.

SOURCE: Translated from Hungarian by Judit Gellérd, in John Erdö, *Transylvanian Unitarian Church* (Chico, CA: Center for Free Religion, 1990). Translation is updated slightly by Judit Gellérd.

FRANCIS DAVID

"Propositions of the Nagyvarad Debate"
1569

The Nagyvarad Debate of 1569 was the final of three debates sponsored by King John Sigismund surrounding controversies over the doctrine of the Trinity within the reform church of Transylvania. Beginning with the first debate in 1566, court preacher Francis David (1510–1579) represented the anti-Trinitarians, articulating the theology of what developed as a separate Unitarian church. The second debate, held in 1568 immediately after the Diet of Torda, led to King Sigismund's personal conversion to Unitarianism. David's arguments in the 1569 debate represent the theological maturation of the new church and contributed to Unitarianism's rapid growth in the following years. His methodology in the debate, a careful opposition to the Trinity on scriptural grounds, reveals the influence of Michael Servetus. David's collaborator in the debates was George Biandrata, the court physician and a religious radical who had earlier cultivated David's own anti-Trinitarianism. In later years, David's theology showed even more progressive influences. These changes alarmed Biandrata, who, sensitive to the hostility directed toward Unitarianism after Sigismund's death, tried to steer the church in a more conservative direction. Betrayed to the state by his old friend Biandrata, David was convicted of the crime of theological innovation and died in prison shortly thereafter. Further Reading: George Huntston Williams, Studies in the Radical Reformation (1517–1618) *(Philadelphia: American Society of Church History, 1958).*

—Susan Ritchie

I. The Trinity held by the pope of Rome is really a belief in four or five Gods; one substance, God, three separate persons each of which are Gods, and one man, Christ. According to Francis David God is only one, that Father from whom and by whom is everything, who is above everything, who created everything through the word of his wisdom and the breath of his mouth. Outside of this God there is no other God, neither three, neither four, neither in substance, neither in persons, because the Scripture nowhere teaches anything about a triple God.

II. One is the Son of God, Jesus Christ, God and man, of whom we cannot say either that he is first born or that he is the only begotten of God because such a person would not be both God and man.

III. The Scripture's God-son who was supposed to have been born of the substance of God from the beginning of eternity is nowhere mentioned, neither a God-son who would be the second person of the Trinity descended from heaven and become flesh. This is only human invention and superstition and as such is to be discarded.

IV. There is no other Son of God than the one who was begotten in the womb of the virgin by the Holy Spirit.

V. Jesus Christ is God and man but he did not create himself, for the Father gave him his divinity, the Father had him begotten by the Holy Spirit, the Father sanctified him and sent him into the world.

VI. The equality of Christ with God is only of a kind which God gave him, God remaining in his divine sovereignty above everyone else.

VII. He [Francis David] does not deny that the Son of God was present in the eternal thought of God because there is no difference in time before God, for God everything is present tense; but the Scriptures nowhere teach that the Son of God would have been born from the beginning of eternity.

VIII. Christ is the Son of God, he was neither purely human nor purely God before the angel announced him to Mary and the shepherds; he was the Son of David in flesh, he was the Son of God in spirit, anointed high priest, judge and Lord above everyone else, he is our hope and fulfillment.

IX. The Holy Spirit is not self-created God, not a third person in the Trinity, but the Spirit of the Father and of the Son, a seal of inheritance, life-giving strength, which the Father realizes in us through the Son, to be seen in ourselves and in our actions.

SOURCE: Francis David, "Propositions of the Nagyvarad Debate" in *Dávid Ferencz emléke: elitéltetése és haláka háromszázados évfordulójára*, ed. Elek Jakab (Budapest, 1879). English version translated by Alexander St.-Ivanyi and reprinted in *The Epic of Unitarianism: Original Writings from the History of Liberal Religion*, ed. David B. Parke (Boston: Skinner House, 1985), 20–22.

A Book Which Showeth the Life and Manners of All True Christians

1582

Robert Browne (1550?–1633) was the first to formalize the basic principles of congregational polity and to gather a church accordingly. Ordained an Anglican priest, under Puritan influences he came to feel that the Church of England was too corrupt to reform from within, thus becoming the first Separatist. Browne held that the centralization of power within the church in the hierarchical rule of bishops, as well as any collaboration of civil and religious power, was inconsistent with both scripture and the church's spiritual and prophetic mission. Instead, he argued that believers had the authority to establish independent congregations by entering into voluntary covenant with God and each other. His teachings were illegal, and some of his followers were executed. He was arrested often, and would have suffered a worse fate if not for his powerful family. His decision to reconcile with the Church of England in 1586 under threat of excommunication was a source of disappointment for his followers. Some of Browne's ideas were included in the Cambridge Platform of 1648 outlining the polity of the New England churches, although that platform departs from Browne in supporting a rule of elders and in reserving a role for the civil magistrate in church affairs. Further Reading: Champlin Burrage, The True Story of Robert Browne, Father of Congregationalism *(Oxford: Oxford University Press, 1906) and Henry Dexter,* The Congregationalism of the Last Three Hundred Years as Seen in Its Literature *(New York: Harper & Brothers, 1880).*

—Susan Ritchie

Question and Answer

35. *What is our calling and leading unto this happiness [promised by Christ]?*

In the new Testament our calling is in plain manner: as by the first planting and gathering of the church under one kind of government.

Also by the further planting of the church according to that government.

But in the Old Testament, our calling was by shadows and ceremonies, as among the Jews.

36. *How must the church be first planted and gathered under one kind of government?*

First by a covenant and a condition, made on God's behalf.
Secondly, by a covenant and condition made on our behalf.
Thirdly, by using the sacrament of Baptism to seal those conditions, and covenants.

37. *What is the covenant, or condition on God's behalf?*

His promise to be the God of our seed, while we are his people.
Also, the gift of his spirit to his children and an inward calling and furtherance of
godliness.

38. *What is the covenant or condition on our behalf?*

We must offer up and give up ourselves to be of the church and people of God.
We must likewise offer up and give up our children and others, being under age, if
they be of our household and we have full power over them.
We must make profession, that we are his people, but submitting ourselves to his laws
and government.

39. *How must Baptism be used, as a seal of this covenant?*

They must be duly presented, and offered to God and to the church, which are to be
Baptized.
They must be duly received into grace and fellowship.

40. *How must they be presented and offered?*

The children of the faithful, though they be infants are to be offered to God and the
church, that they might be baptized.
Also those infants or children which are of the household of the faithful, and under
their full power.
Also all of discretion which are not baptized, if they hold the Christian profession,
and show forth the same.

41. *How must they be received unto grace and fellowship?*

The word must be preached in a holy assembly. The sign or Sacrament must be
applied thereto.

42. *How must the word be preached?*

The preacher being called and met thereto must show the redemption of Christians
by Christ, and the promises received by faith as before.
Also they must how the right use of that redemption, in suffering with Christ to die
unto sin by repentance.

43. *How must the sign be applied thereto?*

The bodies of the parties baptized, must be washed with water, or sprinkled or dipped, in the name of the Father and of the Son and of the holy Ghost, unto the forgiveness of sins, and dying thereto in one death and burial with Christ.

The preacher must pronounce those to be baptized into the body and government of Christ, to be taught and profess his laws, that by his mediation and victory, they might rise again with him in holiness and happiness forever. The church must give thanks for the party baptized, and pray for his further instruction and training unto salvation.

44. *How must [the church] be further built, according unto church government?*

First by the communion of the graces and offices in the head of the church, which is Christ.

Secondly by the communion of the graces and offices in the body, which is the church of Christ.

Thirdly by using the Sacrament of the Lord's supper, as a seal of this communion.

45. *How has the church the communion of those graces and offices, which are in Christ?*

It has the use of his priesthood: because he is the high Priest thereof.

Also his prophecy, because he is the Prophet thereof.

Also his kingdom and government: because he is the king and Lord thereof.

46. *What has the church of his priesthood?*

Thereby he is our mediator, and we present and offer up our prayers in his name, because by his entreaty, our sins are forgiven.

Also his is our justification, because by his atonement we are justified.

Also he is our sanctification, because he parts unto us his holiness and spiritual graces.

47. *What has the church of his prophecy?*

He himself has taught us, and given us his laws.

He preaches unto us by his word and message in the mouths of his messengers.

He appoints to every one of them their callings and duties.

48. *What use has the church of his kingly office?*

By that which executes his laws: First, by overseeing and trying out wickedness.

Also by private or open rebuke, or private or open offenders.

Also by separation of the willful, and more egregious offenders.

49. *What use has the church of the graces and offices under Christ?*

It has those which have office for teaching or guiding.

Also those which have office of cherishing and relieving the afflicted and poor.

Also it has the graces of all brethren and people to do good forthwith.

50. *Who has the grace and office of teaching and guiding?*

Some have this charge and office together, which cannot be sundered.

Some have their several charges over many churches.

Some have charge but in one church only.

51. *How have some their charge and office together?*

There be Synods of meetings of sundry churches: which are when the weaker churches seek help of the stronger, for deciding or redressing of matters: or else the stronger look to them for redress.

52. *Who has their several charges over many churches?*

Apostles had charge over many churches.

Likewise, Prophets, which had the revelations or visions.

Likewise, helpers unto these, as Evangelists, and companions of their journeys.

53. *Who has their several charges in one Church only, to teach and guide the same?*

The Pastor, or he who has the gift of exhorting, and applying especially.

The Teacher, or he which has the gift of teaching especially, and less the gift of exhorting and applying.

They which help unto them both in overseeing and counseling, as the most forward or Elders.

54. *Who has the office of cherishing and relieving the afflicted and poor?*

The Relievers, or Deacons, which are to gather and bestow the church's generosity.

The Widows, which are to pray for the church, with attendance to the sick and afflicted thereto.

55. *How has the church the use of those graces which all the brethren and people have to do good forthwith?*

Because every one of the church is made a King, a Priest, and a Prophet under Christ, to uphold and further the kingdom of God, and to break and destroy the kingdom of Antichrist and Satan.

56. *How are we made Kings?*

We all must watch one another, and try out all wickedness.

We must privately and openly rebuke the private and open offenders. We must also separate the willful and more egregious offenders, and withdraw ourselves from them, and gather the righteous together.

57. *How are all Christians made Priests under Christ?*

They present and offer prayers unto God, for themselves and for others.

They turn others from inequity, so that atonement is made in Christ unto justification.

58. *How are all Christians made prophets under Christ?*

They teach the laws of Christ, and talk and reason for the sake of them.

They exhort, move, and stir up to the keeping of his laws. They appoint, counsel, and tell one another of their duties.

110. *What special furtherance of the kingdom of God is there?*

In talk to edify one another by praising God and declaring his will by rebuke or exhortation.

In doubt and controversy to swear by his name on just occasion, and to use lots.

Also to keep the meetings of the church, and especially with our friends for spiritual exercise.

112. *Which be the duties of the righteous concerning man?*

They either be more bound, as the general duties in government between governors and inferiors:

Or else they be more special duties for each other's name, and avoiding covetousness.

113. *What be the duties of Governors?*

They consist in the entrance of that calling.

And in the due execution thereof by ruling well.

114. *How must Superiors enter and take their calling?*

By assurance of their gift.

By special charge and commandment from God to put it in practice.

By agreement of men.

115. *What gift must they have?*

All Governors must have forwardness before others, in knowledge and godliness, as able to guide.

And some must have age and eldership.

And some must have parentage and birth.

116. *What charge or commandment of God must they have to use their gift?*

They have first the special commandment of furthering his kingdom, by edifying and helping others, where there is occasion and persons be worthy.

Also some special prophecy and foretelling of their calling, or some general commandment for the same.

Also particular warnings from God unknown to the world, as in old times by vision, dream, revelations, and now by a special working of God's spirit in our consciences.

117. *What agreement must there be of men?*

For church governors there must be an agreement of the church.

For civil Magistrates, there must be an agreement of the people or Commonwealth.

For Householders, there must be agreement of the households. As Husbands, Parents, Masters, Teachers, or Schoolmasters, etc. . . .

118. *What agreement must there be of the church, for the calling of church governors?*

They must try their gifts and godliness.

They must receive them by obedience as their guides and teachers, where they plant or establish the church.

They must receive them by choice where the church is planted.

The agreement also for the calling of civil magistrates should be like unto this, expecting their pomp and outward power, and orders established meet for the people.

119. *What choice should there be?*

The prayers and humbling of all, with fasting and exhortation, that God may be chief in the choice.

The consent of the people must be gathered by the Elders or guides, and testifying by voice, presenting, or naming of some, or other tokens, that they approve of them as meet for that calling.

The Elders or forwardest must ordain, and pronounce them, with prayer and imposition of hands, as called and authorized of God, and received of their charge to that calling.

Yet imposition of hands is no essential point of their calling, but it ought to be left, when it is turned into pomp or superstition.

120. *What agreement must there be in the households, for the government of them?*

There must be an agreement of Husband and Wife, of Parents and Children: Also of Master and Servant, and likewise of Teachers and Schoolers, etc. . . .

This agreement between parents and children is of natural desert and duty between them:

But in the other there must be a trial and judgment of each other's fitness for their linkage and calling, as is shown before.

Also there must be a due covenant between them.

SOURCE: Robert Browne, *A Book Which Showeth the Life and Manners of All True Christians* (Middleburg, the Netherlands, 1582). Edited and language modernized by Susan Ritchie.

Racovian Catechism

1605

Faustus Socinus (1539–1604) was an Italian theologian. Influenced by early anti-Trinitarians including his uncle Laelius Socinus, he further developed their ideas into modern Unitarianism, which is still often synonymous with Socianism. He lived among the (unitarian) Polish Brethren of the Minor Reform Church from 1579 until his death, refining their theology and resolving internal conflicts over matters such as conscientious objection and the invocation of Jesus in prayer. He was the first reformer to argue the radical humanity of Jesus (that there was no preexistence of Christ prior to the birth of the human person Jesus). He also held that Christ's living example was more important than his death, and he rejected original sin. His methodology was as important as his conclusions: Believing that humanity is not innately religious but chooses it in free will, he held that all revelation must be closely examined using every human resource, especially reason. The press operated by the Polish Brethren published The Racovian Catechism *after Socinus's death. While drafted by others, it contains some of Socinus's own language and reflects the degree to which the church adopted his teachings. Widely translated, for generations it served as a vital link between unitarian movements across Europe. It is one of the few remnants of the Polish Brethren (expelled in 1658). Further Reading: Stanisław Kot,* Socinianism in Poland: The Social and Political Ideas of the Polish Antitrinitarians in the Sixteenth and Seventeenth Centuries *(Boston: Starr King Press, 1957).*

—Susan Ritchie

Of the holy Scriptures.

QUESTION: *I Would fain learn of you what the Christian Religion is.*

ANSWER: The Christian Religion is the way of attaining eternal life, discovered by God.

Q. *But where is it discovered?*

A. In the Holy Scriptures, especially that of the new Covenant.

Q. *Is there then any other Holy Scripture, besides that of the New Covenant?*

A. Yes.

Q. *What is it?*

A. The Writings of the old Covenant.

* * *

Touching the sufficiency of the holy Scriptures.

Q. *That the sacred Scriptures are firm and certain, you have sufficiently proved, I would therefore further learn, whether they be so sufficient as that in things necessary to eternal life we ought to rest in them only?*

A. They are altogether sufficient for that, inasmuch as Faith on the Lord Jesus Christ, and obedience to these Commandments (which twain are the requisites of eternal life) are sufficiently delivered and explained in the Scripture of the very New Covenant.

Q. *If it be so, then what need is there of Traditions, which the Church of Rome holdeth to be necessary until eternal life, calling them the unwritten Scripture?*

A. You rightly gather that they are unnecessary to eternal life.

Q. *What then must we think of them?*

A. Not only that they were fancied and invented without just cause and necessity, but also to the great hazard of the Christian Faith.

Q. *What may that hazard be?*

A. Because those Traditions give men an occasion of turning aside from divine Truth to falsehood, and the imaginations of men.

Q. *But they seem to assert those Traditions from the very Scripture.*

A. Those testimonies which they produce out of Scripture to assert those Traditions, do indeed demonstrate that Christ and the Apostles spake and did certain things which are not comprehended in the holy Scriptures, but no ways prove that they were delivered from hand to hand by them to be perpetually so conserved, or that those things which are consigned in the holy Scriptures, are not sufficient to Religion and salvation.

✻　✻　✻

Of the knowledge of Christ.

Touching the Person of Christ.

Q. *Inasmuch as you have said that those things have been discovered by Jesus Christ, that concern the will of God as it properly belongeth unto them, who shall obtain eternal life, I would entreat you to declare those things to me concerning Jesus Christ, which are needful to be known.*

A. I am content. First therefore you must know that those things partly concern the Essence, partly the Office of Jesus Christ.

Q. *What are the things that concern his Essence or Person?*

A. Only that he is a true man by nature, as the holy Scriptures frequently testify concerning that matter, and namely, I Tim. 2.5: "There is one Mediator of God and men, the man Jesus Christ." And I Cor. 15.21. "Since by man came death, by man also came the Resurrection from the dead." And indeed such a one God heretofore promised by the Prophets, and such a one the Apostles Creed, acknowledged by all Christians, confesseth Jesus Christ to be.

Q. *Is the Lord Jesus then a mere man?*

A. By no means. For he was conceived of the Holy Spirit, and born of the Virgin Mary, and therefore is from his very conception and birth the Son of God, as we read, Luke 1.35. where the Angel thus speaketh to the Virgin "Mary, The Holy Spirit shall come upon thee, and the power of the Highest shall overshadow thee, therefore also that Holy Thing Generated shall be called the Son of God." That I may omit other causes, which you shall afterwards discover in the Person of Jesus Christ, and most evidently show, that the Lord Jesus ought by no means to be reputed a mere man.

Q. *You said a little before that the Lord Jesus is a man by nature, hath he not also a divine Nature?*

A. At no hand; for that is repugnant not only to sound Reason, but also to the holy Scriptures.

Q. *Show me how if is repugnant to sound Reason.*

A. First, because two substances indued with opposite properties cannot combine into one Person, and such properties are mortality and immortality; to have beginning, and to be without beginning; to be mutable, and immutable. Again, two Natures, each whereof is apt to constitute a several person, cannot be huddled into one Person. For instead of one, there must of necessity arise two persons, & consequently become two Christs, whom all men without controversy acknowledge to be one, and his Person one.

Q. *But when they allege that Christ is so constituted of a divine and humane Nature, as a man is of a body and soul, what answer must we make to them?*

A. That in this case there is a wide difference; for they say that the two Natures in Christ are so united that Christ is both God and Man. Whereas the soul and body in a man are so conjoined, as that a man is neither soul nor body. For neither doth the soul nor the body severally constitute a Person. But as the divine Nature doth by itself constitute a Person, so must the humane by itself of necessity also constitute.

Q. *Show how it is also repugnant to the Scripture that Christ should have a divine Nature.*

A. First, because the Scripture proposeth to us but one God by nature, whom we formerly demonstrated to be the Father of Christ. Secondly, the same Scripture witnesseth that Jesus Christ is a man by nature as was formerly shown. Thirdly, because whatsoever divine excellency Christ hath, the Scripture testifieth that he hath it by gift of the Father. John 3.35. John 5.19, 20, 21, 22, 23, 26, 27. John 10.25. John 12.3. John 14.10. Acts 2.33. Rev. 2.26, 27. 2 Pet. 1. 17. Finally, because the Scripture doth most evidently show, that Jesus Christ doth perpetually ascribe all his Divine acts not to himself, or any Divine nature of his own, but to the Father; who seeth not that such a Divine nature as the Adversaries imagine in Christ, would have been altogether idle, and of no use?

*　*　*

Q. *I perceive that Christ hath not a divine nature, but is a true man, now tell me of what avail unto salvation the knowledge hereof will be?*

A. From the knowledge of this, that Christ is a true man, a sure and well grounded confirmation of our hope doth follow, which by the contrary opinion is exceedingly shaken, and almost taken away.

Q. *How so?*

A. Because it followeth from the adverse opinion, that Christ is not a true man, for since they deny that there is in Christ the person of a man, who seeth that they with one and the same labour deny him to be a true man, in that he cannot be a true man, who wanteth the person of a man, but if Christ had not been a true man, he could not die, and consequently not rise again from the dead, whereby our hope which resteth on the resurrection of Christ, as on a firm basis, and foundation, may be easily shaken, and well nigh thrown down, but that opinion, which acknowledgeth Christ to be a true man, who conversing in the world, was obedient to the Father, even unto death, doth assert, and clearly determine that the same died, and was by God raised from the dead, and indued with immortality, and so in a wonderful manner, supporteth, and proppeth, our hope concerning eternal life, setting before our eyes the very image of that thing, and assuring us thereby, as it were with a pledge, that we also though we be mortal and die; shall notwithstanding in due time rise from death, to come into the society of the same blessed immortality, whereof he is made partaker if we tread in his steps.

*　*　*

Touching the confirmation of the Divine Will.

Q. *How Jesus declared unto us the Divine Will, hath been explained, I would now have it also explained how he confirmed the same?*

A. There are three things of Christ that did confirm the Divine Will which he declared; first, the absolute innocency of his life, John 8.46. I John 3.5. Secondly, his great, and innumerable Miracles, John 15.24. John 21.25. Thirdly, his death, I Tim. 2.6. chap. 6.13. All these three are united in that noted place of John, I Epist. 5.8. There are three that bear record on Earth, The Spirit, the Water, and the Blood. For by the Spirit, without question the holy Spirit is meant, by whose Virtue the Miracles of Christ were wrought, Acts 10.38. As by Water is understood the Purity of his life, and by Blood, his Bloody death.

34

Q. *What was the Innocency of Christ's Life, and how was the Will of God confirmed thereby?*

A. The Innocency of his Life was such, that he not only committed no sin, neither was guile found in his mouth, nor could he be convicted of any crime, but he lived so transcendently pure as that none, either before or after, did equalize him, so that he came next to God himself in Holiness, and was therein very like to him. Whence it followeth that the Doctrine delivered by him was most true.

Q. *What were his Miracles, and how did they confirm the Divine Will?*

A. The Miracles were so great, as none before him ever did; and so many, as that had they been set down in particular, the world would not contain the Books. And these Miracles do therefore make to confirming of the will of God, in that it is not imaginable that God would invest any one with such power, as was truly Divine, who had not been sent by him.

Of Christ's Death.

Q. *What was the Death of Christ, and how did it confirm the Will of God?*

A. Such a death, as had all sorts of afflictions ushering it in, and was of it self most bitter and ignominious, so that the Scripture thereupon testifieth that he was made like to his brethren in all things, Heb. 2.17.

SOURCE: Faustus Socinius, *The Racovian Catechisme* (Amsterdam, 1652), B, 8–9, 27–29, 70–71, 120–22. As excerpted by David B. Parke in *The Epic of Unitarianism* (Boston: Skinner House, 1985). Spelling modernized.

The Salem Covenant and the Enlarged Covenant
1629, 1636

Francis Higginson and Samuel Skelton arrived in Salem, Massachusetts, in 1629. Even though both men were previously ordained by the Church of England and had been appointed by the Massachusetts Bay Company to serve the settlers' spiritual needs, the Salem church elected and ordained Higginson and Skelton as Teacher and Pastor, respectively, in Congregationalist fashion. The church had formally gathered just prior to that election around this 1629 covenant, authored by Higginson. Its simplicity is common to the earliest Congregational covenants, and it is similar to those used in Separatist churches previously formed in London. The expanded revision of 1636 partially reflects the congregation's desire to recovenant after divisions arose among them under the controversial ministry of Roger Williams. Williams openly contested the role of the colonial government in church affairs, but unlike the settlers in Plymouth, the people of Salem did not think of themselves as Separatist and many were concerned about keeping peace with the Crown. Even in churches without controversy, covenants became more complicated over time as increasing suspicion in England regarding the orthodoxy of the New England churches prompted them to explain themselves. This sometimes led to the inclusion of creed-like statements in these later covenants, unlike in earlier covenants, in which doctrinal agreement was presupposed. Further Reading: Williston Walker, The Creeds and Platforms of Congregationalism *(Boston: Pilgrim Press, 1960).*

—Susan Ritchie

The Covenant of 1629

We Covenant with the Lord and with one another; and do bind ourselves in the presence of God, to walk together in all his ways, according as he is pleased to reveal himself unto us in his Blessed word of truth.

The Enlarged Covenant of 1636

Gather my Saints together unto me that have made a Covenant with me by my sacrifice (Psalms 50:5). We whose names are here underwritten, members of the present Church of Christ in Salem, having found by sad experience how dangerous it is to sit loose in the Covenant we make with our God; and how apt we are to wander into byways, even to the loosening of our first aims in entering into Church fellowship: Do therefore solemnly in the presence of the Eternal God, both for our own comforts and those which shall or may be joined unto us, renew that Church Covenant we find this Church bound unto at their first beginning, viz: That We Covenant with the Lord and with one another; and do bind ourselves in the presence of God, to walk together in all his ways, according as he is pleased to reveal himself unto us in his Blessed word of truth. And do more explicitly in the name and fear of God, profess and protest to walk as follows through the power and the grace of our Lord Jesus.

1. First we avow the Lord to be our God, and ourselves his people in the truth and simplicity of our spirits.
2. We give ourselves to the Lord Jesus Christ, and the word of his grace, for the teaching, ruling and sanctifying of us in matters of worship, and Conversation, resolving to cleave to him alone for life and glory; and oppose all contrary ways, canons and constitutions of men in his worship.
3. We promise to walk with our brethren and sisters in this Congregation with all watchfulness and tenderness, avoiding all jealousies, suspicions, backbitings, censurings, provokings, secret risings of the spirit against them; but in all offenses to follow the rule of the Lord Jesus, and to bear and forebear, give and forgive as he has taught us.
4. In public or in private, we will willingly do nothing to the offense of the Church but we will be willing to take advice for ourselves and ours as occasion shall be presented.
5. We will not in the Congregation be forward either to show our own gifts or parts in speaking or scrupling, or there discover the failing of our own brethren or sisters but attend an orderly call there unto; knowing how much the Lord may be dishonored, and his Gospel in the profession of it, slighted, by our distempers, and weakness in public.
6. We bind ourselves to study the advancement of the Gospel in all truth and peace, both in regard of those that are within, or without, no way slighting our sister Churches, but using their counsel as need shall be: nor laying a stumbling block before any, nor not the Indians, whose good we desire to promote, and so to converse, as we may avoid the very appearance of evil.
7. We hereby promise to carry ourselves in all lawful obedience, to those that are over us, in Church or Commonwealth, knowing how well pleasing it will be to the Lord, that they should have encouragement in their places, by our not grieving their spirits through our Irregularities.

8. We resolve to approve ourselves to the Lord in our particular callings, shunning idleness as the bane of any state, nor will we deal hardly, or oppressingly with any, wherein we are the Lord's stewards.

9. Also promising to our best abilities to teach our children and servants, the knowledge of God and his will that they may serve him also; and all this, not by any strength of our own, but by the Lord Christ, whose blood we desire may sprinkle this our Covenant made in his name.

SOURCE: "The Covenant of 1629" and "The Enlarged Covenant of 1636" in *The Creeds and Platforms of Congregationalism*, ed. Williston Walker (Boston: Pilgrim Press, 1960), 116–18. Language modernized by Susan Ritchie. Note: According to Walker, copies of the original version of the 1629 covenant are no longer extant. The earliest copy of the covenant from 1636 can be found in a document entitled "A COPY of Church-Covenants which have been used in the Church of SALEM," which was printed for J. F. in Boston in 1680.

Twelve Arguments Drawn
out of the Scripture

1644

John Biddle (Bidle) (1615–1662) was an English lay preacher, teacher, and biblical scholar, frequently jailed for his advocacy of anti-Trinitarianism. He first attracted the attention of the state when the manuscript for Twelve Arguments *was given to a magistrate by a disloyal friend. He is one of the few English reformers who continued to be outspoken until his death. In addition to writing and speaking, he gathered a settled congregation in 1652, variously referred to as Biddlers, Socianians, and Unitarians. In 1655, Oliver Cromwell ordered him to exile in Sicily to spare him the death sentence after yet another prosecution for heresy. In 1658, powerful friends enabled his return to England, on the condition he remain obscure in the countryside. Biddle nonetheless went to London to preach in 1662, was arrested again, and died shortly thereafter in prison.* Twelve Arguments *displays the biblical basis for his anti-Trinitarianism as well as his rejection of original sin and eternal damnation, and shows the heavy influence of Polish theologian Faustus Socinus, whose works he translated. Further Reading: Michael Watts,* The Dissenters, *vol. 1,* From the Reformation to the French Revolution *(Oxford: Clarendon Press, 1978); Sarah Mortimer,* Reason and Religion in the English Revolution: The Challenge of Socinianism *(Cambridge: Cambridge University Press, 2014).*

—Susan Ritchie

Twelve ARGUMENTS *Drawn out of the Scripture, Wherein the commonly received Opinion touching the Deity of the Holy Spirit is clearly and fully refuted.*

To the impartial READER.

⁕ ⁕ ⁕

I know many men (as well as myself) will be ready to cry out Blasphemy, Blasphemy, at the first view of the Title Page, yet I could wish that they would embrace the Apostles' counsel, *Prove all things, holding fast that which is good:* Call all things to a serious examine, and reject nothing hand over-head, take nothing upon trust, without a fore-examining of every circumstance, lest in the one, they should reject truth instead of error; and in the other, embrace error instead of truth.

The Author hath a long time waited upon learned men for a satisfactory answer to these Arguments, but hath received none; his hopes are that the publishing of them will be a means to produce it, that he may receive satisfaction, and others may be held no longer in suspense, who are in travel with an earnest expectation of a speedy resolution, as well as he. . . . I number myself expecting an Answer to these ensuing Arguments; and that God will be with him that undertakes it, and give in a spirit of meekness, and of wisdom, in the revelation and knowledge of truth, shall be the matter of his prayers, who desires truth may be cleared up, and shine like the noon-day, and all error confounded, and vanish before truth, like a mist before the Sun.

* * *

Argument 1.

HE that is distinguished from God is not God; The holy Spirit is distinguished from God: Ergo. The Major is evident: for if he should be both God, and distinguished from God, he would be distinguished from himself; which implieth a contradiction. The Minor is confirmed by the whole current of the Scripture, which calleth him the Spirit of God, and saith that he is sent by God, and searcheth the depths of God, &c. Neither let any man here think to fly to that ignorant refuge of making a distinction between the Essence and Person of God, saying that the Holy Spirit is distinguished from God, taken Personally, not Essentially. For this wretched distinction (to omit the mention of the Primitive Fathers) is not only unheard of in Scripture, and so to be rejected, it being presumption to affirm anything of the unsearchable nature of God, which he hath not first affirmed of himself in the Scripture; but is also disclaimed by Reason. For first, it is impossible for any man, if he would but endeavor to conceive the thing, and not delude both himself and others with empty terms and words without understanding, to distinguish the Person from the Essence of God, and not to frame two beings or things in his mind, and consequently two Gods. Secondly, if the person be distinct from the Essence of God, then it is either something or nothing; if nothing, how can it be distinguished, since nothing hath no accidents? If something, then either some finite or infinite thing; if finite, then there will be something finite in God, and consequently, since by the confession of the adversaries everything in God is God himself, God will be finite, which the adversaries themselves will likewise confess to be absurd. If infinite, then there will be two infinites in God, to wit, the Person and Essence of God, and consequently two Gods; which is more absurd then the former. Thirdly, to talk of God taken only Essentially, is ridiculous, not only because there is no example thereof in Scripture, but because God is the name of a Person, and signifieth him that ruleth over others: and when it is put for the most high God, it denoteth him who with Sovereign and absolute authority ruleth over all; but none but a person can rule over others, all actions being proper to persons: wherefore to take God otherwise than personally is to take him otherwise than he is, and indeed to mistake him.

SOURCE: John Biddle, *Twelve Arguments Drawn out of the Scripture* (London, 1647), 5–7. Some spelling and punctuation modernized.

The Cambridge Platform
1648

The Cambridge Platform of 1648 was the first formal constitution outlining the principles of government and discipline for the churches of New England. It was the result of a Synod, although the document itself was written by Richard Mather, who used many materials from John Cotton. Although it is often heralded as the gold standard of congregational polity within Unitarian Universalist circles, many laity, as well as clergy defenders of congregational polity in the style of Robert Browne, were disappointed in the Platform insofar as it did not advocate for a complete separation of church and state and gave more power to church officers than to the laity as a body. Still, it did commit the churches to a number of basics of congregational polity: the gathering of the church by covenant, the need for churches to counsel together, the autonomy of the local church, and the right of the churches to select and ordain ministers. And of course, primarily, it promoted the notion that there is no larger or greater church than the gathered congregation. Further Reading: James Cooper, Tenacious of Their Liberties: The Congregationalists in Colonial Massachusetts *(Oxford: Oxford University Press, 1999).*

—Susan Ritchie

Of The form of Church-Government; and that it is one, immutable, and prescribed in the Word of God.

1. Ecclesiastical polity, or church government or discipline, is nothing else but that form and order that is to be observed in the church of Christ upon earth, both for the constitution of it, and all the administrations that therein are to be performed.

* * *

3. The parts of church government are all of them exactly described in the Word of God being parts or means of instituted worship according to the second commandment. . . . So that it is not left in the power of men, officers, churches, or any state in the world to add, or diminish, or alter any thing in the least measure therein.

* * *

Of the nature of the catholic church in general, and in special of a particular visible church.

* * *

6. A congregational church is by the institution of Christ a part of the militant visible church, consisting of a company of saints by calling, united into one body by a holy covenant, for the public worship of God, and the mutual edification of one another in the fellowship of the Lord Jesus.

Of the matter of the visible church, both in respect of Quality And Quantity.

1. The matter of the visible church are saints by calling.
2. By saints, we understand:
   I. Such as have not only attained the knowledge of the principles of religion, and are free from gross and open scandals, but also do, together with the profession of their faith and repentance, walk in blameless obedience to the Word, so as that in charitable discretion they may be accounted saints by calling. . . .
   II. The children of such who are also holy.

* * *

4. The matter of the church, in respect of its quantity, ought not to be of greater number than may ordinarily meet together conveniently in one place; nor ordinarily fewer than may conveniently carry on church work. . . .
5. . . . There is no greater church than a congregation which may ordinarily meet in one place.

Of the Form of A Visible Church and of Church Covenant.

1. Saints by calling must have a visible political union amongst themselves, or else they are not yet a particular church. . . .
2. Particular churches cannot be distinguished one from another but by their forms. . . .
3. This form is the visible covenant, agreement, or consent, whereby they give up themselves unto the Lord, to the observing of the ordinances of Christ together in the same society, which is usually called the "church covenant" for we see not otherwise how members can have church power over one another mutually.

* * *

4. This voluntary agreement, consent or covenant (for all these are here taken for the same) although the more express and plain it is, the more fully it puts us in mind of our mutual duty; and stirs us up to it, and leaves less room for the questioning of the truth of the church estate of a company of professors, and the truth of membership of particular persons; yet we conceive the substance of it is kept where there is real agreement and consent of a company of faithful persons to meet constantly together in one congregation, for the public worship of God, and their mutual edification; which real agreement and consent they do express by their constant practice in coming together for the public worship of God and by their religious subjection

43

unto the ordinances of God there: then rather, if we do consider how Scripture covenants have been entered into, not only expressly by Word of mouth, but by sacrifice, by handwriting and seal; and also sometimes by silent consent, without any writing or expression of words at all.

✳   ✳   ✳

Of the first subject of church power; or, to whom church power doth first belong.

1. The first subject of church power is either supreme, or subordinate and ministerial. The supreme (by way of gift from the Father) is the Lord Jesus Christ. The ministerial is either extraordinary, as the apostles, prophets and evangelists; or ordinary, as every particular Congregational church.

2. Ordinary church power is either power of office, that is, such as is proper to the eldership, or power of privilege, such as belongs unto the brotherhood. The latter is in the brethren formally and immediately from Christ, that is, so as it may, according to order, be acted or exercised immediately by themselves: the former is not in them formally or immediately, and therefore cannot be acted or exercised immediately by them, but is said to be in them, in that they design the persons unto office, who only are to act or to exercise this power.

✳   ✳   ✳

Of Ruling Elders And Deacons.

1. The ruling elder's office is distinct from the office of pastor and teacher; the ruling elders are not so called to exclude the pastors and teachers from ruling, because ruling and governing is common to these with the other; whereas attending to teach and preach the Word is peculiar unto the former.

2. The ruling elder's work is to join with the pastor and teacher in those acts of spiritual rule which are distinct from the ministry of the Word and sacraments committed to them; of which sort these be as follows:

   I. To open and shut the doors of God's house, by the admission of members approved by the church; by ordination of officers chosen by the church and by excommunication of notorious and obstinate offenders renounced by the church, and by restoring of penitents forgiven by the church.

   II. To call the church together when there is occasion, and seasonably to dismiss them again.

   III. To prepare matters in private, that in public they may be carried and end with less trouble, and more speedy dispatch.

   IV. To moderate the carriage of all matters in the church assembled, as to propound matters to the church. To order the season of speech and silence, and

44

to pronounce sentence according to the mind of Christ with the consent of the church.

v. To be guides and leaders to the church in all matters whatsoever pertaining to church administrations and actions.

vi. To see that none in the church live inordinately, out of rank and place without a calling, or idly in their calling.

vii. To prevent and heal such offenses in life or in doctrine as might corrupt the church.

viii. To feed the flock of God with a word of admonition.

ix. And, as they shall be sent for, to visit and pray over their sick brethren. . . .

3. The office of a deacon is instituted in the church by the Lord Jesus; sometimes they are called helps. . . . The office and work of a deacon is to receive the offerings of the church, gifts given to the church, and to keep the treasury of the church, and therewith to serve the tables, which the church is to provide for, as the Lord's table, the table of the ministers, and of such as are in necessity, to whom they are to distribute in simplicity.

✻ ✻ ✻

7. The Lord has appointed ancient widows (where they may be had) to minister in the church, in giving attendance to the sick, and to give succor unto them and others in the like necessities.

Of the Election of Church Officers.

1. No man may take the honor of a church officer unto himself but he that was called of God, as was Aaron.

2. Calling unto office is either immediate, by Christ himself; such was the call of the Apostles And Prophets; this manner of calling ended with them, as has been said: or Mediate, by the church.

3. It is meet that, before any be ordained or chosen officers, they should first be tried and proved, because hands are not suddenly to be laid upon any, and both elders and deacons must be of both honest and good report.

✻ ✻ ✻

5. Officers are to be called by such Churches whereunto they are to minister. . . .

6. A Church being free cannot become subject to any but by a free election; Yet when such a people do choose any to be over them in the Lord, then do they become subject, and most willingly submit to their ministry in the Lord, whom they have chosen.

7. And if the church have power to choose their officers and ministers, then, in case of manifest unworthiness and delinquency, they have power also to depose them. . . .

45

8. We judge it much conducing to the well being and communion of the churches, that, where it may conveniently be done, neighbor churches be advised withal, and their help be made use of in trial of church officers, in order to their choice.

9. The choice of such Church-officers belongs not to the civil magistrates as such, or diocesan-bishops, or patrons: for of these, or any such like, the Scripture is wholly silent, as having any power therein.

Of Ordination and Imposition of hands.

1. Church officers are not only to be chosen by the church, but also to be ordained by imposition of hands and prayer, with which at the ordination of elders, fasting also is to be joined.

2. This ordination we account nothing else but the solemn putting a man into his place and office in the church, whereunto he had right before by election, being like the installing of a magistrate in the commonwealth. Ordination therefore is not to go before, but to follow election, the essence and substance of the outward calling of an ordinary officer in the church does not consist in his ordination, but in his voluntary and free election by the church, and his accepting of that election; whereupon is founded that relation between pastor and flock, between such a minister and such a people.

*　*　*

6. Church officers are officers to one church, even that particular over which the Holy Ghost has made them overseers. Insomuch as elders are commanded to feed not all flocks, but the flock which is committed to their faith and trust, and depends upon them. . . .

7. He that is clearly loosed from his office-relation unto that church whereof he was a minister cannot be looked at as an officer, nor perform any act of office in any other church, unless he be again orderly called unto office; which, when it shall be, we know nothing to hinder; but imposition of hands also in his ordination ought to be used towards him again. . . .

Of the power of the church and its presbytery.

*　*　*

3. This government of the church is a mixed government (and so has been acknowledged, long before the term of independency was heard of); in respect of Christ, the head and king of the church, and the Sovereign Power residing in him, and exercised by him, it is a monarchy; in respect of the body or brotherhood of the church, and power from Christ granted unto them it resembles a democracy, in respect of the presbytery and power committed unto them, it is an aristocracy.

*　*　*

5. The power granted by Christ unto the body of the church and brotherhood, is a prerogative or privilege which the church does exercise:

    i. In choosing their own officers, whether elders or deacons.

    ii. In admission of their own members; and therefore there is great reason they should have power to remove any from their fellowship again. . . .

6. In case an elder offend incorrigibly, the matter so requiring, as the church had power to call him to office, so they have power according to order (the counsel of other churches, where it may be had, directing thereto) to remove him from his office. . . .

*   *   *

8. The power which Christ has committed to the elders is to feed and rule the church of God, and accordingly to call the church together upon any weighty occasion; when the members so called, without just cause, may not refuse to come, nor when they are come, depart before they are dismissed, nor speak in the church before they have leave from the elders, nor continue so doing when they require silence; nor may they oppose or contradict the judgment or sentence of the elders without sufficient and weighty cause, because such practices are manifestly contrary unto order and government, and inlets of disturbance, and tend to confusion.

9. It belongs also unto the elders to examine any officers or members before they be received of the church; to receive the accusations brought to the church, and to prepare them for the churches' hearing. In handling of offenses and other matters before the church, they have power to declare and publish the counsel and will of God touching the same, and to pronounce sentence with the consent of the church. Lastly, they have power, when they dismiss the people, to bless them in the name of the Lord.

10. This power of government in the elders does not any wise prejudice the power of privilege in the brotherhood; as neither the power of privilege in the brethren prejudices the power of government in the elders, but they may sweetly agree together. . . .

11. From the premises, namely, that the ordinary power of government belonging only to the elders, power of privilege remaining with the brotherhood (as the power of judgment in matters of censure and power of liberty in matters of liberty), it follows that in an organic church and right administration, all church acts proceed after the manner of a mixed administration, so as no church act can be consummated or perfected without the consent of both.

*   *   *

Of Admission of members into the Church.

1. The doors of the churches of Christ upon earth do not by God's appointment stand so wide open that all sorts of people, good or bad, may freely enter therein at

47

their pleasure; but such as are admitted thereto, as members, ought to be examined and tried first whether they be fit and meet to be received into church society or not. . . .

2. The things which are requisite to be found in all church members are repentance from sin, and faith in Jesus Christ; and therefore these are the things whereof men are to be examined at their admission into the church, and which then they must profess and hold forth in such sort as may satisfy "rational charity" that the things are there indeed. . . .

3. The weakest measure of faith is to be accepted in those that desire to be admitted into the church, because weak Christians, if sincere, have the substance of that faith, repentance and holiness which is required in church members; and such have most need of the ordinances for their confirmation and growth in grace.

*   *   *

5. A personal and public confession and declaring of God's manner of working upon the soul is both lawful, expedient and useful, in sundry respects and upon sundry grounds.

*   *   *

7. The like trial is to be required from such members of the church as were born in the same, or received their membership, or were baptized in their infancy or minority by virtue of the covenant of their parents, when being grown up unto years of discretion, they shall desire to be made partakers of the Lord's Supper; unto which, because holy things must not be given unto the unworthy . . .

*   *   *

Of Church members . . .

*   *   *

5. To separate from a church, either out of contempt of their holy fellowship, or out of covetousness, or for greater enlargements, with just grief to the church, or out of schism, or want of love; and out of a spirit of contention in respect of some unkindness, or some evil only conceived or intended in the church, which might and should be tolerated and healed with a spirit of meekness, and of which evil the church is not yet convinced (though perhaps himself be) nor admonished; for these or the like reasons, to withdraw from public communion in word or seals, or censures, is unlawful and sinful. . . .

*   *   *

Of the communion of churches one with another.

1. Although churches be distinct, and therefore may not be confounded one with another, and equal, and therefore have not dominion one over another; yet all the churches ought to preserve church communion one with another, because they are

all united unto Christ, not only as a mystical, but as a political head; whence is derived a communion suitable thereunto.

2. The communion of churches is exercised sundry ways.

    I. By way of mutual care in taking thought for one another's welfare.

    II. By way of consultation one with another, when we have occasion to require the judgment and counsel of other churches, touching any person or cause, wherewith they may be better acquainted than ourselves. . . . If a church be rent with divisions among themselves, or lie under any open scandal, and yet refuse to consult with other churches for healing or removing of the same, it is matter of just offense, both to the Lord Jesus and to other churches, as betraying too much want of mercy and faithfulness, not to seek to bind up the breaches and wounds of the church and brethren; and therefore the state of such a church calls aloud upon other churches to exercise a fuller act of brotherly communion, to wit, by way of admonition.

    III. A third way, then, of communion of churches is by way of admonition. . . .

    IV. A fourth way of communion with churches is by way of participation; the members of one church occasionally coming unto another. . . .

* * *

    VI. A sixth way of church communion is in case of need to minister relief and succor one unto another, either of able members to furnish them with officers, or of outward support to the necessities of poorer churches. . . .

3. When a company of believers purpose to gather into church fellowship, it is requisite for their safer proceeding and the maintaining of the communion of churches that they signify their intent unto the neighbor churches, walking according to the order of the gospel, and desire their presence and help, and right hand of fellowship; which they ought readily to give unto them, when there is no just cause of excepting against their proceedings.

4. Besides these several ways of communion, there is also a way of propagation of churches; when a church shall grow too numerous, it is a way, and fit season to propagate one church out of another, by sending forth such of their members as are willing to remove, and to procure some officers to them, as may enter with them into church estate among themselves. . . .

Of Synods.

1. Synods, orderly assembled, and rightly proceeding according to the pattern, Acts. 15., we acknowledge as the ordinance of Christ . . . necessary to the well being of churches, for the establishment of truth and peace therein.

2. Synods, being spiritual and ecclesiastical assemblies, are therefore made up of spiritual and ecclesiastical causes. The next efficient cause of them, under Christ, is

the power of the churches sending forth their elders and other messengers, who being met together in the name of Christ, are the matter of the Synod; and they in arguing, debating and determining matters of religion, according to the Word, and publishing the same to the churches it concerns, do put forth the proper and formal acts of a Synod; to the conviction of errors, and heresies, and the establishment of truth and peace in the churches, which is the end of a synod.

*   *   *

6. Because it is difficult, if not impossible, for many churches to come altogether in one place, in all their members universally; therefore they may assemble by their delegates or messengers, as the church of Antioch went not all to Jerusalem, but some select men for that purpose. . . . Synods are to consist both of elders and other church members, endued with gifts, and sent by the churches, not excluding the presence of any brethren in the churches.

Of the Civil Magistrate's power in matters Ecclesiastical.

*   *   *

2. Church government stands in no opposition to civil government of commonwealths, nor any way entrenches upon the authority of civil magistrates in their jurisdictions; nor any whit weakens their hands in governing, but rather strengthens them, and furthers the people in yielding more hearty and conscionable obedience unto them. . . .
3. The power and authority of magistrates is not for the restraining of churches or any other good works, but for helping in and furthering thereof. . . .

*   *   *

5. As it is unlawful for church officers to meddle with the sword of the magistrate, so it is unlawful for the magistrate to meddle with the work proper to church officers.

*   *   *

8. Idolatry, blasphemy, heresy, venting corrupt and pernicious opinions that destroy the foundation, open contempt of the Word preached, profanation of the Lord's Day, disturbing the peaceable administration and exercise of the worship and holy things of God, and the like, are to be restrained and punished by civil authority.
9. If any church, one or more, shall grow schismatical, rending itself from the communion of other churches, or shall walk incorrigibly and obstinately in any corrupt way of their own, contrary to the rule of the Word; in such case, the magistrate is to put forth his coercive power, as the matter shall require.

SOURCE: *A platform of church discipline gathered out of the Word of God* (Cambridge, MA, 1649), 1, 3–20, 23–29. Some punctuation modernized.

"The Mystery of God, Concerning the whole Creation, Mankind"

1648

Gerrard Winstanley (1609–1676) is best known as the leading figure in the Diggers, a radical movement of the English Civil War whose members repudiated private property and protested the enclosure of the commons by farming on recently privatized land in Walton-on-Thames and Cobham, England, in 1649 and 1650. During the difficult winter of 1648–1649, Winstanley experienced a trance in which he heard the words "Work together; Eat bread together; declare this all abroad" and began publishing pamphlets espousing economic and social equality. In the months before that experience, he had written on a number of heterodox religious topics, among them universal salvation. This text, one of the first explicit endorsements of universal salvation in the English language, echoes Origen in its argument that God cannot be permanently alienated from God's creation. But Winstanley differs from Origen in his claim that the "Serpent" is not truly God's creation and thus will not be saved—a position that would later be expressed by John Murray and Judith Sargent Murray. Further Reading: "Biographical Introduction" to The Complete Works of Gerrard Winstanley, *ed. Thomas N. Corns, Ann Hughes, and David Loewenstein, vol. 1. (Oxford: Oxford University Press, 2009), p. 1–81.*

—Dan McKanan

Dear Country men, when some of you see my name subscribed to this ensuing Discourse, you may wonder at it, and it may be despise me in your heart, . . . but know that God's works are not like men's, he doth not always take the wise, the learned, the rich of the world to manifest himself in, . . . but he chooseth the despised, the unlearned, the poor, the nothings of the world, and fills them with the good things of himself, when as he sends the other empty away. I have writ nothing but what was given me of my Father, and at the first beholding of this mystery, it appeared to be so high above my reach that I was confounded and lost in my spirit. . . . And this I speak in experience, that many truths of God, wherein I now see beauty, my heart at the first hearing rose against them, and could not bear them; and therefore, if what I have writ meet with such hard entertainment in any of your hearts, it is no wonder. . . . Therefore, as you desire that God would manifest love to you, and make you free, be not offended to hear, that God, who is love it self, hath a season to manifest his love to others that are lost, and quicken them that were killed, while you were made alive, and that fell further under death, when you that were lost are redeemed an hour or two before them.

* * *

And after God had made *Adam*, he put him into a Garden, called *Eden*. . . .

Yet thereby God declares that *Adam* himself, or that living flesh, Mankind, is a Garden which God hath made for his own delight, to dwell and walk in, wherein he had planted variety of Herbs, and pleasant Plants, as love, joy, peace, humility, knowledge, obedience, delight, and purity of life.

But all these being created qualities, and a being distinct from the being of God; God knew and saw, that there would spring up as a weed, and the first fruits of it likewise, an inclinable principle, or spirit of self-love aspiring up in the midst of this Created, living Garden, and in the midst of every plant therein, which is indeed, an aspiring to be as God.

* * *

God is pleased to lead us to see a little into these two mysteries: First, the mystery of iniquity, or work of the serpent, which was the aspiring fruit of pride, and self-love, that sprung up in the created being, to be as God, and so to be an absolute being of himself . . . and if that spirit of self-love could not be destroyed . . . God would suffer much dishonor. . . .

Then secondly, God leads us to the mystery of himself, and makes us able to see into the knowledge of that great work that he is in working: and that is, to destroy this Serpent out of flesh, and all beings, that is enmity against him, and to swallow up his creature man into himself, that so there may be but one only pure, endless, and infinite Being, even God himself all in all, dwelling and walking in this Garden Mankind, in which he will plant pleasant fruit trees, and pluck up all weeds.

* * *

Since God revealed his son in me, he lets me see, that those things wherein I did take pleasure, were my death, my shame, and the very power of darkness, wherein I was held, as in a prison; . . . and the more I used means to beat him down, as I thought, the more did this power of darkness appear in me. . . .

And so I continued till God was pleased to pull me out of selfish striving, and selfish actings, and made all means lie dead before me. . . . And so made me to lie down at his feet, & to wait upon him, & to acknowledge, that unless God did swallow me up into his own being, I should never be delivered. . . .

And likewise God causes me to see, with much joy, and peace of heart, into this mystery of himself, that his eternal counsel, which was grounded upon the law of love, himself, was not to destroy me, nor any of his own creation; but only the Serpent, which is my work, or the first fruit that sprung up out of the creation; which is our bondage, and that he himself will become my self, and liberty, and the life and liberty of his whole creation. And in these two things he hath caused me greatly to rejoice.

First, I see and feel that God hath set me free from the dominion and over-ruling power of that body of sin. It reigns not as a King, though sometimes it appears creeping in like a slave, that is easily whipped out of doors by strength of God.

Secondly, I rejoice in perfect hope and assurance in God, that although this serpent, or murderer do begin, by reason of any temptation, or outward troubles, to arise, . . . [he] shall never rise to rule and enslave me as formerly, for God thereby takes the occasion to call me up higher into himself, and so makes me to see and possess freedom. . . .

And as God is pleased thus to deal with me, or with any branch of *Adam*, in the same kind; so he hath caused me to see, and to rejoice in the sight, that he will not lose any of his work, but he will redeem his own whole Creation to himself, and dwell and rule in it himself, and subdue the Serpent under his feet, and take up all his creation, Mankind, into himself, and will become the only, endless, pure, abso-lute, and infinite being. . . . But this mystery of God is not to be done all at once, but in several dispensations, some whereof are past, some are in being, and some are yet to come; but when the mystery of God is absolutely finished, or, as the Scriptures say, The Son hath delivered up the Kingdom to the Father, this will be the upshot or conclusion, that God's work shall be redeemed, and live in God, and God in it; but the creature's work without God, shall be lost and perish. Man, *Adam*, or whole Creation of mankind, which is God's work, shall be delivered from Corruption, Bondage, Death, and Pain, and the serpent that caused the fall shall only perish, and be cast into the lake; and God will be the same in the latter end, accomplishing what in the beginning he promised, that is, to bruise the serpent's head, and subdue him under the feet of his Son, the Human Nature, wherein he will walk, as a Garden of pleasure, and dwell himself for ever.

SOURCE: Gerrard Winstanley, *The Mysterie of God, Concerning the whole Creation, Man-kinde* (London, 1648), A1–A4, 2, 7–8, 12–16. Spelling and punctuation modernized.

JOHN LOCKE

A Letter Concerning Toleration
1689

John Locke (1632–1704) was an English philosopher, a leading Enlighten-
ment thinker credited with developing the first outlines of modern, liberal
social and political theory. His Letter Concerning Toleration *emerged out of*
his conviction that the religious violence common to Europe since the Refor-
mation could only be alleviated by allowing for difference rather than by
attempts to legally homogenize faith. While Locke's commitment to scientific
reason marks him as obviously modern and secular, some scholars have begun
to investigate the degree to which he was also influenced by radical Reforma-
tion thinking. He was certainly well acquainted with anti-Trinitarian argu-
ments, not only in the British literature but from the churches in Poland
and Transylvania as well. While some have tried to claim him as an early
unitarian, Locke remained within the Church of England his entire life. His
Letter Concerning Toleration *served as the philosophical background for*
Parliament's Act of Toleration issued in the same year. The Act of Toleration,
after Locke's recommendations, extended freedom of worship to Protestants
dissenting from the Church of England, but not to Catholics, atheists, or anti-
Trinitarians. Further Reading: John Marshall, John Locke: Tolerance and
Early Enlightenment Culture *(Cambridge: Cambridge University Press,*
2010); Joseph Loconte, God, Locke, and Liberty: The Struggle for Religious
Freedom in the West *(Lanham, MD: Lexington Books, 2014).*

—Susan Ritchie

Honored Sir,

Since you are pleased to inquire what are my thoughts about the mutual toleration of Christians in their different professions of religion, I must needs answer you
freely, that I esteem that toleration to be the chief characteristical mark of the true
Church. For whatsoever some people boast of the antiquity of places and names, or
of the pomp of their outward worship; others, of the reformation of their discipline;
all, of the orthodoxy of their faith (for every one is orthodox to himself); these things,
and all others of this nature, are much rather marks of men striving for power and
empire over one another than of the Church of Christ. Let any one have never
so true a claim to all these things, yet if he be destitute of charity, meekness, and
good-will in general towards all mankind, even to those that are not Christians, he

is certainly yet short of being a true Christian himself. "The kings of the Gentiles exercises lordship over them," said our Savior to disciples, "but ye shall not be so" (Luke 22: 25). The business of true religion is quite another thing. It is not instituted in order to the erecting of an external pomp, nor to the obtaining of ecclesiastical dominion, nor to the exercising of compulsive force; but to the regulating of men's lives according to the rules of virtue and piety.

*   *   *

I esteem it above all things necessary to distinguish exactly the business of civil government from that of religion, and to settle the just bounds that lie between the one and the other.

*   *   *

First, because the care of souls is not committed to the civil magistrate, any more than to other men. It is not committed unto him, I say, by God; because it appears not that God has ever given any such authority to one man over another, as to compel any one to his religion. Nor can any such power be vested in the magistrate by the *consent of the people*, because no man can so far abandon the care of his own salvation, as blindly to leave it to the choice of any other. . . .

In the second place, the care of souls cannot belong to the civil magistrate, because his power consists only in outward force; but true and saving religion consists in the inward persuasion of the mind, without which nothing can be acceptable to God. And such is the nature of the understanding, that it cannot be compelled to the belief of any thing by outward force. Confiscation of estate, imprisonment, torments, nothing of that nature can have any such efficacy as to make men change the inward judgment that they have framed of things.

*   *   *

But after all, the *principal consideration*, and which absolutely determines this controversy, is this. Although the magistrate's opinion in religion be sound, and the way that he appoints be truly evangelical, yet if I be not thoroughly persuaded thereof in my own mind, there will be no safety for me in following it. No way whatsoever that I shall walk in, against the dictates of my conscience, will ever bring me to the mansions of the blessed.

*   *   *

It is not the diversity of opinions (which cannot be avoided), but the refusal of toleration to those that are of different opinions (which might have been granted), that has produced all the bustles and wars, that have been in the Christian world, upon account of religion. The heads and leaders of the Church, moved by avarice and insatiable desire for dominion, making use of the immoderate ambition of magistrates and the credulous superstition of the giddy multitude, have incensed and animated them against those that dissent from themselves, by preaching unto them, contrary to the laws of the Gospel and to the precepts of charity, that schismatics and heretics are to be outed of their possessions, and destroyed. And thus have they mixed together and confounded two things that are in themselves most different, the Church and the Commonwealth.

SOURCE: John Locke, *A Letter Concerning Toleration: Humbly Submitted* (London, 1689), 1–2, 6–8, 26, 55. Some spelling and punctuation modernized.

The Enochian Walks with God
and A Fountain of Gardens
1694, 1696

Jane Leade (1624–1704) lived in England. In her forties, she joined a group of pious, mystical Christians organized by John Pordage, an Anglican priest who was attracted to the ideas of Jakob Böhme. After Pordage's death, Leade led the Philadelphian Society for twenty years. Her mystical visions and writings became central to the group's teachings and spiritual goals. Her visions of a lush, abundant, sensuous paradise recalled Eden and foretold of a New Earth to come. Led and guided by the generative and loving spirit of Jesus, whom Leade believed to contain the Divine Wisdom Sophia within him, the Philadelphians were steadfast in their spiritual practice and witness to the universal love of God's kingdom. Leade proclaimed universal restoration, after a period of accountability for sins, for people of all faiths and non-believers. Her legacy lived on through the German Pietists and Emanuel Swedenborg, who read her works in Dutch. Further Reading: Julie Hirst, Jane Leade: Biography of a Seventeenth-Century Mystic *(Burlington, VT: Ashgate, 2005).*

—Sheri Prud'homme

From *The Enochian Walks with God* (1694):

As my mind was environed with a Divine Light which opened the great design of God's Love in the Redemption of the fallen lapsed State of all Mankind: That Scripture being set before me in *Corinth.* 15.43., *Rom.* 5.12. to the end. *The first Man was made a Living Soul; the second from the Lord from Heaven, was made a Quickening Spirit.* And so as from hence it was shown to me, that the first created Image, and Form was never intended for an Abiding-State; if admit he had continued as he was first created, God from before the Foundation of the World purposed far higher, and more excelling glory; for as much as a Spirit transcend in its Quality and Essence more than That which is of a Soul in its consistency. Christ the Lord being one Eternal Spirit, in and by Which we are raised out of the Fall, and quickened into Spirit, whereby we come to partake of an United Purity, Wisdom, Power, and Glory with him.

But here it may be said, this now is not evident, or come forth to all the whole World, which seemeth yet to lie in an Apostatized State. *Io.* 2.2.

It must be so, for a time, and time, and half time, and then the finishing of the Transgression and Sin will be: *For then will Christ the eternal Root of Righteousness,* in all, and over all, spring: So, as an Universal Restoration to all fallen Angels and Spirits, in Bodies, and out, will by Christ the quickening Spirit be set free. *Eph.* 1. to 10.

But of This Jubilee, an allowance of time will be for the working out this more general Salvation, for many are the degrees of purifying, which all Souls must pass through, and such as do neglect their Day, during the time of this Life, as to the New-Birth, and Regeneration; there is a Law of Necessity for them to go through it, after the time of this Life, in Centers and Regions, which are provided in other Worlds, which are to be passed through.

But herefrom ariseth an Objection, that if it be so that the Grace of God be of this Latitude as to save All, Universally, it may open a door for giving a presumptuous Liberty to some. . . .

Now as to This, let all know, that it is a Punishment and Hell enough to see their Fellow-Creatures entered into Rest and Joy; and they in Labour and Work, having all to do, that tends to a Renovation; and how long they may be in Punishment, It will be according as the Wickedness of their living Here have been, in all manner of Evil, and Sin, Numerous years may spend away. All which time, they live excluded from the Lord's Presence of Joy: All which may be Argument and Motive unto all to improve their Mortal day . . . while abiding in this very World, which is a forerunner, and sure Pledge of what, after the Dissolution of the Body, shall be entered upon.

From *A Fountain of Gardens* (1696):

Now give me leave to tell you the Beginning of my Way that the Spirit first led me into. In the first place then, after some Years that I had lived in some good Degree of an Illuminated Knowledge, setting under the Visible Teachings of Men, that could give no further Light than that they had arrived from others, through all of which I traced as a wandering Spirit that could find no Rest: but something still I found within my self that did open to draw in from a more pure Air, than I could meet without me: Whereupon I introverted more into my own Inward Deep, where I did meet with that which I could not find elsewhere. . . . For I myself found all other Grounds and Pastures dry and barren, as a parched Desert, until I came to this Fruitful *Lebanon*, where all Variety of sweet scented Flowers, did as another *Eden* flourish pleasantly. Which were known and enjoyed by giving up to the Teaching of the Holy Unction, which as the Waters of the Sanctuary, will never cease springing, till they become an Overwhelming River, which is the true Baptizing Water of Life. This you will find to be true, as you seriously apply your self to this Way and Method of God's Immediate Teaching: Which then you shall find to open in the Center of your own Soul.

SOURCE: Jane Leade, *The Enochian Walks with God* (London, 1694), 21–22. Jane Leade, *A Fountain of Gardens*, vol. 1 (London, 1696), 6–7. Some spelling and punctuation modernized.

CHARLES CHAUNCY

Seasonable Thoughts on the State of Religion in New-England

1743

Charles Chauncy (1705–1787) was the most outspoken opponent of the revival methods of the Great Awakening and helped precipitate the formation of a coalition of rational clergy within the Standing Order of Massachusetts. Chauncy was the son of a merchant who died when Charles was only six. After he received a B.A. and M.A. from Harvard, the position of assistant minister at Boston's First Church became available, and Chauncy was called there in 1727. He stayed for sixty years, using the position to achieve prominence among his colleagues. Under his watch, the congregation adopted liberal tendencies, including accepting the Half-Way Covenant to allow children's baptisms for all and rejecting confessions of faith as a requirement for church membership. But Chauncy was more concerned with challenges to congregational order than with theological hair-splitting. This was evident as he became embroiled in the controversies of the Great Awakening. In this, his most famous work, Chauncy objected to how revivalist methods disturbed the peace and order of the established churches. He also worried about itinerants moving from town to town, threatening both the institutional stability of the churches and the established system of settled ministers. For Chauncy, each individual gradually grew into a state of grace rather than experiencing an immediate, ecstatic conversion. In 1758, he publicly rejected original sin and began to formulate his ideas on universal salvation. He was reluctant to go public with such radical beliefs, and his thoughts were later published anonymously in The Mystery Hid from Ages and Generations *(1784). Further Reading: Edward M. Griffin,* Old Brick: Charles Chauncy of Boston, 1705–1787 *(Minneapolis: University of Minnesota Press, 1980); Charles H. Lippy,* Seasonable Revolutionary: The Mind of Charles Chauncy *(Chicago: Nelson-Hall, 1981).*

—Mark W. Harris

PART I. Particularly pointing out the Things of a *bad* and *dangerous Tendency*, in the late *religious Appearance* in NEW-ENGLAND

There is not a Man, in the Country, in the sober exercise of his Understanding, but will acknowledge, that the late religious *Stir* has been attended with many

59

Irregularities and *Disorders*. These, some are pleased to call, *Imprudencies, human Frailties, accidental Effects* only, such as might be expected, considering the Remains of Corruption in good Men, even among those in whom a *remarkable Work of Grace* is carrying on: Others are in the Opinion, they make a *main Part* of the *Appearance* that has been so much talk'd of, and have arisen unavoidably, in the natural Course of Things, from the *Means* and *Instruments* of this *Appearance*; and that it could not reasonably be suppos'd, it should have been otherwise.

I shall particularly show what these *bad* and *dangerous* Things are; making such Remarks (as I go along) as may be thought needful to set Matters in a just and true Light.

Among the *bad* Things attending *this Work*,

I shall *first* mention *Itinerant Preaching*. This had its *Rise* (at least in these Parts) from Mr. WHITEFIELD; though I could never see, I own, upon what Warrant, either from *Scripture* or *Reason*, he went about Preaching from one *Province* and *Parish* to another, where the Gospel was already preach'd, and by Persons as well qualified for the Work as he can pretend to be. I charitably hope, his Design herein was good: But might it not be leavened with some undesirable Mixture? Might he not, at first, take up this Practice from a mistaken Thought of some *extraordinary Mission* from GOD? Or, from the undue Influence of *too high an Opinion* of his own *Gifts* and *Graces*? And when he had got into this Way, might he not be too much encouraged to go on in it, from the *popular Applauses*, everywhere, so liberally heaped on him? If he had not been under too strong a Bias from something or other of this Nature, why so fond of preaching always himself, to the Exclusion, not of his *Brethren* only, but his *Fathers*, in *Grace* and *Gifts* and *Learning*, as well as *Age*? And why-so ostentatious and assuming as to alarm so many Towns, by proclaiming his Intentions, in the *publick Prints*, to preach such a Day in such a *Parish*, the next Day in such a one, and so on, as he passed through the Country and all this, without the Knowledge, either of *Pastors* or *People* in most Places? What others may think of such a Conduct I know not; but to me, it never appeared the most indubitable Expression of that Modesty, Humility, and preferring others in Love, which the *Scriptures* highly recommend as what will adorn the *Minister's*, as well as the Christian's Character.

✻　✻　✻

And if, in the *first Days* of Christianity, when the State of Things was such as to require the *travelling* of the *Apostles* and *others* from Place to Place, to preach the Gospel; I say, if, in these Times, even an *Apostle* thought it *disorderly* to go out of his *own Line*, and enter upon *other Men's Labours*, 'tis much more so in the *present settled State of the Church*. The Pastor has now his *special* Charge. He is devoted to the Service of the LORD JESUS CHRIST, in a *particular* Place, and over a *particular* People. His Work, as a Minister, does not lie at large; but is restrain'd within certain Boundaries. I don't mean, that he mayn't use his Office, in other Places, within the

60

Rules of Order, upon *special* Occasions, and where there may be a just Call: But his stated, constant Business is with his *own People*. These have been committed to his Care; these, he has solemnly engaged, before GOD, and the LORD JESUS CHRIST, and *holy Angels*, to do all the Duties of a *Pastor* to. And can he be faithful to his *Ordination Vow*, or the Command of GOD, which says, *Feed the Flock over which the HOLY GHOST hath made thee an Overseer* (Acts 20. 28.), while he leaves his People one Week and Month after another, bestowing his Labours upon those, he has no *particular* Relation to? Are not the Souls of his *own* People as precious as the Souls of others? Han't he Work enough, among his own people that he need seek for it elsewhere? That Man knows little of the Work of a Minister, that does not know how to employ all his Time, & Strength, and Thought, for the Good of those of his own Charge. He may here spend all his Zeal, and be as abundant in Labours, *in Season and out of Season*, as he judges proper. And I should think, *extraordinary* Pains are as suitable among a Minister's *own* People, as *Strangers*; and would be as evidential of his Love to Souls, and Desire of their Salvation.

* * *

And what is the Language of this going into *other Men's Parishes*? Is it not obviously this? The *Settled Pastors* are Men, not qualified for their Office, or not *faithful* in the Execution of it; They are either *unfit* to take the Care of Souls, or *grossly negligent* in doing their Duty to them: Or, the Language may be, we are Men of *greater Gifts, Superior Holiness, more Acceptableness to GOD*; or have been in an *extraordinary* Manner sent by him. *Some* of these *Itinerants*, 'tis evident, have travelled about the Country preaching, under the full Persuasion of an *immediate* Call from GOD: And as to *most* of them, it may be feared, the *grand Excitement*, at the Bottom, has been, an *overfond* Opinion of themselves, and an *unchristian* on of their Brethren. It has therefore been their Practice, too commonly, not only to *boast of their own Superior Goodness*, wherever they have gone; but to insinuate suspicions against the *fixed Pastors*, if not to preach against them, and pray for them, as *poor, carnal, unconverted* Men: Nay, mere *Candidates* for the ministry; yea, *illiterate Exhorters, raw, weak, young* Men, or *Lads*, have too frequently taken upon them, openly to judge and censure their *Ministers*; as I shall have Occasion, afterwards, to show at large.

Moreover, what is the Tendency of this Practice, but Confusion and Disorder? If one Pastor may neglect his *own* People to take Care of *others*, who are already taken Care of; and, it may be much better than he can take care of them: I say, if one Pastor may do thus, why not another, and another still, and so on, 'till there is no such Thing as *Church Order* in the Land? One Minister hast he same Right to enter into *other Men's Parishes* as another, and may vindicate his Conduct upon the same Principles: And if this should become the general Practice, what might be expected, as the Effect, but an entire Dissolution of our *Church State*? This *Itinerant*

61

Preaching, it is my firm Persuasion, naturally tends to it in the course of Things; yea, and the Principles, upon which it is supported will disband all the Churches in the World, and make the *Relation* between *Pastors* and *People* a *mere Nothing,* a *Sound without Meaning.*

*   *   *

The *next* Thing I shall take Notice of, as what I can't but think of dangerous Tendency, is *that Terror* so many have been the Subjects of; Expressing itself in *Strange Effects* upon the *Body,* such as *swooning away* and *falling to the Ground,* where Persons have lain, for a Time, speechless and motionless; bitter *Shriekings* and *Screamings; Convulsion-like Tremblings* and *Agitations, Strugglings* and *Tumblings,* which in some Instances have been attended with Indecencies I shan't mention: None of which Effects seem to have been *accidental,* nor yet peculiar to some *particular Places* or *Constitutions;* but have been common all over the Land. There are few Places where there has been any considerable religious Stir, but it has been accompanied, more or less, with these Appearances. Numbers in Congregation, 10, 20, 30, would be in this Condition at a Time; Nay, hundreds in some Places, to the opening such a *horrible Scene* as can scarce be described in Words.

*   *   *

Another Thing that very much lessens my Opinion of these *religious Fears,* with the *strange Effects* of them is, that they are produced by the *Exhorters;* and this, in all Parts of the Land; and it may be, in more numerous Instances, than by the *Ministers* themselves. And if these *bodily Agitations* arise from the Influence of the SPIRIT, when produc'd by the *Ministers,* they are so when produced by the *Exhorters.* The Appearance is the same in both Cases; the like *inward Distress* is effected, and discovers it self in like *Cryings* and *Swoonings:* Nor is there any Reason to think well, in the general, of the one, and not of the other. And yet, some of the best Friends of *this Work,* both among the *Clergy* and *Laity,* think ill of these Things, as brought forward by the *Exhorters:* Nay, one of the greatest Friends to the *good Work,* among the Ministers in Town, freely declar'd concerning one of these *Exhorters,* who came into this Place, and began the *Outcries* we were before Strangers to, that he feared the Hand of Satan was in his coming here to throw Disgrace on the Work of GOD. . . .

*   *   *

The next Thing to be considered, as what I can't but look upon to be of *dangerous* Tendency is that *sudden Light and Joy* so many of late claim to be the Subjects of. Not that I question whether there is such a Thing as *religious Joy.* The *Bible* often speaks of *rejoicing in GOD,* and in *Hope of the Glory to be hereafter revealed.* The *Kingdom of GOD* is said to consist in *Joy,* as well as Peace and Righteousness; And Joy is reckon'd among the *Fruits* of the SPIRIT: And this Joy is said to be *unspeakable, and full of Glory;* yea, 'tis called the *Peace of God which passeth all Understanding.*

62

But then, there is a *false*, as well as *true* Joy; the Joy of the *Hypocrite*, as well as of the *real Christian*; a Joy that has its Rise in *animal Nature*, as well as from the HOLY GHOST. And though I would hope, a Number of late have been made Partakers of *true Joy*, the *Joy there is in Believing*; yet, there may be Reason for Fear, lest the Joy that has been so much boasted of, should be no other in the general than the Joy those may experience, who are Christians more in *Appearance* than *Reality*, in *Word* than *Deed*.

* * *

This of *Laughing*, so far as I am acquainted with the History of the Church, is a Method of expressing *religious Joy* peculiar to the present Times: Nor can I think from whence it should take Rise, unless from Mr. WHITEFIELD and TENNENT. The *former of these Gentlemen* was sometimes observed to speak of the Affairs of Salvation, with a *Smile in his Countenance*; but 'tis generally known of the *latter*, that he could scarce hear of the Person's being under the slightest Conviction, but he would *laugh*. And if told of any that were in *great Spiritual Distress*, he would fall into a *broad Laugh*. This always appear'd shocking to some who were Witnesses of it, as I have often heard them say: But as it was the Gentleman's Practice, he might be imitated by others in this Imperfection, and from them by others still, and so the Humour be propagated 'till it became general. I can't, for myself, give an Account of the Rise of this Practice from any other Cause. But from whatever Cause it sprang, 'tis certainly one of the most incongruous Ways of *expressing religious Joy*. It favours of too much Levity, as it has to do with Matters of infinite and eternal Moment. It discovers the Want of a due Reverence towards the *divine Majesty*; and seems inconsistent with that *holy Fear* and *Caution*, which must be thought reasonable, where the Salvation of the Soul is the Thing it is conversant about.

Nor is this all, but these *Raptures* and *Ectasies* have, in too many Instances, come to *Visions*, and *Trances*, and *Revelations*. There are few Places, where this Joy, in all its Height, has prevailed, but it has ended, in a greater or less Number of Persons, in these Things. I could fill many Pages with the Accounts I have had of the *Trances* Persons have been in, from different Parts of the Country.

* * *

The next Thing that is amiss, and very much so, in these Times, is that *Spirit of rash, censorious*, and *uncharitable Judging*, which has been so prevalent in the Land. This appear'd first of all, in Mr. W——D, who seldom preach'd, but he had something or other, in his Sermon, against *unconverted Ministers*: And what he delivered; especially, at some certain Times, had an evident Tendency to fill the Minds of People with *evil Surmisings* against the *Ministers*, as tho' they were, for the most Part, *carnal, unregenerate* Wretches. He often spake of them, in the Lump, as *Pharisees, Enemies of CHRIST JESUS*, and the *worst Enemies* he had: And in Truth, the *Spirit* of his Preaching, upon this Head, was unhappily calculated to leaven the

63

Minds of People with Prejudices against the *standing Ministers*; alienating their Hearts from them, and by this Means, in the most effectual Manner, obstructing their Usefulness. And as though he had not done enough, in *Preaching*, to beget in People an ill Opinion of the *Ministers*, he expresses his *Fear*, in his *Journal* of NEW-ENGLAND, lest "*many, nay, the most that "preach do not experimentally know* CHRIST." This Reflection he immediately levels against the *Ministers*, in *this* Land: And it's the more rash and uncharitable, as he past through the Country in *Post-Haste*, having neither Opportunity nor Advantage, to know the real Character of one tenth Part of the Ministers he thus freely condemns. I don't think this *Gentleman* had it in his *Intention*, by his thus *preaching and writing*, to do an Injury to the Interest of Religion in these Churches; but if this had really been his Design, what more effectual Method could he have taken, than to represent the *Body of the Clergy* as *out of CHRIST*. i.e. *carnal* and *uncontroverted*? And if so, as unfit according to his other Doctrine, to be the Instruments of converting *Spiritually* dead Souls, as a *naturally* dead Man is to beget living Children. What is the Tendency of such a Conduct at this but to set People against their Ministers as not fit to preach to them, and in this Way, to sow among them the Seeds of Contention and Separation?

SOURCE: Charles Chauncy, *Seasonable Thoughts on the State of Religion in New-England* (Boston, 1743), 35–57, 47–48, 50–51, 76–77, 101–102, 119–20, 126–27, 140–41. Spelling and punctuation modernized.

"Men, Endowed with Faculties Proper for Discerning the Difference betwixt Truth and Falsehood"

1748

Jonathan Mayhew (1720–1766) was born on the island of Martha's Vineyard, Massachusetts, where his father, Experience Mayhew, carried on a family tradition of missionizing the Native Americans. His mother, Remember Bourne, was Experience's second wife, and Jonathan was their fifth child and the last to survive. Jonathan had little formal schooling when he entered Harvard College at the age of 19. His theology was in flux at the time of the Great Awakening, but as he read of the excesses of emotional response, he began to distrust the revival techniques that had become popular. Mayhew was called to be minister at the West Church in Boston in 1747, although his ordination had to be postponed after most of the Boston churches boycotted the council meeting, fearing that the radical new minister would destroy their fragile ecclesiastical peace. Once ordained, Mayhew became a leader of the Arminian faction in Puritan Massachusetts along with Ebenezer Gay and Charles Chauncy. Mayhew argued that all people can use reason to discern religious truth. The present document is part of a series of seven sermons delivered in 1748, in which Mayhew asserts that creeds are "imperious and tyrannical: and contrary to the spirit and doctrines of the gospel. They are an infringement upon those rights of conscience, which ought to be sacred." Mayhew refused to submit to any yoke of bondage and urged his congregants to exercise private judgment in religion. Caught up in controversies throughout his ministerial career, he protested the right of the governor of Massachusetts to issue charters, vigorously opposed the Church of England, and delivered election sermons in 1750 and 1754 espousing liberty and resistance to tyranny. Further Reading: Charles W. Akers, Called unto Liberty: A Life of Jonathan Mayhew, 1720–1766 *(Cambridge, MA: Harvard University Press, 1964);* John Corrigan, The Hidden Balance: Religion and the Social Theories of Charles Chauncy and Jonathan Mayhew *(Cambridge: Cambridge University Press, 2006).*

—Mark W. Harris

"And he said also to the people, When ye see a cloud rise out of the west, straightway ye say, There cometh a shower; and so it is. And when ye see the south-wind blow, ye say, There will be heat; and it cometh to pass. Ye hypocrites, ye can discern the face of the sky, and of the earth: but how is it, that ye do not discern this time? Yea, and why even of yourselves judge ye not what is right?"

—LUKE 12:54–57.

The *second* thing proposed, was to show,

II. That as there is a natural difference betwixt truth and falsehood, right and wrong; so men are naturally endowed with faculties proper for the discerning of these differences.

This is evidently implied in my text—"How is it that ye do not discern this time? Yea, and why even of yourselves judge ye not what is right?"

It must be acknowledged that the *Pyrrhonists*, who demand great encomiums for teaching men (not to *know* anything, but) to *doubt* of everything, have not generally carried their *Scepticism* any farther than to deny all certainty in a *relative* sense, or with *respect to us*. To the most of them it appears too gross to affirm that there is no difference in things themselves; and so no such thing as truth and right absolutely, in opposition to error and wrong conduct. What they principally insist upon is, that all things are totally incomprehensible by us; that there is no *criterion* of truth and right; by which they may be distinguished from error and wrong action: so that although there be, in nature, a difference between them, yet *we* have no faculties for discovering it. . . .

Such is the dark and unhappy condition in which the *sceptical* doctrine supposes mankind: doomed to total ignorance, and wandering from the right path. Or, if in any case, they think and act right, it is by mere *chance*; nor can they have the pleasure of knowing it if they happen to be in the right. But it is to be hoped that the Author of our being has not been so sparing of his favours to us as to leave us at such uncertainties about everything, especially about what concerns our own welfare. However, were this really our case, one would think that those who are sensible it is so, instead of deriding the doctrine of a supernatural revelation (as is the practice of modern *Sceptics*), should accommodate the words of David to their own case and circumstances—"Who will show us any good? Lord, lift thou up the light of thy countenance upon us!" [Psalm 4:6]. The blinder we are naturally, the more need we have of supernatural light and instruction.

The doctrine of our total *incapacity* to distinguish between truth and falsehood, right and wrong, has much the same aspect upon common life, civil society, philosophy and religion, with that of the absolute indifference of all things *in their own nature*, and the like absurdities will follow from it. Thus (for example) it follows that there is no difference at all in men with respect to wisdom and knowledge. For in order to constitute such a difference, it is not only necessary that there should be a natural distinction between truth and falsehood, but also, that some at least should have faculties for discovering it. Knowledge, if there be any such thing, consists in *seeing* or *perceiving* truth. But if no men have a capacity for this, all men must be entirely destitute of knowledge, as destitute of it as if there were in nature no distinction between truth and error. . . .

Upon this supposition, he that denies his own existence, and commits murder, adultery and robbery, has as much to say in his own vindication as he that asserts a circle is not a square, and saves his country from ruin. And from hence it appears that those who carry their *scepticism* no farther than to question the abilities of men to discover truth and right in all cases, are guilty of the same inconsistency with those who explode the whole notion of a real distinction between truth and right, and their contraries. For why will they attempt to investigate truth? Or why will they plume themselves upon their supposed discovery of this notable truth: that men are unable to discover truth? Why will they upbraid their antagonists with ignorance? . . . There are many dogmatists about the world, who allow themselves only to be the proper judges of truth and right, which is arrogant enough. But no bigoted dogmatist is half so absurd and insolent as the Sceptic.

*   *   *

But to come more directly to the point—Some things are in themselves so evidently true that no *criterion* is necessary in order to our knowing them with *certainty*. Thus, for example, that we exist is what we have an immediate and intuitive certainty of. And the same may be said concerning the *reality* of all our own *ideas* and *perceptions*. That we experience pleasure and pain, that we converse with various objects which assist us in a different manner, that colour is one thing, and sound another, and that smelling is not tasting—these things are self-evident and no *medium* can make them plainer. But it will perhaps be said that all this is only fantasy and imagination, there being no archetypes existing *without* us, of which these perceptions are the *images* or *representations*. Be it so: still the perceptions and ideas themselves are *real*—this we are *certain* of, whether there be anything *external* of which they are the antitypes, or not, so that certainty may be had in some respects at least. And this is sufficient to our present purpose, for we are not speaking concerning the *extent*, but the *certainty*, of human knowledge.

Of the truth of other things we may be certain in a different manner, *viz.* by reason, deducing them from other truths of which we have an intuitive knowledge. Thus it is that a thousand mathematical truths are demonstrated, and with a certainty little or nothing inferior to those first principles from which they are deduced, the connection in every step through the whole process being so apparent that to suppose the contrary would be a plain contradiction and amount to the denying a thing to be what it is acknowledged to be. And in the same way many moral and religious truths may be demonstrated also—as the being of a God, his power, wisdom, goodness and providence, and our obligation to obey him.

For the truth of many other things we can, indeed, have no more than *probable* evidence, but which is, in many cases, almost as satisfactory to the mind as *intuitive* and *demonstrative* certainty. Thus who doubts but that the sun will set in a few hours?—that the sea will ebb and flow tomorrow, as usual?—that autumn will succeed to summer, winter to autumn, and spring to winter, as in times past? But of these things there is no certainty. For God has power to put a stop to the usual course of nature, and we cannot be certain that he will not do it the next moment. Thus also probable evidence is all we can have for the truth of facts recorded in ancient history. Men may possibly deceive us. But whoever has been in such a doubting humour as to question whether there have been such men as Alexander the Great and Julius Caesar, whether they fought and triumphed, etc. Indeed we can have no more than probable evidence that food and sleep will refresh us for the future, as heretofore. Our whole institution of life, as it relates to the present world, is grounded upon evidence of this sort, and not upon intuitive or demonstrative certainty. Such evidence is easy to be had and is sufficient to the purposes of life, as daily experience shows us. We may, if we please, perplex ourselves about the nature of *time, place* and *motion*. But men who are no philosophers find the way *home* at *one o'clock* without any difficulty. . . .

Nor is there more room for scepticism in relation to morals and religion than in common life, nor indeed so much with regard to the principal branches of our *duty*. But however it comes to pass, men take more pains to doubt in one case than in the other. We have stronger evidence for the proof of the chief articles of religion than we have for most other things of which we are fully satisfied. The being and perfections of God may be known without much difficulty; and these being known, it is as easy to know how we ought to conduct ourselves towards him in general, as it is for a servant to know how to please a master whose temper and character he is acquainted with. And it is at least as plain that the Sovereign of the world will make a distinction between the righteous and the wicked, as that a wise and good prince will make a distinction between dutiful subjects and rebels.

Thus it appears, in general, that men are able to distinguish between truth and falsehood, right and wrong. But I shall now make several observations upon this proposition, in order to farther explain the real intention of it, to obviate some objections against it, and to guard it against those abuses to which it may appear liable. And

1. It is not intended in this assertion, that all men have *equal abilities* for judging what is true and right. The whole creation is diversified, and men in particular. There is a great variety in their intellectual faculties. That which principally

distinguishes some men from the beasts of the field is the different formation of their bodies. Their bodies are *human*, but they are in a manner *brute* all beside. Whether the difference that there is in the natural powers of men proceeds from the original make of their minds, or from some difference in those bodily organs upon which the *exercise* of the rational faculties may be supposed to depend, it is apparent that there is, in fact, such a difference. And therefore when it is said that men are able to judge what is true and right, it must be understood in such a sense as is consistent with this fact. Those of the lower class can go but a little way with their inquiries into the natural and moral constitution of the world. But even these may have the power of judging in *some degree*. However, upon supposition that some were wholly ignorant of their own existence, it does not follow that all must be so, any more than that all bodies must be round, because some are of that particular figure. . . .

2. As a farther limitation of this assertion, I would observe that it does not imply that *the same persons* are equally adequate judges of truth and right in all conditions and circumstances. There is a great difference in the powers of different men. But no one differs more from another than he does from himself, considered in childhood and mature life, before and after his mind is cultivated by study and exercise. The *man* knows what the *child* was ignorant of. We come into the world ignorant of everything. But he that in his natural, rude and uncultivated state is unqualified to judge what is true and right, unless it be in a few obvious cases, is capable of considerable improvements by study and experience. Our intellectual faculties were given us to improve; they rust for want of use, but are brightened by exercise. Exercise strengthens and invigorates our mental faculties as well as our bodily. And the more a man habituates himself to intellectual employments, the greater will be his aptness and facility in discovering truth, and detecting error. . . .

The alteration which time and study make in the abilities of men for judging concerning truth and right is sufficient to account for the diversity of sentiments entertained by *the same persons* at different periods of their life, without having recourse to *scepticism* or supposing all our notions, from first to last, to be mere fancy and illusion. A man may err once without erring always. Nor can we argue from the reveries of youth, and the absurd conceits of the illiterate, that all mankind are but a mighty nation of fools and lunatics, pleasing themselves with idle dreams and delusive appearances, instead of realities.

3. That men are able "even of themselves to judge what is right" does not imply that they can receive no assistance from books and the conversation of learned men, or that they may judge as well without these helps, as with them. Although all men are capable of discerning truth and right in some degree by the bare exercise of their own natural faculties, it does not follow that they can stand in no need of any foreign aid, in order to their judging in a more perfect manner. The more knowing may be helpful to others in their pursuit of knowledge. And the abilities of men for reasoning

justly, and judging truly, may depend, in a great measure, upon the method of their education, the books they read, and the genius and abilities of the persons they converse with. Who will pretend that the natives of Greenland, or the Cape of Good Hope, enjoy the same, or equal, means of knowledge with those that are born in the polite and learned nations of Europe? Who imagines that one brought up at the plough is as likely to form right notions or things, as if he had been educated at a university? Or that a man who has conversed only with ordinary mechanics has the same advantages with those who have enjoyed the familiarity of the greatest proficients in literature? To suppose these things is to contradict daily experience. . . .

4. It is not implied in this doctrine that men's intellectual powers have *no bounds at all*, or that they are equally able to determine upon *all points*, although they should improve all the helps to knowledge and cultivate their reason in the best manner possible. There are many cases wherein the wisest of men are unable to form any judgment at all—difficulties which they cannot solve—heights which they cannot climb—depths which they cannot fathom. Some may, perhaps, think this a reflection upon human understanding. And indeed it is so, if it be any reflection upon it to say that it is not infinite like that of God, but not otherwise. To say that human reason is confined to a certain sphere, beyond which it cannot penetrate, is, in reality, no more than to assert that man is a finite, and not an infinite, being, a creature and not the Creator. There are probably created intelligences much superior to man even *in his best estate*; but it is no derogation from their real dignity to say they are not omniscient. Why then should man grasp at omniscience? imagine he may know everything because he may know some? and look upon it as a reproach, when it is said that his reason, and all his other faculties are circumscribed?

We may know what is proper to be known by beings of our rank, so as to fill our place and answer the design of our creation, without being able to comprehend all things. We may know that *this earth* is inhabited by creatures, the law of whose nature is virtue, and its end happiness, although we cannot certainly tell whether the *planets* are inhabited, or not, or, if they are, by what kind of beings, and what their condition and circumstances. We may know, in general, what tends to health and felicity in this world, although the real essences of things should be beyond our reach. We may know that whatever *came into existence* (as it is demonstrable that everything did which we behold) must have some *invisible* cause adequate to it, although we were not able to form a clear idea of creative power, or the manner of its exertion. We may know that beauty, order, harmony and design, in the works of nature, presuppose a *designer* or intelligent artificer, although we cannot comprehend the system of the universe. We may know that a constitution of things, actually tending to happiness, must be the product of goodness, although we are not able exactly to define beforehand that system, the correspondent parts of which shall be so adjusted as to effect the greatest possible good. We may know in general that the

Author of the world must be a wise and good being, although the final causes of some things which we see in it are beyond our sight. In fine we may know that "God is, and that he is a rewarder of them that diligently seek him" (Heb. 11:6), although we cannot "by searching find out the Almighty unto perfection" (Job 11:7) or comprehend his nature, or see through the whole scheme of his works, government and providence. . . .

5. When it is said we are able "even of ourselves to judge what is right," this is not designed to suggest that our intellectual faculties are so capacious as to render a *supernatural revelation* of *no use* or *importance* to us. Certainly we cannot suppose this to be the intention of him that uttered the words of our text, since one of the titles which he took upon himself was that of a *Prophet*, or a *Teacher sent from God*. And indeed it necessarily follows from the supposition of our rational faculties being *limited*, that there is *room* for our being instructed by revelation. If one man may instruct another, much more may we suppose it possible for "him that is perfect in knowledge" (Job 37:16) to supply the natural defects of human reason by a supernatural communication of light and knowledge. When, and how far, it is expedient for him to do this, he only knows. However upon supposition of such a revelation, we must be supposed to be able to see the evidence of its being such. It is the proper office of reason to determine whether what is proposed to us under the notion of a revelation from God be attended with suitable attestations and credentials or not. So that even in this case, we may "of ourselves judge what is right." If there be no rational evidence of its coming from God, no rational man can receive it as such. And, on the other hand, if it be accompanied with rational evidence, no reasonable man can reject it. Indeed what Jesus Christ particularly blames the Jews for in the text is their not exercising their reason in this way. He had sufficiently proved his divine mission; but they would not "discern the time, nor judge what was right," being under the influence of prejudice, and not of reason. Moreover, it is the proper office of reason to determine the meaning of the particular parts of a revelation, after the divine authority of it in general is established and allowed. And this men's natural faculties qualify them for, much in the same manner that they qualify them for interpreting other writings. If God gives men a revelation, he gives it to be understood by men. And if he gives it to be understood by men, he must give it in human language and accommodate it to human capacity. For otherwise, a second revelation would be necessary to explain the first. And then, why not a third to explain the second, and so on *in infinitum?* And so nothing would be really *revealed* after all.

I shall just add in the

6th, and *last place*, as a farther limitation of the proposition before us, that it does not intend that we are able to determine, with an *equal degree of certainty*, all points which we are capable, in some sense, of coming to a conclusion about. Although truth does not admit *of degrees*, yet the evidence of truth does, so that of

71

various propositions equally true in themselves, some may be known with greater certainty than others. Probable evidence is indeed all that can be had in most cases, as was observed before. It is by virtue of this that that the intercourse of man with man and all the business and commerce of the world is carried on. Experience shows that such evidence is sufficient in *secular* affairs, and it may be sufficient in *religious* affairs also, in those cases where absolute certainty cannot be had.

I shall now conclude this head concerning the certainty and sufficiency of human knowledge with the words of Mr. *Locke*: "If any one," says he, "will be so skeptical as to distrust his senses, and to affirm that all we see and hear, feel and taste, think and do, during our whole being, is but the series and deluding appearances of a long dream, whereof there is no reality; and therefore will question the existence of all things, or our knowledge of anything, I must desire him to consider that if all be a dream, then he doth but dream that he makes the question; and so it is not much matter that a waking man should answer him. But yet, if he pleases, he may dream that I make him this answer, that the certainty of things existing *in rerum natura*, when we have the testimony of our senses for it, is not only as great as our frame can attain to, but as our condition needs. . . . So that this evidence is as great as we can desire, being as certain to us as our pleasure or pain, i.e., happiness or misery, beyond which we have no concernment, either of knowing or being."

Thus it appears that men are naturally endowed with faculties proper for distinguishing between truth and error, right and wrong. And hence it follows that the doctrine of a total ignorance and incapacity to judge of moral and religious truths, brought upon mankind by the apostasy of our *First Parents*, is without foundation. How much brighter and more vigorous our intellectual faculties were in Adam, six thousand years before we had any existence, I leave others to determine. It is sufficient for my purpose to consider mankind as they are at present, without inquiring what they were before they had any being. And it appears that they have now a natural power to judge what is true and right, with the restrictions mentioned above. But it is, nevertheless, the manner of vain Enthusiasts, when the absurdity of their doctrines is laid open, to fall a railing, telling their opposers that they are in a *carnal state*, *blind*, and unable to judge, but that themselves are *spiritually illuminated*. . . .

We see that our Blessed Saviour did not suppose that the minds of men had suffered any such total eclipse, or were wholly overspread with darkness. He addresses the unbelieving Jews as if they had proper faculties for judging of religious truths, and blames them for not exerting them—"why even of yourselves judge ye not what is right?" . . .

Let us retain a suitable sense of the dignity of our nature in this respect. It is by our reason that we are exalted above the beasts of the field. It is by this that we are allied to angels and all the glorious intelligences of the heavenly world: yea, by this we resemble God himself. It is principally on account of our reason that we are said to have been "created in the image of God" (Gen. 1:27). So that how weak soever our intellectual faculties are, yet to speak reproachfully of reason in general is nothing less than blasphemy against God. Let us, therefore, instead of contemning this inestimable gift in which consists the glory of our nature, employ it to the ends for which it was designed, in the service of the great Father of our spirits.

But we have had occasion, in this discourse to speak of the imperfection, as well as of the strength, of human reason. He that is not sensible of this imperfection is so far from being the wisest of men that he "knoweth nothing yet as he ought to know it" (1 Cor. 8:2). . . . The knowledge of our own ignorance is the most important and beneficial of all sciences. This will naturally lead us to humility and excite us to improve, with gratitude and diligence, all the means of knowledge which we are savoured with, especially that revelation which God has given us by his Son, whom he has sent from heaven to be "a light unto the Gentiles" (Isa. 42:6) as well as "the glory of his people Israel" (Luke 2:32). A sense of our ignorance would also teach us modesty in criticising the works of nature and providence. The scheme of God's government is vast; our understandings are narrow and not proportioned to it. . . . And instead of boldly censuring the author of the universe, as taking wrong measures in any respect, it becomes us to use that humble language, not only of a great man, but an inspired *apostle*: "O the depths of the riches both of the wisdom and knowledge of God! How unsearchable are his judgments, and his ways past finding out! (Rom. 11:33)—"Now to the King eternal, immortal, invisible, the only wise God, be honour and glory for ever, through Jesus Christ our Lord. Amen" (1 Tim. 1:17).

SOURCE: Jonathan Mayhew, *Seven Sermons upon the Following Subjects* (Boston, 1749), 22–40. Some punctuation modernized.

A Discourse Concerning Unlimited Submission and Non-Resistance to the Higher Powers

1750

Jonathan Mayhew (1720–1766) laid much of the groundwork for revolutions in both religious and political freedom. In 1750, he preached his most famous sermon, "A Discourse Concerning Unlimited Submission and Non-Resistance to the Higher Powers." Here Mayhew argues that it is not Christian duty to submit always to rulers but only to good rulers; that it is our duty to rebel against tyrants; and that rebellion is right when a monarch exercises arbitrary power. Delivered on the hundredth anniversary of the execution of Charles I (January 30, 1649/50), the day's historical context served as a powerful backdrop to the sermon. Years later John Adams referred to this sermon as indicative of those principles that produced the Revolution. But Mayhew's involvement in political controversies reached a climax in the Stamp Act Crisis, when he expressed his opposition to the British Government in the context of a state of slavery, where the "slaves labor for the pleasure and profit of others." He delivered "The Snare Broken," the most widely circulated sermon on the repeal of the Stamp Act, in 1766, but he died suddenly that year and did not live to see the American Revolution that many credited him with fomenting.

—Mark W. Harris

If we calmly consider the nature of the thing itself, nothing can well be imagined more directly contrary to common sense than to suppose that *millions* of people should be subjected to the arbitrary, precarious pleasure of *one single man* (who has *naturally* no superiority over them in point of authority) so that their estates, and everything that is valuable in life, and even their lives also shall be absolutely at his disposal, if he happens to be wanton and capricious enough to demand them. What unprejudiced man can think that God made ALL to be thus subservient to the lawless pleasure and frenzy of ONE so that it shall always be a sin to resist him! Nothing but the most plain and express revelation from Heaven could make a sober impartial man believe such a monstrous, unaccountable doctrine; and, indeed, the thing itself appears so shocking—so out of all *proportion*, that it may be questioned whether all the *miracles* that ever were wrought could make it credible that this doctrine *really* came from God. At present, there is not the least syllable in Scripture which gives any countenance to it. The hereditary, indefeasible, divine right of kings, and the doctrine of non-resistance, which is built upon the supposition of such a right, are altogether as fabulous and chimerical, as transubstantiation; or any of the most absurd reveries of ancient or modern visionaries. These notions are fetched neither from divine revelation nor human reason; and if they are derived from neither of those sources, it is not much matter from *whence they come, or whither they go*. Only it is a pity that such doctrines should be propagated in society, to raise factions and rebellions, as we see they have, in fact, been both in the last, and in the *present*, REIGN.

But then, if unlimited submission and passive obedience to the *higher powers* in all possible cases, be not a duty, it will be asked, "How far are we obliged to submit? If we may innocently disobey and resist in some cases, why not in all? Where shall we stop? What is the measure of our duty? This doctrine tends to the total dissolution of civil government; and to introduce such scenes of wild anarchy and confusion as are more fatal to society than the worst of tyranny."

After this manner, some men object; and, indeed, this is the most plausible thing that can be said in favor of such an absolute submission as they plead for. But the worst (or rather the best) of it is that there is very little strength or solidity in it. For similar difficulties may be raised with respect to almost every duty of natural and revealed religion. — To instance only in two, both of which are near akin, and indeed exactly parallel, to the case before us. It is unquestionably the duty of children to submit to their parents; and of servants, to their masters. But no one asserts that it is their duty to obey and submit to them in all supposable cases, or universally a sin to resist them. Now does this tend to subvert the just authority of parents and masters? Or to introduce confusion and anarchy into private families? No. How then does the same principle tend to unhinge the government of that larger family, the body politic? We know, in general, that children and servants are obliged to obey their parents and masters respectively. We know also, with equal certainty, that they are not obliged to submit to them in all things without exception, but may, in some cases, reasonably, and therefore innocently, resist them. These principles are acknowledged upon all hands, whatever difficulty there may be in fixing the exact limits of submission. Now there is at least as much difficulty in stating the measure of duty in these two cases, as in the case of rulers and subjects. So that this is really no objection, at least no reasonable one, against resistance to the *higher powers*: Or, if it is one, it will hold equally against resistance in the other cases mentioned. — It is indeed true, that turbulent, vicious-minded men may take occasion from this principle, that their rulers may, in some cases, be lawfully resisted, to raise factions and disturbances in the state; and to make resistance where resistance is needless, and therefore, sinful. But is it not equally true, that children and servants of turbulent, vicious minds, may take occasion from this principle, that parents and masters may, in some cases, be lawfully resisted, to resist when resistance is unnecessary, and therefore, criminal? Is the principle in either case false in itself, merely because it may be abused and applied to legitimate disobedience and resistance in those instances, to which it ought not to be applied? According to this way of arguing, there will be no true principles in the world; for there are none but what may be wrested and perverted to serve bad purposes, either through the weakness or wickedness of men.

We may very safely assert these two things in general, without undermining government: One is, That no civil rulers are to be obeyed when they enjoin things that are inconsistent with the commands of God: All such disobedience is lawful and glorious; particularly if persons refuse to comply with any *legal establishment of religion*, because it is a gross perversion and corruption (as to doctrine, worship, and discipline) of a pure and divine religion brought from heaven to earth by the *Son of God*, (the only King and Head of the *christian* church) and propagated through the world by his inspired apostles. All commands running counter to the declared will of the Supreme Legislator of heaven and earth are null and void: and therefore disobedience to them is a duty, not a crime. . . . Another thing that may be asserted with equal truth and safety is that no government is to be submitted to at the *expense* of that which is the *sole end* of all government,—the common good and safety of society. Because, to submit in this case, if it should ever happen, would evidently be to set up the *means* as more valuable, and above the *end*: than which there cannot be a greater solecism and contradiction. The only reason of the institution of civil government; and the only rational ground of submission to it is the common safety and utility. If, therefore, in any case, the common safety and utility would not be promoted by submission to government, but the contrary, there is no ground or motive for obedience and submission, but, for the contrary. . . .

A PEOPLE really oppressed to a great degree by their sovereign cannot well be insensible when they are so oppressed. And such a people (if I may allude to an ancient *fable*) have, like the *hesperian* fruit, a DRAGON for their *protector* and *guardian*: nor would they have any reason to mourn, if some HERCULES should appear to dispatch him—For a nation thus abused to arise unanimously, and to resist their prince, even to the dethroning him, is not criminal but a reasonable way of vindicating their liberties and just rights; it is making use of the means, and the only means, which God has put into their power for mutual and self-defense. And it could be highly criminal in them, not to make use of this means. It would be stupid tameness, and unaccountable folly for whole nations to suffer *one* unreasonable, ambitious and cruel man to wanton and riot in their misery. And in such a case it would, of the two, be more rational to suppose that they did NOT *resist*, than that they who did, would *receive to themselves damnation*.

SOURCE: Jonathan Mayhew, A *Discourse Concerning Unlimited Submission and Non-Resistance to the Higher Powers* (Boston, 1750), 34–40. Some punctuation modernized.

JAMES RELLY

Union: or, a Treatise of the Consanguinity and Affinity between Christ and his Church

1759

James Relly (ca. 1722–1778) began his preaching career as a disciple of George Whitefield, leader of the Calvinist branch of the Methodist move-ment in Britain. Like Whitefield, Relly held a radical view of divine grace, that fallen human beings can contribute absolutely nothing to their own sal-vation. But Relly broke with Whitefield when he became convinced that grace extends to all humanity, not only to those predestined to salvation. In Union, he offered a novel argument for universalism. While Origen had appealed to the ontological continuity between Creator and creation, Relly stressed the union between Christ and humanity. This logic allowed him and his influen-tial disciple John Murray to retain an essentially Calvinist view of the atone-ment and of divine sovereignty while preaching universal salvation.

—Dan McKanan

The *Union* of *Christ*, and his *Church*, appears to me, a Truth of such importance, that I can see no consistency in the Doctrine of Salvation by *Jesus*, without it. My present design, is to render, with as much plainness of Speech as possible, the rea-sons of my Ideas; intending thereby to prove at once, the necessity, and utility of this Grace.

I. I apprehend it necessary to the harmony of the Divine Perfections. For, as all the hopes, and expectations, of the Creature from the Creator, are founded upon the supposition of his goodness; Men of every sentiment, will agree to this proposition, God is Good.

And, that we may rightly conceive of him under this character, it is as necessary we should see him *Justice*, *Holiness*, and *Truth*; as *Mercy* and *Love*: since all those Properties must unite, and act in perfect Harmony, to constitute real goodness.

* * *

For as in *Adam all die, even so in Christ shall all be made alive.* (I Cor. xv. 22.) (Besides proving the general resurrection) the Apostle explains in those words, the matter whereof I am treating. As all died, and were lost in *Adam* when *he* was caught in toils of sin, and Death, it is evident *they* were then in *him*, then *united* to him, so that *his* sin, was *their* sin; *his* Death, *their* Death. As in *Adam*, so in *Christ*, *united* in *him*, in all *he* did, and suffered: saved in *him*, crucified with *him*, risen with *him*, ascended and seated with *him*, in heavenly places, *&c.* Why may not our salvation in *Christ*, from *union* with *him*, in *his* obedience, and Death, be judged as reasonable as our condemnation in *Adam*, from *union* with *him*, in *His* sin and Misery? I acknowledge the *latter* is more familiar, when *I would do good evil is present with me*: Whilst the *former* is more remote from our senses, and only manifest when *we look not to the things which are seen, but to the things which are not seen*. But, if laying sensible things aside, as that which is temporary, we attend wholly to the testimony of the scriptures; having the anointing to guide us, we shall enter into truth, and spiritual things will be manifest.

✻ ✻ ✻

So truely through Faith we understand our *Union* with *Christ*; yet it is not our Faith that makes it.

But if it is not true until our believing, and by means thereof; then doth believing make that a truth, which was not a truth; and faith creates its own object, and then embraces it. This looks like the heathen idolatry, first making their Gods, and then trusting in them.

✻ ✻ ✻

If it is not our faith, or believing, that makes this *Union*, then it is an act of eternal Love, the *purpose, and grace, which was given us in Christ Jesus before the world began*; The Antiquity of which is obvious, nor may its Date be fixed, because exceeding the Limits of Time. And what hath been from everlasting, will be unto to everlasting . . . It is easy to see, that if our *Union* with *Christ* was dependant on our Faith, or believing it would be changeable; except it appear that we are perfect, and unchangeable in the Faith.

✻ ✻ ✻

I would now consider the objections generally made unto the Grace of *Union*. . . .

The old trite objection, of its tending unto Licentiousness, leads the way, saying, if *Union* with *Christ* is the ground of our acceptance with God, and our security in his favour; then the doctrine of rewards and punishments is overthrown; and man hath nothing left to stimulate him to virtue.

Answ. To work from an expectation of being rewarded, is to make it of Debt; and not of Grace: But the nature of the Deity is so infinitely pure; so holy, just, and true his Laws; that it is impossible Man should make him his Debtor: Nay, it would be the highest arrogance to pretend it . . .

But the obedience of fear, is diametrically opposite unto the obedience of faith: the former hath its rise and maintenance from a *Lie*: from that habit, and principle, which makes God a *Liar*; by not believing the record which he hath given of his Son.

78

But the latter springs from a belief of the *truth*, from a full persuasion of the love of God, and of his being reconciled in *Christ Jesus*.

SOURCE: James Relly, *Union: or, a Treatise of the Consanguinity and Affinity between Christ and his Church* (London, 1759), 2–4, 21–22, 55, 58–59, 60–61. Spelling and punctuation modernized.

"Natural Religion, as Distinguished from Revealed"

1759

Ebenezer Gay (1696–1787) has been called the "father of American Unitarianism." He was born in Dedham, Massachusetts, and showed a natural inclination for scholarly achievement early in life. After graduating from Harvard and a few years of working as a teacher, he was called to the parish church in Hingham, Massachusetts, in December 1717. Though his theology was somewhat evangelical in the early years of his ministry, during the Great Awakening he became a leader of the liberal faction, stressing both the covenant of works and the covenant of grace. Because of his scholarly bent, he became known as an important mentor for aspiring ministers, including his most famous and controversial student, Jonathan Mayhew. Historian Alan Heimert called Gay's 1759 Dudleian Lecture the "manifesto of Congregational Liberalism." Reason, Gay said, was humankind's "original excellence," and he declared that it should not be "subjected to the Sway of brutish Appetites and blind Passions." His belief in natural religion, and a benevolent God, led him to the radical conclusion that humans have an innate capacity for goodness. The human ability to act on this nature was the "Power of Self-determination," and he thus rejected the Calvinist "mechanical Engine," for the free will of Arminianism. With his long ministry of nearly seventy years in Hingham, Gay became a symbol for community solidarity, even though he was an acknowledged Tory during the American Revolution. Further Reading: Robert J. Wilson III, The Benevolent Deity: Ebenezer Gay and the Rise of Rational Religion in New England, 1696–1787 *(Philadelphia: University of Pennsylvania Press, 1984); Alan Heimert,* Religion and the American Mind: From the Great Awakening to the Revolution *(Cambridge, MA: Harvard University Press, 1966).*

—Mark W. Harris

For when the Gentiles, which have not the Law, do by Nature the Things contained in the Law; these having not the Law, are a Law unto themselves: Which show the Work of the Law written in their Hearts, their Conscience also bearing witness, and their Thoughts the mean while accusing, or else excusing one another.

—ROM. II. 14, 15.

The Belief of GOD's Existence is most essentially fundamental to all Religion, and having been at the first of the *Dudleian* Lectures established; the moral Obligation which it induceth upon the Nature of Man, may be the Subject of our present Inquiry.

A devout *Hermit* being asked, How he could profit in Knowledge, living in a Desert, without Men and Books? answered, "I have one Book which I am always studying, and turning over Day and Night: The Heavens, the Earth and the Waters, are the Leaves of which it consists." The Characters of the Deity are plainly legible in the whole Creation around us: And if we open the Volume of our own Nature, and look within, we find there a Law written;—a Rule of virtuous Practice prescribed.

Religion and Law (divine) are Words of promiscuous Use; denoting in the general Signification thereof, *An Obligation lying upon Men to do those Things which the Perfections of God, relative unto them, do require of them.* In this Definition (whether exact and full, or not,) I mean to imply all Things incumbent on such reasonable Creatures as Men are, toward all Beings with which they are concerned, GOD, the supreme, one another, and themselves; and which are incumbent on them, by virtue of the Perfections of God, in the Relation there is betwixt Him and them: other Obligation which can be supposed to any of the same Things, not being of the religious Kind. And in the doing those Things to which Religion is the Obligation, are included, besides the actual Performance, the Principles, Motives and Ends thereof; all that is necessary to render any Acts of Men, whether internal or external, such as the Perfections of the Deity require.

Religion is divided into natural and revealed:—*Revealed* Religion is that which God hath made known to Men by the immediate Inspiration of his Spirit, the Declarations of his Mouth, and Instructions of his Prophets: *Natural*, that which bare Reason discovers and dictates: As 'tis delineated by the masterly Hand of St. *Paul*, the Apostle of the Gentiles, in the Words of holy Scripture now read—Which I take as a proper and advantageous Introduction to my intended Discourse on this Head, Viz.

That Religion is, in some measure, discoverable by the Light, and practicable to the Strength, of Nature; and is so far fitly called *Natural* by Divines and learned Men. The Religion which is possible to be discover'd by the Light, and practis'd by the Power of Nature, consists in rend'ring all those inward and outward Acts of Respect, Worship and Obedience unto God, which are suitable to the Excellence of his all-perfect Nature, and our Relation to Him, who is our Creator, Preserver, Benefactor, Lord, and Judge;—And in yielding to our Fellow-Men that Regard, Help and Comfort, which their partaking of the same Nature, and living in Society with us, give them a Claim to;—And in managing our Souls and Bodies, in their respective Actions and Enjoyments, in a way agreeable to our *Make*, and conducive to our Ease and Happiness: And doing all from a Sense of the Deity, imposing the Obligation, and approving the Discharge of it. For 'tis a Regard to Him in every moral Duty that consecrates it, and makes it truly an Act of Religion. These Things, indeed, are contained in the Revelation of God, which affords the chief Assistance to our knowing and doing of them; and yet they belong to the Religion of Nature, so far as Nature supplies any Light and Strength to the Discovery and Practice of them.

I. That Religion is in some measure, discoverable by the Light of Nature. The Obligation lying on us to do those Things which the Perfections of God, as related to us, require, is discernable in the Light of natural Reason. This Faculty of the human Soul, exercised in the Contemplation of the universal Frame of Nature, or of any Parts thereof; and in the Observation of the general Course of Providence, or of particular Events therein, may convince Men of the Existence and Attributes of God, the all-wise, powerful and good Maker, Upholder, and Governor of all Things. It may be questioned whether the reasoning Faculty, as it is in the Bulk of Mankind, be so acute and strong, as from the necessary eternal Existence of the Deity (which is as evident and incontestable, as that any Thing is) to prove all other Perfections do belong to God in an infinite Degree. . . . They may discern the Wisdom and Goodness of their Maker, in designing and fitting them for a social Life in this World, and thence the sacred Engagements they are under to mutual Benevolence, commutative Justice, and all such Demeanour in their various Stations and Relations, as tends to promote the common Welfare, and the Good of Individuals.—Their Souls may know right well, how wonderfully God hath made them with Powers and Faculties superior to any bodily Endowments; which should not therefore be subjected to the Sway of brutish Appetites and blind Passions. Reason may know its divine Right to govern, to maintain its Empire in the Soul, regulating the Passions and Affections; directing them to proper Objects, and stinting them to just Measures. Nature affords considerable Light for the Discovery, and Arguments for the Proof, of such Parts of Religion. There is an essential Difference between Good and Evil, Right and Wrong, in many Cases that relate to moral Conduct toward our Maker, Mankind, and ourselves, which the Understanding (if made use of) cannot but discern. The obvious Distinction is founded in the Natures and Relations of Things: And the Obligation thence arising to choose the Good, and do that which is Right, is not (as I conceive) antecedent to any Law or Institution, enjoining this upon us. It primarily originates from the Will and Appointment of the Author of those Natures, and Founder of those Relations, which are the Grounds and Reasons of it. And his Will is signified by his apparently wise and good Constitution of Things, in their respective Natures and Relations. The Law of Nature is given by the God of Nature, who is Lord of all. He enacted it by creating and establishing a World of Beings in such Order, as he hath done. He publishes it to rational Creatures (as is necessary to its binding them) in making them capable to learn from his Works, what is good, and what is required of them. Natural Conscience is his Voice, telling them their Duty. This (in part) is the *work of the Law in their Hearts*. . . . In the due Exercise of their natural Faculties, Men are capable of attaining some Knowledge of God's Will, and their Duty, manifested in his Works, as if it were written in legible Characters on the Tables of their Hearts. And 'tis on this Account, that any Part of Religion is called Natural; and stands distinguished, in *Theology*, from that which is revealed.

II. That Religion is, in some Measure, practicable to the Strength of Nature. There is doing, as well as knowing, by Nature, the Things contained in the Law of it. Knowing them is but in order to the doing them: And the Capacity to know them would be in vain, (which nothing in Nature is) if there was no Ability to do them. Whoever observes the divine Workmanship in human Nature, and takes a Survey of the Powers and Faculties with which it is endowed, must needs see that it was designed and framed for the Practice of Virtue: That Man is not merely so much lumpish Matter, or a *mechanical* Engine, that moves only by the Direction of an impelling Force; but that he hath a Principle of Action within himself, and is an Agent in the strict and proper Sense of the Word. The special Endowment of his Nature, which constitutes him such, is the Power of Self-determination, or Freedom of Choice; his being possessed of which is as self-evident, as the Explanation of the Manner of its operating is difficult: He feels himself free to act one Way, or another: And as he is capable of distinguishing between different Actions, of the moral Kind; so is he likewise of choosing which he will do, and which leave undone. Further to qualify our Nature for virtuous or religious Practice (which necessarily must be of Choice) the Author of it hath annexed a secret Joy or Complacence of Mind to such Practice, and as sensible a Pain or Displicence to the contrary. . . .

There may be something in the intelligent moral World analogous to Attraction in the material System—something that inclines and draws Men toward God, the Centre of their Perfection, and consummate Object of their Happiness; and which, if its Energy were not obstructed, would as certainly procure such Regularity in the States and Actions of all intelligent Beings in the spiritual World, as that of Attraction doth in the Positions and Motions of all the Bodies in the material World.—"Created intelligent Beings (says Dr. *Cheyne*) are Images of the SUPREME INFINITE, as he calleth God. In Him there is an infinite Desire and Ardor of possessing and enjoying Himself, and his own infinite Perfections, in order to render Him happy: He himself is the sole Object of his own, and of the Felicity of all his Creatures. There must therefore be an Image of this his infinite Desire after Happiness in all his intelligent Creatures—a Desire after Happiness in a Re-union with Him. An intelligent Being, coming out of the Hands of infinite Perfection, with an Aversion, or even Indifferency, to be reunited with its Author, the Source of its utmost Felicity, is such a Shock, and Deformity in the beautiful Analogy of Things, such a Breach and Gap in the harmonious Uniformity, observable in all the Works of the Almighty, and that in the noblest and highest Part of his Works, as is not consistent with finite Wisdom and Perfection, much less with the supremely infinite Wisdom of the ALL-PERFECT.—This Principle was most certainly implanted in the Creation of intelligent Beings, in the very Fund and Substance of their Natures, tho' there remains but few Footsteps and Instances of it's Being or Effects. . . . There is observable in Man a *natural Proclivity* (as *Origen* termeth it) towards his Maker; to acknowledge God; especially on Occasions of Need or Distress to have recourse unto Him. And from hence ariseth so universal a Consent of Mankind in paying some Homage to the Deity, which is not always directed to the true, because so many blindly follow natural Inclination, without consulting Reason, which should be its Guide. There is such a Disposition in human Nature as makes Religion agreeable to it; so that Divines of great Name have affirm'd it to be essential thereto, and that which raises it above the Brutal; and Philosophers, from what is innate to Man, have defined him a *Creature capable of Religion.*—Whoever attends to this inward Furniture of our Nature for Religion, may easily perceive it to be God's Workmanship, primarily created unto good Works, that Men might walk in them. His Formation of them qualifies them, in a measure, for religious Practice; as his Regeneration, or Renovation of them doth more so. And his fitting them by Nature therefor, is a Work of his, to which the Work of Sanctification, in his furnishing them with Grace to evangelical Obedience, beareth Analogy. The former is the Work of the Law written in their Hearts, that they may do, as well as know, what it enjoins: The latter is the Impression of the Gospel upon them, that, thro' Christ's strengthening them, they may do what it requires. And by doing the Things contained in the Law of Nature, Men *show the Work of the Law written in their Hearts, and are a Law unto themselves,* as truly and plainly, as regenerate Christians, by doing the Things contained in the Gospel, are *manifestly declared to be the Epistle of Christ, written, not with Ink, but with the Spirit of the living God, not in Tables of Stone, but in fleshly Tables of the Heart.* . . .

The Law of Nature is purely a Law of Works, and requires perfect Obedience, which the Transgressors of it, as all Men are, cannot yield to it: And whether that which is wanting in their Obedience may be supplied by Repentance and Humility in them, and by Mercy and Pardon in God, cannot be certainly known without a Revelation of his Will, on which it wholly depends. The Goodness of God, in the general Course of his Providence, toward sinful Mankind, showeth Him to be placable, and leadeth them to Repentance; but doth not assure them of Pardon upon it, much less of the Reward of eternal Life, for imperfect, tho' it should be sincere, Obedience. If Reason doth not see and pronounce it inconsistent with the Perfections of God to pardon Sinners, on the sole Condition of their Repentance; yet it cannot infer from them, that he will:—All that it can say, is in the Words of a Heathen King, *Who can tell if the Lord will turn from his Anger, that we perish not?* . . .

84

1. We should not depreciate and cry down Natural Religion, on Pretence of advancing the Honour of Revealed—as if they were two opposite Religions, and could no more stand together in the same Temple than Dagon and the Ark of God. Whatever Distinction we observe between them, there is no Contrariety in the one to the other: They subsist harmoniously together, and mutually strengthen and confirm each other. Revealed Religion is an *Additional* to Natural; built, not on the Ruins, but on the strong and everlasting Foundations of it. . . . The Law of Nature, like that of *Moses*, may be serviceable unto Men, *as a School-Master to bring them to Christ*, for higher Instruction; especially where the Means of such are afforded; and so usher them into a State of Grace. Notwithstanding the Insufficiency of natural Religion to their Salvation, yet it may, in some Measure, prepare them to be Partakers of the Benefit, without any Diminution of the Glory of the Gospel, which is the Grant of it, or Detraction from the Merits of our blessed Redeemer, who is the Author of it. It is only by Grace that sinful Men can be saved; yet, by making some good Use of their rational Powers (weakened as they be) in the Study and Practice of natural Religion, they may be in a better Preparation of Mind to comply with the Offers and Operations of divine Grace, than if they wholly give up themselves to the Conduct of sensual Appetites & Passions.

* * *

2. We should not magnify and extol natural Religion, to the Disparagement of Revealed. We cannot say, that the Light and Strength of Nature, how great soever, in its original State of Rectitude, had no Assistance from Revelation, toward the first Man's actual Knowledge and Performance of his Duty to his Maker. At the first opening of his Eyes and Understanding, he might not, by one intuitive View, have a clear and full Discernment of the Perfections of God stamped on his Works, and the moral Obligations engraved in his Heart.—God made Himself and his Will known to *Adam* in some other Way beside that of his Creation. There was some *other* Voice of the Lord, beside that of universal Nature's declaring his Being and Pleasure to him; and by which more might be spoken for his Instruction, than we have an Account of in the Mosaic History. And perhaps such Manifestation as God more immediately made of Himself to Man, put his Reason in Exercise for all the Discoveries it was capable of making afterwards from the Works of Creation. Had Man, with all his natural Endowments in their perfect Order and Strength, been placed in this World, and no Notice given him of its Maker, might he not have stood wondering some Time at the amazing Fabric, before he would have thence, by Deductions of Reason, argued an invisible Being, of eternal Power, Wisdom and Goodness, to be the Author of it and him; to whom he was therefore obliged to pay all Regards suitable to such glorious Excellencies? Would he so soon and easily have made those Discoveries, which are necessary to the Perfection of natural Religion, understood and practic'd by him in Paradise, till he eat of *the Tree of Knowledge of*

Good and Evil? If his being Created after the Image of God imports more than his Formation with a sufficient Capacity in his Nature for, and entire Disposition to, even the actual Possession and Use of all that Knowledge, Righteousness and true Holiness, of which the Religion of Nature, consists; yet his falling into Sin, and effacing the divine Image in his Soul, greatly alter'd the Case, with respect to him, and his Posterity, and made Revelation a necessary Supplement of supernatural Light and Strength, for the Discovery and Performance of acceptable and available Religion.

✻ ✻ ✻

The Gospel of Christ hath to be sure been *a Light to lighten the* modern deistical *Gentiles:* For the juster Notions they have of the divine Attributes, and moral Duties than the ancient, they are greatly indebted to that Revelation which they decry. Not to say any Thing of those heavenly Truths and important Duties, which are taught only in the Bible; 'tis there we learn the Religion of Nature in its greatest Purity; which, if there were nothing more to be said in its Commendation might be enough to raise our Esteem of it. And the Grace of God appears in assisting Reason by Revelation in those Discoveries, which it possibly could, but never did, nor would make, without such Help.—And the same is true, with respect to the Performances of Duty: *In thy Light we see Light.* It is in the Light of Revelation, added to that of Nature, that Things are so plain and easy to our discerning, as that we are ready to think bare Reason must discover them to all Mankind, and that we, un-enlightened by the Gospel, should have known as much of the Principles and Duties of Natural Religion. . . . By Means of Revelation we have the right Use of Reason, in Matters of Religion: And, by the due Exercise of Reason, so excited and directed, we have the inestimable Benefit of Revelation. Both are *good Gifts,*—Rays from *the Father of Lights,* to *enlighten every Man that cometh into the World.*—The Mind hath great Satisfaction in observing the harmonious Agreement between them, and the Objects of religious Knowledge and Faith appear the more beautiful and amiable in this double Light: And the better we understand and practise the Religion of Nature, the wiser and better Christians shall we be.

✻ ✻ ✻

It concerns us all to make Proficiency in Religion, answerable to our Capacities therefor, and the Means and Helps afforded us thereto—That having the Foundations of it well laid in our Minds, by convincing Reasons, and authentic Testimonies of Scripture, we go on to Perfection: Which that we may do;—Let us, as the Discourse now had, admonishes us, have a due Respect both to natural and revealed Religion: And not suffer our Zeal to swell so high, and move in so strong a Current towards the one, as shall prove a Drain from, and lower the Regard, which we owe to the other—Let us faithfully improve all the Light and Strength which natural Reason and divine Revelation supply, toward our knowing and doing *whatsoever*

Things are true—honest—just—pure—lovely—and of good Report—in which there is any Virtue, and any Praise; and so make continual Advance in Religion, 'till we come unto *a perfect Man,* in the redintegrated State of Nature—*unto the Measure of the Stature of the Fulness of CHRIST.*

AMEN.

SOURCE: Ebenezer Gay, "N*atural* religion, as distinguished from *revealed*: A sermon preached at the annual *Dudleian*-lecture, at Harvard-College in Cambridge, *May* 9. 1759" (Boston, 1759), 5–17, 19–21, 23–25, 30–34. Spelling and punctuation modernized.

The Apology of Theophilus Lindsey, M. A., on Resigning the Vicarage of Cattarick, Yorkshire

1774

Theophilus Lindsey (1723–1808) was a clergyman ordained in the Anglican Church, who later became a heretic and eventually an apostate. As a heretic, Lindsey attempted to reform the Church of England from within through political channels. When this proved unsuccessful, Lindsey became an apostate, establishing the first avowedly Unitarian congregation in England, the Essex Street Chapel, in 1774. Many dignitaries, including Joseph Priestley and Benjamin Franklin, attended the opening ceremony of the Chapel. Lindsey introduced a Book of Common Prayer purged of the 39 Articles and Trinitarianism, based on the work of Dr. Samuel Clarke. In turn this work became the basis for James Freeman's liturgy at King's Chapel, the first avowedly Unitarian congregation in America. Lindsey hoped to appeal to others compelled by their consciences to leave the Church of England. Lindsey is generally considered one of the three fathers of modern British Unitarianism, along with his biographer, Thomas Belsham, and his friend, Joseph Priestley. Further Reading: G. M. Ditchfield, ed., The Letters of Theophilus Lindsey, *vol. 1, 1747–1788 (Woodbridge, UK: Boydell Press, 2007); Phillip Hewett, "The Heretic from Puddletown," paper presented at the Unitarian Universalist Collegium in 2009.*

*—*Meg Schellenberg Richardson

Firmly persuaded, upon such evidence as he thinks no fair mind can resist, that the Lord Jesus came from God, in the writing of these sheets he hath been all along under the most serious impressions of the relation he bears, and the obligations he owes to this divinely commissioned Savior, *who loved him* (Galat. ii. 20.) *and gave himself for him*; the appointed judge of quick and dead, by whom his future lot is to be decided, and who hath given his faithful followers hope, after death, of living under his virtuous rule, beholding his glory, and being for ever with him (John xvii. 24.).

But he dares not advance him to an equality with his God and heavenly Father, who himself came to teach men, that the Father was the only true God; and whose highest aim, glory and felicity was to be the beloved son and chosen messenger of the Father, and to be employed by him in teaching his will to men.

* * *

Sincerity and integrity are things final in religion; right opinions are of inferior consideration, and instrumental only. Earnestly as it is to be wished for and endeavoured that our solemn public address to almighty God, and worship of him, were framed and conducted in the most perfect manner . . . yet as any great degree of perfection is not to be attained in human appointments, or but by slow degrees; it seems a duty to acquiesce in the public forms of religious worship, though faulty and imperfect, and not to make them a cause of separation from our Christian brethren, where we can innocently comply with them.

* * *

But the matter becomes infinitely more serious and important to the individual, when the worship enjoined in the liturgy is esteemed to be directed to a wrong object, and *sinful*; sinful, I mean, to his apprehension, who is convinced from the sacred scriptures, that God, the Father, is alone the object of religious worship, and that prayer ought not to be addressed to any other being or person whatsoever. To join constantly in forms of devotion, that are directed to one or more other persons, will appear, more or less, an approbation of such worship, and must influence him to wish for some other forms which he can more approve, and in which he may not worship God amiss.

* * *

But, however things may appear to those who occupy the place of hearers, who have no office or authority in the church and may not suppose themselves to give their assent to any thing they hear, any farther than it is inwardly approved by them, it can hardly be reckoned a matter of indifference to those who lead the devotions of the congregation, and thereby make them much more their own, to put themselves to the necessity of continual double meaning and collusion, in addressing prayer sometimes to the Son, sometimes to the Spirit, as *no less God than the Father*, all the while that they are convinced, that there is but one person, the object of prayer, the One God, the Father, to whom alone it is to the addressed. And this brings the matter home to the particular case and situation of the writer.

SOURCE: Theophilus Lindsey, *The Apology of Theophilus Lindsey, M. A., on Resigning the Vicarage of Catterick, Yorkshire* (London, 1774), 5–6, 192–94, 201. Some punctuation modernized.

A True and Most Remarkable Account of Some Passages in the Life of Mr. George de Benneville

1782

George de Benneville (1703–1793), the son of Huguenot refugees of noble birth, grew up at the British royal court. He spent two decades preaching as a missionary in France, Germany, and Holland, while also training as a physician. During a near-death experience, he had a vision of the eventual restoration of all creatures. One of the most interesting features of his account of this "trance" is his description of salvation as "self-annihilation" and being "swallowed up in the ocean of [God's] love." Soon afterward, in 1741, he migrated to America to minister to the bodies and spirits of the Schwenkfelders and Huguenots there. In Pennsylvania and in nearby New Jersey, he preached to religious communities that allowed the possibility of universal salvation. Thus he may have helped to prepare the ground for Thomas Potter's reception of John Murray in 1770. From 1781 to 1787, de Benneville accompanied the Universalist evangelist Elhanan Winchester on preaching tours. Winchester said of him, "I bless God that I was ever acquainted with Dr. George de Benneville, for such an humble, pious, loving man I have scarcely ever seen in my pilgrimage through life." Further Reading: Albert Bell, The Life and Times of Dr. George de Benneville, *1703–1793 (Boston: Dept. of Publications of the Universalist Church of America, 1953); Thomas Whittemore,* The Modern History of Universalism: From the Era of the Reformation to the Present Time, *2nd ed., vol. 1 (Boston, 1860).*

—Peter Hughes

Being arrived at the age of twelve years, I was very wild, thinking myself to be of another mass than mankind in general; and by this fond imagination I was self-exalted, and believed myself to be more than others; but God soon made me know the contrary.

As it was designed that I should learn navigation, I was sent to sea in a vessel of war, which constituted part of a little fleet sent to the coast of Barbary, to carry presents and renew the peace with Algiers, Tunis, and Tripoli. Being arrived at Algiers, as I walked upon deck I saw some Moors, who brought refreshments to sell; one of them slipping down, bruised his leg, and two of his comrades having laid him upon deck, each, one after the other kissed the wound, then both shed tears upon it, and turning towards the rising sun, they cried in such a manner, that being moved with anger at their noise, I ordered my servant to bring them before me.

On my interrogating them with regard to the disturbance, they perceived that I was angry, and asked pardon for having offended me, telling me the cause was that one of their brethren had hurt his leg in falling, and that they kissed the wound in order to sympathize with him, and also in that they shed tears upon it, they took part with him, and as tears were salt, they were a good remedy to heal the same; and the reason of their turning towards the rising sun, was to invoke Him who created the sun to have compassion upon their poor brother, and that he would be pleased to heal him. Here I felt an inward conviction, which affected me so much that I thought my heart would burst, and terminate my existence; my eyes were melted in tears, and self-condemnation operated so powerfully upon me, that I was obliged to cry out, "Are these Heathen? No; I confess before God, they are Christians, and I myself am an Heathen."

Behold the first conviction that the grace of our sovereign GOOD employed; he was pleased to convince a white person by blacks; one who carried the name of a Christian by a Pagan, and who was obliged to confess himself to be but a Heathen.

*   *   *

My conversion made a great noise among the people, for they saw me praising and adoring my divine Saviour on all occasions, and before all companies where I came, without exception, calling and exhorting each one to submit to the love of Jesus, just as they found themselves, and although their sins were many and great, his grace was greater to receive and to pardon; but that we must come as we are to our Jesus, for he is the beginning, the middle, and the end of the conversion of all the human species, and whosoever is not converted by him, and to him, is not converted at all.

The French ministers were very uneasy at what they heard concerning me, doubting that I was not a true Protestant, and therefore they demanded a written confession of my faith. I told them paper would suffer any thing to be written upon it, truth or falsehood; but that I was not ashamed to confess with my mouth, what I believed in my heart; and if they would let me know when they would meet together, I was ready to appear before them, to give an account of my faith, and the wonders which the most Holy Trinity had wrought within me.

The time was fixed, and I appeared before them; they asked me many questions, but we could not agree, for they held predestination, and I held the restoration of all souls, because having myself been the chief of sinners, and that God through Jesus Christ by the efficacy of his Holy Spirit, had granted me mercy, and the pardon of all my sins, and had plucked me as a brand out of Hell, I could not have a doubt but that the whole world would be saved by the same power.

They answered me that I must not take it ill that they could not own me as a member of their church. I answered them that I was very well content to be cast out, and that my consolation was that they were not able to blot my name out of the book of life.

* * *

I was about seventeen years of age when I began to preach in France.

* * *

We were many times taken prisoners during the two years, sometimes by the means of our own brothers, who would go and inform the soldiers of the Marshalsea where we were met together. . . .

At last we were surrounded with soldiers, one day where we were assembled by the side of the Dieppe, where many of us were taken prisoners, among whom I found myself, with Mr. Durant, a young man about 24 years of age, of Geneva.

After a month's imprisonment, we were condemned to die; he to be hanged, and I to have my head cut off. We were conducted together to the place of execution, he was hanged; as he was upon the ladder he sung the 116th psalm, and died joyfully.

I was then conducted upon the scaffold, and my eyes were ordered to be bound to prevent my seeing, but upon my earnest request that was omitted.

I then fell upon my knees, and praying the Lord that he would not require my blood at their hands, as they knew not what they did; my soul was filled with exceeding joy. The executioner came and bound my hands in order for the execution, while he was thus employed, a Courier arrived from the King (which was Louis XV) with a reprieve for the criminal. Immediately the joy of my heart left me, and darkness entered into my soul.

I was then re-conducted into prison at Paris, where I remained sometime before I was set at liberty, which was granted to me through the intercession of the Queen.

* * *

After I had passed about 18 years in Germany and Holland, I became sickly of a consumptive disorder, occasioned by being greatly concerned for the salvation of souls, and much disquieted, because the greatest part by far walked in the ways of perverseness, and neglected their conversion, which caused me great trouble, and I took it so to heart, that I believed my happiness would be incomplete, while one creature remained miserable. . . .

My fever increased in such a manner as reduced me almost to a skeleton, so that they were obliged to feed me as an infant.

While I lay in this weakness, I was favored through grace, with many visions; in one it appeared to me, that I was conducted into a fine plain, filled with all kinds of fruit trees, agreeable both to the sight and smell, loaded with all kinds of the most delicious fruits, which came to my mouth, and satisfied me as with a river of pleasure, at the same time I beheld the inhabitants, and beautiful they were beyond expression, clothed in garments white as snow; they were filled with humility, and their friendship and love was towards all beings; they saluted me with profound reverence, and the most lovely air, saying, with a voice of love, which penetrated me through and through, "Dear soul, take courage, be comforted, for in a little time you shall see the wonders of our God, in the restoration of all the human species without exception."

The weakness of my body so increased, that I was certain of dying. I exhorted my dear brethren to be faithful unto death, to be steadfast, unmovable, and to be always turning inward with an enlivening faith, to behold with a fixed attention the Lamb of God, with believing eyes, and to hearken to his eternal word within them, and that then they should receive of the fullness of Christ, grace upon grace, by which they should be strengthened to abide steadfast unto the end.

I had fellowship with many assemblies of brethren, but in particular with that connected with my dear brother Marsay, and the brethren there had a vision of my death, and sent brother Marsay to visit me.

When he arrived he found me in the agonies of death, and embraced me with a kiss of peace and love, and saluted me in the name of the brethren, who recommended themselves to me, and desired that I would remember them before the throne of God and the Lamb.

He then took leave of me, and I felt myself die by degrees, and exactly at midnight I was separated from my body; and seeing the people occupied in washing me, according to the custom of the country, I had a great desire to be freed from the sight of my body; and immediately I was drawn up as in a cloud, and beheld great wonders where I passed, impossible to be written or expressed. Presently I came to a place which appeared to my eyes as a level plain, so extensive that my sight was not able to reach its limits, filled with all sorts of delightful fruit trees, agreeable to behold, and which sent forth such fragrant odours, that all the air was filled as with incense.

In this place I found that I had two guardians, one at my right hand, and the other at my left, exceeding beautiful beyond expression, whose boundless friendship and love seemed to penetrate through all my inward parts. They had wings, and resembled angels, having shining bodies, and white garments.

He that was at my right hand, came and stood before me and said, "My dear soul, and my dear brother, take good courage, the Most Holy Trinity hath favoured you to be comforted with an everlasting, and universal consolation, by discovering to you, how, and in what manner he will restore ALL his creatures, without exception, to the praise of his glory, and their eternal salvation; and you shall be the witness of this, and shall rejoice in singing, and triumph with all the children of God, as a reward for the friendship and love that you have borne for your neighbours, on whose account you have had many extreme griefs, and shed many tears, which shall be all wiped away from your eyes by God himself, who shall turn all your griefs to exceeding great gladness."

Then he took his place at my right hand. After that the second guardian who was at my left hand, appeared before me, and thus he spake, "My dear soul, my dear brother, be of good cheer, you shall be strengthened and comforted after your griefs, with an universal and eternal consolation: you must be prepared to pass through the seven habitations of the damned; be of good courage, and prepare yourself to feel something of their sufferings, but be turned inward deeply during the time, and you shall thereby be preserved."

Then he took his place at my left hand. Immediately we were lifted up in the air, and after some time we arrived in a dark and obscure place, where nothing but weeping, lamentation, and gnashing of teeth could be understood. A dreadful place, as being the repository of all sorts of damned souls, under condemnation and judgments of all sorts, enduring the torments, pains, griefs and sufferings which their sins had merited, for each one had his works follow him in death. All iniquities and sins were reduced to seven classes or habitations. There was an eternal confusion there, that which one made the other destroyed.

The duelist in his fire of anger burnt against his enemy, and they pass as a flame and firebrand of Hell, one through the other.

You might see fornicators, idolaters, adulterers, the effeminate, thieves, the covetous, drunkards, slanderers, ravishers, &c. each labouring and being employed with his sins and iniquities.

One might also see all kinds and conditions of men, divines, judges, lawyers, &c. and in a word, one might discover whatsoever any of them had committed upon earth. But in each habitation I discovered that those who were abased, and that appeared sorrowful for their sins, were as it were separated from the others of their sort, that were not yet so. . . .

It is impossible to describe my condition, as I had great compassion towards the sufferers, inasmuch as I had part of their sufferings.

After we had passed through, we were lifted up some distance from the place, where we reposed ourselves; and a messenger was sent to us . . . "My dear soul, and my dear brother, (addressing himself to me, saying) the Most Holy Trinity always works wonders in all times within his poor creatures, without exception, and he will order for a little time and half a time, that you shall return into your earthly tabernacle, to publish, and to proclaim to the people of the world an universal Gospel, that shall restore in its time all the human species, without exception, to its honour, and to the glory of the Most Holy Trinity. Hallelujah."

※　※　※

And as the multitudes approached, the glory caused us to fall down, and to adore in spirit and in truth the Son of the living God, who marched in the midst of the multitudes. . . .

When we arrived in the place of the seven habitations of the damned, one could perceive no more darkness, obscurity, pains, torments, lamentations, afflictions, nor gnashing of teeth; but all were still and quiet.

Then all the heavenly hosts shouted with one voice, and said, "An eternal and everlasting deliverance, an eternal and everlasting restoration, an universal and everlasting restitution of all things." . . .

Presently they passed through the seven habitations of the damned, and a multitude were delivered from each, and being clothed in white robes, they followed the heavenly hosts, praising and glorifying the most High for their deliverance. One might know them amongst the others; and all retired by another way than they came in.

* * *

O my Lord and my God, what great wonders hast thou caused to pass before mine eyes! who am I, O my God? dust and ashes, an ungrateful and rebellious creature; I should not dare to lift mine eyes towards Heaven, if the blood of Jesus Christ, thy Son, did not plead for me.

My soul rejoices, and is glad, she shouts for joy. O my God, whom I adore, love, and revere, before whom I desire to be without ceasing self-annihilated at thy feet. O my Lord, and my LOVE, the Seraphim and Cherubim burning with the fire of thy holy love, adore and honour thee; give me thy grace also O my God, that I may be consumed before thee, while I sing the majesty, glory, and the fame of God who hath created and redeemed me. I would praise him incessantly, not in appearance only, but in reality and truth. I would continue devoted to thee, and always be swallowed up in the ocean of love, without a wish to leave it.

* * *

Then my guardians took me up, and re-conducted me to the house whence I came, where I perceived the people assembled to my funeral, and discovering my body in the coffin, I was re-united with the same, and found myself lodged in my earthly tabernacle. And coming to myself, I knew my dear brother Marsay, and many others; who gave me an account that I had been 24 hours in the coffin, and that I lay 17 hours before they put me in my coffin; which altogether made 41 hours; but to me they seemed as many years.

Beginning to preach the universal Gospel, I was presently put into prison, but soon set at liberty again.

I visited all my brethren, preaching the Gospel, and taking leave of them all, because that my God, and Sovereign GOOD, called me to go into America, and preach the Gospel there.

I took my departure for America in the 38th year of my age, where I arrived, and have now dwelt 41 years. The 26th day of next July, I shall be 79 years of age. Blessed be the name of the Lord for ever.

SOURCE: George de Benneville, *A True and Most Remarkable Account of Some Passages in the Life of Mr. George de Benneville*, trans. Elhanan Winchester (London, 1791), 8–9, 14–16, 18–19, 22–29, 34, 36. Some punctuation modernized.

Some Deductions from the System Promulgated in the Page of Divine Revelation, Ranged in the Order and Form of a Catechism

1782

Judith Sargent Murray (1751–1820) was born to a prominent family from Gloucester, Massachusetts. Her father, Winthrop Sargent, first read the Universalist James Relly's Union *in 1769 and gathered the congregation that called John Murray as its minister in 1774. Judith's first marriage, to John Stevens of Gloucester at the age of eighteen, was emotionally unrewarding and financially disastrous. In 1780, John Stevens brought into the household two orphaned nieces. Judith, faced with raising these girls, began to commit to paper her thoughts on the religious upbringing of the young. In 1782, these thoughts were published anonymously in this catechism, an early statement of Universalist belief and an early religious education tool. Further Reading: Sharon M. Harris, ed.,* Selected Writings of Judith Sargent Murray *(New York: Oxford University Press, 1995); "Judith Sargent Murray Society," www.jsmsociety.com.*

—Gordon Gibson

QUESTION: *I wish my Preceptor would inform me to what purpose I came into this world?*

ANSWER: Your heavenly Father, my child, certainly placed you here for his glory and your own good.

Q. *Will my revered friend tell me how I am to be assured of this matter?*

A. Read, my child, those pages which we have every reason to believe dictated by the divine Author of veracity, and you will find there that God is said to be the parent of our spirits; in those writings too, he is clothed with that authority which constitutes the very essence of Godhead. From whence we rationally conclude, that his parental character will lead him to consult the good of his family, while his omnipotence will enable him to pursue every step which his sacred wisdom plans.

Q. *But what idea (give me leave to ask) ought I to form of a Being whom I have never seen?*

A. The Deity is invisible, incomprehensible; it is impossible, my dear, for a finite being to form an idea of infinite perfection.

A. Perhaps every injunction or prohibition may be either expressed, or implied, in the ten commandments; however, of this we may be certain, that there is to be found in the holy scriptures, a complete transcript of the moral beauty of the divine Being: a perfect system which comprehends all the laws of rectitude and harmony.

Q. *Is it possible for any one to keep those laws?*

A. No certainly! If Adam, in a state of innocence, could not continue in honor, consider my child, can his fallen sons answer the plan of rectitude given by the divine mind.

* * *

Q. *To what end then were the commandments given?*

A. For two reasons. 1. To give an exhibition of divine perfection. 2. To convince mankind of sin, of their own impotency, and thereby to induce them to rely *wholly* upon their Redeemer.

Q. *How is our breach of those commands to be punished?*

A. To disobey our Sovereign Law Giver is sin, and God hath declared, *the soul that sinneth, shall die.*

Q. *How then can any of the human race escape?*

A. The whole posterity of Adam, must inevitably have sunk into everlasting perdition, had not the second character of the glorious Trinity, condescended to the depth of our humiliation; he was made under the law; born of a woman; fulfilled every divine precept, and finally, (as being the Head of every man,) he *tasted death for every man!*

Q. *Was it not strange that God should punish the innocent for the guilty, or how could the sufferings of the just One make atonement for our iniquities?*

A. The scriptures speak of a *union* subsisting between Christ and the lost nature, antecedent to the fall; which union they hold up to us, under the apt similitudes of a vine and its branches, a husband, and wife, a head and its members, with many other striking figures: from thence we learn, that we were chosen in Christ before the foundation of the world; that though he himself knew no sin, yet was he made sin for us; all our iniquities were laid upon him.

* * *

Q. *But were we not threatened with eternal misery? how then were those three days accepted as satisfactory?*

A. The infinite Majesty of the sufferer, and his consequent infinite capacity for pain, was more than equivalent to an eternity of those agonies, under which a finite being *could* exist.

Q. *And yet I have been told that this atonement was made but for a few. Do the scriptures say it was satisfactory for the sins of all mankind?*

A. The sacred writings abound with positive declarations to this effect; the consolatory promise was made to Adam, before he was expelled the garden of God: it was afterwards repeated to many, chosen for that purpose. God said to Abraham, *in thee shall all the families of the earth be blessed*, and again, *in thy seed shall all the nations of the earth be blessed.*

* * *

Q. *How ought I to conceive of election according to the scriptures?*

A. I think the most consistent idea is, that there is a few chosen out of the world to bear witness to the truth, with whom the secret of the Lord is, from the rest, for wise reasons, it is hid; but there is a day coming when the veil shall be taken from all hearts, and in the mountain of the Lord of hosts, the feast of fat things shall be made for all people.

* * *

Q. *I heard one say the other day, that the 25th of Matthew, was sufficient to prove the doctrine of universal redemption false—doth it not contain a description of the last judgment?*

A. No doubt it does, all worlds are then collected before the throne of God.

Q. *Who are those upon the right hand of the Judge?*

A. They are every son and daughter of Adam, sheep are every where in the inspired writings held up as a figure of mankind, like lost sheep they once went astray, but they shall then return to the true shepherd and bishop of souls.

Q. *Can it be proved, that the whole race of man are upon the right hand?*

A. That there are two characters upon the right hand is plainly expressed, for God speaks *to* some, who had administered relief, and *of* others, to whom the relief had been administered; those latter, he calls the least of *his* brethren; now, who these least were, a foregoing section in the same book may inform us, where our blessed Lord says, whoever shall break one of these least commandments, and shall teach men to, he shall be called *the least in the kingdom of Heaven.*

Q. *Who are those upon the left hand?*

A. As the sheep is an emblem of human nature, so the goat, in many places, is given as a figure of the fallen Angelic nature; those envious spirits blending with humanity, deters them from feeding the hungry, clothing the naked, visiting the sick, or administering to the prisoners: Therefore, after God hath separated them one from the other (for every human being has an evil spirit, who is influential upon his conduct), as a shepherd divideth the sheep from the goats, he proceeds to address the Angelic nature; he passes sentence upon them, he consigns them over to misery, to the kingdom prepared for them: While the people for whom he had laid down his life, he receives into the kingdom of his Father.

98

Q. *How ought I to conceive of water baptism?*

A. As a figure of that washing wherewith we are cleansed by the blood of Jesus.

Q. *Is there any propriety in using it at this day?*

A. No certainly, the substance being manifested, our regard to the figure should cease.

Q. *But were not the disciples of John baptized?*

A. They were, but they were under the law, we are under grace.

Q. *Was not our Saviour himself baptized?*

A. He was, for he also was under the law, and he says, it became him thus to fulfill all righteousness.

Q. *Did not our Saviour practice water baptism?*

A. The scriptures expressly declare he baptized no one. . . .

Q. *But did not the disciples before the crucifixion use water baptism?*

A. Yes, the end of that dispensation was not fully come, under the jews, diverse washings were enjoined, as figurative of the great cleansing by the blood of Jesus.

Q. *Doth not the Redeemer, after his resurrection, command his disciples to go forth baptizing all Nations?*

A. He does, but *water* is not here mentioned. No, it was his own baptism to which he refers.

* * *

Q. *What think you of the Lord's supper?*

A. Not as of a figure of the sufferings of the Redeemer, for those were held forth in the paschal Lamb, who was to be roasted with fire, eaten with bitter herbs, a bone of whom was not to be broken.

Q. *What then does it hold forth?*

A. A doctrine the most consolatory that can be imagined, as the break which he break, was a gathering together of the many grains constituting one lump in which all distinctions were lost, and of which he says this is my body; so, in him are collected the scattered individuals of humanity, forming a complete man, and constituting the comprehensive character of our Lord.

Q. *What is the cup which he drank?*

A. As the collection of grains figured the body of the Redeemer in his complex character, so the many grapes pressed together constituting one wine, holds up to us the *oneness* of the soul of Jesus with the spirits of the human race, and in that he says this is my blood, we behold our mysterious union with him.

* * *

Q. *Doth not the church ordain that the bread and wine should be consecrated and received in a place appointed for public worship?*

A. She does, but this seems entirely a mode of human invention, and of which no trace is to be found in sacred writ. . . .

Q. *How will a christian now receive them?*

A. Wherever he beholds bread and wine, he will receive it with thankful gratitude, and he will be led from the figure to adore the grace contained therein.

* * *

Q. *What does a christian conceive of hell?*

A. As a place of darkness, from which he is exempt, by the son of man's descending into it; for which deliverance his adorations constantly arise and his soul is fraught with ceaseless gratitude to that righteous man, *the God man*, whose intercessory prayer for him, availeth much.

Q. *What think you of prayer?*

A. That it is an inestimable privilege, wherein we can pour forth our souls to God, and make known to him all our complaints; being assured that as a father, he heareth, and hath compassion upon us.

SOURCE: *Some Deductions from the System Promulgated in the Page of Divine Revelation: Ranged in the Order and Form of a Catechism: Intended as an Assistant to the Christian Parent or Teacher* (Portsmouth, NH, 1782), 5, 10–14, 18–19, 23–26, 31. Some spelling and punctuation modernized.

ETHAN ALLEN

Reason, the Only Oracle of Man
1784

Revolutionary hero Ethan Allen (1738–1789) offered a classically deist theology in this book, known to Allen's fellow Vermonters as "Ethan Allen's Bible." Rejecting all supernatural revelation, he drew conclusions about God, the world, and humanity based entirely on natural reason. In his third chapter, Allen attacked two mainstays of Puritan theology: the idea that humanity's sin against God is infinite in character and the related claim that humans not predestined to salvation will be punished eternally for this sin. Both of his arguments would soon influence Hosea Ballou's scripturally based defense of universal salvation. Further Reading: Darline Shapiro, "Ethan Allen: Philosopher-Theologian to a Generation of American Revolutionaries," William and Mary Quarterly 21, no. 2 (1964): 236–255; Michael Bellesiles, Revolutionary Outlaws: Ethan Allen and the Struggle for Independence on the Early American Frontier *(Charlottesville: University of Virginia Press, 1993).*

— Dan McKanan

The DOCTRINE *of the* INFINITE EVIL *of* SIN *considered.*

That God is infinitely good in the eternal displays of his providence, has been argued in the seventh section of the second chapter, from which we infer, that there cannot be an infinite evil in the universe, inasmuch as it would be incompatible with infinite good; yet there are many who imbibe the doctrine of the infinite evil of sin, and the maxim on which they predicate their arguments in its support, are that the greatness of sin, or adequateness of its punishment, is not to be measured . . . by the capacity and circumstances of the offender, but by the capacity and dignity of the being against whom the offence is committed; and as every transgression is against the authority and law of God, it is therefore against God; and as God is infinite, therefore, sin is an infinite evil, and from hence infer the infinite and vindictive wrath of God against sinners, and of his justice in dooming them, as some say to infinite, and others say to eternal misery. . . .

Admitting this maxim for truth, that the transgressions or sins of mankind are to be estimated . . . by the dignity and infinity of the divine nature, then it will follow that all sins would be equal . . . so that the sin would be the same to kill my neighbor as it would be to kill his horse.

* * *

The Moral GOVERNMENT *of* GOD *incompatible with eternal* PUNISHMENT.

❊   ❊   ❊

We may for certain conclude, that such a punishment will never have the divine approbation, or be inflicted on any intelligent being or beings in the infinitude of the government of God. For an endless punishment defeats the very end of its institution, which in all wise and good governments is as well to reclaim offenders, as to be examples to others; but a government which does not admit of reformation and repentance, must unavoidably involve its subjects in misery; for the weakness of creatures will always be a source of error and inconstancy, and a wise Governor, as we must admit God to be, would suit his government to the capacity and all other circumstances of the governed; and instead of inflicting eternal damnation on his offending children, would rather interchangeably extend his beneficence with his vindictive punishments, so as to alienate them from sin and wickedness, and incline them to morality . . . [and] give them occasion to *glorify* GOD *for the wisdom and goodness of his government* . . . But we are told that the eternal damnation of a part of mankind greatly augments the happiness of the elect, who are represented as being vastly the less numerous, (a diabolical temper of mind in the elect:) Besides, how narrow and contracted must such notions of infinite justice and goodness be? Who would imagine that the Deity conducts his providence similar to the detestable despots of this world? O *horrible* most *horrible impeachment* of DIVINE GOODNESS!

SOURCE: Ethan Allen, *Reason, the Only Oracle of Man: Or, A Compendious System of Natural Religion* (Bennington, VT, 1784), 110–11, 114, 117–19. Some spelling and punctuation modernized.

King's Chapel Prayer Book
1785

James Freeman (1759–1835), an unordained Congregationalist, was ill pre-
pared to revise a 235-year-old Anglican liturgy when called by King's Chapel
to be its lay reader in 1782. He had, however, a copy of the prayer book from
Theophilus Lindsey's breakaway church in London, and a disciple of Lindsey
to advise him. Supported by these and the vestry, he radically revised the
Anglican prayer book, justifying his actions with citations from the Thirty-
Nine Articles and other Church of England documents. Like earlier Unitari-
ans and rational Anglican contemporaries, Freeman removed the Gloria
Patri, prayers to Christ, and all Trinitarian references except for two specifi-
cally scriptural references: the Pauline benediction (2 Cor. 13:14) and the bap-
tismal formula (Matt. 28:19). He changed priest *to* minister *and* sacrament
to ordinance. *He changed the minister's pronouncement of forgiveness to a*
prayer for forgiveness. The communion, once focused on Christ's real pres-
ence, became a largely memorial celebration. The Athanasian Creed disap-
peared from the first edition and the Nicene Creed from the second. Italicized
portions of the psalms, depicting a vengeful God, were no longer read. Free-
man hoped that no Christian could take offense at this revision, yet many
did, and some litigiously. King's Chapel survived this storm of controversy
and others to follow. Further Reading: Charles Forman and Carl Scovel,
Journey Toward Independence: King's Chapel's Transition to Unitarianism
(Boston: Skinner House, 1993); Margaret Barry Chinkes, James Freeman
and Boston's Religious Revolution *(Glade Valley, NC: Glade Valley Books,*
1991); Henry Wilder Foote, "Religious Opinion in the Eighteenth Century"
and "The Ministry of James Freeman," Chaps. XX and XXI in The Annals of
King's Chapel from the Puritan Age to the Present Day, *vol. 2, ed. Henry H.*
Edes *(Little, Brown and Company, 1896).*

—Carl Scovel

The Preface.

Many truly great and learned men, of the Church of England, as well divines as
laymen, have earnestly wished to see their Liturgy reformed; but hitherto all attempts
to reform it have proved ineffectual. The late happy revolution here hath forever
separated all the Episcopal Societies, in the United States of America, from the

Church of England, of which the King of that country is the supreme head, and to whom all Arch-Bishops, Bishops, Priests, and Deacons of that Church are obliged to take an oath of allegiance and supremacy, at the time of their consecration or ordination. Being torn from that King and Church, the Society for whose use this Liturgy is published, think themselves at liberty, and well justified even by the declarations of the Church of England, in making such alterations, as "the exigency of the times and occasions hath rendered expedient," and in expunging everything which gave, or might be suspected to give, offence to tender consciences; guiding themselves however by "the holy scriptures, which" they heartily agree with the Church of England, "contain all things necessary to salvation," and that "whatsoever is not read therein, nor can be proved thereby, is not to be required of any man, that it should be believed as an article of faith, or be thought requisite or necessary to salvation." In the 34th of the Articles of the Church of England, it is declared, That "it is not necessary that traditions and ceremonies be in all places one, or utterly like; for at all times they have been diverse, and may be changed according to the diversity of countries, times, and men's manners, so that nothing be ordained against GOD's word." And by the 20th of those Articles it is declared, That "the Church hath power to decree rites and ceremonies, and authority in controversies of faith." What is there meant by the word Church, will appear from the 19th of those Articles, which declares "The visible Church of Christ is a Congregation of faithful men, in which the pure word of GOD is preached, and the sacraments be duly ministered, according to CHRIST's ordinance, in all those things that of necessity are requisite to the same. As the Church of Hierusalem, Alexandria, and Antioch have erred, so also the Church of Rome hath erred, not only in living, and manner of ceremonies, but also in matters of faith." At the Reformation, when the Book of Common Prayer of the Church of England was compiled, the Committee appointed to execute that business were obliged to proceed very tenderly and with great delicacy, for fear of offending the whole body of the people, just torn from the idolatrous Church of Rome; and many things were then retained which have, in later times, given great offence to many, truly pious, Christians.

The Liturgy contained in this volume is such that no Christian, it is supposed, can take offence at, or had his conscience wounded in repeating. The Trinitarian, the Unitarian, the Calvinist, the Arminian will read nothing in it which can give him any reasonable umbrage. GOD is the sole object of worship in these prayers; and as no man can come to GOD but by the one Mediator, JESUS CHRIST, every petition is here offered in his name, in obedience to his positive command. The Gloria Patri, made and introduced into the Liturgy of the Church of Rome by the decree of Pope Damasus, towards the latter part of the fourth century, and adopted into the Book of Common Prayer, is not in this Liturgy. Instead of that doxology, doxologies from the pure word of GOD are introduced. It is not our wish to make proselytes to any particular system or opinions of any particular sect of Christians. Our earnest desire is to live in brotherly love and peace with all men, and especially with those who call themselves the disciples of JESUS CHRIST.

In compiling this Liturgy great assistance hath been derived from the judicious corrections of the Reverend Mr. Lindsey, who hath reformed the Book of Common Prayer according to the Plan of the truly pious and justly celebrated Doctor Samuel Clarke. Several of Mr. Lindsey's amendments are adopted entire. The alterations which are taken from him, and the others which are made, excepting the prayers for Congress and the General Court, are none of them novelties; for the have been proposed and justified by some of the first divines of the Church of England.

A few passages in the Psalter, which are liable to be misconstrued or misapplied, are printed in Italics, and are designed to be omitted in repeating the Psalms.

SOURCE: "The Preface," in *A Liturgy, Collected Principally from the Book of Common Prayer, for the Use of the First Episcopal Church in Boston*, ed. James Freeman (Boston, 1785). Some spelling and punctuation modernized.

An Appeal to the Impartial Public by the Society of Christian Independents, congregating in Gloucester

1785

The British Universalist John Murray (1741–1815) arrived in North America in 1770 and soon settled in Gloucester, Massachusetts. In 1779, his follow-ers organized themselves into the Independent Church of Christ and soon began refusing to pay taxes for the support of the local parish church. When the authorities seized their possessions and jailed one member, they sued, citing a passage in the Massachusetts Bill of Rights (adopted in 1780). Even unincorporated religious communities, the Universalists argued, could claim exemption from church taxes. The Supreme Judicial Court of Massachusetts decided in their favor in a precedent-setting 1786 decision, and Universalists remained in the forefront of the struggle that culminated in Massachusetts's disestablishment in 1833. This pamphlet, prepared by Epes Sargent, presents their argument and offers a glimpse into early Universalist congregational life. Further Reading: Richard Eddy, Universalism in Gloucester, Mass. *(Gloucester, MA: Proctor Brothers, 1892).*

— Dan McKanan

Friends and Countrymen,

In our appeal to you, we feel a confidence, which in an address to the rulers of a tyrannical government, we could never possess. . . .

We should be far from giving our countrymen the trouble of attending to an appeal from a society, so small and inconsiderable as ours, had we not been drawn before a civil tribunal, in defence of what we suppose to be our just, invaluable and constitutional rights. A question has been agitated respecting us, the decision of which, ultimately regards every citizen of the Commonwealth, and instantly affects the several religious orders of Episcopalians, Baptists, Presbyterians, Sandamanians, Quakers, and every other denomination of Christians, who in this State have been called Sectaries. . . .

In the year 1779, we associated for the purpose of public worship, by a covenant whereof we have caused to be herewith submitted to the public eye.

Though we are united in a mode of worship, and a form of discipline, yet in our association, we have carefully avoided the establishment of it, because we are fully convinced that our blessed Redeemer left no particular form to his followers, but submitted all to their own wisdom and prudence. We conceive that a voluntary agreement, in religious matters, ought to be departed from, the moment the individual who is party to it, conceives that he has done wrong; and where those religious forms have been established by laws, we find by the best history of Ecclesiastical matters, that they have only tended to fetter the human understanding, and have been the unhappy means of substituting the form for the substance of religion.

We did not in our agreement, associate for the beliefs of any particular tenets, or peculiar doctrines, because we conceived that all conviction must rise from evidence rationally applied to the understanding; and we could not suppose that the same evidence would strike every mind in the society with the same force. We therefore concluded that confessions of faith with us, might do what we believe they have done in other societies, where those of human invention have been introduced, oblige men, either to submit their faith to the control of others, and believe without examining, or to profess to believe that which they have never fully considered or understood. With that humility which we find inculcated in every part of the Gospel, we humbly hoped, that it would be sufficient for us to believe the Holy Scriptures, and to adopt the system of morals therein contained, *as the rule of our Conduct, and the man of our Counsel.*

* * *

The articles of faith commonly called the Platform, and made in the year 1646, has ever shackled the freedom of the people in New-England; but blessed be God, the liberty now happily established by our Constitution, has given a fatal stab to all religious oppression in this state.

The evil which we find to have accrued from the establishment of creeds of human invention, we hope will make us sufficiently cautions, and prevent or forming any other mode of expression for articles of faith than the gospel, in its own language, and in its own form. . . .

We find that the Sects of Christians in New-England, have ever been distinguished from each other by their form of church-discipline, and their mode of administering the ordinances: the doctrines, or articles of faith, held by all being as nearly similar, as that of individuals in the same church have generally been. We distinguish ourselves from the church under the instruction of Mr. Forbes, by our not using baptism as an external rite.

* * *

The third article in the declaration of rights, provides, that "all monies paid by the subject to the support of public worship, and of the public teachers aforesaid, shall, if he require it, be uniformly applied to the support of the public teacher or teachers of his own religious sect or denomination, provided there be any on whose instructions he attends." . . . For the reasons before-mentioned, we consider ourselves a *Sect* different from those who attend upon the ministry of Mr. Forbes; and we therefore are of opinion, that the money raised upon us ought to be applied to the support of the teacher of our own religious sect, there being one on whose instructions we attend. But it was objected that the teacher who is intitled to receive the money paid by his hearers, must be a teacher of piety, religion and morality: this we concede, but we are not convinced that the question, whether he is a teacher of piety, religion, and morality, can be determined from a revision of the motives he offers as to the rewards and punishments which are to be bestowed or inflicted in another world. We believe that the question must be decided by the evidence of his urging the people to piety and morality, as the foundation of the greatest good which their natures are capable of, and as a compliance with the will of their almighty Creator and preserver, without going into an inquiry of his opinion respecting the quantity of punishment in a future state.

That God will punish men for sin, in such a manner as will far over-balance the pleasures which can be derived from vice in this world, is so clearly pointed out in the gospel, that we are compelled to believe it; but whether the opinion of some learned and good men, who imagine that the wicked will be annihilated, or whether that of the learned Doctor Chauncy, Doctor Priestly, and many others, who believe that there is a temporary hell prepared for the ungodly, which is another state of probation, or any other opinion respecting that subject is best, every one must determine for himself. . . .

The idea, that it is necessary to the good order of civil government, that the Teachers of Religion should thunder out the doctrine of everlasting punishment, to deter men from atrocious crimes, which they may otherwise commit in secret, has long been hackneyed in the hands of men in power, but without any warrant from reason, or revelation for doing of it. . . . It was not till the Christian Church was illegally wedded to state-policy, that men in power dared to hurl the Thunders of the Most High at those who offended against government.

SOURCE: *An Appeal to the Impartial Public by the Society of Christian Independents, congregating in Gloucester* (Boston: Benjamin Edes & Sons, 1785), 3–6, 12–13, 16–18.

ELHANAN WINCHESTER

The Universal Restoration, Exhibited in a Series of Dialogues

1788

Elhanan Winchester (1751–1797) was the most wide-ranging and successful of early Universalist evangelists. Born near Boston, he became a Baptist revivalist in South Carolina, ministering to both white and black congregations. His success in converting large numbers of people caused him to doubt the Calvinist doctrine that severely limited the number of the elect. In 1780, he became minister to the First Baptist Church of Philadelphia. Influenced by European universalist works and having talked with George de Benneville, Winchester became a believer in "Universal Restoration" and, in consequence, was expelled from his church in 1781. The majority of the membership went with him to found the Society of Universal Baptists. Winchester made trips to New England in 1785 and 1794, taking important parts in Universalist conventions. For seven years, 1787 to 1794, he evangelized in London and throughout England. While there he wrote his most influential book, Dialogues on the Universal Restoration (1788), *which extended his influence long past his lifetime and made many converts to Universalism in the nineteenth century. Further Reading: Thomas Whittemore,* The Modern History of Universalism, *vol. 1, 2nd ed. (Boston, 1860).*

—Peter Hughes

Friend. But if the Spirit of God dwelling in us, and thereby causing us to adhere to Christ, and to follow him through all trials, makes our union to him so perfect, that nothing shall be able to separate us from him to all eternity; since we are confirmed in habits of goodness by free choice, and by oft repeated exercises; why, by the same rule, shall not the misery of the wicked be endless, seeing that they have chosen and adhered to evil through life, and by constant practice are confirmed therein? . . .

Minister. Your reasoning would be conclusive, upon the supposition that *there are two eternal principles,* viz. *good* and *evil*; if it can be proved that evil is coexistent with goodness, that it has always been: then, the absolute eternity of sin and misery may easily be inferred. This is the true foundation of *endless misery,* and it came from Pagan theology: The Heathens believed in *two eternal principles,* ever warring against each other, and neither fully prevailing; that men had the liberty of enlisting under which they pleased; and that those who in life chose virtue, should enjoy endless felicity; while those who chose, and adhered to vice, should eternally remain under its dominion, and of consequence be always miserable. Thus, the infernal deities being judged by the poor Pagans to be as eternal as the good gods, and more powerful; they sacrificed more to the evil principle than to the good, out of fear, and to appease the anger of those abhorred, malevolent agents; hence, the frequency of human sacrifices.

Now, when the Christian religion triumphed over Paganism in the Roman empire, many of the philosophers embraced and professed it, but withal, retained many of their Pagan notions; among which was the *eternity* of these two opposite principles: hence there arose the ancient sect of the Manichees, who believed not only the eternal existence of two contrary eternal Gods, one good and the other evil; but also, that all visible things were created by the devil; and upon this principle, they might argue the universality of damnation, with as much ease and certainty, as we, upon the contrary, may argue the certainty of the universal Restoration, according to the glorious promise of God, Isaiah lvii. 16, 17, 18, 19. "For I will not contend for ever, neither will I be always wroth."

*   *   *

Friend. It is said that it is the nature of God to lay the highest possible restraint upon sin, and, therefore, he has threatened it with eternal, or *endless* punishment; and this is even found too weak the prevailing of iniquity. What a flood of impiety, therefore, would overflow the world, if it should be generally believed, that after some ages of suffering, mankind should be restored to some degree of happiness?

*   *   *

Minister. . . . I. It is not quite clear to me, that it is the nature of God to lay the highest possible restraint upon sin; and that he always does so, in all his dispensations. He sometimes has higher designs in view, than barely to restrain sin: he sometimes, perhaps, suffers it to prevail for a time, that his power might be more manifest in destroying it. . . . Perhaps, if the punishment of sins immediately followed the commission of them, it would be a stronger and more effectual restraint than any threatenings of future misery. . . . There is no doubt, but if the awful punishments of the future state were made visible to our senses, by any means, they would prove a powerful restraint to sin; yet God has not thought fit to restrain it by those, and perhaps many other possible ways: Wherefore, I have a right to doubt the premises; for, if the strongest possible restraints were laid upon sin, it might not be so consistent with a state of probation, as those reasonable restraints which God hath thought fit to lay upon it.

2. But it may be questioned whether there is not something in the idea of limited, yet certain punishment, so just, equitable, reasonable, and evident, that is much more calculated to produce belief, and consequently more effectual to destroy false

110

hopes of escaping it, and also to check that daring presumption, which rises out of the idea of *endless misery*, than can be found in the contrary doctrine. . . . I have heard of numbers that had no better excuse for sinning greedily, than this, *viz.* that there was no hopes of their being saved; that, therefore, they were determined to sin as much as possible, since it could make no difference. I have reason to say, from what I know of mankind, that more persons refuse to believe in Divine Revelation, because it is commonly thought to contain the doctrine of *endless misery*, than from any other cause. . . .

3. Whether it is, that *endless damnation* is too unnatural to be believed, and that *limited punishments*, being more reasonable, seem more certain; or whether it be, that by considering they shall be punished, either without end, or not at all; and every one thinking that endless punishment is more than they deserve, but is only reserved for some greater sinners, and therefore they have nothing to fear from it, I shall not pretend to determine; but certain it is, that where the idea of endless misery prevails, it has not prevented iniquity, in the measure that might have been expected, on the supposition of its being the truth of GOD.

4. The great number of Heathens that die without ever being favoured with the light of the gospel, and certainly without ever hearing of endless misery; the many that die in the state of infancy and childhood; together with the instances of idiots, and persons born deaf; all convince me, more than any logical arguments, that God has many ways of instructing and reclaiming his creatures, in another state that we are at present unacquainted with.

SOURCE: Elhanan Winchester, *The Universal Restoration, Exhibited in a Series of Dialogues* (London, 1788), 29–31, 118, 148–51.

JUDITH SARGENT MURRAY
"On the Equality of the Sexes"
1790

Judith Sargent Murray (1751–1820) became, with this essay, the first published American advocate for women's rights. Here, in other published works, and throughout her extensive correspondence, two preeminent concerns appeared and were often intertwined: universal salvation and the rights and status of women. Judith was born to a prominent Gloucester, Massachusetts, family. Widowed in 1787, she married the Rev. John Murray in 1788. The two had known each other for fourteen years, exchanging frequent letters ranging from the theological to the mundane. Their marriage opened both partners to new prospects, including expanded writing and publication for Judith, one of whose pseudonyms, as seen in the example here, was Constantia. Further Reading: Sharon M. Harris, ed., Selected Writings of Judith Sargent Murray *(New York: Oxford University Press, 1995); "Judith Sargent Murray Society," jsmsociety.com.*

—Gordon Gibson

To the Editors of the Massachusetts Magazine,

Gentlemen,

The following ESSAY *is yielded to the patronage of Candour. — If it hath been anticipated, the testimony of many respectable persons, who saw it in manuscripts as early as the year 1779, can obviate the imputation of plagiarism.*

> THAT minds are not alike, full well I know,
> This truth each day's experience will show;
> To heights surprising some great spirits soar,
> With inborn strength mysterious depths explore;
> Their eager gaze surveys the path of light,
> Confest it stood to Newton's piercing sight.
> Deep science, like a bashful maid retires,
> And but the *ardent* breast her worth inspires;
> By perseverance the coy fair is won.
> And Genius, led by Study, wears the crown.
> But some there are who wish not to improve,

Who never can the path of knowledge love,
Whose souls almost with the dull body one,
With anxious care each mental pleasure shun;
Weak is the level'd, enervated mind,
And but while here to vegetate design'd.
The torpid spirit mingling with its clod,
Can scarcely boast its origin from God;
Stupidly dull—they move progressing on—
They eat, and drink, and all their work is done.
While others, emulous of sweet applause,
Industrious seek for each event a cause,
Tracing the hidden springs whence knowledge flows,
Which nature all in beauteous order shows.
Yet cannot I their sentiments imbibe,
Who this distinction to the sex ascribe,
As if a woman's form must needs enrol,
A weak, a servile, an inferiour soul;
And that the guise of man must still proclaim,
Greatness of mind, and him, to be the same:
Yet as the hours revolve fair proofs arise,
Which the bright wreath of growing fame supplies;
And in past times some men have *sunk* so *low*,
That female records nothing *less* can show.
But imbecility is still confin'd,
And by the lordly sex to us consign'd;
They rob us of the power t'improve,
And then declare we only trifles love;
Yet haste the era, when the world shall know,
That such distinctions only dwell below;
The soul unfetter'd, to no sex confin'd,
Was for the abodes of cloudless day design'd.
Mean time we emulate their manly fires,
Though erudition all their thoughts inspires,
Yet nature with *equality* imparts,
And *noble passions*, swell e'en *female hearts*.

Is it upon mature consideration we adopt the idea, that nature is thus partial in her distributions? Is it indeed a fact, that she hath yielded to one half of the human species so unquestionable a mental superiority? I know that to both sexes elevated understandings, and the reverse, are common. But, suffer me to ask, in what the minds of females are so notoriously deficient, or unequal. May not the intellectual powers be ranged under these four heads—imagination, reason, memory and judgment. The province of imagination hath long since been surrendered up to us, and we have been crowned and undoubted sovereigns of the regions of fancy. Invention is perhaps the most arduous effort of the mind; this branch of imagination hath been particularly ceded to us, and we have been time out of mind invested with that creative faculty. Observe the variety of fashions (here I bar the contemptuous smile) which distinguish and adorn the female world: how continually are they changing, insomuch that they almost render the wise man's assertion problematical, and we are ready to say, *there is something new under the sun*. Now what a playfulness, what an exuberance of fancy, what strength of inventine imagination, doth this continual variation discover? Again, it hath been observed, that if the turpitude of the conduct of our sex, hath been ever so enormous, so extremely ready are we, that the very first thought presents us with an apology, so plausible, as to produce our actions even in an amiable light. Another instance of our creative powers, is our talent for slander; how ingenious are we at inventive scandal? what a formidable story can we in a moment fabricate merely from the force of a prolifick imagination? how many reputations, in the fertile brain of a female, have been utterly despoiled? how industrious are we at improving a hint? suspicion how easily do we convert into conviction, and conviction, embellished by the power of eloquence, stalks abroad to the surprise and confusion of unsuspecting innocence. Perhaps it will be asked if I furnish these facts as instances of excellency in our sex. Certainly not; but as proofs of a creative faculty, of a lively imagination. Assuredly great activity of mind is thereby discovered, and was this activity properly directed, what beneficial effects would follow. Is the needle and kitchen sufficient to employ the operations of a soul thus organized? I should conceive not, Nay, it is a truth that those very departments leave the intelligent principle vacant, and at liberty for speculation. Are we deficient in reason? we can only reason from what we know, and if an opportunity of acquiring knowledge hath been denied us, the inferiority of our sex cannot fairly be deduced from thence. . . .

"But our judgment is not so strong—we do not distinguish so well."—Yet it may be questioned, from what doth this superiority, in this determining faculty of the soul, proceed. May we not trace its source in the difference of education, and continued advantages? Will it be said that the judgment of a male of two years old, is more sage than that of a female's of the same age? I believe the reverse is generally observed to be true. But from that period what partiality! how is the one exalted, and the other depressed, by the contrary modes of education which are adopted! the one is taught to aspire, and the other is early confined and limitted. As their years increase, the sister must be wholly domesticated, while the brother is led by the hand through all the flowery paths of science. Grant that their minds are by nature equal, yet who shall wonder at the *apparent* superiority, if indeed custom becomes *second nature*; nay if it taketh place of nature, and that it doth the experience of each day will evince. At length arrived at womanhood, the uncultivated fair one feels a void, which the employments allotted her are by no means capable of filling. What can she do? to books she may not apply; or if she doth, *to those only of the novel kind*, lest she merit the appellation of a *learned lady*; and what ideas have been affixed to this term, the observation of many can testify. . . . Meantimes she herself is most unhappy; she feels the want of a cultivated mind. Is she single, she in vain seeks to fill up time from sexual employments or amusements. Is she united to a person whose soul nature made equal to her own, education hath set him so far above her, that in those entertainments which are productive of such rational felicity, she is not qualified to accompany him. She experiences a mortifying consciousness of inferiority, which embitters every enjoyment. Doth the person to whom her adverse fate hath consigned her, possess a mind incapable of improvement, she is equally wretched, in being so closely connected with an individual whom she cannot but despise. Now, was she permitted the same instructors as her brother, (with an eye however to their particular departments) for the employment of a rational mind an ample field would be opened. In astronomy she might catch a glimpse of the immensity of the Deity, and thence she would form amazing conceptions of the august and supreme Intelligence. In geography she would admire Jehovah in the midst of his benevolence; thus adapting this globe to the various wants and amusements of its inhabitants. In natural philosophy she would adore the infinite majesty of heaven, clothed in condescension; and as she traversed the reptile world, she would hail the goodness of a creating God. A mind, thus filled, would have little room for the trifles with which our sex are, with too much justice, accused of amusing themselves, and they would thus be rendered fit companions for those, who should one day wear them as their crown. . . . Females would become discreet, their judgments would be invigorated, and their partners for life being circumspectly chosen, an unhappy Hymen would then be as rare, as is now the reverse.

Will it be urged that those acquirements would supersede our domestick duties. I answer that every requisite in female economy is easily attained; and, with truth I can add, that when once attained, they require no further *mental attention*. Nay, while we are pursuing the needle, or the superintendency of the family, I repeat, that our minds are at full liberty for reflection; that imagination may exert itself in full vigor; and that if a just foundation is early laid, our ideas will then be worthy of rational beings. If we were industrious we might easily find time to arrange them upon paper, or should avocations press too hard for such an indulgence, the hours allotted for conversation would at least become more refined and rational. Should it still be vociferated, "Your domestick employments are sufficient" — I would calmly ask, is it reasonable, that a candidate for immortality, for the joys of heaven, an intelligent being, who is to spend an eternity in contemplating the works of the Deity, should at present be so degraded, as to be allowed no other ideas, than those which are suggested by the mechanism of a pudding, or the sewing the seams of a garment? Pity that all such censurers of female improvement do not go one step further, and deny their future existence; to be consistent they surely ought.

Yes, ye lordly, ye haughty sex, our souls are by nature *equal* to yours; the same breath of God animates, enlivens, and invigorates us; and that we are not fallen lower than yourselves, let those witness who have greatly towered above the various discouragements by which they have been so heavily oppressed; and though I am unacquainted with the list of celebrated characters on either side, yet from the observations I have made in the contracted circle in which I have moved, I dare confidently believe, that from the commencement of time to the present day, there hath been as many females, as males, who, by the *mere force of natural powers*, have merited the crown of applause; who, *thus unassisted*, have seized the wreath of fame. I know there are who assert, that as the animal power of the one sex are superiour, of course their mental faculties also must be stronger; thus attributing strength of mind to the transient organization of this earth born tenement. But if this reasoning is just, man must be content to yield the palm to many of the brute creation, since by not a few of his brethren of the field, he is far surpassed in bodily strength. Moreover, was this argument admitted, it would prove too much, for occular demonstration evinceth, that there are many robust masculine ladies, and effeminate gentlemen. . . .

I AM aware that there are many passages in the sacred oracles which seem to give the advantage to the other sex; but I consider all these as wholly metaphorical. Thus David was a man after God's own heart, yet see him enervated by his licentious passions! behold him following Uriah to the death, and shew me wherein could consist the immaculate Being's complacency. Listen to the curses which Job bestoweth upon the day of his nativity, and tell me where is his perfection, where his patience—*literally* it existed not. David and Job were types of him who was to come; and the superiority of man, as exhibited in scripture, being also emblematical, all arguments deduced from thence, of course fall to the ground. The exquisite delicacy of the female mind proclaimeth the exactness of its texture, while its nice sense of honour announceth its innate, its native grandeur. . . .

CONSTANTIA.

By way of supplement to the foregoing pages, I subjoin the following extract from a letter, wrote to a friend in the December of 1780

And now assist me, O thou genius of my sex, while I undertake the arduous task of endeavouring to combat that vulgar, that almost universal errour, which hath, it seems, enlisted even Mr. P— under its banners. The superiority of your sex hath, I grant, been time out of mind esteemed a truth incontrovertible; in consequence of which persuasion, every plan of education hath been calculated to establish this favourite tenet. Not long since, weak and presuming as I was, I amused myself with selecting some arguments from nature, reason, and experience; against this so generally received idea. I confess that to sacred testimonies I had not recourse. I held them to be merely metaphorical, and thus regarding them, I could not persuade myself that there was any propriety in bringing them to decide in this *very important debate*. However, as you, sir, confine yourself entirely to the sacred oracles, I mean to bend the whole of my artillery against those supposed proofs, which you have from thence provided, and from which you have formed an intrenchment *apparently* so invulnerable. And first, to begin with our great progenitors; but here, suffer me to premise, that it is for mental strength I mean to contend, for with respect to animal powers, I yield them undisputed to that sex, which enjoys them in common with the lion, the tyger, and many other beasts of prey; therefore your observations respecting the *rib, under the arm, at a distance from the head,* &c. &c. in no sort militate against my view. Well, but the woman was first in the transgression. Strange how blind *self love* renders you men; were you not wholly absorbed in a partial admiration of your own abilities, you would long since have acknowledged the force of what I am now going to urge. It is true some ignoramuses have absurdly enough informed us, that the beauteous fair of paradise, was seduced from her obedience, by a malignant demon, *in the guise of a baleful serpent*; but we, who are better informed, know that the fallen spirit presented himself to her view, *a shining angel still*; for thus, saith the criticks in the Hebrew tongue, ought the word to be rendered. Let us examine her motive—Hark! the seraph declares that she shall attain a perfection of knowledge; for is there aught which is not comprehended under one or other of the terms *good* and *evil*. It doth not appear that she was governed by any one sensual appetite; but merely by a desire of adorning her mind; a laudable ambition fired her soul, and a thirst for knowledge impelled the predilection so fatal in its consequences. Adam could not plead the same deception; assuredly he was not deceived; nor ought we to admire his superiour strength, or wonder at his sagacity, when we so often confess that example is much more influential than precept. His gentle partner stood before him, a melancholy instance of the direful effects of disobedience; he saw her not possessed of that wisdom which she had fondly hoped to obtain, but he beheld the once blooming female, disrobed of that innocence, which had heretofore rendered her so lovely. To him then deception became impossible, as he had proof positive of the fallacy of the argument, which the deceiver had suggested. What then could be his inducement to burst the barriers, and to fly directly in the face of that command, which *immediately* from the mouth of deity *he* had received, since, I say, he could not plead that fascinating stimulous, the accumulation of knowledge, as indisputable conviction was so visibly portrayed before him. What mighty cause impelled him to sacrifice myriads of beings yet unborn, and by one impious act, which *he saw* would be productive of such fatal effects, entail undistinguished ruin upon a race of beings, which he was yet to produce. Blush, ye vaunters of fortitude; ye boasters of resolution; ye haughty lords of the creation; blush when ye remember, that he was influenced by no other motive than a bare pusilianimous attachment to a woman! by sentiments so exquisitely soft, that all his sons have, from that period, when they have designed to degrade them, described as highly feminine. Thus it should seem, that all the arts of the grand deceiver (since means adequate to the purpose are, I conceive, invariably pursued) were requisite to mislead our general mother, while the father of mankind forfeited his own, and relinquished the happiness of posterity, merely in compliance with the blandishments of a female. The subsequent subjection the apostle Paul explains as a figure; after enlarging upon the subject, he adds, *"This is a great mystery; but I speak concerning Christ and the church."* Now we know with what consummate wisdom the unerring father of eternity hath formed his plans; all the types which he hath displayed, he hath permitted *materially* to fail, in the very virtue for which *they* were famed. The reason for this is obvious, we might otherwise mistake his economy, and render that honour to the creature, which is due only to the creator. I know that Adam was a figure of him who was to come. The grace contained in this figure, is the reason of my rejoicing, and while I am very far from prostrating before the shadow, I yield joyfully in all things the preeminence to the second federal head. Confiding faith is prefigured by Abraham, yet he exhibits a contrast to affiance, when he says of his fair companion, she is my sister. Gentleness was the characteristick of Moses, yet he hesitated not to reply to Jehovah himself, with unsaintlike tongue he murmured at the waters of strife, and with rash hands he break the tables, which were inscribed by the finger of divinity. David, dignified with the title of the man after God's own heart, and yet how stained was his life. Solomon was celebrated for wisdom, but folly is wrote in legible characters upon his almost every action. Lastly, let us turn our eyes to man in the aggregate. He is manifested as the figure of strength, but that we may not regard him as any thing more than a figure, his soul is formed in no sort superiour, but every way equal to the mind of her who is the emblem of weakness and whom he hails the gentle companion of his better days.

SOURCE: Constantia [Judith Sargent Murray], "On the Equality of the Sexes," *Massachusetts Magazine*, 2 (1790): 132–35, 223–26.

"Articles of Faith and Plan of Church Government"

1790

The Philadelphia Convention of Universalists was the first national orga-
nization for believers in universal salvation, but it never achieved a strong
institutional basis. Its first gathering, held in 1790 at the meetinghouse of
Elhanan Winchester's Society of Universal Baptists, attracted seven ministers
and ten laymen. John Murray represented the congregations in Gloucester
and Boston, but all other participants came from Pennsylvania, New Jersey,
and Virginia. By 1792, fifteen societies were in fellowship with the convention,
although it declined quickly thereafter and ceased meeting in 1809. Mean-
while, the New England Convention of Universalists, which first gathered
in 1793, grew steadily into a genuine national denomination. In light of the
many paths that brought people to Universalism, the Philadelphia Conven-
tion's "Articles of Faith" were designed to protect theological and liturgical
diversity. The accompanying recommendations reflect the social reform vision
of Benjamin Rush, a prominent Philadelphia physician and signer of the
Declaration of Independence who was a close ally of Winchester. Further
Reading: Russell E. Miller, The Larger Hope, vol. 1: The First Century of
the Universalist Church in America, 1770–1870 *(Boston: Unitarian Univer-*
salist Association, 1979); Ann Lee Bressler, The Universalist Movement in
America, 1770–1880 *(New York: Oxford, 2001).*

—Dan McKanan

Articles of Faith and Plan of Church Government
composed and adopted by the churches believing in the Salvation of All Men, met
in Philadelphia on the 25th of May, 1790 to which are added, Sundry Recommendations, and a Circular Letter addressed to the churches in the United States, believing
the same doctrine.

INTRODUCTION.

Under a deep sense of the unchangeable, and universal love of God to mankind in
a Redeemer, and in humble thankfulness to his kind providence in permitting us to
assemble and deliberate, agreeably to the dictates of our consciences, without fear of

civil or ecclesiastical power; WE, the representatives of sundry Societies in the United States, believing in the Salvation of all Men, convened on the 25th of May, 1790, in the city of Philadelphia, by an invitation from the brethren in said city, holding the same doctrine, and having implored the direction and blessing of God upon our endeavours to extend the knowledge of his Name, have adopted the following Articles, and Plan of Church Government.

ARTICLES of FAITH.

Of the HOLY SCRIPTURES.

We believe the Scriptures of the Old and New Testaments to contain a revelation of the perfections and will of God, and the rule of faith and practice.

Of the SUPREME BEING.

We believe in ONE GOD, infinite in all his perfections; and that these perfections are all modifications of infinite, adorable, incomprehensible and unchangeable LOVE.

Of the MEDIATOR.

We believe that there is ONE MEDIATOR between God and man, the man Jesus Christ, in whom dwelleth all the fulness of the Godhead bodily; who, by giving himself a ransom for all, hath redeemed them to God by his blood; and who, by the merit of his death, and the efficacy of his Spirit, will finally restore the whole human race to happiness.

Of the HOLY GHOST.

We believe in the HOLY GHOST, whose office it is to make known to Sinners the truth of their [this] salvation, through the medium of the Holy Scriptures, and to reconcile the hearts of the children of men to God, and thereby dispose them to genuine holiness.

Of GOOD WORKS.

We believe in the obligation of the moral law, as to the rule of life; and we hold, that the love of God manifest to man in a Redeemer, is the best means of producing obedience to that law, and promoting a holy, active, and useful life.

PLAN of CHURCH GOVERNMENT.

Of a CHURCH.

We conceive a Church to consist of a number of believers, united by covenant, for the purposes of maintaining the public worship of God, the preaching of the Gospel, ordaining Officers, preserving Order and Peace amongst its Members, and relieving the Poor.—Each Church possesses within itself all the powers of self-government.

Of the OFFICERS of a CHURCH.

The Officers of a Church are two, *viz.* BISHOPS and DEACONS. The terms Bishop, Elder, Minister, Pastor, and Teacher, we conceive to be the same, and intended only to express the different capacities in which the same Officer is called to act. For the duty of Bishops we refer to the 28th chapter of Matthew, and the 19th and 20th verses; and for the qualifications and duty of both Bishops and Deacons, we refer to the 3d and 4th chapters of the first epistle to Timothy.

Of the CALL and ORDINATION of the OFFICERS of the CHURCH.

Such persons as possess those qualifications and gifts, which the Holy Scriptures prescribe for a Bishop, and who wish to devote themselves to God in the ministry, shall be invited to preach before the members of the Church; and if after trial, they shall appear to be under the influence of the spirit of the Gospel, and to possess such endowments as are requisite for the profitable exercise of the duty of a Bishop or Minister, the Church shall solemnly set apart and ordain such persons; and a certificate of such appointment shall be to them a sufficient ordination to preach the gospel, and to administer such ordination, herein after-mentioned, as to them may seem proper, wherever they may be called by Divine Providence.

And as the great design of forms in ordaining Ministers, is to prevent weak, and immoral persons from exercising the ministerial office, we admit Ordination by any Church in which such forms have been observed, to be valid, and when persons so Ordained, shall apply to become members of any of our Churches, they shall (if otherwise qualified) be admitted not only as Members, but Ministers also.

DEACONS shall be chosen by the members of the Church, and ordained in like manner as Bishops or Ministers. Their business (besides receiving and applying the pious and charitable contributions of the Church for the support of the labourers of the Gospel, and the relief of the poor), shall be to attend to the secular affairs of the church, to keep an exact register of all the persons who shall be born, baptized, admitted to communion, married, or who shall remove or die, belonging to the Society; also, an account of the admission and dismission of members, and of all the business of the Church.

Of DIVINE WORSHIP.

Each church shall meet statedly one day in seven for the worship of God, and the preaching of the Gospel. And as we have no rules laid down in the word of God to direct us in our choice of a mode or form of public worship, it is recommended to each Church to use such modes and forms of prayer, and to sing such psalms, hymns, and spiritual songs, as to them shall appear most agreeable to the word of God, or best suited to promote order, and spiritual edification.

Of ORDINANCES.

Whereas a great diversity of opinions has prevailed in all ages of the Church upon the subjects of Baptism and the Lord's Supper; as also upon the subject of Confirmation, the Washing of Feet, Love Feasts, and the anointing the Sick with oil, &c. and as this diversity of opinions has often been the means of dividing Christians, who were united by the same spirit in more essential articles, we agree to admit all such persons who hold the articles of our faith, and maintain good works, into membership, whatever their opinions may be as to the nature—form—or obligations of any or all of the above named ordinances. If it shall so happen that an application shall be made to a Minister to perform any of the said of ordinances, who does not believe in the present obligations of Christians to submit to them; or if he shall be applied to to perform them at a *time*, or in a *way* that is contrary to his conscience, in such a case a neighbouring Minister, who shall hold like principles respecting the ordinance or ordinances required by any member, shall be invited to perform them; or if it be thought more expedient, each Church may appoint or ordain one of their own members to administer the ordinances in such a way as to each Church may seem proper.

Of the ADMISSION and EXCLUSION of MEMBERS.

All persons who subscribe our articles of faith and lead sober and moral lives shall be considered members of a Church. A departure from those articles, or an immoral life, shall subject a member to private admonition by the Minister, or a brother member only, according to Matth. xviii, 18, 21 and Luke xvii. 3, and 4. If what we conceive to be error, or if what all Christian Churches agree to be vice, is persisted in, the offending member shall be admonished a second time by any two or three members of the Church. If after these steps, he continue disobedient, his name be publically erased from the list of members, but he shall be exhorted at the same time to attend public worship, and the preaching of the Gospel; and he shall be restored in love, after he exhibits such signs of a return to his former faith or practice, as shall be deemed satisfactory to the Church.

Of MARRIAGE.

Marriages are to be performed in such way as the laws of the particular States have made necessary; Ministers of the Gospel belonging to our Church are at liberty to celebrate this ordinance.

Of the INSTRUCTION of CHILDREN.

We believe it to be the duty of all parents to instruct their children in the principles of the Gospel, as the best means to inspire them with the love of virtue, and to promote in them good manners, and habits of industry and sobriety. As a necessary introduction to the knowledge of the Gospel, we recommend the institution of a school, or schools, to be under the direction of every church; in which shall be taught reading, writing, arithmetic, and psalmody. We recommend, further, that provision be made for instructing poor children, in the said schools, *gratis*. As the fullest discovery of the perfections and will of God, and the whole duty of man, is contained in the BIBLE, we wish that Divine Book to be read by the youth of our Churches as early and frequently as possible; and that they should be instructed therein at state meetings appointed for that purpose.

Of the COMMUNION of CHURCHES.

The Churches shall convene together for the purpose of more effectually spreading the Gospel, and assisting and edifying each other. A Convention of the Churches shall be held annually by deputies or messengers, to enquire into, and to report, the state of each Church, respecting the admission of members, and the progress of the Gospel; to consult and act for the common benefit of all Churches; and to send forth ministers to propagate the Gospel in places where it had not been regularly preached, and thereby to form and establish new Churches. — No Acts of this Convention shall be supposed to invade the freedom or sovereignty of a particular Church. Each Church reserves to itself full and exclusive power to judge of all matters relating to faith or practice (as established by our Articles) among its own members. — All of the general Acts of the convention which relate to the interests of particular Church shall be issued only by way of advice, or recommendation.

RECOMMENDATIONS

Of WAR.

Although a defensive war may be considered lawful, yet we believe that there is a time coming when the light and universal love of the Gospel, shall put an end to all wars. We recommend, therefore, to all the Churches of our Communion, to cultivate the spirit of peace, and brotherly love, which shall lead them to consider all mankind as brethren; and to strive to spread among them the knowledge of their common Saviour and Redeemer, who came into the world, "not to destroy men's lives but to save them."

Of going to LAW.

We hold it unbecoming for Christians, who are members of the same Church, to appeal to Courts of Law for the settlement of disputes. Such appeals too often engender malice, beget idleness, and produce a waste of property. They are, therefore, contrary to the spirit of the Gospel. In disputes of all kinds, and with all persons, we recommend appeals to Arbitrators appointed by both parties, where it is practicable, in preference to Courts of Law.

Of holding SLAVES.

We believe it to be inconsistent with the union of the human race in a common Saviour, and the obligations to mutual and universal love, which flow from that union, to hold any part of our fellow-creatures in bondage. We therefore recommend a total refraining from the African trade, and the adoption of prudent measures for the gradual abolition of the slavery of the negroes in our country, and for the instruction and education of their children in English literature, and in the principles of the Gospel.

Of OATHS.

We recommend it to all the members of our Churches to enquire, whether Oaths do not lessen the frequency of truth in common life—whether they do not increase profane swearing—whether they are not contrary to the commands of our Saviour, and the apostle James; and lastly, whether they do not lessen the dignity of the Christian name, by obliging the professors of Christianity to yield to a suspicion of being capable of declaring a falsehood. And as we are indulged by the Laws of all our States, with the privilege of giving testimony by simple affirmation, we submit it to the consciences of our members, whether that mode of declaring the truth should not be preferred to any other.

Of SUBMISSION to GOVERNMENT.

We recommend to all the members of our Churches a peaceful submission to the higher powers, not for wrath, but for conscience sake, &c. We enjoin, in a particular manner, a regard to truth, and justice, in the payment of such duties or taxes, as shall be required by our rulers, for the maintenance of order, and the support of government.

Signed by order, and in behalf of the Convention, by
WILLIAM WORTH, MODERATOR.
ATTEST. ARTIS SEAGRAVE, Clerk.
June 8th, 1790.

CIRCULAR LETTER.

The Elders and Brethren, in the belief of the Universal Salvation of all men, thro' our Lord Jesus Christ, met in Convention in Philadelphia, on the 25th of May, and continued by adjournment, until the 8th of June, 1790.

To the Elders and Brethren in the same Belief throughout the United States of America, we wish Health, Peace, and Happiness.

Beloved in our Common Lord and Saviour,

We herewith send you a copy of the Articles of Faith, and Plan of Church Government, which we have, with uncommon love and unanimity, agreed upon in Convention. The Articles are few, but they contain the essentials of the Gospel. We thought it improper to require an assent to opinions that are merely speculative, or to introduce *words*, in expressing the articles of our belief, which have been the cause of unchristian controversies. The plan of Church Government is nearly that of the Congregational Church. We conceive it to be most friendly to Christian Liberty, and most agreeable to the word of God. We have submitted several matters of consequence to your consideration, under the title of 'RECOMMENDATIONS.' They form as yet no part of our system of Faith or Practice as a Church; but we hope the time is not very distant, when the progressive light of the Gospel shall banish all error and vice, which are the sources of the present disorders and miseries of human Society.

We rejoice in the progress of the long imprisoned truth of God's Universal Love to Mankind, and that he hath, in his infinite goodness, raised up so many faithful witnesses of late years, to declare it in many parts of our country. We hope and pray that this glorious truth may continue to prevail against anti-christian darkness and error; and that all who profess to believe it, may be led by the inward manifestation of God's love, to live soberly, righteously, and godly in this present world, and thereby to confute the objections that are urged against us, by those who deny the infinite extent of the mercy and power of God.

We request that such of you as are formed into Churches, would send deputies or messengers to meet in the Convention to be held in Philadelphia on the 25th of next May; and that such of you as are not formed into Churches, would associate for that purpose, and concur in sending Representatives to the Convention.

Signed by order and in behalf of the Convention, by
WILLIAM WORTH, Moderator.
Attest. ARTIS SEAGRAVE, Clerk.

source: *Articles of Faith, and Plan of Church Government, Composed and Adopted by the Churches Believing in the Salvation of All Men* (Philadelphia, 1790). Some spelling modernized.

MARY WOLLSTONECRAFT
A Vindication of the Rights of Woman
1792

Mary Wollstonecraft (1759–1797) was an English educator, writer, philosopher, and advocate of women's rights. She was a member of the Unitarian Church in Newington Green, London, drawn there by the preaching of Dr. Richard Price, a moral philosopher active in radical and republican causes and a friend of Franklin, Jefferson, Paine, and Adams. Her treatise, A Vindication of the Rights of Woman, aimed, as she expressed it, "to persuade women to endeavor to acquire strength, both of mind and body, and to convince them that the soft phrases, susceptibility of heart, delicacy of sentiment, and refinement of taste, are almost synonymous with epithets of weakness." Basing her argument on an appeal to natural rights, Wollstonecraft claimed that it is morally unjust for one segment of society to enjoy rights it denies to another segment and insisted that women be given an equal opportunity to contribute to society. Further Reading: Claire Tomalin, The Life and Death of Mary Wollstonecraft, *rev. ed. (London: Penguin Books, 1992); Claudia L. Johnson, ed.* The Cambridge Companion to Mary Wollstonecraft *(Cambridge: Cambridge University Press, 2002).*

—Barry Andrews

Will moralists pretend to assert, that . . . one half of the human race should be encouraged to remain with listless inactivity and stupid acquiescence? Kind instructors! what were we created for? To remain, it may be said, innocent; they mean in a state of childhood. —We might as well never have been born, unless it were necessary that we should be created to enable man to acquire the noble privilege of reason, the power of discerning good from evil, whilst we lie down in the dust from whence we were taken, never to rise again. —

It would be an endless task to trace the variety of meannesses, cares, and sorrows, into which women are plunged by the prevailing opinion, that they were created rather to feel than reason, and that all the power they obtain, must be obtained by their charms and weakness:

'Fine by defect, and amiably weak!'

And, made by this amiable weakness entirely dependent, excepting what they gain by illicit sway, on man, not only for protection, but advice, is it surprising that, neglecting the duties that reason alone points out, and shrinking from trials calculated to strengthen their minds, they only exert themselves to give their defects a graceful covering, which may serve to heighten their charms in the eye of the voluptuary, though it sink them below the scale of moral excellence?

Fragile in every sense of the word, they are obliged to look up to man for every comfort. In the most trifling dangers they cling to their support, with parasitical tenacity, piteously demanding succour; and their *natural* protector extends his arm, or lifts up his voice, to guard the lovely trembler—from what? Perhaps the frown of an old cow, or the jump of a mouse; a rat, would be a serious danger. In the name of reason, and even common sense, what can save such beings from contempt; even though they be soft and fair?

These fears, when not affected, may be very pretty; but they show a degree of imbecility that degrades a rational creature in a way women are not aware of—for love and esteem are very distinct things.

I am fully persuaded that we should hear of none of these infantile airs, if girls were allowed to take sufficient exercise, and not confined in close rooms till their muscles are relaxed, and their powers of digestion destroyed. . . . It is true, they could not then with equal propriety be termed the sweet flowers that smile in the walk of man; but they would be more respectable members of society, and discharge the important duties of life by the light of their own reason. 'Educate women like men,' says Rousseau, 'and the more they resemble our sex the less power will they have over us.' This is the very point I aim at. I do not wish them to have power over men; but over themselves.

SOURCE: Mary Wollstonecraft, *A Vindication of the Rights of Woman: With Strictures on Political and Moral Subjects* (London, 1792), 131–34.

A General View of the Arguments for the Unity of God

1794

Joseph Priestley (1733–1804) was a founder of Unitarianism and its organized church in England. He carried his views to the United States for the last decade of his life. Both a prominent minister and scientist, he believed that a moral and religious enlightenment would occur through rational thinking and an intertwining of the two realms, resulting in a new millennium of reason. As a reformer and Dissenter, and in alliance with Theophilus Lindsey, he wrote theological works focused on a humanistic reading of the scriptures and approach to religious practice. His A General View of the Arguments for the Unity of God *was a seminal work calling for a reexamination of the concept of the Trinity, especially the divinity of Jesus, based on a close reading of scriptures and the historical development of doctrine as compiled by the Church over the centuries. Calling the Doctrine of the Trinity a "corruption," Priestley argued for a simplicity of doctrinal belief (supporting those he labeled as Primitive Christians), challenging the established Church of England, Catholicism, and even fellow Dissenters and reformers whose contortions created even more contradictory views. Further Reading: J. D. Bowers,* Joseph Priestley and English Unitarianism in America *(University Park: Pennsylvania State University Press, 2007); Robert Schofield,* The Enlightened Joseph Priestley: A Study of His Life and Work from 1773 to 1804 *(University Park: Pennsylvania State University Press, 2004).*

—J. D. Bowers

I. Arguments from reason against the trinitarian hypothesis.

THAT the doctrine of the trinity could ever have been suggested by anything in the course of *nature* (though it has been imagined by some persons of a peculiarly fanciful turn, and previously persuaded of the truth of it) is not maintained by any persons to whom my writings can be at all useful. I shall therefore only address myself to those who believe the doctrine on the supposition of its being contained in the *Scriptures*, at the same time maintaining, that, though it is *above*, it is not properly *contrary* to reason; and I hope to make it sufficiently evident, either that they do not hold the doctrine, or that the opinion of *three divine persons constituting one God* is strictly speaking an *absurdity*, or *contradiction*; and that it is therefore incapable of any

proof, even by miracles. With this view, I shall recite in order all the distinct modifications of this doctrine, and shew that, upon any of them, there is either no proper
unity in the divine nature, or no proper *trinity*.

If, with . . . [those] who are reckoned the strictest Athanasians . . . it be supposed
that there are three persons, properly equal, and that no one of them has any sort of
superiority over the rest, they are, to all intents and purposes, three distinct Gods. For
if each of them, separately considered, be possessed of all divine perfections, so that
nothing is wanting to compile divinity, each of them must be as properly *a God* as
any being possessed of all the properties of man must be a man, and therefore *three
persons* possessed of all the attributes of divinity must be as properly *three Gods* as
three persons possessed of all human attributes must be three men.

✳   ✳   ✳

II. Arguments from reason against the arian hypothesis.

The Arian doctrine, of the world having been made and governed not by the supreme
God himself, but by Christ, the Son of God, though no contradiction in itself, is, on
several accounts, highly improbable.

Our reasoning from effects to causes carries us no further than to the immediate
creator of the visible universe. For if we can suppose that being to have had a cause,
or author, we may suppose that his cause or author had a higher cause, and so on *ad
infinitum*.

✳   ✳   ✳

III. Arguments against the trinitarian and the arian hypotheses from the scriptures.

✳   ✳   ✳

1. The Scriptures contain the clearest and most express declarations that there is
but *one God*, without ever mentioning any exception in favour of a *trinity*, or guard-
ing us against being led into any mistake by such general and unlimited expressions.
Ex. xx. 3. *Thou shalt have no other God before me.* Deut. vi. 4. *Hear, O Israel, the
Lord our God is one Lord.* Mark xii. 29. *The first of all the commandments is, Hear, O
Israel, the Lord our God is one Lord. . . .*

On the other hand, not only does the word *trinity* never occur in the Scriptures,
but it is nowhere said that *there are three persons in this one God*; nor is the doctrine
explicitly laid down in any other direct proposition whatever. Christ indeed says,
John x. 30., *I and my Father are one*; but he sufficiently explains himself by praying
that his disciples might be one with him in the same sense in which he was one with
the Father. John xvii. 21, 22.

✳   ✳   ✳

4. Christ is said expressly to be inferior to the Father, all his power is said to have been given him by the Father, and he could do nothing without the Father. John xvi. 28. *My Father is greater than I.* 1 Cor. iii. 23. *Ye are Christ's, and Christ is God's.* 1 Cor. xi. 3. *The head of Christ is God.* . . .

It is now alleged that Christ did not mean that he was inferior to the Father with respect to his *divine nature*, but only with respect to his *human nature*. But if such liberties be taken in explaining a person's meaning, language has no use whatever. On the same principles it might be asserted that Christ never died, or that he never rose from the dead, secretly meaning his divine nature only.

* * *

IV. Arguments from History against the Divinity and Pre-existence of Christ; or a summary view of the evidence for the primitive christians having held the doctrine of the simple humanity of Christ.

* * *

2. The great objection that jews have always made to christianity in its present state is, that it enjoins the worship of more gods than one; and it is a great article with the christian writers of the second and following centuries to answer this objection. But it does not appear in all the book of Acts, in which we hear much of the cavils of the jews, both in Jerusalem and in many parts of the Roman empire, that they made any such objection to Christianity *then*; nor do the apostles either there, or in their epistles, advance anything with a view to such an objection. It may be presumed, therefore, that no such offence to the jews had then been given by the preaching of a doctrine so offensive to them as that of the divinity of Christ must have been.

* * *

8. All those who were deemed *heretics* in early times were cut off from the communion of those who called themselves the *orthodox* christians, and went by some particular name, generally that of their leader. But the unitarians among the gentiles were not expelled from the assemblies of christians, but worshipped along with those who were called orthodox, and had no particular name till the time of Victor. . . .

9. The *Apostles Creed* is that which was taught to all catechumens before baptism, and additions were made to it from time to time, in order to exclude *those* who were denominated *heretics*. Now though there are several articles in that creed which allude to the gnostics, and tacitly condemn them, there was not, in the time of Tertullian, any article in it that alluded to the unitarians; so that even then any unitarian, at least one believing the miraculous conception, might have subscribed it.

SOURCE: Joseph Priestley, *A General View of the Arguments for the Unity of God* (London, 1794), 3–4, 7, 10–13, 17–18, 20–21.

DANIEL SHUTE AND HENRY WARE, SR.

A Compendious and Plain Catechism

1794

Rev. Daniel Shute (1722–1802) served the Third Parish of Hingham, Massachusetts, from 1746 until his death. (The congregation was renamed as Second Parish when Cohasset was incorporated as a distinct town.) Like First Parish's pastor, Ebenezer Gay, Shute espoused the liberal or "Arminian" theology typical of eighteenth-century ministers educated at Harvard. After Henry Ware, Sr. (1764–1845) succeeded Gay in 1787, he and Shute prepared this catechism for the use of families in Hingham, using Isaac Watts's Plain and Easy Catechisms for Children *as a model. Shute and Ware departed from Watts's text by affirming that God created the world for "the communication of happiness" and by eliminating explicit references to original sin, hell, the substitutionary atonement, and the Trinity. They also expressed the Arian view that Christ was "with God before the world was made." When Ware was appointed Hollis Professor at Harvard in 1805, his opponents called attention to these departures from Puritan orthodoxy. Further Reading: Conrad Wright,* The Beginnings of Unitarianism in America *(Boston: Beacon Press, 1955).*

—Dan McKanan

The First Part.

1 Q. *Can you tell me, child, who made you?*
   A. The great God, who made heaven and earth.
2 Q. *Why did the great God make you and all other creatures?*
   A. Perfectly happy in himself, his infinite goodness led him to make me, together with all other creatures, for the communication of happiness.

*   *   *

The Second Part.

*   *   *

41 Q. *By what methods will you be most likely to guard against the practice of vice and wickedness?*
   A. By early checking sinful thoughts and desires, by correcting every thing amiss in heart and life before I become accustomed to it, by avoiding wicked and profane company, by carefully guarding against those vices, to which I am

most exposed, and feel myself most inclined, and by praying earnestly and frequently to God, to enable me to resist temptation, and to strengthen and confirm my good resolutions.

42 Q. *Have you never yet broken the commands of God, and sinned against him?*

A. My conscience tells me, I have often broken God's holy commands, and sinned against him in thought, in word, and in deed.

43 Q. *Whence came it to pass that you have been such a sinner?*

A. I became so by an unguarded and foolish indulgence of my irregular appetites and passions, in opposition to the law written in my heart, and to the plain dictates of the Holy Scriptures.

44 Q. *But why have you indulged your irregular appetites and passions? was it not your duty to resist them, when you knew they led to that which is evil?*

A. I ought to have resisted every inclination to evil, and therefore I have no sufficient excuse for myself before the great God.

45 Q. *What do you deserve because of your sins?*

A. For my sins I deserve the displeasure and wrath of God.

46 Q. *Is not the displeasure of God, in its ruinous and destructive effects termed his wrath, terrible and greatly to be dreaded?*

A. From our natural desire of happiness, and aversion to misery, it is indeed terrible and greatly to be dreaded; as his displeasure against our sins, if they are persevered in, will deprive us of every thing good and happy, and terminate in the second death, when his wrath will come upon us to the uttermost.

47 Q. *Have you any reason to hope that you may escape the wrath of God?*

A. Through the mercy of God I have; for he has sent his Son into the world to save sinners, as the Gospel teaches.

The Third Part.

1 Q. *What is the Gospel?*

A. It is the good tidings of salvation through a Redeemer, first made known to Adam, immediately after his violation of the holy law of God, gradually unfolded afterward from age to age, and at last completely revealed by Jesus Christ and his Apostles.

2 Q. *Who is Jesus Christ?*

A. He is the Son of God, who was with God before the world was made; but, in the fullness of time, he became the son of man, and dwelt among men, on this earth, for their benefit.

3 Q. *What did Jesus Christ do on earth for the benefit of mankind?*

A. He more clearly made known to men the will of God, and enforced obedience to it by the highest motives; he set them a perfect pattern of holiness; he more fully revealed a future state of rewards and punishments; and obtained the pardon of sin and everlasting life for them by his obedience unto death.

4   *Q. How could Christ obtain pardon and life for us by his doing and suffering?*

    A. By the gracious appointment of the Father, who was pleased to accept the obedience of Christ unto death, as a vindication of his righteous government, in granting pardon to penitent sinners, and raising them to a happy immortality.

SOURCE: Daniel Shute and Henry Ware, Sr., *A Compendious and Plain Catechism, Designed for the Benefit of the Rising Generation* (Boston, 1794), 5, 16–20.

"Profession of Belief" (*The Winchester Profession*)

1803

*In 1803, the New England Universalist General Convention, which held its
meeting that year in Winchester, New Hampshire, needed a creedal document to support its claim as a proper denomination in the eyes of the law. To
that end, the delegates discussed a "Profession of Belief and Plan of General
Association," which had been written by the Vermont evangelist Walter Ferriss.
Although the profession was well received by most delegates, it was strenuously
opposed by a few, including Noah Murray (no relation to John Murray), who
said, "It is harmless now—it is a calf, and its horns have not yet made their
appearance, but it will soon grow older—its horns will grow, and then it will
begin to hook." When it was agreed that nothing would be added to it in future,
the opponents backed down and the profession was passed unanimously. A
"liberty" clause was included, allowing individual churches to make additional
specifications, as long as these did not conflict with the general profession.
After the Winchester Profession began to be applied as a creedal test in the late
nineteenth century, the Universalist Convention specified in 1899 that "neither
[the Winchester Profession], nor any other precise form of words, is required
as a condition of fellowship." Further Reading: The Winchester Centennial,
1803–1903 (Boston: Universalist Publishing House, 1903); Nathaniel Stacy,
Memoirs of the Life of Nathaniel Stacy (Columbus, PA, 1850).*

—Peter Hughes

The Churches and Societies of Universalists of the New England States, assembled in General Convention, holden at Winchester, New Hampshire, on the 21st
and 22nd of September, A.D. 1803,

To the individuals of the several Churches and Societies, and to all persons
whom it may concern;—Greeting.

Brethren and Friends:

Whereas, the diversities of capacity and of opportunity for obtaining information, together with many attendant circumstances, have occasioned, among the sincere professions of the Abrahamic faith, some diversities of opinion concerning some
points of doctrine and modes of practice. We therefore think it expedient, in order to

prevent confusion and misunderstanding, and to promote the edifying and building up of the Church together in love, to record and publish that profession of belief, which we agree in as essential; and that plan of ecclesiastical fellowship and general subordination which we, as a christian association, conceive we ought to maintain.

Profession of Belief.

Article 1. We believe that the Holy Scriptures of the Old and New Testament contain a revelation of the character of God, and of the duty, interest, and final destination of mankind.

Article 2. We believe that there is one God, whose nature is Love; revealed in one Lord Jesus Christ, by one Holy Spirit of Grace; who will finally restore the whole family of mankind to holiness and happiness.

Article 3. We believe that holiness and true happiness are inseparably connected; and that believers ought to maintain order, and practice good works, for these things are good and profitable unto men.

As we believe these to be truths which deeply concern the honor of the Divine Character, and the interests of man, we do hereby declare that we continue to consider ourselves and our societies in fellowship, a denomination of christians, distinct and separate from those who do not approve the whole of this profession of belief, as expressed in the *three* above articles.

And as a distinct denomination, we continue to claim the authority of exercising among ourselves, that order for the glory of God in the good of the church, which christianity requires.

And we continue to claim the external privileges, which, according to the free constitution of our country, every denomination is entitled to enjoy.

Yet, while we, as an Association, adopt a general profession of belief, and plan of church government, we leave it to the several churches and societies, or to smaller associations of churches, if such should be formed within the limits of our general association, to continue or adopt, within themselves, such more particular articles of faith, or modes of discipline, as may appear to them best, under their particular circumstances; provided they do not disagree with our general profession and plan.

And while we consider that every church possesses, within itself, all the powers of self-government, we earnestly and affectionately recommend it to every church, society, or particular association, to exercise the spirit of christian meekness and charity towards those who have different modes of faith or practice; that where the brethren cannot see alike, they may agree to differ; and let every man be fully persuaded in his own mind.

SOURCE: "Profession of Belief and Plan, of the General Association of the Universal Churches and Societies, of the New-England States," *Universalist Magazine*, November 19, 1825, 85.

A Treatise on Atonement

1805

Influenced by Ethan Allen's Reason, the Only Oracle of Man *(1784), as well
as by Caleb Rich and Elhanan Winchester, Hosea Ballou (1771–1852) led
the way in the development of Universalist theology, convincing almost all of
his fellow Universalists to adopt a unitarian theology as well as his version of
the moral influence theory of atonement. He rejected the view, held by most
Roman Catholics and Protestants, that sin was an infinite crime against God
that called for an infinite satisfaction through the sacrifice of God himself.
Instead he proposed that Christ called humanity to atonement with God
by demonstrating God's love and giving an example of godly life. Ballou's*
Treatise on Atonement *was one of the most widely read American Universalist works. Ballou did not venture to settle in Boston while John Murray was
alive out of respect for the patriarch, who could not abide the younger man's
theology. In 1817, he accepted the call of Second Universalist, which had been
founded especially to bring him to Boston. Further Reading: Ernest Cassara,*
Hosea Ballou: The Challenge to Orthodoxy *(Boston: Universalist Historical
Society, 1961);* Thomas Whittemore, Life of Rev. Hosea Ballou, *4 vols. (Boston, 1854–1855).*

—Peter Hughes

I have, from my early youth, been much in the habit of inquiring into the things of
religion, and religious sentiments; and have, for a number of years, seen, or thought
I saw, great inconsistencies in what has for a long time passed for orthodoxy in
divinity.

The ideas, that sin is infinite, and that it deserves an infinite punishment; that
the law transgressed is infinite, and inflicts an infinite penalty; and that the great
Jehovah took on himself a natural body of flesh and blood, and actually suffered
death on a cross to satisfy his infinite justice, and thereby save his creatures from
endless misery, are ideas which appear to me to be unfounded in the nature of reason, and unsupported by divine revelation. . . . One particular object, therefore, in
this work, is, if possible, to free the scripture doctrine of atonement from those
incumbrances which have done it so much injury; and open a door, at least, for the
subject to be investigated on reasonable grounds, and by fair argument.

* * *

Christian divines, in general, have agreed in supposing sin to be an *infinite evil*, being a violation of an *infinite law*, and, therefore, that the law required an *infinite sacrifice*; short of which no atonement could be made; that the transgression of Adam brought the whole human race into the same situation of sin and misery, and subjected them all to the *infinite penalty* of an *infinite law*, which they had violated in their parent, before they individually existed.

* * *

The plan of redemption, as held by many, may be reduced to the following compendium. God, from all eternity, foreseeing that man would sin, provided a Mediator for a certain part of his posterity, who should suffer the penalty of the law for them, and that these elect ones, chosen by God from the rest of mankind, will alone be benefitted by the atonement; that, in order that the sacrifice might be adequate to the crime, for which, the sinner was condemned to *everlasting* or end-less suffering, God himself assumed a body of flesh and blood, such as the delin-quent was constituted in, and suffered the penalty of the law by death, and arose from the dead. By this process, the demand of the law was completely answered, and the debt due to Divine Justice, by the elect, was fully and amply paid. But that this atonement does not affect those who were not elected as objects of mercy, but that they are left, to suffer *endlessly* for what Adam did, before they were born. It is true, that they are a little cautious about saying, that *God himself absolutely died!* But they say, that Christ, who was crucified, was *really God himself*, which must, in effect, amount to the same thing. And in fact, if the Infinite did not suffer death, the whole plan falls, for it is by an *infinite sacrifice* that they pretend to *satisfy* an *infinite dissatisfaction*.

Why the above ideas should ever have been imbibed, by men of understanding and study, I can but scarcely satisfy myself; their absurdities are so glaring that it seems next to impossible that men of sobriety and sound judgment should ever imbibe them, or avoid seeing them.

I have already sufficiently refuted the idea of an infinite sin, which opens to a plain path, in which the mind may run, and run clear of all those perplexities which have served to confuse, rather than enlighten mankind.

If sin be not infinite, the dissatisfaction occasioned by sin is not infinite; there-fore, an infinite sacrifice is not required. But, for the sake of illustration, we will, for a moment, admit, that the doctrine of atonement stands on the ground over which we have just gone. I will state it, as it is often stated by those who believe it, which is by the likeness of debt and credit. The sinner owed a debt to Divine Justice, which he was unable to discharge; the Divine Being cannot, consistently with his honor, dispense with the pay, but says, I must have my due; but as the debtor has not ability to pay the smallest fraction, Divine Wisdom lays a deep concerted mysterious plan for the debt to be discharged. And how was it? Why, for God to pay it himself!

137

My neighbor owes me a hundred pounds; time of payment comes, and I make a demand for my dues. Says my neighbor, my misfortunes have been such that I am not the possessor of the smallest fraction of property in the world; and as much as I owe you I am worse than nothing. I declare to him, positively, that I will not lose so much as a fraction of the interest, and leave him. A friend calls and asks me how I succeeded in obtaining my dues of my neighbor; I reply, my neighbor is not, nor will he ever be able to pay me any part of my demand. My friend says, he is sorry that I should lose the debt. I answer, I shall not lose it. I have very fortunately, in my meditations on the subject, thought of a method by which I can avail myself of the whole, to my full satisfaction; and I think it is a method which no person in the world, but myself, could have ever discovered. My friend is curious, and impatient to know the mighty secret, never before found out. The reader may guess his confusion, on my telling him, that, as I have the sum already by me, I am now going to pay up the obligation, before the interest is any larger! This has been called the gospel plan, which contains the depths of infinite wisdom.

*   *   *

Atonement signifies *reconciliation*, or *satisfaction*, which is the same. It is a being *unreconciled to truth and justice*, which needs *reconciliation*; and it is a *dissatisfied being* which needs *satisfaction*. Therefore, I raise my inquiry on the question, Is God the *unreconciled* or *dissatisfied party*, or is it *man*?

*   *   *

To say, that God loved man any less, after transgression, than before, denies his *unchangeability*; but, to say, that man was wanting in love to God, places him in his real character. As God was not the unreconciled party, no atonement was necessary for his reconciliation. Where there is dissatisfaction, it presupposes an *injured* party; and can it be hard to determine which was *injured* by *sin*, the *Creator*, or the *sinner*? If God were unreconciled to man, the atonement was necessary to *renew* his *love* to his *creature*; but if *man* were the *unreconciled*, the atonement was necessary to *renew* his *love* to his *Creator*. The matter is now stated so plainly that no person, who can read, can mistake.

*   *   *

The belief, that the great Jehovah was offended with his creatures to that degree, that nothing but the death of Christ, or the endless misery of mankind, could appease his anger, is an idea that has done more injury to the christian religion than the writings of all its opposers, for many centuries. The error has been fatal to the life and spirit of the religion of Christ in our world; all those principles which are to be *dreaded* by men, have been believed to *exist* in God; and professors have been moulded into the image of their Deity, and become more cruel than the uncultivated Savage! A persecuting inquisition is a lively representation of the God which professed christians have believed in, ever since the apostacy. It is every day's

138

practice to represent the Almighty so offended with man, that he employs his infinite mind in devising *unspeakable tortures*, as retaliations on those with whom he is offended. Those ideas have so obscured the whole nature of God from us, that the capacious region of the human mind has been darkened with the almost impenetrable cloud; even the tender charities of nature have been frozen with such tenets, and the natural friendship common to human society, has, in a thousand instances, been driven from the walks of man. But, says the reader, is it likely that persecution ever rose from men's believing, that God was an enemy to wicked men? Undoubtedly; for, had all professors of christianity believed, that God had compassion on the ignorant, and those who are out of the way, how could they have persecuted those whom they believed in error? But, with contrary views, those who professed to believe in Christ, who professed to be the real disciples of him who taught his disciples to *love* their *enemies*, have been the fomenters of persecution; they have persecuted, *even unto death*, those who could not *believe all the absurdities in orthodox creeds*. It may be asked, if those animosities did not arise from pride, ambition and carnal mindedness? I answer, yes; and so does the *God* in whom *persecuting christians believe*, for they form a God altogether like unto themselves; therefore, while they vainly fancy they are in the service of the true God, they are following the dictates of pride and unlawful ambition, the natural production of a carnal mind; and atonement is the only remedy for the evil.

Men are dissatisfied with the Almighty and his providence; they are dissatisfied with, and are enemies of, one another; whereas our true happiness consists in loving God, and our neighbors. Men in possession of vile appetites, pursue with greediness, their gratification; but still, they retain their wants, their souls are allied to heaven and holiness, and can never be happy without them. They are conscious of sin, and feel condemnation resting on their minds; they look forward to the awful scene of dissolution, and their souls start back with horror. *Death* is the *King of terrors* to the unreconciled; how awful are the thoughts of death to those whose hopes are only the feeble productions of their fears and wants, unsupported with divine evidence! O, how necessary is atoning grace, on such an occasion, whereby a divine confidence may by enjoyed; the value thereof cannot be estimated by earthly treasures; all the shining dust of India, and the riches of the south, are poverty, when compared with the riches of a reconciled mind.

Without atonement, God's glorious design, in the everlasting welfare of his offspring, man, could never be effected; the ordination of an infinitely merciful God could never be carried into effect. The Almighty must not be deprived of the means of accomplishing his gracious designs. We read of his *covenant* with day and night, which cannot be broken; but it would be broken at once, should the causes cease that produce their changes. So of the covenant of eternal mercy, the testament of eternal life, it must be put in force by the death of the testator, and its life and immortal glory be brought to light through his resurrection. Let it be understood, that it is man who receives the atonement, who stands in need of reconciliation, who, being dissatisfied, needs satisfaction; and not place those imperfections and wants in him who is infinite in his fulness; and the doctrine of atonement may be sought for in the nature of things, and found to be rational to the understanding.

*   *   *

Let it be asked by what means are we brought to love God? Answer, "We love him, because he first loved us." God's love to us is antecedent to our love to him, which refutes the notion of God's receiving the atonement; but the idea, that the manifestation of God's love to us, causes us to love him, and brings us to a renewal of love... is perfectly consonant to the necessity of atonement, it shows us what atonement is, and the power which the Mediator must have and exercise, in order to reconcile all things to God.

The method by which we are brought to love any object, whatever, is, by seeing, or thinking we see, some beauty in the object; and our love is always in proportion to the apparent good qualities of the object seen.

*   *   *

When a sinner views God as an enemy, and grumbles concerning his being hard and austere, when he feels an aversion to him and wishes to avoid his presence, it is certain the Son hath not revealed the Father to that soul. The ideas thus entertained of God are altogether wrong, and the mind that entertains them has no just conceptions of the Almighty. But blessed be the expressed image of the Invisible; he hath power to reveal the true character of the Father, to remove the veil from the heart, and to let the sun-beams of divine light gently into the understanding; then God appears altogether lovely, and the chiefest among ten thousand, while the soul in ecstacy embraces the brightness of his glory, crying, "My Lord, and my God." But the idea of the *letter* is so fixed in the minds of christian people, in general, that the *veil* of the *law* is as fully on their minds, as it was on the Pharisees of old, which caused them to be blind to their Messiah when he came.

Christians have for a long time, believed, that the *temporal death* of Christ made an atonement for sin, and that the *literal blood* of the man who was crucified, has efficacy to cleanse from guilt; but surely this is carnality, and carnal mindedness, if I have any knowledge of the apostle's meaning, where he says, "To be carnally minded is death." The *letter killeth*, but the *spirit giveth life*. The apostles were made able ministers of the new testament, not of the *letter*, but of the *spirit*. Christ saith, "Except ye *eat my flesh*, and *drink my blood* ye have no *life* in you." Must we understand this in a *literal* sense? If we do, how shall we understand what he further says of this matter? "The *flesh* profiteth nothing: the words that I speak unto you, they are *spirit* and they are life."

*   *   *

140

There is nothing in heaven above, nor in the earth beneath, that can do away sin, but love; and we have reason to be eternally thankful that love is stronger than death, that many waters cannot quench it, nor the floods drown it; that it hath power to remove the moral maladies of mankind, and to make us free from the law of sin and death, to reconcile us to God, and to wash us pure in the blood, or life, of the everlasting covenant. O love, thou great Physician of souls, what a work hast thou undertaken! All souls are thy patients; prosperous be thy labors, thou bruiser of the head of carnal mind.

In this view of the subject, we may see how the divine grace of reconciliation may be communicated to those who have never been privileged with the volume of divine revelation, and who have never heard the name of a Mediator proclaimed, as the only way of life and salvation. I have no doubt but thousands, whose education has taught them to look on the christian religion as an imposture, may possess a good degree of this love, which is the spirit of life in Christ Jesus; and though none can feel or experience this divine animation, only through the medium of the second Adam, I do not conceive that its agency is confined particularly to names, sects, denominations, people or kingdoms.

The *word*, which is nigh us, even in our hearts and mouths, is every where, operating, in some degree, in all hearts. The enmity which God put between the seed of the serpent and the seed of the woman is every where felt, and the two are struggling in every breast. When the creature-like nature, or the carnal mind, which is enmity against God, leads the whole man captive, it is then that the soul is in a state of unreconciliation and death; but when the heavenly child, which, after God, is created in righteousness and true holiness, binds the strong man armed and whispers heavenly invitations to the soul, revealing himself in the understanding, the soul immediately ceases to confer with flesh and blood, beholds with inexpressible admiration the heavenly beauties of the new nature, is moulded into its likeness and experimentally become a child of God; the flaming sword is removed from the place of light; the way to the tree of life is opened, and the soul enters by the anchor of hope within the veil, where the cherubims are disarmed of the flaming sword, and stand looking down on the mercy seat, where God communes with his people. Thus, by the spirit of the word, the soul is brought to a sweet communion with God; it feels its eternal sonship, and rejoices therein; with joy unspeakable and full of glory.

*　*　*

Before you found peace, you thought you could see the justice of God in your eternal exclusion from heaven and happiness. Now I ask, can you find that God ever gave a law to man which required endless misery in case of disobedience? Sure I am, that the scriptures speak of none, neither do the dictates of good reason admit of its existence. Perhaps my opponent may say, we are not to use our *reason* in matters of religion. I answer, if we are not to understand the things of God, by scripture and reason, we are at a loss to know how to come at them. I have before argued this point particularly, in order to show that such a penalty does not exist in the law of God. Did you think an exclusion from heaven and happiness would be an exclusion from holiness and righteousness? Did you ever see the justice of God in your being sinful, unholy and impure? You answer, no. Then you never saw the justice of God in your endless exclusion from heaven and happiness.

*   *   *

Atonement by Christ, was never intended to perform impossibilities; therefore, it was never designed to make men agree, and live in peace, while they are destitute of love one to another; but it is calculated and designed to inspire the mind with that true love which will produce peace in Jesus. As atonement is a complete fulfilment of the law of the heavenly man, it causes its recipient to love God and his fellow creatures, in as great a degree as he partakes of its nature. Ask one brought out of darkness into the marvellous light of the gospel, how God appears to him; and he will answer, more glorious than he can describe. Ask him, how he feels towards his fellow men; and he will say, even of his enemies, he wishes them no worse than to enjoy the blessings of divine favor. In times of refreshing, how many thousands have been heard to speak of the goodness of the Lord, and of the infinite fulness of his grace; and with what love, affection, and fervency have they invited their fellow men to the rich provisions of the gospel!

*   *   *

Atoning grace produces all which the bible means by conversion, or being born of the Spirit; it brings the mind from under the power and constitution of the earthly Adam, to live by faith on the Son of God, and to be ruled and governed, even in this life, in a great measure, by the law of the spirit of life, in Christ Jesus. It opens eternal things to our view and contemplation; it brings heaven into the soul, and clothes the man in his right mind; it inspires the soul with divine meekness and boldness at the same time. It was this that enabled the apostles of our Lord to preach the gospel, in defiance of the rage of their enemies, and gave them immortal consolations in their sufferings for the cause of truth. It causes the christian to love all God's rational creatures, and to wish their saving knowledge of the truth; it produces good works in their purity, and all the morality worth the name is founded on it. Its divine power is stronger than any possible opposition, and the gates of hell cannot prevail against it; it opens a door of everlasting hope, and conducts the soul, by way of the cross, to immortality and eternal life. This dispensation of atonement is manifested through Christ, for the reconciliation of all things to God, in his glorious kingdom of holiness and happiness.

SOURCE: Hosea Ballou, A Treatise on Atonement (Randolph, VT, 1805), front matter, 67–69, 98–99, 103–105, 116–120, 122–23, 126–27, 130–31.

JEDIDIAH MORSE

"The True Reasons on which the Election of a Hollis Professor . . . Was Opposed"

1805

When Harvard College appointed Rev. Henry Ware, Sr. (1764–1845), as Hollis Professor of Divinity, Rev. Jedidiah Morse (1761–1826) of Charlestown launched a vigorous campaign of opposition. Ware was unwilling, Morse argued, to profess either a clear belief in the divinity of Christ or a Calvinist view of original sin. As such, his appointment violated the terms of the oldest endowed professorship in America, which specified that only a person "of sound or orthodox principles" could serve. Morse's protest launched what is generally known as the "Unitarian Controversy," a twenty-year period during which orthodox ministers refused to exchange pulpits with liberals, and pamphlets were written on both sides. In 1808 Morse and other orthodox ministers founded Andover Seminary as an alternative to Harvard, which responded by organizing its own Divinity School in 1816. The controversy concluded with the creation of the American Unitarian Association in 1825. Further Reading: Conrad Wright, ed., A Stream of Light: A Short History of American Unitarianism, 2nd ed. (Boston: Skinner House, 1989); Sydney E. Ahlstrom and Jonathan S. Carey, eds., An American Reformation: A Documentary History of Unitarian Christianity (San Francisco: International Scholars Publications, 1998).

—Dan McKanan

Things being so, when called upon at the Board of Overseers to concur with the Corporation in their choice of a Hollis Professor of Divinity, it was conceived proper and necessary to inquire, Does the candidate possess the qualifications required by the founder? Is he of *sound or orthodox* principles? . . . It was particularly asked by one of the honorable members of the Senate, whether the candidate was a believer in that important doctrine, the divinity of the Lord Jesus Christ? The reply conveyed no precise or satisfactory answer on that point. While thus ignorant of the *"principles"* of the candidate, how could the board determine whether or not they were *"sound or orthodox,"* whatever be the meaning of these terms? From the catechism published by the Candidate, it was inferred, that he was not a Calvinist; that his sentiments on important points, such as the depravity of human nature, the impotency of man, the character of Jesus Christ, and the future state of the wicked, were widely different from those of Dr. Watts, whose catechism he professedly followed as his "model." . . .

＊　＊　＊

We have seen the singular anxiety and caution of Mr. *Hollis* by his *letters*, and by a *bond* to secure the object of his Foundation, and to guard his professorship against error and innovation in all future time. Now if barriers so sacred can be removed, what guard can be devised, which shall secure any bequest against violation? . . . What effect this change in the religious character of the Professorship, and of the University will gradually and ultimately produce in the state of our Churches, and on the religious and moral character of our citizens, cannot with so much certainty be foreseen. In respect to New England, it is an untried experiment. GOD forbid, that this change should be injurious and ruinous; that in consequence, the faith of our churches should become less pure, their discipline less strict, the standard of christian morality lowered, the difference lessened between those, who professedly serve God, and those who avowedly serve him not; till at length the spirit and power of our religion shall have evaporated, and its very forms be abolished.

SOURCE: Jedidiah Morse, *The True Reasons on which the Election of a Hollis Professor of Divinity in Harvard College, was opposed at the Board of Overseers, Feb. 14, 1805* (Charlestown, MA, 1805), 19–20, 27–28.

"To a friend, who could not believe in the final holiness and happiness of all mankind"

1809

Lucy Barns (1780–1809) was the daughter of Thomas Barns (1749–1816), the first Universalist preacher in Maine. At age nineteen she was converted in a Methodist revival, but soon thereafter embraced the Universalist faith of her father. As asthma weakened her body, she relied more and more on poetry and letter-writing to spread the Universalist gospel. Her writings were collected and published by Universalists immediately after her death. Further Reading: Laura Horton, "Lucy Barns's The Female Christian: A Universalist Treasure Rediscovered (Again)," *The Unitarian Universalist Christian* 58: 77–90 (2003).*

—Dan McKanan

Honored Madam,

I must humbly beg your pardon for thus presuming to address you by letter; which I hope and trust your goodness will not fail to grant. As I have not a convenient opportunity for verbal conversation, and have long wished to converse with you on a subject of the greatest importance that ever occupied the human mind: which is the doctrine of endless misery. As we do not understand the scriptures alike, and being too feeble to write lengthy, I shall not attempt to quote much scripture, but will endeavor to take reason for my guide. . . .

The scriptures declare that God is love, that he is a good Being, that he is no respecter of persons, but is good to all, and that his tender mercies are over all his works; and that he has all power in his own hand, and worketh all things after the counsel of his own will All nature, likewise, proclaims aloud this blessed and divine truth, and also bespeaks his wisdom to be infinite. He kindly condescends to call us his children, & permits us to address him by the endearing appellation of Father! Is it possible that so good, so kind and loving a Father, can punish his tender and beloved offspring with the most exquisite misery, to the endless ages of eternity, for their disobedience to him, and even for the most trivial faults? . . . Shall we presume to impute those hateful passions to the Almighty, which he himself has taught us to despise in each other and which we absolutely abhor even in a savage, who is not contented merely with the death of his enemy, but puts him to the most cruel death which malice and revenge can possibly invent, roasting him alive in such a moderate manner, as to prolong his life and misery to the utmost extent of his power! But what is that when compared with endless misery? You are a mother, and doubtless possessed of as tender feelings as ever warmed the heart of a parent: and was I to say that you could with pleasure behold your children punished with such exquisite misery, even for an age, you would think that I was either beside myself, or entertained a most unjust opinion of you. But if you could not endure the sight but for one age, what reason have you to suppose that the tenderest, most loving and best of fathers could endure the shocking scene to endless ages of eternity: But perhaps you will say that those who are to suffer thus, are not the offspring of God, but the children of the devil. I know the wicked on account of their disobedience are called the children of the wicked one; but if they are so in reality, we cannot reasonably expect they will be punished so severely, for being too obedient to their father Satan, as children are in duty bound to honor and obey their parents, even by a command from the great Eternal himself. . . . It is believed by many, that the parable of the rich man and Lazarus is a real description of heaven and hell, and that it evidently sets forth the misery of those who are damned, roasting inflames of fire, and begging for water, even for one drop to mitigate their sufferings, while those in heaven must incessantly behold their distress, and hear their groans and cries, and dreadful lamentations to all eternity without having the power to relieve them. If that is really the case, what person is there who possess any real love for his fellow creatures, who would not much rather be annihilated, and be as though he never had been, than go to such a heaven!

> What would avail to me the joys of heaven,
> And all the splendor of the golden coast:
> If I must know millions of human souls
> In mis'ry groan, and are forever lost.

But I cannot believe that such a place of misery ever did exist, or ever will, until there is a change wrought in the Almighty himself, and we behold the great wheel of nature rolling backwards!

SOURCE: Lucy Barns, *The Female Christian* (Portland, ME: Francis Douglas 1809), 22–26.

"A Letter to the Reverend Samuel C. Thatcher"

1815

*Standing at the corner of Boylston and Arlington streets at the edge of the
Boston Public Garden is a statue of William Ellery Channing (1780–1842),
one of two statues of Boston clergymen honored in the garden. Considered the
chief spokesperson of the liberal wing of American Congregationalists who
later became the Unitarians, Channing was known for preaching "with spiritual power" and for his dedication to the liberal cause. Channing grew up in
Newport, Rhode Island. His family belonged to Ezra Stiles's Second Congregational Church but also briefly attended Samuel Hopkins's First Congregational. Channing's first position after graduation from Harvard College was
as a tutor in Richmond, Virginia. His time in the South led him to a period
of reflection and deep reading. After returning to Boston, he trained for the
ministry and settled at Federal Street Church. At the time, the leading spokesperson for liberal Congregationalism was Joseph Stevens Buckminster. After
Buckminster's premature death from epilepsy, Channing became the reluctant leader of the liberal movement. He sought to be inclusive, believing there
was enough room in Congregationalism for the liberal and conservative
wings. But in the decade after Henry Ware's appointment to Harvard's Hollis
Chair, conservative attempts to expose and expel liberals from the Congregationalist camp grew stronger. In 1815, Jedidiah Morse published a chapter
from Thomas Belsham's* Life of Theophilus Lindsey *in an attempt to associate the liberals with Unitarianism. Jeremiah Evarts bolstered Morse's attack
with a review in the* Panoplist *that argued for the necessity of breaking fellowship with the liberals. Channing was the logical choice to respond and did so
with an open letter to his friend and colleague the Rev. Samuel Thatcher.
Neither ready nor desiring to break fellowship with the conservatives, Channing deftly defended his perspective, disavowing the Unitarian label while
pointing out that many of the doctrines the conservatives embraced were not
found in Scripture. Further Reading: Gary Dorrien,* The Making of American Liberal Theology: Imagining Progressive Religion 1805–1900 *(Louis-
ville, KY: Westminster John Knox Press, 2001); Andrew Delbanco,* William
Ellery Channing: An Essay on the Liberal Spirit in America *(Cambridge,
MA: Harvard University Press, 1981); Conrad Wright, "The Rediscovery of
Channing," in* The Liberal Christians: Essays on American Unitarian History *(Boston: Beacon Press, 1970).*

—Nicole C. Kirk

My Friend and Brother,

I have recollected with much satisfaction the conversation, which we held the other morning, on the subject of the late *Review* in the *Panoplist* for *June*, of a pamphlet, called "American Unitarianism." I was not surprised, but I was highly gratified, by the spirit with which your spoke of that injurious publication. Grief rather than indignation marked your countenance, and you mourned, that men, who bear the sacred and pacifick name of Christian, could prove so insensible to the obligations of their profession. Our conversation turned, as you recollect, on the *falsehood* of that Review; on its *motives*; and on the *duties* which are imposed on those ministers, whose good name and whose influence it was designed to destroy. . . .

I bring to the subject a feeling, which I cannot well express in words, but which you can easily understand. It is a feeling, as if I were degrading myself by noticing the false and injurious charges contained in this review. I feel as if I were admitting, that we need vindication, that our reputations want support, that our characters and lives do not speak for themselves. My selfrespect too is wounded, by coming into contact with assailants, who not only deny us the name of Christians, but withhold from us the treatment of gentlemen. . . .

The Panoplist Review, though extended over so many pages, may be compressed into a very narrow space. . . .

The *first* assertion to be considered is, that the ministers of this town and vicinity, and the great body of liberal christians are Unitarians, in Mr. Belsham's sense of that word. . . . We both agreed in our late conference, that a majority of our brethren believe, that Jesus Christ is more than man, that he existed before the world, that he literally came from heaven to save our race, that he sustains other offices than those of a teacher and witness to the truth, and that he still acts for our benefit, and is our intercessor with the Father. This we agreed to be the prevalent sentiment of our brethren.

*　*　*

I now come to the *second* charge of the Review: That the ministers of Boston and the vicinity, and the most considerable members of the liberal party "operate in secret; entrust only the initiated with their measures; are guilty of hypocritical concealment of their sentiments." . . . This charge is infinitely more serious than the first. To believe with Mr. Belsham is no crime. But artifice, plotting, hypocrisy *are* crimes; and if we practise them, we deserve to be driven not only from the ministry, not only from the church, but from the society of the decent and respectable.

*　*　*

It is indeed true, as Mr. Wells says, that we seldom or never introduce the Trinitarian controversy into our pulpits. We are accustomed to speak of the Father as God, and of Jesus Christ as his son, as a distinct being from him, as dependent on him, subordinate to him, and deriving all from him. This phraseology pervades all our prayers, and all our preaching. We seldom or never, however, refer to any different sentiments, embraced by other christians, on the nature of God or of Jesus Christ. We preach precisely as if no such doctrine as the Trinity had ever been known. . . . We all of us think it best to preach the truth, or what we esteem to be the truth, and to say very little about errour, unless it be errour of a strictly practical nature. A striking proof of our sentiments and habits on this subject may be derived from the manner in which you and myself have treated Calvinism. We consider the errours which relate to Christ's person as of little or no importance compared with the errour of those who teach, that God brings us into life wholly depraved and wholly helpless, that he leaves multitudes without that aid which is indispensably necessary to their repentance, and then plunges them into everlasting burnings and unspeakable torture, for not repenting. This we consider as one of the most injurious errours which ever darkened the christian world.

* * *

I now come to the third head of the Review, which I propose to consider. The Reviewer, having charged us with holding the opinions of Mr. Belsham, and hypocritically concealing them, solemnly calls on christians who differ from us in sentiment, "to come out and be separate from us, and to withhold communion with us." . . .

Why is it that our brethren are thus instigated to cut us off, as far as they have power, from the body and church of Christ? Let every christian weigh well the answer. It is not because we refuse to acknowledge Jesus Christ as our Lord and Master; it is not because we neglect to study his word; it is not, because our lives are wanting in the spirit and virtues of his gospel. It is, because after serious investigation, we cannot find in the Scriptures, and cannot adopt as instructions of our Master, certain doctrines, which have divided the church for ages, which have perplexed the best and wisest men, and which are very differently conceived even by those who profess to receive them. . . .

SOURCE: William Ellery Channing, A Letter to the Rev. Samuel C. Thatcher, on the Aspersions Contained in a Late Number of the Panoplist, on the Ministers of Boston and the Vicinity (Boston, 1815), 3–7, 10, 13–14, 19–20.

JOHN MURRAY

Records of the Life of the Rev. John Murray
1816

John Murray (1741–1815), a charismatic Methodist evangelist in England,
was converted to Universalism by the teachings of James Relly. After a series
of family tragedies, he took ship to America. The story of his arrival in 1770
on the coast of New Jersey and his first preaching there has become the most
well-known legend of the founding of Universalism in America. (In fact, Uni-
versalism had preceded him to New Jersey and everywhere else he traveled.)
Eventually, in 1775, he settled as minister among a group of Rellyan univer-
salists who were members of the local Standing Order church in Gloucester,
Massachusetts. Splitting away from the parish church, this group, along with
Murray, pioneered Universalist congregational organization and paved the
way for state recognition of Universalist churches. Murray also helped orga-
nize the earliest denominational conventions: at Oxford, Massachusetts, in
1785 and 1793 and at Philadelphia in 1790. Unique among early Universal-
ists, he had connections with persons of influence, such as George Washing-
ton. He had little theological sympathy with the other kinds of Universalism
that had arisen in New England and his Rellyan theology had little influence
upon other Universalists. Because he was venerated personally and treated
as the leading minister in his time, his second church, in Boston, attained
a status approaching that of an episcopal see. Further Reading: Clarence
Skinner and Alfred S. Cole, Hell's Ramparts Fell: The Life of John Murray
(Boston: Boston Universalist Publishing House, 1941); Russell E. Miller, The
Larger Hope, *vol. 1:* The First Century of the Universalist Church in America, 1770–1870 *(Boston: Unitarian Universalist Association, 1979).*

—Peter Hughes

The water was smooth, and our passage pleasant, until we were, as was supposed,
near Sandy Hook; a dense fog then arose which was sufficiently thick to prevent our
seeing the end of our bowsprit. A sloop shot past us, and we inquired how far we were
from Sandy Hook? The answer was *seventy* miles, but we understood *seven*, and we
passed on, and, in a few moments, were in the midst of the *breakers*; the vessel struck
upon the bar, but passed over into a place we afterwards learned was called Cran-
berry Inlet. The fog now dispersed and we discovered we were nearly on shore; our
anchors, however, saved us; but we were greatly alarmed, and never expected to get
off again. The sloop, with which we had spoken, entered this inlet before us, and was

light. The captain proposed to engage this sloop to receive on board as much of our cargo as she could contain; thus, by lightening his vessel, to give himself the only probable chance of getting off. This was effectuated, and, night coming on, the captain, with many apologies, requested me to lodge on board the sloop, inasmuch as there were many valuable articles which he was afraid to trust without a confidential person. To this I readily consented, and taking my Bible and my purse, I went on board the sloop. The plan of the captain was, supposing the morning should present no prospect of getting off, to deposit the remainder of his cargo upon the beach; but, if they should get off, we were immediately to follow, the goods were to be replaced, and the sloop dismissed. I went not to bed, and, when the morning dawned, just at high water, the wind blowing from the shore, they got off, making a signal for us to follow; and, with all possible dispatch, we prepared to obey; but the wind, instantly shifting, drove us back and they proceeded on to New York, leaving us in the bay.

It proved, upon examination, we had no provisions on board; we were therefore necessitated to lock up the vessel, and go on shore in search of sustenance. It was the after part of the day before we could effectuate our purpose, when I went with the boatmen to a tavern, and, leaving them there, pursued a solitary walk through the woods, which seemed to surround this place. My mind was greatly agitated. I was now in the new world; and in just such a part of this new world, as had appeared so desirable in prospect. Here I was, as much alone as I could wish, and my heart exclaimed: *O, that I had, in this wilderness, the lodging place of a poor wayfaring man, some cave, some grotto, some place where I might finish my days in calm repose.*

As thus I passed along, thus contemplating, thus supplicating, I unexpectedly reached a small log house, and saw a girl cleaning a fresh fish; I requested she would sell it to me.

"No, sir, you will find a very great plenty at the next house; we want this."

"The next house; what this?" pointing to one in the woods.

"O no, sir, that is a meeting-house."

"A meeting-house here in these woods?" I was exceedingly surprised.

"You must pass the meeting house, sir; and, a little way farther on, you will see the other house, where you will find fish enough."

I went forward. I came to the door; there was indeed a large pile of fish of various sorts, and, at a little distance, stood a tall man, rough in appearance and evidently advanced in years:

"Pray, sir, will you have the goodness to sell me one of those fish?"

"No, sir."

"That is strange, when you have so many, to refuse me a single fish!"

"I did not refuse you a fish, sir. You are welcome to as many as you please, but I do not sell this article; I do not sell fish, sir, I have them for taking up, and you may obtain them the same way.

I thanked him.

"But," said he, "what do you want of those fish?"

I informed him that the mariners who belonged to the sloop at a distance were at a tavern and would be glad if I could procure them something for supper.

"Well, sir, I will send my man over with the fish, but you can tarry here and have some dressed for yourself."

"No, sir, it is proper I should see how they are accommodated."

"Well, sir, you shall do as you please, but, after supper, I beg you would return and take a bed with us; you will be better pleased here than at a tavern."

I gratefully thanked him, and cheerfully accepted his offer. I was astonished to see so much genuine politeness and urbanity, under so rough a form; but my astonishment was greatly increased on my return. His room was prepared, his fire bright, and his heart open.

"Come," said he, "my friend. I am glad you have returned. I have longed to see you. I have been expecting you a long time."

I was perfectly amazed.

"What do you mean, sir?"

"I must go on in my own way, I am a poor ignorant man, I neither know how to read, nor write; I was born in these woods, and my father did not think proper to teach me my letters. I worked, on these grounds, until I became a man, when I went coasting voyages from hence to New York. I was then desirous of becoming a husband, but, in going to New York, I was pressed on board a man of war, and I was taken in Admiral Warren's ship to Cape-Breton. I never drank any rum, so they saved my allowance; but I would not bear an affront, so if any of the officers struck me, I struck them again; but the admiral took my part and called me his new light man. When we reached Louisbourg, I ran away, and travelled barefooted through the country, and almost naked, to New-York where I was known and supplied with clothes and money, and soon returned to this place, when I found my girl married. This rendered me very unhappy, but I recovered my tranquillity and married her sister.

"I sat down to work; got forward very fast; constructed a saw mill; possessed myself of this farm, and five hundred acres of adjoining land. I entered into navigation, became the owner of a sloop, and have got together a large estate. I am, as I said, unable either to write or read, but I am capable of reflection; the sacred Scriptures have been often read to me, from which I gather, that there is a great and good Being to whom we are indebted for all we enjoy. It is this great and good Being who hath preserved and protected me through innumerable dangers, and, as he had given me a house of my own, I conceived I could not do less than to open it to the stranger, let him be who he would, and, especially, if a travelling minister passed this way he always received an invitation to put up at my house and hold his meetings here.

"I continued this practice for more than seven years, and, illiterate as I was, I used to converse with them, and was fond of asking them questions. They pronounced me an odd mortal, declaring themselves at a loss what to make of me: while I continued to affirm that I had but one hope; I believed that Jesus Christ suffered death for my transgressions, and this alone was sufficient for me. At length my wife grew weary of having meetings held in her house, and I determined to build a house for the worship of God. I had no children, and I knew I was beholden to Almighty God for everything which I possessed, and it seemed right I should appropriate a part of what he had bestowed for his service.

"My neighbors offered their assistance. But 'No,' said I, 'God has given me enough to do this work without your aid, and as he has put it into my heart to do so, will I do.' 'And who,' it was asked, 'will be your preacher?' I answered, 'God will send me a preacher, and of a very different stamp from those who have heretofore preached in my house. The preachers we have heard are perpetually contradicting themselves, but that God, who has put it into my heart to build this house, will send one who shall deliver unto me his own truth, who shall speak of Jesus Christ and his salvation.'

"When the house was finished, I received an application from the Baptists, and I told them if they could make it appear that God Almighty was a Baptist, the building should be theirs at once. The Quakers and Presbyterians received similar answers. 'No,' said I, 'as I firmly believe, that all mankind are equally dear to Almighty God, they shall all be equally welcome to preach in this house, which I have built.' My neighbors assured me I never should see a preacher, whose sentiments corresponded with my own; but my uniform reply was that I assuredly should. I engaged the first year with a man, whom I greatly disliked; we parted, and, for some years, we have had no stated minister. My friends often ask me, 'Where is the preacher of whom you spake?' And my constant reply has been, 'He will, by and by, make his appearance.'

"The moment I beheld your vessel on shore, it seemed as if a voice had audibly sounded in my ear: 'There, Potter, in that vessel, cast away on that shore, is the preacher you have been so long expecting.' I heard the voice, and I believed the report; and, when you came up to my door, and asked for the fish, the same voice seemed to repeat: 'Potter this is the man, this is the person whom I have sent to preach in your house!'"

I was astonished, immeasurably astonished, at Mr. Potter's narrative; but yet I had not the smallest idea it could ever be realized. I requested to know what he could discern in my appearance, which could lead him to mistake me for a preacher?

"What," said he, "could I discern when you were in the vessel that could induce this conclusion? No, sir, it is not what I *saw*, or *see*, but what I *feel*, which produces in my mind a full conviction."

"But my dear sir you are deceived, indeed, you are deceived; I never shall preach in this place nor anywhere else."

"Have you never preached? Can you say, you have never preached?"

"I cannot, but I never intend to preach again."

"Has not God lifted up the light of his countenance upon you? Has he not shown you his truth?"

"I trust, he has."

"And how dare you hide this truth? Do men light a candle to put it under a bushel? If God has shown you his salvation, why should you not show it to your fellow men? But I know that you will. I am sure God Almighty has sent you to us for this purpose; I am not deceived, I am sure I am not deceived."

I was terrified as the man thus went on; and I began to fear that God, who orders things according to the counsel of his own will, had ordained, that thus it should be, and my heart trembled at the idea. I endeavored, however, to banish my own fears and to silence the warm hearted man by observing that I was in the place of a super-cargo, that property to a large amount had been entrusted to my care, and that, the moment the wind changed, I was under the most solemn obligations to depart.

"The wind will never change, sir, until you have delivered to us, in that meeting house, a message from God."

Still, I was resolutely determined never to enter any pulpit as a preacher; yet, being rendered truly unhappy, I begged I might be shown to my bed. He requested I would pray with them, if I had no objection. I asked him how he could suppose I had any objection to praying? The Quakers, he said, seldom prayed, and there were others, who visited him, who were not in the habit of praying. "I never propose prayer, sir, lest it should not meet with the approbation of those, with whom I sojourn; but I am always pleased when prayer is proposed to me." I prayed, and my heart was greatly enlarged, and softened. When we parted for the night, my kind host solemnly requested, that I would think of what he had said.

Alas! He need not to have made this request; it was impossible to banish it from my mind. When I entered my chamber, and shut the door, I burst into tears; I would have given the world, that I had never left England. I felt, as if the hand of God was in the events, which had brought me to this place, and I prayed most ardently that God would assist and direct me by his counsel. I presented myself before him as a man bowed down by calamity; a melancholy, outcast, driven by repeated afflictions of body and of mind to seek refuge in *private* life, to seek solitude, amid the wilds of America:

"Thou knowest," said my oppressed spirit, "thou knowest, O Lord, that if it had pleased thee I would have preferred death, as the safest, and most sure retreat; but thou hast not seen fit to indulge my wishes in this respect. In thy providence, thou hast brought me into this new world; thou seest how I am oppressed by solicitations to speak unto the people the words of life; thou knowest, that I am not sufficient for these things. . . . To thee, O thou compassionate Father of my spirit, encouraged by thy gracious promises, I make application. Pity, O pity, the destitute stranger; leave me not, I most earnestly entreat thee, to my own direction."

Thus did I pray; thus did I weep through the greater part of the night; dreading more than death, even supposing death an object of dread, the thought of engaging, as a public character. On the one hand, I discovered, that if there be a ruling power, a superintending providence, the account, given by the extraordinary man, under whose roof I reposed, evinced its operation that, if the heart of the creature be indeed in the hand of the Creator, it was manifest that God had disposed the heart of this man to view me as his messenger, sent for the purpose of declaring the counsel of his peace to his creatures. On the other hand, I recollected, that the heart is deceitful above all things; that the devices of the adversary are manifold; and that, had it been the will of God, that I should have become a promulgator of the gospel of his grace, he would have qualified me for an object of such infinite magnitude. If I testified of Jesus according to the scriptures, I well knew upon what I must calculate; the clergy, of all denominations, would unite to oppose me. . . . I was persuaded, that people in general, being under the dominion of the clergy, would hate where they hated and report what they reported. Acquainted in some measure with human nature, and with divine revelation, I was certain, that, if I appeared in the character of a real disciple of Christ Jesus; if I dared to declare the whole truth of God, all manner of evil would be said of me; and, although it might be *falsely* said, while the *inventor* of the slander would be *conscious of its falsehood*, the majority of those who heard would yield it credit, and I should become the victim of their credulity.

I knew how Mr. Relly had suffered in England, and the apostles in Judea; and, being a believer in the testimony of God, I was assured, if my doctrines were the same, my treatment would be similar. All this rose to my view, and the prospect was tremendous. Thus I passed the night, and the ensuing morning witnessed my indisposition both of body, and mind.

My good friend renewed his solicitations. "Will you, sir, speak to me, and to my neighbors, of the things which belong to our peace?"

Seeing only thick woods, the tavern across the field excepted, I requested to know what he meant by neighbors?

"O, sir, we assemble a large congregation, whenever the meeting-house is opened; indeed, when my father first settled here he was obliged to go twenty miles to grind a bushel of corn, but there are now more than seven hundred inhabitants within that distance."

I was amazed; indeed, everything I saw, and everything I heard, amazed me. Nothing, except the religion of the people, resembled what I had left behind.

My mind continued subjected to the most torturing reflections. I could not bring myself to yield to the entreaties of Mr. Potter, and still I urged the necessity of departing the moment the wind would answer. Mr. Potter was positive the wind would not change, until I had spoken to the people. Most ardently did I desire to escape the importunities of this good man. The idea of a crowd, making a public exhibition of myself, was, to my desolate, woe-worn mind, intolerable, and the suspense in which I was held was perfectly agonizing. I could not forbear acknowledging an uncommon coincidence of circumstances. The hopes and fears of this honest man, so long in operation, yet he evinced great warmth of disposition and was evidently tinctured with enthusiasm; but, after making every allowance for these propensities, it could not be denied that an over-ruling Power seemed to operate, in an unusual, and remarkable manner. I could not forbear looking back upon the mistakes, made during our passage, even to the coming in to this particular inlet, where no vessel, of the size of the brig "Hand-in-Hand," had ever before entered; every circumstance contributed to bring me to this house. Mr. Potter's address on seeing me; his assurance, that he knew I was on board the vessel, when he saw her at a distance: all these considerations pressed with powerful conviction on my mind, and I was ready to say, "If God Almighty has, in his providence, so ordered events as to bring me into this country for the purpose of making manifest the savor of his name, and of bringing many to the knowledge of the truth; though I would infinitely prefer death to entering into a character, which will subject me to what is infinitely worse than death, yet, as the issues of life and death are not under my direction, am I not bound to submit to the dispensations of providence?" I wished, however, to be convinced that it was the will of God that I should step forth in a character, which would be considered as obnoxious, as truly detestable. I was fully convinced it was not by the will of the flesh, nor by the will of the world, nor by the will of the god of this world, all these were strongly opposed thereto. One moment I felt my resolution give way; the path, pointed out, seemed to brighten upon me, but the next, the difficulties, from within and without, obscured the prospect, and I relapsed into a firm resolution to shelter myself, in solitude, from the hopes, and fears, and the various contentions of men.

While I thus balanced, the Sabbath advanced. I had ventured to implore the God, who had sometimes condescended to indulge individuals with tokens of his approbation, graciously to indulge me, upon this important occasion; and that, if it were his will, that I should obtain the desire of my soul, by passing through life in a private character. If it were *not* his will, that I should engage as a preacher of the ministry of reconciliation, he would vouchsafe to grant me such a wind, as might bear me from this shore before the return of another Sabbath. I determined to take the changing of the wind for an answer; and, had the wind changed, it would have borne on its wings full conviction, because it would have corresponded with my wishes. But the wind changed not, and Saturday morning arrived.

"Well," said my anxious friend, "now let me give notice to my neighbours."

"No sir, not yet; should the wind change by the middle of the afternoon, I must depart."

No tongue can tell, nor heart conceive, how much I suffered this afternoon; but the evening came on, and it was necessary I should determine; and at last, with much fear and trembling, I yielded a reluctant consent. Mr. Potter then immediately dispatched his servants, on horseback, to spread the intelligence far and wide, and they were to continue their information, until ten in the evening.

I had no rest through the night. What should I say, or how address the people? Yet I recollected the admonition of our Lord: *"Take no thought, what you shall say; it shall be given you, in that same hour, what you shall say."* Ay, but this promise was made to his disciples. Well, by this, I shall know if I am a disciple. If God, in his providence, is committing to me a dispensation of the gospel, he will furnish me with matter without my thought, or care. If this thing be not of God, he will desert me, and this shall be another sign; on this, then, I rested. Sunday morning succeeded; my host was in transports. I was—I cannot describe how I was. I entered the house; it was neat and convenient, expressive of the character of the builder. There were no pews; the pulpit was rather in the Quaker mode; the seats were constructed with backs roomy, and even elegant. I said there were no pews; there was one large square pew, just before the pulpit, in this sat the venerable man and his family, particular friends, and visiting strangers. In this pew sat, upon this occasion, this happy man, and surely no man, upon this side of heaven, was ever more completely happy. He looked up to the pulpit with eyes sparkling with pleasure; it appeared to him, as the fulfilment of a promise long deferred; and he reflected, with abundant consolation, on the strong faith, which he had cherished, while his associates would tauntingly question, "Well, Potter, where is this minister who is to be sent to you?" "He is coming along, in God's own good time." "And do you still believe any such preacher will visit you?" "O yes, assuredly." He reflected upon all this, and tears of transport filled his eyes; he looked round upon the people, and every feature seemed to say, "There, what think you now?"

When I returned to his house, he caught me in his arms.

"Now, now, I am willing to depart; O, my God! I will praise thee; thou hast granted me my desire. After this truth I have been seeking, but I have never found it until now; I knew that God, who put it into my heart to build a house for his worship, would send a servant of his own to proclaim his own gospel. I knew, he would; I knew the time was come, when I saw the vessel grounded; I knew, you were the man, when I saw you approach my door, and my heart leaped for joy. Visitors poured into the house; he took each by the hand. "This is the happiest day of my life," said the transported man: "There, neighbors, there is the minister God promised to send me; how do you like God's minister?"

I ran from the company, and prostrating myself before the throne of grace, besought my God to take me, and do with me, whatever he pleased. "I am," said I, "I am, O Lord God, in thine hand as clay in the hand of the potter. If thou in thy providence hast brought me into this new world to make known unto this people the grace and the blessings of the new covenant, if thou hast thought proper, by making choice of so weak an instrument, to confound the wise, if thou hast been pleased to show to a babe, possessing neither wisdom nor prudence, what thou hast hid from the wise and prudent, — be it so, O Father, for so it seemeth good in thy sight. But, O my merciful God! Leave me not, I beseech thee, for a single moment; for without thee, I can do nothing. O, make thy strength perfect in my weakness, that the world may see that thine is the power, and that, therefore, thine ought to be the glory." Thus my heart prayed while supplicating tears bedewed my face.

I felt, however, relieved and tranquillized, for I had power given me to trust in the Lord; to stay upon the God of my salvation.

Immediately upon my return to the company, my boatmen entered the house: "The wind is fair, sir."

"Well, then, we will depart. It is late in the afternoon, but no matter. I will embark directly. I have been determined to embrace the first opportunity, well knowing the suspense the captain must be in, and the pain attendant thereon. Accordingly, as soon as matters could be adjusted, I set off; but not till my old friend, taking me by the hand, said: "You are now going to New-York; I am afraid you will, when there, forget the man to whom your Master sent you. But I do beseech you come back to me again as soon as possible."

*   *   *

I had not the least idea of tarrying in New-York a moment longer, than to see the captain, deliver up my charge, and receive my baggage, and I resolved to return by the first opportunity, to my benevolent friend. And thus did I make up my mind: Well, if it be so, I am grateful to God, that the business is thus adjusted. If I must be a promulgator of these glad, these vast, yet obnoxious tidings, I shall however be sheltered in the bosom of friendship, in the bosom of retirement. I will employ myself on the grounds of my friend, thus earning my own support, and health will be a concomitant; while I will preach the glad tidings of salvation, free as the light of heaven. The business thus arranged, I became reconciled to the will of the Almighty, and I commenced with tolerable composure another, and very important, stage of my various life.

*   *   *

My next evening lecture was uninterrupted; but, on the succeeding Sunday evening, the throng was so prodigious that it was with much difficulty I reached the pulpit; and, when I entered, I was nearly suffocated by the strong effluvia arising from the asafoetida with which the tools of the adversary had wet the pulpit and the pulpit cloth, plentifully sprinkling the whole house with the same noxious drug. For some moments I was so much overpowered, as to induce an apprehension, that it would be impossible I should proceed; but the God of my life was abundantly sufficient for me. The demons of confusion were, however, not quite satisfied; many stones were violently thrown into the windows, yet no one received any other injury than the alarm which was created. At length, a large rugged stone, weighing about a pound-and-a-half, was forcibly thrown in at the window behind my back; it missed me. Had it sped as it was aimed, it must have killed me. Lifting it up, and waving it in the view of the people, I observed: "This argument is *solid* and *weighty*, but it is neither *rational* nor *convincing*."

Exclamations, from various parts of the house, were echoed, and re-echoed: "Pray, sir, leave the pulpit; your life is at hazard."

"Be it so," I returned, "The debt of nature must be paid, and I am as *ready* and as *willing* to discharge it now as I shall be fifty years hence. Yet, for your consolation, suffer me to say, I am immortal, while He who called me into existence has any business for me to perform; and, when He has executed those purposes for which He designed me, He will graciously sign my passport to realms of blessedness. With your good leave, then, I will pursue my subject, and while I have a—THUS SAITH THE LORD—for every point of doctrine which I advance, not all the stones in Boston, except they stop my breath, shall shut my mouth, or arrest my testimony."

The congregation was, as I have said, astonishingly large; but order and silence were gradually restored, and I had uncommon freedom in the illustration and defence of those sacred truths, which will be ultimately triumphant. Two or three succeeding lecture evenings were unmolested, when the business of stoning me in the pulpit was again resumed; my friends were in terror, and, after I had closed, forming a strong phalanx around me, they attended me home. Many religious people were violent in their opposition; they insisted that I merited the severest punishment, that the old discipline for heretics ought to be put in force, and I was thus furnished with abundant reason to bless God for the religious liberty of the country of my adoption, else racks and tortures would have been put in operation against me, nor would these holy men moved by the Spirit have stopped short of my destruction Yet was the charge of *heresy* never *proved* against me. I was never silenced either by reason or scripture—I had called upon men every where, clergymen, or laymen, to step forward, and convict me of error; promising immediately upon conviction, to relinquish the obnoxious tenet, whatever it might chance to be, and to adopt that better way which would, in such an event, become luminous before me. Truth, and gratitude, originate the confession, that in *all circumstances* I have hitherto had reason to bless the God of my life, who hath promised he will be with me to the end of the world, and that all things shall work together for good. Amen, and amen.

SOURCE: John Murray, *Records of the Life of the Rev. John Murray* (Boston: Munroe and Francis, 1816), 123–134, 193–94.

Conclusion of *Records of the Life of the Rev. John Murray*
1816

Judith Sargent Murray (1751–1820), a pioneering feminist and a prominent literary voice in New England, was the daughter of the wealthy Glouces-ter merchant Winthrop Sargent, who founded the Universalist study group that eventually called John Murray to be its leader. She wrote poetry, plays, and essays promoting education, equal opportunity, and independence for women. After the death of her first husband, the merchant John Stevens, in 1788 she married John Murray. She supported her husband's ministry and defended his theology, even to the extent of reproving Hosea Ballou when he was a guest in the Boston pulpit. She helped compile John's sermons and completed his autobiography after he died. Further Reading: Sharon M. Harris, ed., Selected Writings of Judith Sargent Murray *(New York: Oxford University Press, 1995); Judith Sargent Murray,* From Gloucester to Phila-delphia in 1790, *ed. Bonnie Hurd Smith, (Cambridge, MA: Judith Sargent Murray Society, 1998); Judith Sargent Murray,* The Letters I Left Behind, *ed. Bonnie Hurd Smith (Salem, MA: Judith Sargent Murray Society, 2005).*

—Peter Hughes

His full soul believed in one GREAT AND INDIVISIBLE FIRST CAUSE, or origin of all created beings; before this great First Cause ONE ETERNAL NOW, WAS, IS, AND WILL BE EVER PRESENT. Every thing which has past, is passing, or shall pass, was ordained in His eternal purpose, and actually passed in review before Him, ere ever the worlds were formed, or countless systems commenced their revolutions.

The God of our Philanthropist was OMNIPOTENT, OMNIPRESENT, and OMNI-SCIENT; consequently he performed all his will; was, is, and will be, present through all space, through time and through eternity. In the prosecution of His plans myriads of angels, in their various orders, were, by his Omnipotent power, commanded into being; these cherubim and seraphim, angels and arch angels, surrounded the throne of the Most High. The morning stars sang together, and all the hosts of Heaven rejoiced.

But, strange as it may appear to our finite understanding, fell discord, with peace-destroying influence, reared his hydra, his tremendous head. Various conjec-tures hover round this phenomenon. The origin of evil has exercised intellects the most profound and erudite; but he, who can develop the arcana of the Almighty, may claim equality with his God. It should be our care not to attribute to Deity a mode of conduct irreconcilable with rectitude; and to keep close to that revelation, which he hath graciously vouchsafed to bestow upon us.

The creation of man succeeded the fall of the angelic nature. God said,— *Let Us* make man, &c. &c." Speaking in the plural, with an eye to the *complexity* of that character He had predetermined to assume, and, as we before observed, past, present, and future constituted, the token of Deity, one complete whole; and, thus, were important occurrences garbed in language suited to the elevation of the Godhead. In process of time, this august Creator was to be enrobed in humanity, and become the SON born; was to be exhibited as a HOLY SPIRIT of consolation, taking of the things of Jesus and exhibiting them to the mind, thus speaking peace. Mr. Murray was at the same time a UNITARIAN and a TRINITARIAN, beholding, constantly beholding the trinity in the unity. "LET US make man in our image, after our own likeness."—*Yea*, verily, man may be considered as made in the image, and after the likeness, of his Creator. The figure is striking: man is a triune being, body, soul, and spirit, yet no individual is considered as *three*, but *one* man, the TRINITY and UNITY. The Almighty, clad in garments of flesh, became the GOD-MAN, and, speaking of himself *as man*, he says, "My Father is greater than I," while, reverting to the divinity, he affirms "the Father and He are ONE." . . . Such were the comprehensive views of Deity, which became more and more luminous to the mental eye of the preacher.

He believed, that the creation of human beings made a part of the divine purpose; in which sacred, uncontrollable, and irreversible purpose, the WHOLE FAMILY OF MAN were originally and intimately united to their august Creator, in a manner MYSTERIOUS, and as much beyond our limited conception, as the Creator is superior to the creature whom HE hath formed.

Adam the first was a figure of Adam the second. Adam the first, the prototype; Adam the second, the substance of the prototype, the Creator of all Worlds, the Lord from Heaven. The sacred scriptures abound with figures of this mysterious, this ennobling, this soul-satisfying UNION; among which, perhaps, none is more expressive than that of the *Head* and *Members* constituting one body, of which Jesus Christ was the immaculate Head. Hence the propriety and necessity, of looking with a *single* eye to Jesus Christ. We are members of the body of Christ, *who is the head of every man*: Should a single member of this mystical body be finally lost, the Redeemer must, through eternity, remain IMPERFECT.

A law was given, to the complete obedience of which everlasting lasting life was annexed; but no *individual member* was ever able to fulfil this law. It was only the head and members *collectively in their glorious head*, that was furnished with abilities adequate to a performance of such vast magnitude. Yea verily, *we* do indeed break the divine Law in thought, in word, and in deed, and the lip of truth declares, he who offends in one point is guilty of all.

Why then was the commandment so exceeding broad? To convince mankind of imbecility: and that the rectitude they had forfeited, could never, in their own individual characters, be regained. But the plan of Deity was without an error; the revolution of time ushered in the great Representative, or more properly speaking, the *Head* of the body, and the forfeit was paid, full atonement was presented, the ransom given, and, in this hour of NATURE'S JUBILEE, the prodigal family restored to their original possessor.

To make this truth manifest was the great business of our Promulgator. He was convinced, that only he, who believed, could be saved; and that he, who believed not, was indubitably damned. Hence, he has frequently said, *he did not believe in universal salvation*, because he saw the majority of mankind were *not saved*. But he was a firm believer in UNIVERSAL REDEMPTION; because that sacred volume, which he steadfastly, and unwaveringly believed to be the word of God, assured him the price was paid, and the whole human family was *redeemed*. . . .

An article of intelligence may be an *established fact*; it may most importantly affect us; but, so long as the mind refuses to admit its authenticity, we are undeniably subjected to all those agonizing apprehensions, which we should endure, if no such fact existed; and it was the salvation from these mental sufferings which Mr Murray supposed consequent upon a preached Gospel; in other words, an exemption from those tortures that consciousness of condemnation, which is most emphatically described when it is said, "He who believeth not, is, or shall, be damned."

Yet it is an established truth, that every *believer* was once an *unbeliever*; every believer, then, was *once damned,* and it was only when he became a believer that he *was saved* from those countless agonies, which erst times pierced him through with many sorrows. But he was *redeemed,* the price was paid, ere ever he was called into existence. Thus, in this view, redemption and salvation are distinct *considerations.*

The preacher unhesitatingly believed *all* who *learned* of the Father would come to Jesus, and that *all* would *finally be taught of* God. He was a decided believer in the doctrine of angels of light, and angels of darkness, of ministering spirits of light, and of demons stimulating to deeds of darkness. He looked forward to a judgment *to come,* when countless numbers, among the children of men, would rise to the resurrection of damnation, and, ignorant of the genuine character of the Redeemer, would call upon the rocks and mountains to fall upon them, and hide them from the WRATH OF THE LAMB; and believing himself a humble instrument in the hand of God, ordained by him to the ministry of reconciliation, he was never so completely happy, as when declaring the gospel to be believed; and calling upon men, every where to receive the glad tidings of salvation. He was persuaded that those, who laid down in sorrow, would continue unhappy wanderers, until the opening of that book, in which every human being, every member of Christ was written; yet he had no idea of any purgation for sin save what was suffered by Christ Jesus, *who, by himself, purged our sins*. Writing of Mr. Winchester to a friend, Mr. Murray thus expressed himself, "Mr Winchester is full with Mr. Law, and, of course, preaches purgatorial *satisfaction*. According to these gentlemen, every man must finally be his own Saviour! If I must suffer as much, in my own person, as will satisfy divine justice, how is, or can Christ Jesus be, my Saviour? If this *purgatorial doctrine be true*, the ministry of reconciliation, committed to the Apostles, *must be false*; "to wit, *God was, in Christ, reconciling the world unto himself, not imputing unto them their trespasses*." In fact, I know no persons further from Christianity, genuine Christianity, than such Universalists.

Mr. Murray supposed the inquietude of unembodied, or departed, spirits a natural effect derived from a cause. As *unbelievers*, they cannot see the things which belong to their peace; but he greatly rejoiced, that however, *at present* enveloped in darkness, there were, and are, things that *did* and *do belong to their peace*, that the day cometh, when *whatsoever is hid shall be revealed*, and that, at the period of the restitution of all things, the word, the oath of Jehovah, was pledged that every eye should see and every tongue confess. The preacher was persuaded that a few, even in the present dispensation, were elected out of the world to embrace the truth previous to their passing out of time. These, judging themselves, are therefore not to be judged; Saints of God, they shall surround the Redeemer at his second coming, or be caught up in the air to meet the GOD-MAN; after which, the whole world shall be summoned at the imperial bar of the Sire of angels and of men, the Creator of all worlds: That a separation will then take place; the Judge, the Redeemer will divide them, as a shepherd divides his sheep from the goats; will separate every individual from that body of sin and death, of which Paul complained, being burdened; from that fallen spirit, which attaches to every individual in such sort, as to the man among the tombs, rendering it a truth, that he who sleepeth, *apparently* alone upon his bed is nevertheless still connected with his tormentor, and will so continue until this glorious day of *separation* and of *restitution*, when these two shall be separated one from another, the one *taken, the other left*. The fallen angels, figured by the goats shall be ranged on the left hand, while the harassed human nature, redeemed by the God who created it, shall be found on the right hand of the MOST HIGH. Thus, after the world is judged, out of the things written in the books; after they are found guilty before God, and every mouth is stopped, THE BOOK OF LIFE SHALL BE OPENED, IN WHICH ALL THE MEMBERS OF THE REDEEMER, EVERY INDIVIDUAL OF THE HUMAN FAMILY, SHALL BE FOUND WRITTEN; and the ransomed of the Lord, shall be declared denizens of that kingdom, where dwelleth felicity uninterrupted.

Such were the leading sentiments of OUR UNIVERSALIST; and he was firmly of opinion that the doctrines of the gospel, rightly understood, would teach men, every where, to be careful of maintaining good works, to love one another, and in all things to regard the best interests of their BROTHER MAN.

SOURCE: John Murray, *Records of the Life of the Rev. John Murray* (Boston: Munroe and Francis, 1816), 245–49.

"War"

1816

The War of 1812 deeply shaped Channing. Outraged by the senseless blood-shed and what he felt was an unnecessary war stoked by the government, he took a firm stance against it by preaching his first sermon against war. In 1815, Channing's friend Noah Worcester organized the Massachusetts Peace Society and recruited Channing for its leadership. This work inspired his 1816 address on war, which offered a sweeping critique of militarism while steering clear of the "uncertain and dangerous ground" of pure pacifism. Further Reading: Valarie H. Ziegler, The Advocates of Peace in Antebellum America *(Bloomington: Indiana University Press, 1992).*

—Nicole C. Kirk

ISAIAH ii. 4: "Nation shall not lift up sword against nation, neither shall they learn war any more."

I have chosen a subject which may seem at first view not altogether appropriate to the present occasion,—the subject of WAR. It may be thought that an address to an assembly composed chiefly of the ministers of religion, should be confined to the duties, dangers, encouragements of the sacred office. But I have been induced to select this topic because, after the slumber of ages, Christians seem to be awakening to a sense of the pacific character of their religion. . . . I resolved to urge on you the duty, and I hoped to excite in you the purpose, of making some new and persevering efforts for the abolition of this worst vestige of barbarism, this grossest outrage on the principles of Christianity. The day, I trust, is coming when Christians will look back with gratitude and affection on those men who, in ages of conflict and blood-shed, cherished generous hopes of human improvement, withstood the violence of corrupt opinion, held forth, amidst the general darkness, the pure and mild light of Christianity, and thus ushered in a new and peaceful era in the history of mankind. . . .

The *miseries* and *crimes* of war, its *sources*, its *remedies*, will be the subjects of our present attention.

In detailing its miseries and crimes, there is no temptation to recur to unreal or exaggerated horrors. No depth of coloring can approach reality. It is lamentable that we need a delineation of the calamities of war to rouse us to exertion. The mere idea of human beings employing every power and faculty in the work of mutual destruction ought to send a shuddering through the frame. But on this subject, our sensibilities are dreadfully sluggish and dead. Our ordinary sympathies seem to forsake us when war is named. The sufferings and death of a single fellow-being often excite a tender and active compassion; but we hear without emotion of thousands enduring every variety of woe in war.

* * *

The influence of war on the morals of society is also to be deprecated. The suspension of industry multiplies want; and criminal modes of subsistence are the resource of the suffering. Commerce, shackled and endangered, loses its upright and honorable character, and becomes a system of stratagem and collusion. In war, the moral sentiments of a community are perverted by the admiration of military exploits. . . . War especially injures the moral feelings of a people, by making human nature cheap in their estimation, and human life of as little worth as that of an insect or a brute.

* * *

Having considered the crimes and miseries of war, I proceed, as I proposed, to inquire into its sources . . . for it is only by a knowledge of the sources that we can be guided to the remedies of war. . . .

One of the great springs of war may be found in a very strong and general propensity of human nature, in the love of excitement, of emotion, of strong interest,— a propensity which gives a charm to those bold and hazardous enterprises which call forth all the energies of our nature.

* * *

I now proceed to another powerful spring of war; and it is the admiration of the brilliant qualities displayed in war. These qualities, more than all things, have prevented an impression of the crimes and miseries of this savage custom. . . . Men seldom delight in war, considered merely as a source of misery. When they hear of battles, the picture which rises to their view is not what it should be, a picture of extreme wretchedness, of the wounded, the mangled, the slain. These horrors are hidden under the splendor of those mighty energies, which break forth amidst the perils of conflict, and which human nature contemplates with an intense and heart-thrilling delight.

* * *

I have thus attempted to unfold the principal causes of war. They are, you perceive, of a moral nature. They may be resolved into wrong views of human glory, and into excesses of passions and desires which, by right direction, would promote the best interests of humanity. From these causes we learn that this savage custom is to be repressed by moral means, by salutary influences on the sentiments and principles of mankind. And thus we are led to our last topic,—the remedies of war. In introducing the observations which I have to offer on this branch of the subject,

166

I feel myself bound to suggest an important caution. Let not the cause of peace be injured by the assertion of extreme and indefensible principles. I particularly refer to the principle that war is absolutely, and in all possible cases, unlawful, and prohibited by Christianity. . . .

We are indeed told, that the language of Scripture is, "Resist not evil." But the Scriptures are given to us as reasonable beings. We must remember that to the renunciation of reason in the interpretation of Scripture we owe those absurdities which have sunk Christianity almost to the level of Heathenism. If the precept to "resist not evil," admit no exception, then civil government is prostrated; then the magistrate must in no case resist the injurious; then the subject must in no case employ the aid of the laws to enforce his rights. The very end and office of government is to *resist* evil men. . . . Without taking this uncertain and dangerous ground, we may and ought to assail war, by assailing the principles and passions which gave it birth, and by improving and exalting the moral sentiments of mankind.

SOURCE: William Ellery Channing, "War: Discourse before the Congregational Ministers of Massachusetts, Boston, 1816," *The Works of William E. Channing, D.D., with an Introduction* (Boston, 1886), 642–43, 645–49.

A Dictionary of All Religions and Religious Denominations

1817

Hannah Adams (1755–1831), an early American writer and Unitarian living in Massachusetts, published the first edition of An Alphabetical Compendium of the Various Sects Which Have Appeared from the Beginning of the Christian Era to the Present Day *in 1784, as a reaction to what she perceived as the unfair treatment of non-Christian religious groups in other religious dictionaries of the time, such as Thomas Broughton's* An Historical Dictionary of All Religions from the Creation of the World to This Perfect Time *(1742), which offered only scathing commentary of unfamiliar traditions. By contrast, Adams aimed to present a group's beliefs in its own words, without preferential treatment. When her publisher retained all proceeds from the book's sell-out first edition, she began to lobby Congress for copyright laws, which were signed into law for the first time in 1790. The text presented here is from the final edition of her compendium of religions, published in 1817.*

—Emily Mace

The reader will be pleased to observe, that the following rules have been carefully adhered to through the whole of this performance.

1. To avoid giving the least preference of one denomination above another: omitting those passages in the authors cited, where they pass their judgment on the sentiments, of which they give an account: consequently the making use of any such appellations, as Heretics, Schismatics, Enthusiasts, Fanatics, &c. is carefully avoided.

2. To give a few of the arguments of the principal sects, from their own authors, where they could be obtained.

3. To endeavor to give the sentiments of every sect in the general collective sense of that denomination.

4. To give the whole, as much as possible, in the words of the authors from which the compilation is made, and where that could not be done without too great prolixity, to take the utmost care not to misrepresent the ideas.

* * *

Mahometans, or Mohammedans, derive their name and doctrine from Mahomet, or Mohammed, who was born in Arabia late in the sixth century. He was endowed with a subtle genius, and possessed of great enterprise and ambition. He aimed at the introduction of a new religion, and began his eventful project by accusing both Jews and Christians with corrupting the revelations that had been made to them from heaven. He maintained that the prophets, and even Christ himself, had foretold his coming.

* * *

This rapid and extensive spread of the Moslem faith has not only been urged as an argument in its favour, but been brought into competition with the propagation of Christianity. Two circumstances however must be brought into consideration. Mohammed contrived by the permission of polygamy and concubinage to make his creed palatable to the most depraved of mankind; and at the same time, by allowing its propagation by the sword, to excite the martial spirit of unprincipled adventurers. . . .

The great doctrine of the koran is the *unity of God*: to restore which point, Mohammed pretended, was the chief end of his mission; it being laid down by him as a fundamental truth, that there never was, nor can be, more than one true religion. For though particular laws or ceremonies are temporary, and subject to alteration according to divine direction; yet, the substance of religion being truth, continues immutable. And he taught, that whenever this religion became neglected, or essentially corrupted, God informed and admonished mankind thereof by prophets, of whom Moses and Jesus were the most distinguished, till the appearance of Mohammed.

The koran asserts Jesus to be the true Messiah, the word and breath of God, a worker of miracles, a preacher of heavenly doctrines, and an exemplary pattern of a perfect life. . . . They believe that his religion was improved and completed by Mohammed, who was the *seal* of the prophets.

SOURCE: Hannah Adams, *A Dictionary of All Religions and Religious Denominations* (New York and Boston, 1817), 1, 156–58.

"On Future Misery"
1817–1818

Friendship soured between Hosea Ballou and Edward Turner (1776–1853), his circuit-preaching partner in central Massachusetts, when Turner accepted the call of the church in Charlestown, Massachusetts, in 1814, a pulpit that Ballou coveted. In Charlestown, across the bridge from Boston, Turner became friendly with Ballou's rival Paul Dean, John Murray's trinitarian associate and successor. This widened the rift between the two old friends. Although Turner had forced Ballou to concede in 1812 that 1 Peter 3:18–20 could only be interpreted as describing punishment in the afterlife, Ballou was not satisfied. Their 1817–1818 debate in the short-lived magazine The Gospel Visitant *began in a cooperative spirit, but the result further strained the relationship between two old friends. In 1823, the Turner-Dean party, called the Restorationists, published a manifesto that Ballou's partisans portrayed as a breach of fellowship. Soon afterward Turner was dismissed from his church in Charlestown. Blaming Ballou for his misfortune, Turner sought an apology, which Ballou would not give. Unhappy, Turner became a Unitarian. The controversy continued after his 1828 departure from Universalist ministerial fellowship, leading the remaining Restorationists to secede from the Universalist denomination in 1831. That Ballou's position as the leading Universalist minister in New England was never in doubt, even in the time of controversy, may be attributed to his political acumen, his control of the leading denominational newspaper (the* Universalist Magazine, *which he helped establish in 1819), and his willingness to travel to help organize and defend local Universalist churches and associations. The following rearrangement and condensation of the text in the published letters that Ballou and Turner sent to each other gathers the main threads of argument together in a small compass. Further Reading: Richard Eddy,* Universalism in America: A History *(Boston: Universalist Publishing House, 1884–86), 2:260–342; Peter Hughes, "The Restorationist Controversy: Its Origin and First Phase, 1801–1824," Journal of Unitarian Universalist History 27 (2000): 1–57*

— Peter Hughes

HOSEA BALLOU: The question whether the doctrine of a future state of punishment be a doctrine taught in the scriptures, is proposed for candid discussion. . . . No doubt considerable success might attend the well-directed researches of an individual unassisted by a fellow labourer; but as the human mind never becomes acquainted with its own resources, until opposition and difficulties call them into action, it is believed that in the proposed investigation "two are better than one."

Though at first thought, it might seem, that the two who are to conduct this investigation, should be of opposite sentiments on the subject to be argued, on more mature consideration a thought suggests itself, that the enquiry would be more likely to be kept free from improper warmth or injudicious zeal, were the parties of the same opinion, than if they were of opposite sentiments.

Another circumstance, which could not fail greatly to favor the contemplated attempt, would be realized in a long habitual attachment reciprocated between the parties, together with their union of sentiment on the general system of the gospel. . . .

Should the foregoing suggestions have the weight in your mind as they bear in mine, you have the privilege of choosing the side of the proposed question that you should prefer to vindicate, and come as directly to the merits of the argument as you think proper, and leave the other to be vindicated by me.

EDWARD TURNER: I will frankly acknowledge, that I have ever been inclined more to the doctrine of a future punishment, than to the opposite idea; hence, as I shall not succeed VERY well as an argumentator in any way, and wishing to do as well as possible, I shall endeavor to prove that there is a balance of evidence for believing in a future state of punishment.

HOSEA BALLOU: I am equally as well satisfied with the part your selection has allotted me, as I should have been had your choice been different, feeling a determination to pursue the enquiry with reference to nothing but the result of candid reasoning, dictated and sanctioned by the divine testimony.

EDWARD TURNER: Perhaps it will be most proper for you to assume a position, or state a proposition, which being proved, the point will be gained. You will pardon this intimation. I do not mean to prescribe the method in which you shall conduct your plan. But it occurs to me, that this subject is resolvable into one point, which being settled, the question is put to rest. If it can be proved from reason and scripture, that "death NECESSARILY produces such a moral change in the mind of the sinner, as to make him at once a willing, obedient and happy subject of the moral kingdom;" then it will follow that the doctrine of future punishment is proved false; but if it cannot be proved, I conceive the aforesaid doctrine stands upon good ground.

HOSEA BALLOU: Were it possible to prove that "death necessarily produces such a moral change in the mind of the sinner, as to make him at once a willing, obedient and happy subject of the moral kingdom," would the perpetuity of this desirable condition follow as a necessary consequence? Is it not observable in changeable beings, that willing obedience, together with corresponding happiness, is frequently transitory? . . . If in a future state there grows a forbidden fruit, and a tempter be there, whose deceitful arts may prove as successful as did the serpent's with our first parents, however pure, however innocent, however willing, obedient, and happy, man may be, when he enters that unknown world, his rectitude and felicity may be as transitory as was Adam's at first. On the other hand, must it not be allowed that this prohibition, this artful tempter, and this liability to be led into sin, are all necessary, in order to maintain a state of misery?

EDWARD TURNER: I am quite conscious that I can be a sufferer today, for sins committed a year ago, without supposing the occurrence of a new temptation between that period on the present. I can as easily conceive that a sinner, dying in a state of irreconciliation to God, may continue under the power, and suffer the consequences of his unreconciledness in another world, and yet without supposing any fresh temptation to take place.

HOSEA BALLOU: That the mental powers of man should remain for a year without temptation, and without being led into sin, and without being liable to be led into sin, and yet suffer for sins committed before this period, surely requires some evidence, either from actual experience, from some known law of moral nature, or from the faithful testimony of divine revelation.

EDWARD TURNER: The "faithful testimony of divine revelation" is a record of "actual experience and the known laws of moral nature." When the ten brethren knew Joseph in Egypt as the man they had persecuted heretofore, and when they felt the "compunctious visitings of conscience," was this sensation of anguish the effect of sins committed subsequent to their conduct to Joseph, but anterior to their discovering him; or was it the consequence of a crime committed long before? For if it WAS the latter, the case is the same as if they had not transgressed at all between the period of selling Joseph, and his making himself known to them. St. Paul adverts, more than once, to the circumstance of his persecuting the church of God; and the language is such as to carry the idea, that he was filled with sincere regret and sorrow at this part of his conduct; now, were Paul's sensations, on this review of his past life, the effect of the sin of persecuting the church, or were they the consequences of continued habits of transgression, subsequent to his conversion? If Paul's regret at his former persecuting conduct, was the effect of his particular conduct in that respect, whatever other sins he might have committed in the intervening time; the case is the same as if he had not been tempted or led astray in all the intervening time.

HOSEA BALLOU: REGRET and GUILT are very different. [Paul], no doubt, regretted the blindness of his brethren the Jews, but that he felt any condemnation for their blindness, may not necessarily follow.

EDWARD TURNER: I am willing also to grant that in many instances "regret and guilt are very different." But to me it is evident that much of this difference arises from the difference in the subjects. Paul might, as he did, deeply regret the blindness of his countrymen, but there was no possible view of the case, in which he could be guilty. Their blindness was their own act or condition of mind; Paul's 'REGRET' was *his* own condition, and as far as he had conducted sinfully in persecuting the Church, was, as it appears to me, a consequence of his own act. And, besides, I wish to enquire, wherein the great difference is between this regret and guilt of the Apostle, unless the regret be the child of the guilt? If Paul had never done what was wrong, why should he feel any regret for past persecuting measures? If no guilt, why any condemnation? And if no condemnation, why should he say, 'I obtained mercy?' I will only add, that, if Paul's regret was the production of his persecuting conduct in times past, and if it gave him mental uneasiness, then, it strikes me, that his regret, though a relation, in ever so distant a remove from the original act, was a consequence of a sinful act.

HOSEA BALLOU: Every ordinance of divine wisdom must have a desirable object to effect; when the object is effected, the means to produce such an effect may cease without injury. The sensation of guilt and condemnation for sin, was undoubtedly ordained by divine wisdom, to check the growth of moral evil; but when sin or moral evil becomes extinct, why the sensation of guilt should continue, is not understood. . . .

I will submit for our mutual consideration, the question, Whether the doctrine of future punishment be necessarily embraced in the faith of the gospel; leaving all other questions relative to the subject, to be discussed when it shall be thought necessary. . . .

If the particular question above submitted for investigation, be acceptable to you, it will remain for you to prove that the doctrine of future punishment is in fact embraced in the faith of the gospel, and to disprove the arguments which I may find to oppose it; of which the following are here suggested.

The promise made to Abraham is adverted to in the New Testament, as containing the substance of the gospel; and his faith in that promise is distinguished in the writings of St. Paul, as the approved pattern of Gospel faith. But in this promise, variously expressed, and several times communicated to the FATHERS, there appears to be no intimation of the doctrine which we are endeavoring to investigate. If it be necessary for the Christian to believe in the doctrine of future punishment, why was it not equally necessary for the father of the faithful to embrace this indispensable article? May it not be contended, that Abraham was the fit person for this doctrine to be communicated to, and likewise that the time would have been well chosen, so that whenever the Abrahamic faith was adverted to in after ages, the plainly expressed doctrine of future punishment, should strike the mind as one of its essential articles?

Secondly. In all the cloud of testimonies borne by the prophets concerning the Messiah and his dispensation, there appears to be nothing plainly laid down respecting a state of future punishment. Will it not be difficult to account for this general silence through the prophetic ages of the Jewish Church, on an essential article of the faith of the gospel?

Thirdly. If the belief of this particular tenet be required in the gospel faith, would it have been omitted in the preaching of Jesus himself? Or will it be contended, that so far from omitting this particular, our Saviour has laid it down in direct, positive language; that he has insisted on this point of doctrine with all his usual plainness on great and momentous subjects? Let it be here premised, that FORCED and FAR-FETCHED explanations of the parables of Jesus, can never be admitted in proof of the doctrine in question. And as it does not appear that the divine teacher ever made this doctrine a subject of a single discourse which he delivered in all his ministry, it remains for proof to be brought from some other source to substantiate it.

Fourthly. May we not justly suppose, that the preaching of Jesus was a plain and luminous comment on the law and the prophets? And furthermore, that the preaching of the Apostles of Jesus was a well digested comment on the doctrine and preaching of their divine master? If so, and the design of the law, the prophets, and of Jesus, had been to inculcate the doctrine of a future punishment, would the apostles have been silent upon it? . . .

Fifthly. When the CREATOR proposed the prohibition of the forbidden tree to our first parents in the garden, and laid down the consequence of transgression for their admonition, how can his silence on the subject of future punishment be accounted for in any other way, than by supposing that the ALMIGHTY FATHER saw no necessity of Adam's believing in it? And let it be further noticed, that after the transgression, when the CREATOR delineated the effects and consequences of sin to his unhappy children, he mentioned particular circumstances relative to their mortal existence in this world, but said not a word concerning this future punishment, which is the subject of our enquiry. How is this to be accounted for? Furthermore, when Cain had risen up against his brother and taken his life, God called him to an account for his wicked act, and announced his punishment, but intimated nothing concerning this punishment in a future state. Was neither the sin of Adam, nor the sin of Cain, a subject to justify the denunciation of this doctrine? Can we reasonably conceive of a better time, or a more proper occasion, than one of these, to justify a declaration of it?

If it were possible to give even a plausible reason why this doctrine was omitted on the foregoing occasions, could we assign a sufficient one for its total omission in all the dreadful threatenings denounced against the rebellious house of Israel, in all the writings of Moses?

Having noticed the first declarations found in the word of God, on the subject of the punishment of sin, and finding no intimations of a future state of misery, there seems to be a propriety in looking at the "last plagues" contained in the wrath of God, as laid down in the books of Revelations. But here again we find all confined to this mortal state.

EDWARD TURNER: It was certainly the design of the promise to Abraham, of much of the prophetical writings, of a considerable portion of our Saviour's discourses, and of most of the Apostolic letters, and the sermons of the Apostles which we find on record, to prove a DELIVERANCE FROM SIN AND MISERY. This being admitted, a reason may be offered, why a FUTURE punishment, or indeed punishment of any DEFINITE duration, should not be an EXPRESS article of such writings. If the subjects of a prince had rebelled, and the prince was pleased to grant a full pardon to all offenders, and a perfect deliverance from all the consequences of the revolt; the edict which should announce these "glad tidings," and call upon the subjects to believe in the mercy of the prince, would not NECESSARILY embrace this article of faith, viz: "some of my subjects will continue rebellious beyond such a period of time," and then noting the period expressly.

The gospel preached to Abraham, and by Christ and his Apostles, as well as Prophets, is mainly conversant with the final deliverance of mankind from the power of sin and death; but this deliverance has not, as I recollect, any specific period allotted it. The Apostle uses this general language, "the dispensation of the fulness of times." And were it justifiable, on principles of reasoning, might I not employ your own mode of argument, and say, If the doctrine of a deliverance from sin and its consequences, in the article of death, be an evangelical truth, should we not expect to find it plainly expressed, in the before mentioned departments of scripture? And if it be not there expressed, is not the conclusion logical, that such a doctrine is without competent authority?

But I am not certain, however, that the prophetic and christian scriptures are SILENT on the subject of future punishment, though they are not so direct upon the point, as upon some others, (for reasons above mentioned) and though they do not notice it so often as other subjects. I will say, it is difficult for me to understand the text, 1st Pet. 3: 19–20—[For Christ also hath once suffered for sins, the just for the unjust, that he might bring us to God, put to death in the flesh, and quickened

175

by the Spirit: by which also he went and preached unto the spirits in prison; which sometime were disobedient, when once the long-suffering of God waited in the days of Noah]—and also, chap. 4, 5th and 6th verses, without admitting a future punishment as suffered by the persons mentioned by the Apostle.

HOSEA BALLOU: The opinion that Christ went to a place where the spirits of the literally dead were imprisoned for the purpose of preaching the gospel to them, which opinion has been founded on this passage in Peter, is subject to many objections, some of which are the following:

1st. This event, which must be considered, if true, of equal moment with any particular circumstances attending the ministry of Jesus Christ was never once mentioned by him, that we have any account of. 2nd. No mention is made by any of the prophets, who spake of the glorious things the Messiah should do. 3rd. No writer of the New Testament has mentioned this thing except St. Peter.

EDWARD TURNER: What is the argument itself, which is here employed to disprove the above interpretation? It seems to me to be this; an argument from what is *not*, in all or many places, to the conclusion, that it is *no* place. The idea of preaching to departed spirits, in prison, is not in the prophets, is not in the discourses of Christ to his apostles; and therefore it is no where. And when we think, that one Christian writer has, as far as circumstances and grammatical construction go, favoured a particular idea, we are still not to believe it, because the same is not found in the writings of all, or some of the rest.

HOSEA BALLOU: . . . "The particular subject to which the apostle alluded when he spake of Christ's preaching to the spirits in prison, in consequence of being put to death in the flesh, and being quickened by the spirit, is thought to be this, viz. "he went and preached to the gentiles who were dead in trespasses and sins, and of a character similar to those abominable people who were destroyed by the flood." . . . "During the life of Jesus, he *confined* his ministry to the Jews, charged his disciples to go to none of the cities of the Gentiles, and said that he was sent to the lost sheep of the house of Israel. But after his resurrection he enlarged the mission of the gospel and ordered it to be preached to every creature."

Now, if we duly consider that St. Peter was writing a general epistle to Christian professors, throughout Pontus, Galatia, Cappadocia, Asia and Bithynia, comprehending multitudes of the Gentile believers as well as converts from among the Jews, the application of our text already suggested will appear the more probable. It was saying to the Gentiles; Christ has suffered in the flesh for you; although he was a just and holy character, for your sakes, to bring you to God, to the true God, and away from your idols, he was led as a lamb to the slaughter. And being quickened by the spirit, he comes to the Gentile world with the gospel of peace and salvation.

EDWARD TURNER: You doubt, that our Lord, in his disembodied state, preached to the inhabitants of the old world because no writer but Peter takes any notice of such an event. Let us then apply the argument to this "enlargement of the gospel Mission." If Peter had received such a commission to preach to a gentile family, is it not strange that others have not received the same? That no particular mention has been made of any such thing to any other but only to Peter? And therefore conclude, that either Peter had received no such commission, in words, or if he had mistaken their meaning.

I must take liberty to say, that I know not, by what rule, or by what authority you have used the word "similar," in the above sentence. The apostle is not presenting similarities, nor making comparisons between men who lived at some former time, and such as lived then. Nor does he convey any idea usually employed in cases of comparison; much less does he intimate that the character of the inhabitants of the old world was so like that of men in the day in which he wrote, that the former might be identified with the latter; or that the two were so "similar," that the former could stand for the latter. Yet your explanation imports as much; and really I think, that without this consideration, without the use of the word "similar," it would have been much less plausible. And still upon recurring to the text, we find nothing like similarity. It is not, "he went and preached to spirits in prison" of *similar* character to the people in Noah's time; but to this same people themselves, "who were sometimes disobedient, when once the long suffering of God waited in the days of Noah."

HOSEA BALLOU: Notwithstanding the effort you make to disallow the propriety of the word *similar*, which I used to carry the sense of the passage from the people of Noah's time to the gentiles of Peter's day, I am persuaded that as by allowing this transfer, every thing relative to the whole subject may be clearly understood, and understood perfectly analogous with so general a topic of scripture testimony, the eye of candour, on due reflection, will see some thing more than mere plausibility in the argument.

SOURCE: Hosea Ballou and Edward Turner, *The Gospel Visitant*, July 1817, October 1817, January 1818.

"Unitarian Christianity"
1819

"Unitarian Christianity," also known as the Baltimore Sermon, is Channing's most famous sermon. Delivered at the ordination of Jared Sparks in May of 1819 at the First Independent Church of Baltimore, Channing abandoned his pattern of playing down differences by unapologetically claiming the title Unitarian. The sermon laid out a liberal approach rooted in Scripture, the importance of reason, the absence of the Trinity in Scripture, and an elevated understanding of human nature. The sermon's boldness was no accident. It became the platform of the Congregationalist liberals, and arrangements had already been made to publish it before it was preached. More than ten thousand copies were sold. The setting of Baltimore, moreover, presaged the 1825 founding of the American Unitarian Association, which worked to extend liberal Congregationalism beyond its New England roots. Further Reading: Conrad Wright, "Introduction," in Three Prophets of Religious Liberalism: Channing, Emerson, Parker *(Boston: Beacon Press, 1961).*

—Nicole C. Kirk

The peculiar circumstances of this occasion not only justify but seem to demand a departure from the course generally followed by preachers at the introduction of a brother into the sacred office. It is usual to speak of the nature, design, duties, and advantages of the Christian ministry; and on these topics I should now be happy to insist, did I not remember that a minister is to be given this day to a religious society whose peculiarities of opinion have drawn upon them much remark, and, may I not add, much reproach. Many good minds, many sincere Christians, I am aware, are apprehensive that the solemnities of this day are to give a degree of influence to principles which they deem false and injurious. The fears and anxieties of such men I respect; and, believing that they are grounded in part on mistake, I have thought it my duty to lay before you, as clearly as I can, some of the distinguishing opinions of that class of Christians in our country who are known to sympathize with this religious society. I must ask your patience, for such a subject is not to be despatched in a narrow compass. I must also ask you to remember that it is impossible to exhibit, in a single discourse, our views of every doctrine of revelation, much less the differences of opinion which are known to subsist among ourselves. I shall confine myself to topics on which our sentiments have been misrepresented, or which distinguish us most widely from others. May I not hope to be heard with candor? God deliver us all from prejudice and unkindness, and fill us with the love of truth and virtue!

There are two natural divisions under which my thoughts will be arranged. I shall endeavour to unfold, 1st, The principles which we adopt in interpreting the Scriptures; and 2dly, Some of the doctrines, which the Scriptures, so interpreted, seem to us clearly to express.

I. We regard the Scriptures as the records of God's successive revelations to mankind, and particularly of the last and most perfect revelation of his will by Jesus Christ. Whatever doctrines seem to us to be clearly taught in the Scriptures; we receive without reserve or exception. We do not, however, attach equal importance to all the books in this collection. Our religion, we believe, lies chiefly in the New Testament. The dispensation of Moses, compared with that of Jesus, we consider as adapted to the childhood of the human race, a preparation for a nobler system, and chiefly useful now as serving to confirm and illustrate the Christian Scriptures. Jesus Christ is the only master of Christians, and whatever he taught, either during his personal ministry, or by his inspired Apostles, we regard as of divine authority, and profess to make the rule of our lives.

This authority which we give to the Scriptures is a reason, we conceive, for studying them with peculiar care, and for inquiring anxiously into the principles of interpretation by which their true meaning may be ascertained. The principles adopted by the class of Christians in whose name I speak need to be explained, because they are often misunderstood. We are particularly accused of making an unwarrantable use of reason in the interpretation of Scripture. We are said to exalt reason above revelation, to prefer our own wisdom to God's. Loose and undefined charges of this kind are circulated so freely, that we think it due to ourselves, and to the cause of truth, to express our views with some particularity. Our leading principle in interpreting Scripture is this, that the Bible is a book written for men, in the language of men, and that its meaning is to be sought in the same manner as that of other books. We believe that God, when He speaks to the human race, conforms, if we may so say, to the established rules of speaking and writing. How else would the Scriptures avail us more than if communicated in an unknown tongue? . . .

Were the Bible written in a language and style of its own, did it consist of words which admit but a single sense, and of sentences wholly detached from each other, there would be no place for the principles now laid down. We could not reason about it, as about other writings. But such a book would be of little worth; and perhaps, of all books, the Scriptures correspond least to this description. The word of God bears the stamp of the same hand which we see in his works. It has infinite connections and dependences. Every proposition is linked with others, and is to be compared with others, that its full and precise import may he understood. Nothing stands alone. The New Testament is built on the Old. The Christian dispensation is a continuation of the Jewish, the completion of a vast scheme of providence, requiring great extent of view in the reader. Still more, the Bible treats of subjects on which we receive ideas from other sources besides itself,—such subjects as the nature, passions, relations, and duties of man; and it expects us to restrain and modify its language by the known truths which observation and experience furnish on these topics.

We profess not to know a book which demands a more frequent exercise of reason than the Bible.

*　*　*

We object strongly to the contemptuous manner in which human reason is often spoken of by our adversaries, because it leads, we believe, to universal skepticism. If reason be so dreadfully darkened by the fall, that its most decisive judgments on religion are unworthy of trust, then Christianity, and even natural theology, must be abandoned; for the existence and veracity of God, and the divine original of Christianity, are conclusions of reason, and must stand or fall with it.

*　*　*

To the views now given, an objection is commonly urged from the character of God. We are told that God being infinitely wiser than men, his discoveries will surpass human reason. In a revelation from such a teacher we ought to expect propositions which we cannot reconcile with one another, and which may seem to contradict established truths; and it becomes us not to question or explain them away, but to believe and adore, and to submit our weak and carnal reason to the divine word. To this objection we have two short answers. We say, first, that it is impossible that a teacher of infinite wisdom should expose those whom he would teach to infinite error. . . .

We answer again, that if God be infinitely wise, He cannot sport with the understandings of his creatures. A wise teacher discovers his wisdom in adapting himself to the capacities of his pupils, not in perplexing them with what is unintelligible, not in distressing them with apparent contradictions, not in filling them with a sceptical distrust of their own powers. An infinitely wise teacher, who knows the precise extent of our minds and the best method of enlightening them, will surpass all other instructors in bringing down truth to our apprehension, and in showing its loveliness and harmony. . . .

II. Having thus stated the principles according to which we interpret Scripture, I now proceed to the second great head of this discourse, which is, to state some of the views which we derive from that sacred book, particularly those which distinguish us from other Christians.

1. In the first place, we believe in the doctrine of God's UNITY, or that there is one God, and one only. To this truth we give infinite importance, and we feel ourselves bound to take heed lest any man spoil us of it by vain philosophy. The

180

proposition that there is one God seems to us exceedingly plain. We understand by it that there is one being, one mind, one person, one intelligent agent, and one only, to whom underived and infinite perfection and dominion belong. We conceive that these words could have conveyed no other meaning to the simple and uncultivated people who were set apart to be the depositaries of this great truth, and who were utterly incapable of understanding those hair-breadth distinctions between being and person which the sagacity of later ages has discovered. We find no intimation that this language was to be taken in an unusual sense, or that God's unity was a quite different thing from the oneness of other intelligent beings.

We object to the doctrine of the Trinity, that, whilst acknowledging in words, it subverts in effect, the unity of God. . . .

We do, then, with all earnestness, though without reproaching our brethren, protest against the irrational and unscriptural doctrine of the Trinity. "To us," as to the Apostle and the primitive Christians, "there is one God, even the Father." With Jesus, we worship the Father, as the only living and true God. We are astonished, that any man can read the New Testament and avoid the conviction that the Father alone is God.

*   *   *

We have further objections to this doctrine, drawn from its practical influence. We regard it as unfavorable to devotion, by dividing and distracting the mind in its communion with God. It is a great excellence of the doctrine of God's unity, that it offers to us ONE OBJECT of supreme homage, adoration, and love, One Infinite Father, one Being of beings, one original and fountain, to whom we may refer all good, in whom all our powers and affections may be concentrated, and whose lovely and venerable nature may pervade all our thoughts. True piety, when directed to an undivided Deity, has a chasteness, a singleness, most favorable to religious awe and love.

*   *   *

2. Having thus given our views of the unity of God, I proceed, in the second place, to observe that we believe in the unity of Jesus Christ. We believe that Jesus is one mind, one soul, one being, as truly one as we are, and equally distinct from the one God. We complain of the doctrine of the Trinity, that, not satisfied with making God three beings, it makes Jesus Christ two beings, and thus introduces infinite confusion into our conceptions of his character. This corruption of Christianity, alike repugnant to common sense and to the general strain of Scripture, is a remarkable proof of the power of a false philosophy in disfiguring the simple truth of Jesus.

*   *   *

We are also told, that Christ is a more interesting object, that his love and mercy are more felt, when he is viewed as the Supreme God, who left his glory to take humanity and to suffer for men. That Trinitarians are strongly moved by this

181

representation, we do not mean to deny; but we think their emotions altogether founded on a misapprehension of their own doctrines. They talk of the second person of the Trinity's leaving his glory and his Father's bosom to visit and save the world. But this second person, being the unchangeable and infinite God, was evidently incapable of parting with the least degree of his perfection and felicity. At the moment of his taking flesh, he was as intimately present with his Father as before, and equally with his Father filled heaven, and earth, and immensity. This Trinitarians acknowledge; and still they profess to be touched and overwhelmed by the amazing humiliation of this immutable being! But not only does their doctrine, when fully explained, reduce Christ's humiliation to a fiction, it almost wholly destroys the impressions with which his cross ought to be viewed. According to their doctrine, Christ was comparatively no sufferer at all. It is true, his human mind suffered; but this, they tell us, was an infinitely small part of Jesus, bearing no more proportion to his whole nature than a single hair of our heads to the whole body, or than a drop to the ocean. The divine mind of Christ, that which was most properly himself, was infinitely happy at the very moment of the suffering of his humanity. Whilst hanging on the cross, he was the happiest being in the universe, as happy as the infinite Father; so that his pains, compared with his felicity, were nothing. This Trinitarians do, and must, acknowledge. It follows necessarily from the immutableness of the divine nature which they ascribe to Christ; so that their system, justly viewed, robs his death of interest, weakens our sympathy with his sufferings, and is, of all others, most unfavorable to a love of Christ, founded on a sense of his sacrifices for mankind. We esteem our own views to be vastly more affecting. It is our belief that Christ's humiliation was real and entire, that the whole Saviour, and not a part of him, suffered, that his crucifixion was a scene of deep and unmixed agony. As we stand round his cross, our minds are not distracted, nor our sensibility weakened, by contemplating him as composed of incongruous and infinitely differing minds, and as having a balance of infinite felicity. We recognize in the dying Jesus but one mind. This, we think, renders his sufferings, and his patience and love in bearing them, incomparably more impressive and affecting than the system we oppose.

3. Having thus given our belief on two great points, namely, that there is one God and that Jesus Christ is a being distinct from and inferior to God, I now proceed to another point, on which we lay still greater stress. We believe in the *moral perfection of God*. We consider no part of theology so important as that which treats of God's moral character; and we value our views of Christianity chiefly as they assert his amiable and venerable attributes. . . .

We conceive that Christians have generally leaned towards a very injurious view of the Supreme Being. They have too often felt as if He were raised, by his greatness and sovereignty, above the principles of morality, above those eternal laws of equity and rectitude, to which all other beings are subjected. We believe that in no being is the sense of right so strong, so omnipotent, as in God. We believe that his almighty power is entirely submitted to his perceptions of rectitude; and this is the ground of our piety. It is not because He is our Creator merely, but because He created us for good and holy purposes; it is not because his will is irresistible, but because his will is the perfection of virtue, that we pay him allegiance. We cannot bow before a being, however great and powerful, who governs tyrannically. We respect nothing but excellence, whether on earth or in heaven. We venerate not the loftiness of God's throne, but the equity and goodness in which it is established.

We believe that God is infinitely good, kind, benevolent, in the proper sense of these words, — good in disposition as well as in act; good not to a few, but to all; good to every individual, as well as to the general system.

We believe, too, that God is just; but we never forget that his justice is the justice of a good being, dwelling in the same mind, and acting in harmony, with perfect benevolence. By this attribute we understand God's infinite regard to virtue or moral worth expressed in a moral government; that is, in giving excellent and equitable laws, and in conferring such rewards, and inflicting such punishments, as are best fitted to secure their observance. God's justice has for its end the highest virtue of the creation, and it punishes for this end alone; and thus it coincides with benevolence; for virtue and happiness, though not the same, are inseparably conjoined. . . .

To give our views of God in one word, we believe in his parental character. We ascribe to him not only the name, but the dispositions and principles of a father. We believe that He has a father's concern for his creatures, a father's desire for their improvement, a father's equity in proportioning his commands to their powers, a father's joy in their progress, a father's readiness to receive the penitent, and a father's justice for the incorrigible. We look upon this world as a place of education, in which He is training men by prosperity and adversity, by aids and obstructions, by conflicts of reason and passion, by motives to duty and temptations to sin, by a vari-ous discipline suited to free and moral beings, for union with himself, and for a sublime and ever-growing virtue in heaven.

Now, we object to the systems of religion, which prevail among us, that they are adverse, in a greater or less degree, to these purifying, comforting, and honorable views of God; that they take from us our Father in heaven, and substitute for him a being whom we cannot love if we would, and whom we ought not to love if we could. We object, particularly on this ground, to that system, which arrogates to itself the name of Orthodoxy, and which is now industriously propagated through our country. This system indeed takes various shapes, but in all it casts dishonor on the Creator. According to its old and genuine form, it teaches that God brings us into life wholly depraved, so that under the innocent features of our childhood is hidden a nature averse to all good and propense to all evil, a nature which exposes us to God's displeasure and wrath, even before we have acquired power to understand our duties or to reflect upon our actions. . . .

This system also teaches that God selects from this corrupt mass a number to be saved, and plucks them, by a special influence, from the common ruin; that the rest of mankind, though left without that special grace which their conversion requires, are commanded to repent, under penalty of aggravated woe; and that forgiveness is promised them on terms which their very constitution infallibly disposes them to reject, and in rejecting which they awfully enhance the punishments of hell. These proffers of forgiveness and exhortations of amendment, to beings born under a blighting curse, fill our minds with a horror which we want words to express.

That this religious system does not produce all the effects on character which might be anticipated, we most joyfully admit. It is often, very often, counteracted by nature, conscience, common sense, by the general strain of Scripture, by the mild example and precepts of Christ, and by the many positive declarations of God's universal kindness and perfect equity. But still we think that we see its unhappy influence. It tends to discourage the timid, to give excuses to the bad, to feed the vanity of the fanatical, and to offer shelter to the bad feelings of the malignant. By shocking, as it does, the fundamental principles of morality, and by exhibiting a severe and partial Deity, it tends strongly to pervert the moral faculty, to form a gloomy, forbidding, and servile religion, and to lead men to substitute censoriousness, bitterness, and persecution, for a tender and impartial charity. We think, too, that this system, which begins with degrading human nature, may be expected to end in pride; for pride grows out of a consciousness of high distinctions, however obtained, and no distinction is so great as that which is made between the elected and abandoned of God.

The false and dishonorable views of God which have now been stated, we feel ourselves bound to resist unceasingly. Other errors we can pass over with comparative indifference. But we ask our opponents to leave to us a GOD worthy of our love and trust, in whom our moral sentiments may delight, in whom our weaknesses and sorrows may find refuge. We cling to the divine perfections. We meet them everywhere in creation, we read them in the Scriptures, we see a lovely image of them in Jesus Christ; and gratitude, love, and veneration call on us to assert them. Reproached, as we often are, by men, it is our consolation and happiness that one of our chief offences is the zeal with which we vindicate the dishonored goodness and rectitude of God.

4. Having thus spoken of the unity of God; of the unity of Jesus, and his inferiority to God; and of the perfections of the divine character; I now proceed to give our views of the mediation of Christ, and of the purposes of his mission. With regard to the great object which Jesus came to accomplish, there seems to be no possibility of mistake. We believe, that he was sent by the Father to effect a moral or spiritual

deliverance of mankind; that is, to rescue men from sin and its consequences, and to bring them to a state of everlasting purity and happiness. We believe, too, that he accomplishes this sublime purpose by a variety of methods, —by his instructions respecting God's unity, parental character, and moral government, which are admirably fitted to reclaim the world from idolatry and impiety, to the knowledge, love, and obedience of the Creator; by his promises of pardon to the penitent, and of divine assistance to those who labor for progress in moral excellence; by the light which he has thrown on the path of duty; by his own spotless example, in which the loveliness and sublimity of virtue shine forth to warm and quicken as well as guide us to perfection; by his threatenings against incorrigible guilt; by his glorious discoveries of immortality; by his sufferings and death; by that signal event, the resurrection, which powerfully bore witness to his divine mission, and brought down to men's senses a future life; by his continual intercession, which obtains for us spiritual aid and blessings; and by the power with which he is invested of raising the dead, judging the world, and conferring the everlasting rewards promised to the faithful.

We have no desire to conceal the fact that a difference of opinion exists among us in regard to an interesting part of Christ's mediation, —I mean, in regard to the precise influence of his death on our forgiveness. Many suppose that this event contributes to our pardon, as it was a principal means of confirming his religion, and of giving it a power over the mind; in other words, that it procures forgiveness by leading to that repentance and virtue, which is the great and only condition on which forgiveness is bestowed. Many of us are dissatisfied with this explanation, and think that the Scriptures ascribe the remission of sins to Christ's death with an emphasis so peculiar that we ought to consider this event as having a special influence in removing punishment, though the Scriptures may not reveal the way in which it contributes to this end.

Whilst, however, we differ in explaining the connection between Christ's death and human forgiveness, —a connection which we all gratefully acknowledge, —we agree in rejecting many sentiments which prevail in regard to his mediation. The idea which is conveyed to common minds by the popular system, that Christ's death has an influence in making God placable or merciful, in awakening his kindness towards men, we reject with strong disapprobation. We are happy to find that this very dishonorable notion is disowned by intelligent Christians of that class from which we differ. We recollect, however, that, not long ago, it was common to hear of Christ as having died to appease God's wrath, and to pay the debt of sinners to his inflexible justice; and we have a strong persuasion that the language of popular religious books, and the common mode of stating the doctrine of Christ's mediation, still communicate very degrading views of God's character. They give to multitudes the impression that the death of Jesus produces a change in the mind of God towards man, and that in this its efficacy chiefly consists. No error seems to us more pernicious. We can endure no shade over the pure goodness of God. We earnestly maintain that Jesus, instead of calling forth, in any way or degree, the mercy of the Father, was sent by that mercy to be our Saviour; that he is nothing to the human race but what he is by God's appointment; that he communicates nothing but what God empowers him to bestow; that our Father in heaven is originally, essentially, and eternally placable, and disposed to forgive; and that his unborrowed, underived, and unchangeable love is the only fountain of what flows to us through his Son. We conceive that Jesus is dishonored, not glorified, by ascribing to him an influence which clouds the splendor of divine benevolence.

We farther agree in rejecting, as unscriptural and absurd, the explanation given by the popular system of the manner in which Christ's death procures forgiveness for men. This system used to teach, as its fundamental principle, that man, having sinned against an infinite Being, has contracted infinite guilt, and is consequently exposed to an infinite penalty. We believe, however, that this reasoning, if reasoning it may be called, which overlooks the obvious maxim that the guilt of a being must be proportioned to his nature and powers, has fallen into disuse. Still the system teaches that sin, of whatever degree, exposes to endless punishment, and that the whole human race, being infallibly involved by their nature in sin, owe this awful penalty to the justice of their Creator. It teaches that this penalty cannot be remitted, in consistency with the honor of the divine law, unless a substitute be found to endure it or to suffer an equivalent. It also teaches that, from the nature of the case, no substitute is adequate to this work, save the infinite God himself; and accordingly, God, in his second person, took on him human nature, that he might pay to his own justice the debt of punishment incurred by men, and might thus reconcile for-giveness with the claims and threatenings of his law. Such is the prevalent system. Now, to us, this doctrine seems to carry on its front strong marks of absurdity; and we maintain that Christianity ought not to be encumbered with it, unless it be laid down in the New Testament fully and expressly. We ask our adversaries, then, to point to some plain passages where it is taught. We ask for one text in which we are told that God took human nature that he might make an infinite satisfaction to his own justice; for one text which tells us that human guilt requires an infinite substi-tute; that Christ's sufferings owe their efficacy to their being borne by an infinite being; or that his divine nature gives infinite value to the sufferings of the human. Not *one word* of this description can we find in the Scriptures; not a text which even hints at these strange doctrines. They are altogether, we believe, the fictions of theologians.

*　　*　　*

5. Having thus stated our views of the highest object of Christ's mission, that it is the recovery of men to virtue, or holiness, I shall now, in the last place, give our views of the nature of Christian virtue, or true holiness. We believe that all virtue has

its foundation in the moral nature of man, that is, in conscience, or his sense of duty, and in the power of forming his temper and life according to conscience. We believe that these moral faculties are the grounds of responsibility, and the highest distinctions of human nature, and that no act is praiseworthy any farther than it springs from their exertion. We believe that no dispositions infused into us without our own moral activity are of the nature of virtue, and therefore we reject the doctrine of irresistible divine influence on the human mind, moulding it into goodness as marble is hewn into a statue. Such goodness, if this word may be used, would not be the object of moral approbation, any more than the instinctive affections of inferior animals, or the constitutional amiableness of human beings.

By these remarks, we do not mean to deny the importance of God's aid or Spirit; but by his Spirit, we mean a moral, illuminating, and persuasive influence, not physical, not compulsory, not involving a necessity of virtue.

*   *   *

We would not, by these remarks, be understood as wishing to exclude from religion warmth, and even transport. We honor, and highly value, true religious sensibility. We believe that Christianity is intended to act powerfully on our whole nature, on the heart as well as the understanding and the conscience. We conceive of heaven as a state where the love of God will be exalted into an unbounded fervor and joy; and we desire, in our pilgrimage here, to drink into the spirit of that better world. But we think that religious warmth is only to be valued when it springs naturally from an improved character, when it comes unforced, when it is the recompense of obedience, when it is the warmth of a mind which understands God by being like him, and when, instead of disordering, it exalts the understanding, invigorates conscience, gives a pleasure to common duties, and is seen to exist in connection with cheerfulness, judiciousness, and a reasonable frame of mind. When we observe a fervor called religious in men whose general character expresses little refinement and elevation, and whose piety seems at war with reason, we pay it little respect. We honor religion too much to give its sacred name to a feverish, forced, fluctuating zeal, which has little power over the life.

*   *   *

I have thus given the distinguishing views of those Christians in whose names I have spoken. We have embraced this system not hastily or lightly, but after much deliberation; and we hold it fast, not merely because we believe it to be true, but because we regard it as purifying truth, as a doctrine according to godliness, as able to "work mightily" and to "bring forth fruit" in them who believe. That we wish to spread it, we have no desire to conceal; but we think that we wish its diffusion because we regard it as more friendly to practical piety and pure morals than the opposite doctrines, because it gives clearer and nobler views of duty, and stronger motives to its performance, because it recommends religion at once to the understanding and the heart, because it asserts the lovely and venerable attributes of God, because it tends to restore the benevolent spirit of Jesus to his divided and afflicted church, and because it cuts off every hope of God's favor except that which springs from practical conformity to the life and precepts of Christ. We see nothing in our views to give offence save their purity, and it is their purity which makes us seek and hope their extension through the world.

SOURCE: William Ellery Channing, "Unitarian Christianity," *The Works of William E. Channing, D.D., with an Introduction* (Boston, 1886), 367–73, 375–83.

Baker et al. v. Fales
(The Dedham Decision)

1820

As the Unitarian controversy raged, many Massachusetts congregations found themselves divided between liberals and orthodox. Disagreements typically came to a head over the appointment of new ministers. In Massachusetts's "Standing Order" of tax-supported congregations, each "church" (composed of full members who had testified to an orthodox experience of conversion) chose a minister with the concurrence of the "parish" (composed of all tax-paying town citizens). Often the mostly female church members preferred an orthodox minister while the parish wanted a liberal. In a precedent-setting case involving the First Parish of Dedham, the Massachusetts Supreme Court ruled that a church can exist only in relation to a parish (or "society") and thus that the preference of the parish should prevail in cases of conflict. When congregations divided, as a consequence, it was usually the Unitarian group who retained the property.

—Dan McKanan

Probably there was no very familiar distinction at that time [of the founding of Dedham and its church] between the church and the whole assembly of Christians in the town. We have had no evidence that the inhabitants were divided into two bodies, of church and society or parish—keeping separate records, and having separate interests; but if the fact be otherwise than is supposed, there is no doubt that most of the inhabitants of the town were church members at that time. . . . The presumption is violent then, that almost if not quite all of the adult inhabitants of *Dedham* and other towns were church members, and a grant to *the church*, under such circumstances, could mean nothing else than a grant to the town.

* * *

Considering then that the land granted was for the beneficial use of the assembly of Christians in *Dedham*, which were no other than the inhabitants of that town who constituted the religious society, within which the church was established, these inhabitants were the *cestui que trusts* [beneficiaries of the trust]—and the equitable title was vested in them, as long as they continued to constitute the assembly denominated the church in the grants.

* * *

No particular number is necessary to constitute a church, nor is there any established quorum . . . A diminution of its numbers will not affect its identity. A church may exist, in an ecclesiastical sense, without any officers as will be seen in the [Cambridge] platform. . . . The only circumstance therefore, which gives a church any legal character, is its connexion with some regularly constituted society; and those who withdraw from the society cease to be members of that particular church, and the remaining members continue to be the identical church.

* * *

We consider then the non-concurrence of the church in the choice of the minister, and in the invitation to the ordaining council, as in no degree impairing the constitutional right of the parish.—That council might have refused to proceed, but the parish could not by that have been deprived of their minister. It was right and proper, as they could not proceed according to ancient usage, because of the dissent of the church, to approach as near to it as possible by calling a respectable council, and having their sanction in the ordination. And it was certainly wise in that council, finding that the points of disagreement were such as would be likely to cause a permanent separation, to yield to the wishes of the parish, and give their sanction to proceedings, which were justified by the constitution and laws of the land. They ordained him over the parish only: but by virtue of that act, founded upon the choice of the people, he became not only the minister of the parish, but of the church still remaining there, notwithstanding the secession of a majority of the members.

* * *

Having established the point necessary to settle this cause, *viz.* that the property sued for belongs to the first church in *Dedham, sub modo*; that is, to be managed by its deacons under the superintendence of the church, for the general good of the inhabitants of the first parish, in the support of the publick worship of God:—that the members of the church, now associated and worshipping with the first parish, constitute the first church:—and that the plaintiffs are duly appointed deacons of that church; it follows that the verdict of the jury is right, and that judgment must be entered accordingly.

SOURCE: *Reports of Cases Argued and Determined in the Supreme Judicial Court of the Commonwealth of Massachusetts*, vol. 16 (Boston, 1821), 498, 500, 504, 513–14, 522.

DAVID REED

"To the Public"
1821

The Christian Register *was founded at the height of the Unitarian controversy and functioned as the Unitarian denominational journal until the time
of consolidation, when it merged with the* Universalist Leader *to form what is
now* UU World. *Founder David Reed (1790–1870) edited the* Register *for its
first forty-five years. In his inaugural editorial, Reed stressed the importance
of "free and independent religious inquiry" for liberal Christianity.*

—Dan McKanan

The present period is distinguished above any other since the first settlement of our
country, for the general prevalence of a spirit of free religious inquiry. Amongst all
classes of the community, there has been discovered of late, an increasing desire to
understand better, and to bring into practical exercise, the genuine principles and
spirit of Christianity. And it is with much satisfaction, that the friends of enlightened
piety have perceived, that whilst this spirit of inquiry has been exercised with a considerable degree of freedom and boldness, it has, at the same time, been so effectually guarded by good sense, and chastened by piety, that the cause of truth, instead
of suffering detriment, has been greatly promoted, by the light that has been thrown
upon the true doctrines and principles of our religion.

It will, however, no doubt, be generally admitted that something remains still to
be done, to increase the purity of our Christian faith, and to promote its genuine
practical influence upon the heart and life. It seems important, not only that the
spirit of inquiry that is abroad, should be kept alive, but that exertions be made, to
assist and guide the inquiries of those who are honestly seeking the truth. . . .

The subscriber proposes, therefore, to publish weekly in Boston, the CHRIS-
TIAN REGISTER, a work, which, in its doctrines and temper, shall harmonize with
the Christian Disciple, but which shall be more *elementary*, and better adapted to
the taste and wants of those whose advantages of reading and inquiry have been less
extensive. The great object of the Christian Register will be to inculcate the principles of a rational faith, and to promote the practice of genuine piety. To accomplish
this purpose, it will aim to excite a spirit of free and independent religious inquiry,
and to assist in ascertaining and brining into use, the true principles of interpreting
the scriptures. It will urge the importance and duty of subjecting our faith to the test
of enlightened reason, and of rejecting for our creed, not only what is *contrary* to the

general language of the scriptures, but everything that is not plainly and explicitly taught there. It will also enforce the duty, of a serious and practical regard, to the moral precepts of Christianity, by showing that the final favour of God toward us, is to depend not so much upon what has been done *to* us or *for* us by another, as upon the temper of mind we have ourselves cherished, and the course of moral conduct we have pursued. And it will earnestly recommend to all, the cultivation of the mild and amiable spirit of the gospel toward those who differ from them, from the belief that genuine piety is not confined to any sect, but exists in a greater or less degree amongst all, and that he is the *best* Christian, not whose speculations are in nearest accordance with the faith of the majority, but whose life and temper are most perfectly and habitually under the influence of the precepts and spirit of the gospel.

It is believed that a work of this kind, if conducted with ability and candor, might render an important service to the cause of *truth, piety and Christian love*, by diffusing religious knowledge, by giving enlargement and catholicism to the view and feeling of men, and by inculcating those true and rational principles of religion, which are so important to our virtue and happiness. . . .

To render the work, as far as possible, satisfactory to subscribers, each number shall contain a summary of the important foreign and domestic news, both political and miscellaneous.—Political discussions, however, shall never be admitted.

The *Theological* department shall contain articles original and extracted on various subjects, doctrinal, critical and practical, with occasional biography and poetry, and sketches of ecclesiastical history. It shall also contain such well authenticated intelligence as may be obtained, respecting the moral and religious state of different parts of the world, with accounts of the character, operations and success, of the various societies and institutions, in this and other countries, for moral and benevolent purposes.

SOURCE: David Reed, "To the Public," *Christian Register*, April 20, 1821.

THOMAS JEFFERSON

Letter to James Smith

1822

Thomas Jefferson (1743–1826), third president of the United States and author of the Declaration of Independence, is frequently claimed as a Unitarian, although he never joined a Unitarian congregation or relinquished his membership in the Episcopal Church. While in Philadelphia, however, he attended services at the Unitarian congregation established by his friend Joseph Priestley—suggesting that his comments about Unitarianism in this letter may refer more to the Priestleyan congregations in Pennsylvania than to their more politically conservative counterparts in New England. Further Reading: Edwin Gaustad, Sworn on the Altar of God: A Religious Biography of Thomas Jefferson *(Grand Rapids, MI: Wm. B. Eerdmans, 1996); David Holmes,* The Faiths of the Founding Fathers *(New York: Oxford University Press, 2006); Thomas Jefferson,* Jefferson's Extracts from the Gospels: "The Philosophy of Jesus" and "The Life and Morals of Jesus," *Dickinson Adams, ed. (Princeton, NJ: Princeton University Press, 1983).*

—Dan McKanan

Sir,—I have to thank you for your pamphlets on the subject of Unitarianism, and to express my gratification with your efforts for the revival of primitive Christianity in your quarter. No historical fact is better established, than that the doctrine of one God, pure and uncompounded, was that of the early ages of Christianity; and was among the efficacious doctrines which gave it triumph over the polytheism of the ancients, sickened with the absurdities of their own theology. Nor was the unity of the Supreme Being ousted from the Christian creed by the force of reason, but by the sword of civil government, wielded at the will of the fanatic Athanasius. The hocus-pocus phantasm of a God like another Cerberus, with one body and three heads, had its birth and growth in the blood of thousands and thousands of martyrs. And a strong proof of the solidity of the primitive faith, is its restoration, as soon as a nation arises which vindicates to itself the freedom of religious opinion, and its external divorce from the civil authority. The pure and simple unity of the Creator of the universe, is now all but ascendant in the eastern States; it is dawning in the west, and advancing towards the south; and I confidently expect that the present generation will see Unitarianism become the general religion of the United States. . . .

I write with freedom, because, while I claim a right to believe in one God, if so my reason tells me, I yield as freely to others that of believing in three. Both religions, I find, make honest men, and that is the only point society has any right to look to. Although this mutual freedom should produce mutual indulgence, yet I wish not to be brought in question before the public on this or any other subject, and I pray you to consider me as writing under that trust. I take no part in controversies, religious or political. At the age of eighty, tranquility is the greatest good of life, and the strongest of our desires that of dying in the good will of all mankind.

SOURCE: Thomas Jefferson, "Letter to James Smith, December 8, 1822," in *The Writings of Thomas Jefferson: being his autobiography, correspondence, reports, messages, addresses, and other writings, official and private*, vol. 7, ed. H. A. Washington (Washington, DC: Taylor & Maury, 1854), 269–70.

A New-England Tale; Or, Sketches of New-England Character and Manners

1822

Catharine Sedgwick (1789–1867) was the preeminent American author of sentimental novels in the 1820s and 1830s. Drawing inspiration from such British writers as Maria Edgeworth and Anna Barbauld, Sedgwick created literary models that were in turn emulated by Harriet Beecher Stowe, Lydia Maria Child, and dozens of others. Raised in the preeminent Federalist family of Berkshire County, Massachusetts, Sedgwick embraced the nascent Unitarian movement at the time of its founding, befriended William Ellery Channing, and began her first novel as a Unitarian tract. The heroine of A New-England Tale, *Jane Elton, is a virtuous orphan who is raised by a Calvinist aunt. The selected passages, culminating when Jane confronts her aunt after her cousin has been arrested for robbery, illustrate what William Ellery Channing called "the moral argument against Calvinism." Predestinarian doctrine, Sedgwick believed, led some to self-righteous hypocrisy and others to despair or infidelity. Further Reading: Mary Kelley,* Private Woman, Public Stage: Literary Domesticity in Nineteenth-Century America *(New York: Oxford University Press, 1984); Philip Gura,* Truth's Ragged Edge: The Rise of the American Novel *(New York: Farrar, Straus and Giroux, 2013).*

—Dan McKanan

Mrs. Wilson had fancied herself one of the subjects of an awakening at an early period of her life; had passed through the ordeal of a church-examination with great credit, having depicted in glowing colours the opposition of her natural heart to the decrees, and her subsequent joy in the doctrine of election. She thus assumed the form of godliness, without feeling its power. Are there not many such: some who, in those times of excitement, during which many pass from indifference to holiness, and many are converted from sin to righteousness, delude themselves and others with vain forms of words, and professions of faith?

Mrs. Wilson was often heard to denounce those who insisted on the necessity of good works, as Pharisees;—she was thankful, she said, that she should not presume to appear before her Judge with any of the 'filthy rags of her own righteousness;'— it would be easy getting to heaven if the work in any way depended on ourselves;—

any body could 'deal justly, love mercy, and walk humbly.' How easy it is, we leave to those to determine, who have sought to adjust their lives by this divine rule.

Mrs. Wilson rejected the name of the Pharisee, but the proud, oppressive, bitter spirit of the Jewish bigot was manifest in the complacency with which she regarded her own faith, and the illiberality she cherished towards every person, of every denomination, who did not believe what she believed, and act according to her rule of right. As might be expected, her family was regulated according to 'the letter,' but the 'spirit that giveth life' was not there. Religion was the ostensible object of every domestic arrangement; but you might look in vain for the peace and good will which a voice from heaven proclaimed to be the objects of the mission of our Lord.

Mrs. Wilson's children produced such fruits as might be expected from her culture. The timid among them had recourse to constant evasion, and to the meanest artifices to hide the violation of laws which they hated; and the bolder were engaged in a continual conflict with the mother, in which rebellion often trampled on authority.

Jane had been gently led in the bands of love. She had been taught even more by the example than the precepts of her mother.

*   *   *

If Mrs. Wilson had not been blinded by self-love, she might have learnt an invaluable lesson from the melancholy results of her own mal-government. But she preferred incurring every evil, to the relinquishment of one of the prerogatives of power. Her children, denied the appropriate pleasures of youth, were driven to sins of a much deeper die, than those which Mrs. Wilson sought to avoid could have had even in her eyes; for surely the very worst effects that ever were attributed to dancing, or to romance-reading, cannot equal the secret dislike of a parent's authority, the risings of the heart against a parent's tyranny, and the falsehood and meanness that weakness always will employ in the evasion of power; and than which nothing will more certainly taint every thing that is pure in the character.

*   *   *

Mrs. Wilson was scrupulous in exacting the attendance of every member of her family at her morning and evening devotions. With this requisition Jane punctually and cheerfully complied, as she did with all those that did not require a violation of principle. But still she had often occasion secretly to lament, that where there was so much of the form of worship, there was so little of its spirit and truth; and she sometimes felt an involuntary self reproach, that her body should be in the attitude of devotion, while her mind was following her aunt through earth, sea, and skies, or pausing to wonder at the remarkable inadaptation of her prayers to the condition and wants of humanity, in general, and especially to their particular modification in her own family.

196

Mrs. Wilson was fond of the bold and highly figurative language of the prophets; and often identified herself with the Psalmist, in his exultation over his enemies, in his denunciations, and in his appeals for vengeance.

We leave to theologians to decide, whether these expressions from the king of Israel are meant for the enemies of the church, or whether they are to be imputed to the dim light which the best enjoyed under the Jewish dispensation. At any rate, such as come to us in 'so questionable a shape,' ought not to be employed as the medium of a Christian's prayer.

✻   ✻   ✻

Still anxious that some effort should be made for David, she said to Mrs. Wilson, "Is there, then, nothing to be done for your unhappy son?"

"Nothing, child, nothing; he has gone out from me, and he is not of me; his blood be upon his own head; I am clear of it. My 'foot standeth on an even place.' My case is not an uncommon one," she contined, as if she would by this vain babbling, silence the voice within. "The saints of old—David, and Samuel, and Eli, were afflicted as I am, with rebellious children. I have planted and I have watered, and if it is the Lord's will to withhold the increase, I must submit."

"Oh, aunt!" exclaimed Jane, interrupting and advancing towards her, "do not—do not, for your soul's sake, indulge any longer this horrible delusion. You have more children," she continued, falling on her knees, and taking one of her aunt's hands in both hers, and looking like a rebuking messenger from Heaven, "be pitiful to them; be merciful to your own soul. You deceive yourself. You may deceive others; but God is not mocked."

Mrs. Wilson was conscience stricken. She sat as motionless as a statue; and Jane went on with the courage of an Apostle to depicture, in their true colours, her character and conduct. She made her realize, for a few moments at least, the peril of her soul. She made her feel, that her sound faith, her prayers, her pretences, her meeting-goings, were nothing—far worse than nothing in his sight, who cannot be deceived by the daring hypocrisies, the self-delusions, the refuges of lies, of his creatures. She described the spiritual disciple of Jesus; and then presented to Mrs. Wilson so true an image of her selfishness, her pride, her domestic tyranny, and her love of money, that she could not but see that it was her very self. There was that in Jane's looks, and voice, and words, that was not to be resisted by the wretched woman; and like the guilty king, when he saw the record on the wall, her "countenance was changed, her thoughts were troubled, and her knees smote one against the other."

SOURCE: Catharine Sedgwick, A New-England Tale: Or, Sketches of New-England Character and Manners, (New York: E. Bliss & E. White, 1822), 31–33, 72, 158–59, 246–47.

First Annual Report of the
Executive Committee

1826

The American Unitarian Association (AUA) was founded on May 25, 1825,
twenty years after open conflict between liberal and orthodox Christians had
broken out over the appointment of Henry Ware, Sr., as Hollis Professor at
Harvard. Its institutional precursors included Harvard Divinity School, orga-
nized in 1816 as a distinct unit of Harvard for the education of liberal minis-
ters, and the Berry Street Conference, an annual gathering of liberal ministers
in Massachusetts that began in 1820. The AUA's intellectual leader was
undoubtedly William Ellery Channing, but Channing declined the presi-
dency, leaving much of the organizational work to his assistant, Ezra Stiles
Gannett, who served as the AUA's founding secretary. An association of indi-
viduals rather than of congregations, the AUA had little direct influence over
the Standing Order churches of Massachusetts, but as these excerpts from its
first annual report suggest, it had an ambitious plan for spreading Unitari-
anism to other regions. Further Reading: Charles C. Forman, "Elected Now
By Time: The Unitarian Controversy 1805–1835," in Conrad Wright, ed., A
Stream of Light: A Short History of American Unitarianism *(Boston: Skin-*
ner House, 1975).

—Dan McKanan

THE Executive Committee of the American Unitarian Association in offering their
first annual report, cannot but express their gratification at the circumstances under
which it is presented. They behold in the numbers and character of those who compose this meeting, not only a proof of interest in the Association, but evidence of
its stability, and the promise of its future usefulness. In reviewing the past year, the
Committee find much to encourage, and nothing to dishearten them; and this anniversary is welcomed by them with feelings of satisfaction, which a few months since
they did not dare to anticipate. This Association was organized under some disadvantages. Its plan was suggested by a few gentlemen on the evening preceding the last
election, at too late an hour to secure the advice and cooperation of many of those
whose judgment would be useful in forming, and whose influence would be important in strengthening such a society. The time for a more general and effective concert seemed, however, to have arrived; and the presences of many Unitarians from

distant towns, who annually assemble in this city, showed the necessity of an immediate effort for the accomplishment of this object. It would have been impossible to ascertain in a few hours the sentiments of the great body of Unitarian Christians, in relation to the measures, which they should adopt for the diffusion of pure religion. The friends of more united efforts than had hitherto been employed, trusted to their own convictions of duty, and to their belief that an occasion only was needed to call forth zeal and energy among us. From the circumstances, to which allusion has been made, the meeting at which the project of this Association was discussed, and its constitution adopted, was necessarily small. Notice could only be given at the close the Berry Street Conference on Wednesday morning, that such a meeting would be held in the afternoon. At that meeting, it was unanimously voted, that it is expedient to form a society to be called the American Unitarian Association. At an adjourned meeting, held the next morning, a constitution, reported by a committee appointed for the purpose, was accepted, and the officers required by the constitution were elected. This brief statement will explain the fact, that the existence of this society was unknown to most Unitarians in this city and commonwealth, until some weeks after its organization; and will also show under what doubtful prospects of support it was commenced. The expectations of its early friends have not been disappointed, and the Committee hope, in the sketch, which they shall now give of their labours and success, to satisfy all inquiries respecting the utility of this institution, or the favour which has been bestowed upon it. . . .

The Committee have been gratified by the sympathy expressed for them in the prosecution of their duties by Unitarians near and at a distance. . . . In all these letters the same interest is exhibited in the efforts which the Association promises to make for the diffusion of pure Christianity. Many of them have contained interesting accounts of the state of religion in different places, and especially correspondents have furnished the Committee with ample details respecting the history and condition of Unitarians in Pennsylvania. . . . The existence of a body of christians in the Western States, who have for years been Unitarians, have encountered persecution on account of their faith, and have lived in ignorance of others east of the mountains, who maintained many similar views of christian doctrine, has attracted the attention of the Committee. Measures have been taken to ascertain more correctly the situation and character of this fraternity, who have adopted various names significant of their attachment to freedom of inquiry, and to a purer gospel than that embraced by other sects, and who, though they have refused to assume the title, openly avow themselves Unitarians. With two ministers of this body a correspondence has been continued for some time. The Committee have watched with peculiar interest the growth of the Christian Connexion, which is daily becoming more numerous and respectable. From members of that body, they have received expressions of fraternal regard; and although there should not be a more intimate union between these disciples and ourselves, than now exists, yet we rejoice that they have the same great work at heart, and we doubt not will prosecute it perseveringly and successfully. . . . Of New England it would be difficult to speak with certainty. There are in almost every town Unitarians, in many towns of Massachusetts they constitute the majority, in many more they have respectable, though not large churches, but in far the greater number of parishes in New England they are still blended with other sects, and either from a distrust for their own strength, or from a reluctance to disturb the quiet of a religious society, or from local reasons, they make small exertions to secure such an administration of the gospel, as may accord with their convictions of truth. The number of these silent Unitarians is increasing, and at the same time, more are manifesting a determination to assert their rights as citizens and as christians.

*   *   *

At the last of these meetings a committee was appointed to address a circular to the standing committees of the several parishes, inviting their cooperation in advancing the interests of the Association in their several societies. From this circular we beg leave to extract the following remarks: —

"The American Unitarian Association has been established from a persuasion, that the time has arrived, when it is necessary for those who profess the simple Unity of God, to adopt measures differing, in some respects, from those which they have heretofore pursued. By this we do not mean, that Unitarians should lay aside those means of support and defence upon which they have heretofore relied; or divest themselves of that charity, which they have always cherished towards those, who differ from them in sentiment. By a difference of measures we mean, that the circumstances of the times require a more systematic union, and a 'concentration of labours, by which interest may be awakened, confidence inspired, and efficiency produced.' The want of union among Christians of our denomination, is felt to be a great evil by those, who have directed their attention to this subject. Living in an age of unusual religious excitement, surrounded by numerous sects, all of which are zealously employed in disseminating their peculiar tenets, we should be wanting in duty to ourselves, and be doing injustice to the doctrines we profess, if we should allow them to fail in exercising their due influence, for the want of a corresponding zeal and interest. Our exertions have not been apparent, because insulated; and the contributions of many of our friends have been thrown into the treasuries of other denominations of Christians, from the want of some proper objects among ourselves, upon which they could be bestowed. We feel confident, that there are among us men of zeal and energy, who are both willing and able to exert themselves in the cause of religion; and that others, who are now indifferent to the subject, might by sympathy and encouragement be excited to similar exertions. All that is required, is, that they be brought together, and be made acquainted with each other's view and feelings; that they be allowed to unite their labours in one common field, and for one common end, and thereby warm each others' hearts and strengthen each others' hands. To produce this concert among Unitarians is one of the objects of the American Unitarian Association."

* * *

The thoughts of the Committee have been turned to their brethren in other lands. A correspondence has been opened with Unitarians in England, and the coincidence is worthy of notice, that the British and Foreign Unitarian Association and the American Unitarian Association were organized on the same day, for the same objects and without the least previous concert. Our good wishes have been reciprocated by the directors of the British Society. Letters received from gentlemen, who have recently visited England, speak of the interest which our brethren in that country feel for us, and of their desire to strengthen the bonds of union. A constant communication will be preserved between the two Associations, and your committee believe it will have a beneficial effect, by making us better acquainted with one another, by introducing the publications of each country into the other, by the influence which we shall mutually exert, and by the strength which will be given to our separate, or it may be, to our united efforts for the spread of the glorious gospel of our Lord and Saviour. Letters have also been forwarded to Unitarians in India, although your Committee did not consider this Association instituted for the diffusion of Christianity in foreign lands, and have only requested that a friendly correspondence might ensue, which would enable them to communicate intelligence interesting to Unitarian Christians in this country. With the same views they are taking measures to open a correspondence with Unitarians on the continent of Europe, and are especially desirous to establish friendly relations with their brethren in France, Switzerland, and Transylvania, of whom they hope to obtain more accurate information than they now possess, from a gentleman, whose return to his people may be expected in a few weeks.

* * *

While the Committee congratulate the officers and members on the degree of favour, which has been shown to it, they mean not to deny that objections have been started, and that some have been reluctant to add their names to the list of its supporters. They have laboured to show the futility of these objections, and to dissipate the fears expressed by good men, and decided Unitarians, that the new Society might be a source of evil rather than of good, of division rather than of harmony. They have strenuously opposed the opinion, that the object of its founders was to build up a party, to organize an opposition, to perpetuate pride and bigotry. Had they believed that such was its purpose, or such would be its effect, they would have withdrawn themselves from any connexion with so hateful a thing. They thought otherwise, and experience has proved that they did not judge wrongly, They have witnessed an increased zeal for purse and undefiled religion, the religion not of this man nor that party, but of Jesus Christ, our Master and Redeemer, brought into action, if it were not inspired, by the influence of this Association. . . .

The Executive Committee beg leave to close their Report with two suggestions concerning the means of increasing the extent and efficiency of this Association.

It is essential that a general cooperation should be produced, and for this end, they propose the formation of an auxiliary association in every Unitarian congregation. They would press this on the attention of every person present at this meeting; and would express their strong persuasion, that this will be the most simple, permanent, and effectual method of accomplishing the purposes of the Association.

The Committee also advise that measures be taken to effect a union of the existing Unitarian Societies, viz. The Society for the Promotion of Christian Knowledge, Piety and Charity, the Evangelical Missionary Society, and the Publishing Fund, with the American Unitarian Association. Such a union will prevent any interference of one Society with another, and any impression which may be received, that they are hostile or unfriendly to one another. It will also render the operations of these societies more useful, will prevent an unnecessary waste of labour, and will make the information acquired by one, common to all.

SOURCE: *First Annual Report of the Executive Committee of the American Unitarian Association* (Boston: Isaac R. Butts, 1826), 6–11, 14–17, 23–25.

JOSEPH TUCKERMAN

A Letter on the Principles of the Missionary *Enterprise* and Semiannual Reports

1826, 1831, 1832

Joseph Tuckerman (1778–1840), a nineteenth-century Unitarian minister, is widely regarded as the "founding father" of Unitarian Universalist community ministry. In the nineteenth century, this was termed "ministry-at-large," similar in meaning to today's ministry beyond the parish walls, particularly visiting the poor, sick, or imprisoned. His sole biographer to date, a Catholic priest with ecumenical interest in this particular Unitarian, also deemed him a "pioneer in American social work." Tuckerman naturally combined a "social work micro needs focus" on individuals and families with a "social work macro transformative lens" on the larger society, or in religious language, Tuckerman uniquely intertwined the pastoral and the prophetic in his ministry. Of particular historical interest in the first selection is Tuckerman's theological anthropology: God created human beings with a natural empathic interdependence, a precursor to psychology's focus today on neuroaffective attachment as well as to the contemporary Universalist theological message of the power of love. As seen in the second selections, Tuckerman's theological anthropology and Christian belief in the moral power of connection also led him at times to more radical language in his call for the church to eliminate a "caste" system and to integrate the social classes, as well as to hold the rich accountable for the scientific study and elimination of poverty through their immersion in community with the poor. Tuckerman's brief ministry-at-large began in 1826 at the urging of his good friend William Ellery Channing and under the employ of the American Unitarian Association. Ultimately his ministry was international in scope and led in 1834 to the founding of the Benevolent Fraternity of Unitarian Churches, which today is known as the Unitarian Universalist Urban Ministry in Boston. The first selection helped launch the ministry-at-large; the remaining passages are drawn from semiannual reports submitted by Tuckerman in 1831 and 1832. Further Reading: Daniel T. McColgan, Joseph Tuckerman: Pioneer in American Social Work *(Washington, DC: Catholic University of America Press, 1940); Jedediah Mannis,* Joseph Tuckerman and the Outdoor Church *(Eugene, OR: Pickwick Publications, 2009).*

—Michelle Walsh

From "A Letter on the Principles of the Missionary Enterprise" (1826)

That man should sympathize with man, that he should feel an interest, deep and strong, in the condition of his fellow-men; and, especially, that we should be affected, and strongly affected, by the wants and sufferings, not alone of those around us, but of our whole race, I fear not to say is as much a law of our nature, as it is that we should feel a deep and strong interest in those, who are immediately connected with us, in the nearest relations of life; or, as it is, that we should love ourselves . . . there are occasions in the life of every one, whose heart has not been shut up by bands of brass, or iron . . . when this feeling, chilled and dead as it may have seemed to be, is warmed into life, and puts forth its strength, and breaks from its enclosures, and speaks in a language not to be misunderstood; . . . demonstrating that it is the purpose of God, that man shall be his instrument for the communication of all possible blessings to man. I need not refer you to the effects, which are produced within us, while we are reading narratives of real, or of imaginary scenes and circumstances of distress. These effects alone demonstrate, not only that God has made us for one another, but that, in an important sense, he has made each one of us for the whole of our species . . . that we should feel a strong interest in others, and not only in the wants and the happiness of our family, our neighborhood, our country and our age, but in those too of men in every country, and in all time, than it is that we should love ourselves. I say not, that one principle is as strong, and steady, and active at all times, or that it is as generally manifested in human conduct, as is the other. It is not. In many it is bound in the chains of a sordid avarice. In many, it is kept in subjection by a miserable ambition. . . . But the principle of sympathy . . . with the cause of human nature, of human good and happiness,—dead and buried as it sometimes seems to be, does also sometimes rise, and manifest itself; and, with an electric influence, at once animate, and give new vigor, to thousands, and millions. How has the thrill of its power been felt, in the cause of the abolition of the slave trade?

From Tuckerman's Semiannual Reports

Let any one look about him, and ask, who were the grandfathers and the fathers of our rich men? and who were the fathers and grandparents of our paupers and criminals? and he will find, that it is not poverty alone which produces poverty. . . . The rich are in truth accountable for much of the abject poverty of the world; and that right sentiments, Christian sentiments of property, and of human relations and duties, among the rich, are to be among the most effectual of the means of salvation from pauperism and crime.

* * *

I would say, therefore, in the first place, that if a few of our most intelligent and philanthropic men, men of leisure and influence, would unite for the study of these subjects; not merely, or principally, by consulting books, but by an extensive personal communication with the poor and with criminals; if these gentlemen would meet frequently,—for example, one evening in every week,—to bring together their facts and to compare their opinions; if they would occasionally publish these facts and opinions, with the sanction of their names; and when they shall see clearly what are the demands of justice, of humanity, and of religion, if they would combine their efforts, now for the suppression of one, and now of another, of the springs of evil, and now to obtain one, and now another establishment, for the salvation and greatest happiness of those, who must otherwise be irretrievably lost to all the higher purposes of their being; a great and glorious reform might soon be effected in our city. Am I told that the plan of such an association is impracticable? I ask, why? And I appeal to the sober judgment of the intelligent, the affluent, and influential. . . . A few judicious and energetic minds, combined and resolved to accomplish all which they may for the suppression of pauperism and crime, would accumulate for themselves in this work a better treasure than all their wealth, let them be as rich as they may; and, in a few years, might do more for the advancement of society than, without these services, would probably be accomplished in half a century.

*   *   *

It is a very important purpose of the ministry for which I plead, to bring the classes of society into a new, and Christian union with each other; and it is greatly to be regretted, that our religious societies are constituted as they now are, in respect to the accommodation of any but proprietors in their places of public worship. The poor, who would gladly unite with them, but who cannot pay for the privilege, in the largest number of our places of worship have at best a very narrow space appropriated for them; and there they must sit apart, as "the class of the poor." This is a practice not less inconsistent with our political principles, than it is with the spirit of Christianity. Under other governments, where distinctions of rank and of rights are universally recognized, the poor feel themselves to be, and revolt not at being treated, both politically and religiously, as *a caste*. . . . Let nothing, then, be done by this ministry, by which the poor shall be made to feel that the very religion, which is intended to be a bond of union between them and their fellow-men, is itself an instrument of their separation from the more favored classes of their fellow-beings.

SOURCE: Joseph Tuckerman, *A Letter on The Principles of the Missionary Enterprise* (Boston, 1826); *Mr. Tuckerman's Eighth Semiannual Report of His Service as a Minister at Large in Boston* (Boston, 1831), 26, 34–35; *Mr. Tuckerman's Ninth Semiannual Report of His Service as a Minister at Large in Boston* (Boston, 1832), 21–22. See also Joseph Tuckerman, *On the Elevation of the Poor: A Selection from His Reports as Minister at Large in Boston* (1874; rept. New York: Arno Press, 1971).

"Narrative of Elder Caleb Rich"

1827

Caleb Rich (1750–1821), born in Sutton, Massachusetts, migrated north to Warwick, Massachusetts, near the New Hampshire border, as a young man. After having visions that convinced him not to fear hell, he was expelled from the Baptist church. He, his brother, and a friend formed their own religious society. At the beginning of the Revolutionary War, Rich was called up to participate in the siege of Boston. Given a furlough, he visited his cousins, members of the Davis family, in Oxford, Massachusetts. Finding that they also questioned orthodox doctrine, he found a substitute to serve out his enlistment and joined them in a preaching tour in Connecticut. In 1778, back home in Warwick, he had another vision, assuring him that all human beings would be saved and calling him to preach. Among the families in his preaching circuit were the Ballous of Richmond, New Hampshire. Perhaps his greatest accomplishment was to introduce Hosea Ballou to Universalism. Rich's theology, later further developed by Ballou, was independent of the thinking of Murray and Winchester and, together with the ideas promoted by his cousins, represented an indigenous and independent emergence of Universalism in New England's hill country. Further Reading: Stephen Marini, Radical Sects of Revolutionary New England (*Cambridge, MA: Harvard University Press, 1982); Peter Hughes, "Early New England Universalism: A Family Religion,"* The Journal of Unitarian Universalist History, *Vol. 26, pp. 93–113 (1999).*

—Peter Hughes

I was born in Sutton, county of Worcester, and state of Mass. on the 12th day of August, in 1750. My Father and Mother joined a Congregational church in early life; had thirteen children that lived to be upward of 21 years of age, and had them all sprinkled by the Priest; and after the strictest manner of the Religion of that day, they trained them up in the nurture and admonition of their Lord. They taught us that Christ would have but few, yea but very few as trophies of his Mission into the world, while his antagonist would have his countless millions to play the tyrant over as long as God existed. My Minister and School Master taught me the same, and I was not more than 9 or 10 years old before I had the most serious and shocking reflections on my hard fortune, to be born of Adam's vice. My situation appeared more precarious than a ticket in a lottery, where there was an hundred blanks to one prize. I often looked upon insects and poison reptiles, thinking how much better their lot was in this world than mine. . . .

Father was converted from a Congregationalist to a Baptist, then he seemed to double his diligence to teach and to admonish and warn us in the fear of endless damnation, setting forth our imminent danger. Now as our Father was a Baptist, and went to meeting with them, and our Mother remained as before, we children divided our time—part of our time we went to meeting with our Father, and part with our Mother, resolved if possible to find out which was in the right way. One Sunday noon as we were at the Baptist meeting, I went out with my Brothers and a number of other young men, to converse by ourselves upon the important concerns of religion. One of them observed that he wished he knew which was right, the Baptists or the Congregationalists, for if we did not embrace the true Religion in this world we never could be saved. I seconded him, and it was the settled opinion of us all, but one who replied as follows: "How do you know that either of them are right? there are more than an hundred different denominations of christians, who all take their Religion from the Bible, and we have never heard but two, and there can be but one right way among them all, and we have but a forlorn hope of selecting the right way out of them when we have no acquaintance with only two. Now I believe there is one right way and only one, for God has not left himself without a witness, and must we certainly conclude that either the Baptists or the Congregationalists are that one." These words were louder to me than thunder; never in all my life had I heard anything from the lips of man that had such a deep and lasting impression on my mind. I was so stunned at these words, I could say no more, my mind was so swallowed up in contemplation, that I gave but little heed to what any body said: few indeed thought I, will ever find the strait gate.—Sometimes I thought hard of God for ever suffering the world to be thus enveloped in such a dilemma, and overwhelmed in such impenetrable darkness. I went to no person for instruction, but spent my time in ruminating on the awful situation in which mankind were plunged. I came to a firm and fixed resolution not to believe nor disbelieve any man's testimony any more or less for their word, but if possible to see and understand for myself. . . .

About this time I became 21 years of age, and had to leave my Father's family, and go to Warwick about sixty miles to occupy a new farm, and to seek my fortune there. And as I bid farewell to parents and younger brothers and sisters, I felt an uncommon impression of gloomy melancholy, which I never before had experienced, sorrowing most of all that my parents and brethren would see my face no more except as a visitor. . . . I boarded with my brother who also professed to believe in the Baptist constitution and articles of faith, and I had much agreeable conversation with him on religious topics. It happened one evening that our conversation turned on the subject of the day of grace. My brother did not agree with me in that point; for I believed thus: that God had limited a certain time to strive with man, setting heaven before them to draw them, and hell to drive them; and if they outstood that time, he gave them over to hardness of heart and blindness of mind. At that time the source of my christian consolation was from two considerations. 1st, that I should be numbered among the chosen few, who were to escape the pit of destruction.—2nd, with shame I confess I anticipated with seeming joy, the day when I should see all nations gathered before the Judge of quick and dead; and hear my opposers sentenced, "*depart ye cursed,*" and see them dragged down by devils to the bottomless pit. He made a reply to what I had said, setting forth the nature and extent of grace; "do you think, said he, mortals can withstand God in the day of his power," &c. Altho' I received no light as to the nature of grace, yet it served thoroughly to convict me that I was a consummate hypocrite. I then retired alone in the most racking distress of mind that ever before I had experienced, and after a long time of serious meditation, I came to a firm resolution not to give sleep to my eyes, until I had found mercy; but determined to pray without ceasing.

Accordingly I went to a secret place, & began my secret prayer. . . . a great calm overspread my mind and my passions all subsided. Instantly I saw a vision, as it appeared to me. I was walking a straight road with a celestial guide at my right hand. The sun appeared to be about two hours high in the morning, shining through a hazy cloud, cast a beautiful red and yellow color on the ground. I saw a stone wall on the right hand not quite finished; and I saw a stone lying on the ground near the wall suitable to help finish the wall, here we stopt; my guide said to me, "by what means will this stone ever get placed into this wall?" I answered, "if the owner of the premises judges the stone fit for the building and is self-moved to put it into the wall, it will be done; otherwise it never will." My guide said that I had answered discreetly, and then said to me, "thou art as that stone & you can do no more toward influencing God to put you into his building, than this stone can the owner to lay it into this wall; and you (said he) was placed by unerring wisdom into God's building before the foundation of the world." From that moment I have firmly believed without a tormenting fear or doubt, that if I had died any moment from the day of my birth to that day, I should have been as secure as any stone in his building. I immediately entered into rest and ceased from my own work—my joy was unspeakable. . . . Never since can I bear to hear the fears of death or the torments of hell or future judgment bro't up to influence people to be religious, but to use no other means than the simplicity of the gospel of good news, by hearing of which, faith may come, which produces good works. The next thing which I recollect that arrested my attention was, I felt an unusual love for every person that occurred to mind. I said within myself, what manner of salvation can this be? (surely I can think of those that will not appear to be such lovely beings,) but those who before appeared hateful to me now appeared as lovely as my best friends. Then I concluded it was Christ in me that loved them with such impartiality as induced him to cry while expiring on the cross, "Father forgive them for they know not what they do." . . .

The next thing of importance to me was in a vision of the night when deep sleep had fallen upon me. It appeared to me that I was suddenly awakened at the west end of a straight path, in a very thick wilderness where the trees were so thick behind me and at my right and left hand that I could see but a few steps any way, except to the east where the light shone in its usual brightness as far as my eyes could reach. The ground was almost level where I stood, and kept a gradual ascent until near the east end of the road where growing steeper it reached to the top of a mountain, over which the clear sky appeared. The road through the wilderness, was as straight as a line, not a single branch from the forest hung over the strait and narrow way which was about twenty feet wide and filled with small bushes; except in the middle of the road was a foot path just wide enough for one person to walk in. In this was neither briers nor bushes, nor any thing to stumble over, not the least crook in it from one end to the other. At the west end of this road, I found myself as one just brought into existence with a celestial friend holding me erect on my feet by the right arm.

Not knowing from what part of the wilderness or by what means I was brought to that spot, I asked my guide from what part of the forest and by what means I was conveyed here. He did not answer me as I expected—he gave me no account of any way to the path, but answered me in scriptural language, which was, "he leadeth in the blind, in a way they knew not." He informed me that was the straight and narrow way that led to mount zion; and that I had no strength only what I received when I was brought into it: then putting a staff into my right hand which he called faith, without which, said he, "you can neither stand nor go." Then letting go my right arm bid me walk, saying, "we walk by faith and not by sight." Then I understood the functions of each member. Although my eyes by the help of the light could see to the end of my journey, yet I could not move without the exercise of my feet and they could not exercise without the staff of faith, and having a steadfast hope that I should not run in vain, but obtain the prize which inspired me with zeal, and thus I went on my way rejoicing. Then casting my eyes to the ground I discovered new tracks of travellers; I knew whose they were, and they were all Baptists. Then I was careful to step into their tracks. My guide soon admonished me for it, for purposely stepping into their tracks, "you must follow no man any further (said he) tho' they follow Christ, if you continue so doing you will soon get out of this way, and will again be lost in the wilderness. Now (said he) I will shew you the mark, on which if you keep your eyes you will never lose the way, and pointing to the east he shewed me a bright light directly over the middle of the top of Mount Zion, resembling the sun through a foggy cloud. I could see the form of it without dazzling my eyes, I thought it was a sun but not our natural sun, for there it gave light at all times, and there was no night in the way, nor on Mount Zion. "That mark (said he) is exactly over this straight way, keep your eyes upon it, and walk towards it; and your feet cannot miss the way. There is no occasion for your looking down to see other men's footsteps, by which means you will be sure to lose the way." Thus fixing my eyes on the mark I travelled with great delight and more speed for a considerable distance; although the ascent gained, yet I arose more in advancing one step now, than in many when I first set out. I observed to my guide that my strength was increased, that I could go much faster and easier. He replied "as your day is, so your strength shall be." I then cast my eyes on the ground to see whether I could discover any new tracks, not in order to walk in them but to see if any traveller had thus far advanced, as I was then fast ascending the hill of Zion. And I saw no sign of any recent traveller. Then said I to my guide (which had kept at my right hand to give me all the information necessary for the journey and guide me into all truth) "I see no footsteps of the Baptists thus far advanced." He replied "no, the Baptists have never travelled so far as this. They are all at present in wilderness between this and the place where we first set out. Their carcasses have fallen in the wilderness as many of the children of Israel did. And they have lost sight of this way." I still advanced, my joy and speed increasing until I arrived at the summit of the mountain. Here we stopped when I viewed with great transport and delight the sun which had lighted me all the way, and the beautiful situation of the mountain for delights, when my guide exclaimed with an *Emphasis* "this is no less than the house of God and the Gate of Heaven." At this I instantly awoke with joyful surprise the words still resounding in my ears for a long time. . . . Yet it was not made known to me that every soul that came of Adam's loins would be restored to holiness and happiness; for I was yet imperfect in the knowledge of the scriptures, and doubtless am yet.

*   *   *

Joseph Goodell, Nathaniel and Caleb Rich were dissenters from the Congregationals, and were cast out of the Baptist Societies—not suffered to pray or exhort or publicly speak among them, of course necessarily become a distinct society themselves, not knowing of a fourth person to join them in that vicinity. Here I notice, that the U. States of America, were then British Colonies, and the laws obliged all dissenters from the congregational order to bring them annual certificates to clear them from taxation by them or otherwise pay them, as they claimed all the nothingarians to help support them. Accordingly we three set up a warrant to notify and warn each other to meet at a certain time and place to proceed according to law to organize ourselves into a religious society, and when met we made choice of three of our principal members as a committee to give certificates to our society, and when chosen (curious to relate) it took the whole of our society to make out our committee according to law, however we made out our certificates, carried them in, which served to clear us from being taxed by any other religious society.

And in one year our society had increased to the number of ten, and in the second year (if I mistake not) the Revolutionary War broke out, when I with many others was called upon in the alarm to go down to Lexington, where we saw many of the houses and the ground stained with the first blood that was shed in that war. I tarried there about three weeks, my officers refusing to let me return. I then enlisted for eight months, then got a furlow for three weeks to visit my friends in Sutton andOxford; in that time I had an opportunity of exchanging places with a man my brother-in-law, had hired. And in these eight months that I lived with my Brother-in-law [probably his cousin and brother-in-law, Samuel Davis, Jr.], as I had a convenient opportunity and by night and day improved every hour I could spare to propagate this new doctrine as it was then called, and had great success; for I had three Brothers-in-law in Oxford [the brothers Samuel Davis, Jr., Elijah Davis, and Learned Davis, all married to Rich's sisters], and one natural Brother in Sutton [Ebenezer Rich] who were well versed in Scripture and men of argument. These being fully established in the same sentiment with me, we appointed meetings on Sundays to read and expound the scriptures. We sometimes had as many as thirty hearers, and some came 6 or 8 miles. We taught from house to house and often continued our speech until midnight and break of day, contending earnestly for the fulfilment of the promise made to Abraham, Isaac and Jacob; and often reading the 11th ch. of Romans. In this time I went one tour to Thomson, in Connecticut. The people heard of my coming and collected together, and desired me to preach a sermon to them. I replied that I never preached in the usual form, but I was willing to expound the scripture to them which I did a great part of one day and night, and gained some proselytes; and when my time with my Brother-in-law had expired, our Brethren in Sutton, Oxford, Charlton, Dudley, and Douglass amounted, as I judge, to 40 or 50 persons. Then I returned to Warwick and found my Brethren there steadfast in the Faith. . . .

And in April next, in the evening, soon after I went to rest, at the foreside of the bed, with my face towards the out-side door, a person, or a likeness of one, opened the door, stepped into the house and shut the door after him—stepped to the hearth and looking me in the face with a bible in his hand. It was not very light in the house, yet I could plainly see his face, his form, and his bible; but could not discover his features so as to have known him, if he had been one of my acquaintance. And he addressed me as follows, saying, "I am come to preach to you." I replied, "I shall be glad to hear you." And I believe that never was the attention of any person more seriously and earnestly engaged. . . .

The free woman had four names; as free woman, covenant, Jerusalem, which is above and mother of us all. And he mentioned several more appelations in the sequal of his discourse, as Zion, Church, City of the living God; and last of all he said she was that power that brought again our Lord Jesus from the dead, that great

Shepherd of the sheep and he was the first born Son, and that never had been one man born again in that sense that Christ spoke to Nicodemus until our Lord was born from the tomb; who was the first born from the dead, and the first born among many Brethren; & even the 1st born of every creature. He also mentioned that Sarah was a type of Zion as much while she was barren as when she become the joyful mother of a son, for she was barren 30 years, and Zion was barren 4000 years, even from the foundation of the world until by her the stone was rolled from the door of the sepulchre and brought forth a man child, and that the whole human family was as much born in him as they fell in Adam. . . .

Then speaking of the mother of us all, he brought in the 7th verse of the 26th chap. of Isaiah, "Before she travelled she bro't forth; before her pains came she was delivered of a man child." And said that Man Child was Christ born from the dead. Then brought in the 8th verse, "who hath heard of such a thing, who hath seen such a thing? Shall the earth be made to bring forth in one day, or shall a Nation be born at once? For as soon as Zion travelled she brought forth her children." Here are children spoken of in the plural, therefore the whole of Adam's race was then born and made alive in Christ in the same sense that they fell or died in Adam.—Here for the first time I found my mistake concerning an addition to Adam's loins after the fall compared to thorns, thistles, and ceased to exist at death. Being informed by my Preacher that the multiplication spoken of to Eve after her transgression did not imply additional number after the first creation than that which was spoken to Abraham that God would greatly multiply his seed even as the stars in heaven, or the sand of the sea shore, &c. Here I was confirmed in the restoration and salvation of every man made in the image of God, as in any one of the human race. . . .

But I was astonished at his doctrine for he taught as one who perfectly knew what he taught, and as I had learned in the sequel of his discourse that the Lord had assuredly called upon me in a public manner to proclaim the same gospel, without a second in those parts; only I had heard that a Mr. Murray preached Universal Salvation in Cape Ann, but had never seen him, nor had any communication from him. The next day as I contemplated on these things which were painted in my thoughts, I found them precisely consonant to what I had been taught of God before I viewed with great emotion the bewildered situation of fallen Christendom; feeling the ponderous weight of these important things, the responsibility towards God that rested on me, who had vouchsafed in his rich mercy to communicate to me in such a marvelous way, that I felt as it were a shock of electricity, my lips quivered, my flesh trembled, and felt a tremour throughout my whole frame for several days, which was noticed by my wife; but before I undertook to preach in a public manner in the usual form, I was endowed with more confidence.

* * *

Soon after I began to preach in Warwick, there was a considerable addition to our society there. Soon I was called to preach in Richmond at stated times and collected a considerable of a society there. A man by the name of Thomas Barnes came from the town of Jaffrey [late 1783 or early 1784] to hear me out of curiosity and he was caught in the gospel net and invited me to come over to Jaffrey to help them, which I did, and considerable numbers gathered there. Then we called a general society meeting in Richmond to organize ourselves into a regular church and society, at which I was made choice of as their minister, and we appointed three of our members deacons, one from Warwick, one from Richmond, and one from Jaffrey, and set up church discipline and stated society meetings to be holden annually at Richmond. After I had preached about three years it was agreed at one of our annual meetings, that brother C. Rich should receive public ordination as minister of the united society of Warwick, Richmond and Jaffrey, and wherever he should be called by divine Providence. We sent for Elder Adam Streeter to assist at said ordination. Said Streeter had been ordained to the baptist order. His faith was increased until it became Abrahamic and accordingly the ordination was attended in Richmond, accompanied with about 300 people, and as I considered myself legally authorised, I scrupled not to solemnize the ordinance of marriage. . . .

As our annual meetings served the same as our conventions do now, we gave letters of licence and ordained preachers, &c. and in the year 1785 I received a circular letter from Oxford signed Dr. Fisk, requesting me, in behalf of that society to give said letter circulation to all the societies where I had labored to meet in convention at Oxford, which was done accordingly in September following. When met we organized ourselves into a convention, and if my memory serves, Eld. Adam Streeter was Moderator, and Dr. Fisk, Clerk. Brother Zepheniah Laythe was present at that meeting, but was conscientiously scrupulous in putting his hand to a paper covenant. He said it savoured too much of formality and therefore he did not act with us; and so there was only two public speakers that acted in said convention, viz. brother A. Streeter and myself. We adjourned to meet again at Oxford, in 1786, at which meeting our brethren John Murray, Elhanan Winchester, Z. Laythe joined and acted with us. We again adjourned to 1787 to meet in Oxford again at which brother Hosea Ballou met with us who has attended all our general conventions ever since and must be possessed of much more information from that time than myself.

SOURCE: Caleb Rich: "A Narrative of Elder Caleb Rich," *Candid Examiner*, April 30, 1827, May 14, 1827, May 28, 1827, and June 18, 1827.

"Likeness to God"
1828

Though many liberals were deeply influenced by the empiricist philosophy of John Locke, Channing drank more deeply from Scottish Common Sense philosophy and from Neoplatonism, traditions that affirmed a continuity between the divine and the human that could be glimpsed through introspection. Channing's mature expression of this theology came in an 1828 ordination sermon. His words inspired both Transcendentalists, who found in them a reason to emphasize divine humanity at the expense of revealed religion, and social reformers, who were inspired to cherish the divine likeness in slaves, prisoners, alcoholics, and social outcasts. Further Reading: Dan McKanan, Identifying the Image of God: Radical Christians and Nonviolent Power in the Antebellum United States *(New York: Oxford, 2003).*

—Dan McKanan

Ephesians v. 1: "Be ye therefore followers of God, as dear children."
The text calls us to follow or imitate God, to seek accordance with or likeness to him, and to do this, not fearfully and faintly, but with the spirit and hope of beloved children. The doctrine which I propose to illustrate, is derived immediately from these words, and is incorporated with the whole New Testament. I affirm, and would maintain, that true religion consists in proposing, as our great end, a growing likeness to the Supreme Being. Its noblest influence consists in making us more and more partakers of the Divinity. For this it is to be preached. Religious instruction should aim chiefly to turn men's aspirations and efforts to that perfection of the soul, which constitutes it a bright image of God. . . .

The likeness to God, of which I propose to speak, belongs to man's higher or spiritual nature. It has its foundation in the original and essential capacities of the mind. In proportion as these are unfolded by right and vigorous exertion, it is extended and brightened. In proportion as these lie dormant, it is obscured. In proportion as they are perverted and overpowered by the appetites and passions, it is blotted out.

* * *

It is only in proportion to this likeness that we can enjoy either God or the universe. That God can be known and enjoyed only through sympathy or kindred attributes, is a doctrine which even Gentile philosophy discerned. That the pure in heart can alone see and commune with the pure Divinity, was the sublime instruction of ancient sages as well as of inspired prophets. It is indeed the lesson of daily experience. To understand a great and good being, we must have the seeds of the same excellence. . . . God becomes a real being to us, in proportion as his own nature is unfolded within us. To a man who is growing in the likeness of God, faith begins even here to change into vision. He carries within himself a proof of a Deity, which can only be understood by experience.

* * *

That man has a kindred nature with God, and may bear most important and ennobling relations to him, seems to me to be established by a striking proof. This proof you will understand by considering, for a moment, how we obtain our ideas of God. . . . We derive them from our own souls. The divine attributes are first developed in ourselves, and thence transferred to our Creator. The idea of God, sublime and awful as it is, is the idea of our own spiritual nature, purified and enlarged to infinity. In ourselves are the elements of the Divinity. God, then, does not sustain a figurative resemblance to man. It is the resemblance of a parent to a child, the likeness of a kindred nature.

We call God a Mind. He has revealed himself as a Spirit. But what do we know of mind but through the unfolding of this principle in our own breasts? . . . God is another name for human intelligence raised above all error and imperfection, and extended to all possible truth.

The same is true of God's goodness. How do we understand this, but by the principle of love implanted in the human breast? . . .

The same is true of all the moral perfections of the Deity. . . .

I am aware, that it may be objected to these views, that we receive our idea of God from the universe, from his works, and not so exclusively from our own souls. The universe, I know, is full of God. The heavens and earth declare his glory. In other words, the effects and signs of power, wisdom, and goodness, are apparent through the whole creation. But apparent to what? Not to the outward eye; not to the acutest organs of sense; but to a kindred mind, which interprets the universe by itself. . . .

I shall now be met by another objection, which to many may seem strong. It will be said, that these various attributes of which I have spoken exist in God in infinite perfection, and that this destroys all affinity between the human and the divine mind. To this I have two replies. In the first place, an attribute by becoming perfect does not part with its essence. . . .

But I would offer another answer to this objection, that God's infinity places him beyond the resemblance and approach of man. I affirm, and trust that I do not speak too strongly, that there are traces of infinity in the human mind; and that, in this very respect, it bears a likeness to God.

* * *

The views which I have given in this discourse respecting man's participation of the Divine nature, seem to me to receive strong confirmation from the title or

215

relation most frequently applied to God in the New Testament; and I have reserved this as the last corroboration of this doctrine, because, to my own mind, it is singularly affecting. In the New Testament God is made known to us as a Father. . . . And what is it to be a Father? It is to communicate one's own nature, to give life to kindred beings; and the highest function of a Father is to educate the mind of the child, and to impart to it what is noblest and happiest in his own mind. . . .

What, then, is religion? I answer; it is not the adoration of a God with whom we have no common properties; of a distinct, foreign, separate being; but of an all-communicating Parent. . . .

I regard this view of religion as infinitely important. It does more than all things to make our connection with our Creator ennobling and happy; and, in proportion as we want it, there is danger that the thought of God may itself become the instrument of our degradation. That religion has been so dispensed as to depress the human mind, I need not tell you; and it is a truth which ought to be known, that the greatness of the Deity, when separated in our thoughts from his parental character, especially tends to crush human energy and hope. To a frail, dependent creature, an omnipotent Creator easily becomes a terror, and his worship easily degenerates into servility, flattery, self-contempt, and selfish calculation. Religion only ennobles us, in as far as it reveals to us the tender and intimate connection of God with his creatures, and teaches us to see in the very greatness which might give alarm the source of great and glorious communications to the human soul. You cannot, my hearers, think too highly of the majesty of God. But let not this majesty sever him from you.

*   *   *

I do and I must reverence human nature. Neither the sneers of a worldly scepticism nor the groans of a gloomy theology, disturb my faith in its godlike powers and tendencies. I know how it is despised, how it has been oppressed, how civil and religious establishments have for ages conspired to crush it. I know its history. I shut my eyes on none of its weaknesses and crimes. I understand the proofs by which despotism demonstrates that man is a wild beast, in want of a master, and only safe in chains. But, injured, trampled on, and scorned as our nature is, I still turn to it with intense sympathy and strong hope. The signatures of its origin and its end are impressed too deeply to be ever wholly effaced. I bless it for its kind affections, for its strong and tender love. I honor it for its struggles against oppression, for its growth and progress under the weight of so many chains and prejudices, for its achievements in science and art, and still more for its examples of heroic and saintly virtue. These are marks of a divine origin and the pledges of a celestial inheritance; and I thank God that my own lot is bound up with that of the human race.

SOURCE: William Ellery Channing, "Likeness to God," *The Works of William E. Channing, D.D., with an Introduction* (Boston, 1886), 291–97, 299.

A Dialogue on Some of the Causes of Infidelity

1828

A Dialogue on Some of the Causes of Infidelity *was one of five tracts writ-ten by Mrs.* Dorcas Hiller Cleveland (1773–1850) *as a series of conversations between members of a family in which the mother served as theological expert and spiritual guide. The American Unitarian Association (AUA) published Cleveland's work anonymously between 1827 and 1829. Cleveland convened early nineteenth-century parlor conversations on education reform and theol-ogy in her home in Lancaster, Massachusetts. She mentored budding Unitar-ian educators and ministers, including Elizabeth Peabody, Jared Sparks, and George B. Emerson. According to Peabody, participants at the Cleveland salon regularly discussed "the heroic ideal of inspiring children with the power to educate themselves." A rare example of nineteenth-century women's public theology, Cleveland's* Dialogues *are unique in presentation and well versed in liberal and orthodox doctrine. Asserting the authority of personal experi-ence as theological source across the lifespan, Cleveland's work provided a method for teaching a "life-giving" Christianity that would serve as a middle way between orthodox Calvinism and apostate deism. Cleveland's approach to spiritual development—encouraging each seeker to search her heart, exam-ine her ego, and remain open to transformation—is as relevant today as it was almost two hundred years ago. Further Reading: Abijah P. Marvin,* History of the Town of Lancaster, Massachusetts: From the First Settlement to the Present Time: 1643–1879 *(Lancaster, 1879).*

—Megan Lloyd Joiner

MRS. HENDERSON sat alone at work one evening, when Mr. Henderson entered the parlour, having been taking a walk, as was his custom, to refresh himself after the labours of the day.

"I have been talking with George again," said he, as he seated himself on the sofa, "and I am altogether out of patience with him." Mr. Henderson looked dis-turbed; and his wife's countenance immediately manifested sympathetic emotions.

"What has the poor boy been doing now?" she inquired in a tone of anxiety.

"I do not feel as if he were entitled to pity," said Mr. Henderson. "He is wilful and perverse, and I am more angry than grieved with him."

"Whatever be his fault, my dear," replied Mrs. Henderson mildly, "young as he is, I think he is to be pitied; and the more wilful he is, the more I grieve for him, because I know he is only treasuring up future anguish for himself. What has he been doing?"

*   *   *

"He has not done any thing wrong, that I know of," replied Mr. Henderson. "I do not mean to find fault with his conduct; but you know he has got his head full of deistical nonsense. And he is so wilful and headstrong, he thinks he knows more than any body ever did before; there is no arguing him out of his infidel notions. He will not listen to reason."

Mrs. Henderson sighed gently, and remained some time silent.

"It is in vain," at length she said, "to attempt to reason against opinions that have been formed by feeling and association, without any reason to support them. I have long been watching the progress of George's character with great anxiety. I have seen the tendency to this state of mind from its commencement, and have done what I could under existing circumstances to counteract it. But though we cannot induce him to yield to argument, and though you cannot alarm him by representing to him the dangers of his errors, yet I do indulge a hope, that, after a while, our anxiety will be relieved by a change in his sentiments, and a better state of mind."

*   *   *

"He has heard and learned more of all the doctrinal points and sectarian views, than I knew till long after we were married," said Mr. Henderson. "And I was more astonished than I can express, to find him entertaining such opinions. I think Tom Paine will have to answer for more mischief than can easily be computed."

"There are other causes beside deistical writers," said Mrs. H., "that have served to lead George's mind astray, and such as have, in my opinion, made more infidels than all the open attacks upon christianity, that have ever been made by professed deists."

*   *   *

"Do you not recollect," continued his wife, "that I said, you were going to place your son under the influence of people, whom we both believed had embraced many pernicious errors in their religious creed, and that I was afraid his young and ductile mind would be drawn into a state of unnatural and injurious excitement, and that lasting evils would follow from it."

*   *   *

"But," inquired Mr. Henderson, "how could his going there,—where the danger was, as you apprehended, that he would be made to believe in Calvinistic tenets— how could that have any thing to do with his now being a deist."

*   *   *

"You know, my dear," said his wife, "that it has been a principle which has governed me, and which you have approved, that when instructing our little children, religion should be presented to them in the simplest and plainest manner. We strove to give them the deepest, the highest, and the most expanded ideas of the character of God; and to dwell particularly on his infinite benevolence, as the quality best calculated to inspire confidence and devout affection in their young hearts. The beauty of holiness, and every divine quality manifested by Jesus Christ, were pointed out in a way to captivate them, and fix their strongest feelings on what we deemed the fundamental principles of revelation. But we avoided initiating them into what are called the mysteries of religion, thinking it wisest and best to keep the clouds and darkness, which the human mind has thrown over this beautiful and heavenly system, quite out of their view; believing, that when their hearts were imbued with the pure spirit of the gospel, and their understandings enlightened by its wisdom at a mature period of life, they would be able to grapple with the dogmas they might learn, and resist the falsehood offered as divine truth." Mrs. Henderson paused, and looked earnestly in her husband's face.

"Well, go on," said he.

* * *

"What were the several states of mind, which you think have led to this?" asked Mr. Henderson. "I really have not observed them."

"The first impression that he received, after being placed in your brother's family, was excessive ennui and disgust, in consequence of being debarred so many of his accustomed amusements, and compelled to attend so many, and such long religious exercises, which, as he could not understand them, were naturally very tedious." . . .

"The second change of his feelings," continued Mrs. Henderson, in a tone that manifested regret and sorrow, "was that of fear and horror, on account of the inevitable and dreadful sufferings he was taught to believe he was doomed to endure eternally, unless the irresistible grace of God were vouchsafed to save him. This terror was renewed as often as the least natural reaction of his spirits had allayed it; and at length such a nervous excitement was produced as threw him into a slow fever." . . .

"He started from his broken slumbers one night, thinking he heard his name called; he thought he opened his eyes, and saw his chamber full of sparkling stars which were in continual motion; he was greatly alarmed and cried aloud. His uncle and aunt, who anxiously watched over him, in the hope of a happy change, on hearing his terrified voice, when to his room, and listened to the account. They told him, in so many words, that he was hanging over hell, as by a single hair."

* * *

"It was not long before he was again aroused by a similar affection of the nervous system, a sickly dream, which was very natural in his situation, which indeed is very common in such a state of the body, and should, therefore, be treated altogether as a symptom of disease. I have very often experienced similar impressions, and so have others, without imagining it in any way connected with religion, or observing any mental effect afterwards."

"Certainly," said Mr. Henderson, "How could any one think otherwise?"

"Your brother and sister believed it was the voice of God, and so they told George, and that he might now pour out his heart in hallelujahs and praises to his Maker for his unmerited goodness in saving a lost soul, and granting such an abundant entrance into his heavenly kingdom. George gladly laid hold of these bright prospects; and the sudden relief, from excessive fear to hope and joy, caused such a reaction of the spirits, that it produced a highly active stage of fever; and he became as raving with delight as he had previously been with horror. By this time, it was discovered by those around him, that he was really diseased, and burning with fever. They became alarmed, and sent for the village physician, who pronounced him dangerously ill. The poor boy was several days on the borders of the grave. When he became convalescent, I wished to take him home, to recover his strength, and the proper tone of mind; but circumstances prevented."

"What circumstances?" asked Mr. H. "I cannot conceive how I could consent to leave him there after that."

"These things appeared less important to you then," replied Mrs. Henderson, "than they do now. You felt, and treated the subject of religion, with much greater indifference, and made little discrimination as to the truth or falsehood of the different doctrines professed. You looked upon many of the notions of your brother and sister as so wholly absurd and irrational, that you could not imagine them to be seriously believed; and therefore thought, as George's health was restored, he could be in no danger of being affected by them. You conceived his sickness to be the cause, and not the effect of the state of mind he had been in; and the whole matter made little impression on your mind."

        *   *   *

"What was the effect on George?" asked Mr. Henderson. "I do not recollect attending to the subject after our return."

"The effect was such as might naturally be expected," replied Mrs. H. "When his strength and natural vivacity were restored, and his mind had recovered its rational and elastic action, he was led to reflect on what had taken place, and review the changes he had passed through. An unconquerable aversion to the subject of religion took possession of his feelings. Its association with his sufferings was strong, and the recollection of every scene he had experienced, extremely painful and disgusting to him. The views of the divine character daily presented to him by his uncle and aunt, and also by his teachers, who neglected no opportunity to instil their peculiar sentiments, were so opposed to those his own reflections suggested when contemplating the beauty and majesty of nature, that they became more and more abhorrent to him. Sometimes, as he has since told me, when his mind had been disturbed and bewildered by the sophistry he had listened to, he would go into a corner, and secretly express the aversion he felt for a being, so powerful and so malignant as he conceived God to be. Then, when he plunged into the woods, and cooled his heated head in the pure brook, and soothed his excited feelings in the sweet and solemn tranquility of rural scenes, his heart expanded with gratitude and love to the God, who spoke to his soul in the pure language of nature, and declared himself to be as benevolent as he is wise and powerful. Such was the effect of the course pursued with him, that he became impatient to cast off the whole of revealed religion."

SOURCE: "A Dialogue on Some of the Causes of Infidelity," *Tracts of the American Unitarian Association*, first series, vol. 2 (Boston: Leonard Bowles, 1829), 219–31.

"Trust Deed of Adi Brahmo Samaj"
1830

Raja Rammohun Roy (1774–1833) was the primary founder of the Brahmo Samaj, a Bengali reform movement that was early Unitarianism's most important partner on the Indian subcontinent. Committed to the Vedanta philosophy found in the Upanishads, *but also impressed by the monotheism of Islam and the commitment of Christian missionaries, Rammohun strove to purge Indian religion of polytheism, animal sacrifice, the burning of widows, rigid caste distinctions, and the use of images in worship. His* Precepts of Jesus *(1820) offered an ethical interpretation of Christianity that drew the support of British and American Unitarians, and the Brahmo Samaj's ties to Unitarianism were renewed when missionary Charles Dall befriended leader Keshub Chandra Sen in 1855, ultimately sparking schism within the movement. In 1900, the Brahmo Samaj became a founding member of the International Council of Unitarian and Other Liberal Religious Thinkers and Workers (now the International Association for Religious Freedom). Its spirituality is often represented in Unitarian Universalist worship through the writings of Rabindranath Tagore. Further Reading: Amiya P. Sen,* Rammohun Roy: A Critical Biography *(New Delhi: Penguin Books, 2012).*

—Dan McKanan

This indenture made the eighth day of January in the year of Christ one thousand eight hundred and thirty. . . .

To have and to hold the said Messuage Building . . . land tenements hereditaments and premises with their appurtenances to be used occupied enjoyed applied and appropriated as and for a place of public meeting of all sorts and descriptions of people without distinction as shall behave and conduct themselves in an orderly sober religious and devout manner for the worship and adoration of the Eternal Unsearchable and Immutable Being who is the Author and Preserver of the Universe, but not under or by any other name designation or title peculiarly used for and applied, to any particular Being or Beings by any man or set of men whatsoever, and that no graven image statue or sculpture carving painting picture portrait or the likeness of anything shall be admitted within the said messuages building land tenements hereditaments and premises and that no sacrifice offering or oblation of any kind or thing shall ever be permitted therein, and that no animal or living creature shall within or on the said messuage building land tenements hereditaments and premises be deprived of life either for religious purposes or for food and that no eating or drinking (except such as shall be necessary by any accident for the preservation of life) feasting or rioting be permitted therein or thereon and that in conducting the said worship and adoration no object animate or inanimate that has been or is or shall hereafter become or be recognized as an object of worship by any man or set of men shall be reviled or slightingly or contemptuously spoken of or alluded to either in preaching prayer or in the hymns or other mode of worship that may be delivered or used in the said messuage or building and that no sermon preaching discourse prayer or hymn be delivered made or used in such worship but such as have a tendency to the promotion of the contemplation of the Author and Preserver of the Universe to the promotion of charity morality piety benevolence virtue and the strengthening the bonds of union Between men of all religious persuasions and creeds, and also that a person of Good repute and well known for his knowledge piety and morality be employed by the said Trustees or the survivors or survivors of them or the heirs of such survivor or their or his assigns as a resident superintendent and for the purpose of superintending the worship so to be performed as in hereinbefore stated and expressed, and that such worship be performed daily or least as often as once in seven days.

SOURCE: *The English Works of Raja Rammohun Roy, with an English Translation of "Tuhfatul Muwahhiddin"* (Allahabad: Panini Office, 1906), 213–16.

HENRY WARE, JR.

On the Formation of the
Christian Character

1831

Henry Ware, Jr. (1794–1843) carried on the family tradition of teaching at
Harvard Divinity School. Whereas his father's appointment to the esteemed
Hollis Chair precipitated the Unitarian controversy, Ware's invitation to join
the faculty as the inaugural Professor of Pastoral Care and Pulpit Eloquence
in 1830 caused little uproar. In his monograph on the formation of Chris-
tian character, which the Unitarian Book and Pamphlet Society liberally
distributed throughout Boston, Ware depicts Christ as a model more than as
a martyr—a divine instructor who educates humans on account of their
imperfection, rather than redeeming them from their depravity. This Chris-
tology informs Ware's implicit and, at times, explicit contention that Chris-
tianity must be true not only in the abstract but as it is lived in day-to-day life.
Ware is said to have embodied this ethic himself. On his retirement, his stu-
dents offered the following words: "Your example, beloved Sir, even more than
your instructions, has taught us the greatness and beauty of a Christian life."
Further Reading: John Ware, Memoir of the Life of Henry Ware, Jr. *(Boston,*
1846).

—Erik Martinez Resly

The Nature of Religion, and What We Are to Seek.

In order to the intelligent and successful pursuit of any object, it is necessary, first
of all, to have a definite conception of what we desire to effect or obtain. This is
especially important in the study of Religion, both because of the extent and variety of the subject itself, and because of the very different apprehensions of men
respecting it. Many are disheartened and fail, in consequence of setting out with
wrong views and false expectations. From which cause religion itself suffers; being
made answerable for failures, which are entirely owing to the unreasonable antici-
pations and ill-directed efforts of those who enlisted in her service, but did not persevere in it.

Let us begin, then, with considering what is the object at which we aim when
we seek a religious character.

Religion, in a general sense, is founded on man's relation and accountableness
to his Maker; and it consists in cherishing the sentiments and performing the duties

which thence result, and which belong to the other relations to other beings which God has appointed him to sustain.

Concerning these relations, sentiments, and duties, we are instructed in the Scriptures, especially in the New Testament. Religion, with us, is the *Christian* religion. It is found in the teachings and example of Jesus Christ. It consists in the worship, the sentiments, and the character, which he enjoined, and which he illustrated in his own person.

What you are to seek, therefore, is, under the guidance of Jesus Christ, to feel your relation to God, and to live under a sense of responsibility to him; to cultivate assiduously those sentiments and affections which spring out of this responsible and filial relation, as well as those which arise out of your connexion with other men as his offspring; to perform all the duties to Him and them, which appertain to this character and relation; and to cherish that heavenward tendency of mind, which should spring from a consciousness of possessing an immortal nature. He who does all this is a religious man, or, in other words, a Christian.

You desire to be a Christian. To this are requisite three things: belief in the truths which the gospel reveals; possession of the state of mind which it enjoins; and performance of the duties which it requires: or, I may say, the subjection of the mind by faith, the subjection of the heart by love, the subjection of the will by obedience. This universal submission of yourself to God is what you are to aim at. This is Religion.

Observe how extensive a thing it is. It is a principle of the mind; founded upon thought, reflection, inquiry, argument; and leading to devotion and duty as most reasonable and suitable for intelligent beings.

It is a sentiment or affection of the heart; not the cold judgment of the intellect alone, in favor of what is right; but a warm, glowing feeling of preference and desire; a feeling, which attaches itself in love to the Father of all and to all good beings; which turns duty into inclination, and pursues virtue from impulse; which prefers and delights in that which is well pleasing to God, and takes an affectionate interest in the things to which the Saviour devoted himself.

It is a rule of life; it is the law of God; causing the external conduct to correspond to the principle which is established, and the sentiment which breathes, within; bringing every action into a conformity with the divine will, and making universal holiness the standard of the character.

*　*　*

The Means of Religious Improvement.

The means to be used in order to render permanent your religious impressions, and promote the growth of your character, are now to be considered. They may be arranged under the following heads:—Reading, Meditation, Prayer, Hearing the word preached, and the Lord's Supper.

I. Reading.

I begin with the more private means; and I speak of reading first, because it is in the perusal of the Scriptures that the beginning of religious knowledge is to be found. It is they which testify of Christ, and have the words of eternal life. It is they which make wise unto salvation. And it is through a devout acquaintance with them, that the mind and heart grow in the knowledge and love of God, and that the dispositions are formed which prepare for heaven. Every one may read the Bible, and, such is its plainness and simplicity in all matters pertaining to life and godliness, that if he be able to read nothing else, he may yet learn all that is essential to duty and acceptance. Hence it has happened, that many, to whom circumstances have interdicted all general acquaintance with books, have gathered, from their solitary study of the Bible alone, a wisdom which has expanded and elevated their minds, and a peace which has raised them above the darkness and trials of an unhappy worldly lot.

* * *

II. Meditation.

This is a great and essential means of improvement. It is essential to self-examination and self-knowledge, without which the hope of progress and of virtue is vain. No one can know his own character, or be aware of the dispositions, feelings and motives by which he is actuated, except by means of deep and searching reflection. In the crowd of business and the hurry of the world, we are apt to rush on without weighing, as we should, the considerations which urge us; we are liable to neglect that close inspection of ourselves, and that careful reference of our conduct to the unerring standard of right, which are requisite both to our knowing where we are, and to our keeping in the right way. It is necessary that we sometimes pause and look around us, and consider our ways; that we take observation of the course we are running, and the various influences to which we are subjected, and be sure that we are not driven or drifted from the direction in which we ought to be proceeding. Without this there is no safety.

* * *

III. Prayer.

As there is no duty more frequently enjoined in the New Testament by our Saviour and the Apostles, so there is none which is a more indispensable and efficacious means of religious improvement, than Prayer; for which reasons it demands particular attention.

The practice of devotion is a sign of spiritual life, and a means of preserving it. No one prays heartily without some deep religious sentiment to actuate him. This sentiment may be but occasionally felt; it may be transient in duration; but the exercise of it in acts of devotion tends to render it habitual and permanent, and its frequent exercise causes the mind at length to exist always in a devout posture. He who truly prays, feels, during the act, a sense of God's presence, authority and love; of his own obligations and unworthiness; of his need of being better. He feels grateful, humble, resigned, anxious for improvement. He who prays often, often has these feelings, and by frequent repetition they become customary and constant. And thus prayer operates as an active, steady, powerful means of Christian progress.

*　*　*

Having, then, your stated times, if you would make them in the highest measure profitable, observe the following rules. First of all, when the hour has arrived, seek to excite in your mind a sense of the divine presence, and of the greatness of the act in which you are engaging. Summon up the whole energy of your mind. Put all you power upon the stretch. Do not allow yourself to utter a word, to use an expression, thoughtlessly, nor without setting before yourself, in a distinct form, its full meaning. Remember the words of Ecclesiasticus: "When you glorify the Lord, exalt him as much as you can; for even yet will he far exceed: and when you exalt him, put forth all your strength, and be not weary; for you can never go far enough." Pour your whole soul, the utmost intensity of your feelings, into your words. One sentence uttered thus is better than the cold repetition of an entire liturgy. For this reason, let your prayer be preceded by meditation. In this way make an earnest effort after a devout temper. While you thus muse, the fire of your devotion will kindle, and then you may "speak with your tongue;" then you may breathe out the adoring sentiments of praise and thanksgiving, the holy aspirations after excellence and grace, the humble confessions of your contrite spirit, the glowing emotions of Christian faith. As you proceed, you will probably find yourself increasing in warmth and energy; especially if you give way to the impulse of your feelings, and do not check them by watching them too closely. To do this chills the current of devotion, and changes your prayer from the simple expression of desire and affection, into an exercise of mental philosophy. Wherefore, having warmed your mind, give it free way, and let its religious ardor flow on. But if, as will often be the case, you find your thoughts wander and your feelings cool, then pause, and by silent thought bring back the mind to its duty; and thus intermix meditation with prayer, in such manner that you shall never fall into the mechanical, unmeaning repetition of mere words.

SOURCE: Henry Ware, Jr., *On the Formation of the Christian Character: Addressed to Those Who Are Seeking to Lead a Religious Life* (Cambridge, MA: Hilliard and Brown, 1831), 5–8, 47–48, 68–69, 82–83, 89.

ADIN BALLOU

"Epistle General to Restorationists"

1831

*Adin Ballou (1803–1890), famous for being a pacifist and the founder of a
utopian community, was in his early years more interested in theological
issues than social ones. Born in Rhode Island, he was raised as a General
Baptist and in the Christian Connexion. When he came of age, Ballou defied
his father—and attended the urgings of his mother-in-law—by converting to
Universalism. Told that he did not have to adopt Hosea Ballou's "no future
punishment" doctrine, he accepted a call to the Universalist church in Milford, Massachusetts. In 1828, he became disillusioned by Hosea's conduct
in financial negotiations with a church in New York City, but it was only
after the death of his first wife, Abigail, followed by a severe illness and his
remarriage (all in 1829) that he began openly to rebel against the theological
dominance of Hosea Ballou. The following year he preached a pro-future
punishment sermon, "The Inestimable Value of Souls." This led to the loss of
his pulpit and to his being driven into the camp of Hosea's enemies. Providing new energy to this Restorationist faction, Adin helped them create a new
denomination in 1831, the Massachusetts Association of Universal Restorationists, and founded and edited their newspaper,* The Independent Messenger. *In the "Epistle General to Restorationists," printed in the first issue,
he laid out his story and his case. Further Reading: Adin Ballou,* The Autobiography of Adin Ballou, 1803–1890 *(Lowell, MA, 1896); Peter Hughes,
"The Second Phase of the Restorationist Controversy: Disciplinary Crisis and
Schism, 1824–1831,"* Journal of Unitarian Universalist History *28, no. 2 (2001):
28–91.*

—Peter Hughes

In the year 1822, after much anxious inquiry, and many trying exercises of mind, I at
length found repose in the full persuasion, that God through Jesus Christ will finally
restore the whole human family to holiness and happiness. An honest avowal of this
persuasion involved me in the censure of my former religious friends, and resulted
in my exclusion from their fellowship. Soon after, having received intimations that
the denomination of Universalists would give me a friendly admission into their
connexion, I made application and met a cordial welcome. I entered into this new
connexion with the confident expectation of enjoying fraternal countenance and
protection, without sacrificing my religious liberty. . . .

228

The commencement of my acquaintance with Universalists was with several of the most conspicuous advocates of the doctrine of no future punishment. Against these men, and their distinguishing tenets, my prejudices had formerly been very strong; nor as yet, had I entirely divested myself of their influence. I was, however, received and treated by them with so much courtesy, kindness and apparent friendship, that my unfavorable impressions were soon exchanged for those of confidence and respect. I seemed to find them persons of sounder heads and better hearts than I had anticipated, and before I was well aware, passed from suspicious dread to an extravagant credulity. I presently arrived at that easy, unsuspecting frame of mind, in which all distrust subsides, and everything is allowed to pass at its nominal value.

My new associates took care to improve their opportunity for gradually doctrinating me into their views. They solemnly assured me, that although they believed the doctrine of no future punishment to be more sound and consistent than that of limited future retribution, as held by Restorationists, yet they had not the least inclination on this account to treat their brethren of that faith with unkindness or disrespect. That all were Universalists, who believed in universal salvation, whether holding to limited future or no future punishment, and as such bound to consider themselves under mutual obligations to preserve the rights of each from violation. Hence that Restorationism subjected no member of the order to any disadvantage whatever; and might be as freely enjoyed as any other doctrine. This assurance, being perfectly satisfactory to my mind, went far towards preparing it for an entire surrender to their direction.

Knowing, however, that there had recently arisen a somewhat serious disturbance between certain eminent Restorationists, and the leading members of the no future punishment class, I desired some explanation of its cause and object. It was replied, with some circumlocution but much apparent candor, that very unhappy difficulties had indeed taken place; but that they originated, not in a conscientious regard to particular doctrinal views, so much as in personal rivalry, envy, and hatred. It was gravely represented that the Rev. Edward Turner, Paul Dean, and Jacob Wood, principal men of the disaffected party, had been aspiring to the most influential rank in the order—but that upon finding the Rev. Hosea Ballou perpetually in advance of them, both with respect to talents and the good opinion of the laity, they had conceived an envious ill will to wards that gentleman, and conspired his overthrow. That in pursuance of their design they had availed themselves (for the sake of a convenient pretext) of the difference which existed in the faith of Universalists on the question of punishment, intending to excite an evil prejudice, in relation to his well known doctrine, which should prostrate his reputation among the societies. That in reality the disaffected cared not whether their doctrine or the other were uppermost; provided they themselves could stand at the head of the order. And finally, that the whole scheme of operations was a contrivance of hypocritical wickedness, from which every well-disposed man in the denomination could but recoil with abhorrence.

This representation went down into my soul cold and bitter as the dregs of death; yet there was so much semblance of truth in the numerous circumstantial criminations which were made against the accused, and all was delivered with so many appearances of injured innocence, that I could not allow myself to doubt its correctness. I was too far carried away to think of inquiring, as I ought to have done, what the accused could offer in justification of themselves—and from that time forward, deemed it not only a dictate of prudence but of duty, to stand aloof from such dangerous men. I abstained purposely from all intimacy, and only interchanged such civilities with them as seemed unavoidable. . . .

I was now considered on good ground by the no future punishment class, and in a fair way to obtain the whole truth in due time. With all around me the grand watchword was, "research and improvement." Many were becoming enamored with the discovery of new truths, and I began to fear, that without better efforts I should discover myself a dull scholar. I therefore read with solicitude a multitude of different publications in favor of the doctrine of no future punishment. In most of these I found it a leading business of their authors, not to prove from scripture and reason by direct testimony, that all mankind would certainly be happy upon their entrance into the future state, but to show that there was no proof that any part would be miserable or suffer punishment in that state. Numerous passages of scripture, generally understood to teach future retribution, were examined, explained, and elaborately shown to have no reference to the future state. Indeed I know of no important text relating to future judgment, or punishment, which had not undergone such an explanation.

The writings of Rev. Hosea Ballou, whom I had learned to look upon with extraordinary reverence, contained many of those expositions of scripture, several of which for a time I regarded as extremely plausible. And if I rightly recollect, that gentleman himself expressed privately and publicly his settled conviction, that not a single passage of scripture fairly interpreted, either declared or intimated the doctrine of retribution in the future state. To hear a man for whom I entertained so elevated a respect, deliberately declare such a conviction, with so much confidence in its truth, was well calculated to impress me with the idea that possibly he might be right. In a few instances, I endeavored, in private conversation with him, to obtain more perfect explanations of his views concerning universal salvation; but was never so happy as to receive anything more explicit or satisfactory, than I had read in his works. This was a circumstance that rather perplexed me, and the more so, as I did not find all that freedom which I needed, in order to propose my doubts and difficulties. Yet I suffered it not to diminish my deference for the man; and applied with double diligence to his writings for more thorough information.

Rev. Walter Balfour's first Inquiry came out with an imposing importance, as a learned and valuable work; and I read it with high raised expectations of deriving satisfaction on many points, concerning which I had been perplexed. I had been informed that he was a thorough scholar, particularly in the original languages of the Bible, a man of sterling sense, a strong reasoner, and withal remarkably candid. I consequently read his work with interest, and with a prejudice in his favor. Indeed I had grown so respectful to the no future punishment scheme, and was so intimate with its influential friends, that I greatly desired to be convinced of its soundness, and was if possible too willing to find sufficient evidence in its support. Yet even in this frame of mind, all I had read came short of affording me the desired proof. Mr. Balfour's work just noticed, though the most able and candid of all his Universalist productions, and though embracing much on the subjects discussed which deserved respectful consideration, did by no means settle the queries which chiefly agitated my mind. I however thought tolerably well of it, as I endeavored to do of all the works I had examined on that side of the question.

But as my Restorationism had now become silent, my neutrality was little better than partiality to ultra Universalism. And while in my preaching I said nothing directly in support of future retribution, I went as far as I could with those who were its opposers. I never preached the no future punishment scheme at full length, for I never believed it true. . . .

As to the style of my preaching, it had insensibly become remotely imitative of that which distinguished the leading Universalists. Although irony, satire and witticism was never pleasing to me, and therefore not indulged in my discourses, yet in other respects I went too far. In following the example of those who use their texts by way of accommodation to smite at the prevailing sects, I have since thought I sometimes erred. Those preachers, who had become most acceptable to the laity, distinguished themselves by often selecting texts, which with an ingenious treatment would enable them to cast the severest reflections upon their opponents with the best grace. If I fell into this practice it was only to a brief extent, for which I can plead no other excuse, than it was the fashion of my associates and therefore difficult wholly to avoid. . . .

In devotion to the denomination, I was not a whit behind the foremost—an enemy to that which was denominated faction, alarmed at any thing which portended disunion, and proud to deserve the credit of a peaceable brother. I deprecated that "bad spirit," which tended to "make difficulty in the order," and thought of nothing but success and prosperity to the common cause. In the meantime the disaffected Restorationists were considered as defeated, silenced, humbled and rendered harmless. They were indeed treated externally as brethren, on the ground that the difficulties they had excited were settled, yet both they and their doctrine had evidently fallen into discredit with a majority of the societies; which majority evinced their determination, not only to befriend the no future punishment clergy, but to discountenance any thing that deviated from their distinguishing tenets. This influence seemed to be fatal against Restorationism, and necessitated its preachers to keep their doctrine chiefly to themselves, or seek a new field for its dissemination.

I had now arrived at the twenty-fourth year of my age, and was passing the perihelium of my proximity to ultra Universalism. Up to this time I had persuaded myself that my preaching, and that of my brethren, exerted or tended to exert, a salutary influence upon the moral condition of society, and believed that when fully proved in its effect it would vindicate itself against all reproach. I knew well that some, who pretended to propagate Universalism, were too rough and vulgar to do any great good either for their own cause or any other (and such I could have wished might remain silent) but as the clergy generally promised better things, for such I accordingly hoped. Henceforth, however, I perceived so much bitterness indulged, so much labor bestowed to show that the Bible teaches no future judgment or retribution, so much ridicule of the religion of professing Christians, and so much smart witticism, even in the preaching of those who were thought most eminent, that I began seriously to doubt whereunto things would grow. Close moral, practical and evangelical preaching seemed to be going out of date, and when occasionally I struck into a vein of it, I found that it was evidently unwelcome to those ears, which were so much delighted with a different style and subject. This troubled me exceedingly, and was an evil which I knew not how to remedy. I learned that to declaim against the superstition, bigotry, hypocrisy and fanaticism of the various religious sects entertained a certain class of people very agreeably, yet without ever producing the effect to reform them of a single vice. In contemplating the faults and follies of their neighbors, as described by an ingenious speaker, those people would evince the highest gratification; but the certain result, I observed always to be, a growing disrelish of all serious religion, and a forgetfulness of their own sinfulness in denouncing that of others. I looked to my elders in the ministry, those who had it in their power to give tone to the taste and feelings of the laity, but I soon ascertained that they were as far from the mark at which I was aiming, as any of the people. Gradually entering into their secrets, I began to discover some doctrines, practices and feelings not altogether consistent with the good opinion I had formed of their moral and intellectual worth. I found them disposed to think lightly of that kind of preaching called moral. They would speak of it as a sort of weakly, insipid, tiresome repetition, calculated to reflect no great honor upon the preacher, and to do no essential good to the hearer. It would do well enough for those whose gifts fitted them for nothing higher—but doctrine, and exposure of the errors of the Church should be mainly attended to, by all who wished to attain celebrity.

Family devotion—asking blessings and returning thanks at table, etc. etc. they considered well enough for those who thought proper to observe them, but on the whole, as idle ceremonies which could be beneficial neither to God nor man. With regard to a future state of existence, many of them disbelieved that mankind will in that state possess any consciousness of having previously existed in the present. Some of them also, privately confessed their disbelief in the existence of angelic beings of a higher nature than human. These and other similar skepticisms, which from time to time leaked out, occasioned me much bitter anxiety for the issue. Then in relation to the Restorationist doctrine of limited future retribution, I found the whole ultra party, both clergy and laity, to hold it in abhorrence and contempt. As I was supposed to have got over that childish notion, its opposers laid aside their reserve, and gave me an opportunity to discover their real feelings. I found the doctrine regarded as a relic of heathenish superstition—a weak and silly whim—an indication wherever held of a shallow mind—and finally, as a serious detriment to the reputation of young preachers among the societies. It would do well enough for people who had just been released from the dungeon of error, whose mental vision could not at once endure the full light of day. It was, perhaps, a necessary evil, which as a convenient stepping stone into the knowledge of the truth, must be tolerated. But as a permanent ground of faith, no man of intelligence could long rest upon it—for if any misery were admitted to exist in the future state, it was far more consistent to believe it would be endless. Hence the man who should presume to urge it upon public attention, in distinction from their Universalism, could expect no less than to be denounced by them as an emissary of discord, and a promoter of "difficulty in the order." Such indeed, they appeared to esteem everyone, who had independence enough to say anything in its vindication.

All these things I carefully observed, without appearing to do so, and along with many a painful pang locked them up in my own bosom. Feeling that I was inextricably involved in the net which enclosed me, I resolved to make the best of my case, and to wait in silence for better times. Yet even in this situation of mind I was a doubtful neutral, and thought it an almost impossible task to disprove the reasoning employed by Messrs. Ballou and Balfour to show that the scriptures do not teach the doctrines of future judgment and punishment. But I no longer felt any anxiety to be persuaded of the soundness of their peculiar opinions; having become quite disposed to be content with whatever might finally appear most conformable to divine truth and reason. . . .

During this period, I was invited to the pastoral charge of the Universalist Society in Prince Street, New York. This I accepted, but remained with the society only about nine months. The Rev. Abner Kneeland was then flourishing at the head of a society in that city, part of whom had followed him from Prince Street, which he had left a short time before my arrival. He was on the highway from ultra Universalism to Atheism, and had reduced things to such a state of confusion that I soon became convinced of my incompetency to restore them to wholesome order. Party feuds, personal animosities, jealousy, envy and strife, with obvious symptoms of skepticism, even in some of the most respectable individuals, reigned on all sides among those who called themselves Universalists. I endured this state of things till I could neither hope for better times, nor successfully withstand existing evils—then asked dismission and returned to Milford, whither I had been earnestly invited by my former friends.

While in New York I became acquainted with Rev. E. Mitchell, Pastor of the Society of United Christian Friends, a Restorationist who had long stood aloof from the denomination of Universalists. I found him a man of sound moral principle, devoted piety and sincere Christian feeling. He had stood amid the swelling surges of skepticism and infidelity firm as a rock of the ocean, and notwithstanding ultra Universalism had somewhat diminished the number of his society, he still retained a respectable congregation. I have since fully appreciated his motives in declining the fellowship of Universalists as a denomination, and do not in the least wonder at the course he has pursued. He has proved himself a genuine friend of the Christian religion, of moral order, and practical godliness. And as a faithful minister of Christ, an independent minded man, and an uncompromising opponent of all sorts of licentiousness, he will receive the approbation of every good man.

I returned from New York deeply disgusted with Atheism, libertinism, Kneelandism, and I may add ultra Universalism. I had seen so much in the management of those who were distinguishing themselves as the friends of these isms, which did not meet the approbation of either my conscience or understanding, that I resolved henceforth to think and act wholly for myself. I immediately examined all my opinions, reviewed the whole pathway of my mind since I first became a neutral, searched the scriptures with renewed diligence, analyzed the doctrines and arguments of the ultras, and in the course of a few months settled down into a firm belief of Restorationism, as I first received it in the year 1822. My mind has since remained undisturbedly satisfied of the soundness and truth of that doctrine. . . .

I applied myself studiously to criticism on all the writings of modern Universalists within my reach, and to close observation of the effects of the doctrine on its warmest advocates. I discerned daily in these writings what appeared to me to be irreconcilable inconsistencies and contradictions. Absurdities, which I had before no apprehension of finding, stood forth in bold relief; and I felt an indescribable mortification in reflecting that the ancient doctrine of Restorationism must be suffocated by such errors. Yet nothing could be done without making "difficulty in the order;" because there was no medium of fair public investigation through which to act successfully against false doctrine. I once addressed a few queries to the editor of the *Trumpet*, concerning his exposition of the sin against the Holy Ghost, which though he published, his reply was such as to satisfy me, that he meant to evade the leading difficulties, and stand aloof from discussion. I made no further attempt towards public investigation till within the last year. . . .

Another injustice that aggrieved me was the frequent statements which appeared in the *Trumpet* and elsewhere, of the faith of our order. Universalists were set down in the aggregate as believing all the tenets of the ultras, and the impression thereby sent abroad among the uninformed, that no man could be a Universalist, without holding those tenets. I had preserved the original idea, given me upon my first acquaintance with the denomination, and always inculcated it; i.e. that all men were Universalists who believed in universal salvation—as much those who held the doctrine of future retribution, as those who rejected it. But I found by the statements alluded to, that I was a believer in universal salvation, and yet not a Universalist. . . .

Added to all this was the occasional discovery of a deep disgust at everything said in our general meetings not conformable to all their improved notions. I have known an ultra Universalist preacher, upon hearing a Restorationist speak in the pulpit of "appearing in the presence of God," of "standing at the judgment seat of Christ," or of "suffering the retributions of a future state"—signify his contempt and dislike by sneers and whisperings. Such things added fuel to the fire shut up in my bones, and urged me on to independence. I have attended but few Associations, and only one General Convention of Universalist ministers. The General Convention of 1829, at Winchester, N.H., was the only session of that body, and the last general meeting of clergymen at which I have been present. I saw there a spirit in the ultras, which made me resolve it should be the last time I would meet with them on any such occasion. There Brother Paul Dean was prohibited by a vote of the Convention from inviting Brother David Pickering to pray with him in the desk. When I found such a vote about to pass, I left the meeting with grief and astonishment. . . .

In June the Southern Association of Universalists held a session at Berlin, Connecticut. At that Association, Rev. Hosea Ballou, Thomas Whittemore and others, procured the passage of resolutions denouncing the Providence Association—and virtually prohibiting those brethren, who had of late met with it, from giving it their further countenance, on pain of excommunication from the General Convention. Although I was not then a member of the Providence Association, and had never happened to be present at one of its sessions, yet I considered the passage of these resolutions an unwarrantable assumption of ecclesiastical authority—and an aggression upon all the Restorationists in the Convention, which if passively endured, must involve the ultimate surrender of their most sacred rights.

Soon after this, early in July, the editor of the *Trumpet* came out in his paper against a sermon of mine just published at his office entitled "The Inestimable Value of Souls." This sermon had been delivered before my friends in Medway, and by their particular request a copy furnished for the press. They carried the copy directly to the *Trumpet* office, and contracted to have it printed. Its great design was to illustrate and establish the doctrine of Universal Restoration in opposition to that of endless misery. But as I did not construe scripture according to the light of modern Universalism, and distinctly inculcated the faith of future limited retribution, Mr. Whittemore and his brethren could not silently brook my independence. He therefore, in accordance with the advice of his counselors, lost no time in testifying his disapprobation of the sermon and the presumption of its author. Ere the sermon reached me in print the number of the *Trumpet* containing Mr. W.'s strictures was laid before me. Those strictures breathed a spirit of censorious intolerance and hostility, warm from the fountain of ultra Universalism, which left no room to doubt the feelings and designs with which they were given to the world. They virtually denounced me and my production as unworthy the respect and confidence of the denomination of Universalists. The public was cautioned against receiving the sentiments of the sermon as those of American Universalists. I was accused of having shown great irreverence towards my elders in the ministry; of having construed my text and other passages of scripture in contempt of better light; and finally as being, in Mr. W.'s opinion, "certainly far behind the orthodox in rescuing the sacred writings from perversion." My sentiments, motives, and conduct were so misrepresented, misjudged and censured, that I considered the article no less than a ban of outlawry. . . .

I now prepared and forwarded to the editor of the *Trumpet* a vindication of myself against his attack, and requested that he would give it immediate publicity in his paper, or if he decided not to publish it at all, to return it to me within four days. About a week afterwards he returned it, without note or comment. He refused to publish it, gave no notice that he had received any reply from me, and deigned not even so much as to signify his reasons for returning it. But I soon learned that he and his coadjutors were industriously circulating a report in private circles, that my article was so fiery, bitter, and abusive, as to be unfit to appear in print. To others it was pretended to be an act of friendship towards me, to suppress an article, which, if laid before the public, would certainly reflect deep disgrace upon my name. But among the uninformed ultras abroad, the conclusion seemed to be readily drawn, that Mr. Whittemore's rod had taught me silence. They presumed I should in future take care to respect my betters. Thus was I accused, denounced and condemned without a hearing.

This sealed the protest of my utter separation. I immediately announced to my society from the pulpit, my views, feelings, and determination, in the most undisguised terms—offering to receive dismission from their pastoral charge, at any moment, declaring that I considered others as free to withhold their fellowship and support from me, as I was to enjoy and propagate my own honest opinion. I assured them that compromise with my ultra Universalist persecutors could never take place, consistently with my sense of duty to myself, to God and my fellow men—and that if I should stand entirely alone in the religious world, I would be an independent Restorationist. Several of the most valuable of my friends assured me, they thought none the worse of me for my frankness, and should not be in haste to dismiss me from their service. The disaffected probably meditated other things, without choosing to express them. But whatever might be meditated gave me no concern, as I had made up my mind to count all things dross for the sake of duty and truth. After this I came out without reserve in defense of my doctrine, and of course in opposition to modern Universalism. The excitement was everywhere great, and I had full opportunity to know how much abhorrence and contempt the real ultras felt towards Restorationists and their faith. The more coarse and immoral poured out their profanity upon and denounced me most heartily, together with what they were pleased to denominate my "hell junior," "tophet" and "purgatory." In these vituperations they have been encouraged by at least some of their preachers. Some contented themselves with saying that they had as lief hear orthodox preaching as mine, and that there was no true Universalism about me. But others, who are distinguished for their greater candor and moderation, though inclined to the side of modern Universalism, have treated me with respect, and say that they are ready to hear, read and consider whatever Restorationists have to offer in support of their views. With such men I have no contention. As to decided Restorationists, and those who are friendly to the upbuilding of their cause, I have found for my encouragement many more than at first I had any anticipation—and I now feel fully persuaded that God will not suffer me to travel in solitude to the grave.

With respect to an entire separation from the no future punishment Universalists, I had only to join the Providence Association, and share the impending fate of its members—viz., be cut off from the General Convention, by the probable vote of our opposers in that body. I accordingly became a member with the brethren of that Association, and at the session of the General Convention holden in Lebanon, N.H. during September last—we were virtually excluded from the Universalist order. The separation has thus been consummated, and I shall henceforth govern myself accordingly.

When this separation was foreseen to be inevitable, it became an object of the highest importance to have a periodical publication, through which to speak to the world in our defense. As no one came forward to undertake such a publication I engaged in it myself; and now after much care and expense have at length commenced the work under more favorable auspices than I at first expected.

Since the Prospectus went out, every effort has been made by my opposers to hedge up my way. Not one of their papers, to my knowledge, has given my prospectus a favorable notice—several of them none at all—and one or two have appeared in opposition. The old cry has been raised, in which I once ignorantly joined, "he is making difficulty in the order," "exciting disunion, discord and strife among brethren," etc. Slander is everywhere privately whispered against me by those who have not courage to utter it publicly; I am represented as acting under the influence of delusion, envy and revenge—and it seems to have become with some a righteous thing to prejudice as many as possible against me, that they may thereby hinder the circulation of my paper. Those people dread nothing so much as that Restorationism and its friends should have a full hearing.

The editor of the *Trumpet*, finding that this publication would inevitably issue, has latterly proclaimed himself a man of peace, a friend of union, concord and good fellowship; and with grave professions of devoting his paper to the interests of the "whole order," calls upon all to sustain him. He deprecates disunion among Universalists, and warns them against the emissaries of discord. It were well if men like him and others, who are such friends of union and good feeling, had always exercised that justice and moderation towards their brethren, which is the only basis and security of uninterrupted peace. . . .

With the help of God these columns will be devoted to an unfettered discussion of the doctrines which divide ancient and modern Universalists. Through them I shall assign to the world the reasons which have led me to reject the interpretations of Scripture, doctrines, opinions etc. of the ultras; and whosoever reads it will in due time know whether Restorationism is susceptible of self defense or not. But never as its editor will I treat my opponents with the injustice of prohibiting them an opportunity to defend themselves on any point wherein I assail them. And if I lay unsparing hands in the way of review upon all influential modern Universalist writings—if I oppose them ever so strenuously, they shall find me as honorable, open and fair an opponent as I am severe and uncompromising.

SOURCE: Adin Ballou, "Epistle General to Restorationists," *Independent Messenger*, January 1, 1831.

"Author's Preface to the Fifth Edition
of A *Treatise on Atonement*"

1832

Hosea Ballou (1771–1852) published A Treatise on Atonement *as a young man and continued to revise it throughout his career. In this preface to the fifth edition, he highlighted the two major ways in which his theology had developed: He was now fully convinced that all souls go directly to heaven after death, and he embraced the Socinian or Priestleyan view of Jesus Christ as an ordinary human being rather than a semi-divine person who was created prior to the creation of the material world.*

—Dan McKanan

As this edition of the treatise on atonement, in several respects, varies from former editions, the author feels that he owes it to the public to offer some reason for such variations.

It has pleased God to continue his life, until this work has passed through four editions, with all the imperfections which it contained when first published, nearly thirty years ago. For a number of years he has seen reasons to doubt the correctness of some of the opinions which he entertained at the time he wrote the work; and also the propriety of the use he then made of certain passages of scripture.

* * *

But be it known, and duly considered, that in no particular has the author's views, undergone any change unfavorable to the main doctrine, to the support of which the treatise was devoted.

The main points, in relation to which his views now differ from those he entertained when he first wrote the following work, relate to the pre-existence of Christ, of man's existence before his corporeal organization; and the application of some passages of scripture *solely* to the purifying operations of divine truth in man's understanding which passages he now believes embraced, in their true sense, all the temporal judgments with which a most perverse and wicked generation was visited.

Although he as fully believed in the dependence of Christ on his God and Father, as he now does, he entertained the opinion that he had a sentinent [sic] existence before he was manifested in flesh; and he then thought that certain passages of scripture evidently supported that opinion. These passages, though they seem to favor such a sentiment, do not appear altogether sufficient, fully to warrant the belief of it. Could the opinion now be fully supported that Christ existed in a sentinent state before he was manifested in the flesh, it would not be difficult to yield to a belief that Adam also had an existence before he was formed of the dust of the ground. However these things are, in fact, they now appear to the author as points of mere speculation, much too obscure to be laid down as matters of faith. . . .

To the foregoing it may be proper to add, that the doctrine of a future disciplinary state, and the application of certain passages of scripture to that state of suffering which were left in suspense, undecided, in the treatise originally, were so left on account of the author's mind being then undecided in relation to these subjects. He was, however, as well convinced then as now, that the doctrine of a future retribution could be supported on no other hypothesis than that of the continuance of sin in a future state; but he was not then so fully satisfied, that all which the scriptures say about sin, and the punishment of it, relates solely to this mortal state as he now is.

SOURCE: Hosea Ballou, "The Author's Preface to the Fifth Edition," *A Treatise on Atonement* (Boston, 1832), 11–12.

RALPH WALDO EMERSON
"The Lord's Supper"
1832

Following the death of his wife in 1831, Ralph Waldo Emerson (1803–1882) began having second thoughts about the ministry. He had come to reject the Christian scheme of redemption and felt constrained by the traditional role of the minister. "I have sometimes thought that in order to be a good minister it was necessary to leave the ministry," he confided to his journal at the time. "The profession is antiquated. In an altered age, we worship in the dead forms of our forefathers." He went on to insist that religion is neither belief nor ritual but life: "It is not something else to be got, to be added, but is a new life of those faculties you have." Emerson resigned his position as minister of Boston's Second Church, in part because of conscientious scruples about serving communion. Yet he remained, in James Freeman Clarke's estimation, "essentially a preacher to the end of his days." Suggested reading: J. Frank Schulman, "Emerson and the Ministry," Minns Lectures, 1983; David Robinson, Apostle of Culture: Emerson as Preacher and Lecturer *(Philadelphia: University of Pennsylvania Press, 1982).*

— Barry Andrews

In the history of the Church no subject has been more fruitful of controversy than the Lord's Supper. There never has been any unanimity in the understanding of its nature nor any uniformity in the mode of celebrating it. Without considering the frivolous questions which have been hotly debated as to the posture in which men should partake or whether mixed or unmixed wine should be served, whether leavened or unleavened bread should be broken, the questions have been settled differently in every church, who should be admitted to partake, and how often it should be prepared. . . .

Having recently paid particular attention to this subject, I was led to the conclusion that Jesus did not intend to establish an institution for perpetual observance when he ate the passover with his disciples; and, further to the opinion that it is not expedient to celebrate it as we do. . . .

Now observe the facts. Two of the evangelists (namely, Matthew and John) were of the twelve disciples and were present on that occasion. Neither of them drops the slightest intimation of any intention on the part of Jesus to set up any thing permanent. John especially, the beloved disciple, who has recorded with minuteness the conversation and the transactions of that memorable evening, has quite omitted such a notice.

Neither did it come to the knowledge of Mark who relates the other facts. It is found in Luke alone, who was not present. . . .

Still we must suppose that the expression—This do in remembrance of me—had come to the ear of Luke from some disciple present. What did it really signify? It is a prophetic and an affectionate expression. Jesus is a Jew sitting with his countrymen celebrating their national feast. He thinks of his own impending death and wishes the minds of his disciples to be prepared for it and says to them, "When hereafter you shall keep the passover it will have an altered aspect in your eyes. . . ." I see natural feeling and beauty in the use of such language from Jesus, a friend to his friends. I can readily imagine that he was willing and desirous that when his disciples met, his memory should hallow their intercourse, but I cannot bring myself to believe that he looked beyond the living generation, beyond the abolition of the festival he was celebrating and the scattering of the nation, and meant to impose a memorial feast upon the whole world.

* * *

This mode of commemorating Christ is not suitable to me. That is reason enough why I should abandon it. If I believed that it was enjoined by Jesus on his disciples, and that he even contemplated to make permanent this mode of commemoration every way agreeable to an Eastern mind, and yet on trial it was disagreeable to my own feelings, I should not adopt it.

* * *

Freedom is the essence of Christianity. It has for its object simply to make men good and wise. Its institutions should be as flexible as the wants of men. That form out of which the life and suitableness have departed should be as worthless in its eyes as the dead leaves that are falling around us.

* * *

It is my desire, in the office of a Christian minister, to do nothing which I cannot do with my whole heart. Having said this, I have said all. I have no hostility to this institution. I am only stating my want of sympathy with it. Neither should I ever have obtruded this opinion upon other people, had I not been called by my office to administer it. That is the end of my opposition, that I am not interested in it. I am content that it stand to the end of the world if it please men and please heaven, and shall rejoice in all the good it produces.

As it is the prevailing opinion and feeling in our religious community that it is an indispensable part of the pastoral office to administer this ordinance, I am about to resign into your hands that office which you have confided to me. It has many duties for which I am feebly qualified. It has some which it will always be my delight to discharge according to my ability wherever I exist. And whilst the thought of its claims oppresses me with a sense of my unworthiness, I am consoled by the hope that no time and no change can deprive me of the satisfaction of pursuing and exercising its highest functions.

SOURCE: Ralph Waldo Emerson, "CLXII," in *The Complete Sermons of Ralph Waldo Emerson*, ed. Wesley T. Mott (Columbia: University of Missouri Press, 1992), 4:185–87, 192–94.

An Appeal in Favor of that Class of Americans Called Africans

1833

Lydia Maria Child (1802–1880) was an influential writer, editor, abolition-ist, and anti-racist. Inspired by her friendships with Indian neighbors, Child protested the country's disregard for Indians' land rights and became a best-selling author with the publication of her novel Hobomok *about the mar-riage of a Puritan woman and an Indian man. As a self-supporting woman, she was left in financial ruin when sales plummeted after the publication of her* Appeal in Favor of that Class of Americans Called Africans, *which documented the horrors of slavery, urged emancipation, and argued that the North was even more racist than the South. However, Child continued to write prolifically on antiracist themes and edited the* National Anti-Slavery Standard *for two years. Several abolitionist leaders, including Wendell Phil-lips and Charles Sumner, credited her with converting them to the cause. After emancipation she sought to help freedpeople become recognized as fully equal American citizens. Further Reading: Carolyn Karcher,* The First Woman in the Republic: A Cultural Biography of Lydia Maria Child *(Durham, NC: Duke University Press, 1994); Lori Kenschaft,* Lydia Maria Child: The Quest for Racial Justice *(New York: Oxford University Press, 2002).*

—Lori Kenschaft

In almost all great evils there is some redeeming feature—*some* good results, even where it is not intended. . . . But slavery is *all* evil—within and without—root and branch,—bud, blossom and fruit!

In order to show how dark it is in every aspect—how invariably injurious both to nations and individuals,—I will select a few facts from the mass of evidence now before me.

In the first place, its effects upon *Africa* have been most disastrous. . . . The soil of Africa is rich in native productions, and honorable commerce might have been a blessing to her, to Europe, and to America; but instead of that a trade has been sub-stituted, which operates like a withering curse, upon all concerned in it.

* * *

We will now follow the poor *slave* through his wretched wanderings, in order to give some idea of his physical suffering, his mental, and moral degradation.

Husbands are torn from their wives, children from their parents, while the air is filled with the shrieks and lamentations of the bereaved. . . .

The poor wretches are stowed by hundred, like bales of goods, between the low decks, where filth and putrid air produce disease, madness, and suicide. Unless they die in *great* numbers, the slave captain does not even concern himself enough to fret.

*   *   *

We next come to the influence of this diabolical system on the *slave-owner*; and here I shall be cautioned that I am treading on delicate ground, because our own countrymen are slaveholders. But I am yet to learn that wickedness is any better for being our own.—Let the truth be spoken . . .

The following is the testimony of Jefferson, who had good opportunities for observation, and who certainly had no New-England prejudices: "There must, doubtless, be an unhappy influence on the manners of the people, produced by the existence of slavery amongst us. The whole commerce between master and slave is a perpetual exercise of the most boisterous passions; the most unremitting despotism on the one part, and degrading submission on the other. . . . The man must be a prodigy, who can retain his morals and manners undepraved in such circumstances."

In a community where all labor is done by one class, there must of course be another class, who live in indolence; and we all know how much people that have nothing to do are tempted by what the world calls pleasures; the result is, that slave-holding states and colonies are proverbial for dissipation. Hence too the contempt for industry, which prevails in such a state of society. Where none work but slaves, usefulness becomes degradation.

*   *   *

The negro woman is unprotected either by law or public opinion. She is the property of her master, and her daughters are his property. They are allowed to have no conscientious scruples, no sense of shame, no regard for the feelings of husband, or parent; they must be entirely subservient to the will of their owner, on pain of being whipped as near unto death as will comport with his interest, or quite to death, if it suit his pleasure.

Those who know human nature would be able to conjecture the unavoidable result, even if it were not betrayed by the amount of mixed population. Think for a moment, what a degrading effect must be produced on the morals of both blacks and whites by customs like these!

Considering we live in the nineteenth century, it is indeed a strange state of society where the father sells his child, and the brother puts his sister up at auction!

*   *   *

It is commonly urged against emancipation that white men cannot possibly labor under the sultry climate of our most Southerly states. This is a good reason for not sending the slaves out of the country, but it is no argument against making them free. No doubt we need their labor; but we ought to pay for it. Why should their presence be any more disagreeable as hired laborers, than as slaves? In Boston, we continually meet colored people in the streets, and employ them in various ways, without being endangered, or even incommoded. There is no moral impossibility in a perfectly kind and just relation between the two races.

*   *   *

The constant threat of the slave-holding States is the dissolution of the Union; and they have repeated it with all the earnestness of sincerity, though there are powerful reasons why it would not be well for them to venture upon that untried state of being. In one respect only, are these threats of any consequence—they have familiarized the public mind with the subject of separation, and diminished the reverence, with which the free States have hitherto regarded the Union.

*   *   *

In order to decide what is our duty concerning the Africans and their descendants, we must first clearly make up our minds whether they are, or are not, human beings—whether they have, or have not, the same capacities for improvement as other men.

The intellectual inferiority of the negroes is a common, though most absurd apology, for personal prejudice, and the oppressive inequality of the laws; for this reason, I shall take some pains to prove that the present degraded condition of that unfortunate race is produced by artificial causes, not by the laws of nature.

In the first place, naturalists are universally agreed concerning "the identity of the *human* type;" by which they mean that all living creatures, that can, by any process, be enabled to perceive moral and intellectual truths, are characterized *by similar peculiarities of organization*. They may differ from each other widely, but they still belong to the same class.

*   *   *

While we bestow our earnest disapprobation on the system of slavery, let us not flatter ourselves that we are in reality any better than our brethren of the South. Thanks to our soil and climate, and the early exertions of the Quakers, the *form* of slavery does not exist among us; but the very *spirit* of the hateful and mischievous thing is here in all its strength. The manner in which we use what power we have, gives us ample reason to be grateful that the nature of our institutions does not intrust us with more. Our prejudice against colored people is even more inveterate than it is at the South. The planter is often attached to his negroes, and lavishes caresses and kind words upon them, as he would on a favorite hound: but our cold-hearted, ignoble prejudice admits of no exception—no intermission.

The Southerners have long continued habit, apparent interest and dreaded danger, to palliate the wrong they do; but we stand without excuse. They tell us that

246

Northern ships and Northern capital have been engaged in this wicked business; and the reproach is true. Several fortunes in this city have been made by the sale of negro blood. If these criminal transactions are still carried on, they are done in silence and secrecy, because public opinion has made them disgraceful. But if the free States wished to cherish the system of slavery forever, they could not take a more direct course than they now do. Those who are kind and liberal on all other subjects, unite with the selfish and the proud in their unrelenting efforts to keep the colored population in the lowest state of degradation; and the influence they unconsciously exert over children early infuses into their innocent minds the same strong feelings of contempt. . . .

In the first place, an unjust law exists in this Commonwealth, by which marriages between persons of different color is pronounced illegal. I am perfectly aware of the gross ridicule to which I may subject myself by alluding to this particular; but I have lived too long, and observed too much, to be disturbed by the world's mockery. In the first place, the government ought not to be invested with power to control the affections, any more than the consciences of citizens. A man has at least as good a right to choose his wife, as he has to choose his religion.

* * *

A fierce excitement prevailed, not long since, because a colored man had bought a pew in one of our churches. I heard a very kind-hearted and zealous democrat declare his opinion that "the fellow ought to be turned out by constables, if he dared to occupy the pew he had purchased." Even at the communion-table, the mockery of human pride is mingled with the worship of Jehovah. Again and again have I seen a solitary negro come up to the altar, meekly and timidly, after all the white communicants had retired.

* * *

It merely requires an earnest wish to overcome a prejudice, which has "grown with our growth and strengthened with our strength," but which is in fact opposed to the spirit of our religion, and contrary to the instinctive good feelings of our nature. When examined by the clear light of reason, it disappears. Prejudices of all kinds have their strongest olds in the minds of the vulgar and the ignorant. In a community so enlightened as our own, they must gradually melt away under the influence of public discussion. There is no want of kind feelings and liberal sentiments in the American people; the simple fact is, they have not *thought* upon this subject.—An active and enterprising community are not apt to concern themselves about laws and customs, which do not obviously interfere with their interests or convenience; and various political and prudential motives have combined to fetter free inquiry in this direction. Thus we have gone on, year after year, thoughtlessly sanctioning, by our silence and indifference, evils which our hearts and consciences are far enough from approving.

It has been shown that no other people on earth indulge so strong a prejudice with regard to color, as we do.

*　*　*

Pride will doubtless hold out with strength and adroitness against the besiegers of its fortress; but it is an obvious truth that the condition of the world is rapidly improving, and that our laws and customs must change with it.

Neither ancient nor modern history furnishes a page more glorious than the last twenty years in England; for at every step, free principles, after a long and arduous struggle, have conquered selfishness and tyranny. Almost all great evils are resisted by individuals who directly suffer injustice or inconvenience from them; but it is a peculiar beauty of the abolition cause that its defenders enter the lists against wealth, and power, and talent, not to defend their own rights, but to protect weak and injured neighbors, who are not allowed to speak for themselves.

Those, who have become interested in a cause laboring so heavily under the pressure of present unpopularity, must expect to be assailed by every form of bitterness and sophistry. At times, discouraged and heart-sick, they will perhaps begin to doubt whether there are in reality any unalterable principles of right and wrong. But let them cast aside the fear of man, and keep their minds fixed on a few of the simple, unchangeable laws of God, and they will certainly receive strength to contend with the adversary.

SOURCE: Lydia Maria Child, *An Appeal in Favor of that Class of Americans Called Africans* (Boston, 1833), 3, 6–7, 17–19, 102, 125, 155, 208–209, 217, 222–24.

"Remember the Slave"
1834

Eliza Lee Cabot Follen (1787–1860) was the daughter of a prominent Boston family, a friend of novelist Catharine Sedgwick, and a Sunday school teacher at William Ellery Channing's Federal Street Church. In 1828, she married the German political refugee Charles Theodore Christian Follen, a Harvard professor and Unitarian minister with whom she shared a strong abolitionist commitment. Though Follen's best-remembered work may be "Three Little Kittens Who Lost Their Mittens," she also wrote extensively on slavery and social justice. "Remember the Slave" exemplifies the sentimental worldview of liberal reformers. She sought to elicit sympathy for enslaved persons by reminding her readers of their own family ties and vulnerability to suffering. Further Reading: Dan McKanan, Identifying the Image of God: Radical Christians and Nonviolent Power in the Antebellum United States *(New York: Oxford University Press, 2002).*

—Dan McKanan

Mother, when around your child
You clasp your arms in love,
And when with grateful joy you raise
Your eyes to God above,—

Think of the negro mother, when
Her child is torn away,
Sold for a little slave,—oh then
For that poor mother pray!

Father, whene'er your happy boys
You look upon with pride,
And pray to see them, when you're old,
All blooming by your side;—

Think of that father's wither'd heart,
The father of a slave,
Who asks a pitying God to give
His little son a grave.

Brothers and sisters! who with joy
Meet round the social hearth,
And talk of home and happy days,
And laugh in careless mirth; —

Remember too the poor young slave
Who never felt your joy;
Who, early old, has never known
The bliss to be a boy.

Ye Christians! ministers of him
Who came to make men free,
When at the Almighty Maker's throne,
You bend the suppliant knee; —

From the deep fountains of your soul,
Then let your prayers ascend,
For the poor slave, who hardly knows
That God is still his friend.

Let all who know that God is just,
That Jesus came to save,
Unite in the most holy cause
Of the forsaken slave!

SOURCE: Eliza Lee Cabot Follen, "Remember the Slave," in Lydia Maria Child, ed., *The Oasis* (Boston, 1834), 19–20.

Speech Delivered before the Supreme Court of the City of Boston

1834

Abner Kneeland (1774–1844) was the last man jailed for blasphemy in the United States. Raised in Massachusetts, he was converted to Universalism by the writings of Elhanan Winchester and then to both unitarianism and ultra-universalism by his personal friendship with Hosea Ballou. He was a prominent denominational leader for two decades before gravitating to the freethinking socialism of Robert Owen and Frances Wright. As minister of Boston's Society of Free Enquirers and editor of the Boston Investigator, *Kneeland published scathing and satirical critiques of biblical Christianity, occasionally using sexually explicit language. He also engaged in ongoing debate with his former Universalist colleagues, writing to editor Thomas Whittemore that "Universalists believe in a god which I do not; but believe that their god, with all his moral attributes (aside from nature itself), is nothing more than a chimera of their own imagination." These words, coupled with his sexual and social radicalism, led to a trial for blasphemy in which both prosecutor and judge were Unitarians—hence Kneeland's sly argument that the Unitarian* Christian Examiner *had published an article as blasphemous as his own. Kneeland's speech in his own defense was both a plea for freedom of speech and an exposition of the pantheistic infidelity that critics of Ralph Waldo Emerson would soon see in the Divinity School Address. Emerson, Theodore Parker, Bronson Alcott, and George Ripley all signed the petition for Kneeland's pardon that was initiated by William Ellery Channing. Further Reading: Stephan Papa,* The Last Man Jailed for Blasphemy *(Franklin, NC: Trillium Books, 1998).*

—Dan McKanan

Gentlemen. It is not so much for myself that I shall plead, as it is for the cause of Truth, in which I profess to be engaged, and the Liberty of my country, both civil and religious, which I hold dearer to my heart for the sake of my children and posterity, than I do my own individual life.

I shall contend, gentlemen, that I have not, in any thing that I have either said or written, nor in any thing that I have published, (save in the choice of words in point of delicacy and taste) gone beyond the bounds of fair argument, honorable criticism, or justifiable satire and ridicule. And if I can show this to your satisfaction, gentlemen, as I have no doubt I shall, then I have no fears as to the result. But if christians, or those who call themselves such, are to be allowed the most unbridled latitude in speaking even of other christian sects, and more especially in speaking of unbelievers whom they term Atheists and Infidels, and unbelievers are not allowed to meet them on their own ground, and contend against them with their own weapons, then where is the liberty of speech and of the press? It is gone, or else it never has had any thing more than a mere name to live. If this be the case, in vain our fathers fought for American freedom; in vain have we attempted to rear a monument on yonder height in honor of one who fell at the very threshold of such a laudable struggle; we had better demolish than attempt to finish it, and convert its ruins into the tomb of *the genius of liberty!* . . .

As it respects the first article named in the indictment . . . I hope I shall be able to convince you what is literally the fact, that I never knew it. . . .

As it respects the second article, I expect to show that it has been misunderstood. . . .

As respects the third article, I shall prove by a document that was not introduced in either of the former trials, that I am not an Atheist; that I have not denied the existence of God, or of any thing else which does in reality exist; but have professed my belief in God, and in the only true God, in the very letter, for a part which, it is now attempted to prove me an Atheist. . . .

Gentlemen. Having proceeded thus far, the next thing to which I wish to call your attention, is the meaning of the word *blasphemy*. . . . It is the intention of the heart, and not the words spoken, that constitutes blasphemy. . . . My opinions may or may not be erroneous; but whether they are or are not, I come not here to defend them. I only come to defend my rights and privileges, which I hold in common with every free citizen of these United States and of this Commonwealth. . . .

Gentlemen. How often have your feelings and mine been mortified, by being reproached with the fact of our being the descendants of those who hung the witches; hung or banished the Quakers; and whipped or banished the Baptists? And will posterity, think ye, a century hence, think any better of us? . . .

I shall now call your attention to the third article named in the indictment.

This, gentlemen, is an article of my own. There is no mistake on my part about it. It means all that it was intended to mean, and it means nothing more; notwithstanding the grand jury, or whoever framed the indictment, the attorney of the commonwealth, and even the Court on the former trials, have all, not very ingenuously, as I think, tried to make it mean what was never intended by the writer, and what the words in fact do not mean. In proof of this, I shall now introduce my creed. . . .

I believe in the existence of a universe of suns and planets, among which there is one sun belonging to our planetary system; and that other suns, being more remote, are called stars; but that they are indeed suns to other planetary systems. I believe that the whole universe is NATURE, and that the word NATURE embraces the whole universe, and that God and Nature, so far as we can attach any rational idea to either, are perfectly synonymous terms. Hence, I am not an Atheist, but a Pantheist; that is, instead of believing there is no God, I believe that in the abstract, all is God; and that all power that is, is in God, and that there is no power except that which proceeds from God. I believe that there can be no will or intelligence where there is no sense, and no sense where there are no organs of sense; and hence sense, will, and intelligence, is the effect, and not the cause, of organization. I believe in all that logically results from these premises, whether good, bad or indifferent. Hence, I believe, that God is all in all; and that it is in God we live, move, and have our being; and that the whole duty of man consists in living as long as he can, and in promoting as much happiness as he can while he lives. . . .

Now, is this creed Atheism? And can a believer in this creed be an Atheist? Not in his own estimation, certainly, whatever he may be in the view of others. . . .

Now, gentlemen, let us see what there is in that wonderful line about which there has been so much said, and which is thought to have been so blasphemous. "Universalists believe in a god which I do not; but" &c. Four things are stated in that one line, all designed and intended at the time it was written, to prevent the construction which has been put upon it. . . .

First, observe the indefinite article *a*, "*a* god,' to distinguish it from all other similar gods. . . . Second, "*god*," written with a little *g*, and not begun with a capital, the same as in Judges vi. 31., where Joash says, "if he be a god, let him plead for himself." Third, the omission of a comma after the word god, for the purpose of showing that it was intended that the relative pronoun *which*, should agree with it. Fourth, the relative pronoun *which* is used, instead of *whom*, because we do not know of what gender an imaginary god is, and it was therefore put in the neuter gender.

* * *

Gentlemen. Look at me! What do you see or perceive in me that savors either of vice or malice? You see a man standing before you who is rising of sixty years of age; his head silvered over with the effects of sickness, of trouble, of labor, and of study; who now for the first time in his life, or under the first indictment, is arraigned before a human tribunal for a supposed high crime and misdemeanor—no less than an obscene and blasphemous libel against God. How can you suppose me even capable of being guilty of such an offence? Have I not proved to you that the God in whom I believe, lives in me and I in him? . . .

Little did those who were the cause of getting up this prosecution think where it might end. Little did they imagine that those who profess to be christians, and Christians of high standing too, would so soon publish an article which would cause the Attorney General to be called upon, as he has been in some of the public prints, to prosecute the publisher for the same offence. . . .

The article in the Christian Examiner, for July last, to which I allude, is more clearly within the law, I think, than any thing that I have published. It absolutely asserts that a great portion of the canonical scriptures are NOT the "Holy Word of God;" and also that Jesus Christ assumed a title and character that did not belong to him. What is this but reproaching the "canonical scriptures;" and also reproaching "Jesus Christ," or what is tantamount, of using dissimulation at least, not to say being an imposter? . . . But this comes from a source professedly christian, and therefore is suffered to pass with impunity.

*   *   *

In closing I must say, I feel more for the disgrace that this prosecution has already brought upon my native State, than all that I feel for myself, my children, or my posterity. Say what you will, posterity will view it in the same light as the most discerning view it now; that is, in the light of persecution. There has not been an argument used, nor is there any that can be used in favor of this prosecution, that could not as well be used on a trial for witchcraft. . . .

I wish you not to be biased by the opinions of other men, whether they were for me or against me, but to act your own judgment. Nothing remains for me now, but to thank the Attorney General, that he has permitted me to say all that I have thought it necessary to urge in my behalf; the Judge for his kind indulgence; and you for giving me such a patient and attentive hearing. And if the Shylocks of my accusers, whoever they may be, insist upon it, give them their pound of flesh! but at the same time warn them that if they draw one drop of blood from the life of the Constitution, the consequences may be more serious than they at present imagine.

SOURCE: *Speech of Abner Kneeland, Delivered before the Supreme Court of the City of Boston, in His Own Defence, on an Indictment for Blasphemy* (Boston: J. Q. Adams, 1834), 1–5, 16–17, 27–28, 30–31.

Record of a School

1835

Elizabeth Palmer Peabody (1804–1894) was a writer, educator, bookstore proprietor, publisher, and active participant in the Transcendentalist Movement. Her writings chronicle complex friendships with Channing, Emerson, Hawthorne, Horace Mann, Margaret Fuller, and others. When family financial difficulties forced her to work, she became a teacher, one of the few professions open to women. In 1834, she became Bronson Alcott's assistant at the experimental Temple School, which gave her the chance to apply her deeply held philosophical and religious ideas. Alcott's conversational methodology sought to cultivate the unfolding of the human soul, honoring the innate intellectual, religious, and moral capacities of the child. Although Peabody later fell out with Alcott and came to question some of his methods, she was initially captivated by his work and chronicled his conversations, practices, and events. The following year, Peabody published a detailed account of educational practices in Record of a School. *Further Reading: Megan Marshall,* The Peabody Sisters: Three Women Who Ignited American Romanticism *(Boston: Houghton Mifflin, 2005); Bruce A. Ronda,* Elizabeth Palmer Peabody: A Reformer on Her Own Terms *(Cambridge, MA: Harvard University Press, 1999).*

—Gail Forsyth-Vail

MR. ALCOTT re-commenced his school in Boston, after four years interval, September, 1834, at the Masonic Temple, No. 7.

Considering that the objects which meet the senses every day for years, must necessarily mould the mind, he felt it necessary to choose a spacious room, and ornament it, not with such furniture as only an upholsterer can appreciate, but with such forms as might address and cultivate the imagination and heart.

In the four corners of the room, therefore, Mr. Alcott placed upon pedestals, fine busts of Socrates, Shakspeare, Milton, and Sir Walter Scott. And on a table, before the large gothic window by which the room is lighted, the God of Silence, "with his finger up, as though he said, beware." Opposite this gothic window, is his own table, about ten feet long, whose front is the arc of a circle, and which is prepared with little desks for the convenience of scholars. On this table he placed a small figure of a child aspiring. Behind him is a very large bookcase, with closets below, a black tablet above, and two shelves filled with books. A fine cast of Christ, in basso-relievo, is fixed into this bookcase, so as to appear to the scholars just over Mr. Alcott's head. The bookcase itself is surmounted with a bust of Plato. On the northern side of the room, opposite the door, is the table of the assistant, with a small figure of Atlas, bending under the weight of the world. On a small bookcase behind the assistant's chair, are the figures of a child reading, and a child drawing. Two old pictures; one of Harding's portraits; and some maps hang on the walls. The desks for the scholars, with conveniences for placing all their books in sight, and with black tablets hung over them, which swing forward, when they wish to use them, are placed against the wall round the room, that when in their seats for study, no scholar need look at another. On the right hand of Mr. Alcott, is a sofa for the accommodation of visitors, and a small table, with a pitcher and bowl; and underneath the "table of sense," as this cold water table is called, is a small figure of Bacchus, riding on a barrel. Great advantages have been found to arise from this room; every part of which speaks the thoughts of Genius. It is a silent reproach upon rudeness.

About twenty children came the first day. They were all under ten years of age, excepting two or three girls. I became his assistant, to teach Latin to such as might desire to learn.

Mr. Alcott sat behind his table, and the children were placed in chairs, in a large arc around him; the chairs so far apart, that they could not easily touch each other. He then asked each one separately, what idea she or he had of the object of coming to school? To learn; was the first answer. To learn what? By pursuing this question, all the common exercises of school were brought up—successively—even philosophy. Still Mr. Alcott intimated that this was not all; and at last some one said "to behave well," and in pursuing this expression into its meanings, they at last decided that they came to learn to feel rightly, to think rightly, and to act rightly. A boy of seven years old suggested, and all agreed, that right actions were the most important of these three.

Simple as all this seems, it would hardly be believed what an evident exercise it was to these children, to be led of themselves to form and express these conceptions and few steps of reasoning. Every face was eager and interested. From right actions, the conversation naturally led into the means of bringing them out. And the necessity of feeling in earnest, of thinking clearly, and of school discipline, was talked over. School discipline was very carefully considered; Mr. Alcott's duty, and the children's individual duties, and the various means of producing attention, self-control, perseverance, faithfulness. Among these means, punishment was mentioned; and after a consideration of its nature and issues, they all very cheerfully agreed, that it was necessary, and that they preferred Mr. Alcott should punish them, rather than leave them in their faults, and that it was his duty to do so. Various punishments were mentioned, and hurting the body was decided upon, as necessary and desirable in some instances. It was universally admitted that it was desirable whenever words were found insufficient to command the memory of conscience. After this conversation, which involved many anecdotes, many supposed cases, and many judgments, Mr. Alcott read from Krummacher's fables, a story which involved the free action of three boys of different characters, and questioned them respecting their opinion of these boys, and the principles on which it was seen by analysis that they acted. Nearly three hours passed away in this conversation and reading; and then they were asked, how long they had been sitting? None of them guessed more than an hour. After recess Mr. Alcott heard them read; and after that, spell. All present could read in such a book as Miss Edgeworth's Frank. Then each was asked what he had learned, and having told, they were dismissed one by one. The whole effect of the day seemed to be a combination of quieting influences, with an awakening effect upon the heart and mind.

*   *   *

It was in pursuance of these ideas that Mr. Alcott took so much pains at first, to bring out clearly in the children's consciousness, a conception of the spiritual world, as alone having permanence and reality, not withstanding its invisibleness. And when he read, he constantly asked questions, calculated to keep attention on the ideas in the author's mind, that were clothed with imagery, and signed by words. So successful was he in fixing attention on the spiritual part of any matter, that not only the imagery of poetry, but every incident of a narrative was listened to with an air of thought and investigation, not always seen in adult hearers of reading. To illustrate this fact, I will make an extract in this place from the Journal of February 12th, when Mr. Alcott read from Krummacher, "the birth of the caterpillar."

What is in your mind? Said he, to a boy of eight years old, as soon as he had finished. I cannot express it, he replied. Is it a thought, or a feeling? — Both — it is a belief. What have you learned from this story? said Mr. Alcott to another boy of the same age. It reminds me that when the body dies the soul will live and go to heaven. How long have you had that thought? Ever since I was four years old. Do you remember the time when you did not have it? Yes, when I was very little I thought we did not live after our bodies died. Another boy of the same age said, he never remembered the time when he did not believe in life's going on. Do all believe without a shadow of doubt that they shall live after death has taken place? I believe it, said a boy of nine, but not without a shadow of doubt. A boy of six said, when we die, an angel comes from heaven, and takes us — the shell and all. What is the shell? said Mr. Alcott. The body, said another child of the same age. Do you want to stay in your bodies a-while? Yes, said both, with a smile. What did you think while I was reading this story? said Mr. Alcott to a thoughtful little boy of five. I thought God changed the caterpillar into a butterfly, and then there was an angel that went in, and ascended into heaven, and when it got to heaven the butterfly's body fell again to the earth. But

257

where did the butterfly come from? God changed the caterpillar into a butterfly; the body of the caterpillar was changed into the form of a butterfly. Who made the caterpillar? God. What did God make it of? He made it out of dust. Nothing but dust? Nothing but dust. When did the angel go into the butterfly? When it began to move. Where did the angel come from? I did not think—I must stop to think, said he. In a minute he went on. The angel must have been in the worm—some of it. Where did the angel come from? God sent it. Did the angel help to make the caterpillar into a butterfly? No, but God made the body of the caterpillar into the body of a butterfly, and covered over the angel with it. You see it was not a real butterfly but it seemed so to the eyes. It was made to carry the angel up to heaven with its wings. Do you think every butterfly has an angel in it, like that one? Oh no! Well how came it to be so, that particular time? Why God wanted to show Adam and all of them, an angel going to heaven, and he could not do it without something for their eyes. Why did he want to show them an angel going to heaven? Oh! so that they need not mourn any longer for their brother Abel. I think, said I, that God means to put us in mind of the soul's going to heaven by every butterfly that he makes. *Do you?* said he very slowly, his thoughtful countenance lighting up into a bright smile. (Is not that a mind in the kingdom? said Mr. Alcott to me, after this conversation was over.) What does this story bring to your mind? said he to a girl of twelve. The life of the senses—the change of death—and immortality. In the Bible some one says, *I die daily:*—do you understand that? Yes—It means you daily go more and more away from the senses, into the inward life.

SOURCE: Elizabeth Palmer Peabody, *Record of a School: Exemplifying the General Principles of Spiritual Culture* (Boston: James Munroe, 1835), 1–3, 10–11.

RALPH WALDO EMERSON

Nature

1836

His first published work, Emerson's Nature *is a manifesto of the Transcendentalist movement. It is an example of what Carlyle termed "natural supernaturalism," or the substitution of nature for the Bible as the source of revelation. As Emerson expresses it, "the noblest ministry of nature is to stand as an apparition of God." In moments of rapture, "the currents of Universal Being" circulate through us and we feel that we are part and parcel of the whole. As it stands, however, we are estranged from nature. We relate to it in a utilitarian manner, mastering it "by a penny-wisdom." The problem lies in our lack of perception. As Emerson writes, "The ruin or blank that we see when we look at nature is in our own eye." However, with new eyes we may come to see not a dualism but a unity. Emerson was convinced that a resolution of this dichotomy would be tantamount to a revolution in all areas of life. Further Reading: Robert D. Richardson, Jr., "Emerson and Nature,"* in The Cambridge Companion to Ralph Waldo Emerson, *ed. Joel Porte and Saundra Morris (New York: Cambridge University Press, 1999), 97–105;* David Robinson, Apostle of Culture: Emerson as Preacher and Lecturer *(Philadelphia: University of Pennsylvania Press, 1982).*

—Barry Andrews

Introduction

Our age is retrospective. It builds the sepulchres of the fathers. It writes biographies, histories, and criticism. The foregoing generations beheld God and nature face to face; we, through their eyes. Why should not we also enjoy an original relation to the universe? Why should not we have a poetry and philosophy of insight and not of tradition, and a religion by revelation to us, and not the history of theirs? Embosomed for a season in nature, whose floods of life stream around and through us, and invite us by the powers they supply, to action proportioned to nature, why should we grope among the dry bones of the past, or put the living generation into masquerade out of its faded wardrobe? The sun shines to-day also. There is more wool and flax in the fields. There are new lands, new men, new thoughts. Let us demand our own works and laws and worship.

✳ ✳ ✳

Nature

To speak truly, few adult persons can see nature. Most persons do not see the sun. At least they have a very superficial seeing. . . . The lover of nature is he whose inward and outward senses are still truly adjusted to each other; who has retained the spirit of infancy even into the era of manhood. His intercourse with heaven and earth, becomes part of his daily food. In the presence of nature, a wild delight runs through the man, in spite of real sorrows. Nature says,—he is my creature, and maugre all his impertinent griefs, he shall be glad with me. . . . Crossing a bare common, in snow puddles, at twilight, under a clouded sky, without having in my thoughts any occurrence of special good fortune, I have enjoyed a perfect exhilaration. Almost I fear to think how glad I am. In the woods, too, a man casts off his years, as the snake its slough, and at what period soever of life, is always a child. In the woods, is perpetual youth. Within these plantations of God, a decorum and sanctity reign, a perennial festival is dressed, and the guest sees not how he should tire of them in a thousand years. In the woods, we return to reason and faith. There I feel that nothing can befal me in life,—no disgrace, no calamity, (leaving me my eyes,) which nature cannot repair. Standing on the bare ground,—my head bathed by the blithe air, and uplifted into infinite space,—all mean egotism vanishes. I become a transparent eye-ball. I am nothing. I see all. The currents of the Universal Being circulate through me; I am part or particle of God. The name of the nearest friend sounds then foreign and accidental. To be brothers, to be acquaintances,—master or servant, is then a trifle and a disturbance. I am the lover of uncontained and immortal beauty. In the wilderness, I find something more dear and connate than in streets or villages. In the tranquil landscape, and especially in the distant line of the horizon, man beholds somewhat as beautiful as his own nature.

The greatest delight which the fields and woods minister, is the suggestion of an occult relation between man and the vegetable. . . .

Yet it is certain that the power to produce this delight, does not reside in nature, but in man, or in a harmony of both.

✻ ✻ ✻

Spirit

But when, following the invisible steps of thought, we come to inquire, Whence is matter? and Whereto? many truths arise to us out of the recesses of consciousness. We learn that the highest is present to the soul of man, that the dread universal essence, which is not wisdom, or love, or beauty, or power, but all in one, and each entirely, is that for which all things exist, and that by which they are; that spirit creates; that behind nature, throughout nature, spirit is present; that spirit is one and not compound; that spirit does not act upon us from without, that is, in space and time, but spiritually, or through ourselves. Therefore, that spirit, that is, the Supreme

260

Being, does not build up nature around us, but puts it forth through us, as the life of the tree puts forth new branches and leaves through the pores of the old. As a plant upon the earth, so a man rests upon the bosom of God; he is nourished by unfailing fountains, and draws, at his need, inexhaustible power. Who can set bounds to the possibilities of man? Once inhale the upper air, being admitted to behold the absolute natures of justice and truth, and we learn that man has access to the entire mind of the Creator, is himself the creator in the finite.

* * *

Prospects

At present, man applies to nature but half his force. He works on the world with his understanding alone. He lives in it, and masters it by a penny-wisdom; and he that works most in it, is but a half-man, and whilst his arms are strong and his digestion good, his mind is imbruted, and he is a selfish savage. His relation to nature, his power over it, is through the understanding; as by manure; the economic use of fire, wind, water, and the mariner's needle; steam, coal, chemical agriculture; the repairs of the human body by the dentist and the surgeon. . . .

The problem of restoring to the world original and eternal beauty is solved by the redemption of the soul. The ruin or the blank, that we see when we look at nature, is in our own eye. The axis of vision is not coincident with the axis of things, and so they appear not transparent but opake. The reason why the world lacks unity, and lies broken and in heaps, is, because man is disunited with himself. He cannot be a naturalist until he satisfies all the demands of the spirit. . . .

So shall we come to look at the world with new eyes. . . . Then shall come to pass what my poet said; "Nature is not fixed but fluid. Spirit alters, moulds, makes it. The immobility or bruteness of nature, is the absence of spirit; to pure spirit, it is fluid, it is volatile, it is obedient. Every spirit builds itself a house; and beyond its house, a world; and beyond its world, a heaven. Know then, that the world exists for you. For you is the phenomenon perfect. What we are, that only can we see. All that Adam had, all that Caesar could, you have and can do. Adam called his house, heaven and earth; Caesar called his house, Rome; you perhaps call yours, a cobler's trade; a hundred acres of ploughed land; or a scholar's garret. Yet line for line and point for point, your dominion is as great as theirs, though without fine names. Build, therefore, your own world. As fast as you conform your life to the pure idea in your mind, that will unfold its great proportions. A correspondent revolution in things will attend the influx of the spirit. . . ."

SOURCE: Ralph Waldo Emerson, *Nature, The Collected Works of Ralph Waldo Emerson* (Cambridge, MA: Harvard University Press, 1971), 1:7, 9–10, 38, 42–45.

ADIN BALLOU

A Discourse on the Subject of American Slavery

1837

When Adin Ballou was expelled from his Universalist pulpit in Milford, Massachusetts, in 1830, he was almost immediately invited to commence a new ministry with the Unitarian church in nearby Mendon. Along with a number of other Restorationist ministers, he found himself with at least one foot in the Unitarian denomination. While some university-trained Unitarians despised self-taught Universalists, one group of Unitarian ministers, mostly settled to the west of Boston, welcomed the Restorationists and warmly extended fellowship. Among these was Samuel J. May, an ardent abolitionist and pacifist, who introduced Ballou to William Lloyd Garrison. In 1837, having retired from the future punishment controversy, Ballou came out openly as an abolitionist. He took the first opportunity to make an important statement against slavery in this Fourth of July speech delivered in Mendon. Further Reading: Adin Ballou, The Autobiography of Adin Ballou, 1803–1890 *(Lowell, MA, 1896); Donald Yacovone,* Samuel Joseph May and the Dilemmas of the Liberal Persuasion, 1797–1871 *(Philadelphia: Temple University Press, 1991).*

—Peter Hughes

I need not inform you that a *remedy* has been proposed and is now before the people of this Union for consideration. I need not inform you that though the great majority of the nation, have as yet disdained seriously to discuss the merits of the remedial proposition, it has been warmly embraced by thousands of Christians, philanthropists and patriots. That proposed remedy, which is, *immediate emancipation of all the enthralled slaves,* has commended itself to my understanding and conscience as the only *just, safe, practicable,* effectual one for this horrible malady. If, however, a better can be proposed, I shall be happy to adopt it. But all the lights of divine revelation, reason, history and experience, concur in my mind, to establish the conclusion, that this is the *remedy sought.* It was the privilege of thousands of enlightened and generous spirits to embrace this proposition, before the light of its excellency illuminated my darker mind. It is no doubt equally true, that other thousands of illustrious men, at whose feel it might become such an one as myself to sit for instruction, remain to be convinced of what appears to me unquestionable truth. But I am

262

persuaded that all the truly wise and good will ultimately come to the one conclusion. Under this impression, I cannot understand why there should be so much reluctance, in some of the high places of religion and learning, to come manfully to the investigation of this question. It must be met. Something must be done. And the least that any man, however doubtful he may be, can with propriety do, is to promote discussion and research. Without these the progress of human improvement never has been and never can be sustained.

And now, lest you should not clearly understand the terms and application of the proposed remedy for slavery—*Immediate* Emancipation—I will explain. You have observed, that the slavery of the United States, is not the mere creature of chance and lawless custom; but the long since adopted child of statute enactments. It is asserted, sanctioned, and guarantied on every side, by legislative and judicial authority. Chance and usage, without express law, gave birth to and sustained it for a while. But now the iron bond of constitutional, legal and judicial prescription maintains its dreadful ascendancy. If slavery were now, as at first in this country, only the tolerated creature of accident, resting wholly on primary public opinion and usage, the task of its abolition would be comparatively easy. But, as matters now stand, the most unjust and anti-christian laws must be repealed—laws which are deeply rooted in a corrupt public opinion. We have not only to persuade masters to free their slaves, but also to get the consent of the body politic, in the form of law. We cannot go to the slave and invite him to be a man, and act like a man; but we are first obliged to procure the repeal of a host of laws, which declare him and his posterity mere animal property. There is no chance for him to rise, till the pressure of an unrighteous legislation is taken off. The fundamental particulars of immediate emancipation are these:—

1. The restoration of manhood to the slave. He is now brute property, divested of all the necessary attributes of an intelligent soul. Let all those laws, which declare and hold the slave such property, be immediately repealed; and let him be legally re-converted into, what he is by nature, a *human being*. Give him a chance to rise, if he *will*—and give his friends a chance to make something of him, if they *can*. This is laying the axe at the root of the tree.

2. Let all those laws, which make the slave incapable of marriage, be immediately repealed, and others enacted in their stead, establishing the marriage relation, with all its rights and sanctions. Then would families be organized, and a home created; and all the conjugal, parental and filial obligations of religion, would be brought to bear upon the colored population.

3. Let all those laws, which exclude the slaves from the lights of education and moral instruction, be immediately repealed. And let others be enacted in their stead, providing every possible means for their enlightenment in useful knowledge, religion and morals.

4. Let all those laws, which declare slaves incapable of receiving, acquiring, holding and bequeathing property, be immediately blotted from the statute book. And let other laws be passed, encouraging them to industry and economy, and securing them in the possession of all their honest earnings.

5. Let all those laws, which incapacitate the slave to petition the civil authorities for redress under his wrongs—and all those laws which exclude his testimony against white persons—and all those laws which deny him the right to bring actions at law—and all those laws which expose him to be tried by prejudiced and interested judges—be immediately abolished. And in lieu of them, let laws be enacted, guaranteeing to all men, without exception, the right of petition, the right of giving testimony, the right of suing at the bar of public justice, and the right of an impartial trial under accusation.

6. Let all laws, which make any distinction between men, on account of their color, or any similar imaginary incapacitation, be immediately abolished. And let there be one common level of merit and demerit, of qualification and disqualification, for *all*. Let worth be deemed to "make the *man*, and want of it the *fellow*." If a black, red, or white person, is *non compos*, let him be provided for as such. If a black, red or white person needs to be instructed, or needs to be put under guardianship, or needs to be withholden from the exercise of the elective franchise, or is really disqualified for office, let one law of justice and equity answer for all. If a black, red, or white person, becomes a nuisance in society, or violates the wholesome laws of the State, or any how deservedly incurs punishment, let there be one law, and one course of treatment for *all*, without respect of persons, and with *sole* respect to those considerations, which divine justice takes into account in its awards. So on the other hand, let the privilege of electing and being elected to office, be conferred on all the truly worthy, according to some scale of even-handed justice. If one man is more meritorious than another, has more real worth and capacity than another, let honor be rendered to whom honor is due.

*   *   *

Obj. 8. The negroes are an inferior race. They are incapable of freedom and civil government. It is of no use to attempt their improvement. They are fit only for a state of slavery.

Ans. I pity the man who can seriously urge such an objection as this. I must deem his head or his heart, or both, disordered. It is but the groundless assertion of men, who themselves need a guardian, or a keeper. A thousand historical facts, a thousand facts of our own times, the contrivances of the slave system to prevent the rise of its victims, reason, revelation, and observation, are all against this insane conclusion. The Africans are *men*—created by the same God, and of one blood with ourselves. They are capable of respectable attainments in all the arts, sciences, and

264

morals of civilized life. Jesus Christ died for them, as well as for us. Heaven is as accessible to them as to us. They will stand before the same judgment-seat with us, before a Judge, who will give the master no preference over his slave. If the degradation of slavery has sunk the colored people of our country below their natural level, and *ever* so far below *us*, *that* is no reason why we should add wrong to wrong, by treading them still deeper in the mire. On the other hand, it is a good reason, why we should undo our wrongs, and endeavor to restore their broken nature to soundness. I disdain to go into arguments showing our obligations to provide for, protect, instruct, encourage, reform and elevate these our unfortunate brethren. This is too plain to require argument. And we may rest assured, that we can never discharge our obligations, nor accomplish any thing to the purpose, without first terminating slavery.

✻ ✻ ✻

Obj. 11. If the blacks must be emancipated, let them be shipped off to their own country. Let them go where they belong; we do not want them here; the two races can never dwell together; send them to Africa and let them civilize it.

Ans. Although such emigrants would hardly be qualified for the work of civilization; yet we have no objection to their colonizing Africa, if they please. They have the same liberty to go to Africa, that their European brethren have to go to Europe; and probably they would carry as much human improvement into their father continent, as their masters would into theirs.

But, say you, "Let them be shipped off, whether they are willing or not—send them home—we have had enough of them." You mean, that having extorted from them all we can, and stripped them of every thing but life, we have no further use for them. Very generous and kind, indeed! Where did we learn such a morality as this? The southern landholders, however, tell us, that if we take away their blacks, we shall also take away their country, since the blacks *only* can cultivate the soil. Perhaps, we had better retain enough to do their work, at fair wages. And as for the rest, they are as much in their own country, as we are. They are not Aboriginal Americans; neither are we. Their ancestors came from Africa, ours from Europe; and *here*, we are in the red man's country. If there is to be any shipping off without consent, we had better let the Indian say who shall be sent home. I dare say he would colonize Europe quite as liberally as we would Africa. At all events, he would be justified in making room to spread his blanket and dig him a grave, among the bones of his progenitors. My friends, when we look at it, just as it is, there is something quite as ludicrous as there is wicked, in this notion of transporting the colored people to their *own country*. No man can reflect a moment, without seeing that *this* is as much *their* country as ours; that Europe is as much our home as Africa is theirs; and that there is no more justice in shipping them to *their* father land, than in shipping their master's to *theirs*. We had better make up our minds "to do justly, love mercy and walk humbly with God," when undoubtedly the Almighty will take care that we are not stifled by disagreeable odors, nor crazed by unseemly colors.

SOURCE: Adin Ballou, A Discourse on the Subject of American Slavery, Delivered in the First Congregational Meeting House in Mendon, Mass. July 4, 1837 (Boston: Isaac Knapp, 1837), 29–33, 56–57, 60–62.

RALPH WALDO EMERSON

"Divinity School Address"

1838

Emerson's celebrated "Divinity School Address" was delivered in 1838, six years after he resigned from Second Church in Boston. His remarks on the idea that religious sentiment is innate and intuitive in human experience stirred considerable debate between orthodox Unitarians and the Transcendentalists. As he argued that ministers make religion vital not by worshipping Jesus or venerating the Bible but by leading parishioners to look within for divine revelation and guidance in ethical living, he challenged Unitarian theology, which was grounded in the Bible and validated by the miracles of Jesus. Harvard professor Andrews Norton denounced Emerson's rejection of miracles as the "latest form of infidelity." Norton's response provoked heated exchanges between conservative Unitarians and proponents of the "new views," including Theodore Parker and George Ripley, that continued for months afterward. Further Reading: William R. Hutchison, The Transcendentalist Ministers: Church Reform in the New England Renaissance *(New Haven, CT: Yale University Press, 1959).*

—Barry Andrews

In this refulgent summer it has been a luxury to draw the breath of life. The grass grows, the buds burst, the meadow is spotted with fire and gold in the tint of flowers. The air is full of birds, and sweet with the breath of the pine, the balm-of-Gilead, and the new hay. Night brings no gloom to the heart with its welcome shade. Through the transparent darkness the stars pour their almost spiritual rays. Man under them seems a young child, and his huge globe a toy. The cool night bathes the world as with a river, and prepares his eyes again for the crimson dawn. The mystery of nature was never displayed more happily.

*   *   *

A more secret, sweet, and overpowering beauty appears to man when his heart and mind open to the sentiment of virtue. Then instantly he is instructed in what is above him. He learns that his being is without bound; that, to the good, to the perfect, he is born, low as he now lies in evil and weakness. That which he venerates is still his own, though he has not realized it yet. *He ought.* He knows the sense of that grand word, though his analysis fails entirely to render account of it. . . .

The sentiment of virtue is a reverence and delight in the presence of certain divine laws. . . . These laws refuse to be adequately stated. They will not by us or for us be written out on paper, or spoken by the tongue. They elude, evade our persevering thought, and yet we read them hourly in each other's faces, in each other's actions, in our own remorse. . . .

The intuition of the moral sentiment is an insight of the perfection of the laws of the soul. These laws execute themselves. They are out of time, out of space, and not subject to circumstance. Thus; in the soul of man there is a justice whose retributions are instant and entire. He who does a good deed, is instantly ennobled himself. He who does a mean deed, is by the action itself contracted. . . .

See how this rapid intrinsic energy worketh everywhere, righting wrongs, correcting appearances, and bringing up facts to a harmony with thoughts. Its operation in life, though slow to the senses, is, at last, as sure as in the soul. By it, a man is made the Providence to himself, dispensing good to his goodness, and evil to his sin. Character is always known. Thefts never enrich; alms never impoverish; murder will speak out of stone walls. The least admixture of a lie,—for example, the smallest mixture of vanity, the least attempt to make a good impression, a favorable appearance,—will instantly vitiate the effect. But speak the truth, and all nature and all spirits help you with unexpected furtherance. Speak the truth, and all things alive or brute are vouchers, and the very roots of the grass underground there, do seem to stir and move to bear you witness. . . .

These facts have always suggested to man the sublime creed, that the world is not the product of manifold power, but of one will, of one mind; and that one mind is everywhere active, in each ray of the star, in each wavelet of the pool; and whatever opposes that will, is everywhere baulked and baffled, because things are made so, and not otherwise. Good is positive. Evil is merely privative, not absolute. It is like cold, which is the privation of heat. All evil is so much death or nonentity. Benevolence is absolute and real. So much benevolence as a man hath, so much life hath he. For all things proceed out of this same spirit, which is differently named love, justice, temperance, in its different applications, just as the ocean receives different names on the several shores which it washes. All things proceed out of the same spirit, and all things conspire with it. Whilst a man seeks good ends, he is strong by the whole strength of nature. In so far as he roves from these ends, he bereaves himself of power, of auxiliaries; his being shrinks out of all remote channels, he becomes less and less, a mote, a point, until absolute badness is absolute death.

The perception of this law of laws awakens in the mind a sentiment which we call the religious sentiment, and which makes our highest happiness. . . .

This sentiment is divine and deifying. It is the beatitude of man. It makes him illimitable. Through it, the soul first knows itself. It corrects the capital mistake of the infant man, who seeks to be great by following the great, and hopes to derive advantages *from another,* — by showing the fountain of all good to be in himself, and that he, equally with every man, is an inlet into the deeps of Reason. . . .

This sentiment lies at the foundation of society, and successively creates all forms of worship. The principle of veneration never dies out. . . . This thought dwelled always deepest in the minds of men in the devout and contemplative East; not alone in Palestine, where it reached its purest expression, but in Egypt, in Persia, in India, in China. Europe has always owed to oriental genius, its divine impulses. What these holy bards said, all sane men found agreeable and true. And the unique impression of Jesus upon mankind, whose name is not so much written as ploughed into the history of this world, is proof of the subtle virtue of this infusion.

Meantime, whilst the doors of the temple stand open, night and day, before every man, and the oracles of this truth cease never, it is guarded by one stern condition; this, namely; it is an intuition. It cannot be received at second hand. Truly speaking, it is not instruction, but provocation, that I can receive from another soul. What he announces, I must find true in me, or wholly reject; and on his word, or as his second, be he who he may, I can accept nothing. On the contrary, the absence of this primary faith is the presence of degradation. As is the flood so is the ebb. Let this faith depart, and the very words it spake, and the things it made, become false and hurtful. Then falls the church, the state, art, letters, life. The doctrine of the divine nature being forgotten, a sickness infects and dwarfs the constitution. Once man was all; now he is an appendage, a nuisance. And because the indwelling Supreme Spirit cannot wholly be got rid of, the doctrine of it suffers this perversion, that the divine nature is attributed to one or two persons, and denied to all the rest, and denied with fury.

*   *   *

Jesus Christ belonged to the true race of prophets. He saw with open eye the mystery of the soul. Drawn by its severe harmony, ravished with its beauty, he lived in it, and had his being there. Alone in all history, he estimated the greatness of man. One man was true to what is in you and me. He saw that God incarnates himself in man, and evermore goes forth anew to take possession of his world. He said, in this jubilee of sublime emotion, "I am divine. Through me, God acts; through me, speaks. Would you see God, see me; or, see thee, when thou also thinkest as I now think." But what a distortion did his doctrine and memory suffer in the same, in the next, and the following ages! There is no doctrine of the Reason which will bear to be taught by the Understanding. The understanding caught this high chant from the poet's lips, and said, in the next age, "This was Jehovah come down out of heaven. I will kill you, if you say he was a man." The idioms of his language, and the figures of his rhetoric, have usurped the place of his truth; and churches are not built on his principles, but on his tropes. Christianity became a Mythus, as the poetic teaching of Greece and of Egypt, before. He spoke of miracles; for he felt that man's life was a miracle, and all that man doth, and he knew that this daily miracle shines, as the man is diviner. But the word Miracle, as pronounced by Christian churches, gives a false impression; it is Monster. It is not one with the blowing clover and the falling rain. . . .

1. In thus contemplating Jesus we become very sensible of the first defect of historical Christianity. Historical Christianity has fallen into the error that corrupts all attempts to communicate religion. As it appears to us, and as it has appeared for ages, it is not the doctrine of the soul, but an exaggeration of the personal, the positive, the ritual. It has dwelt, it dwells, with noxious exaggeration about the *person* of Jesus. The soul knows no persons. It invites every man to expand to the full circle of the universe, and will have no preferences but those of spontaneous love. But by this eastern monarchy of a Christianity, which indolence and fear have built, the friend of man is made the injurer of man. . . .

That is always best which gives me to myself. The sublime is excited in me by the great stoical doctrine, Obey thyself. That which shows God in me, fortifies me. That which shows God out of me, makes me a wart and a wen. There is no longer a necessary reason for my being. Already the long shadows of untimely oblivion creep over me, and I shall decease forever.

The divine bards are the friends of my virtue, of my intellect, of my strength. They admonish me, that the gleams which flash across my mind, are not mine, but God's; that they had the like, and were not disobedient to the heavenly vision. So I love them. Noble provocations go out from them, inviting me also to emancipate myself; to resist evil; to subdue the world; and to Be. And thus by his holy thoughts, Jesus serves us, and thus only. To aim to convert a man by miracles, is a profanation of the soul. . . .

2. The second defect of the traditionary and limited way of using the mind of Christ is a consequence of the first; this, namely; that the Moral Nature, that Law of laws, whose revelations introduce greatness,—yea, God himself, into the open soul, is not explored as the fountain of the established teaching in society. Men have come to speak of the revelation as somewhat long ago given and done, as if God were dead. The injury to faith throttles the preacher; and the goodliest of institutions becomes an uncertain and inarticulate voice. . . .

To this holy office, you propose to devote yourselves. I wish you may feel your call in throbs of desire and hope. The office is the first in the world. It is of that reality, that it cannot suffer the deduction of any falsehood. And it is my duty to say to you, that the need was never greater of new revelation than now. From the views I have already expressed, you will infer the sad conviction, which I share, I believe, with numbers, of the universal decay and now almost death of faith in society. The soul is not preached. The Church seems to totter to its fall, almost all life extinct. On this occasion, any complaisance, would be criminal, which told you, whose hope and commission it is to preach the faith of Christ, that the faith of Christ is preached. . . .

This great and perpetual office of the preacher is not discharged. Preaching is the expression of the moral sentiment in application to the duties of life. In how many churches, by how many prophets, tell me, is man made sensible that he is an infinite Soul; that the earth and heavens are passing into his mind; that he is drinking forever the soul of God? . . . The test of the true faith, certainly, should be its power to charm and command the soul, as the laws of nature control the activity of the hands,—so commanding that we find pleasure and honor in obeying. The faith should blend with the light of rising and of setting suns, with the flying cloud, the singing bird, and the breath of flowers. But now the priest's Sabbath has lost the splendor of nature; it is unlovely; we are glad when it is done. . . .

Whenever the pulpit is usurped by a formalist, then is the worshipper defrauded and disconsolate. We shrink as soon as the prayers begin, which do not uplift, but smite and offend us. We are fain to wrap our cloaks about us, and secure, as best we can, a solitude that hears not. I once heard a preacher who sorely tempted me to say, I would go to church no more. Men go, thought I, where they are wont to go, else had no soul entered the temple in the afternoon. A snowstorm was falling around us. The snowstorm was real; the preacher merely spectral; and the eye felt the sad contrast in looking at him, and then out of the window behind him, into the beautiful meteor of the snow. He had lived in vain. He had no one word intimating that he had laughed or wept, was married or in love, had been commended, or cheated, or chagrined. If he had ever lived and acted, we were none the wiser for it. The capital secret of his profession, namely, to convert life into truth, he had not learned. Not one fact in all his experience, had he yet imported into his doctrine. This man had ploughed, and planted, and talked, and bought, and sold; he had read books; he had eaten and drunken; his head aches; his heart throbs; he smiles and suffers; yet was there not a surmise, a hint, in all the discourse, that he had ever lived at all. Not a line did he draw out of real history. The true preacher can be known by this, that he deals out to the people his life,—life passed through the fire of thought. But of the bad preacher, it could not be told from his sermon, what age of the world he fell in; whether he had a father or a child; whether he was a freeholder or a pauper; whether he was a citizen or a countryman; or any other fact of his biography.

It seemed strange that the people should come to church. . . .

And now, my brothers, you will ask, What in these desponding days can be done by us? The remedy is already declared in the ground of our complaint of the Church. We have contrasted the Church with the Soul. In the soul, then, let the redemption be sought. Wherever a man comes, there comes revolution. . . . The stationariness of religion; the assumption that the age of inspiration is past, that the Bible is closed; the fear of degrading the character of Jesus by representing him as a man; indicate with sufficient clearness the falsehood of our theology. It is the office of a true teacher to show us that God is, not was; that He speaketh, not spake. . . .

Let me admonish you, first of all, to go alone; to refuse the good models, even those most sacred in the imagination of men, and dare to love God without mediator or veil. . . .

Yourself a newborn bard of the Holy Ghost,—cast behind you all conformity, and acquaint men at first hand with Deity. Look to it first and only, that you are such; that fashion, custom, authority, pleasure, and money, are nothing to you,—are not bandages over your eyes, that you cannot see,—but live with the privilege of the immeasurable mind. Not too anxious to visit periodically all families and each family in your parish connexion,—when you meet one of these men or women, be to them a divine man; be to them thought and virtue; let their timid aspirations find in you a friend; let their trampled instincts be genially tempted out in your atmosphere; let their doubts know that you have doubted, and their wonder feel that you have wondered. By trusting your own heart, you shall gain a greater confidence in other men. For all our penny-wisdom, for all our soul-destroying slavery to habit, it is not to be doubted, that all men have sublime thoughts; that all men do value the few real hours of life; they love to be heard; they love to be caught up into the vision of principles. We mark with light in the memory the few interviews, we have had in the dreary years of routine and of sin, with souls that made our souls wiser; that spoke what we thought; that told us what we knew; that gave us leave to be what we inly were. Discharge to men the priestly office, and, present or absent, you shall be followed with their love as by an angel.

*   *   *

And now let us do what we can to rekindle the smouldering, nigh quenched fire on the altar. The evils of the church that now is, are manifest. The question returns, What shall we do? I confess, all attempts to project and establish a Cultus with new rites and forms, seem to me vain. Faith makes us, and not we it, and faith makes its own forms. All attempts to contrive a system, are as cold as the new worship introduced by the French to the goddess of Reason,—to-day, pasteboard and fillagree, and ending to-morrow in madness and murder. Rather let the breath of new life be breathed by you through the forms already existing. For, if once you are alive, you shall find they shall become plastic and new. The remedy to their deformity is, first, soul, and second, soul, and evermore, soul. A whole popedom of forms, one pulsation of virtue can uplift and vivify. Two inestimable advantages Christianity has given us; first; the Sabbath, the jubilee of the whole world; whose light dawns welcome alike into the closet of the philosopher, into the garret of toil, and into prison cells, and everywhere suggests, even to the vile, the dignity of spiritual being. Let it stand forevermore, a temple, which new love, new faith, new sight shall restore to more than its first splendor to mankind. And secondly, the institution of preaching,—the speech of man to men,—essentially the most flexible of all organs, of all forms. What hinders that now, everywhere, in pulpits, in lecture-rooms, in houses, in fields, wherever the invitation of men or your own occasions lead you, you speak the very truth, as your life and conscience teach it, and cheer the waiting, fainting hearts of men with new hope and new revelation?

I look for the hour when that supreme Beauty, which ravished the souls of those Eastern men, and chiefly of those Hebrews, and through their lips spoke oracles to all time, shall speak in the West also. The Hebrew and Greek Scriptures contain immortal sentences, that have been bread of life to millions. But they have no epical integrity; are fragmentary; are not shown in their order to the intellect. I look for the new Teacher, that shall follow so far those shining laws, that he shall see them come full circle; shall see their rounding complete grace; shall see the world to be the mirror of the soul; shall see the identity of the law of gravitation with purity of heart; and shall show that the Ought, that Duty, is one thing with Science, with Beauty, and with Joy.

SOURCE: Ralph Waldo Emerson, "The Divinity School Address," *The Collected Works of Ralph Waldo Emerson* (Cambridge, MA: Harvard University Press, 1971), 1:71–86, 89–90, 92–93.

"The Personality of the Deity"
1838

Ware rebuilt Second Church in Boston into a thriving parish in the 1820s and welcomed Ralph Waldo Emerson as his assistant and eventual successor. While the two shared a belief in divine immanence, the idea that God could and should be directly encountered in everyday life, Ware took issue with Emerson's depiction of how God appears. In response to Emerson's infamous "Divinity School Address," Ware preached this sermon at the beginning of the next term. More tactful than Emerson's other critics and never mentioning Emerson by name, Ware nevertheless warned against Emerson's impulse to reduce God into an abstract and impersonal set of cosmic laws.

—Erik Martinez Resly

"He is the living God and an everlasting King." —JEREMIAH 10:10

In treating the doctrine respecting God, the mind is deeply impressed with a sense of its importance in its bearing on human duty and happiness. It is the doctrine of a Creator, the Governor and Father of man. The discussion relates not merely to the laws of the universe and the principles by which its affairs are directed, but to the character and dispositions of the Being, who presides over those laws, and by whose will those affairs are determined. It teaches, not only that there is a wise and holy order to which it is for every man's interest to conform, but that that order is ordained and upheld by an active, overruling Intelligence; and that hence virtue is not merely conformity to a rule, but allegiance to a rightful Lawgiver; and happiness not the result merely of obedience to a command, but of affectionate subjection to a Parent.

The importance of this consideration to a true and happy virtue cannot be over-estimated. The difference between conformity to a statute and obedience to a father is a difference not to be measured in words, but to be realized in the experience of the soul. It is slightly represented in the difference between the condition of a little child that lives in the presence of a judicious and devoted mother, an object of perpetual affection, and of another that is placed under the charge of a public institution, which knows nothing but a set of rules. Each is alike provided for and governed; but the one enjoys the satisfactions of a trusting and loving heart, while the other, deprived of the natural objects of affection, knows nothing but a life of order and restraint. Take away the Father of the universe, and, though every ordinance remain unchanged, mankind becomes but a company of children in an orphan asylum; clothed, fed, governed, but objects of pity rather than congratulation because deprived of those resting-places for the affections, without which the soul is not happy.

Our representations of the being and perfections of God are therefore incomplete, until we have taken into consideration the additional view now suggested. The idea of personality must be added to that of natural and moral perfection, in order to the full definition of the Deity. Without this he is but a set of principles or a code of laws. Yet by some philosophers at various times it has been speculatively denied, and by too many in common life it is practically lost sight of. It may be well, then, in connexion with our preceding discussion, to consider a little particularly the doctrine of the Divine Personality; to state what it is; to show the grounds on which it is established; and to survey the evils which must result from a denial of it.

I begin with stating what is meant by the Personality of the Deity.

A *person* is an intelligent, conscious agent; one who thinks, perceives, understands, wills, and acts. What we assert is, that God is such. It is not implied, that any distinct form or shape is necessary to personality. In the case of man, the bodily form is not the person. That form remains after death; but we no longer call it a person, because consciousness and the power of will and of action are gone. The personality resided in them. So also in the case of the Deity; consciousness, and the power of will and of action constitute him a person. Shape, form, or place make no part of the idea.

The evidence of this fact is found in the works of design with which the universe is filled. They imply forethought, plan, wisdom, a designing mind; in other words, an Intelligent Being who devised and executed them. If we suppose, that there is no conscious, intelligent person, we say that there is no plan, no purpose, no design; there is nothing but a set of abstract and unconscious principles. And, strange as it may seem to Christian ears, which have been accustomed to far other expressions of the Divinity, there have been those who maintain this idea; who hold, that the principles which govern the universe constitute the Deity; that power, wisdom, veracity, justice, benevolence, are God, that gravitation, light, electricity, are God. Speculative men have been sometimes fond of this assertion, and in various forms have set up this opposition to the universal sentiment; sometimes with the design of removing the associations of reverence and worship, which make men religious; sometimes under the supposition, that they thereby elevate the mind to a conception of the truth more worthy of its exalted subject. But it will be evident upon a little inquiry that, in either case, the speculation is inconsistent with just and wholesome doctrine.

1. For, in the first place, one of the most observable and least questionable principles, drawn from our observation of man and nature, is, that the person, the

conscious being, is the chief thing, for the sake of which all else is, and subservient to which all principles operate. The person, the conscious, intelligent, active, enjoying, suffering being, is foremost in importance and honor; principles and laws operate for its support, guidance, and well-being; and therefore are secondary. Some of these principles and laws have their origin in the relations which exist amongst intelligent, moral agents; most of them come into action in consequence of the previous existence of those relations. If there were no such agents, there either would be no such principles, or they would have no operation. Thus, for example, veracity, justice, love, are sentiments or obligations which spring up from the relations subsisting between different beings, and can exist only where there are persons. We may say, indeed, that they exist abstractly, in the nature of things; but if there be no beings to recognise them, no agents to conform to or violate them, they would be as if they were not. They are qualities of being; and like all qualities have no actual existence independent of the substances in which they inhere. They have relation to acts, — voluntary acts of truth, justice, goodness; and acts belong to persons. If there existed no persons in the universe, but only things, there could be neither the act nor the sentiment of justice, goodness, truth; these are qualities of persons, not of things; of actions, not of substances. Suppose the Deity to exist alone in the universe which he has made. Then, from the conscious enjoyment of his own perfections and the exercise of his power in the physical creation, He must dwell in bliss; but, as he has no relations to other conscious existences, he cannot exercise justice, or truth, or love; they lie in the infinite bosom as if they were not; they have only a contingent existence. But the instant he should *create* various tribes, they spring into actual existence; they no longer may be, they are; they rise out of the new relations which are created, and are the expression of sentiments and duties which had not before been possible.

Or make another supposition. Upon the newly created earth one man is placed alone. He knows no other conscious existence but himself. What are truth, justice, charity, to him? They are nothing to him. He cannot have ideas of them. They are sentiments that belong to certain relations between beings, which relations he does not stand in, and knows nothing of. To him, therefore, they do not exist. Now send him companions, and the relations begin, which give those sentiments birth and make their expression possible. He is in society; and those principles, which make the strength and order of society, immediately come into action. The necessities of conscious being call them forth.

Thus what is chiefest in the universe, is conscious, active mind; abstract principles are but the laws of its various relations. . . .

2. It also, in the next place, amounts to a virtual denial of God. Indeed, this is the only sense in which it seems possible to make that denial. No one thinks of denying the existence of principles and laws. Gravitation, order, cause and effect, truth,

benevolence,—no one denies that these exist; and, if these constitute the Deity, he has not been, and cannot be, denied. The only denial possible is by this exclusion of a personal existence. There can be no atheism but this; and this is atheism. If the material universe rests on the laws of attraction, affinity, heat, motion, still all of them together are no Deity; if the moral universe is founded on the principles of righteousness, truth, love, neither are these the Deity. There must be some Being to put in action these principles, to exercise these attributes. To call the principles and the attributes *God*, is to violate the established use of language and confound the common apprehensions of mankind. It is in vain to hope by so doing to escape the charge of atheism; there is no other atheism conceivable. There is a personal God, or there is none. . . .

3. Further, to exclude personality from the idea of God is, in effect, to destroy the object of worship, and thus to annihilate that essential duty of religion. The sentiment of reverence may, undoubtedly, be felt for a principle, for a code of laws, for an institution of government. But worship, which is the expression of that sentiment, is applicable only to a conscious being; as all the language and customs of men signify. It is praise, thanks, honor, and petition, addressed to one who can hear and reply. If there be no such one,—if the government of the world be at the disposal of unconscious power and self-executing law,—then there can be no such thing as worship. . . .

4. In the next place, this notion removes the sense of responsibility, and so puts in jeopardy the virtue of man, as we have just seen that it trifles with his happiness. The idea of responsibility implies someone, to whom we are responsible, and who has a right to treat us according to our fidelity. We indeed sometimes use the word with a little different application; we say that a man is responsible to his country, to posterity, to the cause of truth; but this is plainly employing the word in a secondary sense; it is not the original, literal signification. We hear it said, also, that a man is responsible to his own conscience; and this is sometimes spoken of as the most solemn responsibility.In one point of view, justly; since it is responsibility to that person whose disapprobation is nearest to us, and whose awards are of the highest consequence to our peace. We are not, therefore, to speak lightly of the tribunal within the breast. But why is it terrible? Because it is thought to represent and foreshadow the decisions of the higher tribunal of God. Let a man believe that it is ultimate, and he can learn to brave it; and how many accordingly have hardened themselves against it, and persevered in sin, as if it were not! Or let him think that the retributions of guilt are simply the accomplishment of natural laws, which go on mechanically to execute themselves, unattended by any sentiment of approbation or disapprobation, and he can, without great difficulty, defy them. They do not address his moral sensibility. This is the case with the improvident, the miserly, the intemperate; they are perfectly aware that grievous ill consequences will pursue their folly,

yet they are not restrained thereby; if they have a mind to risk them, whose concern is it? they will judge for themselves what makes their happiness. But, if they had been made sensible to the disapprobation of a Living Father, if they had realized that the sentence against their iniquities was to be executed by Him to whom they owe everything, then they would have paused in their bad career. . . .

6. Further still, it destroys the possibility of a revelation, in any intelligible sense of the word. A revelation is a message, or a direct communication, from the Infinite mind to the human mind. But in order to this, there is required a conscious and individual action on the part of the communicator; and this implies personality. So that this doctrine virtually accuses the Scriptures of imposture, since they purport to contain a revelation from God, which in the nature of things is impossible. Nay, let us see the worst of it;—it accuses the apostles of Christ, and the blessed Saviour himself, of deliberate fraud and imposition; since they and he declared, with the most solemn asseverations, that he was directly sent by God, the Father of mankind, when, if there be no such Being, but only certain principles and laws, he could not have been sent by him. Their language in that case is altogether deceptive. It seems to mean one thing, when it really means something quite the reverse. When Jesus declares again and again, that he came from the Father and speaks his word, he does not intend what the words assert, but only what is equally true, in a degree, of all men. . . . This is the result at which the doctrine arrives. It destroys the possibility of a revelation in any sense which makes it peculiar and valuable by making all truth a revelation, and all men revealers. It takes away all special divinity and authority from the Gospel, reduces it to a level with any other wisdom, and thus robs it of its power over the earth. Its pure and holy author becomes a pretender; for he professed to be sent from God and to bring his message; he worshipped him, and spoke of holding continual personal intercourse with him; and by such means he gained a hearing and an influence among men,—gained them, however, only by deceiving the world, if there be, after all, no personal God.

By thus tracking this doctrine through its various bearings and observing its tendencies, we come to a clear discernment of its falseness and mischievousness. We see, that it opposes what is taught in nature by all the marks of design which cover the works of creation;—it sets aside the fundamental fact, that conscious, intelligent being, in its various relations, is the chief interest of the universe, for the sake of which everything else is;—it is a virtual denial of God, and a consequent overthrow of worship and devotion;—it injures happiness by taking from the affections their highest object, and virtue by enfeebling the sense of responsibility;—it contradicts the express lessons of the Bible, excludes the possibility of a revelation in any proper sense of the word, and denies to the Gospel its right to authority and power.

Of course, it will not happen that all these disastrous consequences will follow from this doctrine in the case of every individual who may receive it. To the pure all things are pure; and some men will dwell forever in the midst of abstraction and falsehood without being injuriously affected. Express infidelity is not vice, and may exist together with great integrity and purity of life. Atheism is not immorality, and may consist with an unblemished character. But, however it may be with individuals, living in the midst of a believing and worshipping community, it is not to be doubted that a community, unbelieving and godless, would rush to evil unmitigated and hopeless. A philosopher here and there, by his science and skill, might perhaps live without the sun; but strike it out from the path of all men, and despair and death ensue.

SOURCE: Henry Ware, Jr., *The Personality of the Deity: A Sermon Preached in the Chapel of Harvard University, September 23, 1838* (Boston, 1838), 5–11, 13–14, 16–22.

ANDREWS NORTON

"The Latest Form of Infidelity"

1839

History has not been especially kind to Andrews Norton (1786–1853). Dubbed the "hard-headed Unitarian Pope" by those who preferred a more liberal interpretation of religious authority, Norton devoted his life to developing a Unitarian mode of reading and interpreting the Bible, particularly the gospels. As Harvard's Dexter Professor of Sacred Literature (1819–1830) and with the publication of his Unitarian apology, The Evidences of the Genuineness of the Gospels *(1837, 1844), Norton cemented his legacy as the greatest Unitarian Bible scholar of his day. However, his belief in the primacy of the Bible as the touchstone of Unitarian identity came under critique in the late 1830s, primarily by Transcendentalists such as Ralph Waldo Emerson, whose "Divinity School Address" would precipitate the composition of the following treatise. In light of the growing skepticism concerning the Bible's authority, particularly its claims to confirmation by miracles, Norton seeks in this excerpt to revive the biblical, Christian roots of Unitarianism and undermine the true culprit of this "latest form of infidelity," German philosophical idealism. Further Reading: Allen R. Clark,* Andrews Norton: A Conservative Unitarian, *A.B. Thesis, Harvard College, 1942; Robert D. Habich, "Emerson's Reluctant Foe: Andrews Norton and the Transcendentalist Controversy,"* New England Quarterly 65, *no. 2 (June 1992): 208–37; Lydia Willsky-Ciollo,* American Unitarianism and the Protestant Dilemma: The Conundrum of Biblical Authority *(Lanham, MD: Lexington Books, 2015).*

—Lydia Willsky-Ciollo

I address you, Gentlemen, and our friends who are assembled with us, on an occasion of more than common interest; as it is your first meeting since joining together in a society as former pupils of the Theological School in this place. . . .

We meet in a revolutionary and uncertain state of religious opinion, existing throughout what is called the Christian world. Our religion is very imperfectly understood, and received by comparatively a small number with intelligent faith. In proportion as our view is more extended, and we are better acquainted with what is and what has been, we shall become more sensible of the great changes that have long been in preparation, but which of late have been rapidly developed. The present state of things imposes new responsibilities upon all who know the value of our faith and have ability to maintain it. Let us then employ this occasion in considering some of the characteristics of the times and some of those opinions now prevalent, which are at war with a belief in Christianity.

By a belief in Christianity, we mean the belief that Christianity is a revelation by God of the truths of religion; and that the divine authority of him whom God commissioned to speak to us in his name was attested, in the only mode in which it could be, by miraculous displays of his power. . . .

The latest form of infidelity is distinguished by assuming the Christian name, while it strikes directly at the root of faith in Christianity, and indirectly of all religion, by denying the miracles attesting the divine mission of Christ. The first writer, so far as I know, who maintained the impossibility of a miracle was Spinoza, whose argument . . . is . . . that the laws of nature are the laws by which God is bound, Nature and God being the same, and therefore laws from which Nature or God can never depart. The argument is founded on atheism. The denial of the possibility of miracles must involve the denial of the existence of God, since, if there be a God, in the proper sense of the word, there can be no room for doubt, that he may act in a manner different from that in which he displays his power in the ordinary operations of nature. It deserves notice, however, that in Spinoza's discussion of this subject we find that affectation of religious language, and of religious reverence and concern, which is so striking a characteristic of many of the irreligious speculations of our day, and of which he, perhaps, furnished the prototype; for he has been regarded as a profound teacher, a patriarch of truth, by some of the most noted among the infidel philosophers and theologians of Germany. "I will show from Scripture," he says, "that the decrees and commands of God, and consequently his providence, are nothing but the order of nature." . . . So strong a hold has religion upon the inmost nature of man, that even its enemies, in order to delude their followers, thus assume its aspect and mock its tones. . . .

To deny that a miracle is capable of proof, or to deny that it may be proved by evidence of the same nature as establishes the truth of other events, is, in effect, as I have said, to deny the existence of God. A miracle can be incapable of proof, only because it is physically or morally impossible; since what is possible may be proved. To deny that the truth of a miracle may be established, involves the denial of creation; for there can be no greater miracle than creation. It equally implies, that no species of being that propagates its kind ever had a commencement; for if there was a first plant that grew without seed, or a first man without parents, or if of any series of events there was a first without such antecedents as the laws of nature require, then there was a miracle. So far is a miracle from being incapable of proof, that you can escape from the necessity of believing innumerable miracles only by believing that man, and all other animals, and all plants, have existed from eternity upon this earth, without commencement of propagation, there never having been a first of any species. No one, at the present day, will maintain with Lucretius that they were generated from inanimate matter, by the fermentation of heat and moisture. Nothing can seem more simple or conclusive than the view we have taken; but we may render it more familiar by an appeal to fact. The science of geology has shown us, that man is but a late inhabitant of the earth. The first individuals of our race, then, were not produced as all others have been. They were formed by a miracle, or, in other words, by an act of God's power, exerted in a different manner from that in which it operates according to the established laws of nature. Creation, the most conspicuous, is at the same time the most undeniable, of miracles.

*　*　*

Gentlemen, I have addressed your understandings, not your feelings. But the subject of Christianity is one which cannot be rightly apprehended without the strongest feeling; not the transient excitement existing for an hour, and then forgotten, but a feeling possessing the whole heart, and governing our lives. Of the form of infidelity, which we have been considering, there can be but one opinion among honest men. . . . It is a truth, which few among us will question, that, for any one to pretend to be a Christian teacher, who disbelieves the divine origin and authority of Christianity, and would undermine the belief of others, is treachery towards God and man. If I were to address such a one, I would implore him by all his remaining self-respect, by his sense of common honesty, by his regard to the well-being of his fellow-men, by his fear of God, if he believe that there is a God, and by the awful realities of the future world, to stop short in his course; and, if he cannot become a Christian, to cease to be a pretended Christian teacher, and to assume his proper character.

SOURCE: Andrews Norton, A *Discourse on the Latest Form of Infidelity Delivered at the Request of the Association of the Alumni of the Cambridge Theological School on the 19th of July, 1839, with Notes* (Cambridge, 1839), 3–5, 11–12, 14–16, 36–37.

JAMES MARTINEAU

"Christianity Without Priest, and Without Ritual"

1839

James Martineau (1805–1900) was a British Unitarian minister, educator, ethicist, and theologian. His pulpits were in Dublin, Liverpool, and London, but the longest association of his career was with Manchester College, where he directed Unitarian ministers' education for forty-five years. Martineau's three most significant books are commonly described as a systematic Unitarian theology. However, for Martineau, the central aspect of religion was worship and, accordingly, he composed liturgies, prayers, hymns, and sermons. Martineau believed that an individual may be a Unitarian but also that the church as a whole should be Christian, to be more inclusive. Ironically, his liturgies eliminated references to Jesus as Christ or Messiah. This selection is the final sermon Martineau delivered as part of the Liverpool Controversy, an attack on Unitarianism by thirteen orthodox clergyman of the Church of England. The three Unitarians who defended their faith were also known as the British Transcendentalists. Further Reading: Frank Schulman, James Martineau: This Conscience-Intoxicated Unitarian *(Chicago: Meadville Lombard Theological School, 2002).*

—Meg Schellenberg Richardson

Surely it must be admitted that the general spirit of our Lord's personal life and ministry was that of the Prophet, not of the Priest; tending directly to the disparagement of whatever priesthood existed in his country, without visibly preparing the substitution of anything at all analogous to it. The sacerdotal order felt it so; and with the infallible instinct of self-preservation, they watched, they hated, they seized, they murdered him. The priest in every age has a natural antipathy to the prophet, dreads him as kings dread revolution, and is the first to detect his existence. The solemn moment and the gracious words, of Christ's first preaching in Nazareth, struck with fate the temple in Jerusalem. To the old men of the village, to the neighbours who knew his childhood, and companions who had shared its rambles and its sports, he said, with the quiet flush of inspiration; "The Spirit of the Lord is upon me, because he hath anointed me to preach the gospel to the poor: he hath sent me to heal the broken-hearted, to preach deliverance to the captives, and recovering of sight to the blind; to set at liberty them that are bruised, to preach the acceptable year of the

Lord." The Spirit of the Lord in Galilee! speaking with the peasantry, dwelling in villages, and wandering loose and where it listeth among the hills! This would never do, thought the white-robed Levites of the Holy City; it would be as a train of wild-fire in the Temple. And were they not right? When it was revealed that sanctity is no thing of place and time, that a way is open from earth to heaven, from every field or mountain trod by human feet, and through every roof that shelters a human head; that amid the crowd and crush of life, each soul is in personal solitude with God, and by speech or silence (be they but true and loving) may tell its cares and find its peace; that a divine allegiance might *cost nothing*, but the strife of a dutiful will and the patience of a filial heart; how could any priesthood hope to stand? See how Jesus himself, when the Temple was close at hand, and the sunshine dressed it in its splendor, yet withdrew his prayers to the midnight of Mount Olivet. He entered those courts to teach, rather than to worship; and when there, he is felt to take no consecration, but to give it; to bring with him the living spirit of God, and spread it throughout all the place. When evening closes his teachings, and he returns late over the Mount to Bethany, did he not feel that there was more of God in the night-breeze on his brow, and the heaven above him, and the sad love within him, than in the place called "Holy" which he had left? And when he had knocked at the gate of Lazarus the risen and become his guest; when, after the labours of the day, he unburthened his spirit to the affections of that family, and spake of things divine to the sisters listening at his feet; did they not feel, as they retired at length, that the whole house was full of God, and that there is no sanctuary like the shrine, not made with hands, within us all? In childhood, he had once preferred the temple and its teachings to his parents' home: now, to his deeper experience, the temple has lost its truth; while the cottage and the walks of Nazareth, the daily voices and constant duties of this life, seem covered with the purest consecration. True, he vindicated the sanctity of the temple, when he heard within its enclosure the hum of traffic and the chink of gain, and would not have the house of prayer turned into a place of merchandise: because in this there was imposture and a lie, and Mammon and the Lord must ever dwell apart. In nothing must there be mockery and falsehood; and while the temple stands, it must be a temple true.

Our Lord's whole ministry then (to which we may add that of his apostles) was conceived in a spirit quite opposite to that of priesthood. A missionary life, without fixed locality, without form, without rites; with teaching free, occasional and various, with sympathies ever with the people, and a strain of speech never marked by invective, except against the ruling sacerdotal influence;—all these characters proclaim him, purely and emphatically, the Prophet of the Lord.

* * *

All Unitarian writers maintain the Moral Perfection and Fatherly Providence of the Infinite Ruler; the Messiahship of Jesus Christ, in whose person and spirit there

is a Revelation of God and a Sanctification for Man; the Responsibility and Retributive Immortality of men; and the need of a pure and devout heart of Faith, as
the source of all outward goodness and inward communion with God. These great
and self-luminous points, bound together by natural affinity, constitute the fixed
centre of our religion. And on subjects beyond this centre, we have no wider divergences than are found among those who attach themselves to an opposite system.
For example, the relations between Scripture and Reason, as evidences and guides
in questions of doctrine, are not more unsettled among us, than are the relations
between Scripture and Tradition in the Church. Nor is the perpetual authority of the
"Christian rites" so much in debate among our ministers, as the efficacy of the Sacraments among the clergy. In truth, our diversities of sentiment affect far less *what*
we believe, than the question *why* we believe it. Different modes of reasoning, and
different results of interpretation, are no doubt to be found among our several
authors. We all make our appeal to the records of Christianity: but we have voted no
particular commentator into the seat of authority. And is this not equally true of our
opponents' church? Their articles and creeds furnish no textual expositions of Scripture, but only results and deductions from its study. And so variously have these
results been elicited from the sacred writings, that scarcely a text can be adduced in
defence of the Trinitarian scheme, which some witness unexceptionably orthodox
may not be summoned to prove inapplicable. In fine, we have no greater variety of
critical and exegetical opinion than the divines from whom we dissent: while the
system of Christianity in which our Scriptural labours have issued, has its leading
characteristics better determined and more apprehensible, than the scheme which
the articles and creeds have vainly labored to define.

The refusal to embody our sentiments in any authoritative formula appears to
strike observers as a whimsical exception to the general practice of churches. The
peculiarity has had its origin in hereditary and historical associations: but it has its
defence in the noblest principles of religious freedom and Christian communion. At
present, it must suffice to say, that our Societies are dedicated, not to theological
opinions, but to religious worship: that they have maintained the unity of the spirit,
without insisting on any unity of doctrine: that Christian liberty, love, and piety are
their essentials in perpetuity, but their Unitarianism an accident of a few or many
generations;—which has arisen, and might vanish, without the loss of their identity.
We believe in the mutability of religious systems, but the imperishable character of
the religious affections;—in the progressiveness of opinion within, as well as without, the limits of Christianity. Our forefathers cherished the same conviction: and so,
not having been born intellectual bondsmen, we desire to leave our successors free.
Convinced that uniformity of doctrine can never prevail, we seek to attain its only
good,—peace on earth and communion with heaven,—without it. We aim to make
a true Christendom,—a commonwealth of the faithful,—by the binding force, not

of ecclesiastical creeds, but of spiritual wants, and Christian sympathies: and indulge the vision of a Church that "in the latter days shall arise," like "the mountain of the Lord," bearing on its ascent the blossoms of thought proper to every intellectual clime, and withal massively rooted in the deep places of our humanity, and gladly rising to meet the sunshine from on high.

And now, friends and brethren, let us say a glad farewell to the fretfulness of controversy, and retreat again, with thanksgiving, into the interior of our own venerated truth. Having come forth, at the severer call of duty, to do battle for it, with such force as God vouchsafes to the sincere, let us go in to live and worship beneath its shelter. They tell you, it is not the true faith. Perhaps not: but then, you think it so; and that is enough to make your duty clear, and to draw from it, as from nothing else, the very peace of God. May be, we are on our way to something better, unexistent and unseen as yet; which may penetrate our souls with nobler affection, and give a fresh spontaneity of love to God and all immortal things. Perhaps there cannot be the truest life of faith, except in scattered individuals, till this age of conflicting doubt and dogmatism shall have passed away. Dark and leaden clouds of materialism hide the heaven from us: red gleams of fanaticism pierce through, vainly striving to reveal it; and not till the weight is heaved from off the air, and the thunders roll down the horizon, will the serene light of God flow upon us, and the blue infinite embrace us again. Meanwhile, we must reverently love the faith we have: to quit it for one that we have not, were to lose the breath of life, and die.

SOURCE: *Unitarianism Defended, A Series of Lectures by Three Protestant Dissenting Ministers of Liverpool in Reply to a Course of Lectures, Entitled Unitarianism Confuted by Thirteen Clergymen of the Church of England* (London, 1839), 27–29, 51–53.

ADIN BALLOU

"Standard of Practical Christianity"

1839

In 1838 Adin Ballou attended a Peace Convention, organized by William Lloyd Garrison, Samuel J. May, and other pacifist abolitionists, at which they formed the New England Non-Resistance Society. Ballou was initially shocked by the convention's Declaration of Sentiments, which declared, "We cannot acknowledge allegiance to any human government." On reflection, however, he decided that the requirements of the Kingdom of Heaven did indeed outweigh allegiance to any "sword-sustained" government. Shortly after adopting the non-resistant position, Ballou composed the "Standard of Practical Christianity," which would become the founding document of the Hopedale Community. It was modeled on the convention's Declaration of Sentiments, but presented a more comprehensive vision of the good life. Its followers were to "be perfect as our Father in heaven is perfect, in all possible respects." In addition to prohibiting all forms of violence, it prohibited economic sins, such as covetousness and extravagance; social sins, such as rudeness and ingratitude; and sins of the flesh, such as intemperance and licentiousness. When Ballou presented the Standard at the annual meeting of the Massachusetts Association of Universal Restorationists in 1839, it split the association. The four ministers and two laymen who signed the Standard went on to form the Hopedale Community. The more conservative members, Ballou later wrote, "gave us up as impracticable fanatics, with whom they could go no further." Further Reading: Adin Ballou, History of the Hopedale Community *(Lowell, MA: Thompson & Hill, 1897); Edward K. Spann,* Hopedale: From Commune to Company Town, 1840–1920 *(Columbus: Ohio State University Press, 1992).*

—Lynn Gordon Hughes

Humbly desirous of promoting Christian piety and morality in their primitive purity, the undersigned do solemnly acknowledge the Principles, Sentiments, and Duties declared in the following Standard, viz.:

We are Christians. Our creed is the New Testament. Our religion is love. Our only law is the will of God. Our grand object is the restoration of man, especially the most fallen and friendless. Our immediate concern is the promotion of useful knowledge, moral improvement, and Christian perfection. We recognize no Spiritual Father but God; no master but Christ. We belong to that kingdom of "righteousness, peace, and joy" which is "not of this world"; whose throne is holiness, whose scepter is truth, whose greatness is humility, whose preeminence is service, whose patriotism is love of enemies, whose heroism is forbearance, whose glory is self-sacrifice, whose wealth is charity, whose triumphs are salvation. Therefore, we can make no earthly object our chief good, nor be governed by any motive but the love of *Right*, nor compromise duty with worldly convenience, nor seek the preservation of our property, our reputation, our personal liberty, or our life, by the sacrifice of Conscience. We cannot live merely to eat, drink, sleep, gratify our sensual appetites, dress, display ourselves, acquire property, and be accounted great in this world; but to do good.

All that we are and have, with all that God shall ever bestow upon us, we unreservedly dedicate to the cause of universal righteousness, expecting for ourselves in the order of divine providence only a comfortable subsistence until death, and in the world to come eternal life.

Placing unlimited confidence in our Heavenly Father, we distrust all other guidance. We cannot be governed by the will of man, however solemnly and formally declared, nor put our trust in an arm of flesh. Hence we voluntarily withdraw from all interference with the governments of this world. We can take no part in the politics, the administration, or the defense of those governments, either by voting at their polls, holding their offices, aiding in the execution of their legal vengeance, fighting under their banners, claiming their protection against violence, seeking redress in their courts, petitioning their legislatures to enact laws, or obeying their unrighteous requirements. Neither can we participate in any rebellion, insurrection, sedition, riot, conspiracy, or plot against any of these governments, nor resist any of their ordinances by physical force, nor do anything unbecoming a peaceable submission to the existing powers; but will quietly pay the taxes levied upon us, conform to all innocent laws and usages, enjoy all righteous privileges, abstain from all civil commotions, freely express our opinions of governmental acts, and patiently endure whatever penalties we may for conscience's sake incur.

We cannot employ carnal weapons nor any physical violence whatsoever to compel moral agents to do right, or to prevent their doing wrong—not even for the preservation of our lives. We cannot render evil for evil, railing for railing, wrath for wrath, nor revenge insults and injuries, nor lay up grudges, nor be overcome of evil, nor do otherwise than "love our enemies, bless them that curse us, do good to them that hate us, and pray for them that despitefully use us and persecute us."

We cannot indulge the lust of dominion, nor exercise arbitrary authority, nor cherish bigotry, nor be egotistical, nor receive honorary titles, nor accept flattery, nor seek human applause, nor assume the place of dignity. We cannot be pharisaical, self-righteous, nor dogmatical. We cannot do evil that good may come. We cannot resent reproof, nor justify our faults, nor persist in wrong-doing.

We cannot excommunicate, anathematize, or execrate an apostate, heretic, or reprobate person otherwise than withdrawing our fellowship, refusing our confidence, and declining familiar intercourse.

We cannot be cruel, even to the beasts of the earth. We cannot be inhuman, unmerciful, unjust, unkind, abusive, or injurious to any being of our race. We cannot be indifferent to the sufferings of distressed humanity, nor treat the unfortunate with contempt. But we hold ourselves bound to do good, as we have opportunity, unto all mankind; to feed the hungry, clothe the naked, minister to the sick, visit the imprisoned, entertain the stranger, protect the helpless, comfort the afflicted, plead for the oppressed, seek the lost, lift up the fallen, rescue the ensnared, reclaim the wandering, reform the vicious, enlighten the benighted, instruct the young, admonish the wayward, rebuke the scornful, encourage the penitent, confirm the upright, and diffuse a universal charity.

We cannot go with a multitude to do evil, nor take part with the mighty against the feeble, nor excite enmity between the rich and the poor, nor stand aloof from the friendless, nor abandon them that take refuge with us, nor court the great, nor despise the small, nor be afraid of the terrible, nor take advantage of the timid, nor show respect of persons, nor side with a friend in what is wrong, nor oppose an enemy in what is right, nor forbid others to do good because they follow not us, nor set up names and forms above personal holiness, nor refuse to cooperate with any man, class, or association of men on our own principles in favor of righteousness, nor contemn any new light, improvement, excellence, which may be commended to our attention from any direction whatsoever.

We cannot make a trade or emolument of preaching the gospel, nor be supported therein by unwilling contributions, nor keep back any truth thereof which ought to be declared, nor consent to preach anything more or less than God directs us, nor encourage religious devotion in mere worldly show, nor pursue any course of conduct whereby the money, the smiles, or the frowns of corrupt men may overrule the divine law and testimony. We cannot surrender the right of serving God according to the dictates of our own conscience, nor interfere with others in their exercise of the same liberty.

We hold it impossible to cherish a holy love for mankind without abhorring sin. Therefore, we can give no countenance, express or implied, to any iniquity, vice, wrong, or evil, on the ground that the same is established by law, or is a source of pecuniary profit to any class of men, or is fashionable in high life, or is popular with the multitude; but we hold ourselves bound so much the more to testify plainly, faithfully, and fearlessly against such sins. Hence, we declare our utter abhorrence of war, slavery, intemperance, licentiousness, covetousness, and worldly ambitions in all their forms. We cannot partake in these sins nor apologize for them, nor remain neutral concerning them, nor refrain from rebuking their various manifestations; but must forever abstain from and oppose them.

We cannot promote our own advantage at the expense of others by deceiving, defrauding, corrupting, degrading, overbearing, or impoverishing them. We cannot take away their good name by defamation, nor by retailing the scandal of their enemies, nor by spreading abroad evil reports on mere hearsay authority, nor by wantonly publishing their failings. We cannot be busybodies in other people's affairs, nor tale-bearers of domestic privacy, nor proclaimers of matters unsuitable for the public ear. We cannot rashly judge men's motives, nor raise evil suspicions against them, nor join in condemning the accused without a hearing, nor delay reparation to the injured, nor make any one's necessity our advantage, nor willingly render ourselves burdensome to others, nor cause any one a single unnecessary step for our mere gratification; but we will always deem it "more blessed to give than to receive," to serve than to be served—sacrificing nothing of holy principle, though, if need be, everything of personal convenience.

We cannot live in idleness, nor be careless or extravagant, nor on the other hand avaricious, parsimonious, or niggardly. We cannot indulge a feverish anxiety in any of our temporal concerns, nor fret ourselves under disappointment, nor repine at anything that marks our lot. We cannot be austere, morose, or rude; nor capricious, ungrateful, or treacherous. We cannot practice dissimulation, nor offer fulsome compliments, nor use a flattering courtesy. We cannot follow pernicious fashions, nor encourage theatrical exhibitions, nor join in frivolous amusements, nor countenance games of chance, nor array ourselves in costly apparel, nor wear useless ornaments, nor put on badges of mourning, nor distinguish ourselves by any peculiar formalities of raiment or language.

We cannot indulge to excess in eating, drinking, sleeping, re creation, labor, study, joy, or sorrow, nor permit our passions to tyrannize over our reason. We cannot harbor pride, envy, anger, malice, wrath, ill-will, sullenness, or peevishness; nor cherish any unholy lusts, imaginations, or tempers.

We cannot swear by any matter of oath, nor make any rash vows, nor offer any extraordinary protestations of our innocence, sincerity, or veracity; nor utter any blasphemy, imprecation, falsehood, obscene expression, foolish jest, or profane exclamation.

We cannot enter into the state of matrimony without grave deliberation and an assurance of divine approbation. We cannot neglect or abuse our families, nor evince any want of natural affection towards our bosom companion, our aged parents, or our helpless offspring. We cannot imbrute our children by disregarding their education, nor by setting them an evil example, nor by over-fondness, nor by harshness and severity, nor by corporeal punishment, nor by petulance and scolding.

We cannot neglect our brethren in their adversity, nor call anything our own when their necessities demand relief, nor be silent when they are unjustly accused or reproached. We cannot speak of their faults in their absence without first having conferred with and admonished them; nor then if they have promised amendment.

We cannot over-urge any person to unite with us, nor resort to undignified artifices of proselytism, nor seek debate with unreasonable men, nor protract a controversy for the sake of the last word, nor introduce sacred subjects for discussion in a company of scorners. Yet we will hold ourselves ready to give an answer to every one that asketh of us a reason for our faith, opinion, or conduct, with meekness, frankness, and patience.

Finally, as disciples of Jesus Christ, before whose judgment seat all must appear, we acknowledge ourselves bound by the most sublime, solemn, and indispensable obligations to be perfect as our Father in heaven is perfect, in all possible respects; and whereinsoever we come short thereof to take shame to ourselves, confess our sins, seek divine pardon, repair to the utmost our delinquencies, and bring forth fruits meet for repentance. And for all this, our sufficiency is of God, to whom be glory, world without end. Amen.

Adin Ballou, David R. Lamson, Daniel S. Whitney, Wm. H. Fish, *Ministers.*
Charles Gladding, Wm. W. Cook, *Laymen Concurring.*

SOURCE: Adin Ballou, "Standard of Practical Christianity," *The Practical Christian*, April 1, 1840.

Prospectus for *The Dial:*
A Magazine for Literature,
Philosophy, and Religion
1840

As the leading journal for the Transcendentalist movement, The Dial was edited by Margaret Fuller, Ralph Waldo Emerson, and (briefly) Henry David Thoreau. Though it lasted only four years and attracted only three hundred subscribers, it published important works by its editors and by Bronson Alcott, Lydia Maria Child, James Freeman Clarke, Frederic Henry Hedge, James Russell Lowell, Theodore Parker, Elizabeth Palmer Peabody, George and Sophia Ripley, and many others. The prospectus, probably written by George Ripley, conveys the spirit of what would become the United States' most widely recognized philosophical movement. Further Reading: Joel Myerson, The New England Transcendentalists and the Dial: A History of the Magazine and Its Contributors *(Rutherford, NJ: Fairleigh Dickinson University Press, 1980).*

—Dan McKanan

The purpose of this work is to furnish a medium for the freest expression of thought on the questions which interest earnest minds in every community.

It aims at the discussion of principles, rather than at the promotion of measures; and while it will not fail to examine the ideas which impel the leading movements of the present day, it will maintain an independent position with regard to them.

The pages of this Journal will be filled with contributors, who possess little in common but the love of intellectual freedom, and the hope of social progress; who are united by sympathy of spirit, not by agreement in speculation; whose faith is in Divine Providence, rather than in human prescription; whose hearts are more in the future than in the past; and who trust the living soul rather than the dead letter. It will endeavor to promote the constant evolution of truth, not the petrifaction of opinion. . . .

In literature, it will strive to exercise a just and catholic criticism, and to recognise every sincere production of genius; in philosophy, it will attempt the reconciliation of the universal instincts of humanity with the largest conclusions of reason; and in religion, it will reverently seek to discover the presence of God in nature, in history, and in the soul of man.

The DIAL, as its title indicates, will endeavor to occupy a station on which the light may fall; which is open to the rising sun; and from which it may correctly report the progress of the hour and the day.

SOURCE: *The Dial*, July 1840, wrapper.

ORESTES BROWNSON
"The Laboring Classes"
1840

Orestes Augustus Brownson (1803–1876) was born into a Universalist family, but was largely raised by Congregationalist foster parents. After a brief period as a Presbyterian, in 1825 he studied for the Universalist ministry and then served several small Universalist societies in New York State. While a Universalist minister, Brownson adopted increasingly radical beliefs. In 1829, beset by controversy with other Universalist ministers and having been dismissed from his position as editor of a Universalist newspaper, he turned to political journalism. In 1831 he returned to the ministry, this time as a Unitarian. Five years later, with the assistance of George Ripley and other members of the Transcendentalist movement, he founded the Society for Christian Union and Progress in Boston, whose mission was to develop a form of liberal Christianity that would be meaningful to the urban poor and working classes. Brownson wrote "The Laboring Classes" during this period. He was deeply disillusioned by the negative response to his essay and by the outcome of the 1840 presidential election, the first in which advertising played a significant role. Convinced that liberal religion and democracy were inadequate to resist the growing power of moneyed interests and the mass media they controlled, Brownson became a conservative in both religion and politics. In 1844 he converted to Catholicism, eventually becoming a leading American Catholic journalist and essayist. Further Reading: Patrick W. Carey, Orestes A. Brownson: American Religious Weathervane *(Grand Rapids, MI: Wm. B. Eerdmans, 2004); Patrick W. Carey, ed.,* The Early Works of Orestes A. Brownson, *7 volumes (Milwaukee: Marquette University Press, 2000–2007).*

—Lynn Gordon Hughes

What we would ask is, throughout the Christian world, the actual condition of the laboring classes, viewed simply and exclusively in their capacity of laborers? They constitute at least a moiety of the human race. We exclude the nobility, we exclude also the middle class, and include only actual laborers, who are laborers and not proprietors, owners of none of the funds of production, neither houses, shops, nor lands, nor implements of labor, being therefore solely dependent on their hands. We have no means of ascertaining their precise proportion to the whole number of the race; but we think we may estimate them at one half. In any contest they will be as two to one, because the large class of proprietors who are not employers, but laborers on their own lands or in their own shops will make common cause with them.

Now we will not so belie our acquaintance with political economy, as to allege that these alone perform all that is necessary to the production of wealth. We are not ignorant of the fact, that the merchant, who is literally the common carrier and exchange dealer, performs a useful service, and is therefore entitled to a portion of the proceeds of labor. But make all necessary deductions on his account, and then ask what portion of the remainder is retained, either in kind or in its equivalent, in the hands of the original producer, the working-man? All over the world this fact stares us in the face, the working-man is poor and depressed, while a large portion of the non-workingmen, in the sense we now use the term, are wealthy. It may be laid down as a general rule, with but few exceptions, that men are rewarded in an inverse ratio to the amount of actual service they perform. Under every government on earth the largest salaries are annexed to those offices, which demand of their incumbents the least amount of actual labor either mental or manual. And this is in perfect harmony with the whole system of repartition of the fruits of industry, which obtains in every department of society. Now here is the system which prevails, and here is its result. The whole class of simple laborers are poor, and in general unable to procure anything beyond the bare necessaries of life.

In regard to labor two systems obtain; one that of slave labor, the other that of free labor. Of the two, the first is, in our judgment, except so far as the feelings are concerned, decidedly the least oppressive. If the slave has never been a free man, we think, as a general rule, his sufferings are less than those of the free laborer at wages. As to actual freedom one has just about as much as the other. The laborer at wages has all the disadvantages of freedom and none of its blessings, while the slave, if denied the blessings, is freed from the disadvantages. We are no advocates of slavery, we are as heartily opposed to it as any modern abolitionist can be; but we say frankly that, if there must always be a laboring population distinct from proprietors and employers, we regard the slave system as decidedly preferable to the system at wages. It is no pleasant thing to go days without food, to lie idle for weeks, seeking work and finding none, to rise in the morning with a wife and children you love, and know not where to procure them a breakfast, and to see constantly before you no brighter prospect than the almshouse. Yet these are no unfrequent incidents in the lives of our laboring population.

* * *

Now the great work for this age and the coming, is to raise up the laborer, and to realize in our own social arrangements and in the actual condition of all men, that equality between man and man, which God has established between the rights of one and those of another. In other words, our business is to emancipate the proletaries, as the past has emancipated the slaves.

We admit the importance of what Dr. Channing in his lectures on the subject we are treating recommends as "self-culture." Self-culture is a good thing, but it cannot abolish inequality, nor restore men to their rights. As a means of quickening moral and intellectual energy, exalting the sentiments, and preparing the laborer to contend manfully for his rights, we admit its importance, and insist as strenuously as any one on making it as universal as possible; but as constituting in itself a remedy for the vices of the social state, we have no faith in it. As a means it is well, as the end it is nothing.

The truth is, the evil we have pointed out is not merely individual in its character. It is not, in the case of any single individual, of any one man's procuring, nor can the efforts of any one man, directed solely to his own moral and religious perfection, do aught to remove it. What is purely individual in its nature, efforts of individuals to perfect themselves, may remove. But the evil we speak of is inherent in all our social arrangements, and cannot be cured without a radical change of those arrangements. Could we convert all men to Christianity in both theory and practice, as held by the most enlightened sect of Christians among us, the evils of the social state would remain untouched. Continue our present system of trade, and all its present evil consequences will follow, whether it be carried on by your best men or your worst. Put your best men, your wisest, most moral, and most religious men, at the head of your paper money banks, and the evils of the present banking system will remain scarcely diminished. The only way to get rid of its evils is to change the system, not its managers. The evils of slavery do not result from the personal characters of slave masters. They are inseparable from the system, let who will be masters. Make all your rich men good Christians, and you have lessened not the evils of existing inequality in wealth. The mischievous effects of this inequality do not result from the personal characters of either rich or poor, but from itself, and they will continue, just so long as there are rich men and poor men in the same community. You must abolish the system or accept its consequences. No man can serve both God and Mammon. If you will serve the devil, you must look to the devil for your wages, we know no other way.

Let us not be misinterpreted. We deny not the power of Christianity. Should all men become good Christians, we deny not that all social evils would be cured. But we deny in the outset that a man, who seeks merely to save his own soul, merely to perfect his own individual nature, can be a good Christian. The Christian forgets himself, buckles on his armor, and goes forth to war against principalities and powers, and against spiritual wickedness in high places. No man can be a Christian who does not begin his career by making war on the mischievous social arrangements from which his brethren suffer. He who thinks he can be a Christian and save his soul, without seeking their radical change, has no reason to applaud himself for his proficiency in Christian science, nor for his progress towards the kingdom of God. Understand Christianity, and we will admit, that should all men become good Christians, there would be nothing to complain of. But one might as well undertake to dip the ocean dry with a clam-shell, as to undertake to cure the evils of the social state by converting men to the Christianity of the Church.

* * *

The next step in this work of elevating the working classes will be to resuscitate the Christianity of Christ. The Christianity of the Church has done its work. We have had enough of that Christianity. It is powerless for good, but by no means powerless for evil. It now unmans us and hinders the growth of God's kingdom. The moral energy which is awakened it misdirects, and makes its deluded disciples believe that they have done their duty to God when they have joined the church, offered a prayer, sung a psalm, and contributed of their means to send out a missionary to preach unintelligible dogmas to the poor heathen, who, God knows, have unintelligible dogmas enough already, and more than enough. All this must be abandoned, and Christianity, as it came from Christ, be taken up, and preached, and preached in simplicity and in power. . . .

No man can be a Christian who does not labor to reform society, to mould it according to the will of God and the nature of man; so that free scope shall be given to every man to unfold himself in all beauty and power, and to grow up into the stature of a perfect man in Christ Jesus. No man can be a Christian who does not refrain from all practices by which the rich grow richer and the poor poorer, and who does not do all in his power to elevate the laboring classes, so that one man shall not be doomed to toil while another enjoys the fruits; so that each man shall be free and independent, sitting under "his own vine and figtree with none to molest or to make afraid."

SOURCE: Orestes Brownson, "The Laboring Classes," *Boston Quarterly Review*, July 1840, reprinted as a pamphlet, *The Laboring Classes* (Boston, 1840), 10, 13–15, 21.

The Plain Guide to Universalism

1840

*Thomas Whittemore (1800–1861) was one of the greatest denominational orga-
nizers in Universalist history. Mentored in his youth by Rev. Jedidiah Morse,
Whittemore was converted to Universalism by Hosea Ballou and served congregations in Milford and Cambridge, Massachusetts, before devoting himself full time to editing and writing at age thirty-one. Whittemore established
his* Trumpet and Universalist Magazine *as the leading denominational journal and also published a catechism, a hymnal, a history of Universalism, a
biography of Hosea Ballou, biblical commentaries, and this* Plain Guide *to
his chosen tradition. The passages presented here emphasize the antiquity of
universalist doctrine, refute those who would conflate it with infidelity, and
address the concerns of those who worry that belief in universal salvation
might lead to immorality. Further Reading: John Greenleaf Adams,* Memoir
of Thomas Whittemore *(Boston: Universalist Publishing House, 1878).*

—Dan McKanan

Universalists are those who believe in the eventual holiness and happiness of all the
human race, as revealed to the world in the Gospel of the Lord Jesus Christ.

They are supposed by some to be of a very recent origin; but it is well known,
that there have been Universalists in almost every age, since the word of God was
revealed to the children of men.

*   *   *

It is also worthy of remark, that the Christian Fathers defended Universalism as
the doctrine of the sacred Scriptures. Clemens of Alexandria, the renowned Origen,
Gregory, of Nyssa, and others, quoted much the same texts to prove that sentiment,
that are now quoted for that purpose by Universalists of the present age. They used
the words *eternal* and *everlasting*, not to signify endless duration when applied to
punishment, but they used them in a limited sense. It was not until nearly four hundred years after the death of Christ, that Universalism was regarded as worthy of
condemnation, and it was not formally condemned by any general council, until the
meeting of the Fifth General Council, in 553. . . .

Let it be observed, also, that Universalism was not put down, by reason, by argument, by appeals to the word of God, but it was crushed by the arm of power. It was
the arm of usurped power that crucified the Son of God; it was the arm of usurped

power that persecuted the infant church; and it was the arm of usurped power that condemned and crushed Univesalism, in 553. During the dark ages, when the Pope held undisturbed dominion, and the whole Christian world trembled at his nod,—when the light of science almost expired, and wickedness of every description stalked abroad at noonday; then little was known of Universalism; while the contrary doctrine of endless misery flourished abundantly. . . . But we have shown, that no sooner was the arm of usurped power broken, than Universalism once more appeared. . . .

The sentiment by which Universalists are distinguished is this: *that at last every individual of the human race shall become holy and happy.* This does not comprise the whole of their faith; but merely that feature of it, which is peculiar to them, and by which they are distinguished from the rest of the world.

Universalists are not infidels. It is sometimes very indiscreetly said that Universalism is but a species of infidelity; that Universalists are not Christians, and cannot be so considered. We shall have no lengthened argument on this point; but we desire one question settled, touching this matter. If the doctrine of Jesus concerning the resurrection of the dead is not true, how is the doctrine of Universalism to be established? It evidently cannot be. If the doctrine of Jesus concerning a future life fails, what becomes of Universalism? It is gone like a dream. Why, then, should Universalism be called infidelity? If it cannot rest unless it rest on Christianity, is it not a very singular kind of infidelity? It is just such *infidelity* as Jesus taught, when he said, the dead shall become as the angels of God in heaven, neither shall they die any more, but shall be the children of God, being the children of the resurrection.

*　*　*

What are the peculiar duties of Universalists? It is but seldom that we now hear the objection urged against Universalism, which was formerly urged with frequency and confidence that it had a licentious influence on those who believed it. We are inclined to attribute the disrespect into which this charge against Universalism has fallen, to reflection in the opponent, who is convinced, that Universalists are not what he has often represented them to be; and, moreover, that a doctrine of love and mercy must have a benign and salutary tendency.

The Universalist now maintains, as he has always maintained, that the doctrine in which he believes, so far from exerting an injurious influence, is, in fact, of all doctrines advocated by Christians, the most pure and holy,—exciting the sweetest and most generous sentiments in the human heart; and he goes further, and declares, that, so far as any doctrine is really opposed to the doctrine of Universalism, it must exert a paralyzing influence on the benevolent affections of the human soul. There is nothing in any creed under heaven which is calculated to make men love God and one another, but what is found in the sublime and heavenly doctrine of universal grace.

*　*　*

The love of God is a soul-inspiring theme. The heart is softened by this subject. O happy Universalists! ye are the only people on the earth who believe in a God whose perfection may be safely imitated. You can *love*, and imitate your God; but others, to imitate their God, must *hate*. You can find peace and joy in obeying the injunction of our great Master,—"Be ye, therefore, perfect, even as your Father in heaven is perfect." Remember, brethren, there is no other way to be perfect, but that in which God is perfect. Universalists, having so reasonable and benevolent a doctrine, are laid under more sacred obligations to be virtuous than any other class of men.

SOURCE: Thomas Whittemore, *The Plain Guide to Universalism* (Boston, 1840), 7, 13–15, 282–83, 288–89.

RALPH WALDO EMERSON

"Self-Reliance"
1841

*Emerson preached the doctrine of self-reliance all his life, from his earliest
sermons to his last lectures; it was at the core of his spiritual teaching and his
political philosophy. But it has often been misinterpreted. By self-reliance
Emerson did not mean individualism, rugged or otherwise. He was well aware
of the perils of individualism resulting from a distorted understanding of the
true nature of the self. The self that he refers to is not the ego or the isolated
self of modern psychology, but rather the soul, which, though individually
incarnated in each person, is nevertheless commonly shared by all human
beings as an expression of the One. Thus self-reliance is not reliance on the
self in isolation but the self in relation to that larger Self which "makes us
receivers of its truth and organs of its activity." And because all selves are
equally related to this larger Self, each person possesses inherent worth and
dignity. In essence, Emerson reads the first Unitarian Universalist Principle
through the lens of the seventh. Further Reading: Lawrence Buell,* Emerson
(Cambridge, MA: Harvard University Press, 2003); Barry M. Andrews, Emerson as Spiritual Guide: A Companion to Emerson's Essays for Personal
Reflections and Group Discussion *(Boston: Skinner House, 2003).*

—Barry Andrews

To believe your own thought, to believe that what is true for you in your private
heart, is true for all men,—that is genius. Speak your latent conviction, and it shall
be the universal sense; for the inmost in due time becomes the outmost,—and our
first thought is rendered back to us by the trumpets of the Last Judgment. Familiar as
the voice of the mind is to each, the highest merit we ascribe to Moses, Plato, and
Milton, is that they set at naught books and traditions, and spoke not what men but
what they thought. A man should learn to detect and watch that gleam of light which
flashes across his mind from within, more than the lustre of the firmament of bards
and sages. Yet he dismisses without notice his thought, because it is his. In every work
of genius we recognize our own rejected thoughts: they come back to us with a certain alienated majesty. . . .

There is a time in every man's education when he arrives at the conviction that
envy is ignorance; that imitation is suicide; that he must take himself for better, for
worse, as his portion; that though the wide universe is full of good, no kernel of nour-
ishing corn can come to him but through his toil bestowed on that plot of ground

which is given to him to till. The power which resides in him is new in nature, and none but he knows what that is which he can do, nor does he know until he has tried. . . .

Trust thyself: every heart vibrates to that iron string. Accept the place the divine Providence has found for you; the society of your contemporaries, the connexion of events. Great men have always done so, and confided themselves childlike to the genius of their age, betraying their perception that the absolutely trustworthy was seated at their heart, working through their hands, predominating in all their being. And we are now men, and must accept in the highest mind the same transcendent destiny; and not minors and invalids in a protected corner, not cowards fleeing before a revolution, but guides, redeemers, and benefactors, obeying the Almighty effort, and advancing on Chaos and the Dark.

☆ ☆ ☆

Whoso would be a man must be a nonconformist. He who would gather immortal palms must not be hindered by the name of goodness, but must explore if it be goodness. Nothing is at last sacred but the integrity of your own mind. Absolve you to yourself, and you shall have the suffrage of the world. I remember an answer which when quite young I was prompted to make to a valued adviser who was wont to importune me with the dear old doctrines of the church. On my saying, What have I to do with the sacredness of traditions, if I live wholly from within? my friend suggested—"But these impulses may be from below, not from above." I replied, "They do not seem to me to be such; but if I am the Devil's child, I will live then from the Devil." No law can be sacred to me but that of my nature. Good and bad are but names very readily transferable to that or this; the only right is what is after my constitution, the only wrong what is against it. . . . If malice and vanity wear the coat of philanthropy, shall that pass? If an angry bigot assumes this bountiful cause of Abolition, and comes to me with his last news from Barbadoes, why should I not say to him, "Go love thy infant; love thy wood-chopper: be good-natured and modest: have that grace; and never varnish your hard, uncharitable ambition with this incredible tenderness for black folk a thousand miles off. Thy love afar is spite at home." Rough and graceless would be such greeting, but truth is handsomer than the affectation of love. Your goodness must have some edge to it—else it is none. The doctrine of hatred must be preached as the counteraction of the doctrine of love when that pules and whines. I shun father and mother and wife and brother, when my genius calls me. I would write on the lintels of the door-post, *Whim.* I hope it is somewhat better than whim at last, but we cannot spend the day in explanation. Expect me not to show cause why I seek or why I exclude company. Then, again, do not tell me, as a good man did to-day, of my obligation to put all poor men in good situations. Are they *my* poor? I tell thee, thou foolish philanthropist, that I grudge the dollar, the dime, the cent, I give to such men as do not belong to me and to whom

I do not belong. There is a class of persons to whom by all spiritual affinity I am bought and sold; for them I will go to prison, if need be; but your miscellaneous popular charities; the education at college of fools; the building of meeting-houses to the vain end to which many now stand; alms to sots; and the thousandfold Relief Societies;—though I confess with shame I sometimes succumb and give the dollar, it is a wicked dollar which by and by I shall have the manhood to withhold. . . .

What I must do, is all that concerns me, not what the people think. This rule, equally arduous in actual and in intellectual life, may serve for the whole distinction between greatness and meanness. It is the harder, because you will always find those who think they know what is your duty better than you know it. It is easy in the world to live after the world's opinion; it is easy in solitude to live after our own; but the great man is he who in the midst of the crowd keeps with perfect sweetness the independence of solitude.

The objection to conforming to usages that have become dead to you, is, that it scatters your force. It loses your time and blurs the impression of your character. If you maintain a dead church, contribute to a dead Bible-Society, vote with a great party either for the Government or against it, spread your table like base housekeepers,—under all these screens, I have difficulty to detect the precise man you are. And, of course, so much force is withdrawn from your proper life. But do your work, and I shall know you. Do your work, and you shall reinforce yourself. A man must consider what a blindman's-buff is this game of conformity.

* * *

A foolish consistency is the hobgoblin of little minds, adored by little statesmen and philosophers and divines. With consistency a great soul has simply nothing to do. He may as well concern himself with his shadow on the wall. Speak what you think now in hard words, and to-morrow speak what to-morrow thinks in hard words again, though it contradict every thing you said to-day.—"Ah, so you shall be sure to be misunderstood."—Is it so bad then to be misunderstood? Pythagoras was misunderstood, and Socrates, and Jesus, and Luther, and Copernicus, and Galileo, and Newton, and every pure and wise spirit that ever took flesh. To be great is to be misunderstood.

* * *

Let us affront and reprimand the smooth mediocrity and squalid contentment of the times, and hurl in the face of custom, and trade, and office, the fact which is the upshot of all history, that there is a great responsible Thinker and Actor working wherever a man works; that a true man belongs to no other time or place, but is the centre of things. Where he is, there is nature. He measures you, and all men, and all events. Ordinarily, every body in society reminds us of somewhat else or of some other person. Character, reality, reminds you of nothing else; it takes place of the whole creation. The man must be so much, that he must make all circumstances indifferent. Every true man is a cause, a country, and an age; requires infinite spaces and numbers and time fully to accomplish his design;—and posterity seem to follow his steps as a train of clients. A man Caesar is born, and for ages after, we have a Roman Empire. Christ is born, and millions of minds so grow and cleave to his genius, that he is confounded with virtue and the possible of man. An institution is the lengthened shadow of one man.

* * *

The magnetism which all original action exerts is explained when we inquire the reason of self-trust. Who is the Trustee? What is the aboriginal Self on which a universal reliance may be grounded? What is the nature and power of that science-baffling star, without parallax, without calculable elements, which shoots a ray of beauty even into trivial and impure actions, if the least mark of independence appear? The inquiry leads us to that source, at once the essence of genius, of virtue, and of life, which we call Spontaneity or Instinct. We denote this primary wisdom as Intuition, whilst all later teachings are tuitions. In that deep force, the last fact behind which analysis cannot go, all things find their common origin. For the sense of being which in calm hours rises, we know not how, in the soul, is not diverse from things, from space, from light, from time, from man, but one with them, and proceeds obviously from the same source whence their life and being also proceed. We first share the life by which things exist, and afterwards see them as appearances in nature, and forget that we have shared their cause. Here is the fountain of action and of thought. Here are the lungs of that inspiration which giveth man wisdom, and which cannot be denied without impiety and atheism. We lie in the lap of immense intelligence, which makes us receivers of its truth and organs of its activity. When we discern justice, when we discern truth, we do nothing of ourselves, but allow a passage to its beams. If we ask whence this comes, if we seek to pry into the soul that causes, all philosophy is at fault. Its presence or its absence is all we can affirm. Every man discriminates between the voluntary acts of his mind, and his involuntary perceptions, and knows that to his involuntary perceptions a perfect faith is due. He may err in the expression of them, but he knows that these things are so, like day and night, not to be disputed. . . .

Whenever a mind is simple, and receives a divine wisdom, old things pass away,—means, teachers, texts, temples fall; it lives now and absorbs past and future into the present hour. All things are made sacred by relation to it,—one as much as another. All things are dissolved to their centre by their cause, and, in the universal miracle petty and particular miracles disappear. If, therefore, a man claims to know and speak of God, and carries you backward to the phraseology of some old mouldered nation in another country, in another world, believe him not. Is the acorn better than the oak which is its fulness and completion? Is the parent better than the child into whom he has cast his ripened being? Whence then this worship of the past? . . .

Man is timid and apologetic; he is no longer upright; he dares not say "I think," "I am," but quotes some saint or sage. He is ashamed before the blade of grass or the blowing rose. These roses under my window make no reference to former roses or to better ones; they are for what they are; they exist with God to-day. There is no time to them. There is simply the rose; it is perfect in every moment of its existence. . . . But man postpones or remembers; he does not live in the present, but with reverted eye laments the past, or, heedless of the riches that surround him, stands on tiptoe to foresee the future. He cannot be happy and strong until he too lives with nature in the present, above time.

* * *

Life only avails, not the having lived. Power ceases in the instant of repose; it resides in the moment of transition from a past to a new state, in the shooting of the gulf, in the darting to an aim. This one fact the world hates, that the soul *becomes*; for, that forever degrades the past, turns all riches to poverty, all reputation to a shame, confounds the saint with the rogue, shoves Jesus and Judas equally aside. Why then do we prate of self-reliance? Inasmuch as the soul is present, there will be power not confident but agent. To talk of reliance, is a poor external way of speaking. Speak rather of that which relies because it works and is.

* * *

Insist on yourself; never imitate. Your own gift you can present every moment with the cumulative force of a whole life's cultivation; but of the adopted talent of another, you have only an extemporaneous, half possession. That which each can do best, none but his Maker can teach him. No man yet knows what it is, nor can, till that person has exhibited it. Where is the master who could have taught Shakespeare? Where is the master who could have instructed Franklin, or Washington, or Bacon, or Newton? Every great man is a unique.

* * *

So use all that is called Fortune. Most men gamble with her, and gain all, and lose all, as her wheel rolls. But do thou leave as unlawful these winnings, and deal with Cause and Effect, the chancellors of God. In the Will work and acquire, and thou hast chained the wheel of Chance, and shalt sit hereafter out of fear from her rotations. A political victory, a rise of rents, the recovery of your sick, or the return of your absent friend, or some other favorable event, raises your spirits, and you think good days are preparing for you. Do not believe it. Nothing can bring you peace but yourself. Nothing can bring you peace but the triumph of principles.

SOURCE: Ralph Waldo Emerson, "Self-Reliance," *The Collected Works of Ralph Waldo Emerson* (Cambridge, MA: Harvard University Press, 1979), 2:27–35, 37–40, 47, 50–51.

THEODORE PARKER

"The Transient and Permanent in Christianity"
1841

Rev. Theodore Parker (1810–1860) was the most influential Unitarian minister of his era. A scholarly prodigy reared on the edge of poverty, he was ordained pastor of a tiny congregation in West Roxbury in 1836. There, largely unnoticed, he preached Transcendentalist "heresies": that the Bible was full of contradictions and errors, that Jesus had no miraculous authority, that the biblical miracles were myths, and that society needed radical reform. Yet in 1841, when he delivered this sermon at an ordination in South Boston, he did not intend to start a controversy. He said nothing about social reform, and his main point, that the words of Jesus would live forever, seemed unexceptionable. Three evangelical clergymen in the audience, however, heard only rank deism and were appalled that when Parker finished speaking, the service proceeded as if nothing had happened. A few days later, they issued a challenge in the newspapers, demanding to know which Unitarians shared Parker's views or regarded him as a Christian. The Unitarian leadership responded defensively, criticizing Parker and distancing themselves from him, but his ideas excited ordinary Unitarians, who began snapping up his publications and flocking to hear him lecture and preach. Further Reading: Dean Grodzins, American Heretic: Theodore Parker and Transcendentalism *(Chapel Hill: University of North Carolina Press, 2002), esp. 238–60; Conrad Wright, ed.,* Three Prophets of Religious Liberalism: Channing, Emerson, Parker *(Boston: Beacon Press, 1961), 32–43.*

— Dean Grodzins

"Heaven and earth shall pass away: but my word shall not pass away."
— LUKE XXI.33.

In this sentence we have a very clear indication that Jesus of Nazareth believed the religion he taught would be eternal, that the substance of it would last forever. Yet there are some, who are affrighted by the faintest rustle which a heretic makes among the dry leaves of theology; they tremble lest Christianity itself should perish without hope. . . . Let us, therefore, devote a few moments to this subject, and consider what is *Transient* in Christianity, and what is *Permanent* therein. . . .

Christ says, his Word shall never pass away. Yet at first sight nothing seems more fleeting than a word. It is an evanescent impulse of the most fickle element. It leaves

306

no track where it went through the air. Yet to this, and this only did Jesus entrust the truth wherewith he came laden, to the earth; truth for the salvation of the world. He took no pains to perpetuate his thoughts; they were poured fourth where occasion found him an audience, — by the side of the lake, or a well; in a cottage, or the temple; in a fisher's boat, or the synagogue of the Jews. He founds no institution as a monument of his words. He appoints no order of men to preserve his bright and glad revelations. He only bids his friends give freely the truth they had freely received. He did not even write his words in a book. With a noble confidence, the result of his abiding faith, he scattered them broad-cast on the world, leaving the seed to its own vitality. He knew, that what is of God cannot fail, for God keeps his own. He sowed his seed in the heart, and left it there, to be watered and warmed by the dew and the sun which heaven sends. He felt his words were for eternity. So he trusted them to the uncertain air; and for eighteen hundred years that faithful element has held them good. . . . They make all things ours: Christ our brother; Time our servant; Death our ally and the witness of our triumph. They reveal to us the presence of God, which else we might not have seen so clearly, in the first wind-flower of spring; in the falling of a sparrow; in the distress of a nation; in the sorrow or the rapture of the world. Silence the voice of Christianity, and the world is well nigh dumb.

*   *   *

Looking at the Word of Jesus, at real Christianity, the pure religion he taught, nothing appears more fixed and certain. Its influence widens as light extends; it deepens as the nations grow more wise. But, looking at the history of what men call Christianity, nothing seems more uncertain and perishable. While true religion is always the same thing, in each century and every land, in each man that feels it, the Christianity of the Pulpit, which is the religion taught; the Christianity of the People, which is the religion that is accepted and lived out; has never been the same thing in any two centuries or lands, except only in name. The difference between what is called Christianity by the Unitarians in our times, and that of some ages past, is greater than the difference between Mahomet and the Messiah. The difference at this day between opposing classes of Christians; the difference between the Christianity of some sects, and that of Christ himself; is deeper and more vital than that between Jesus and Plato, Pagan as we call him. . . .

Let us look at this matter a little more closely. In actual Christianity—that is, in that portion of Christianity which is preached and believed—there seem to have been, ever since the time of its earthly founder, two elements, the one transient, the other permanent. The one is the thought, the folly, the uncertain wisdom, the theological notions, the impiety of man; the other, the eternal truth of God. These two bear perhaps the same relation to each other that the phenomena of outward nature, such as sunshine and cloud, growth, decay, and reproduction, bear to the great law of nature, which underlies and supports them all. As in that case, more attention is commonly paid to the particular phenomena than to the general law; so in this case, more is generally given to the Transient in Christianity than to the Permanent therein.

It must be confessed, though with sorrow, that transient things form a great part of what is commonly taught as Religion. An undue place has often been assigned to forms and doctrines, while too little stress has been laid on the divine life of the soul, love to God, and love to man. Religious forms may be useful and beautiful. They are so, whenever they speak to the soul, and answer a want thereof. In our present state some forms are perhaps necessary. But they are only the accident of Christianity; not its substance. They are the robe, not the angel, who may take another robe, quite as becoming and useful. One sect has many forms; another none. Yet both may be equally Christian, in spite of the redundance or the deficiency. They are a part of the language in which religion speaks, and exist, with few exceptions, wherever man is found. In our calculating nation, in our rationalizing sect, we have retained but two of the rites so numerous in the early Christian church, and even these we have attenuated to the last degree, leaving them little more than a spectre of the ancient form. Another age may continue or forsake both; may revive old forms, or invent new ones to suit the altered circumstance of the times, and yet be Christians quite as good as we, or our fathers of the dark ages. Whether the Apostles designed these rites to be perpetual, seems a question which belongs to scholars and antiquarians; not to us, as Christian men and women. So long as they satisfy or help the pious heart, so long they are good. . . .

For, strictly speaking, there is but one kind of religion, as there is but one kind of love, though the manifestations of this religion, in forms, doctrine, and life, be never so diverse. It is through these, men approximate to the true expression of this religion. Now while this religion is one and always the same thing, there may be numerous systems of theology or philosophies of religion. These with their creeds, confessions, and collections of doctrines, deduced by reasoning upon the facts observed, may be baseless and false, either because the observation was too narrow in extent, or otherwise defective in point of accuracy, or because the reasoning was illogical, and therefore the deduction spurious. Each of these three faults is conspicuous in the systems of theology. Now the solar system as it exists in fact is permanent, though the notions of Thales and Ptolemy, of Copernicus and Descartes about this system, prove transient, imperfect approximations to the true expression. So the Christianity of Jesus is permanent, though what passes for Christianity with Popes and catechisms, with sects and churches, in the first century or in the nineteenth century, prove transient also. Now it has sometimes happened that a man took his philosophy of Nature at second hand, and then attempted to make his observations conform to his theory, and Nature ride in his panniers. Thus some philosophers refused to look at the Moon through Galileo's telescope, for, according to their

theory of vision, such an instrument would not aid the sight. Thus their precon-
ceived notions stood up between them and Nature. Now it has often happened that
men took their theology thus at second hand, and distorted the history of the world
and man's nature besides, to make Religion conform to their notions. Their theology
stood between them and God. Those obstinate philosophers have disciples in no
small number. . . .

Any one, who traces the history of what is called Christianity, will see that nothing changes more from age to age than the doctrines taught as Christian, and insisted
on as essential to Christianity and personal salvation. What is falsehood in one province passes for truth in another. The heresy of one age is the orthodox belief and
"only infallible rule" of the next. Now Arius, and now Athanasius is Lord of the
ascendant. Both were excommunicated in their turn, each for affirming what the
other denied. . . . The theological doctrines derived from our fathers seem to have
come from Judaism, Heathenism, and the caprice of philosophers, far more than
they have come from the principle and sentiment of Christianity. The doctrine of
the Trinity, the very Achilles of theological dogmas, belongs to philosophy and not
religion; its subtleties cannot even be expressed in our tongue. . . . If Paul and Jesus
could read our books of theological doctrines, would they accept as their teaching,
what men have vented in their name?

*   *   *

This transitoriness of doctrines appears, in many instances, of which two may be
selected for a more attentive consideration. First, the doctrine respecting the origin
and authority of the Old and New Testament. There has been a time when men
were burned for asserting doctrines of natural philosophy, which rested on evidence
the most incontestable, because those doctrines conflicted with sentences in the Old
Testament. . . . What was originally a presumption of bigoted Jews became an article
of faith, which Christians were burned for not believing. This has been for centuries
the general opinion of the Christian church. . . . Hence the attempt, which always
fails, to reconcile the philosophy of our times with the poems in Genesis writ a thousand years before Christ; hence the attempt to conceal the contradictions in the
record itself. Matters have come to such a pass, that even now he is deemed an infidel, if not by implication an atheist, whose reverence for the Most High forbids him
to believe that God commanded Abraham to sacrifice his Son, a thought at which
the flesh creeps with horror; to believe it solely on the authority of an oriental story,
written down nobody know when or by whom, or for what purpose; which may be
a poem, but cannot be the record of a fact, unless God is the author of confusion
and a lie.

Now this idolatry of the Old Testament has not always existed. Jesus says that
none born of a woman is greater than John the Baptist, yet the least in the kingdom
of heaven was greater than John. Paul tells us the Law—the very crown of the old

309

Hebrew revelation—is a shadow of good things, which have now come; only a schoolmaster to bring us to Christ, and when faith has come, that we are no longer under the schoolmaster; that it was a law of sin and death, from which we are made free by the Law of the spirit of Life. Christian teachers themselves have differed so widely in their notion of the doctrines and meaning of those books, that it makes one weep to think of the follies deduced therefrom. But modern Criticism is fast breaking to pieces this idol which men have made out of the Scriptures. It has shown that here are the most different works thrown together. That their authors, wise as they sometimes were; pious as we feel often their spirit to have been, had only that inspiration which is common to other men equally pious and wise; that they were by no means infallible; but were mistaken in facts or in reasoning; uttered predictions which time has not fulfilled; men who in some measure partook of the darkness and limited notions of their age, and were not always above its mistakes or its corruptions.

The history of opinions on the New Testament is quite similar.

* * *

Another instance of the transitoriness of doctrines, taught as Christian, is found in those which relate to the nature and authority of Christ. One ancient party has told us, that he is the infinite God; another, that he is both God and man; a third, that he was a man, the son of Joseph and Mary,—born as we are; tempted like ourselves; inspired, as we may be, if we will pay the price. . . .

Almost every sect, that has ever been, makes Christianity rest on the personal authority of Jesus, and not the immutable truth of the doctrines themselves, or the authority of God, who sent him into the world. Yet it seems difficult to conceive any reason, why moral and religious truths should rest for their support on the personal authority of their revealer, any more than the truths of science on that of him who makes them known first or most clearly. It is hard to see why the great truths of Christianity rest on the personal authority of Jesus, more than the axioms of geometry rest on the personal authority of Euclid, or Archimedes.

* * *

Now it seems clear, that the notion men form about the origin and nature of the scriptures; respecting the nature and authority of Christ, having nothing to do with Christianity except as its aids or its adversaries; they are not the foundation of its truths. These are theological questions; not religious questions. Their connection with Christianity appears accidental; for if Jesus had taught at Athens, and not at Jerusalem; if he had wrought no miracle, and none but the human nature had ever been ascribed to him; if the Old Testament had forever perished at his birth,— Christianity would still have been the Word of God; it would have lost none of its truths. It would be just as true, just as beautiful, just as lasting, as now it is; though we should have lost so many a blessed word, and the work of Christianity itself would have been, perhaps, a long time retarded.

To judge the future by the past, the former authority of the Old Testament can never return. Its present authority cannot stand. It must be taken for what it is worth. The occasional folly and impiety of its authors must pass for no more than their value;—while the religion, the wisdom, the love, which make fragrant its leaves, will still speak to the best hearts as hitherto, and in accents even more divine, when Reason is allowed her rights. The ancient belief in the infallible inspiration of each sentence of the New Testament is fast changing; very fast. One writer, not a skeptic, but a Christian of unquestioned piety, sweeps off the beginning of Matthew; another, of a different church and equally religious, the end of John. Numerous critics strike off several epistles. The Apocalypse itself it not spared, notwithstanding its concluding curse. Who shall tell us the work of retrenchment is to stop here; that others will not demonstrate, what some pious hearts have long felt, that errors of doctrine and errors of fact may be found in many parts of the record, here and there, from the beginning of Matthew to the end of Acts? . . .

But what if this should take place? Is Christianity then to perish out of the heart of the nations, and vanish from the memory of the world, like the religions that were before Abraham? It must be so, if it rest on a foundation which a scoffer may shake, and a score of pious critics shake down. But this is the foundation of a theology, not of Christianity. That does not rest on the decision of Councils. It is not to stand or fall with the infallible inspiration of a few Jewish fishermen, who have writ their names in characters of light all over the world. It does not continue to stand through the forbearance of some critic, who can cut, when he will, the thread on which its life depends. Christianity does not rest on the infallible authority of the New Testament. It depends on this collection of books for the historical statement of its facts. In this we do not require infallible inspiration on the part of the writers, more than in the record of other historical facts. To me it seems as presumptuous, on the one hand, for the believer to claim this evidence for the truth of Christianity, as it is absurd, on the other hand, for the skeptic to demand such evidence to support these historical statements. I cannot see that it depends on the personal authority of Jesus. He was the organ through which the Infinite spoke. It is God that was manifested in the flesh by him, on whom rests the truth which Jesus brought to light and made clear and beautiful in his life; and if Christianity be true, it seems useless to look for any other authority to uphold it, as for some one to support Almighty God. So if it could be proved,—as it cannot,—in opposition to the greatest amount of historical evidence ever collected on any similar point, that the gospels were the fabrication of designing and artful men, that Jesus of Nazareth had never lived, still Christianity would stand firm, and fear no evil. None of the doctrines of that religion would fall to the ground; for if true, they stand by themselves. But we should lose,—oh, irreparable loss!—the example of that character, so beautiful, so divine, that no human genius could have conceived it, as none, after all the progress and refinement of eighteen centuries, seems fully to have comprehended its lustrous life. If Christianity were true, we should still think it was so, not because its record was written by infallible pens; nor because it was lived out by an infallible teacher,—but that it is true, like the axioms of geometry, because it is true, and is to be tried by the oracle God places in the breast. If it rest on the personal authority of Jesus alone, then there is no certainty of its truth, if he were ever mistaken in the smallest matter, as some Christians have thought he was, in predicting his second coming. . . .

To turn away from the disputes of the Catholics and the Protestants, of the Unitarian and the Trinitarian, of Old School and New School, and come to the plain words of Jesus of Nazareth, Christianity is a simple thing; very simple. It is absolute, pure Morality; absolute, pure Religion; the love of man; the love of God acting without let or hindrance. The only creed it lays down is the great truth which springs up spontaneous in the holy heart—there is a God. Its watchword is, be perfect as your Father in Heaven. The only form it demands is a divine life; doing the best thing, in the best way, from the highest motives; perfect obedience to the great law of God. Its sanction is the voice of God in your heart; the perpetual presence of Him, who made us and the stars over our head; Christ and the Father abiding within us. All this is very simple; a little child can understand it; very beautiful, the loftiest mind can find nothing so lovely. Try it by Reason, Conscience, and Faith—things highest in man's nature—we see no redundance, we feel no deficiency. Examine the particular duties it enjoins; humility, reverence, sobriety, gentleness, charity, forgiveness, fortitude, resignation, faith, and active love; try the whole extent of Christianity so well summed up in the command, "Thou shalt love he Lord they God with all thy heart, and with all thy soul, and with all thy mind—thou shalt love thy neighbor as thyself;" and is there anything therein that can perish? No, the very opponents of Christianity have rarely found fault with the teachings of Jesus. The end of Christianity seems to be to make all men one with God as Christ was one with Him; to bring them to such a state of obedience and goodness, that we shall think divine thoughts and feel divine sentiments, and so keep the law of God by living a life of truth and love. Its means are Purity and Prayer; getting strength from God and using it for our fellow men as well as ourselves. It allows perfect freedom. It does not demand all men to *think* alike, but to think uprightly, and get as near as possible at truth; not all men to *live* alike, but to live holy, and get as near as possible to a life perfectly divine.

*　*　*

Let then the Transient pass, fleet as it will, and may God send us some new manifestation of the Christian faith, that shall stir men's hearts as they were never stirred; some new Word, which shall teach us what we are, and renew us all in the image of God; some better life, that shall fulfill the Hebrew prophecy, and pour out the spirit of God on young men and maidens, and old men and children; which shall realize the Word of Christ, and give us the comforter, who shall reveal all needed things. . . .

Such, then, is the Transient, and such the Permanent in Christianity. What is of absolute value never changes; we may cling round it and grow to it forever. No one can say his notions shall stand. But we may all say, the Truth, as it is in Jesus, shall never pass away.

SOURCE: Theodore Parker, *Critical and Miscellaneous Writings* (Boston, 1843), 136–48, 150–54, 160–61, 165–66.

"The Great Lawsuit. Man *versus* Men. Woman *versus* Women"

1843

Margaret Fuller (1810–1850) called for consciousness-raising: She asked women and men to "sue" for the ideal potential that each might achieve. Such awareness, she hoped, would then move outward from the soul, transforming the gendered inequalities of marriage and religious doctrine and finally bringing forth a new humanity. But she called women themselves to lead. Instead of being buried in the underworld like Eurydice, they must go down and rescue Orpheus. This reversal of patterns typified Fuller's engagement with both Biblical religion and Greco-Roman mythology. "Seek, and ye shall find," she urged, echoing Jesus, but she called on women to seek as well by understanding the ancient goddesses who best represent women's wisdom. Her 1843 essay entered into dialogue with two male mentors, William Ellery Channing and Ralph Waldo Emerson. Fuller honored Channing and his Unitarian circle for their recognition of women's spiritual equality, but she more subversively appropriated Emerson's Transcendental "self-reliance"—represented in the ideal woman Miranda—as a counter-force against dependence on men. Her argument was also positioned within the traditions of democratic revolution and reform, from French and American liberty to contemporary antislavery appeals. The essay, especially as expanded in Woman in the Nineteenth Century, *offered a vital source for the women's rights movement launched in 1848. Further Reading: Megan Marshall,* Margaret Fuller: A New American Life *(Boston: Houghton Mifflin Harcourt, 2013);* The Essential Margaret Fuller, *ed. Jeffrey Steele (New Brunswick, NJ: Rutgers University Press, 1992); Charles Capper,* Margaret Fuller: An American Romantic Life, *2 vols. (New York: Oxford University Press, 1992, 2007).*

—Phyllis Cole and Dorothy May Emerson

This great suit has now been carried on through many ages, with various results. The decisions have been numerous, but always followed by appeals to still higher courts. How can it be otherwise, when the law itself is the subject of frequent elucidation, constant revision? . . .

Yet a foundation for the largest claim is now established.

✻ ✻ ✻

Whatever the soul knows how to seek, it must attain. Knock, and it shall be opened; seek, and ye shall find. . . . However disputed by many, however ignorantly used, or falsified, by those who do receive it, the fact of an universal, unceasing revelation, has been too clearly stated in words, to be lost sight of in thought, and sermons preached from the text, "Be ye perfect," are the only sermons of a pervasive and deep-searching influence.

* * *

Meanwhile, not a few believe, and men themselves have expressed the opinion, that the time is come when Euridice is to call for an Orpheus, rather than Orpheus for Euridice; that the idea of man, however imperfectly brought out, has been far more so than that of woman, and that an improvement in the daughters will best aid the reformation of the sons of this age.

It is worthy of remark, that, as the principle of liberty is better understood and more nobly interpreted, a broader protest is made in behalf of woman. As men become aware that all men have not had their fair chance, they are inclined to say that no women have had a fair chance. The French revolution, that strangely disguised angel, bore witness in favor of woman, but interpreted her claims no less ignorantly than those of man. Its idea of happiness did not rise beyond outward enjoyment, unobstructed by the tyranny of others. The title it gave was Citoyen, Citoyenne, and it is not unimportant to woman that even this species of equality was awarded her. Before, she could be condemned to perish on the scaffold for treason, but not as a citizen, but a subject. The right, with which this title then invested a human being, was that of bloodshed and license. The Goddess of Liberty was impure. Yet truth was prophesied in the ravings of that hideous fever induced by long ignorance and abuse. Europe is conning a valued lesson from the blood stained page. The same tendencies, farther unfolded, will bear good fruit in this country.

* * *

Though the national independence be blurred by the servility of individuals; though freedom and equality have been proclaimed only to leave room for a monstrous display of slave dealing, and slave keeping; though the free American so often feels himself free, like the Roman, only to pamper his appetites and his indolence through the misery of his fellow beings, still it is not in vain, that the verbal statement has been made, "All men are born free and equal." There it stands, a golden certainty, wherewith to encourage the good, to shame the bad. The new world may be called clearly to perceive that it incurs the utmost penalty, if it rejects the sorrowful brother. And if men are deaf, the angels hear.

* * *

Of all its banners, none has been more steadily upheld, and under none has more valor and willingness for real sacrifices been shown, than that of the champions of the enslaved African. And this band it is, which, partly in consequence of a

natural following out of principles, partly because many women have been prominent in that cause, makes, just now, the warmest appeal in behalf of woman.

Though there has been a growing liberality on this point, yet society at large is
not so prepared for the demands of this party, but that they are, and will be for some
time, coldly regarded as the Jacobins of their day.

"Is it not enough," cries the sorrowful trader, "that you have done all you could
to break up the national Union, and thus destroy the prosperity of our country, but
now you must be trying to break up family union, to take my wife away from the
cradle, and the kitchen hearth, to vote at polls, and preach from a pulpit? Of course,
if she does such things, she cannot attend to those of her own sphere. She is happy
enough as she is. She has more leisure than I have, every means of improvement,
every indulgence."

"Have you asked her whether she was satisfied with these indulgences?"

"No, but I know she is. She is too amiable to wish what would make me unhappy,
and too judicious to wish to step beyond the sphere of her sex. I will never consent
to have our peace disturbed by any such discussions."

"'Consent'—you? it is not consent from you that is in question, it is assent from
your wife."

"Am I not the head of my house?"

"You are not the head of your wife. God has given her a mind of her own."

"I am the head and she the heart."

"God grant you play true to one another then. If the head represses no natural
pulse of the heart, there can be no question as to your giving your consent. Both will
be of one accord, and there needs but to present any question to get a full and true
answer. There is no need of precaution, of indulgence, or consent. But our doubt is
whether the heart consents with the head, or only acquiesces in its decree; and it is
to ascertain the truth on this point, that we propose some liberating measures."

Thus vaguely are these questions proposed and discussed at present. But their
being proposed at all implies much thought, and suggests more. Many women are
considering within themselves what they need that they have not, and what they
can have, if they find they need it. Many men are considering whether women are
capable of being and having more than they are and have, and whether, if they are,
it will be best to consent to improvement in their condition.

* * *

It is not surprising that it should be the Anti-Slavery party that pleads for woman,
when we consider merely that she does not hold property on equal terms with men;
so that, if a husband dies without a will, the wife, instead of stepping at once into his
place as head of the family, inherits only a part of his fortune, as if she were a child,
or ward only, not an equal partner.

* * *

316

And, as to men's representing women fairly, at present, while we hear from men who owe to their wives not only all that is comfortable and graceful, but all that is wise in the arrangement of their lives, the frequent remark, "You cannot reason with a woman," when from those of delicacy, nobleness, and poetic culture, the contemptuous phrase, "Women and children," and that in no light sally of the hour, but in works intended to give a permanent statement of the best experiences, when not one man in the million, shall I say, no, not in the hundred million, can rise above the view that woman was made *for man*, when such traits as these are daily forced upon the attention, can we feel that man will always do justice to the interests of woman? . . .

Under these circumstances, without attaching importance in themselves to the changes demanded by the champions of woman, we hail them as signs of the times. We would have every arbitrary barrier thrown down. We would have every path laid open to woman as freely as to man. Were this done, and a slight temporary fermentation allowed to subside, we believe that the Divine would ascend into nature to a height unknown in the history of past ages, and nature, thus instructed, would regulate the spheres not only so as to avoid collision, but to bring forth ravishing harmony.

Yet then, and only then, will human beings be ripe for this, when inward and outward freedom for woman, as much as for man, shall be acknowledged as a right, not yielded as a concession. As the friend of the negro assumes that one man cannot, by right, hold another in bondage, should the friend of woman assume that man cannot, by right, lay even well-meant restrictions on woman. If the negro be a soul, if the woman be a soul, apparelled in flesh, to one master only are they accountable. There is but one law for all souls, and, if there is to be an interpreter of it, he comes not as man, or son of man, but as Son of God. . . .

I was talking on this subject with Miranda, a woman, who, if any in the world, might speak without heat or bitterness of the position of her sex.

* * *

[S]he smilingly replied, And yet we must admit that I have been fortunate, and this should not be. My good father's early trust gave the first bias, and the rest followed of course. . . .

[T]he position I early was enabled to take, was one of self-reliance. And were all women as sure of their wants as I was, the result would be the same.

* * *

The severe nation which taught that the happiness of the race was forfeited through the fault of a woman, and showed its thought of what sort of regard man owed her, by making him accuse her on the first question to his God, who gave her to the patriarch as a handmaid, and, by the Mosaical law, bound her to allegiance like a serf, even they greeted, with solemn rapture, all great and holy women as heroines,

317

prophetesses, nay judges in Israel; and, if they made Eve listen to the serpent, gave Mary to the Holy Spirit. In other nations it has been the same down to our day.

* * *

Whatever may have been the domestic manners of the ancient nations, the idea of woman was nobly manifested in their mythologies and poems, where she appeared as Sita in the Ramayana, a form of tender purity, in the Egyptian Isis, of divine wisdom never yet surpassed. In Egypt, too, the Sphynx, walking the earth with lion tread, looked out upon its marvels in the calm, inscrutable beauty of a virgin's face, and the Greek could only add wings to the great emblem. In Greece, Ceres and Proserpine, termed "the goddesses," were seen seated, side by side. They needed not to rise for any worshipper or any change; they were prepared for all things, as those initiated to their mysteries knew. More obvious is the meaning of those three forms, the Diana, Minerva, and Vesta. Unlike in the expression of their beauty, but alike in this,—that each was self-sufficing.

* * *

Women who speak in public, if they have a moral power, such as has been felt from Angelina Grimke and Abby Kelly, that is, if they speak for conscience' sake, to serve a cause which they hold sacred, invariably subdue the prejudices of their hearers, and excite an interest proportionate to the aversion with which it had been the purpose to regard them.

* * *

The late Dr. Channing, whose enlarged and tender and religious nature shared every onward impulse of his time, though his thoughts followed his wishes with a deliberative caution, which belonged to his habits and temperament, was greatly interested in these expectations for women. His own treatment of them was absolutely and thoroughly religious. He regarded them as souls, each of which had a destiny of its own, incalculable to other minds, and whose leading it must follow, guided by the light of a private conscience. He had sentiment, delicacy, kindness, taste, but they were all pervaded and ruled by this one thought, that all beings had souls, and must vindicate their own inheritance. Thus all beings were treated by him with an equal, and sweet, though solemn courtesy. The young and unknown, the woman and the child, all felt themselves regarded with an infinite expectation, from which there was no reaction to vulgar prejudice. He demanded of all he met, to use his favorite phrase, "great truths." . . .

At one time when the progress of Harriet Martineau through this country, Angelina Grimke's appearance in public, and the visit of Mrs. Jameson had turned his thoughts to this subject, he expressed high hopes as to what the coming era would bring to woman. . . . He seemed to think that he might sometime write upon the subject. That his aid is withdrawn from the cause is a subject of great regret, for on this question, as on others, he would have known how to sum up the evidence and take, in the noblest spirit, middle ground. He always furnished a platform on which opposing parties could stand, and look at one another under the influence of his mildness and enlightened candor.

*   *   *

For woman, if by a sympathy as to outward condition, she is led to aid the enfranchisement of the slave, must no less so, by inward tendency, to favor measures which promise to bring the world more thoroughly and deeply into harmony with her nature. When the lamb takes place of the lion as the emblem of nations, both women and men will be as children of one spirit, perpetual learners of the word and doers thereof, not hearers only.

*   *   *

There are two aspects of woman's nature, expressed by the ancients as Muse and Minerva. . . .

The especial genius of woman I believe to be electrical in movement, intuitive in function, spiritual in tendency. She is great not so easily in classification, or re-creation, as in an instinctive seizure of causes, and a simple breathing out of what she receives that has the singleness of life, rather than the selecting or energizing of art. . . .

Male and female represent the two sides of the great radical dualism. But, in fact, they are perpetually passing into one another. Fluid hardens to solid, solid rushes to fluid. There is no wholly masculine man, no purely feminine woman.

*   *   *

If it has been the tendency of the past remarks to call woman rather to the Minerva side, — if I, unlike the more generous writer, have spoken from society no less than the soul, — let it be pardoned. It is love that has caused this, love for many incarcerated souls, that might be freed could the idea of religious self-dependence be established in them, could the weakening habit of dependence on others be broken up. . . .

If any individual live too much in relations, so that he becomes a stranger to the resources of his own nature, he falls after a while into a distraction, or imbecility, from which he can only be cured by a time of isolation, which gives the renovating fountains time to rise up. . . . It is therefore that while any elevation, in the view of union, is to be hailed with joy, we shall not decline celibacy as the great fact of the time. . . . Union is only possible to those who are units. To be fit for relations in time, souls, whether of man or woman, must be able to do without them in the spirit.

It is therefore that I would have woman lay aside all thought, such as she habitually cherishes, of being taught and led by men. I would have her, like the Indian girl, dedicate herself to the Sun, the Sun of Truth, and go nowhere if his beams did not make clear the path. I would have her free from compromise, from complaisance, from helplessness, because I would have her good enough and strong enough to love one and all beings, from the fulness, not the poverty of being.

319

A profound thinker has said "no married woman can represent the female world, for she belongs to her husband. The idea of woman must be represented by a virgin."

But that is the very fault of marriage, and of the present relation between the sexes, that the woman does belong to the man, instead of forming a whole with him. Were it otherwise there would be no such limitation to the thought.

Woman, self-centred, would never be absorbed by any relation; it would be only an experience to her as to man. It is a vulgar error that love, *a* love to woman is her whole existence; she also is born for Truth and Love in their universal energy. Would she but assume her inheritance, Mary would not be the only Virgin Mother. . . .

And will not she soon appear? The woman who shall vindicate their birthright for all women; who shall teach them what to claim, and how to use what they obtain? Shall not her name be for her era Victoria, for her country and her life Virginia? Yet predictions are rash; she herself must teach us to give her the fitting name.

SOURCE: Margaret Fuller, "The Great Lawsuit. Man *versus* Men. Woman *versus* Women," *The Dial*, July 1843, 1, 4, 7–11, 13–16, 18, 20, 40–45, 47.

Historical Sketches and Incidents
1843

Stephen R. Smith (1788–1850) was a towering figure in the early history of Universalism in New York State. Trained for the ministry by Paul Dean and Richard Carrique, he served six settled pastorates and preached thousands of circuit-riding sermons in two hundred different locations. Near the end of his career, he became the chronicler of the denominational beginnings in his home state. In addition to describing the process by which congregations and ministerial associations were founded, Smith offered colorful sketches of the strengths and weaknesses of the early ministers in New York, among them Maria Cook (1779–1835). Cook was the first Universalist woman preacher in the United States, but by no means the only woman to take up a preaching vocation in upstate New York in the early nineteenth century. Both Mother Ann Lee of the Shakers and Jemima Wilkinson of the Society of Universal Friends had planted communities in the vicinity shortly before the arrival of Universalism. Further Reading: Russell Miller, The Larger Hope: The First Century of the Universalist Church in America, 1770–1870 *(Boston: Unitarian Universalist Association, 1979);* Catherine Brekus, Strangers & Pilgrims: Female Preaching in America, 1740–1845 *(Chapel Hill: University of North Carolina Press, 1998).*

—Dan McKanan

It was not until 1802, that Universalism was preached in the state of New York, beyond the immediate vicinity of the city—unless perhaps, in some of the towns bordering on Vermont. In the summer of this year, Mr. Edwin Ferris—a plain man of Quaker habits, but of very good common sense, visited what is now the town of Butternuts, Otsego County, and delivered to the few and scattered inhabitants, the message of Universal salvation. . . . It is probable that Mr. Ferris never wholly devoted his attention and his labors to the work of the ministry. He appears in the first instance, to have entertained some prejudices against receiving what is called "ministerial support;" and it is certain that the general circumstances of the recent population were favorable to the gratification of his choice in this particular. Much of his time was therefore spent in the improvement and cultivation of a farm. . . . At this time, and during many succeeding years, whatever may have been the peculiarities or prejudices of Mr. Ferris, he faithfully devoted his talents to the interests and advancement of Universalism—cheerfully enduring the ignominy and reproach of its profession, and rejoicing in its triumphs. He entertained high and just views of the necessity of an elevated morality in the professors of religion—and especially in the professors of Universalism.—And he was among those who saw and felt the necessity and propriety of a sound system of discipline—and was vigilant to fastidiousness, of what he deemed the rights of the laity, and of individual congregations. . . .

In the summer of 1804, Mr. Miles T. Wooley, located in the town of Hartwick, Otsego Co.—in the neighborhood of Mr. Ferris, where he also commenced preaching the restitution. This seems to have been a favorable location; and had the capabilities and worth of the preacher been equal to his advantages of place, the best results would have been realized. A successful attempt was made to form a society in this town, sometime in March 1803; and it is believed, that a constitution was adopted and subscribed by about *twenty-five members*. This was undoubtedly the first Universalist society, organized in the state of New York. But the eccentricities and immoralities of Mr. Wooley prevented his usefulness, and must have had an injurious effect upon the society. He was suspended from the fellowship of the order, on the organization of a proper council; and formally expelled in June of the following year.

In 1805, Mr. Nathaniel Stacy—a good man, and a most faithful, persevering and devoted minister, visited and preached in parts of Oneida, Madison, Otsego and Chenango Counties; and in the course of the season, societies were formed in Whitestown, (now New Hartford,) Hamilton and Brookfield. From this time, the affairs of the infant denomination assumed an aspect of order; and early measures were taken for the establishment of a system of discipline and church government.

*   *   *

The original organization of the society in Whitestown, appears to have been under a Confession of Faith and Covenant, which constituted its members *a christian church*. The constitution, or by-laws which it appended, provided accordingly for the regular administration of the *ordinances*—and the Eucharist or Lord's Supper, was usually administered *once in three months*, when the society had a pastor. *Baptism* by affusion or immersion, was sometimes chosen by candidates, either because they had not previously received it, or because some particular mode was preferred. And whenever desired, it was administered in the form pointed out by the candidate. A similar, if not the same compact was adopted by the society in Hamilton; and probably by all. . . . So that nothing could be more slanderous than the oft repeated assertion of the enemies of the restitution, that "Universalists had neither churches nor ordinances." . . .

There is one distinctive and benevolent feature in the constitution of Universalist societies—which if not peculiar to the denomination, is probably not generally known—certainly not by other sects. It is a provision *for the poor*. And so faithfully is this pledge redeemed, that very few instances can be found in which destitute Universalists have been thrown upon the public charities.

322

Application was also made at this session [of the Western Association in 1809] by Mr. William Baker, for a letter of fellowship as a minister of the reconciliation. He was then a preacher in the Methodist connection—probably, what is termed a "local preacher." . . . Mr. Baker appears to have been a well disposed, illiterate and ineffi-cient man—and was probably better qualified for some other field of labor and duty, than the ministry. . . .

In the summer of this year, Mr. Calvin Winslow—a Methodist circuit preacher, renounced his former views, professed his faith in "the restitution of all things," and received the fellowship of the association. He was possessed of strong native talents, of quick apprehension and warm affections,—was a very ready speaker, and pre-served much of the style and energy so characteristic of the preachers of his former connection. His memory was remarkably tenacious, and while he read little, he observed much, which he had the art of turning to very good account in his pub-lic ministrations. Mr. Winslow received ordination the following year. And but for one besetting weakness, by which he was finally overcome,—intemperance—would have been a valuable acquisition. No man loved the truth better,—his heart was in its prosperity through every trial, and every period of life.

* * *

It is probably the fortune or *misfortune* of all newly organized christian commu-nities, to win to their ranks the most discordant materials, and the most eccentric characters. . . .

Fellowship was granted to Mr. Lewis Beers [in 1811], as a minister of the recon-ciliation. He was a gentleman of undoubted worth, of respectable talents, and a firm believer in the restitution. But he held nothing else in common with Universalists. He was a Swedenborgian—and consequently, in the estimation of every proper Uni-versalist, a visionary. Nothing can be farther from the plain, common sense doctrine of the restitution than the forced, and unnatural, and mystical "science of correspon-dencies," maintained by Swedenborg and his admirers. In an age making any pre-tention to reason, Universalism coupled with the endless fancies of such a theory, could not be supposed to make any very intelligible progress. . . .

At the same session of the Association, the Council was honored with the atten-dance of, and the congregation edified by, a discourse from—*a female preacher*. She too, was a Universalist. Miss Maria Cook, was at the time some thirty-five years of age, of genteel and commanding appearance, well educated, and certainly a very good speaker.—From the character of her discourses, it would appear that Universal-ism as a system, was unknown to her; and it was rather the result of her feelings than of an extensive acquaintance with the scriptures, that she had made it the creed of her adoption. Difficult as many found it, to reconcile the ministry of Miss Cook, with their ideas of duty and propriety—they still accorded her their sympathy and their hospitality. She was a Universalist and a preacher of that doctrine—none doubted the purity of her motives, or the sincerity of her heart; and satisfied that she would do no hurt, they yielded her the right of choosing this manner of doing good. And for a time—while the double charm of novelty and singularity furnished its attractions, multitudes crowded to hear her ministrations. But these influences could not, and they did not last long; and she was permitted and encouraged to discontinue her public labors, and to seek a more congenial sphere under the protection of a hospitable private family.—Miss Cook's connections were numerous and respectable; and were by her, represented, as inveterately opposed to Universalism. This was probably true—but there is much reason to believe that their opposition to her, grew out of far other considerations. They were extremely averse to her assumption of the ministerial character; and probably not without grounds of apprehension that so extraordinary an undertaking was an evidence of *mental alienation*. One thing is certain—they received and cherished her; whenever she preferred to avail herself of their protection and kindness.

SOURCE: Stephen R. Smith, *Historical Sketches and Incidents, Illustrative of the Establishment and Progress of Universalism in the State of New York* (Buffalo, NY: Steele's Press, 1843), 8–11, 15–16, 23–24, 29–32.

Constitution of the Brook Farm Association for Industry and Education

1844

Of the dozens of utopian communities established in the 1840s, Brook Farm was the most closely identified with the Transcendentalist movement. Launched by George and Sophia Ripley in 1841, it endured until 1846 and counted Nathaniel Hawthorne as an early member and Margaret Fuller and Theodore Parker as staunch friends. Other community members pursued subsequent careers in journalism, labor organizing, classical music, and (in the case of Isaac Hecker) the creation of a new Roman Catholic religious order, the Paulists. The Constitution was composed as Brook Farm was gravitating toward the utopian theories of Charles Fourier, who taught that giving free rein to individual passions would usher in an age of universal harmony. Further Reading: Sterling Delano, Brook Farm: The Dark Side of Utopia *(Cambridge, MA: Harvard University Press, 2004); Carl Guarneri,* The Utopian Alternative: Fourierism in Nineteenth-Century America *(Ithaca, NY: Cornell University Press, 1991).*

—Dan McKanan

Introduction

The Association at Brook Farm has now been in existence upwards of two years. . . .

Every step has strengthened the faith with which we set out; our belief in a divine order of human society, has in our own minds become an absolute certainty; and considering the present state of humanity and of social science, we do not hesitate to affirm, that the world is much nearer the attainment of such a condition than is generally supposed.

* * *

The following Constitution is the same as that under which we have hitherto acted, with such alterations as on a careful revision seemed needful. All persons who are not familiar with the purposes of Association, will understand from this document that we propose a radical and universal reform, rather than to redress any particular wrong, or to remove the sufferings of any single class of human beings. We do this in the light of universal principles, in which all differences, whether of religion, or politics, or philosophy, are reconciled, and the dearest and most private hope of every man has the promise of fulfilment. Herein, let it be understood, we

325

would remove nothing that is truly beautiful or venerable; we reverence the religious sentiment in all its forms, the family, and whatever else has its foundation either in human nature or the Divine Providence. The work we are engaged in is not destruction, but true conservation: it is not a mere revolution, but, as we are assured, a necessary step in the course of social progress which no one can be blind enough to think has yet reached its limit. We believe that humanity, trained by these long centuries of suffering and struggle, led onward by so many saints and heroes and sages, is at length prepared to enter into that universal order, toward which it has perpetually moved. Thus we recognize the worth of the whole Past and of every doctrine and institution it has bequeathed us; thus also we perceive that the Present has its own high mission, and we shall only say what is beginning to be seen by all sincere thinkers, when we declare that the imperative duty of this time and this country, nay more, that its only salvation, and the salvation of all civilized countries, lies in the Reorganization of Society, according to the unchanging laws of human nature and of universal harmony. . . .

Constitution

In order more especially to promote the great purposes of human culture; to establish the external relations of life on a basis of wisdom and purity; to apply the principles of justice and love to our social organization in accordance with the laws of Divine Providence; to substitute a system of brotherly cooperation for one of selfish competition; to secure to our children and those who may be entrusted to our care the benefits of the highest physical, intellectual, and moral education, which in the progress of knowledge the resources at our command will permit; to institute an attractive, efficient, and productive system of industry; to prevent the exercise of worldly anxiety, by the competent supply of our necessary wants; to diminish the desire of excessive accumulation, by making the acquisition of individual property subservient to upright and disinterested uses; to guarantee to each other forever the means of physical support, and of spiritual progress; and thus to impart a greater freedom, simplicity, truthfulness, refinement, and moral dignity, to our mode of life;—we the undersigned do unite in a voluntary Association, and adopt and ordain the following articles of agreement, to wit:

Article I.

Name and Membership.

Sec. 1. The name of this Association shall be "The Brook-Farm Association for Industry and Education." All persons who shall hold one or more shares in its stock, or whose labor and skill shall be considered an equivalent for capital, may be admitted by the vote of two-thirds of the Association, as members thereof.

Sec. 2. No member of the Association shall ever be subjected to any religious test; nor shall any authority be assumed over individual freedom of opinion by the Association. . . .

* * *

Article III.

Guaranties.

Sec. 1. The Association shall provide such employment for all its members as shall be adapted to their capacities, habits, and tastes; and each member shall select and perform such operations of labor, whether corporal or mental, as shall be deemed best suited to his own endowments and the benefit of the Association.

Sec 2. The Association guaranties to all its members, their children and family dependents, house-rent, fuel, food, and clothing, and the other necessaries of life, without charge, not exceeding a certain fixed amount to be decided annually by the Association; no charge shall ever be made for support during inability to labor from sickness or old age, or for medical or nursing attendance, except in case of shareholders, who shall be charged therefor, and also for the food and clothing of children, to an amount not exceeding the interest due to them on settlement; but no charge shall be made to any member for education or the use of library and public room. . . .

Sec 4. Children over ten years of age shall be provided with employment in suitable branches of industry; they shall be credited for such portions of each annual dividend, as shall be decided by the Association, and on the completion of their education in the Association at the age of twenty, shall be entitled to a certificate of stock to the amount of credits in their favor, and may be admitted as members of the Association.

SOURCE: *Constitution of the Brook Farm Association for Industry and Education* (Boston: I. R. Butts, 1844).

JAMES FREEMAN CLARKE

"The Principles and Methods of the Church of the Disciples"

1845

The charter for the Church of the Disciples, organized by Rev. James Freeman Clarke (1810–1888), was signed in the same West Street parlor where Elizabeth Peabody sponsored many Transcendentalist conversations, just as Brook Farm began its own operation. The principles the charter introduced may be taken for granted now, but in 1841 they were new. Control of the church by all contributing members, not just wealthy pew-owners, was a direct result of the refusal, the previous year, of the leaders at the Federal Street Church to allow Dr. Channing to hold a memorial service for the abolitionist Rev. Charles Follen. Fellow abolitionist Rev. Samuel May gave the eulogy and encouraged Clarke's new church. Charter members included Channing's brothers and niece. Lay participation in worship included lay preaching. Without benefit of ordination, Julia Ward Howe, a later member, founded the first association of women ministers. The social principle meant meetings of members for fellowship, sharing of "joys and concerns," and organizing around social concerns. The Disciples raised the funds to outfit the 54th Massachusetts Volunteers—the first regiment of African-American soldiers in the Union Army, authorized by John Andrew, Civil War Governor of Massachusetts and a lay leader of the Disciples. Further Reading: John Buehrens, Transcendentalist Disciples *(Boston: Beacon Press, 2018).*

—John Buehrens

[It] may be asked, "But why need we have a church at all? . . . Is not religion a matter between the soul and God? . . ."

I reply that there are two reasons for joining a church; we should join it for our own good, and for the good of others. For our own good; because we need such a union for the growth of our spiritual life. . . . We need to commit ourselves by an outward act to the determination we have inwardly taken. . . .

We should also be willing to unite with the church for the sake of others. It is one mode of doing good, for it is strengthening that body which is the open manifestation of Christian principles to the world. . . . So long as Christians remain silent about their convictions, they do not know each other, and are unable to strengthen each other; but when they come together and express their faith, they are able to bind themselves together, and work effectually on society around. . . .

At the time the church was about to be formed in 1841, I proposed three principles to be involved in its operation, which were agreed to. These we called the *Social Principle*, the *Voluntary Principle*, and the Principle of *Congregational Worship*.

1. The *Social Principle* was simply this. . . . To cooperate, we must know each other; and to know each other we must meet. We determined, therefore, to have meetings of a more social character than those of the Lord's day—where subjects of religious and moral interest could be discussed, and where soul could become acquainted with soul. . . .

It is desirable for the intellectual culture of the religious nature. The union of many minds in the earnest investigation of truth will produce deeper and broader results, than the solitary efforts of any individual mind, no matter how superior he is to each of them. . . .

Then we have meetings of another kind, not for discussion, but for the expression of devout thought and religious affections. Here heart meets with heart, as there mind with mind. At these prayer meetings . . . where we endeavor to speak from our inward experience, rather than from our reflections, a holy influence often seems to extend itself, as one speaker after another, in a few simple words, unfolds his deep convictions and trials, joys and hopes. . . . We have a third class of meetings of a more practical character. Some of the ladies of the church meet on two afternoons of every week, during the winter, to cut out and give out work to poor women, who are thus assisted to clothe their children, as they are paid for their work in comfortable clothing, which they could not otherwise procure for a much greater amount of labor. . . .

It is not to be supposed that nothing occurs at our conversational meetings but what is pleasant. . . . Sometimes the remarks made, may be not in perfectly good taste, or may be tedious. But all this we have learned to tolerate. It is itself a good discipline. . . .

We learn to say what we know, not what we have heard. . . .

* * *

2. Our second method we call the *Voluntary Principle*. . . . "That the expenses of the church shall be defrayed by a voluntary subscription, and pews shall not be sold, rented, or taxed." . . .

According to the pew-selling system, our churches become churches for the rich, respectable, and educated classes. The poor and the ignorant are excluded from them. Those who cannot afford to buy a pew, those who are not sufficiently interested in religion to wish to buy one, those who are strangers in the city; young men and young women from the country, with small means and few acquaintances; all these, if not *shut out*, are *left out* by churches on the common system. . . . .

Again, these pew owners are not necessarily the friends of Christian and humane movements. One is a distiller or a retailer of ardent spirits, and he does not like to hear anything said strongly about Temperance. Another owns a plantation in Cuba, or has security on negroes in New Orleans, or his son has married a slaveholding lady in Georgia, and he does not wish to hear anything said against Slavery.

* * *

3. Our third method . . . we called *Congregational Worship*.

By this, we intend a worship in which the congregation shall take an active part . . . modelled in part upon the Episcopal, and in part upon the Methodist and Quaker forms; which we find has interested those who use it, and has this advantage at least, that the whole body of worshippers can take an active part in it. . . .

There is no part of our worship which has been more interesting than the pause for meditation and prayer after the sermon. Though occupying but a few minutes, this has been full of satisfaction. . . .

We by no means profess to have discovered the best form of worship—on the contrary we should be happy to have it superseded by one more rich, more free, more imposing in its majesty, more touching in its simplicity. We should like to borrow from Catholic worship all that is beautiful in its symbols and its art. We should like to have Protestant festivals on which to celebrate, not saints, whose lives are forgotten, but the great events and holy characters of modern as well as of ancient times. . . .

But something more than this variety of forms was intended by us, when we spoke of Congregational worship. We meant that the worship should be conducted by the congregation themselves, as well as by the minister. . . . There is no reason, either, on Protestant principles, why the members of a church should not administer the ordinances when necessary.

* * *

The Church of the Disciples was commenced early in 1841. The subject of such a church had been discussed in an association . . . meeting for religious conversation. . . . I preached on the following subjects:

Jan. 31st. "What shall I do to be saved?"

Feb. 7th. Justification by Faith

Feb. 13th. The Church: as it is, as it ought to be, as it may be.

* * *

The first social meeting was held on March 16th, to consider and determine on the form of worship. At this meeting Dr. Wm. E. Channing, Mr. Samuel J. May and Mr. George Ripley were present, and joined in the conversation.

On the 13th of April, a declaration of faith in Christ and purpose of obedience was adopted as the basis of our church union. . . .

330

It was predicted . . . that it would soon fall apart; it was said that the members were restless people, who would always be dissatisfied; that nothing could suit them long. . . . It was said that we should be made up of Abolitionists and Transcendentalists, and all kinds of Reformers, mixed with Rationalists and Spiritualists, and Orthodox. It was thought that such heterogeneous materials could not hold together long. . . .

But what seemed to be our danger was in fact our salvation. For there was one point of central, higher union among us, and this was in a common longing for SPIRITUAL LIFE as the highest aim. . . . Now there were many members, yet but one body.

* * *

The church for me is the church of the future, not of the past; the church that seeks for unity not in dogma and form, but in faith and love. . . .

In this faith let us put a new spirit into every part of our organization; for organization, without the spirit, is good for nothing.

SOURCE: James Freeman Clarke, *A Sermon on the Principles and Methods of the Church of the Disciples* (Boston, 1846), 17–33.

An Answer to "Questions Addressed to Rev. T. Parker and His Friends"

1845

Theodore Parker's 1841 sermon Transient and Permanent in Christianity *provoked Unitarians to debate whether he was a "Christian" or an "Infidel." Only in 1844–45, however, did they debate whether their liberal principles required them to maintain fellowship with him regardless. The Fellowship Controversy opened a decades-long struggle to define the theological boundaries of Unitarianism when the directors of the Benevolent Fraternity of Churches ordered John Turner Sargent, minister of one of their chapels, not to exchange pulpits with Parker. Sargent resigned in protest. James Freeman Clarke then exchanged pulpits with Parker, which so offended some leaders of his Church of the Disciples, including William Ellery Channing's brother George, that they withdrew from the congregation and formed a new one with a different minister. These and related events alarmed many Unitarians, who believed freedom of speech in Unitarian pulpits was under threat, and prompted a group of "Friends of Theodore Parker" to invite him to preach weekly in Boston. Parker soon moved his ministry there from West Roxbury and began attracting the largest congregation in the city. The controversy also produced many pamphlets. One, probably by George Channing, posed hostile questions to Parker and his supporters. Sargent answered them in this pamphlet of his own. Further Reading: Dean Grodzins,* American Heretic: Theodore Parker and Transcendentalism *(Chapel Hill: University of North Carolina Press, 2002), 415–460.*

— Dean Grodzins

"Is . . . [a] man entitled, *in his own eyes,* to the name of a Christian, who rejects prophecy, who denies that a miracle is or ever was possible, and who holds the resurrection of our Lord to be only a pleasant legend? Who thinks the holy Jesus was not sinless, not without his weaknesses, not free from error?"

Ans:—"Petitio principii"! "What is it to be a Christian"? The question here goes on the supposition, or assumption, that belief in prophecy, the miracles, the resurrection, &c., constitutes a man's claim to be called a Christian, and that without this he is none. Whereas we maintain that a man may believe all these things and yet be no Christian at all, in any right sense. He, and only he, is a Christian, who lives, according to his ability, THE LIFE OF CHRIST. . . .

"Why cling so tenaciously to a name out of which you take the peculiar and distinctive meaning?"

Ans:—Ay! Sure enough! You may well ask that! Why call ourselves "LIBERAL CHRISTIANS," while we belie the title? . . .

"Because Christianity bids mankind,—clergymen included,—love *all* their fellow men, must those clergymen go and exchange with Mormons, Mahometans, Millerites, Tartars, Idiots, Jews, Hindoos, Pantheists or Deists?"

Ans:—The Mormons, Mahometans, Tartars, Idiots, &c., might well teach a lesson of charity to some who profess and call themselves "*liberal* Christians"; but what has inquiry to do with the main question at issue in regard to exchanges with Mr. Parker? He comes, rightly, under neither of the classes above enumerated. He professes to be and he is a UNITARIAN minister, and the question of fellowship is between *Unitarians* as such.

SOURCE: [John Turner Sargent], *An Answer to "Questions Addressed to Rev. T. Parker and His Friends," by a "Friend Indeed"* (Boston, 1845), 7, 8, 23.

HENRY DAVID THOREAU
"Civil Disobedience"
1848

Henry David Thoreau (1817–1862) was still living at Walden Pond in July of 1846, when he was arrested for refusing to pay his poll tax. Thoreau was a Unitarian by birth if not by choice, having "signed-off" from the rolls of Concord's First Parish Church in 1840. Nevertheless, he was a member in good standing of the Transcendental Club, comprised almost exclusively of Unitarian ministers and fellow activists. His falling out with the church was due in part to Thoreau's dissatisfaction with the church's failure to take a stand against slavery, an issue of increasing concern to Thoreau and others in the Transcendentalist circle. The recent war with Mexico, following the statehood of Texas in 1845, threatened to expand slavery westward. Thus, his refusal to pay his tax was in protest of the Mexican War as well as the institution of slavery. First delivered as a lecture, the essay "Civil Disobedience" was originally published in 1849 as "Resistance to Civil Government." Thoreau subsequently changed the title to "Civil Disobedience" in preparation for posthumous publication. In this essay, he promotes the notion of action from principle based on an appeal to conscience, or the "higher law." When as in the case of slavery, the higher law comes into conflict with civil law, the individual is duty bound, Thoreau says, to resist the government, peaceably if possible, but forcibly if necessary. In any event, it is essential not to collude with state-sanctioned injustice and oppression. Further Reading: Robert D. Richardson, Jr., Henry Thoreau: A Life of the Mind *(Berkeley: University of California Press, 1986); Joel Myerson, ed.,* The Cambridge Companion to Henry David Thoreau *(New York: Cambridge University Press, 1995).*

— Barry Andrews

Must the citizen ever for a moment, or in the least degree, resign his conscience to the legislator? Why has every man a conscience, then? I think that we should be men first, and subjects afterward. It is not desirable to cultivate a respect for the law, so much as for the right. The only obligation which I have a right to assume, is to do at any time what I think right.

*   *   *

How does it become a man to behave toward this American government to-day? I answer that he cannot without disgrace be associated with it. I cannot for an instant

334

recognize that political organization as *my* government which is the *slave's* government also.

All men recognize the right of revolution; that is, the right to refuse allegiance to and to resist the government, when its tyranny or its inefficiency are great and unendurable. But almost all say that such is not the case now. But such was the case, they think, in the Revolution of '75. . . . When a sixth of the population of a nation which has undertaken to be the refuge of liberty are slaves, and a whole country is unjustly overrun and conquered by a foreign army, and subjected to military law, I think that it is not too soon for honest men to rebel and revolutionize. What makes this duty the more urgent is the fact, that the country so overrun is not our own, but ours is the invading army.

* * *

How can a man be satisfied to entertain an opinion merely, and enjoy *it*? Is there any enjoyment in it, if his opinion is that he is aggrieved? . . . Action from principle,—the perception and performance of what is right,—changes things and relations; it is essentially revolutionary, and does not consist wholly with anything which was. It not only divides states and churches, it divides families; aye, it divides the *individual*, separating the diabolical in him from the divine.

Unjust laws exist: shall we be content to obey them, or shall we endeavor to amend them, and obey them until we have succeeded, or shall we transgress them at once? Men generally, under such a government as this, think that they ought to wait until they have persuaded the majority to alter them. They think that, if they should resist, the remedy would be worse than the evil. But it is the fault of the government itself that the remedy *is* worse than the evil. *It* makes it worse. Why is it not more apt to anticipate and provide for reform? Why does it not cherish its wise minority? Why does it cry and resist before it is hurt? Why does it not encourage its citizens to be on the alert to point out its faults, and *do* better than it would have them?

* * *

Under a government which imprisons any unjustly, the true place for a just man is a prison. The proper place to-day, the only place which Massachusetts has provided for her freer and less desponding spirits, is in her prisons. . . . It is there that the fugitive slave, and the Mexican prisoner on parole, and the Indian come to plead the wrongs of his race, should find them; on that separate, but more free and honorable ground, where the State places those who are not *with* her, but *against* her,— the only house in a slave-state in which a free man can abide with honor. If any think that their influence would be lost there, and their voices no longer afflict the ear of the State, that they would not be as an enemy within its walls, they do not know by how much truth is stronger than error, nor how much more eloquently and effectively he can combat injustice who has experienced a little in his own person. Cast

335

your whole vote, not a strip of paper merely, but your whole influence. A minority is powerless while it conforms to the majority; it is not even a minority then; but it is irresistible when it clogs by its whole weight. If the alternative is to keep all just men in prison, or give up war and slavery, the State will not hesitate which to choose. If a thousand men were not to pay their tax-bills this year, that would not be a violent and bloody a measure as it would be to pay them, and enable the State to commit violence and shed innocent blood. This is, in fact the definition of a peaceable revolution, if any such is possible. . . . But even suppose blood should flow. Is there not a sort of blood shed when the conscience is wounded? Through this wound a man's real manhood and immortality flow out, and he bleeds to an everlasting death. I see this blood flowing now.

* * *

I have paid no poll-tax for six years. I was put into a jail once on this account, for one night; and, as I stood considering the walls of solid stone, two or three feet thick, the door of wood and iron, a foot thick . . . I could not help being struck with the foolishness of that institution which treated me as if I were mere flesh and blood and bones, to be locked up. . . . I saw that, if there was a wall of stone between me and my townsmen, there was still a more difficult one to climb or break through, before they could get to be as free as I was. I did not for a moment feel confined, and the walls seemed a great waste of stone and mortar. I felt as if I alone of all my townsmen had paid my tax. They plainly did not know how to treat me, but behaved like persons who are underbred. In every threat and in every compliment there was a blunder; for they thought that my chief desire was to stand the other side of that stone wall. I could not but smile to see how industriously they locked the door on my meditations, which followed them out again without let or hindrance, and *they* were really all that was dangerous. . . .

Thus the State never intentionally confronts a man's sense, intellectual or moral, but only his body, his senses. It is not armed with superior wit or honesty, but with superior physical strength. I was not born to be forced. I will breathe after my own fashion. Let us see who is the strongest. What force has a multitude? They only can force me who obey a higher law than I.

SOURCE: Henry David Thoreau, "Resistance to Civil Government," in *Reform Papers*, ed. Wendell Glick (Princeton, NJ: Princeton University Press, 1973), 65, 67, 72–73, 76–77, 79–81.

Correspondence
1849

Lucy Stone (1818–1893) and Antoinette Brown (1825–1921) met as students at Oberlin in 1846, became sisters-in-law when they married brothers Henry and Samuel Blackwell in 1855 and 1856, and were lifelong friends. One fruit of their friendship was women's ordained ministry in the United States. These letters were exchanged in 1849, when Stone was embarking on her career as a women's rights lecturer and Brown was beginning her theological studies at Oberlin College. At the time, Stone saw herself as a Unitarian and a Garrisonian abolitionist, while Brown was an orthodox Congregationalist. Four years later, Brown was ordained by an independent congregation in South Butler, New York, that was aligned with the political abolitionism of the Liberty Party. Long after theological doubts ended her ministry in South Butler, she transferred her ministerial credentials to Unitarianism in 1878. Further Reading: Elizabeth Cazden, Antoinette Brown Blackwell: A Biography *(Old Westbury, NY: Feminist Press, 1983); Sally G. McMillen,* Lucy Stone: An Unapologetic Life *(New York: Oxford University Press, 2015).*

—Dan McKanan

Brown to Stone, February 25, 1849

Dear dear L. when shall I see you again & when shall we walk together & talk together as we used to. . . . Every one is beginning to ask when will Lucy Stone be here. They are anxious to hear you lecture. You would have a house full & overflowing. . . . The people here love & respect you & so they will continue to do while you manifest a noble sweet spirit however much you may differ in sentiment but when you become like Mrs [Abby Kelley] Foster they will think of you as they do of her. O dear! Lucy *don't* imbibe her spirit or fall in with her manner for if you do one half of my love for you will be turned into pitty & you hate to be pittied you know. Yet I am sure your friends would all pity you.

Brown to Stone, March 25, 1849

I do love you dearest Lucy better than ever but I sometimes think of you just as I used to think of my brother Addy—that he was going wrong, all wrong & it makes me feel sad. You don't think it even right to pray that it is wicked & sinful for an enlightened mind at least, & is mockery to God. You dont believe in an overruling Providence.

Well Lucy say what you do believe candedly & honestly & believe with true honesty of heart & we'll all love you just as well but take care that you are not like those we read of in Hebrew yesterday "blind people that had eyes." . . . You talk about cause & effect. I do believe that effect will always follow its cause but I believe also that a God to whom past present & future time is all present to whom eternity is an eternal now can so conditionat[e] certain blessings which he would bestow upon his children upon their asking, that, their asking in a proper state of mind is indispensebly necessary to obtaining.

Stone to Brown, August 1849

I wonder if you have any idea how dreadfully I feel about your studying that old musty theology, which already has its grave clothes on, and is about to be buried, in so deep a grave that no resurrection trump can call it into being, and no Prophet voice, clothe its dry bones with *living* life? . . . The Great *Soul* of the Present, hungering and thirsting, for the bread and water of Life, falters by the wayside, finding no green pastures, or living fountains, that are not all polluted with the horrid stench which goes up from the decaying corpse of such a theology, with which Humanity, and God himself are weary. Yet *my own dear Nette* is spending *three* precious years of her life's young prime, wading through that deep slough, from the stain of which she can never wash herself, and by which I *fear*, her vision will be so clouded that she can only see *men* through *creeds*, while her ear, will only hear God's voice speaking in the *written* book, unconscious of the *unwritten* revelations so grand and glorious which stand out, in "living light" all over God's creation. . . . O Nette it is intolerable and I can think of it with allowance only when I think that the loss of what is *invaluable* in *you* will purchase apparatus to batter down that *wall* of bible, brimstone, church and corruption, which have hitherto hemmed *women* into *nothingness* — The fact that you have entered a field forbidden to women, will be a good to the sex, but I half fear it will be purchased at too dear a rate.

SOURCE: Carol Lasser and Marlene Deahl Merrill, *Friends and Sisters: Letters between Lucy Stone and Antoinette Brown Blackwell, 1846–93* (Urbana: University of Illinois Press, 1987), 48, 49, 53–54.

EDMUND HAMILTON SEARS

"It Came Upon the Midnight Clear"
1849

Edmund Hamilton Sears (1810–1876) was a Unitarian minister, theologian, and poet. Sickly, often depressed, and unable to sustain a heavy parish work-load, he spent much of his time writing. He had an intense Christian piety that many of his Unitarian friends and colleagues found conservative, so much so that, in 1865, the great Unitarian denominational organizer Henry Whitney Bellows wrongly suspected him of being among the ministers who "want to secede and are disposed to deny any fellowship with the looser and more liberal party." But he was actually as averse to traditional Christian theology as any radical Unitarian. His most famous work, the Christmas carol "It Came upon the Midnight Clear," with its message of peace on earth, was written in 1849, shortly after the 1848 revolutions in Europe and the American war with Mexico. In his original wording, Sears omits the theological imagery found in almost all hymns and most carols. When the hymn is sung in most Christian churches, discreet modifications are made to eliminate non-scriptural references (such as "the age of gold") and to supply the missing reference to Christ. His earlier Christmas hymn, "Calm on the Listening Ear of Night," does, in the last verse, mention the Savior's birth. Further Reading: Chandler Robbins, "Memoir of Rev. Edmund Hamilton Sears," Proceedings of the Massachusetts Historical Society, 1891; Erik Routley, The English Carol (London: H. Jenkins, 1958).

—Peter Hughes

It came upon the midnight clear,
That glorious song of old,
From angels bending near the earth,
To touch their harps of gold:
"Peace on the earth, goodwill to men,
From heaven's all-gracious King."
The world in solemn stillness lay,
To hear the angels sing.

Still through the cloven skies they come,
With peaceful wings unfurled,
And still their heavenly music floats

O'er all the weary world;
Above its sad and lowly plains,
They bend on hovering wing,
And ever o'er its Babel sounds
The blessèd angels sing.

Yet with the woes of sin and strife
The world has suffered long;
Beneath the angel-strain have rolled
Two thousand years of wrong;
And man, at war with man, hears not
The love-song which they bring;
O hush the noise, ye men of strife,
And hear the angels sing.

And ye, beneath life's crushing load,
Whose forms are bending low,
Who toil along the climbing way
With painful steps and slow,
Look now! for glad and golden hours
come swiftly on the wing.
O rest beside the weary road,
And hear the angels sing!

For lo!, the days are hastening on,
By prophet bards foretold,
When with the ever-circling years
Comes round the age of gold
When peace shall over all the earth
Its ancient splendors fling,
And the whole world give back the song
Which now the angels sing.

SOURCE: *Christian Register*, December 29, 1849.

340

NATHANIEL STACY

Memoirs

1850

Nathaniel Stacy (1778–1868) was one of the founders of Universalism in upstate New York. Born in Gloucester, Massachusetts, to parents who sympathized with John Murray's teaching, he was raised in New Salem, Massachusetts, and embraced Universalism after hearing Hosea Ballou preach. In 1802, Ballou invited him into his home to learn to be a minister, and Stacy went on to an extensive, circuit-riding career during which (by his report) two hundred new congregations were planted in New York. He proposed and helped found the New York State Convention of Universalists in 1825. These passages from his Memoirs *illustrate the character of Ballou's mentorship and the flavor of early Universalist debates with their opponents. Further Reading: Mark Harris,* Among the Dry Bones: Liberal Religion in New Salem, Massachusetts *(Boston: Unitarian Universalist Association, 1981).*

—Dan McKanan

It was in the month of October, 1802, if I rightly recollect, in the 24th year of my age, that I entered the study of Mr. Ballou. I had been with him not to exceed one month, when, one Sunday morning, being his appointment in Dana, after we had reached the village, and called at the house of our friend Amsden, Mr. Ballou was seized with a violent pain in the head, and came to me with his hand on his forehead, saying, very mournfully, "Brother Stacy, you must preach today; for I am in such violent pain, I can not." . . . "I am glad," he said, "you have no writing with you; it would only be a trouble to you. You must learn to preach extemporaneously; and the better way is to begin in the first place." "But," I answered, "I cannot attempt it to-day; and I never can begin here. I must go among strangers in the first place; I shall feel less embarrassment there, I'm sure. Here every body knows me, and I shall certainly break down under their suspicious gaze." "No," he said, "this is the very place." . . . In a few moments he returned, with some half-dozen of our friends, who surrounded me with, "Brother Stacy! Come, preach to-day;—this is your time to begin—the very best time you ever can have; and when once you have made a beginning, the worst will be over; and the sooner you begin the better." By their united importunity, I was at length led, "like an ox to the slaughter," into the desk! . . . I knew they were friends to the cause, and friends to me. But I felt my own insufficiency, my own nothingness; and the absolute preposterousness of attempting to teach those whose experience was so much greater than mine, and whose knowledge must, consequently, far exceed that of mine. But notwithstanding that, I felt no regret that I had resolved to enter the ministry; no inclination to give up exertions to become a useful laborer in the vineyard, but rather a renewed resolution to persevere; and I devoutly prayed for strength, and boldness in the good cause. The congregation took their seats and I arose, and with a trembling voice read a hymn, or rather a psalm, for we used Watts' psalms and hymns. And here I made a blunder in the outset—I read a psalm and called it a hymn. . . . After the choir had concluded singing, I again arose, and it was well that I had a desk to lay my bible on, and to lean against, otherwise I felt sure I could not have seen a letter, and it is very questionable whether I should have been able to stand up. But I opened the bible and read, I guess, intelligibly, the 8th verse of the 40th chapter of Isaiah: "The grass withereth, and the flower fadeth; but the word of our God shall stand forever." I spoke probably twenty or twenty-five minutes; but I attended to every proposition of my text, and finished my discourse. Mr. Ballou then arose and closed the service; and it appeared to me, that I never heard so fervent and pathetic a prayer uttered by mortal man before. I heard no more of Mr. Ballou's headache—he was well enough, as far as I could discover, when he got me into the desk; for he made no complaint in the afternoon, but preached like an Apostle.

*   *   *

One evening, at the close of a discourse delivered in a well-filled school-house, in the town of Westford, three men came upon me altogether, with their denunciations of the doctrine I had advanced, and in a clamorous manner began to ask me questions. . . . One of them stepped forward and put a number of questions, which I answered as well as I could; and so answered, as at least to confound him. When he drew back, the second came, who also, soon gave place to the third. This was a valiant soldier, filled with holy wrath against such heresy and heretics—his zeal was warmed to a high degree, and his voice trembled with emotion, as he stepped into the arena, with the courage of a Napoleon, determined to have me down, by fair play, or by foul. His arguments were hard almost as brick-bats, but made no impression on me, and very little, I apprehended, on any member of the audience; for they were heated so highly, that they exploded before reaching the object at which they aimed. . . . As defeat seemed to stare him in the face, he resolved to make one bold and irresistible effort . . . and he took (reader, don't be surprised out of your senses) this invulnerable position, which I give in his own unmistakable language: "If you have proved the salvation of all men, you have not proved that all women will be saved!" There, reader! will you ever dare again to open your mouth, in favor of Universal Salvation? Will you not now give it up, and come to the conclusion, almost, that it is right for some people to be endlessly miserable, inasmuch as their attachment to that cherished and beloved dogma is so violent, that they would thrust

342

women into their hell, or even rather go there themselves, than have it fail! . . . [I] replied, "I am truly astonished, sir, that a man professing to be a gentleman, and a Christian, should condescend to resort to so mean a subterfuge. Your remark is unworthy a reply, it merits only contempt: but for the sake of those that stand by, I will merely remark that the Apostle says, 'There is neither Jew nor Greek, there is neither bond nor free, there is neither male nor female; for ye are all one in Christ Jesus.'" The man, manifestly, turned away ashamed; the congregation broke out into a laugh, and the controversy closed.

SOURCE: Nathaniel Stacy, *Memoirs of the Life of Nathaniel Stacy, Preacher of the Gospel of Universal Grace* (Columbus, PA: Abner Vedder, 1850), 71–73, 75–76.

"Speech at the Ministerial Conference"

1851

In 1850, Congress passed the Fugitive Slave Law, which empowered federal court commissioners in the free states to arrest runaway slaves and send them back to the South. Further, it required these commissioners to presume, unless proven otherwise, that slave catchers' claims were valid and that blacks were slaves; did not require alleged fugitives to have legal counsel and forbade them from testifying on their own behalf; and made rescuing fugitives a federal offense, punishable by imprisonment. President Millard Fillmore, a Unitarian from New York, signed the law, and prominent Unitarians endorsed it, among them Rev. Dr. Ezra Stiles Gannett, William Ellery Channing's successor at the Federal (later Arlington) Street Church. His congregation included a "fugitive slave commissioner." By contrast, Theodore Parker's Twenty-Eighth Congregational Society included both free-born blacks and fugitive slaves. Parker vowed to resist the law, which he denounced as legalized kidnapping, both proslavery and immoral. In October 1850, when Gannett's parishioner issued a warrant for the arrest of a fugitive slave who belonged to Parker's congregation, he hid her in his house (she eventually escaped to England). In 1851, at the annual "May meeting" of Unitarian ministers, Gannett defended his position. Parker, who respected Gannett despite their political and theological disagreements, responded.

— Dean Grodzins

I am glad also to hear Dr. Gannett say we have no right to attribute improper motives to any one who differs from us in opinion. It was rather gratuitous, however; no man has done it here to-day. But it is true, no man has a right thus to "judge another." But I will remind Dr. Gannett that a few years ago, he and I differed in opinion on a certain matter of considerable importance, and after clearly expressing our difference, I said: "Well, there is an honest difference of opinion between us," and he said: "Not an *honest* difference of opinion, Brother Parker," for he called me "Brother" then, and not "Mr." as since, and now, when he has publicly said he cannot take my hand *fraternally.* Still there was an honest difference of opinion on his part as well as mine. . . .

I attribute no unmanly motive to Mr. Gannett. I thought him honest when he denied that I was; I think him honest now. I know him to be conscientious, laborious, and self-denying. I think he would sacrifice himself for another's good.

If we do not obey [the Fugitive Slave Law], he says, we shall disobey all laws. It is not so. There is not a country in the world where there is more respect for human laws than in New England; nowhere more than in Massachusetts. . . .

Why are we thus loyal to law? First, because we make the laws ourselves, and for ourselves; and next, because the laws actually represent the Conscience of the People, and help them keep the laws of God. The value of human laws is only this— to conserve the Great Eternal Law of God; to enable us to keep that; to hinder us from disobeying that. So long as laws do this we should obey them; New England will be loyal to such laws.

But the fugitive slave law is one which contradicts the acknowledged precepts of the Christian religion, universally acknowledged. It violates the noblest instincts of humanity; it asks us to trample on the Law of God. It commands what Nature, Religion, and God alike forbid; it forbids what Nature, Religion, and God alike command. It tends to defeat the object of all just human law; it tends to annihilate the observance of the Law of God. So faithful to God, to Religion, to Human Nature, and in the name of Law itself, we protest against this particular statute, and trample it under our feet.

Who is it that oppose the fugitive slave law? Men that have always been on the side of "law and order," and do not violate the statutes of men for their own advantage. This disobedience to the fugitive slave law is one of the strongest guaranties for the observance of any *just* law. You cannot trust a people who will keep law, *because it is law*; nor need we distrust a people that will only keep a law when it is just. The fugitive slave law itself, if obeyed will do more to overturn the power of human law, than all disobedience to it—the most complete.

* * *

I have in my church black men, fugitive slaves. They are the crown of my apostleship, the seal of my ministry. It becomes me to look after their bodies in order to "save their souls." This law has brought us into the most intimate connection with the sin of slavery. I have been obliged to take my own parishioners into my house to keep them out of the clutches of the kidnapper. Yes, gentlemen, I have been obliged to do that; and then to keep my doors guarded by day as well as by night. Yes, I have had to arm myself. I have written my sermons with a pistol in my desk,—loaded, a cap on the nipple, and ready for action. Yea, with a drawn sword within reach of my right hand. . . .

[W]hen a parishioner, a fugitive from slavery, a woman, pursued by the kidnappers, came to my house, what could I do less than take her in and defend her to the last? But who sought her life—or liberty? A parishioner of my Brother Gannett came to kidnap a member of my church; Mr. Gannett preaches a sermon to justify the fugitive slave law, demanding that it should be obeyed; yes, calling on his church members to kidnap mine, and sell them into bondage for ever. Yet all this while Mr. Gannett calls himself "a Christian," and me an "Infidel" . . .

O, my Brothers. . . . You have called me "Infidel." Surely I differ widely enough from you in my theology. But there is one thing I cannot fail to trust; that is the Infinite God, Father of the white man, Father also of the white man's slave. I should not dare violate his laws, come what may come;—should you?

SOURCE: Theodore Parker, *Additional Speeches, Addresses, and Occasional Sermons* (Boston, 1855), 1:7–10, 12–15.

"Substance and Show"

1851

Universalist and Unitarian minister Rev. Thomas Starr King (1824–1864) was born in New York to European-American parents. Instead of a seminary educa- tion, he learned from men such as Hosea Ballou II, Edwin Hubbell Chapin, James Walker, and Frederic Henry Hedge. An early advocate of merger beween the Unitarians and Universalists, King served Charlestown Univer- salist Church before being called to the Unitarian Hollis Street Church. King and his wife, Julia, maintained a vibrant social and intellectual circle of Boston's elites, and King became a luminary on the lyceum circuit. His lec- ture, "Substance and Show," which illuminates the metaphysical underpin- nings of his theology, was one of his most popular in New England as well as in California. Further Reading: Richard Frothingham, A Tribute to Thomas Starr King (Boston: Ticknor and Fields, 1865); Charles W. Wendte, Thomas Starr King: Patriot and Preacher (Boston: Beacon Press, 1921).

—Sheri Prud'homme

I propose to speak on the difference between *substance* and *show*, or the distinction we should make between the facts of the world and life, and the causal forces which lie behind and beneath them. . . .

Most persons, doubtless, if you place before them a paving-stone and a slip of paper with some writing on it, would not hesitate to say that there is as much more substance in the rock than in the paper as there is heaviness. Yet they might make a great mistake. Suppose that the slip of paper contains the sentence, "God is love"; or, "Thou shalt love thy neighbor as thyself"; or, "All men have moral rights by reason of heavenly parentage," then the paper represents more force and substance than the stone. Heaven and earth may pass away, but such words can never die out or become less real.

The word "substance" means that which stands under and supports anything else. Whatever then creates, upholds, classifies anything which our senses behold, though we cannot handle, see, taste, or smell it, is more substantial than the object itself. In this way the soul, which vivifies, moves, and supports the body, is a more potent substance than the hard bones and heavy flesh which it vitalizes. . . .

There is a very general tendency to deny that ideal forces have any practical power. But there have been several thinkers whose skepticism has an opposite direction. "We cannot," they say, "attribute external reality to the sensations we feel." We need not wonder that this theory has failed to convince the unmetaphysical commonsense of people that a stone post is merely a stubborn thought, and that the bite of a dog is nothing but an acquaintance with a pugnacious, four-footed conception. . . .

And yet, by more satisfactory evidence than that which the idealists propose, we are warned against confounding the conception of substance with matter, and confining it to things we can see and grasp. Science steps in and shows us that the physical system leans on spirit. We talk of the world of matter, but there is no such world. Everything about us is a mixture or marriage of matter and spirit. A world of matter simply would be a huge head of sandy atoms or an infinite continent of stagnant vapor. There would be no motion, no force, no form, no order, no beauty, in the universe as it now is; organization meets us at every step and wherever we look; organization implies spirit,—something that rules, disposes, penetrates, and vivifies matter.

SOURCE: Thomas Starr King, *Substance and Show and Other Lectures*, ed. Edwin P. Whipple (Boston: James R. Osgood and Company, 1877), 1–3.

JOHN MURRAY SPEAR

Messages from the Superior State

1852

John Murray Spear (1804–1887) was a Universalist minister, a prominent reformer and opponent of the death penalty, and a spiritualist medium. After he brought back messages from the spirits of John Murray, Thomas Jefferson, and other worthies, he was dropped from Universalist fellowship. He created further controversy by his preaching of free love. But Spear was not the only Universalist intrigued by spiritualism. Adin Ballou became interested after the death of his son and wrote a book, Spirit Manifestations. *Spiritualism also held a special appeal to Universalists in general. The view of the afterlife reported by many mediums was similar to what had been anticipated in the theology of many Universalists, especially those who believed in future punishment. Accordingly spiritualism entered many Universalist churches, not infrequently dividing the congregations over the issue. This deflection from Universalism's main message, and the consequent internal controversy, may have contributed to the slowing of the growth of Universalism in the later nineteenth century. The following two excerpts come from Spear's* Messages from the Superior State, *the first an apology for the physical manifestations common in séances, and the second a portion of one of his messages from the spirit of John Murray. Further Reading: John Buescher,* The Remarkable Life of John Murray Spear: Agitator for the Spirit Land *(Notre Dame, IN: University of Notre Dame Press, 2006); John Buescher,* The Other Side of Salvation: Spiritualism and the Nineteenth-Century Religious Experience *(Boston: Skinner House, 2004).*

—Peter Hughes

A scientific age needs its scientific methods in all things, in the beginning of all new ideas. But what is there scientific in the sounds [the spirit rappings], of which we hear so much?—it will be asked again. Plainly this, that agents, with which science has so much to do, are made the instruments, through which, intelligence from the world above, comes to the world below. These agents are those subtle elements of Nature, with which science has made us familiar, and which we call Electricity and Magnetism. And besides, this new mode of development leads the scientific class of observers, to a scientific classification of its facts; and also to an analysis of its principles, of the most thorough and philosophic character: thus giving the world without, what is true of the world within: a SPIRITUAL SCIENCE, which shall give to all materiality, the soul and life it so much needs.

A grand mistake has been made, on the part of a certain school of reputed wise ones, in relation to the *origin* of these sounds. They have mistaken the *instrument*, or secondary agent, for the primary one, or intelligent actor, in the case. They have, in a sense, *deified* Electricity and Magnetism; and set them to work in the way of talking by sound, while they should have been wise enough to have escaped this pool of a mere material Pantheism. Were they a little wiser, they would see, that however much these imponderables may have to do with, either the sounds that are heard, or with the other modes of manifestation, they are as incapable of independent intelligence, as water, air or earth. They would see, that they may answer very well as *intermediates*, through which intelligent beings of the upper world, may speak to us the word of cheer; while, as the speakers themselves, they fail of possessing an adequate power, or, even any *pretension* to such power. And these remarks apply equally well, in my estimation, to any theory based on mere materialism, as all theories must be, which do not admit an independent intelligence, separate from, and superior to, the merely *human* mind, or any material element, as the active cause of these modern wonders.

But, then, would *spirits* tip over chairs and tables, break furniture, write, speak and play such pranks as we often hear of their doing? Is this the *way—new* though it be—in which they come to us, if they come at all? In reply, I would ask the *reader* a few questions: Are not Spirits, *men*, very much like ourselves? And do not men do such things? Where is the law by which one thing becomes another, on the instant? Even Saul, on his way to Damascus, is only *arrested* instantaneously, while it takes some length of time for him to get the scales from his eyes, and to become Paul.

But would God *permit* Spirits to do such things? Why not? He permits men to do them. Is it not consistent for Him to permit the same things, in beings of the same character, even though a part of them be in the Spirit world, while the other part are here? There is nothing out of character, as I see it, in this moving of furniture, in itself considered. If the *object* of it be evidently a frivolous one; if it be unworthy of true Christian dignity; or, if it be truly wicked and injurious, then let it be condemned as it regards the *object* of it—not, as it respects the thing itself. The latter is a *fact*, which has a deep meaning, and is not to be slightly passed over. The mere fact of communication with beings of another world—though the spirits themselves, with whom we communicate, as well as the mode of address, be of a low order—is nevertheless a fact of very great value. It *demonstrates*, at least, a *future life for the spirit*, and that, low as the means may be by which the thing is made sure, is worth more than all mere human *testimony*, however good, to the same end. Once let it become a matter of *actual knowledge*, that *spirits* do communicate with mortals, then it is sure that Spirits are *real* and *living beings* — that they are immortal beings, and can never die.

from Message IV dictated by the spirit of John Murray

I shall now proceed further to instruct you. The teaching which you now will receive, will be of great importance to the inhabitants of your earth. Naturally, you wish to know more concerning the life of the spirit after its departure from its mortal body. It will afford me, my young friend, it will afford me great pleasure now to instruct you in regard to this most interesting and important subject.

Before, I have spoken to you of victory over death and the grave; and have already said to you, we could truly inquire, "O death, where is thy sting, O grave, where is thy victory?" Death, as you are accustomed to call it, is but a change, from a lower to a higher state. Your own good sense will at once lead you to consider the changes which you perceive going on around you in nature. From the lower to the higher, all things in nature, all are tending upward, as I have said before, in infinite, in *infinite* progression.

Leaving behind the body which I occupied when on your earth, — feeble it was, but poorly answering the purposes of life for a season, — I was able to rise to a more perfect condition. No clear, distinct view, had I enjoyed of the higher life. Of course you already comprehend the thought, that we have no further use for this tabernacle. You already understand the meaning of the passage, "This earthly tabernacle shall be dissolved." Then comes a better building, suited to our wants, and our new and improved state. Each person goes to his own and best place; there to receive that useful knowledge which shall prepare him for a still higher state. This brings to your mind again the thought of infinite, *infinite* progression. There, circumstances being more favorable, more rapidly we can acquire; and, at the same time, impart wisdom, and useful knowledge. Every one, in his place, finds his own work to do.

While in this mortal state, inhabiting my poor body, I had no clear conception of the employment of those who had left your earth. *Teaching* is our favorite work. There we become the most useful, and there we find the greatest happiness; those above teaching those who are below. And O, could I enable the inhabitants of your earth to behold the charming scenes, and the beautiful landscapes, that are spread out before us, in the richest possible variety, your hearts would leap for joy; you would long, long to be with us. At present, it is well that you should be where you now are; where you have your varied work to do; and when that work is completed, then the change comes. And then, my young friend, O, let me impress that thought upon your mind, which shall never be, for a moment, forgotten, — the thought that as you are wise, virtuous, useful in your present state, so shall you be qualified to enter into the next. Keep then, my young friend, keep the thought constantly before you, that in addition to the happiness which you will find in a virtuous and useful life, when on the earth; in addition to that, shall you be able, more perfectly, and immediately, to enjoy the heavenly, the superior state. Let these two thoughts never be separated.

On your earth, you see those now who, to your eye, appear prosperous. They seem to be in possession of much that is desirable. But if these possessions are unwisely obtained; if improperly used, then those very possessions sink them into a lower state. We see, constantly, the inhabitants of your earth leaving their bodies, and we know, we *know* the difference. There may be some poor, silent man, in his humble cot, unknown to the world, who rises far, far higher than he who has enjoyed large possessions. The talents, those *inward* talents, which had been given him, were used for wise purposes. He lived humbly, though he appeared in a high and happy state. And beautifully, beautifully has one said: "God dwells in the high and holy, and with him that is of a humble and contrite spirit." Beautifully was it said: "Learn of *me*, for I am meek and lowly in heart." Such, such are the truly blessed. Such are best qualified to enter into the higher state.

You will not, you will not, my young friend, misunderstand me. I wish you to keep the thought constantly before you, that all goes on in infinite progression. That poor, foolish, unwise man,—he goes into a lower state; and there are those ready to welcome him; to teach him; and, as rapidly as possible, to raise him from that estate to a higher, and more perfect condition: I say a *more* perfect condition; for, with us, we find it exceedingly difficult to speak of perfection; because we are constantly being, *being* perfected. But in comparison with the inhabitants of your earth, when we meet our change, immediately, we are in a perfect state. I say, my young friend, I say, *comparatively*, because that state is so much better than the one in which you now live.

SOURCE: S. C. Hewitt, ed., *Messages from the Superior State: Communicated by John Murray, Through John M. Spear, in the Summer of 1852* (Boston, 1853), 19–22, 116–19.

"Beneath Thine Hammer, Lord, I Lie"

1853

Frederic Henry Hedge (1805–1890) spent four years in a German gymna-
sium *before entering Harvard College, then the Divinity School, to prepare
for Unitarian ministry. Nicknamed* Germanicus Hedge, *he introduced German idealism to the emergent Transcendentalist movement. This hymn uses
biblical imagery (Jer. 23:29) to evoke the soul's yearning for union with God,
which Hedge elsewhere described as a "deliverance from self." For Hedge, this
individual act of self-surrender marked an important step in the progress of
society at large toward a "divine humanity." The hymn can be read, therefore,
as a veiled critique of theologies centered on personal salvation, which Hedge
dismissed as "drawing attention to the self," as well as a timely counterpoint
to materialist philosophies that idolized the hammers of industry over those
of the Lord. Further Reading: Bryan F. LeBeau,* Frederic Henry Hedge,
Nineteenth Century American Transcendentalist: Intellectually Radical,
Ecclesiastically Conservative *(Allison Park, PA: Pickwick Publications, 1985);
Ronald Vale Wells,* Three Christian Transcendentalists: James Marsh,
Caleb Sprague Henry, Frederic Henry Hedge *(New York: Columbia Uni-
versity Press, 1943).*

—Erik Martinez Resly

Beneath thine hammer, Lord, I lie
With contrite spirit prone;
O, mould me till to self I die,
And live to thee alone!

With frequent disappointments sore
And many a bitter pain,
Thou laborest at my being's core
Till I be formed again.

Smite, Lord! thine hammer's needful wound
My baffled hopes confess;
Thine anvil is the sense profound
Of mine own nothingness.

Smite, till from all its idols free,
And filled with love divine,
My heart shall know no good but thee,
And have no will but thine.

SOURCE: Frederic Henry Hedge and Frederic Dan Huntington, eds., *Hymns for the Church of Christ* (Boston, 1853), 460.

"Relation of the North to Slavery"

1854

Ezra Stiles Gannett (1801–1871), colleague and successor to William Ellery Channing at the Federal Street Church in Boston, was in 1825 a principal founder of the American Unitarian Association. Believing, along with many Unitarians of his time, in a special revelation validated by the miracles recorded in the Bible, he opposed Theodore Parker's idea that Christianity was an imperfect expression of absolute religion. Although he encouraged Parker in 1843 to resign from the Boston Association of Ministers and would not exchange pulpits with him, he steadfastly opposed having Parker, or anyone else, expelled from the Unitarian ranks for theological reasons. He was also, for a long time, a moderate opponent of Parker on the question of slavery. While he wished that slavery could be ended, he nevertheless opposed adopting any political position, such as abolition, as a creed of the church. And he believed that radical abolition would result in disunion, which would prevent slaves from ever getting any help from the Northern states. At first he supported the 1850 Fugitive Slave Act on the grounds that federal law had to be obeyed. After an escaped slave, Anthony Burns, was arrested in Boston in 1854 and sent back to the South, he changed his mind and decided that such a law had to be met with civil disobedience. Further Reading: William Channing Gannett, Ezra Stiles Gannett: Unitarian Minister in Boston, 1824–1871 *(Boston, 1875).*

—Peter Hughes

It is the relation which we shall in future hold to Slavery, that was brought before us by the occurrences which so painfully agitated this community for many days, and at last drew tears from the eyes of men, and harsh words form woman's lips; it is the relation in which we shall allow ourselves hereafter to stand towards Slavery, that demands serious and Christian thought. For this is not purely a political question; it has its moral side, and religion and Christianity are entitled to examine it as entering within their domain.

We shall arrive at a just decision more speedily, if we separate the question both from the individuals and from the incidents connected with any particular exhibition of its character. . . .

Another mistake, and more than a mistake, a wrong has been committed, by many who are indignant at wrong-doing on one side and the other, in imputing unworthy motives to men of whose conduct they have disapproved. . . .

The judgment of many at the North on Slavery has been vitiated, and its effect upon the South been impaired, by similar errors. To make the fact of slaveholding conclusive proof against a man's character shows a disregard of one of the plainest lessons taught by human history. That which seems to you or me to be palpably wrong, may be accounted by another whose education has been different, to be justifiable on grounds alike of morality and humanity. I can believe that a Southerner may in good faith use arguments in defence of Slavery which, as I hold, have no foundation in fact or sound reason. He may assert the native inferiority and inevitable dependence of the black race, contradict statements and conclusions which appear to me incontrovertible, maintain that the transportation of the negro from his own continent to this Christian land has been to him and his descendants a blessing, and frame a vindication of ownership in human beings from texts gathered out of the Bible, and I will not only be slow to charge him with wilful sin, I dare not do it. The slave-dealer who traffics in his fellow-beings for the sake of gain, or who treats them with a cruelty which he would not exercise towards a brute, I am justified in pronouncing a bad man, for passion or avarice is his acknowledged motive. But there are thousands of masters at the South who believe Slavery to be a logical deduction from sure premises, and a fair inference from Christian truths.

It is equally wrong to charge upon all masters harsh usage or cold neglect of their slaves. In many families they are treated with uniform kindness. We gain nothing in our address to the consciences or the sensibilities of Southern slaveholders by representing them as destitute of all proper feeling.

*　*　*

To this then we come at last, and till we come to this we fall short of a just consideration of the matter,—the intrinsic character, the inherent vice of slavery. What should we of the North think of it as an institution, and what should we do in regard to it, that the light which is in us may not be darkness?

To the former of the questions I answer, we should think of it as ineradicably wrong and bad.

*　*　*

It does not follow that immediate emancipation, in the sense of absolute freedom for the millions now held in bondage, is the duty of the South, or would be its duty, if the whole South entertained the conviction which I have expressed; since their past life has disqualified the greater portion of the slaves for taking care of themselves. But an immediate adoption of measures for the final liberation of every man, woman and child, now regarded as transferable property, is what a correct view of duty would obtain from the Southern masters.

*　*　*

We are, in the first, place, precluded, by the terms of citizenship under which we enjoy the privileges of the Union, from intermeddling with Slavery in the States

356

which adopt it as a part of their social institutions. So long as we remain under the Constitution of the United States, each State must be left undisturbed in the settlement of its own internal policy. . . .

The law of the land. We are subjects of a government which we, or our fathers on our behalf, have created, as well as freemen who have inherited liberties that we will never alienate. Order is the first condition of a safe or prosperous community. We are prohibited, therefore, from resorting to violence as an expression of our dislike of Slavery. . . .

What then remains for us to do? More than some persons may at first suppose. Four ways are open by which we may signify our repugnance to Slavery, without the breach of any obligation that rests on us as Christians or citizens.

First, we may maintain an inflexible determination to be drawn into no farther support or countenance of this institution, direct or indirect, than we are already obliged to render. . . .

Secondly, we may take all constitutional and lawful methods for securing an abrogation of those enactments, and of those provisions of the fundamental law, which offend our moral convictions. . . .

Thirdly, we may oppose every attempt of the South to extend the institution beyond its present limits. Such opposition we are bound to make by every principle of loyalty to our country, or to the cause of human freedom. Slavery is intrinsically bad, and therefore we have no right to consent that regions in which it does not now exist, and over whose future history we have any control, should be afflicted by its presence. . . .

Fourthly, we may proceed to rescue our own soil from being trampled by those whose attempts to reclaim their fugitive servants are conducted in a manner to wound our sensibilities and provoke our passions. I repeat, that while a law stands in force, we must either consent to its execution or bear the penalty of disobedience. But when the execution of that law not only inflicts a pang on our moral nature, but is made doubly painful by the frequency and zeal with which it is carried into effect, we cannot, or if we can, we ought not to fold our arms and close our lips in patient acquiescence. . . . But if the South evince a determination to put Northern feeling to a trial on this question whenever it shall have an opportunity, Northern men will not consent to witness often such scenes as we were made to endure a few days since. The question will not be simply, whether a law shall be executed or be resisted; a deeper question will arise, when the Southern master shall use the free States as the ground on which to assert the immaculate character of Slavery. The alternative will then present itself, whether we will become ready participants in upholding a system which we abhor, or will seek a dissolution of the bond which holds us and the South together. This is sad language, and fearful. I know what it means, and what it suggests. But the facts which wring such language from us are sad and fearful. I have loved the Union as dearly perhaps as any one. I have clung to it as the guide and hope of the oppressed nations of the world. I have lost friends and been traduced,— that is no matter, except as it shows how I have spoken,—because I maintained that the Union must be preserved at almost any cost. I say so now. But it may cost us too much.

SOURCE: Ezra Stiles Gannett, *Relation of the North to Slavery: A Discourse, Preached in the Federal Street Meetinghouse* (Boston, 1854), 6–10, 12–20.

JOHN CORDNER

"The Foundations of Nationality"
1856

*In 1843, the fledgling Unitarian community of Montreal called as their first
settled minister the Irishman John Cordner (1816–1894), newly ordained by
the Non-subscribing Presbyterian Church of Ireland. By affiliating with this
body, composed of Arminian liberals who had separated from orthodox Pres-
byterianism in 1829, the Canadians hoped to ward off the Transcendentalism
then sweeping through Unitarianism in the United States. The pious and
Bible-centered Cordner fulfilled that hope during a thirty-five year ministry
that placed him at the center of Canadian Unitarianism. He was also a passionate social reformer who opposed slavery, war, and capital punishment,
and worked for women's rights and better treatment of persons with mental
illness. In this address, given during the celebration of the completion of Canada's Grand Trunk Railway, Cordner anticipated the social gospel and many
of the social democratic policies that Canada would adopt in the twentieth
century. Further Reading: Phillip Hewett,* Unitarians in Canada, *2nd ed.
(Toronto: Canadian Unitarian Council, 1995).*

—Dan McKanan

"I will make a man more precious than fine gold; even a man than the
golden wedge of Ophir."

—ISAIAH 13:12

These significant words lie embedded in an ancient prophecy concerning Babylon.
In looking back through the dim vista of the old and far distant civilizations that of
Babylon looms up with profuse grandeur and magnificence.

     ✻ ✻ ✻

 I have adverted to some of the details of the visible greatness of Babylon. And for
what purpose? . . . I did so to the end that ye might take note of the direction in
which the Babylonian civilization put forth its greatest efforts. It sought wide national
domains that it might reap a golden harvest of tribute. It sought to gather to itself the
rich and shining wedges of Ophir. . . .

 The divine law took effect on Babylonia and Egypt. They fell. They thought less
of a man, than of a palace or a pyramid, and they fell.

359

I speak still of our cognate Anglo-Saxon nations, and ask:—As Britain and America in all the wide extent of their domains, and collective strength of their people, and magnitude of their achievements, rise up before us, can we say of a verity that they have wisely taken warning from the fate of Babylon and the nations of antiquity? Can we say that they have come to estimate a man at his right value—at a higher value than the golden wedges of Australia or California, than territory in India or in Mexico, than railroads, and factories, and steamships, than coals, and cotton, and sugar? No. As we look upon these great nations, we see to what extent the Babylonian notion still prevails, and how widely it is still acted upon. We see, and in sadness we see, that man is still depressed and degraded into a mere toiling tool—through which certain ends are to be reached, certain achievements accomplished. Does Britain desire a portion of India, or the American Union a part of Mexico? Men are then sought and valued in proportion to their powers of extermination. A thousand, or ten thousand, or twenty thousand human lives, besides I know not how much degradation to those who survive, will be paid as an equivalent for the coveted territory. . . . Men are made slaves by statute, and sent into the cane brake and cotton field, and valued according to their powers of endurance there, just as the horse or the ox is valued. In all such forms or manifestations of existing human activities we see a great wrong done to man, and therefore a great offence to God. In the system of slavery by statute we see the most deliberate and daring form of degrading men. But I dwell not now on special forms, since it suits my present purpose better to look at the prevailing spirit and tendency of our civilization as a whole. Is this spirit and tendency Babylonian or divine? Here we touch a matter of direct practical interest to us all. We touch a matter of supreme interest to the generations which are to follow us on the stage of human affairs. For it amounts to this:—Shall Britain and America fall as Babylon and Assyria have fallen, and through similar causes?

The giant Accumulation, mounted on the back of humanity, rides it close to death. The weight thereof, crushes and smothers humane sentiment, religious feeling, all nobler thought, all holier aspiration. Labor is a great blessing, but it may be made a great blight. It is a great blessing when rightly used. No man ever yet felt the full enjoyment of life who did not work. But it becomes an awful blight to a manwhen it is abused and exaggerated. A man ceases to be a man when he becomes a mere labor machine. . . . I speak not here of the American slave. Legislation has deliberately and formally ignored his manhood. Let us not forget his wrongs; but we speak just now rather of those who are legally free—their own property, not the property of another. The tendency of the present civilization is to oppress them with labor. . . .

All of this comes from the tendency of our present civilization, and it is not very difficult to see where it would lead. It is not difficult to see that it leads to a partial development of manhood, not a full and just development.

*　*　*

I have spoken of the peril of our present civilization, and would now speak of its promise. And here I say again, that it would be strange indeed if there were no promise in our present civilization, seeing that the leaven of Christianity has been hid and working in the world for eighteen centuries. Through the coming of Jesus a new element of divine power was infused into human society. Hereby, I am convinced, will the world be renovated. Another Babylon can never be raised, where Christianity is known. Nor can another Egypt. . . . They can never be reproduced in the future, I say, though the Babylonian principle may be so far reproduced as to bring decay and downfall to nations nominally Christian.

*　*　*

And it devolves on us as Christians—it devolves on the Christian Church as the working body of Christian believers—to give effect to Christianity in the world—to carry its principles faithfully into the present economy of the world's affairs. Jesus by his coming, his suffering, and dying, to save the human soul from sin, gave the highest emphasis to the value of a man, and it devolves on us to affirm that value, to maintain it, and to insist that the economy of the nations shall be ordered in view thereof. It is not merely that the weak, the poor, and the enslaved, should have our sympathy, advocacy, and aid, (for the Christian obligation here is palpable,) but we should strive, and see to it, that our, *i.e.* the Christian, nations should have for their prevailing economy and policy a basis not Babylonian, but divine. We should strive and see to it that all national management and government should be for the help and elevation of the masses of men and women within the limits of its control, rather than for the extension of territory, the accumulation of wealth, or the erection of huge national structures.

Standing as we are here on the banks of the St. Lawrence—engaged as we are in building up a national structure, let us not so far forget the early days of civilization in this land as to struggle for material prosperity as the only thing worthy of our effort. Let us not forget that among the earliest messengers of civilization to Canada was the Christian missionary, who, for the sake of dark and uninstructed men, braved all the perils of the savages and the wilderness, and pitched his habitation here, enduring hardships betimes, such as we in these days can scarcely understand. . . . In the dogmatic and ecclesiastical system which he brought along with him I have but little faith. It is not a system which aids advancement in widespread material prosperity. . . . But so far as the Catholic missionary came in the self-sacrificing spirit of Christ, and through love of God labored for the good of man—so far as he came

361

in this spirit, through this motive, and for this purpose, he was a pioneer of religion, and it would be a sad commentary on our Protestant order of civilization if it should crush and smother an element like this by the dead weight of mere material achievement.

SOURCE: John Cordner, *The Foundations of Nationality: A Discourse Preached in the Unitarian Church, Montreal, on the Sunday after the Great Railway Celebration, November, 1856* (Montreal: Henry Rose, 1856), 3, 7, 16–17, 19–22, 25–27.

"A False and True Revival of Religion"
1858

In 1857 and 1858, the largest evangelical revival in American history swept the nation. Historians see it as a watershed, when revivalism turned away from earlier concerns with moral transformation of society and toward almost exclusive focus on individual salvation and communal piety. At a Saturday prayer meeting in Boston's Park Street Church in March 1858, several men asked God to convert or silence Theodore Parker, whose congregation met a block away at the Boston Music Hall. Parker responded to these events with this sermon and another on The Revival of Religion Which We Need. *He published them together as a pamphlet, which became a national best-seller. Further Reading: Kathryn Theresa Long,* The Revival of 1857–58: Interpreting an American Religious Awakening *(New York: Oxford University Press, 1998).*

—Dean Grodzins

"But when he saw the multitudes, he was moved with compassion on them, because they fainted, and were scattered abroad, as sheep having no shepherd."

—MATT. IX.36

There is some little difference, I think, between oat meal and strychnine, though they are both called medicine; and there is no less difference between various things called Religion. One is bread—the bread of life; the other is poison—the poison of death.

Look first at some of the deeds that are called Religion. (I will not go out from the Christian and Hebrew Church.) I go back three or four thousand years, and I find an old man—more than seventy years old—standing by a pile of split wood, with a brand of fire beside him; he lays hold of his little son with one hand, and grasps a large, crooked knife with the other. "What are you going to do with the boy, and with that knife?" I ask. "I am going to kill and burn him on that pile of split wood, as an offering to God." "What would you do that for?" "Why, it is Religion. Only three days ago, God said to me, 'Abraham, take thou thine only son, and offer him a burnt offering on one of the mountains I will tell thee of.' This is one of the grandest acts of my life. Glory to God, who demands the sacrifice of my only boy!"

Next I make a long stride, and find a knot of Roman soldiers surrounding a young man they have nailed to a cross. His head has fallen to one side—he is just dead. . . . A wealthy, educated priest stands by, very joyful, and I ask him, "Who is this man?" "O, he is a miserable fellow . . . His name was Jesus." "Why did you kill him? Was he a murderer?" "A murderer! Murder was nothing to his crime. . . . He was an infidel. He said religion was nothing but piety and morality; or as he called it, loving God and your neighbor as yourselves. He said man was greater than the Sabbath, more than this temple, and that Religion would save a man, without burning the blood of goats, and bulls, and sheep. Besides, he spoke against the priesthood— against us. . . . [He] said we were graves, that appear not, and men stumble into them; that we devour widow's houses, and for a pretence make long prayers. . . . Why, to crucify such a man was an act of Religion! . . . Glory to God!"

I come still nearer [to our own time]—I come down to New England. It is Tuesday, the first of June, 1660. The magistrates of Massachusetts—peaked hats on their heads, broad ruffles at their necks—have just hanged a woman on Boston Common; a handsome woman, a milliner, a wife and mother also. Her dead body is swinging in the wind, from one of the branches of yonder elm,—standing still. "Why did you kill her?" I ask of the Rev. John Norton—a tall, gaunt, harsh-looking minister, on a white horse, with a scholar's eyes, and the face of a hangman,— Geneva bands on his neck, a wig on his head—the man who seemed more interested in the proceeding than any other one of the company. "Why did you do this?" "She was a Quaker. She said that magistrates have no right over the consciences of men; that God made revelations now as much as ever, and was just as near to George Fox as to Moses and Paul, and just as near to her as to Jesus Christ; that priests had no right to bind and loose; that we should call no man master on earth; that sprinkling water on a baby's face did it no good, and gave no pleasure to God. Besides, she said war was wicked; and that woman had just as much right as man; and when we bade her hold her peace, she impudently declared that she had as good a right to publish her opinions as we had to publish ours. So we hanged her by the neck, in the name of God and the Puritan Church of New England. It is an act of Religion. Glory to God, and the vine he has planted here in the wilderness!"

I come down still further. It is the same Boston,—the month of March, 1858. Saturday afternoon, in a meeting house, I find men and women met together for prayer, and conference;—honest-looking men, and respectable—I meet them every day in the street. Most exciting speeches are made, exciting stories are told, exciting hymns are sung, fanatical prayers are put up. Half the assembly seem a little beside themselves, out of their understanding,—more out of their conscience, still more out of their affections. . . . Prayers are made for individual men, now designated by description, then by name. One obnoxious minister is singled out, and set up as a mark to be prayed at, and the petitions riddle that target as they will. One minister asks God to convert him, and if he cannot do that, to remove him out of the way, and let his influence die with him. Another asks God to go into his study this very afternoon, and confound him, so that he will not be able to finish the sermon—which has been writ five days before; or else meet him next day in the pulpit, and confound him so that he shall not be able to speak. Another prays that God will put a hook into that man's jaws, so that he cannot preach. . . .

One step more I take, into surroundings a little different. By the full moonlight . . . in a little chamber not far off, a woman lays aside her work, not quite done. "I will finish that to-morrow morning, before breakfast," she says, " 'twill be ready five hours before the wedding, and I only promised it one hour before." She looks up at the great moon walking in beauty, and silvering her little chamber, with a great star or two beside her—the little stars had been put to bed long before the moon was full. She thinks of the infinite soul who watches over the slumbering earth, the wakeful moon, the great stars and the little, and her own daily life. "The moon serves thee by making beauty in the night, the sun in the day, both of them heavenly bodies," quoth she, "I only an earthly body. Can I also serve by making bonnets?" And out from the great human heart, the Divine soul answers, "Not less; each in its order; the sun in his, the milliner in hers." She lays down on her own bed, her limbs full of weariness, her eyes full of sleep, her heart full of trust in that God, who fills the earth with his love, as the moon fills her window with its beauty.

* * *

Not far off, a little company of men and women are assembled, to consult upon the welfare of mankind. "We must end slavery; we must abolish drunkenness; we must educate the people; woman must be emancipated, and made equal with man; then prostitution will end, and many another woe. War must pass away, society be constructed anew, so that creative love shall take the place of aggressive lust, and repressive fear. The family, the community, the nation, the world, must be organized on justice, not on covetousness, fraud, and violence, as now; and, above all things, the ecclesiastical idea of religion must be improved. We must have a true theology, with a just idea of God, of man, of religion; and so direct aright the strongest faculty in man. What can we do to promote this blessed revolution? This must be our service to God, and we must not let this generation pass away, until we have mended all this. No matter what it costs us. Think what it cost our fathers, the Christian martyrs, nay, Jesus of Nazareth, to do their work! Ministers will pray against us—it will hurt nobody but themselves. . . . A few grand lives will bless this whole age, for the nations look up and ask to be guided."

* * *

365

See what a difference between these various examples that I have given, yet they are all called Religion. Some of them spring from the very highest emotions in man; some of them spring from the meanest, the cowardliest, and the most sneaking of the passions that God has given human nature.

* * *

When I hear of a Revival of Religion, I always ask, what do they mean to revive? What feeling, what thinking, what doing, what being? Is it a religion that shall kill a boy . . . crucify a prophet . . . torture a woman for her opinion, and that opinion a true one? Or is it a religion that will make me a better man, husband, brother, friend; a better minister, mechanic, president, street-sweeper, king—no matter what—a better man in any form?

Just now there is a "Revival of Religion," so called, going on in the land. The newspapers are full of it. Crowds of men and women throng the meeting houses. They cannot get preaching enough. The poorer the article, the more they want of it. Speeches and sermons of the most extravagant character are made. Fanatical prayers are put up. Wonderful conversions are told of. The innermost secrets of men's and women's hearts are laid bare to the eye of the gossip and the pen of the newspaper reporter. The whole is said to be the miraculous outpouring of the Holy Ghost, the direct interposition of God. You look a little more closely, and you find the whole thing has been carefully got up, with the utmost pains. Look at the motive. Ecclesiastic institutions decay in England and America. This is well known. The number of church members in the United States is quite small—only three and a quarter millions. There are sixteen negro slaves to thirteen church members; the slaves increase, the church members do not. For two hundred years, the number was never so small a fraction of the whole people. The number of births increases rapidly; the number of baptisms falls off. Belief in the ecclesiastical theology is fading out of the popular consciousness.

* * *

Attempts at Revivals are no new things—the experiment has often been tried. A few winters ago, some Unitarians tried it in Boston but they toiled all winter, and caught nothing—enclosing nothing but a few sprats and minnows, who ran out through the broad meshes of their net, before it could be hauled into their boat. Other ministers, who are the wisest and the most religious part of that valuable sect, would have nothing to do with it.

* * *

A real Revival of Religion—it was never more needed. Why are men and women so excited now? Why do they go to the meeting houses, and listen to doctrines that insult the common sense of mankind? They are not satisfied with their religious condition. They feel their want. "They are as sheep having no shepherd." This movement shows how strong is the religious faculty in man. In the name of Democracy, politicians use the deep, patriotic feeling of the people to destroy the best institutions of America and the world; and in the name of God, ministers use this mightiest religious feeling to impose on us things yet more disastrous. Let you and me remember that Religion is wholeness, not mutilation; that it is life, and not death; that it is service with every limb of this body, every faculty of this spirit; that we are not to take this world on halves with God, or on sevenths, giving him only the lesser fraction, and taking the larger ourselves: it is to spread over and consecrate the whole life, and make it divine.

SOURCE: Theodore Parker, *A False and True Revival of Religion* (Boston, 1858), 3–9, 12.

"Saints and Their Bodies"

1858

Soldier, minister, abolitionist, and editor Thomas Wentworth Higginson
(1823–1911) wrote this article for the March 1858 Atlantic Monthly *to promote*
a new vision of religion that was strong and robust physically. Higginson's
article excoriated the sedentary boy who was "pallid, puny . . . lifeless," while
celebrating boys who were "ruddy, the brave and the strong." He wondered
why the pallid and puny boy would represent the minister in popular culture
while the ruddy and strong boy was "assigned to a secular career!" Higginson
argued that healthy religious life was fully embodied and offered the prescrip-
tion of exercise and spending time outdoors. Shortly after publishing this
article, Higginson joined the Civil War effort as colonel of the 1st South Car-
olina Volunteers, a regiment for formerly enslaved African Americans. His
ideas about embodiment were echoed in the final years of the nineteenth
century, as rapid urbanization and immigration gave rise to anxiety over
white men's bodies and their moral character and generated a response that
scholars call "muscular Christianity." Further Reading: Howard N. Meyer,
ed., The Magnificent Activist: The Writings of Thomas Wentworth Higginson *(New York: Da Capo Press, 2000).*

—Nicole C. Kirk

Ever since the time of that dyspeptic heathen, Plotinus, the saints have been
"ashamed of their bodies." What is worse, they have usually had reason for the
shame. Of the four famous Latin fathers, Jerome describes his own limbs as mis-
shapen, his skin as squalid, his bones as scarcely holding together; while Gregory
the Great speaks in his Epistles of his own large size, as contrasted with his weakness
and infirmities. Three of the four Greek fathers—Chrysostom, Basil, and Gregory
Nazianzen—ruined their health early, and were wretched invalids for the remainder
of their days. Three only of the whole eight were able-bodied men,—Ambrose,
Augustine, and Athanasius; and the permanent influence of these three has been far
greater, for good or for evil, than that of all the others put together.

* * *

Indeed, the earlier some such saints cast off their bodies the better, they make
so little use of them. Chittagutta, the Buddhist saint, dwelt in a cave in Ceylon.
His devout visitors one day remarked on the miraculous beauty of the legendary

paintings, representing scenes from the life of Buddha, which adorned the walls. The holy man informed them, that, during his sixty years' residence in the cave, he had been too much absorbed in meditation to notice the existence of the paintings, but he would take their word for it. And in this non-intercourse with the visible world there has been an apostolical succession, extending from Chittagutta, down to the Andover divinity-student who refused to join his companions in their admiring gaze on that wonderful autumnal landscape which spreads itself before the Seminary Hill in October; but marched back into the Library, ejaculating, "Lord, turn thou mine eyes from beholding vanity!"

It is to be reluctantly recorded, in fact, that the Protestant saints have not ordinarily had much to boast of, in physical stamina, as compared with the Roman Catholic. They have not got far beyond Plotinus. We do not think it worth while to quote Calvin on this point, for he, as everybody knows, was an invalid for his whole lifetime. But we do take it hard, that the jovial Luther, in the midst of his ale and skittles, should have deliberately censured Juvenal's *mens sana in corpore sano*, as a pagan maxim!

If Saint Luther fails us, where are the advocates of the body to look for comfort? Nothing this side of ancient Greece, we fear, will afford adequate examples of the union of saintly souls and strong bodies. Pythagoras the sage we doubt not to have been identical with Pythagoras the inventor of pugilism, and he was, at any rate, (in the loving words of Bentley,) "a lusty proper man, and built as it were to make a good boxer." Cleanthes, whose sublime "Prayer" is, to our thinking, the highest strain left of early piety, was a boxer likewise. Plato was a famous wrestler, and Socrates was unequalled for his military endurance. Nor was one of these, like their puny follower Plotinus, too weak-sighted to revise his own manuscripts.

* * *

But, happily, times change, and saints with them. Our moral conceptions are expanding to take in that "athletic virtue" of the Greeks . . . which Dr. Arnold, by precept and practice, defended. . . .

This is as it should be. One of the most potent causes of the ill-concealed alienation between the clergy and the people, in our community, is the supposed deficiency on the part of the former, of a vigorous, manly life. It must be confessed that our saints suffer greatly from this moral and physical *anhaemia*, this bloodlessness, which separates them, more effectually than a cloister, from the strong life of the age. What satirists upon religion are those parents who say of their pallid, puny, sedentary, lifeless, joyless little offspring, "He is born for a minister;" while the ruddy, the brave, and the strong are as promptly assigned to a secular career! Never yet did an ill-starred young saint waste his Saturday afternoons in preaching sermons in the garret to his deluded little sisters and their dolls, without living to repent it in maturity. These precocious little sentimentalists wither away like blanched potato-plants in a cellar; and then comes some vigorous youth from his out-door work or play, and grasps the rudder of the age, as he grasped the oar, the bat, or the plough. . . .

Everybody admires the physical training of military and naval schools. But these same persons never seem to imagine that the body is worth cultivating for any purpose, except to annihilate the bodies of others. Yet it needs more training to preserve life than to destroy it. The vocation of a literary man is far more perilous than that of a frontier dragoon. The latter dies at most but once, by an Indian bullet; the former dies daily, unless he be warned in time, and take occasional refuge in the saddle and the prairie with the dragoon. What battle-piece is so pathetic as Browning's "Grammarian's Funeral"? Do not waste your gymnastics on the West Point or Annapolis student, whose whole life will be one of active exercise, but bring them into the professional schools and the counting-rooms. Whatever may be the exceptional cases, the stern truth remains, that the great deeds of the world can be more easily done by illiterate men than by sickly ones. Wisely said Horace Mann, "All through the life of a pure-minded but feeble-bodied man, his path is lined with memory's gravestones, which mark the spots where noble enterprises perished, for lack of physical vigor to embody them in deeds." And yet more eloquently it has been said by a younger American thinker, (D.A. Wasson,) "Intellect in a weak body is like gold in a spent swimmer's pocket, — the richer he would be, under other circumstances, by so much the greater his danger now."

* * *

For, after all, the secret charm of all these sports and studies is simply this, — that they bring us into more familiar intercourse with Nature. They give us that *vitam sub divo* in which the Roman exulted, — those out-door days, which, say the Arabs, are not to be reckoned in the length of life. Nay, to a true lover of the open air, night beneath its curtain is as beautiful as day. The writer has personally camped out under a variety of auspices, — before a fire of pine logs in the forests of Maine, beside a blaze of faya-boughs on the steep side of a foreign volcano, and beside no fire at all, (except a possible one of Sharp's rifles,) in that domestic volcano, Kansas; and every such remembrance is worth many nights of indoor slumber. We never found a week in the year, nor an hour of day or night, which had not, in the open air, its own special beauty. We will not say, with Reade's Australians, that the only use of a house is to sleep in the lee of it; but there is method in even that madness. As for rain, it is chiefly formidable indoors. Lord Bacon used to ride with uncovered head in a shower, and loved "to feel the spirit of the universe upon his brow"; and we once knew an enthusiastic hydropathic physician who loved to expose himself in thunder-storms at midnight, without a shred of earthly clothing between himself and the atmosphere. Some prudent persons may possibly regard this as being rather an extreme, while yet their own extreme of avoidance of every breath from heaven is really the more extravagantly unreasonable of the two.

370

It is easy for the sentimentalist to say, "But if the object is, after all, the enjoyment of Nature, why not go and enjoy her, without any collateral aim?" Because it is the universal experience of man, that, if we have a collateral aim, we enjoy her far more. He knows not the beauty of the universe, who has not learned the subtle mystery, that Nature loves to work on us by *indirections*. Astronomers say that, when observing with the naked eye, you see a star less clearly by looking at it, than by looking at the next one. Margaret Fuller's fine saying touches the same point, — "Nature will not be stared at." Go out merely to enjoy her, and it seems a little tame, and you being to suspect yourself of affectation. We know persons who, after years of abstinence from athletic sports or the pursuits of the naturalist or artist, have resumed them, simply in order to restore to the woods and the sunsets the zest of the old fascination. Go out under pretence of shooting on the marshes or botanizing in the forests; study entomology, the most fascinating, most neglected of all the branches of natural history; go to paint a red maple-leaf in autumn, or watch a pickerel-line in winter; meet Nature on the cricket ground or at the regatta; swim with her, ride with her, run with her, and she gladly takes you back once more within the horizon of her magic, and your heart of manhood is born again into more than the fresh happiness of the boy.

SOURCE: "Saints and their Bodies," *Atlantic Monthly*, March 1858, 582–85, 594–95.

THEODORE PARKER

Theodore Parker's Experience as a Minister
1859

*In early 1859, Theodore Parker collapsed from tuberculosis. He fled the Bos-
ton winter, traveling first to Cuba and Santa Cruz, then Europe. He died
in Florence, Italy, in 1860, at the age of forty-nine. While in Santa Cruz, he
rallied his strength enough to write a remarkable thirty-eight-thousand-word
letter to his congregation. It was the farewell sermon he never got to preach: a
spiritual autobiography, a reform manifesto, a Transcendentalist confession
of faith. He did not give it a title or even ask that it be published, but his
congregation immediately did publish it, bestowing on it the title by which it
is still known,* Theodore Parker's Experience as a Minister. *In this passage,
Parker passed judgment on the mainstream Unitarianism of his day, which
he had been battling for most of his career.*

—Dean Grodzins

I count it a great good-fortune that I was bred among religious Unitarians, and
thereby escaped so much superstition. But I felt early that the "liberal" ministers did
not do justice to simple religious feeling; to me their preaching seemed to relate too
much to outward things, not enough to the inward pious life; their prayers felt cold;
but certainly they preached the importance and the religious value of Morality as no
sect, I think, had done before. Good works, the test of true Religion, noble character,
the proof of salvation, if not spoken, were yet implied in their sermons, spite of their
inconsistent and traditionary talk about "Atonement," "Redeemer," "Salvation by
Christ," and their frequent resort to other pieces of damaged phraseology. The effect
of this predominant Morality was soon apparent. In Massachusetts, the head-quar-
ters of the Unitarians, not only did they gather most of the eminent intellect into
their ranks, the original talent and genius of the most intellectual of the States, but
also a very large proportion of its moral talent and moral genius, most of the eminent
conscience and philanthropy. Leaving out of sight pecuniary gifts for theological and
denominational purposes, which come from peculiar and well-known motives,
where the Trinitarians are professedly superior, I think it will be found that all the
great moral and philanthropic movements in the State—social, ecclesiastical, and
political—from 1800 to 1840, have been chiefly begun and conducted by the Unitarians. Even in the Anti-Slavery enterprise, the most profound, unrespectable and
unpopular of them all, you are surprised to see how many Unitarians,—even

ministers, a timid race—have permanently taken an active and influential part. The Unitarians certainly once had this moral superiority, before the free, young, and growing party became a Sect, hide-bound, bridled with its creed, harnessed to an old, lumbering, and crazy chariot, urged with sharp goads by near-sighted drivers, along the dusty and broken pavement of tradition, noisy and shouting, but going nowhere.

But yet, while they had this great practical excellence, so obvious once, I thought they lacked the deep, internal feeling of piety, which alone could make it lasting: certainly they had not that most joyous of all delights. This fact seemed clear in their sermons, their prayers, and even in the hymns they made, borrowed, or "adapted." Most powerfully preaching to the Understanding, the Conscience and the Will, the cry was ever, "Duty, Duty! Work, Work!" They failed to address with equal power, the Soul, and did not also shout "Joy, Joy! Delight, Delight!" . . .

This defect of the Unitarians was a profound one. Not actually, nor consciously, but by the logic of their conduct, they had broke with the old ecclesiastic Supernaturalism, that with its whip of fear yet compelled a certain direct, though perverted, action of the simple religious element in the Trinitarians: ceasing to fear "the great and dreadful God" of the Old Testament, they had not quite learned to love the All-Beautiful and Altogether Lovely of the Universe. But in general they had no theory which justified a more emotional experience of religion. Their philosophy, with many excellences, was sure of no great Spiritual Truth. . . . Surely, a party with no better philosophy . . . could not produce a deep and continuous action of the religious element in the mass of its members, when left individually free: nor, when organized into a sect, with the discipline of a close corporation, could it continue to advance, or even to hold its own, and live long on its "Statement of Reasons for not believing the Trinity." Exceptional men—like Henry Ware, Jr., who leaned strongly towards the old supernaturalism, or like Dr. Channing, whose deeper reflection or reading supplied him with a more spiritual philosophy—might escape the misfortune of their party; but the majority must follow the logic of their principle. The leaders of the sect, their distinctive creed only a denial, always trembling before the Orthodox, rejected the ablest, original talent born among them; nay, sometimes scornfully repudiated original genius, each offering a more spiritual philosophy, which they mocked at as "transcendental," and turned off to the noisy road of other sects, not grateful to feet trained in paths more natural. After denying the Trinity, and the Deity of Christ, they did not dare affirm the Humanity of Jesus, the Naturalness of Religion to man, the actual or possible Universality of Inspiration, and declare that Man is not amenable to ecclesiastic authority, either the oral Roman Tradition, or the written Hebrew and Greek Scriptures; but naturally communing with God, through many faculties, by many elements, has in himself the Divine Well of Water, springing up full of Everlasting Life, and sparkling with Eternal Truth, and so enjoys continuous revelation.

373

Alas! after many a venturous and profitable cruise, while in sight of port, the winds all fair, the little Unitarian bark, o'ermastered by its doubts and fears, reverses its course and sails into dark, stormy seas, where no such craft can live. Some of the fragments of the wreck will be borne by oceanic currents where they will be used by the party of progress to help to build more sea-worthy ships; whilst others, when water-logged, will be picked up by the great Orthodox fleet, to be kiln-dried in a revival, and then serve as moist, poor fuel for its culinary fires. It is a dismal fault in a religious party, this lack of Piety, and dismally have the Unitarians answered it; yet let their great merits and services be not forgot.

SOURCE: *Theodore Parker's Experience as a Minister, with Some Account of His Early Life and Education for the Ministry; Contained in a Letter from Him to the Members of the Twenty-Eighth Congregational Society of Boston* (Boston, 1859), 107–112.

HENRY WHITNEY BELLOWS

"The Suspense of Faith"

1859

Called "our Bishop, our Metropolitan" at the time of his death by Frederic Henry Hedge, Henry Whitney Bellows (1814–1882) was a leading Unitarian minister in the mid-nineteenth century who helped institutionalize and revitalize American Unitarianism. For forty years he led an ambitious congregation, one of the first to emerge outside of New England, First Congregational Church (later All Souls Church) in New York City. Bellows was widely respected for his leadership capabilities. Congregations looking for ministers and ministers looking for congregations regularly relied on him as a one-man clearinghouse and matchmaker. He founded the Christian Inquirer, *an important weekly, in 1846. During the Civil War, Bellows served as the president of the U.S. Sanitary Commission. Following the Civil War, he turned his organizational acumen to Unitarianism by organizing a National Conference of Unitarian Churches in April of 1865. This was the first Unitarian denominational body composed of congregations rather than of individuals. In "The Suspense of the Faith," delivered to Harvard alumni in 1859, Bellows analyzed the strains upon religion in the mid-nineteenth century and proposed a course of action to mitigate those strains. He argued for building an institution joined by shared ritual and practice and a core theological understanding. By ending his speech with a call for "a new catholic church," Bellows inadvertently prompted a vast misunderstanding and set off a maelstrom of criticism. Surprised by the controversy, he spent the next decade clarifying his comments for his supporters and opponents while simultaneously bringing his vision to life through the National Conference. Further Reading: Walter Kring,* Henry Whitney Bellows *(Boston: Skinner House, 1979); Conrad Wright, "Henry W. Bellows and the Organization of the National Conference," in* The Liberal Christians: Essays on American Unitarian History *(Boston: Beacon Press, 1970), 81–109.*

—Nicole C. Kirk

What, then, is the present condition of our Unitarian body? . . . Our ministers, churches, charities, public gatherings, manifestations of all sorts, were never so numerous and so popular as at present.

And yet, spite of increasing numbers and increasing moral vitality, of growing earnestness and activity, of larger acceptance and easier advance, there is an undeniable chill in the missionary zeal, an undeniable apathy in the denominational life of the body; with general prosperity, in short, there is despondency, self-questioning, and anxiety. It is a singular, and, to many, perhaps an unaccountable phenomenon.

What is the explanation of it? . . .

I. Is it not largely due, in the first place, and particularly, to the fact, that our missionary and denominational work, through the changed aspects of the theological world—the decay of intolerance, the softening of the current creed of Christendom, and the spread of mild and practical views of religious duty—has lost much of its urgency and point? Is not the work of emancipating the community from bigotry and superstition, so much more rapidly and successfully carried on by political and democratic life, literature, and the public press, that our vocation in this direction is mostly gone? . . . The propagandism of Unitarian ideas is essentially paralyzed by the feeling that they are sowing themselves broadcast, not in the formal, but the essential religious thought of the country and the time; and the indifference to increasing our ministers and our churches is very much due to the conviction that many ministers and churches, of all names and orders, are now doing our work, if less directly, yet more thoroughly than we could do it ourselves.

❊ ❊ ❊

II. But in the second place, to come to the *general* reason. There is a broader view to be taken of the general cause of the pausing posture and self-distrust of our Body. Since we began our career, a fact of decisive influence upon our destiny has unexpectedly disclosed itself. The underlying principles and sentiments of the Unitarian body have turned out to be the characteristic ideas and tendencies of the religious epoch we live in. Protestantism produced us, not we it. Whatever is good or bad in our spirit and direction was latent in the Reformation, and is fast becoming patent in the whole product of that world-movement. . . . Thus no criticism of Unitarianism is radical which is not also a criticism of Protestantism.

❊ ❊ ❊

If, then, with logical desperation, we ultimate the tendencies of Protestantism, and allow even the malice of its enemies to flash light upon their direction, we may see that the sufficiency of the Scriptures turns out to be the self-sufficiency of man, and the right of private judgment an absolute independence of Bible or Church. No creed but the Scriptures, practically abolishes all Scriptures but those on the human heart; nothing between a man's conscience and his God, vacates the Church; and with the Church, the Holy Ghost, whose function is usurped by private reason: the Church lapses into what are called Religious Institutions; these into Congregationalism, and Congregationalism into Individualism—and the logical end is the abandonment of the Church as an independent institution, the denial of Christianity

376

as a supernatural revelation, and the extinction of worship as a separate interest. There is no pretence that Protestantism, as a body, has reached this, or intends this, or would not honestly and earnestly repudiate it; but that its most logical product is at this point it is not easy to deny. Nay, that these are the *tendencies* of Protestantism is very apparent.

Let us not be too much alarmed at this statement, assuming it to be true. Tendencies are not always ultimate. They encounter resistance. They meet and yield to other tendencies. The tendencies of an epoch, religious or political, do not decide its whole character. There are forces in humanity stronger than any epochal powers—the permanent wants, the indestructible instincts of our nature. It is safe, and it ought not to be alarming, to see and confess that the tendencies of political and religious speculation and sentiment, in the universal Church of our day, are to the weakening of the external institutions of Christianity, the extinction of the ministry, and the abandonment of any special interest in religion, as a *separate* interest of man or society. If our Unitarian body understands this better than the inner ranks of Protestantism, it is only because the squadrons behind have pressed it nearer the brink towards which they are unconsciously advancing. . . . The Unitarian body, not as being more learned or more thoughtful than other Protestant bodies in its leaders and ministry, but as having a laity on the same intellectual level with its leaders, and no dead weight of mere instinct and affection to drag along with it, has carried out and experienced in its denominational life, what no other Protestant sect has yet been sufficiently conscious of itself, and enough under the dominion of its own ideas fully to experience. We have shown the world the finest fruits and the rankest weeds of the Protestant soil; we have most freely felt and most plainly indicated the main Protestant current; and the criticisms we have suffered from our Protestant brethren have owed much of their edge, to the anxiety of fellow-passengers, bitterly upbraiding the officers of the ship because they could not resist the force of the stream that set towards the rapids and the precipice. The same sympathy, taking often the form of antipathy, that connects the conservative and historical rank of our own body, with the front-rank of avowed rationalists, connects us all, as the front-rank of Protestantism, with the whole body behind; and we must pardon the severity of its criticism upon us, when we consider that it is an unconscious self-criticism—a parent's blame of the hereditary taint it has communicated to its child.

* * *

Nor is this all. It is not only an unreligious age, but it is becoming more and more unreligious. For religious institutions and ideas in our day flourish mainly in the strength of their roots in a religious past, a strength which is constantly diminishing. As respect for rank in England, the remnant of an honest aristocratic system ages in power, is the wholesome *vis inertia* which prevents the democratic instincts of the age in that country from hurrying precipitately to their inevitable goal, so the genuine religiousness of ages gone by, whose flavor lingers in our blood, is the most vigorous support the worship of this age enjoys. Whatever public nourishment besides, distinctive and essential religion has in our generation, is due to the exceptional devoutness of spirits born out of due time, and to the *esprit de corps* so characteristic of the day—the love of joint action, the fondness for educational, moral and ethical institutions, the emulation of communities with each other, the partisan rivalry of sects, and the fact that, under the name of religious institutions, we sustain a vast and valuable system of adult education, in thought, humanity and manners. Our churches, to a great extent, and constantly more and more so, are lecture-foundations—in which the interest is less and less religious, more and more political, social and ethical. The one thing the people are interested in is life, themselves, each other, and the relation of the inside to the outside—of man to his dwelling, of man to man, of man to himself. To make a religion out of self-respect, right-living, self-culture—to insist that aspiration is worship, that truth is God, that goodness is religion—is the highest ambition of our modern pulpit. I do not say it in blame, nor in scorn; for, under the circumstances, it is an honorable ambition, laid upon men by the necessity of justifying their own faith to themselves.

* * *

I have been speaking, you will observe, not wholly, yet mainly, of tendencies; and tendencies may be dangerous and extravagant, and yet necessary and providential—a wholesome reaction upon other tendencies still more alarming. There have been perilous tendencies to excess of ritual and positive religion in Oriental regions, in past eras, ending in paralysis of the private will, and deterioration of humanity. At times, even in the Christian world, there has been too much worship, too constant and formal a reference to God's will to admit of a proper degree of human freedom. You will not understand me, then, as generally questioning the merits of the age we live in, by calling it an unreligious age, or as disparaging Protestantism, as if it had not been, and were not still, until honestly exhausted, a valuable and indispensable movement. And for a psychological reason of the utmost importance, to explain which is the third step in our journey. I have shown, first, the particular, and next, the general historical reason of the pause of faith; I wish now to set forth the still more fundamental or psychological reason of this pause—the *universal* reason.

III. There are two motions of the spirit in relation to God, his Creator and upholder, essential to the very existence of generic or individual Man—a centrifugal and centripetal motion—the motion that sends man away from God, to learn his freedom, to develop his personal powers and faculties, relieved of the over-awing and predominating presence of his Author; and the motion that draws him back to God, to receive the inspiration, nurture, and endowment, which he has become strong

378

enough to hold. For man, though a creature of faculties, is still more characteristically, a creature of capacities; and his capacities must be developed before they can be filled—his vessel shaped before it can go to the fountain. He must have freedom before he can yield obedience; he must possess a will before he can surrender it; affections, trained to love visible objects, before they can love the unseen Source; intellectual and moral independence, to make his loyalty significant, and his service blessed. Accordingly, the origin and history of the race exhibits the care with which God has hidden himself away from his creatures in the infancy of their existence, let they should be scorched and shriveled in the glory of his presence. And yet his whole purpose is to create a race that can live in his conscious society, without losing their individuality and freedom in gaining his inspiration and guidance. The whole vexed question of the tardiness of the great Dispensations, and of the necessity of Revelation itself, is to be solved only in the light of this law, the sistole or diastole, or double motion of our spirits. Man is not made acquainted with God by nature, and God does not come into his earliest stages of existence with distinctness, because spiritual creation must precede spiritual salvation. The first man is of the earth, earthy; the second man, is the Lord from heaven: the first Adam was created a living soul; the second Adam a quickening spirit. Man's creation is not complete at his birth, but continues on in his development as an intellectual and moral being; and this development is primarily more important than the use to which his faculties are put; as the life, health, and growth of our children are more important than any thing they can do for us, or any affections they manifest towards us, in their infancy and youth. If we view the history of the race in a comprehensive way, we shall observe that it has been providentially occupied in all its earlier eras with itself, establishing what may be called its self-hood; and that what is termed natural religion—which is only an inverted self-worship, in which man makes his own deity to suit his tastes and feelings, and of course, does not make him too strong for his own self-will—is then the only witness of the living God—a witness so meek, as not to interfere with the providential process of setting man up in his own right and liberty. Revealed religion—the only religion that ever has had authority, or which, by the nature of the case, can have power to awe, restrain, and elevate man, or to overcome he congenital bias of his nature—being something outside of, and independent of his personality—has necessarily been subsequent to his creation; confined to special representative races and eras; and has applied itself through the slow form of institutional influences, in order to gain a greater power in the end, because over a more freely and fully developed being, surrendering himself voluntarily to a control which enlarges his true freedom, and accepting a liberty in divine dependence, of which his previous independence has been only a fictitious foreshadowing.

* * *

Is it not plain, then, that as Protestants of the Protestants, we are at the apogee of our orbit; that in us the centrifugal epoch of humanity has for this swing of the pendulum, at least reached its bound. For one cycle we have come, I think, nearly to the end of our self-directing, self-asserting, self-developing, self-culturing faculties; to the end of our honest interest in this necessary, alternate movement. . . . And this is the painful pause—this the suspended animation, seen and felt throughout Christendom—especially throughout Protestant Christendom—and more particularly throughout our own more Protestantized province of the Church. Why is it that the moment we find ourselves in possession of men, whom genius, character, and scholarship fit to lead us in our logical career to new victories and the extension of our faith, they almost uniformly become paralyzed by doubts and scruples, and lose their interest in the progress they might assure? It is simply because the small elevation which gives them command of us, reveals to them the absence of any more road, in the direction we have been going.

* * *

If, however, universal history is to be heeded, if the great common instincts of humanity are prophetic, if religion be the earliest and latest, the deepest and the highest interest of man, then we may trust that the sense of want, the yearning for rest, the longing for legitimate authority, the expectation of relief, the general feeling throughout the devouter portion of Protantism of dissatisfaction with the existing attitude of things, with a secret faith that God or Christ is about to interpose for its relief, indicates the conception—I do not say the birth—of a new religious epoch, to be distinguished as much by faith, as the last has been by doubt—an epoch in which the temple that man has been building and beautifying shall be occupied by its Lord—in which the passive side of humanity shall enjoy its long-neglected rights; and when, instead of seeking God as the solar system is seeking the star *Aries* in the constellation Hercules, He shall seek us, as the shepherd in the parable, leaving the ninety and nine of the flock, sought the lost lamb and folded it in his arms; and in place of self-assertion, self-abnegation and life in God, shall again become the type of human experience.

* * *

The particular, the general, the universal reason for the suspense of faith, we have now successively set forth. It remains only, in conclusion, to look at the form in which we may hope that faith will rally and go on. And this brings us face to face, at last, with what we have been secretly envisaging all the time, the Church question, which is the real question of the earnest, religious thought of the time, and agitates itself and us, under all sorts of disguises. . . .

Who does not see that the fatal misgiving at the bottom of the mind of Protestantism is this—Have the external institutions of religion any authority but expediency?

do they stand for and represent any thing but one portion of the human race educating another portion of the human race, which, in the last analysis, is self-culture? And if they stand only for self-culture, on what other basis do they stand than schools and colleges? . . .

* * *

In his individual capacity, as an inorganic, unrelated, independent being, a man has not, and cannot have, the affections, internal experiences and dispositions, or the powers and blessings, which we can, and may, and will receive in his corporate capacity—in either or any of the great departments of his Humanity, the family, the State, the Church. Nor is there any complete and satisfactory, perhaps no real way, to come into this corporate capacity, except through a publicly recognized and legitimate organization, whether domestic, political, or religious. "The powers that be are ordained of God";—the laws governing the family order, are, in each country for the time, divinely empowered, to shield what society did not make and cannot unmake; and the Historical Church for the time being, and the place in which it organizes the Word of God, and institutes the channel of divine grace, is a divine institution, connection with which is the normal, not the only, condition of salvation. I am not to be driven from this ground by arguments drawn from the number and variety of churches, or the profitless character of many of them, or their often imperfect and miserable administration; any more than the unhappy marriages, or the wretched laws applicable to them, should drive me from my reverence for the family, as a divine institution and order. I recognize the fact that in all Christian countries the main channel of the religious life of the people is an external organization. I know that the whole Gospel cannot be taught to individuals as individuals. I believe that the Holy Spirit communicates with Humanity, and not with private persons. God speaks to men, individual men, through their consciences; but the Holy Spirit is God coming into the world through his Word, a living word, but still a word, a spoken, taught, published word, which is neither communicated to individuals, nor from individuals, but from the Church to Humanity. This doctrine does not deny open relations between individual men and their Maker; does not deny spiritual influences to private souls; but it denies that the Holy Ghost is to be confounded with these private whispers, or that the religious life of the world is mainly due to these independent and inorganic suggestions.

* * *

Let the Church feel that it has a sphere quite as important as it can fill, in maintaining the worshipful and God-fearing affections—in supplying the purely religious wants of the people. I would have it undertake less, in order to do more; it would exert a larger influence in the end by confining its work to the illumination of the spiritual interior, the communication of the Holy Ghost.

381

If we imagine this to be a short, a vague, a monotonous work, it is only because we have not considered that the communication of the contents of revelation, the supply of the Holy Spirit, and the publishing of the Word, the conversion, regeneration, and sanctifying of the souls of men, involves the perpetual reproduction of Christ's life, precepts, history, and spirit. I know how degenerate a sense of Christianity the so-called advanced feeling about the Gospel is. The words of the Bible pass for the Word of God, which that Bible is; the words of Jesus, for Jesus himself—the Word that came down from heaven. But God's Word is God's power, God's Wisdom, God's love made known in the great language of natural and supernatural events. God talks in creation, in history, in revelation. Nations are his alphabet, epochs his syllables, humanity his discourse. The Bible is God's Word, because it is the record of his dealings with nations and ages—the religious and priestly nations and ages. More especially, and in the most pregnant and peculiar sense, Christ is the Word of God; not what he said but what he was and did and suffered, and thus showed and taught; and his words and promises and precepts are only part and parcel of his life and death, his resurrection, and perpetual epiphany in the Church. Christ must be formed in us, the hope of glory. God speaks peculiarly and savingly to every soul in whom he makes Christ live. And the work or the Church is so to speak to the world in the orotund of great historic incidents; so to preach by emphasizing the commemorative days, and illuminating the holy symbols—and pausing on the successive events which made the doctrines of Christianity—as gradually to thunder into the deaf ear of humanity the saving lesson of the Gospel.

No lecture-room can do this; no preaching-man can do this; no thin, ghostly individualism or meagre congregationalism can do this. It calls for the organic, instituted, ritualized, impersonal, steady, patient work of the Church—which, taking infancy into its arms, shall baptize it, not as a family custom, but a Church sacrament; which shall speak to the growing children by imaginative symbols and holy festivals—and not merely by Sunday-school lessons and strawberry-feasts; which shall confirm them and take them into the more immediate bosom of the Church as they attain adult years, and are about to step beyond the threshold of domestic life; which shall make both marriage and burial rites of the immediate altar—and give back to the communion-service the mystic sanctity which two centuries has been successfully striving to dispel, without gaining by this rationality any thing except the prospect of its extinction. A new Catholic Church—a Church in which the needed but painful experience of Protestantism shall have taught us how to maintain a dignified, symbolic, and mystic church-organization without the aid of the State, or the authority of the Pope—their support being now supplied by the clamorous wants of our starved imaginations and suppressed devotional instincts—this is the demand of the weary, unchurched humanity of our era. How to remove the various obstacles, how to inaugurate the various steps to it—is probably more than any man's wisdom is adequate to direct just now. But to articulate, or even to try to articulate the dumb wants of the religious times, is at least one step to it. It is a cry for help, which God will hear, and will answer by some new word from the Holy Ghost, when humanity is able and willing to bear it.

SOURCE: Henry Whitney Bellows, *The Suspense of Faith: An Address to the Alumni of the Divinity School of Harvard University* (New York, 1859), 4–6, 8–12, 15–20, 22–23, 25, 32–33, 38–39, 44–46.

"A Plea for Captain John Brown"

1859

John Brown's shocking raid on Harper's Ferry in October 1859, intended to ignite slave uprisings in the South, was regarded by many as the work of a madman. Not so, argued Thoreau and Emerson in passionate defense of Brown's heroism. Both likened him to Christ and portrayed him as a martyr for the cause of emancipation. Thoreau's "Plea for Captain John Brown"— widely reported in the press—outraged Brown's opponents and inspired his supporters. In the view of historian David Reynolds and others, Thoreau and Emerson's endorsements divided the Northern and Southern wings of the Democratic Party and, in doing so, significantly contributed to the election of Abraham Lincoln in 1860. Further Reading: David S. Reynolds, John Brown, Abolitionist: The Man Who Killed Slavery, Sparked the Civil War, and Seeded Civil Rights *(New York: Knopf, 2005); Jack Turner, ed.,* A Political Companion to Henry David Thoreau *(Lexington: University Press of Kentucky, 2009).*

—Barry Andrews

Little as I know of Captain Brown, I would fain do my part to correct the tone and the statements of the newspapers, and of my countrymen generally, respecting his character and actions.

* * *

He was by descent and birth a New England farmer, a man of great common sense, deliberate and practical as that class is, and tenfold more so. He was like the best of those who stood at Concord Bridge once, on Lexington Common, and on Bunker Hill, only he was firmer and higher principled than any that I have chanced to hear of as there. . . .

He did not go to the college called Harvard, good old Alma Mater as she is. . . . But he went to the great university of the West, where he sedulously pursued the study of Liberty, for which he had early betrayed a fondness, and having taken many degrees, he finally commenced the public practice of Humanity in Kansas, as you all know. Such were his *humanities*, and not any study of grammar. He would have left a Greek accent slanting the wrong way, and righted up a falling man.

* * *

A man of rare common sense and directness of speech, as of action; a transcendentalist above all, a man of ideas and principles,—that was what distinguished him.

It was his peculiar doctrine that a man has a perfect right to interfere by force with the slaveholder, in order to rescue the slave. I agree with him. . . . I shall not be forward to think him mistaken in his method who quickest succeeds to liberate the slave. I speak for the slave when I say, that I prefer the philanthropy of Captain Brown to that philanthropy which neither shoots me nor liberates me. . . . I do not wish to kill nor to be killed, but I can foresee circumstances in which both these things would be by me unavoidable. We preserve the so-called "peace" of our community by deeds of petty violence every day. Look at the policeman's billy and hand cuffs! Look at the jail! Look at the gallows! . . . So we defend ourselves and our hen roosts, and maintain slavery. I know that the mass of my countrymen think that the only righteous use that can be made of Sharps' rifles and revolvers is to fight duels with them, when we are insulted by other nations, or to hunt Indians, or shoot fugitive slaves with them, or the like. I think that for once the Sharps' rifles and the revolvers were employed in a righteous cause. The tools were in the hands of one who could use them.

The same indignation that is said to have cleared the temple once will clear it again. The question is not about the weapon, but the spirit in which you use it. No man has appeared in America as yet who loved his fellow man so well, and treated him so tenderly. He lived for him. He took up his life and he laid it down for him.

* * *

Who is it whose safety requires that Captain Brown be hung? Is it indispensible to any Northern man? . . . Think of him—of his rare qualities! such a man as it takes ages to make, and ages to understand; no mock hero, nor the representative of any party. A man such as the sun may not rise upon again in this benighted land. To whose making went the costliest material, the finest adamant; sent to be the redeemer of those in captivity. And the only use to which you can put him is to hang him at the end of a rope! You who pretend to care for Christ crucified, consider what you are about to do to him who offered himself to be the savior of four millions of men. . . .

I am here to plead his cause with you. I plead not for his life, but for his character—his immortal life; and so it becomes your cause wholly, and is not his in the least. Some eighteen hundred years ago Christ was crucified; this morning, perchance, Captain Brown was hung. These are two ends of a chain which is not without its links. He is not Old Brown any longer; he is an Angel of Light.

SOURCE: Henry David Thoreau, "A Plea for Captain John Brown," in *Reform Papers*, ed. Wendell Glick (Princeton, NJ: Princeton University Press, 1973), 111–13, 115, 132–33, 136–37.

"The Broad Church"

1860

*In response to the growing schism between Transcendentalists and advocates
of Christian Unitarianism, Frederic Henry Hedge (1805–1890) joined with
Henry Whitney Bellows and James Freeman Clarke to form the Broad Church
movement. In this Berry Street Essay of 1860, Hedge described the preservation of "ecclesiastical continuity" as both an institutional and metaphysical
necessity. Comparing it to the "spinal cord of humanity," Hedge viewed the
Church as the primary vehicle through which God pushes history forward.
The diversity within Unitarianism therefore evidenced rather than threatened
its exceptionalism. Insofar as Unitarians could cultivate a "catholic spirit"
within the denomination, they would lead other sects into the kingdom of God.*

—Erik Martinez Resly

And they shall come from the east, and from the west, and from the north,
and from the south, and shall sit down in the kingdom of God.

—LUKE XIII. 29.

WE all know how utterly and astonishingly this prediction was verified in the first
centuries of the Christian Church, which is what is here meant by the kingdom of
God. Fifty days after the death of Christ, in whose tomb it was seemingly extinct, and
whose resurrection was then the private persuasion of a few friends, the soul of that
kingdom burst forth again with irrepressible vehemence at Jerusalem. It swept the
city with a rushing mighty wind from heaven, and a demonstration of fiery tongues,
inaugurating the new heavens and the new earth of the Christian ages. Three thousand souls sat down in the kingdom by invitation of Peter that day. East, west, north,
and south were all represented. For there were dwelling at Jerusalem at that time
Jewish proselytes "out of every nation under heaven," providentially gathered to the
feast of the tribes,—Parthians, Medes, Elamites, from the east; people from the parts
of Libya about Cyrene, strangers of Rome, Cappadocians, Phrygians, from the west
and the north; and dwellers in Mesopotamia from the south. When this rushing
mighty wind struck them it lodged a seed of the kingdom in their souls, which they
took with them to their proper homes, and sowed in their several lands, where it grew
to be a heavenly plantation, a spiritual oasis amid the perishing polytheisms of the
Empire and the droning synagogues of the Dispersion.

So mightily grew the Word, and prevailed; so it was that geographically east and west and north and south sat down in the kingdom of God. And in our day, though other religions may number more disciples, there is none so widely diffused as the Christian,—none that can vie with it in geographical extent,—none which embraces so many latitudes and longitudes and differing nationalities. A few meridians include the boasted millions of Hinduism and of Islamism. When daylight dies along the waves of the Caspian, it disappears to all the worshippers of Buddha; when "sets the sun on Afric's shore, that instant all is night" to the followers of Mohammed; but Christendom is a kingdom on which the sun never sets, where east and west and north and south sit down together, and earth's extremities join hands.

But the prophecy of our Lord has another meaning and fulfillment besides the geographical one we have been discussing. The kingdom of God has other distinctions and relations, divergences and approximations, than those of space. The spiritual horizon has its polarities as well as the material. There are cardinal points of the spirit, as decided in their peculiarities as east and west and north and south, and, like these divisions of the compass, organic constituents of the spiritual world, necessary each to its orbed completeness and indispensable to its very being. Viewing the prophecy in this light, it expresses the spiritual completeness of the kingdom of God, or the Christian Church, as well as its geographical extent. East, west, north, south, may be regarded as typifying different tendencies and qualities of the spirit,—the east, stability, conservativism; the west, mobility, progress; the north internal activity, the inner life, idealism, mysticism; the south, exterior productiveness, ritualism, symbolism, ecclesiastical organization.

* * *

If now we come to the world of our own time, to the Protestant Christendom of to-day, we find there also—regarding Protestantism externally and historically as one movement—a complete church, in which east and west and north and south are all represented. Protestant Christendom is bounded on the east by the Rocky Mountains of immovable Orthodoxy, on the west by the River of Free Inquiry, on the north by the White Sea of Mysticism, on the south by the Gulf of Prelacy, which divides it from the Church of Rome. In other words, Calvinism at one extremity, and Universalism at the other, Quakerism and Spiritism on this hand, and Episcopacy on that, define this spiritual kingdom and attest its completeness. But though Protestantism as a whole, externally and historically considered, exhibits this compass and variety, it is one of the evils of Protestantism that, internally and practically, it is not a whole, but a chaos of disunited, independent states, having no ecclesiastical fellowship with one another. The Protestant Christian, however catholic his own temper and views, is practically shut up within the fold of a sect which, if liberal, is excluded by all the rest, and which, if illiberal, excludes them. If a native of the east, it is not lawful for him to sit down with them of the west; if he come from the west, he is an offence to the saints of the east; if inclined to the north, he is cut off from the sympathies of the south; if reared in the south, he is early imbued with a holy horror of the north. The only way to obviate this evil in each particular communion is by individual tolerance to strive for completeness within that fold. Each sect should seek, so far as practicable, to be a catholic, complete church. A sect is then in a healthy state when a due admixture of conservatism and liberality, of speculation and activity, of idealism and formalism, answering the condition and satisfying the necessities of different minds, supplies all the elements of ecclesiastical edification, and completes the spiritual horizon. East, west, north, and south must unite in every kingdom of God, and every sect is in theory such a kingdom.

*   *   *

These four, represented by and representing the fourfold completeness of the spiritual horizon, east, west, north, and south,—stability and progress, ideal and ritual,—are the cardinal constituents of a true church. To which we must add, as the complement and crown of the whole, the Charity which binds and pervades and harmonizes all,—that supreme grace of the Christian dispensation, Love manifest in works of social reform, in ministrations to the poor and suffering, in health to the sick, and light to them that sit in darkness, and the opening of prison to them that are bound. The church in which these elements unite is a broad church, though numbering its disciples not by millions, but by hundreds or by tens. A holy catholic church it is, though the smallest sect in Christendom, and excommunicated by all the rest. I believe in the Broad Church thus defined. According to the creed of the Fathers, "I believe in the Holy Catholic Church,"—not that which consists in masses and indulgences, in manipulations and genuflexions, and infallibility and a breaden God, but that which consists in faith and progress and devotion and love. Let each church labor in its place and kind to develop and assert this catholicity, and the boundary lines which divide the sects shall be washed clean out in the gracious life that shall flood them all, and fuse them all into one prevailing kingdom of God, whose unshut gates shall exclude none that desire to enter, and where east and west and north and south shall meet in peace and join in praise.

SOURCE: Frederic Henry Hedge, "The Broad Church," in *Sermons* (Boston, 1891), 150–51, 153–55, 157–59, 169–70.

THOMAS STARR KING

"Sermon on Yosemite" and
"Lessons from the Sierra Nevada"
1860, 1863

*Thomas Starr King (1824–1864) set the course for liberal religion in Cali-
fornia with his Christian Transcendentalism, which found in California's
natural beauty an affirmation of the new state's importance in the nation and
of God's infinite love and power. As the minister of San Francisco's Unitarian
church, King was instrumental in securing California for the Union cause
and raising money for the Sanitary Commission. He promoted racial equality
as part of a democratic, Protestant society he believed was destined to stretch
from the Pacific to the Atlantic. His theology emphasized not only the personality of God but also nature as the expression of God's wisdom, power, and
love; the reality and substance of the spiritual world; and the absolute necessity of moral conduct. King made the trek to Yosemite Valley three months
after arriving in San Francisco, about which he wrote a series of letters for the
Boston Evening Transcript. Many scholars consider these letters as instrumental in acquainting New Englanders with the wonders of Yosemite Valley. King's two most popular nature sermons were "Living Waters from Lake
Tahoe" and "Lessons from the Sierra Nevada," both reproduced in a widely
read collection of his sermons. Both reveal key elements of the role of nature
in King's liberal Christianity. Further Reading: Glenna Matthews,* The
Golden State in the Civil War: Thomas Starr King, the Republican Party,
and the Birth of Modern California *(New York: Cambridge University Press,
2012); Sandra Sizer Frankiel,* California's Spiritual Frontiers: Religious Alter-
natives in Anglo-Protestantism, 1850–1910 *(Berkeley: University of California
Press, 1988).*

— Sheri Prud'homme

From "Sermon on Yosemite," 1860

A fresh impression of the marvels of nature always awakens a religious emotion. I
thought of this more seriously than ever before, when, about two weeks ago, I first
looked down from the Mariposa trail into the tremendous fissure of the Sierras. The
place is fitly called "Inspiration Point." The shock to the senses there, as one rides out
from the level and sheltered forest, up to which our horses had been climbing
two days, is scarcely less than if he had been instantly borne to a region where the

389

Creator reveals more of himself in his works than can be learned from the ordinary scenery of this world. . . . A vast trench, cloven by Omnipotence amid a tumult of mountains, yawned beneath us. The length of it was seven or eight miles; the sides of it were bare rock, and they were perpendicular. . . .

All this, no doubt, seems tame enough in the wording; and even if a vivid picture of the actual scene could be given here by an adequate description, some of you might say that it is only a pile of rock overhanging a river-course—not very remarkable, and certainly not religiously suggestive.

But I do not think that there was one in our party who had the feeling, when that surprising view first broke upon us, that he was looking merely upon a freak of natural forces, or a patch of chaos. I am sure we all felt that something more than matter was shown to us—a clearer gleam of the Infinite Majesty. I believe that the impression was, in some degree, like that which the Israelites felt amid the passes of Sinai, when the Divine glory was on the mount. If the emotion which that first view excited could remain with us, I am sure that all life would be more reverent and loyal.

And that is a large portion of the value of such impressive wonders in nature. They break in, for a moment, if no more, upon our materialistic and skeptical estimate of the world, and show us that it is penetrated with Divine meaning—that it is an expression of Infinite power and thought.

From "Lessons from the Sierra Nevada," 1863

This, brethren, is the spirit out of which the most efficient knowledge grows, this is the spirit which acquaintance with the works of God should ever deepen and feed. I meet you to-night that we may together bow reverently before the mountains that guard the eastern frontier of our State, with whose majesty I have been permitted, of late, to form an intimate acquaintance. Love of nature has its root in wonder and veneration, and it issues in many forms of practical good. There can be no abounding and ardent patriotism where sacred attachment to the scenery of our civil home is wanting; and there can be no abiding and inspiring religious joy in the heart that recognizes no presence and touch of God in the permanent surrounding of our earthly abode.

The great bane of modern life is materialism,—the divorce of spirit from power, order, bounty, and beauty in our thought of the world. We look upon nature as a machine, a play of forces that run of necessity and of course. We do not bow before it with wonder and awe as the manifestation of a present all-animating will and art. Whatever leads us to such feelings towards the universe puts us on the road to Christian faith, helps character, and lifts the plane of the privilege of life. I believe that if, on every Sunday morning before going to church, we could be lifted to a mountain-peak and see a horizon line of six hundred miles enfolding the copious splendor of the light on such a varied expanse; or if we could look upon a square mile of flowers representing all the species with which the Creative Spirit embroiders a zone; or if we could be made to realize the distance of the earth from the sun, the light of which travels every morning twelve millions of miles a minute to feed and bless us, and which the force of gravitation pervades without intermission to hold our globe calmly in its orbit and on its poise; if we could fairly perceive, through our outward senses, one or two features of the constant order and glory of nature, our materialistic dullness would be broken, surprise and joy would be awakened, we should feel that we live amid the play of Infinite thought; and the devout spirit would be stimulated so potently that our hearts would naturally mount in praise and prayer.

SOURCE: Oscar Tully Shuck, *The California Scrap-Book* (San Francisco: H. H. Bancroft and Company, 1869), 446–48; Thomas Starr King, *Christianity and Humanity*, ed. Edwin P. Whipple (Boston: Houghton, Osgood, and Company, 1880), 286–287.

Report of the Convention of Unitarian Churches Held in New York
1865

Through his leadership of the Sanitary Commission, Henry Whitney Bellows (1814–1882) became convinced that liberal Christianity had the potential to grow into a truly national movement—if it had the right denominational apparatus. Bellows believed the American Unitarian Association, which was centered in Massachusetts and comprised of individuals rather than congregations, was inadequate to the task. He proposed a new body, which he initially hoped would be called The Liberal Church of America. Delegates from three quarters of all Unitarian congregations in the United States settled instead on "National Conference of Unitarian and other Christian Churches." In other respects, they honored Bellows's Broad Church vision for the body, which was designed to accommodate both traditional Christian Unitarians and moderate Transcendentalists. It failed to satisfy the most radical heirs of Emerson and Parker, who created a rival Free Religious Association a few years later. Included here are both the address that opened the convention and the constitution on which the delegates agreed. Further Reading: Conrad Wright, "'Salute the Arriving Moment': Denominational Growth and the Quest for Consensus, 1865–1895," in Conrad Wright, ed., A Stream of Light: A Short History of American Unitarianism *(Boston: Skinner House, 1975), 62–94.*

—Dan McKanan

"Address to the Churches"

New York, Feb. 10, 1865.

Dear Brethren:

You have recently received a call, inviting you to represent your Church and Society, by its Pastor and two male delegates, in the General Convention of our Unitarian Body, to be held in the City of New York, on April 5th, 1865. The General Committee created by the A.U.A. to issue that call, appointed us a sub-Committee, to prepare an Address to the Churches on the urgent importance of the occasion.

The great agitation through which our country has been passing during the last four years, has shaken down many sectarian lines and prejudices; brought into view and acquaintance with each other, those long separated and unknown; tested the worth of opinions, and shown what was practically inspiring and efficient in the beliefs of Christians; thrown open many doors of mental imprisonment, and enlarged the whole area of our moral and intellectual life as a nation. We have seen social and political prejudices of the most fixed and hopeless character, giving way before the majestic power of God's providence, and disappearing like a mist. Such vast changes in our political, economical, social, and intellectual life, must inevitably be accompanied by great changes in the religious life and theological opinions of the American people. It is impossible that an adjustment should not take place between their altered views on all other subjects, and their old views on the subject of the Christian Faith, and it is almost inevitable that a revolution in the theological life of the nation, as great as that taking place in its civil and political life, should follow upon it.

Now, we have always been claiming, as Unitarians, that our theological opinions, besides being the simplicity of the Gospel, represented the spirit and wants of the nineteenth century, and that nothing but the cramping power of ecclesiastical authority, or prescriptive creeds, with the mighty force of old customs and old expressions, kept down the popular utterance of a Christian faith, essentially like our own. So effectually, however, have these or other influences suppressed our growth as an organized body, represented by visible churches, that we barely maintain our place, and have been making for many years almost no progress in the country at large. We had to bear the stigma of having reared in our bosom the moral radicalism which produced the war. We were feared and systematically discouraged, and warned off the more productive fields of labor, and have been objects alike of political, social, and theological jealousy throughout the nation.

But all this has now changed. What was so long our past shame is likely enough to become our future glory. That crust of ecclesiastical and theological usage, so long thickening with undisturbed possession of the surface, and which we could not puncture, has been broken up, as the ice is broken by the spring freshet. Men's minds and hearts are emancipated, at least for this noble hour, from the dominion of mere usage. There is a longing for light, a hospitality toward truth, a willingness to hear, and do, and accept new things, with a courage, faith, and aptitude for large and generous enterprises.

Shall not the Unitarian denomination take advantage of this high-tide in the national life, to float itself over its old obstructions, out of its side-channel, into the ain current of the religious feeling and Christian activity of the nation? Can that denomination much longer claim to have any right to live, much less any large prospects in the future, which, with the learning, wealth, moral purity, and spiritual illumination which we claim, is satisfied with a local and limited existence and influence, without popular acceptance, without missionary zeal, without growth, and without nationality? Surely, we must arouse ourselves, and claim our inheritance, assert our place and occupy it, or we shall fitly be left to dwindle and die of faithlessness and isolation.

Want of zeal, and inaptitude for organization, the natural results of toleration and hatred of bondage, have long hindered us from forming into churches that immense body of people in the country, who, in silent indifference to the prevailing creeds, have forsaken all connection with the popular communions, and are now wholly unchurched and in danger of soon being wholly unchristianized. Without in the least trenching upon the great Christian denominations, is there not an immense floating body of intelligence, detached from all ecclesiastical relations, to which we owe the urgent and speedy presentation of our Christian views, and the shelter of our Christian communion? And is there not certain to be, the moment the thoughts of the country turn from the war, a still larger number of dissatisfied, inquiring, earnest, yet courageous and independent minds, to whom no existing organization of Christians offers the same welcome as ours, and whose wants can by no other be so well supplied? Moreover, are not all the popular sects agitated from within by the very questions which fifty years ago disturbed out hearts, and gave birth to our denomination? Is there not abundant evidence, that if the actual state of theological opinion throughout our whole country now had existed in the early days of our movement, not merely Boston and its neighborhood, but all America, would have gone over at one change, where the Unitarian churches then went? Why should they not do it now? And what a blessing for us as well as for themselves, if the nation were enough *at one* in its faith for Christians to withdraw their energies from controversy, and the tactics of jealousy and mutual counteraction, their eyes from dividing walls and distinctive opinions, and devote their united hearts and souls to the positive truth, the positive faith, and the positive work of the gospel of Jesus Christ! We know not what fruit and flowers our liberal faith would produce were it only nationalized, living in the genial climate of public confidence, and with the common people lending their ardent affections, and bringing their great human instincts into its fold. Cold, fastidious, critical, not in itself, but wholly on account of the special class that chance to hold it, it is misunderstood, and has never taken its proper place in the world. Never, until adopted by the people, never, until commonly recognized as the gospel itself, never, until reunited with the blessed traditionary impulses and associations which have always continued with the popular Sects, will liberal Christianity show the world its real character, or indeed, be known by its own professed disciples!

It is to consider the duties of this critical hour in the Religious Life of the nation, that we ask the Unitarian churches to meet in general convention, at 10 A.M. on the 5th of April next, in All Souls' Church, New York. . . .

It is not fitting to anticipate what the action of such a Convention may be. It can of course do nothing to abridge the independence and freedom of our individual churches, nor to force upon any parties to it, any common action which they do not heartily approve. Whatever it does, must and will be done with a tender regard to our congregational principles, and our individual liberty. But it will doubtless strive to discover and set forth the possible grounds of a hearty agreement among ourselves, which abridges the freedom of none; of a stronger and more formal organization; of larger and more consentaneous activity in our missionary works, whether by means of denominational organs, by tracts, or by living messengers; and of the firm establishment of our interests at Antioch and Meadville, and Cambridge.

Begging your prayerful attention to the views of the address, we have, in concluding, only to implore the blessing of God upon your Church and Society, upon our common cause as one Branch of the Christian Vine, and on the Church Universal!

In the fellowship of the faith, and in the Communion of the Lord Jesus Christ, your Christian brethren and servants,

HENRY W. BELLOWS, EDWARD E. HALE, A. P. PUTNAM, *Committee on Address.*

"Constitution of the National Conference of Unitarian and other Christian Churches"

PREAMBLE.—*Whereas* The great opportunities and demands for Christian labor and consecration at this time increase our sense of the obligations of all disciples of the Lord Jesus Christ to prove their faith by self-denial, and by the devotion of their lives and possessions to the service of God and the building-up of the kingdom of his Son,—

ARTICLE I.—Therefore, the Christian churches of the Unitarian faith here assembled unite themselves in a common body, to be known as the National Conference of Unitarian and other Christian Churches, to the end of energizing and stimulating the denomination with which they are connected to the largest exertions in the cause of the Christian faith and work.

ARTICLE II.—This National Conference shall be composed of such delegates, elected once in two years, not to exceed three from any church, including its minister, who shall officially be one, as any of our churches may accredit to it by a certificate of their appointment.

ARTICLE III.—The American Unitarian Association, the Western Conference, and such other theological, academic, or humane organizations in our body as the Conference may see fit to invite, shall be entitled to representation by not more than three delegates each.

ARTICLE IV.—The Conference shall meet biennially at such time and place as it may designate at its successive biennial sessions.

Article V.—Its officers shall consist of a President; six Vice Presidents; three Secretaries—a Statistical, a Recording, and a Corresponding Secretary; a Treasurer; and a Council of ten, half ministers and half laymen; who shall be elected at each meeting, to hold their offices for two years, and until their successors are appointed.

Article VI.—The Council shall have charge, during the intervals of the biennial sessions, of all business having reference to the interests of the Conference, and intrusted to it by that body, which is hereby declared a purely advisory one.

Article VII.—The National Conference, until further advised by its experience, adopts the existing organizations of the Unitarian body as the instruments of its power, and confines itself to recommending them to such undertakings and methods as it judges to be in the heart of the Unitarian denomination.

Article VIII.—This Constitution may be amended at any regular meeting of the Conference, by a vote of not less than two-thirds of the delegates accredited thereto.

Article IX.—To secure the largest unity of the spirit and the widest practical co-operation, it is hereby declared that all the declarations of this Conference, including the Preamble and Constitution, are expressions only of its majority, committing in no degree those who object to them, and dependent wholly for their effect upon the consent they command on their own merits form the churches here represented, or belonging within the circle of our fellowship.

SOURCE: *Report of the Convention of Unitarian Churches Held in New York* (Boston, 1866), vii–xi, 134–35.

"We Are All Bound Up Together"
1866

Frances Ellen Watkins Harper (1825–1911) was the most prominent African-American woman writer of her generation, author of Iola Leroy *and other novels, stories, and poems. She was also an activist who worked tirelessly on behalf of the Women's Christian Temperance Union, the National Association of Colored Women, and the African Methodist Episcopal (AME) Church, the tradition in which she was raised. In 1870, she joined the First Unitarian Church of Philadelphia, after which she maintained a dual commitment to Unitarianism and to the AME. In this speech given at a women's rights convention in New York City, Harper gave vivid testimony about the interlocking oppressions confronting African-American women and called upon white women to practice a deeper solidarity. Further Reading: Frances Smith Foster, ed.,* A Brighter Coming Day: A Frances Ellen Watkins Harper Reader *(New York: Feminist Press at CUNY, 1993).*

— Dan McKanan

I feel I am something of a novice upon this platform. Born of a race whose inheritance has been outrage and wrong, most of my life had been spent in battling against those wrongs. But I did not feel as keenly as others, that I had these rights, in common with other women, which are now demanded. About two years ago, I stood within the shadows of my home. A great sorrow had fallen upon my life. My husband had died suddenly, leaving me a widow, with four children, one my own, and the others stepchildren. I tried to keep my children together. But my husband died in debt; and before he had been in his grave three months, the administrator had swept the very milk-crocks and wash tubs from my hands. I was a farmer's wife and made butter for the Columbus market; but what could I do, when they had swept all away? They left me one thing-and that was a looking glass! Had I died instead of my husband, how different would have been the result! By this time he would have had another wife, it is likely; and no administrator would have gone into his house, broken up his home, and sold his bed, and taken away his means of support.

I took my children in my arms, and went out to seek my living. While I was gone, a neighbor to whom I had once lent five dollars, went before a magistrate and Swore that he believed I was a non-resident, and laid an attachment on my very bed. And I went back to Ohio with my orphan children in my arms, without a single feather bed in this wide world, that was not in the custody of the law. I say, then, that justice is not fulfilled so long as woman is unequal before the law.

We are all bound up together in one great bundle of humanity, and society cannot trample on the weakest and feeblest of its members without receiving the curse in its own soul. You tried that in the case of the Negro. You pressed him down for two centuries; and in so doing you crippled the moral strength and paralyzed the spiritual energies of the white men of the country. When the hands of the black were fettered, white men were deprived of the liberty of speech and the freedom of the press. Society cannot afford to neglect the enlightenment of any class of its members. . . .

This grand and glorious revolution which has commenced, will fail to reach its climax of success, until throughout the length and breadth of the American Republic, the nation shall be so color-blind, as to know no man by the color of his skin or the curl of his hair. It will then have no privileged class, trampling upon and outraging the unprivileged classes, but will be then one great privileged nation, whose privilege will be to produce the loftiest manhood and womanhood that humanity can attain.

I do not believe that giving the woman the ballot is immediately going to cure all the ills of life. I do not believe that white women are dew-drops just exhaled from the skies. . . .

You white women speak here of rights. I speak of wrongs. I, as a colored woman, have had in this country an education which has made me feel as if I were in the situation of Ishmael, my hand against every man, and every man's hand against me. Let me go to-morrow morning and take my seat in one of your street cars—I do not know that they will do it in New York, but they will in Philadelphia—and the conductor will put up his hand and stop the car rather than let me ride.

Going from Washington to Baltimore this Spring, they put me in the smoking car. Aye, in the capital of the nation, where the black man consecrated himself to the nation's defence, faithful when the white man was faithless, they put me in the smoking car! They did it once; but the next time they tried it, they failed; for I would not go in. I felt the fight in me; but I don't want to have to fight all the time. . . .

In advocating the cause of the colored man, since the Dred Scott decision, I have sometimes said I thought the nation had touched bottom. But let me tell you there is a depth of infamy lower than that. It is when the nation, standing upon the threshold of a great peril, reached out its hands to a feebler race, and asked that race to help it, and when the peril was over, said, You are good enough for soldiers, but not good enough for citizens. . . .

We have a woman in our country who has received the name of "Moses," not by lying about it, but by acting it out—a woman who has gone down into the Egypt of slavery and brought out hundreds of our people into liberty. The last time I saw that woman, her hands were swollen. That woman who had led one of Montgomery's most successful expeditions, who was brave enough and secretive enough to act as a scout for the American army, had her hands all swollen from a conflict with a brutal conductor, who undertook to eject her from her place. That woman, whose courage and bravery won a recognition from our army and from every black man in the land, is excluded from every thoroughfare of travel. Talk of giving women the ballot-box? Go on. It is a normal school, and the white women of this country need it. While there exists this brutal element in society which tramples upon the feeble and treads down the weak, I tell you that if there is any class of people who need to be lifted out of their airy nothings and selfishness, it is the white women of America.

SOURCE: Frances Ellen Watkins Harper, "We Are All Bound Up Together," in *Proceedings of the Eleventh Women's Rights Convention* (New York: Robert J. Johnston, 1866), 45–48.

"Why Do I Not Call Myself a Christian?"

1867

Francis William Newman (1805–1897), brother of Roman Catholic cardinal John Henry Newman, was a professor whose interests included linguistics, mathematics, classics, poetry, and religion. His integrity and deeply held convictions led to his commitment to a variety of social justice issues as well, including education for women, temperance, abolition, public health, and vegetarianism. He influenced others on both sides of the Atlantic and was quoted by both William James and Karl Marx. Newman's faith evolved from a casual membership in the Church of England to a youthful period of evangelical fundamentalism, which led him to spend three years as a missionary to Turkey, Syria, and Iraq. His experience explaining Christianity to unbelievers had the opposite effect. He returned to England, where he faced social stigma and estrangement from his family for his nonconformist beliefs. His theism was mystical, yet rational. His disbelief in the afterlife and the moral perfection of Jesus prevented him from calling himself a Unitarian, until 1876. Two years later, he was Vice President of the British and Foreign Unitarian Society. Further Reading: David Hempton, Evangelical Disenchantment: Nine Portraits of Faith and Doubt *(New Haven: Yale University Press, 2009); William Robbins,* The Newman Brothers: An Essay in Comparative Intellectual Biography *(Cambridge, MA: Harvard University Press, 1966).*

—Meg Schellenberg Richardson

First, because it is an extremely ambiguous profession, and professions ought to be intelligible. We want to be understood—not misunderstood. Ninety-nine persons out of a hundred, understand that to profess oneself a Christian means at least to profess that one is a submissive and reverential disciple of Christ: but I am not and cannot be this.

Second, because the admission that Christianity is our religion, draws after it the very vexatious, very difficult, and obscure inquiry: What is Christianity? in which valuable time and talents are wasted. If, for instance, the Indian Theists called themselves Christians, they would inflect upon their successors the curse of Christian controversies, from Romanism to the extremist Unitarian school.

Third, Christianity originally aimed to unite mankind, but is now the potent divider. We, from within, are proud of Christianity, and little realize how hateful it is, seen from without. What more wicked than the conduct of Christians for centuries together to Jews, to Indians, and to all the dark-skinned races? Why am I gratuitously to take on myself all this frightful odium?

Fourth, Jews, Mohammedans, Indians will all join without repugnance in a profession of theism; but they shudder at Christianity. To insist on this name is to claim that they shall forget the past and sacrifice their memories and their just hatred to our pride. By disowning the name Christian, I purge myself of Christian guilt; I profess to these that I have sympathy with their equal claims, and will meet them on a strictly common and neutral platform.

SOURCE: Francis Henry Newman, "Why Do Not I Call Myself a Christian?" *The Radical*, April 1867, 501–02.

"What Is the Aim of the Woman Movement?"
1870

The Woman's Journal was founded in 1870 as the organ of the American Woman Suffrage Association, the wing of the suffrage movement that was willing to support the Fifteenth Amendment, which enfranchised African-American men while leaving women of all races without the vote. Organized by Lucy Stone (1818–1893) in opposition to Elizabeth Cady Stanton and Susan B. Anthony's National Woman Suffrage Association, the AWSA counted such prominent Unitarians as Julia Ward Howe and Thomas Wentworth Higginson among its officers. Universalist Mary Livermore (1820–1905) served as editor of the journal. This unsigned article encapsulates the vision they shared. Further Reading: Sally G. McMillen, Lucy Stone: An Unapologetic Life *(New York: Oxford University Press, 2014).*

—Dan McKanan

We answer, *freedom for woman*. Not a struggle for supremacy, not a vulgar tournament for office-holding, not merely an effort to obtain the ballot *as an end*. But it is a movement to give to woman possession of herself, with the unrestricted use of all her faculties, and the power of deciding for herself what she can do and cannot do in the world—what is and what is not her sphere.

In the past, man has designated woman's sphere for her. . . . What she now demands is perfect freedom to develop *as a woman*, without any legislative or social tyranny on his part to restrain her, to choose her path in life according to her taste and capacity. To this end, she asks the abrogation of all legislation against her, with a chance to legislate for herself, the opening of every field of effort, the unlocking of every means of culture.

It has never yet appeared what the capabilities of woman are, nor what is the peculiar work of the world to which she is fitted. For man has chosen to force all womanhood into one avenue of human existence, and then has proclaimed that she is fit for no other. . . .

But she has felt the general quickening of the age, and has grown with the growth of the civilized world. She has risen to the height of asking complete possession of herself, with freedom to work out her own future, and to decide for herself her place in the world of work. Freedom, education, opportunity, justice—the same as men have—these are her demands to-day. She asks the ballot, as that is the method, in this country, of expressing and getting hold of public opinion. Are these demands unreasonable? Not at all. They are woman's heritage, her birthright, and man in withholding them has greatly wronged her. And in the incompleteness of his own development, in the social disorders and distresses of the age, in the very frivolity, incompetence and weakness of woman, of which man makes loud complaint, in the ill success which has necessarily attended his experiment of running the world with half the wisdom and power God gave for its management—in these penal results the wrong of man's mistake stands confessed.

Is there anything in the woman movement which ought to awaken the hostility of good, wise and just men? Should it not rather command their cooperation?

SOURCE: "What Is the Aim of the Woman Movement?" *The Woman's Journal*, April 9, 1870, 108.

"Mother's Day Proclamation"

1870

Julia Ward Howe (1819–1910) is best known as the author of the "Battle Hymn of the Republic," but she struck a decidedly less martial tone in the proclamation she prepared for the first Mother's Day. Her anti-war message responded to the carnage of the Franco-Prussian War, as well as to the recent memory of the Civil War. Raised an Episcopalian, Howe came to Unitarianism through her friendships with Theodore Parker and James Freeman Clarke. She was a leader in Clarke's Church of the Disciples, as well as in the American Woman's Suffrage Association, the New England Women's Club, and the Association for the Advancement of Women. In 1875, she began hosting conventions of women ministers in conjunction with the annual meeting of the Unitarian denomination, even though she never sought ordination for herself. Further Reading: Valarie Ziegler, Diva Julia: The Public Romance and Private Agony of Julia Ward Howe *(Harrisburg, PA: Trinity Press International, 2003).*

—Dan McKanan

Arise, then, Christian women of this day! Arise, all women who have hearts, whether your baptism be that of water or of tears! Say firmly: We will not have great questions decided by irrelevant agencies. Our husbands shall not come to us, reeking with carnage, for caresses and applause. Our sons shall not be taken from us to unlearn all that we have been able to teach them of charity, mercy and patience. We, women of one country, will be too tender of those of another country, to allow our sons to be trained to injure theirs. From the bosom of the devastated earth a voice goes up with our own. It says: Disarm, disarm! The sword of murder is not the balance of justice. Blood does not wipe out dishonor, nor violence vindicate possession. As men have often forsaken the plough and the anvil at the summons of war, let women now leave all that may be left of home for a great and earnest day of council.

Let them meet first, as women, to bewail and commemorate the dead. Let them then solemnly take council with each other as to the means whereby the great human family can live in peace, man as the brother of man, each bearing after their own time the sacred impress, not of Caesar, but of God.

In the name of womanhood and of humanity, I earnestly ask that a general congress of women, without limit of nationality, may be appointed and held at some place deemed most convenient and at the earliest period consistent with its objects, to promote the alliance of the different nationalities, the amicable settlement of international questions, the great and general interests of peace.

SOURCE: Julia Ward Howe, *Appeal to Womanhood Throughout the World*, broadside, Boston, 1870.

"Fifty Affirmations of Free Religion"
1870

Francis Ellingwood Abbot (1836–1903) was a pioneer in the development of free religious ideas in the latter half of the nineteenth century. After graduating first in his 1859 Harvard class, he studied for the Unitarian ministry. Ordained by the Unitarian congregation in Dover, New Hampshire, he quickly discovered that he had neither the temperament nor the taste for the parish ministry. A brilliant thinker, he espoused Darwinism but believed that religion and God could be demonstrated scientifically. Frustrated by the insistence of the majority that the preamble of the new National Conference of Unitarian Churches should commit the group to an explicitly Christian identity, he joined with his best friend, Rev. William James Potter of New Bedford, and others to organize the Free Religious Association (FRA). With the support of his FRA colleagues, he founded The Index, *a journal of news and ideas. A brilliant and energetic editor, he solicited excellent contributions from distinguished European as well as American authors. The loudest voice, though, was always his own. His "Fifty Affirmations" appeared on the front page of the first issue and was reprinted often in the following years. Further Reading: Creighton Peden,* The Philosopher of Free Religion: Francis Ellingwood Abbot, 1836–1903 *(New York: Peter Lang, 1992).*

—Richard Kellaway

Religion

1. Religion is the effort of man to perfect himself.
2. The root of religion is universal human nature. . . .
5. Every historical religion has thus two distinct elements,—one universal or spiritual, the other special or historical.

✻ ✻ ✻

Free Religion

32. The Protestant Reformation was the birth of Free Religion,—the beginning of the religious protest against authority within the confines of the Christian Church.
33. The history of Protestantism is the history of the growth of Free Religion at the expense of the Christian Religion. As love of freedom increases, reverence for authority decreases.

34. The completion of the religious protest against authority must be the extinction of faith in the Christian Confession.

35. Free Religion is emancipation from the outward law, and voluntary obedience to the inward law.

36. The great faith or moving power of Free Religion is faith in Man as a progressive being.

37. The great ideal end of Free Religion is the perfection or complete development of Man,—the race serving the individual, the individual serving the race.

38. The great practical means of Free Religion is the integral, continuous and universal education of man.

39. The great law of Free Religion is the still, small voice of the private soul.

40. The great peace of Free Religion is spiritual oneness with the infinite One.

41. Free Religion is the natural outcome of every historical religion—the final unity, therefore, towards which all historical religions slowly tend.

Relation of Christianity to Free Religion

42. Christianity is identical with Free Religion so far as its universal element is concerned,—antagonistic to it so far as its special element is concerned.

43. The corner-stone of Christianity is faith in the Christ. The corner-stone of Free Religion is faith in Human Nature.

44. The great institution of Christianity is the Christian Church, the will of the Christ being its supreme law. The great institution of Free Religion is the coming Republic of the World, or Commonwealth of Man, the universal conscience and reason of mankind being its supreme organic law or constitution.

45. The fellowship of Christianity is limited by the Christian Confession; its brotherhood includes all subjects of the Christ and excludes all others. The fellowship of Free Religion is universal and free; it proclaims the great Brotherhood of Man without limit or bound.

46. The practical work of Christianity is to Christianize the world,—to convert all souls to the Christ, and ensure their salvation from the wrath of God. The practical work of Free Religion is to humanize the world—to make the individual nobler here and now, and to convert the human race into a vast Co-operative Union devoted to universal ends.

47. The spiritual ideal of Christianity is the suppression of self and perfect imitation of Jesus the Christ. The spiritual ideal of Free Religion is the free development of self, and the harmonious education of all its powers to the highest possible degree.

48. The essential spirit of Christianity is that of self-humiliation at the feet of Jesus, and passionate devotion to his person. The essential spirit of Free Religion is

that of self-respect and free self-devotion to great ideas. Christianity is prostrate on its face; Free Religion is erect on its feet.

49. The noblest fruit of Christianity is a self-sacrificing love of man for Jesus' sake. The noblest fruit of Free Religion is a self-sacrificing love of man for man's own sake.

50. Christianity is the faith of the soul's childhood; Free Religion is the faith of the soul's manhood. In the gradual growth of mankind out of Christianity into Free Religion, lies the only hope of the spiritual perfection of the individual and the spiritual unity of the race.

SOURCE: Francis Ellingwood Abbot, "Fifty Affirmations of Free Religion," supplement to *The Index*, January 22, 1870.

The Sympathy of Religions

1870

Thomas Wentworth Higginson (1823–1911) is best remembered in America today as a Unitarian minister, author, and lecturer, and as an abolitionist who supported John Brown as one of the "Secret Six" by securing funding for his raid on Harper's Ferry. During the Civil War, Higginson served as an officer and was colonel of the first official regiment of African-American freedmen. He is also widely remembered today as a friend to Emily Dickinson, whose poetry was unknown in her own time. This selection, from an address that Higginson delivered in 1870 at Horticultural Hall in Boston and later published in The Radical, *reveals another central theme in Higginson's career. In "The Sympathy of Religions," he expresses his belief that all religions share a common core, a unity of sentiment and aspiration. Although this idea of cosmopolitanism in religion was considered radical at the time, it has since become a commonplace in contemporary Unitarian Universalism and offers an interesting point of historical comparison. Further Reading: Leigh Eric Schmidt,* Restless Souls: The Making of American Spirituality *(San Francisco: HarperOne, 2005).*

—Emily Mace

Our true religious life begins when we discover that there is an Inner Light, not infallible but invaluable, which "lighteth every man that cometh into the world." Then we have something to steer by; and it is chiefly this, and not an anchor, that we need. The human soul, like any other noble vessel, was not built to be anchored, but to sail. An anchorage may, indeed, be at times a temporary need, in order to make some special repairs, or to take fresh cargo in; yet the natural destiny of both ship and soul is not the harbor, but the ocean; to cut with even keel the vast and beautiful expanse; to pass from island on to island of more than Indian balm, or to continents fairer than Columbus won; or, best of all, steering close to the wind, to extract motive power from the greatest obstacles. Men must forget the eternity through which they have yet to sail, when they talk of anchoring here upon this bank and shoal of time. It would be a tragedy to see the shipping of the world whitening the seas no more, and idly riding at anchor in Atlantic ports; but it would be more tragic to see a world of souls fascinated into a fatal repose and renouncing their destiny of motion.

And as with individuals, so with communities. The great historic religions of the world are not so many stranded hulks left to perish. The best of them are all in motion. All over the world the divine influence moves men. There is a sympathy in religions, and this sympathy is shown alike in their origin, their records, and their progress. Men are ceasing to disbelieve, and learning to believe more. I have worshiped in a Roman Catholic church when the lifting of one finger broke the motionless multitude into twinkling motion, till the magic sign was made, and all was still once more. But I never for an instant have supposed that this concentrated moment of devotion was more holy or more beautiful than when one cry from a minaret hushes a Mohammedan city to prayer, or when, at sunset, the low invocation, "Oh! the gem in the lotus—oh! the gem in the lotus," goes murmuring, like the cooing of many doves, across the vast surface of Thibet. True, "the gem in the lotus" means nothing to us, but it means as much to the angels as "the Lamb of God," for it is a symbol of aspiration.

Every year bring new knowledge of the religions of the world, and every step in knowledge brings out the sympathy between them. They all show the same aim, the same symbols, the same forms, the same weaknesses, the same aspirations. Looking at these points of unity, we might say there is but one religion under many forms, whose essential creed is the Fatherhood of God, and the Brotherhood of Man,— disguised by corruptions, symbolized by mythologies, ennobled by virtues, degraded by vices, but still the same. Or if, passing to a closer analysis, we observe the shades of difference, we shall find in these varying faiths the several instruments which perform what Cudworth calls "the Symphony of Religions." And though some may stir like drums, and others soothe like flutes, and others like violins command the whole range of softness and of strength, yet they are all alike instruments, and nothing in any one of them is so wondrous as the great laws of sound which equally control them all.

✳   ✳   ✳

To say that different races worship different Gods, is like saying that they are warmed by different suns. The names differ, but the sun is the same, and so is God. As there is but one source of light and warmth, so there is but one source of religion. To this all nations testify alike. We have yet but a part of our Holy Bible. The time will come when, as in the middle ages, all pious books will be called sacred scriptures, *Scripturae Sacrae*. From the most remote portions of the earth, from the Vedas and the Sagas, from Plato and Zoroaster, Confucius and Mohammed, from the Emperor Marcus Antoninus and the slave Epictetus, from the learned Alexandrians and the ignorant Galla negroes, there will be gathered hymns and prayers and maxims in which every religious soul may unite,—the magnificent liturgy of the human race.

✳   ✳   ✳

And, as all these inevitably recur, so comes back again and again the idea of incarnation,—the Divine Man. Here, too, all religions sympathize, and, with slight modifications, each is the copy of the other. As in the dim robing-rooms of foreign churches are kept rich stores of sacred vestments, ready to be thrown over every successive generation of priests, so the world has kept in memory the same stately traditions to decorate each new Messiah. He is predicted by prophecy, hailed by sages, born of a virgin, attended by miracle, born to heaven without tasting death, and with promise of return. Zoroaster and Confucius have no human father. Osiris is the Son of God, he is called the Revealer of Life and Light; he first teaches one chosen race; he then goes with his apostles to teach the Gentiles, conquering the world by peace; he is slain by evil powers; after death he descends into hell, then rises again, and presides at the last judgment of all mankind: those who call upon his name shall be saved. Buddha is born of a virgin; his name means the Word, the Logos, but he is known more tenderly as the Savior of Man; he embarrasses his teachers, when a child, by his understanding and his answers; he is tempted in the wilderness, when older; he goes with his apostles to redeem the world; he abolishes caste and cruelty, and teaches forgiveness; he receives among his followers outcasts whom Pharisaic pride despises, and he only says, "My law is a law of mercy to all." Slain by enemies, he descends into hell, rising without tasting death, and still lives to make intercession for man.

✳   ✳   ✳

The one unpardonable sin is exclusiveness. Any form of religion is endangered when we bring it to the test of facts; for none on earth can bear that test. There never existed a person, nor a book, nor an institution, which did not share the merits and the drawbacks of its rivals. Granting all that can be established as to the debt of the world to the very best dispensation, the fact still remains, that there is not a single maxim, nor idea, nor application, nor triumph, that any single religion can claim as exclusively its own.

SOURCE: Thomas Wentworth Higginson, *The Sympathy of Religions: An Address Delivered at Horticultural Hall, Boston, February 6, 1870* (Boston, 1871).

"Hymn"

1870

In 1870, Phebe Ann (Coffin) Hanaford (1829–1921) became the first woman in New England ordained to Universalist ministry. A prolific writer, editor, lecturer and suffragist, Hanaford met Hannah Tobey (Shapleigh) Farmer, usually noted in historical texts as (Mrs.) M. G. Farmer or Mabelle, in 1861. They became friends, both believing in the abolition of slavery and sharing a love of song, poetry, and hymns. (Farmer and her husband harbored runaway slaves in 1845–1846.) Farmer believed in Hanaford's calling, writing, "My dear Mrs. Hanaford, . . . my heart is with you in the work to which you are devoting soul and body." She wrote this hymn for Hanaford's ordination. Further Reading: Augustin Caldwell, The Rich Legacy: Memories of Hannah Tobey Farmer, Wife of Moses Gerrish Farmer (Boston, 1892).

—Patrice K. Curtis

Lay naught but holy hands on her,
Ye servants of our Lord;
Who at His bidding doth declare
The ever-living word.
She brings to this sweet work, we trust,
A consecrated heart,
Where love of fame,—nor worldly pride,
Shall never have a part.

Then welcome her within your fold,
Her joys and trial share;
Help her to train the tender vines
Lest they no fruit shall bear.
"Last at the cross,—first at the grave,"
Was faithful woman found;
Then let her voice proclaim to all
The Gospel's joyful sound!

No earthly cares should come between
To rob God of His due;—
Between our souls and Him will rest

The work we each must do.
Then for Thy Servant, Lord, we crave
Thy blessing and Thy love;
While prayers for her from many a heart
Will find their way above.

SOURCE: *Services at the Ordination and Installation of Rev. Phebe A. Hanaford* (Boston, 1870), 5.

"Hand of Fellowship"

1870

Olympia Brown (1835–1926) was born in 1835 to Universalist parents. Her parents believed in equal education for their daughters and son, which led her to finish college, where she heard her calling to ministry. Throughout her education, including her seminary, she encountered restrictive rules and lower expectations for women. At her ordination in 1863, she was one of the first ordained women in the United States. Universalism and women's rights were her life's work. As a suffragist, Olympia believed that men and women held equal moral responsibilities to the needs of the world. Her ministry was rooted in Universalism, the belief that Jesus Christ recognized the full worth and dignity of women and embodied the characteristics of both women and men. In Phebe Hanaford, Rev. Brown recognized a kindred soul who equalled her own passion for women's rights. In 1866, Olympia asked Phebe to preach for her. That first time became many, and thereby Olympia mentored Phebe in her ministry. At Phebe's ordination two years later, Olympia extended the hand of fellowship in remarks, reflecting her belief that she and Phebe "paved the way for more women to serve as parish ministers." Further Reading: Charlotte Cote, Olympia Brown: The Battle for Equality (Racine, WI: Mother Courage Press, 1988).

—Patrice K. Curtis

My Dear Sister:—It becomes my privilege, as the representative of the order to which we belong, to extend to you the fellowship of the churches, and of the ministers representing our denomination.

You have entered upon a work most important in its results—a work most glorious when contemplated in regard to its final results upon the human race—a work of labor, and often one of trial. You will be called to scenes of sorrow and mourning; it will be yours to weep with those who weep, as well as to rejoice with those who rejoice, to sympathize with suffering in its various forms. And it will be your privilege to do this, and all the duties which fall to you, in reliance upon Him in whom is all your trust. It will be yours to instruct the young. It will be yours, sometimes, to offer words of rebuke; to administer words of warning; for the Gospel comes as a warning against all sin. It knows no respect of persons; when you preach it, you are to preach it fearlessly. Some one has said, "Hew to the line, let the chips fall where they may;"

and this seems to me a fitting precept to be applied to this work. Have no fear, then, in presenting these truths which Jesus taught, but apply them wherever there may be occasion and necessity. Jesus knew no distinction of persons. He used but one code of morals; sin was sin, wherever found, and it is for you to call all to the same standard of excellence which Jesus Christ himself presented. Sin is not to be overlooked because excused by society in a certain class; but men and women, whoever and wherever they be, alike need to be called to purity and holiness of life. Spare no position or sex, but reprove, rebuke, exhort with all long-suffering and doctrine.

As a woman, you stand in some sense as a representative; as one the earliest to assume the high office of the preacher, it is yours to maintain the position in which you now stand. Remember the words which you heard from the Scripture, "Let no man despise you." In your office, show yourself worthy of your high calling. Perfect yourself in the performance of those duties assigned to you. Be faithful, devoted and earnest. Assume every duty, every prerogative which pertains to the minister, and let it be your purpose to discharge them well. Let no one have occasion to say that you have come short in one particular, even the smallest of the duties which pertain to the Christian ministry.

It will be yours, as a woman, to sympathize with and aid suffering woman, who needs the sympathies of her sex.

It will be yours to strengthen those who suffer from the evil influences of the use of intoxicating drinks. Give them the hand of helping, and lift them up out of their sad estate.

Young women will look to you for instruction and guidance—for that sympathy which they have not found in the ministry in the years that are past. Be it yours to call them to a higher life. Jesus died for women—for all—to make known to us the Gospel; to make *us* free in that liberty which the Gospel alone can give. It will be yours to call these young women to the earnest defence of the Word, to awaken in them a true life, to teach them to live for God and humanity. And my prayer is, that you will have opportunity to lead some of the young women of your parish to consecrate themselves to the work of the ministry. I would that you might lead them up, to be sharers with us in this work.

In your work you are not unaided or alone. You are upheld by the most glorious faith that was ever revealed to the children of men; it will be to you inspiration and help. It will enable you to speak with authority because you speak of the same glad tidings that were published by Jesus Christ eighteen hundred years ago. You have always the consciousness of the presence of Jesus, and you may feel, too, that the great cloud of unseen witnesses, spirits of the departed, of the fathers of our faith and of lovers of truth in all ages are hovering near, speaking to your soul.

And more visible, but not more real, stand the great company of living witnesses, the whole household of your faith, dear brothers and sisters, who are praying for our success, earnest preachers of the Gospel who have preceded you in the Lord's work; grave D.D.s who will hail with joy the coming of another devoted laborer; professors in our theological schools who should see in each cultured preacher of the word an added power for education and for truth. Young students of divinity who will look up to you as an example and a leader; all these will be with you in this glorious cause and in the name of all these, as their representative, I to-day offer you the right hand of fellowship of the Universalist denomination. You shall have our co-operation, our sympathy, our best wishes and our prayers.

You are welcome to the work—welcome to the labors, welcome to the triumphs, welcome to the sacrifices (for there are sometimes, yes, oftentimes, sacrifices to be made by the Christian minister), welcome to the rewards and the joys that come from the consciousness of doing good. And may it be that your ministry with us, will be long and richly blest. May God prosper you; may you see the fruits of your work, blossoming here about you like the sweet spring flowers, carrying joy to your heart, and to the heart of every beholder.

Amen.

SOURCE: *Services at the Ordination and Installation of Rev. Phebe A. Hanaford* (Boston, 1870), 29–31.

PHEBE HANAFORD

"The Question Answered"

1871

This poem by Phebe Hanaford centers on an imagined conversation between Antoinette Brown (Blackwell) and Lucy Stone, illustrating the two paths that Hanaford faced herself: Brown became the first female ordained minister in America, while Stone was active in women's suffrage. Politically aware as early as age thirteen, Hanaford also felt called to ministry at a time when women were not accepted as religious leaders. The poem celebrates and claims God as calling women to lead in political and religious realms, a challenge to the practice of using Scripture to control women's public involvement. Further Reading: Loretta Cody, with Sarah Barber-Braun, A Mighty Social Force: Phebe Ann Coffin Hanaford 1829–1921 *(booksurge.com, 2009).*

—Patrice K. Curtis

The evening hour with soothing quiet came;
The silver moon rose slowly up the sky;
Crowned with young womanhood, two friends walked forth,
Communing gladly of Life's purpose high.

The queenly step of one, the taller, ceased:
She turned, and looked full in her friend's clear eye.
"Can woman reach the pulpit?" then she asked.
And waited, with a full heart, the reply.

The answer came; but not a hope was born,
As fell those words upon the querist's heart:
"Woman may labor in full many a field,
But may not hope to act the preacher's part."

She asked of God—that woman brave and pure:
God gave the answer in the wish inspired.
The seed contained the germ; and in God's time
There came the fruitage which the words desired.

Years passed: and she who answered stood full oft
Beneath the shelter of our State-House domes;
And legislators heard her soul-full tones,
Pleading for equal rights in states and homes.

The querist stood in many a pulpit too,
Proclaiming Christ with hope to bless and save;
Her young heart glad with more than human joy,
As there she told of bliss beyond the grave.

Both have wrought nobly where few women toil,
Been pioneers in that cause, pure and high,
Which gives her place to woman by man's side,
With him to lead immortals to the sky.

Their lives have shown that naught can stay the tide
Of God's great purpose in its onward flow;
That where man nobly labors for the race,
There, too, many woman, at God's summons, go.

A quarter-century now hath passed away,
And many a woman in the pulpit stands,
Ordained to do the pastor's noble work
By more than laying on of human hands.

O God! we'll trust thee for the days to come,
Thou who hast guided woman in the Past;
And with a grateful heart thine handmaids sing,
"The day of righteous freedom dawns at last."

SOURCE: Phebe Hanaford, "The Question Answered," *From Shore to Shore and Other Poems* (Boston, 1871), 275–77.

"Transcendental Wild Oats"

1873

Louisa May Alcott (1832–1888) was the preeminent children's author of the nineteenth century. Little Women and its sequels conveyed liberal ideals of parenting and education to the broader American public. The success of the books also restored the finances of Alcott's father, Bronson, one of the most visionary and idiosyncratic members of the Transcendentalist circle. During Louisa's childhood, Bronson and his associate Charles Lane established Fruitlands as an intentional community devoted to principles of absolute nonviolence—even to the point of foregoing wool, silk, and the use of draft animals. Louisa's jaundiced account of the short-lived community reflected both her resentment of Lane (whom she cast as a Lion oppressing her father the Lamb) and her solidarity with her long-suffering mother. Further Reading: John Matteson, Eden's Outcasts: The Story of Louisa May Alcott and Her Father *(New York: W. W. Norton, 2007).*

—Dan McKanan

This prospective Eden at present consisted of an old red farm-house, a dilapidated barn, many acres of meadow-land, and a grove. Ten ancient apple trees were all the "chaste supply" which the place offered as yet; but, in the firm belief that plenteous orchards were soon to be evoked from their inner consciousness, these sanguine founders had christened their domain Fruitlands.

Here Timon Lion intended to found a colony of Latter Day Saints, who, under his patriarchal sway, should regenerate the world and glorify his name for ever. Here Abel Lamb, with the devoutest faith in the high ideal which was to him a living truth, desired to plant a Paradise, where Beauty, Virtue, Justice, and Love might live happily together, without the possibility of a serpent entering in. And here his wife, unconverted but faithful to the end, hoped, after many wanderings over the face of the earth, to find rest for herself and a home for her children.

* * *

"What shall we do for lamps, if we cannot use any animal substance? I do hope light of some sort is to be thrown upon the enterprise," said Mrs. Lamb, with anxiety, for in those days kerosene and camphene were not and gas unknown in the wilderness.

"We shall go without till we have discovered some vegetable oil or wax to serve us," replied Brother Timon, in a decided tone, which caused Sister Hope to resolve that her private lamp should always be trimmed, if not burning.

"Each member is to perform the work of which experience, strength, and taste best fit him," continued Dictator Lion. "Thus drudgery and disorder will be avoided and harmony prevail. We shall arise at dawn, begin the day by bathing, followed by music, and then a chaste repast of fruit and bread. Each one finds congenial occupation till the meridian meal; when some deep-searching conversation gives rest to the body and development to the mind. Healthful labor again engages us till the last meal, when we assemble in social communion, prolonged till sunset, when we retire to sweet repose, ready for the next day's activity."

"What part of the work do you incline to yourself?" asked Sister Hope, with a humorous glimmer in her keen eyes.

"I shall wait till it is made clear to me. Being in preference to doing is the great aim, and this comes to us rather by a resigned willingness than a willful activity, which is a check to all divine growth," responded Brother Timon.

"I thought so." And Mrs. Lamb sighed audibly, for during the year he had spent in her family Brother Timon had so faithfully carried out his idea of "being, not doing," that she had found his "divine growth" both an expensive and unsatisfactory process.

Here her husband struck into the conversation, his face shining with the light and joy of the splendid dreams and high ideals hovering before him.

"In these steps of reform, we do not rely so much on scientific reasoning or physiological skill as on the spirit's dictates. The greater part of man's duty consists in leaving alone much that he now does. Shall I stimulate with tea, coffee, or wine? No. Shall I consume flesh? Not if I value health. Shall I subjugate cattle? Shall I claim property in any created thing? Shall I trade? Shall I adopt a form of religion? Shall I interest myself in politics? To how many of these questions—could we ask them deeply enough and could they be heard as having relation to our eternal welfare—would the response be 'abstain'?"

A mild snore seemed to echo the last word of Abel's rhapsody, for brother Moses had succumbed to mundane slumber and sat nodding like a massive ghost.

*   *   *

With the first frosts, the butterflies, who had sunned themselves in the new light through the summer, took flight, leaving the few bees to see what honey they had stored for winter use. Precious little appeared, beyond the satisfaction of a few months of holy living.

At first it seemed as if a chance to try holy dying also was to be offered them. Timon, much disgusted with the failure of the scheme, decided to retire to the Shakers, who seemed to be the only successful community going.

"What is to become of us?" asked Mrs. Hope, for Abel was heartbroken at the bursting of his lovely bubble.

"You can stay here, if you like, till a tenant is found. No more wood must be cut, however, and no more meal ground. All I have must be sold to pay the debts of the concern, as the responsibility is mine," was the cheering reply.

"Who is to pay us for what we have lost? I gave all I had—furniture, time, strength, six months of my children's lives—and all are wasted. Abel gave himself body and soul, and is almost wrecked by hard work and disappointment. Are we to have no return for this, but leave to starve and freeze in an old house, with winter at hand, no money, and hardly a friend left, for this wild scheme has alienated nearly all we had. You talk much about justice. Let us have a little, since there is nothing else left."

But the woman's appeal met with no reply by the old one: "It was an experiment. We all risked something, and must bear our losses as we can."

With this old comfort Timon departed with his son, and was absorbed into the Shaker brotherhood, where he soon found that the order of things was reversed, and it was all work and no play.

Then the tragedy began for the forsaken little family. Desolation and despair fell upon Abel. As his wife said, his new beliefs had alienated many friends. Some thought him mad, some unprincipled. Even the most kindly thought him a visionary, whom it was useless to help till he took more practical views of life. All stood aloof, saying: "Let him work out his own ideas, and see what they are worth."

He had tried, but it was a failure. The world was not ready for Utopia yet.

SOURCE: Louisa May Alcott, "Transcendental Wild Oats," *The Independent*, December 18, 1873, 1569–71.

WILLIAM JAMES POTTER

"What Is Christianity, and What Is It to Be a Christian?"

1873

William James Potter (1829–1893) accelerated the transformation of Ameri-
can Unitarianism from an insistently Christian denomination into an open
and inclusive movement. As a founder and the mainstay of the Free Religious
Association, he insisted that Unitarianism should not be confined to any par-
ticular theological position but should welcome all who shared its values. The
Association was founded in 1867 as a "spiritual anti-slavery society," welcom-
ing all who wanted to join in the search for religious truth. While the majority
of members were Unitarians, it also included Universalists, Jews, and free-
thinkers. Potter served as the Association's secretary and president, and later
as editor of its journal, The Index. *While he spent his entire ministerial career*
serving the First Congregational Society (Unitarian) in New Bedford, Mas-
sachusetts, he was a nationally known public figure. The so-called Year-
book Controversy erupted when Potter's name was omitted from the American
Unitarian Association's Yearbook listing congregations and their ministers
because he refused to affirm that he was a Christian. Potter addressed the
issue from his pulpit on December 28, 1873. Further Reading: W. Creighton
Peden, Civil War Pulpit to World's Parliament of Religion: The Thought
of William James Potter, 1829–1893 *(New York: Peter Lang, 1996); Richard*
Kellaway, William James Potter from Convinced Quaker to Prophet of Free
Religion: An Epic Spiritual Journey *(Bloomington, IN: Xlibris, 2014–2015).*

—Richard Kellaway

I could not believe that to be a Christian, it was necessary to have faith in the atoning
blood of Jesus, or to adopt any of the other peculiar Orthodox doctrines concerning
him or to pass through any process of so-called "conversion." I did not see, as I do not
today, that Jesus taught any of the theological systems that have been popularly
accepted in the Christian church. . . . It seemed to me that to be a Christian or a follower of Christ was to strive after those gracious spiritual virtues that he possessed, — to
have his disinterested earnestness and devotion, his gentleness, his purity, his power
to rebuke iniquity, his love and self-sacrifice; it was to live like him, to bear witness to
the truth and to go about doing good to one's fellow-men. And doubtless there are
many calling themselves "Christian" today to whom this definition suffices. But when

I came to see that many Jews and Buddhists and Mohammadans and those of other faiths were saying that to be a true Jew, a true Buddhist, a true Mohammadan and so forth, was to have those same qualities in their lives, I saw that there must be some defect in the logic that defined the word "Christian" as synonymous simply with these general qualities exclusively by the name of the religion in which I chanced to be bred.

Therefore latterly I have dropped the use of the word "Christian" as defining my religious position. Since I plant myself on the principles of natural religion and believe that they will suffice to account for all the phenomena of religious history, and since I believe that Christianity, though, considered in all its breadth and elasticity, the greatest and noblest of all the religions, yet came in the natural order of historical development, and in the same way that other religions have arisen, and since I believe that all the religions, though none is infallible, have given expression to valuable spiritual and moral truths, and all have their providential place in the education of mankind, and since I believe that Jesus, though take him all in all, he seems to me greatest of religious teachers and prophets and has left an influence for righteousness that can never die out of world, yet stands a natural man in the natural line of human-ity, one of a company of rare spiritual geniuses, that have appeared in various races and nations, inspired of that universal wisdom which "in all ages entering into holy souls, maketh of them friends of God and prophets"—since I believe these things, I cannot consistently assume a name which appears to me to accord to Jesus an excep-tional and unique position in the world's history as a specially commissioned revealer of religious truth and to set apart the religion which dates itself from his birth and leaving a different authority from that of the other religions of the world. . . . .

The tendency of which I have spoken, is to define the religions by their univer-sal rather than by their special elements, is evidence that the several faiths are advancing towards this era of reconciliation. When such liberal minds. . . . shall come to see that under their different names they are including really the same ideas and aiming at the same practical good, they will not long suffer the names which a reminder of differences no longer existing to keep them apart. The names will drop off, as naturally as leaves are shed in autumn. . . . But meantime, let those who are not yet ready to drop the name, those who for whom the word "Christian" is so spirit-ually vital or has such tender associations that they cannot part with it—let those put into the word all the good, broad, sweet, unsectarian meanings that are possible. . . . And ere long the brave and good meanings will burst the vessels that have been holding them and the sweet incense will be wafted from church to church and from man to man, and by the freed common fragrance they will discover that the faiths so differently named are no longer strangers and enemies, but friends and brothers.

SOURCE: William James Potter, "What Is Christianity, and What Is It to Be a Christian?" *The Index*, January 22, 1874, 38–40.

The Sexes Throughout Nature
1875

*Antoinette Brown Blackwell (1825–1921) had one of the most varied careers of
any woman in nineteenth-century America. After her pathbreaking 1853 ordination and brief ministry in South Butler, New York, she researched poverty
in New York City, lectured on women's rights, parented seven children, and
eventually served as founding minister of the Unitarian Society in Elizabeth,
New Jersey. But her most continuous employment was as a science writer. In
a series of books published over half a century, she challenged Herbert
Spencer's social Darwinism and attempted to use physics to prove the immortality of the soul. In* The Sexes Throughout Nature, *she sought to build a
scientific foundation for women's rights by showing that the female's role in
reproduction does not weaken her physically or intellectually (as Spencer had
suggested) but simply allows her to develop in a complementary manner. This
argument presupposed cooperation, not competition, as the driving force of
evolution. Blackwell's cooperative theory also led her to retain the traditional
argument from design, even as she accepted evolution, and to defend traditional monogamy against proponents of free love. Further Reading: Elizabeth Cazden,* Antoinette Brown Blackwell: A Biography *(Old Westbury, NY:
Feminist Press, 1983).*

—Dan McKanan

It is the central theory of the present volume that the sexes in each species of beings
compared upon the same plane, from the lowest to the highest, are always true
equivalents—equals but not identicals in development and in relative amounts of all
normal force. This is an hypothesis which must be decided upon the simple basis
of fact.

❋ ❋ ❋

The facts of Evolution may have been misinterpreted, by giving undue prominence to such as have been evolved in the male line; and by overlooking equally
essential modifications which have arisen in the diverging female line. It is claimed
that average males and females, in every species, always have been approximately
equals, both physically and mentally. It is claimed that the extra size, the greater
beauty of color, and wealth of appendages, and the greater physical strength and
activity in males, have been in each species mathematically offset in the females by

corresponding advantages—such as more highly differentiated structural development; greater rapidity of organic processes; larger relative endurance, dependent upon a more facile adjustment of functions among themselves, thus insuring a more prompt recuperation after every severe tax on the energies. It is claimed that the stronger passional force in the male finds its equivalent in the deeper parental and conjugal affection of the female; and that, in man, the more aggressive and constructive intellect of the male, is balanced by a higher intellectual insight, combined with a greater facility in coping with details and reducing them to harmonious adjustment, in the female. It is also claimed that in morals—development still modified by the correlative influences of sex—unlike practical virtues and vices and varied moral perceptions, must still be regarded as scientific equivalents.

All characters, being equally transmitted to descendants of both sexes, may remain undeveloped in either, or may be developed subject to sexual modifications; and yet, as a whole, the males and females of the same species, from mollusk up to man, may continue their related evolution, as true equivalents in all modes of force, physical and psychical. If this hypothesis can be shown to have a sufficient basis in nature, then Mr. Spencer and Mr. Darwin are both wrong in the conclusion that, in the process of Evolution, man has become the superior of woman.

* * *

That all Evolution has been carried forward by small successive stages, can hardly be doubted by many persons who will devote the necessary attention to the accumulative evidence on this point. But that all this has been accomplished *without intelligent plan or prevision*, certainly is not a theory essential to the hypothesis of Evolution. On the contrary, that Nature, as we know it, could have originated otherwise than through the natural creation or adaptation of a *co-operative constitution* of things, co-ordinating all substances, sentient and unsentient, is to my apprehension, utterly incredible. Nowhere is there higher evidence of Design, and of the existence of a true sentient force co-operative in every organism, than in the wondrous instincts of insect life.

* * *

If Evolution, as applied to sex, teaches any one lesson plainer than another, it is the lesson that the monogamic marriage is the basis of all progress. Nature, who everywhere holds her balances with even justice, asks only that every husband and wife shall co-operate to develop her most diligently-selected characters. When she has endowed any woman with special talents, the balanced development of such a character requires the amplest exercise of these predominant gifts. Any prevailing tendency is itself evidence that the entire organism is adjusted to promote its superior activity. If it is a quality, just, honorable, desirable to be attained by the race, to hinder its highest development is to retard the normal rate of human progress; to interfere unwarrantably with a fundamental law of evolution. No theory of unfitness,

425

no form of conventionality, can have the right to suppress excellence which Nature has seen fit to evolve. Men and women, in search of the same ends, must co-operate in as many heterogeneous pursuits as the present development of the race enables them both to recognize and appreciate.

* * *

THE supposed law of inverse relations between growth and reproduction was first announced, I think, by Dr. Carpenter, but adopted independently by Mr. Spencer, whose elaborate, forcible arguments have done much to convince many physiologists that a principle so well established may be accepted without further question. But the underlying facts are so various, complex, and unsolved, it is by no means impossible, or even improbable, that some new element yet to be introduced into the premises may partially modify or even reverse the necessary logical conclusion.

* * *

Up to this point one may freely admit the antagonistic relations alleged; but when, in his article on "The Psychology of the Sexes," Mr. Spencer asserts that "a somewhat earlier arrest of individual development in women than in men is necessitated by the reservation of vital force to meet the cost of reproduction," there are so many not yet discounted conditions to be considered that the position cannot be regarded as satisfactorily sustained. *There is* the "earlier arrest" of physical growth; the "rather smaller growth of the nervo-muscular system;" the much longer nutritive tax demanded for the nourishment of foetal and infant life; the "somewhat less of general power or massiveness" in feminine mental manifestations; *there may be,* "beyond this, a perceptible falling short in those two faculties, intellectual and emotional, which are the latest products of human evolution—the power of abstract reasoning, and that most abstract of the emotions, the sentiment of justice." It does not therefore follow that these results, any or all of them are deductions made from the "cost of reproduction." Force modified and readjusted is not force subtracted or destroyed.

The smaller nervo-muscular system, and the diminished power or massiveness of mental action, may be supposed to arise as direct results of the larger nutritive cost of maternity. But the earlier arrest of physical growth may or may not be coupled with an earlier arrest of mental development; and one or both of these may offer to us very marked illustrations—not of process prematurely cut short to be handed over to offspring—but of process quickened by other related antecedents, and therefore more rapidly completed. This need not involve loss or transfer of individual force to offspring; but, rather, a modified system of the transfer of substance ad force from the environment to the reproductive functions and their products.

If it could be shown that men or women who are the parents of many children have thereby lost something of individual power, we might then be forced to admit that the greater cost related to the reproductive system in women must be at their personal expense, not at the expense of the nutriment which they assimilate and eliminate.

The weakness resulting from a too early or an excessive tax of functions belong to a distinct class of considerations. I assume that every balanced constitutional activity, though including loss of nutritive elements, is yet a normal aid to constitutional strength. Every action, physical or psychical, involves either integration or disintegration; every use of faculty belongs to the latter class. There is no more antagonism between growth and reproduction than between growth and thought, growth and muscular activity, growing and breathing. The antagonism is only that of action and reaction, which are but two phases of the same process—opposing phases which exist everywhere, and which must exist, or action itself cease, and death reign universally.

*   *   *

The maternal constitution elaborates nutriment from which it is itself to receive no direct benefit. But do we forget the inexorable conditions which compel the human father to expand equivalent muscular or mental force to feed, not himself, but his dependents? Whenever man does not interfere monogamy seems to be the general order of Nature with all higher organisms. Where the cost of obtaining food is great, the parents sustain commensurate burdens in rearing their young; and, with these claims, I think it will be found that monogamy is the primal condition of reproduction. The warlike duty of defence is also borne chiefly by males, and must often be an immense tax on the energies.

Among the beings of a lower type, plant and animal, all the more recent observations indicate that Nature herself systematically favors the females—the mothers of the destined races. Nature's sturdiest buds and her best-fed butterflies belong to this sex; her female spiders are large enough to eat up a score of her little males; some of her mother-fishes might parody the nursery-song, "I have a little husband no bigger than my thumb." Natural selection, whether the working out of intelligent design or otherwise, would make this result inevitable. We might expect that the neuter bee could be nourished into the queen-mother. If required to judge *a priori*, we should decide if there is no predetermination of sex, that the best-fed embryos would most readily become female; since the one special fact in the feminine organism is the innate tendency to manufacture, and, within certain limits, to store up reserved force for the future needs of offspring.

In women, if there is a greater arrest of individual growth than in men, the difference begins in the foetal life; their comparative weight and size at birth are the same as at maturity; and, if the former finish their growth earlier, it must be because relatively they grow more rapidly. The feminine circulation and respiration are both quicker; and so are the female mental processes. When the whole subject has been quantitatively investigated with sufficient exactness, I believe it will be found that, what man has gained in "massiveness," woman has gained in rapidity of action; and that all their powers of body and mind, *mathematically computed*, are and will continue to be, real and true equivalents. The premises are already sufficiently known to compel me to this condition.

One point more. Physical and psychical growth in man are not arrested simultaneously. After the body has ceased to grow, the brain-system still enlarging and compacting its highly mobile structure, mental power increases long after the more rigid, merely mechanical forces have reached their maximum. The same law applies, at least, in equal degrees to woman. If there is any proof that feminine psychical powers normally reach an earlier cessation of growth than the masculine, then, so far as I can lean, no scientist has yet collated the facts and put them before the world in evidence. On the contrary, so far is the earlier physical maturity of woman from necessitating a corresponding earlier psychical maturity, that in the light of physiological relations, we may deduce the exactly opposite hypothesis.

In woman, maximum mental power should be reached at a considerably later period than in man, because the greater cost of reproduction, though related chiefly to the physical economy, is indirectly psychical; tending to diminish intellectual action also, and to retard its evolution. The cost of all reproductive provisions fully met, and the child-bearing age at an end, the special constitutional tendency to accumulate reserve force will not be immediately destroyed. Functions, active hitherto in the interest of posterity, go on now to accumulate in the interest of the individual. Still further, the naturally less overtaxed intellectual faculties of woman now have *this* advantage also over those of man—an advantage as least as great as the previous disadvantage.

When the vast weight of past social conditions is considered, that women thus far have failed to acquire large powers of abstract thinking and feeling, affords no reason for supposing that there is a corresponding constitutional lack of ability in this direction. They attain an earlier growth, but, that they reach the highest point even of physical vigor earlier than men, we have no evidence. Many facts indicate otherwise. Men and women live to equal ages, retain their vigor to equal ages—those using the greater force more slowly, these the lesser force more rapidly—thus with uneven steps keeping even pace in physical progress; the greater mobility of all womanly functions being less readily stiffened into inactivity. This principle, applied to the nervous system, should prolong the period of greatest mental activity, and hold the balance which measures the working value of the sexes with even justice.

Is it true that average women to-day are less versed than average men in abstract thinking, feeling, or acting? Not in New England! Not in any locality where they have equal education. They have not become *savants*! But circumstances have not yet impelled them to become such. In these days, philosophers grow by steady accretions, like every thing else. No full-armed Minerva can be expected to spring by simple heredity from a paternal Jupiter; but the laws of mental inheritance are too little known to enable us to decide that the daughters of the nineteenth century are less gifted than the sons. When women are convinced that the antagonisms between growth and reproduction, though embracing all personalities, must yet leave them all intact, every thing else may be left to adjust itself, with no solicitude for the ultimate results.

SOURCE: Antoinette Brown Blackwell, *The Sexes Throughout Nature* (New York: G. P. Putnam's Sons, 1875), 11, 20–22, 62, 136–48.

"The Chinese Problem"
1876

California saw an influx of Chinese immigrants to mine for gold, build rail-roads, and fill in the Sacramento River Delta for farmland in the years before the Civil War. But with the economic downturn of the 1870s, politicians fanned the flames of xenophobia among Americans of European descent, and by 1879 most California voters favored Chinese exclusion. Unitarians could be found on all sides of the debate. Two prophetic voices on the issue belonged to local ministers. First Unitarian Church of San Francisco's Horatio Steb-bins was outspoken against Chinese exclusion, quick to condemn both human prejudice and politicians' manipulation of the issue to secure votes. Charles Ames, having served the Unitarian churches in San Francisco and Santa Cruz, used his editorship of the Christian Register *to point out the ways systematically unfair laws created many of the conditions for which Chinese immigrants were chastised in European American presses. The views of Charles Wendte (1844–1931), who attended the San Francisco Unitarian church for six years before entering theological school in 1866, were more problematic and offensive from a contemporary perspective. He was serving the Unitarian Church in Cincinnati at the time he wrote the following article, by that time the longest treatment of these issues in a national Unitarian periodical.*

—Sheri Prud'homme

We have a right to consider the effect of Chinese immigration on our national life, as well as on our private pockets. What is to be the result of this Asiatic graft upon our American stock? It will certainly add a new and not very desirable element to the *olla podrida* of American society, which is already boiling and seething like Hecate's cauldron, with its diversities and antagonisms of race, color, language, custom, and religious belief.

✳   ✳   ✳

The great tendency of American business life is towards consolidation of inter-ests and the centralization of power in a few hands. . . .

Now oppose to this concentrated capital in the hands of a limited number of selfish, ambitious, able men, an ignorant, degraded laboring class like the Chinese; a class which does not grumble or find fault, which does not strike, and which works not eight, but twelve and fourteen hours a day . . . and we have the same order of things which so lately existed at the South,—an oligarchy of capitalists, agriculturalists, manufacturers, and merchants, with complete arbitrary control over the labor of the lower working-classes. . . . Without dwelling here on the demoralizing influence of such a condition of things on California society, it is sufficient to point out how directly it would conflict with the interests of free white labor and small capital as we find them in the more Eastern States.

*　*　*

We cheerfully admit that the Chinaman is a man like ourselves. . . . Still, it must be borne in mind that the Chinese in this country are mainly the off-scourings, the dregs of Asiatic civilization, driven by poverty and wretchedness to our shores. . . .

The Chinese immigrant is doubtless possessed of many remarkable aptitudes and excellent qualities of character. He is tirelessly industrious, very economical, patient, persistent, and courageous in all his enterprises. He is a great lover of everything that is practical, methodical, and useful. He shows remarkable aptitude for business. The cöoperative system, still an experiment with us, has been employed for centuries in China. . . .

These more hopeful traits are accompanied, however, by great defects and vices. As a rule the Chinese in California are a small and stunted race, physically weak, afflicted by terrible and nameless diseases, uneducated, and encompassed by a network of prejudices and superstitions that bar out all higher life. Like other Orientals they are notoriously insincere. Beneath some little gloss of politeness and ceremony, they are essentially coarse and licentious in their tastes, and very filthy in their personal habits. It needs but a single walk through the foul kennels and noisome odors of the Chinese quarter in San Francisco to assure one of this fact. The dirt and vileness are not to be described in words.

*　*　*

What is needed is an organized, aggressive force that will go to the Chinaman, and not wait for the Chinaman to come to it. This moral force, this organized centre of effort, is best found to-day in the Church of America. Political sagacity must be reinforced by moral and religious enthusiasm to succeed in this great work. The nerveless, apathetic Chinaman must be kindled by the glow of a religious sentiment to labor for his own social and moral redemption.

*　*　*

Let the churches persevere in the good work of education and reform, and seek to inspire a profounder sentiment of humanity, patience, and charity in the treatment of this stranger race. May both our private conduct and our public legislation be guided by the spirit of the Golden Rule taught by both Jesus and Confucius, that, amidst the clash of material interests and the strife of politics, there may be no violence done to the sacred causes of national honor and human brotherhood.

SOURCE: Charles Wendte, "The Chinese Problem," *The Unitarian Review and Religious Magazine,* May 1876, 516–18, 521–22, 525, 528.

LYDIA MARIA CHILD

"Aspirations of the World"
1878

Lydia Maria Child (1802–1880) is best remembered today as a Unitarian writer, abolitionist, and women's rights activist, but she also contributed to the nascent discipline of comparative religion. In his 1870 essay "The Sympathy of Religions," Thomas Wentworth Higginson called for the creation of a universal Bible, and by the end of that decade, liberals had responded enthusiastically. One of the more approachable versions of these collections of scriptures was Lydia Maria Child's Aspirations of the World: A Chain of Opals, a collection of scriptural excerpts from both Christian and non-Christian religious sources, including Judaism, Islam, Hinduism, and Buddhism. She organized her selections according to themes such as "Ideas of the Supreme Being," "Immortality," "Temperance," and "Brotherhood," among thirty other categories. The following selection draws from her introduction to the material, in which she lays out her understanding of comparative religion. It is worth comparing her perspective to Higginson's, as well as noting that her interpretation of these sources nonetheless places the different traditions into very Christian categories of understanding, which possibly belies the cosmopolitanism of her project.

—Emily Mace

In this book I have collected some specimens of the moral and religious utterances of various ages and nations; from the remotest known records down to the present time. In doing this, my motive is simply to show that there is much in which all mankind agree. I have, therefore, avoided presenting the theological aspects of any religion. Sentiments unite men; opinions separate them. The fundamental rules of Morality are the same with good men of all ages and countries; the idea of Immortality has been present with them all; and all have manifested similar aspirations toward an infinitely wise and good Being, by whom they were created and sustained. From these three starting points many paths diverge, leading into endless mazes of theology. Into these labyrinths I do not consider it useful to look. I do not assume that any one religion is right in its theology, or that any others are wrong. I merely attempt to show that the primeval impulses of the human soul have been essentially the same everywhere; and my impelling motive is to do all I can to enlarge and strengthen the bond of human brotherhood.

In the Sacred Scriptures of all peoples the performance of moral and religious duties is enjoined, with frequent promises of reward, either here or hereafter. These promises I have systematically omitted, because they seem to me to appeal, more or less, to selfishness; for I think, in our highest spiritual states, we all realize that "the reward is *in* keeping the commandments, not *for* keeping them."

On these pages, antique gems are ranged side by side with modern pearls and crystals; for all the great human family have contributed somewhat to the family-jewels, and left their precious legacies as heir-looms to posterity.

The different names by which the Supreme Being has been addressed in various ages and countries I have uniformly translated into our own language; therein following the rule that is observed with regard to all words translated from foreign tongues into our own. Without the slightest regard to creeds, or the absence of creeds, I have quoted what seemed to me sensible and good, or what seemed to illustrate the state of the human mind at any given epoch. I have done this, because I saw no other way of being perfectly impartial. I have frequently compiled and abridged quotations, for the sake of making a small, unexpensive book; but I have in no case altered the sense of any thing. I am not learned myself, and I have not written for the learned; therefore I have not deemed it necessary to encumber the pages with references to Greek, Latin, and Oriental books. I trust my readers will be satisfied when I assure them, honestly and truly, that I believe there is good authority for every thing I have quoted. Having a dislike to titles, I have called no man Rabbi, Saint, or Reverend; but, as the same rule is applied to all, I hope no one will take offence.

* * *

With regard to three primeval ideas there is observable similarity among all ages and nations. They have all conceived of One Supreme Being, who created and sustained all things; they all believed that man had within his body a soul, which shared the Immortality of the Eternal Source of Being, whence it was derived; and a Natural Law of Justice, the basis of all other laws, early dawned upon all human minds. Ideas of how or where the Divine being existed were vague; and so they remain unto the present day. All the people on earth, from the beginning of time, have been "feeling after God, if haply they might find him;" and still we are obliged to ask, as Job did many centuries ago, "Canst thou by searching find out God?"

SOURCE: L. Maria Child, *Aspirations of the World: A Chain of Opals* (Boston, 1878), 1–3, 13.

"What Shall We Do with Our Daughters?"

1883

During the decades when the Universalists led the way in the ordination of women, the most famous Universalist woman was a non-ordained minister's wife. Mary Livermore (1820–1905) discovered Universalism through her husband, Daniel Livermore, and joined him in his journalistic endeavors and activism on behalf of temperance, abolition, and women's rights. During the Civil War, she led the Northwestern branch of the U.S. Sanitary Commission, mobilizing thousands of women volunteers to work on behalf of Union soldiers. This wartime experience empowered women for other sorts of activism after the war, and Livermore was in the forefront as editor of the Woman's Journal *and as president of the Massachusetts chapter of the Women's Christian Temperance Union. She also held leadership positions in organizations ranging from the Association for Advancement of Women to the Society of Christian Socialists and lectured continually on women's rights and other topics. This speech was delivered hundreds of times in the decade prior to its publication. Further Reading: Wendy Hamand Venet,* A Strong-Minded Woman: The Life of Mary Livermore *(Amherst: University of Massachusetts Press, 2005).*

— Dan McKanan

Nearly forty years ago, Margaret Fuller, standing, as she said, "in the sunny noon of life," wrote a little book, which she launched on the current of thought and society. It was entitled "Woman in the Nineteenth Century;" and as the truths it proclaimed, and the reforms it advocated, were far in advance of public acceptance, its appearance was the signal for an immediate, widespread, newspaper controversy, that raged with great violence. I was young then; and as I took the book from the hands of the bookseller, wondering what the contents of the thin little volume could be, to provoke so wordy a strife, I opened at the first page. My attention was immediately arrested, and a train of thought started, by the two mottoes at the head of the opening chapter, — on underneath the other, one contradicting the other.

The first was an old-time adage, indorsed by Shakespeare, believed in by the world, and quoted in that day very generally. It is not yet entirely obsolete. "Frailty, thy name is Woman." Underneath it, and unlike it was the other, — "The Earth waits for her Queen." The first described woman as she has been understood in the past;

as she has masqueraded in history; as she has been made to figure in literature; as she has, in a certain sense, existed. The other prophesied of that grander type of woman, towards which to-day the whole sex is moving,—consciously or unconsciously, willingly or unwillingly,—because the current sets that way, and there is no escape from it.

No one who has studied history, even superficially, will for a moment dispute the statement, that, during the years of which we have had historic account, there has brooded very steadily over the female half of the human family an air of repression, of limitation, of hindrance, of disability, of gloom, of servitude. If there have been epochs during which women have been regarded equal to men, they have been brief and abnormal. Among the Hindoos, woman was the slave of man, forbidden to speak the language of her master, and compelled to use the *patois* of slaves. The Hebrews pronounced her an afterthought of the Deity, and the mother of all evil. The Greek law regarded her as a child, and held her in life-long tutelage. The Greek philosophers proclaimed her a "monster," "an accidental production." Mediaeval councils declared her unfit for instruction. The early Christian fathers denounced her as a "noxious animal," a "painted temptress," a necessary evil," a "desirable calamity," a "domestic peril." From the English Heptarchy to the Reformation the law proclaimed the wife to be "in all cases, and under all circumstances, her husband's creature, servant, slave." To Diderot, the French philosopher, even in the eighteenth century, she was only a "courtesan;" to Montesquieu, an "attractive child;" to Rousseau, "an object of pleasure to man." To Michelet, nearly a century later, she was a "natural invalid." Mme. De Stael wrote truly, "that, of all the faculties with which Nature had gifted woman, she had been able to exercise fully but one,—the faculty of suffering."

*　*　*

Born and bred for generations under such conditions of hindrance, is has not been possible for women to rise much above the arbitrary standards of inferiority persistently set before them. Here and there through the ages some woman endowed with phenomenal force of character has towered above the mediocrity of her sex, hinting at the qualities imprisoned in the feminine nature. It is not strange that these instances have been rare: it is strange, indeed, that women have held their own during these ages of degradation. And as, by a general law of heredity, "the inheritance of traits of character is persistent in proportion to the length of time they have been inherited," it is easy to account for the conservatism of women to-day, and for the indifference, not to say hostility, with which many regard the movements for their advancement.

For humanity has moved forward to an era where wrong and slavery are being displaced, and reason and justice are being recognized as the rule of life. Science is extending immeasurably the bounds of knowledge and power; art is refining life, giving to it beauty and grace; literature bears in her hands whole ages of comfort and sympathy; industry, aided by the hundred-handed elements of nature, is increasing the world's wealth; and invention is economizing its labor. The age looks steadily to the redressing of wrong, to the righting of every form of error and injustice; and a tireless and prying philanthropy, which is almost omniscient, is one of the most hopeful characteristics of the time.

If the barbaric spirit of war still lingers among the nations, so also does the voice of Charles Sumner, who for thirty years taught that "the true grandeur of nations is peace." If slavery fastens fetters on the bodies and souls of human beings, Garrison and Phillips cry aloud for immediate emancipation: the nation joins in the holy crusade for liberty, and slavery dies. If the cry of the criminal comes up for prisons noisome with filth, and soul with moral pollution, the tendency of the age is, not only to realize the ideal of Howard, that "prisons should be made moral reformatories," but to organize societies for the prevention of crime. If ignorance cowers in darkness in sections of the land, a plea is made for universal, compulsory education, on the tenable ground that a republic cannot live with an illiterate constituency behind it.

*　*　*

It could not be possible in such an era but that women should share in the justice and kindliness with which the time is fraught. A great wave is lifting them to higher levels. The leadership of the world is being taken from the hands of the brutal and low, and the race is groping its way to a higher ideal than once it knew. It is the evolution of this tendency that is lifting women out of their subject condition, that is emancipating them from the seclusion of the past, and adding to the sum total of the world's worth and wisdom, by giving to them the cultivation human beings need. The demand for their education,—technical and industrial as well as intellectual,—and for their civil and political rights, is being urged each year by an increasing host, and with more empathetic utterance.

The doors of colleges, professional schools, and universities, closed against them for ages, are opening to them. They are invited to pursue the same courses of study as their brothers, and are graduated with the same diplomas. Trades, businesses, remunerative vocations, and learned professions seek them; and even the laws which are the last to feel the change in public opinion,—usually dragging a whole generation behind,—even these are being annually revised and amended, and then they fail to keep abreast of the advancing civilization.

All this is but prefatory, and prophetic of the time when, for women, law will be synonymous with justice, and no opportunity for knowledge or effort will be denied them on the score of sex.

As I listen to the debates that attend this progress, and weigh the prophecies of evil always inspired by a growing reform; as I hear the clash of the scientific raid upon women, by the small pseudo-scientists of the day,—who make of "The

436

American Review" catapults for the hurling of their missiles,—my thoughts turn to the young women of the present time. "What shall we do with our daughters?" is really the sum and substance of what, in popular phrase is called "the woman question." For if to-morrow all should be done that is demanded by the wisest reformer, and the truest friend of woman, it would not materially affect the condition of the adult women of society. Their positions are taken, their futures are forecast; and they are harnessed into the places they occupy, not unfrequently, by invisible, but omnipotent, ties of love or duty. Obedience to the behests of duty gives peace, even when love is lacking; and peace is a diviner thing than happiness.

It is for our young women that the great changes of the time promise the most: it is for our daughters—the fair bright girls, who are the charm of society and the delight of home; the sources of infinite comfort to fathers and mothers, and the sources of great anxiety also. What shall we do with them,—and what shall they do with and for themselves? . . .

Let no one, therefore, say this question of the training of our daughters is a small question. No question can be small that relates to half the human race. The training of boys is not more important than that of girls. The hope of many is so centred in the "coming man," that the only questions of interest to them are those propounded by James Parton in "The Atlantic Monthly,"—"Will the coming man smoke?" "Will he drink wine?" and so onto the end of the catechism. But let it not be forgotten, that, before this "coming man" will make his appearance, his mother will precede him, and that he will be very largely what his mother will make him. Men are to-day confessing their need of the aid of women by appointing them on school committees, boards of charities, as prison commissioners, physicians to insane-asylums,—positions which they cannot worthily fill without preparation.

Nor let us forget the vast influence exerted by women upon men, sometimes worthily, and sometimes, alas! disastrously. We often see a man starting in life, lacking largeness of aim and fineness of organization. Left to himself he would drift on the current of society wherever it might bear him. But a kind fate harnesses him, in love or friendship, with a woman of nobler character. Seeing farther than the narrow present, and deeper than the gilded surface, she transfuse him with her own spirit, inspires him with noble purposes, and he becomes a power for good.

* * *

And have we not all known men of rare promise, whose early manhood has glowed with high ambitions, but who, alas! have been made petty, ill-natured, and ignoble by their female companions? These, through physical weakness, mental poverty, and lowness of moral tone, have shut down, like brakes, on the progress of husbands, sons, and brothers, halting them, lowering their ideals, till at last their very manhood has died out, and their faces have become tombstones, written all over with obituaries of dead souls within.

Therefore, not only for their own sakes, but for the sake of the human family, of which women make one-half, should we look carefully to the training of our daughters. Nature has so constituted us, that the sexes act and re-act upon each other, making every "woman's cause" a man's cause, and every man's cause a woman's cause; so that we

> "Rise or sink
> Together, dwarfed or godlike, bond or free."

And they are the foes of the race, albeit not intentional, who set themselves against the removal of woman's disabilities, shut in their faces the doors of education or opportunity, or deny them any but the smallest and most incomplete training. For it is true that "who educates a woman, educates a race."

SOURCE: Mary A. Livermore, *What Shall We Do with Our Daughters? Superfluous Women and Other Lectures* (Boston: Lee and Shepard, 1883), 7–19.

"The Five Points of the New Theology"
1885

James Freeman Clarke (1810–1888) exchanged pulpits with Theodore Parker when all others refused to do so. After the Civil War his became one of the most influential Unitarian voices, and his Church of the Disciples one of the most inclusive and socially active Unitarian churches in Boston. A pioneer university professor of theology and comparative religion at Harvard, he also published twenty-two books, including Ten Great Religions. *His "Five Points of Liberal Theology" were posted prominently in many Unitarian churches for decades. Here, the fifth (and most controversial) point should be read as embracing theological universalism in its restorationist interpretation. Further Reading: Arthur Bolster, Jr.,* James Freeman Clarke: Disciple to Advancing Truth *(Boston: Beacon Press, 1954).*

—John Buehrens

The number five has acquired as great significance in theology as it has in nature. The largest family of plants is that of which the flowers have five petals; and the most popular theology of modern times is that of Calvin with its five points of doctrine. . . .

The theology of the future will dwell on something else than the five points of Calvinism, and I have thought it well to consider the counterparts of this ancient system in five points of the coming theology. . . .

1. I believe the first point of doctrine in the theology of the future will be the *Fatherhood of God*. The essence of this is the love of the father for his children. . . . The justice of God as a Father is not, as in the old theology, an abstract justice, which has no regard to consequences. God's justice is only another form of mercy. It is the wise law which brings good to the universe, and is a blessing to every creature.

Jesus has everywhere emphasized this truth, that God is a father. . . .

We look up out of our sin and weakness and sorrow, not to an implacable law, not to an abstract king, but to an infinite and inexhaustible tenderness. Thus, this doctrine is the source of the purest piety.

2. The second point of doctrine in the new theology will be, I think, the *Brotherhood of Man*.

If men are children of the same father, then they are all brethren. If God loves them all, they must all have in them something lovable. If he has brought them here by his providence, they are here for some important end. Therefore, we must call no man common or unclean, look down upon none, despise none, but respect in all that essential goodness which God has put into the soul, and which he means to be at last unfolded into perfection.

As from the idea of the fatherhood of God will come all the pieties, so from that of the brotherhood of man will proceed . . . purer moralities and nobler charities.

This truth, also, Jesus has taught by his words and his life. . . .

3. The third point of doctrine in the new theology will be, as I think, the *Leadership of Jesus.*

The simplest definition of a Christian is one who follows Christ . . . who takes Jesus as his guide in religion, and who goes directly to his teachings for religious truth.

But hitherto, instead of considering those as Christians who have studied the words of Jesus, and sought to know the truth, the name has usually been given to those who accepted some opinion about him. Not what he himself teaches, but what the Church says he teaches, has been made the test of Christian fellowship. . . . Instead of sending us to the teacher himself, we are sent to our fellow-students. We, therefore, in reality take them, and not Jesus, for our leader. . . .

Of course there is no harm in a creed, when it merely states what a man believes at the present time or what any number of men believe at any particular period. The harm comes from making the creed a perpetual standard of belief, a test of Christian character, and a condition of Christian fellowship. . . .

4. The fourth point of the new theology will be *Salvation by Character.*

Salvation means the highest peace and joy of which the soul is capable. It means heaven here and heaven hereafter. This salvation has been explained as something outside of us,—some outward gift, some outward condition, place, or circumstance. We speak of going to heaven, as if we could be made happy solely by being put in a happy place. But the true heaven, the only heaven which Jesus knew, is a state of the soul. . . . The poor in spirit already possess the kingdom of heaven. The pure in heart already see God. . . . He identifies goodness with heaven, and makes character the essence of salvation. . . .

5. The fifth point of doctrine in the new theology will, as I believe, be the *Continuity of Human Development* in all worlds, or the *Progress of Mankind* onward and upward forever.

Progress is the outward heaven, corresponding to the inward heaven of character. The hope of progress is one of the chief motives to action. Men are contented, no matter how poor their lot, so long as they can hope for something better. And men are discontented, no matter how fortunate their condition, when they have nothing more to look forward to. The greatest sufferer who hopes may have nothing, but he possesses all things: the most prosperous man who is deprived of hope may have all things, but he possesses nothing.

The old theology laid no stress on progress here or progress hereafter. The essential thing was conversion: that moment passed, the object of life was attained. . . . If hope abides, there is always something to look forward to,—some higher attainment, some larger usefulness, some nearer communion with God. And this accords with all we see and know: with the long processes of geologic development by which the earth became fitted to be the home of man; with the slow ascent of organized beings from humbler to fuller life; with the progress of society from age to age; with the gradual diffusion of knowledge, advancement of civilization, growth of free institutions, and ever higher conceptions of God and of religious truth. The one fact which is written on nature and human life is the fact of progress, and this must be accepted as the purpose of the Creator.

Some such views as these may constitute the theology of the future. . . Let us endeavor to see God and nature face to face, confident that whoever is honestly seeking the truth, though he may err for a time, can never go wholly wrong.

SOURCE: James Freeman Clarke, "The Five Points of Calvinism and the Five Points of the New Theology," *Vexed Questions in Theology: A Series of Essays* (Boston, 1886), 9–18.

"Religious Nurture"
1886

In the 1850s, Peabody studied German educator Friedrich Froebel's kindergarten movement, which sought to nurture young children through organized play, drawing out their innate moral, intellectual, and physical capacities while teaching them basic socialization. In 1860, she founded the first English-speaking kindergarten in the United States. She went on to advocate for kindergartens for children growing up surrounded by poverty and urban social problems. These excerpts from Lectures in the Training School for Kindergartners *explain how a teacher should cultivate the religious, moral, and spiritual sensibility already present in young children.*

—Gail Forsyth-Vail

On this last day of communion with you on the Froebel education, I would like to speak with some comprehensiveness and particularity on the subject of religious nurture. Mark me, I say religious *nurture*, not religious teaching. The religion that integrates human education is not to be taught. It is the primeval consciousness of filial relation to GOD, who alone can reveal Himself; for human language has no adequate expression of GOD, founded as it is on the material universe, which is the finite opposite of Creative Being. Every individual child is a momentum of God's creativeness which the human Providence of education must take as its *datum*. . . .

You should talk about GOD as little as possible, after having given Him the name that will excite the child's worshipful aspiration, and limit yourselves carefully to regulating moral manifestations, leading children to act kindly, generously, truthfully, in your own assured faith that GOD is present to inspire the truth, generosity, and loving *will* that is practically prayed for with *good resolution*.

* * *

Now the true religious nurture is to keep the child in the mood of ineffable joy in which he was created, while he is evolving his sense of individuality and free agency by experimenting freely, but more or less painfully, so that he shall not lose sight of the central Sun, to which everything he is slowly learning through his senses and his reflection is related; and this must be begun by giving a name to the central Sun that shall express the character of his inmost consciousness of joy and love, which is his vision of GOD, and needs to be recognized as GOD in the understanding.

In religious conversation children have the advantage of us in their as yet uneclipsed original vision of GOD, and we have an advantage of them in knowledge of outside things and the adaptation of means to ends. By this knowledge of ours we can generally guide them to accomplish their purposes when they are such as will really give them pleasure and do no harm to any one else. They get our knowledge by confidingly doing as we direct, and a confidence in the method which brings about the results they have instinctively foreseen. We save their minds from getting lost or bewildered in the chaos of particulars by winning their attention to the orderly connections of things, and leading them to realize how they connect little things in order to make larger things, and how opposites are connected in the world around about them. To recognize their own little plans and open their eyes to GOD's methods and plans; and because they cause new effects, they realize that all effects have causes, and in the last analysis realize one personal cause. They must believe in themselves as a preliminary to believing in GOD.

∗ ∗ ∗

I do not think it right or wise to suggest to little children that *their* wrong-doings, which are more weaknesses than presumptions, are *sins against God*. Children can comprehend their relations to each other, and the violation of each other's rights to happiness, and can be easily led to sympathize with the pain or inconvenience of those they make suffer, which touches their sense of justice and generosity; they can appreciate wrong and its consequences to their equals and to themselves in the *present life*. But GOD is too great to be injured by them; and to bring GOD to their imagination as personally angry with them, overwhelms thought, and annihilates all sense of responsibility, with all self-respect.

SOURCE: Elizabeth Palmer Peabody, *Lectures in the Training School for Kindergartners* (Boston, 1886), 161–62, 164, 167–68, 170–71.

JABEZ SUNDERLAND

The Issue in the West
1886

Jabez Sunderland (1842–1936) trained as a Baptist minister but his liberal beliefs led him to become a Unitarian. He served churches in Northfield, Massachusetts, and Chicago before being called to the Unitarian Church in Ann Arbor, Michigan, in 1878. While there, he succeeded the first secretary of the Western Unitarian Conference (WUC), Jenkin Lloyd Jones, in 1884. Sunderland considered himself a follower of Theodore Parker's theology, but he felt the lack of Christian and theistic language in the WUC's self-description and in its primary newspaper Unity *inhibited the spread of Unitarianism in its territory. He sought to bring western Unitarians in closer affiliation with the AUA. For the 1886 meeting of the WUC, Sunderland prepared the pamphlet he called* The Issue in the West, *in which he argued an ethical basis of religion was not enough: "To abandon God and Christianity was to abandon religion itself." Sunderland was widely misunderstood to be arguing for a creed. The controversy ended when the WUC adopted a non-theistic statement by William Channing Gannett the next year. Sunderland's later ministry included work with religious liberals in India and support of Indian independence. Further Reading: Charles Lyttle,* Freedom Moves West: A History of the Western Unitarian Conference, 1852–1952 *(Boston: Beacon Press, 1952).*

—Nicole C. Kirk

Plainly, Western Unitarianism has reached a question which it must face. . . . Are we ready to declare that those great faiths—in God, prayer, immortality and the spiritual leadership of Jesus—which have always in the past been at the very heart of Unitarianism, are no longer essential to our movement?

Unitarianism in the past has always been Christian. Nobody thinks of doubting that. Our great historic leaders, the men who have given luster to the Unitarian name—Channing, the Wares, Parker, Dewey, Bellows, to say nothing of those now living—have all stood for Liberal Christianity. Unitarianism in England, Europe, and all foreign lands where it is known does the same today. So does it in New England and the Middle States and the South and on the Pacific Coast. So has it always in the West, without dispute and without a question, until within a very few years. So does it indeed, doubtless, with a great majority of the Unitarians of the West

444

still. But, within a dozen years or so, seemingly as the result of the breaking over the West of the free religious wave of the East, there has been a movement here, at first quite unnoticed, possibly hardly conscious of itself, but becoming more definite in its purpose and more pronounced as it went on, to create a new and different order of Unitarianism in the West. From the beginning, this new Unitarianism has shown an especially warm sympathy with the Free Religious movement, and later, with the Ethical movement; has steadily sought to differentiate itself from the Unitarianism of the East as being something "broader" and "more advanced" than that, has long been averse to the use of the Christian name, and for a few years past has been more and more distinctly moving off from even a theistic basis, until now it declares openly and strongly that even belief in God must no longer be declared an essential of Unitarianism.

To avoid misunderstanding, it should be said at the outset, however, that most of the men who are thus endeavoring to remove the Unitarianism of the West onto this new basis, are themselves, personally, believers in God, prayer and immortality—as they are unquestionably sincere in their expressed wish that all individual Unitarians might be believers in the same. But, they say, all this must be left solely to the individual. Unitarian churches as churches, Unitarian organizations as organizations, the Unitarian denomination as a denomination, must not plant themselves upon these beliefs. Unitarianism must stand for ethical beliefs and beliefs in certain so-called "principles," but not for belief in anything that will commit it to theism or Christianity. The particular beliefs which are most often and most strongly insisted upon by this new school, are four, viz.: Belief in "freedom," belief in "fellowship," belief in "character," and, by implication, belief in "religion." These beliefs are declared to be essential to Unitarianism; but belief in the *Christian* religion, or belief in religion in any such *high form* as distinctly recognizes a *conscious Intelligence* and *Goodness* over the world inviting man's *worship*, this must not be held to be essential. Even for the ordination of men to the ministry—to be recognized teachers and preachers of Unitarianism—theistic belief must not be required; our pulpits and pastorates must be as distinctly open to the agnostic or the atheist as to the theist or the Christian.

※　※　※

1. Let it be clearly understood, the question at issue is not whether the men leading this new Unitarian departure are good men; the question is whether the movement is a good movement. Some of the greatest calamities of history have come as the result of the mistaken action of good men.

2. The issue is not whether we shall make much or little of ethics. All are agreed to put as strong emphasis upon ethics as possible, as Unitarianism has always done. The question is, whether we do not stand for ethics with a *plus*—ethics *and also something else*, namely, belief in God and Worship—these as being both of them

445

important in themselves, and also as being something without which ethics itself loses its highest sanction and impulse.

3. The issue is not between "radicalism" and "conservatism." The claim that it is, is wholly misleading. The position that Unitarianism stands and always must stand for Christian theism finds its supporters as much among the stoutest radicals as among conservatives—as much among Theodore Parker Unitarians as among Channing Unitarians—as much among those who accept most heartily the teachings of science and comparative religion, and the doctrine of evolution as among any class. Indeed the matter before us is one of so grave and vital a character that in its presence all ordinary thought of radicalism or conservatism seems trivial; for the present issue is one that concerns the very life of the Unitarian body. It is a question as to changing the essential character of Unitarianism. It is the question as to whether our movement is or is not to continue to be fundamentally religious. It is the question, shall we keep our churches, really churches? . . .

4. The issue is not that of dogma or non-dogma. In the only sense in which Christian or theistic Unitarians hold to dogmas, our new-departure brethren also hold to dogmas—and just as firmly as we do, and as just as essential to Unitaranism; only their dogmas are solely ethical (or ethical and intellectual), while ours are ethical and theistic.

5. The question at issue in the West is not between freedom and bondage. Nobody insists upon freedom more perfect and entire than do Christian Unitarians. Was not Channing free? Was not Parker? Did not both stand for a freedom as absolute as the thought of man can conceive? Yet both were Christian theists. We would put no fetters upon inquiry. We would have reason exercise itself to the fullest degree. But does this imply that we must wipe out all lines of distinction, and destroy all principles of classification, in the religious world? . . .

6. The issue before the West is not one of creed or no creed. Nobody wants a creed; nobody, so far as I am aware, would have a creed if he could; that is, unless the word creed is to be used in some new and unwarranted sense. What is a creed, in the true sense? According to the historic and practically universal use of the word from as far back as we can go, "a creed" has signified a formulated, systematized statement of theological doctrine, made out and authorized by some supposed ecclesiastical authority—synod, council or other. Using the word in this, its historic and proper signification, Unitarians have always said: We want no creed; we will have no creed. We put little store by elaborated, systematized, theological statements; if any one wants them let him make them for himself, but let him stop there, for we recognize no council or synod or body as having "authority" to impose any formulated or not-to-be-changed statement of doctrine upon any but himself. I say this has always been our position, and it is the same to-day. But this cannot justly be made to imply that we have not stood or do not stand for any doctrinal belief, as

446

a denomination. It only means that we have not been willing to make formulated and authorized and not-to-be-changed definitions and statements of our belief.

* * *

Of course we have a creed, if to have belief is to have a creed. But with that meaning of the word our new-departure brethren have a creed quite as much. We have a creed, if to believe in the reasonableness, practicability and need of religious classification is a creed. But if the physical scientist classifies without being called a credist, why should not the religious scientist? We have a creed, if to hold that Unitarianism is necessarily theistic and Christian is a creed. But if this is a creed, then to believe that Unitarianism is necessarily ethical must also be a creed. . . .

7. The issue that is before the West is not between a Unitarianism which shall set up dogmatic tests of fellowship, and one that shall not. It *is* between a Unitarianism which shall have a *real* fellowship at all, and one that shall have only a *sham* fellowship.

* * *

8. The issue in the West is not between a Unitarianism of "doctrines" and a Unitarianism of "principles," as Mr. Gannett would have us believe. We have been told that Unitarianism in the past has stood partly for doctrines and partly for principles; but that the tendency from the first has been to put more and more emphasis upon principles and less and less upon doctrines, until now the time has come for us to say, frankly, we wholly give up doctrines as essential, and boldly affirm nothing to be essential but principles. This might be convincing were it not for certain discoveries, which we quickly make when we begin looking at the matter with a little care.

The first is that the principles themselves are actually every one of them doctrines, and derive all their value from the fact that they are doctrines. A doctrine is something believed and taught as true. . . . The real line of separation between the two is not at all that between doctrines and principles, it is between *doctrines ethical* (or ethical and intellectual) and *doctrines theistic*; or, if we are to use the word principles at all, it is between *principles ethical* (or ethical and intellectual) and *principles theistic*.

* * *

There are some who seem to think that the issue in the West in some way involves the question as to whether such well-known and honored brethren as Mr. Gannett, Mr. Blake and Mr. Jones are Unitarians, and have a right to a place in the Unitarian body. Where the idea arose that anyone ever questioned the legitimacy of the place of these brethren among us, I do not know. I can only say that even to suggest such a question seems to me preposterous; for these brethren are theists, individually they believe in worship. The question is only as to other men who are not theists, who are not believers in God or worship. Shall we say to such, "Your want of these faiths makes no difference; you are Unitarians just as truly without them

447

as with; you have just as good a right to be Unitarian ministers without them as with?" *This* is where the issue comes. It does not even come necessarily at the case of laymen, certainly not at all at members of congregations as such. Probably there is nobody among us who is not glad to have men of every possible shade of belief, from Catholic or Mormon to Atheist, come freely to our services. . . .

The difficulty, I say, does not come here: the difficulty comes on the side of the pulpit. Shall our pulpits and pastorates be open to known disbelievers in the simple fundamentals of Christian theism? Here I, and certainly a very large number of others with me, say no. I believe our ministers should not ordain, I believe our fellowship committees should not recommend, I believe our churches cannot without disaster call to or maintain in their pulpits men who are known to be devoid of these essential faiths. And yet the need of saying even this comes wholly from the strange condition into which our body in the West has allowed itself to drift—a condition of uncertainty, to some extent, in the eyes of itself and the public, as to whether it is theistic or Christian. The whole matter would solve itself instantly—I say would *solve itself*—if our churches and our denomination stood distinctly on a basis of Christian theism, for then nobody would *want*, certainly nobody would *ask* ordination among us, or pulpits among us, except persons who believed in Christian faith and worship. The trouble all comes when, and only when, we give up our Christian or theistic basis.

* * *

This protest which this paper contains against the abandonment of the theistic position I make not from one consideration, but from many—indeed, I make it in the name of every most important interest connected with or involved in Western Unitarianism.

1. I make it in the name of *truth*. I deny that the simple fundamental doctrines of Christian theism are mere "opinions," as we are told, and that only the doctrines of ethics are real "soul-faiths." I affirm that no voices of the soul are more authoritative than those which declare that man's puny thought isn't the highest intelligence in the universe, or man's bungling and baby justice the highest righteousness.

* * *

2. I make my protest against abandoning the distinct Christian theistic character of the denomination, *in the interest of unity and harmony*. If we cannot live in harmony on this basis, it is clear as the sun in the sky we cannot on any other. . . .

3. I deprecate all attempts to destroy the Christian, and especially the theistic character of our body because of the necessarily *evil effects* of the same upon our *missionary* and *church extension work*. . . .

4. I protest against the de-Christianizing of Unitarianism in the name of *every commonest principle of business intelligence*. Every business man knows that any enterprise which attempts to embrace everything, succeeds in nothing. . . .

5. I protest against the de-Christianizing of Unitarianism in the West, in the name of *progress* and *evolution*. The position that Unitarianism should lift no banner but that of ethics, and should stand before the world for only "freedom, fellowship and character in religion," claims to be an advanced position. I believe it to be a seriously retrograde position. I believe it to be a mistaking of revolution for evolution. . . .

6. I deprecate the non-Christian attitude which a portion of Western Unitarianism is taking, because it puts our movement *out of line* with the *great Christian army*,—that army which, with all its faults, is yet the most powerful force operating in our day against sin, and in favor of the higher life of men. . . .

7. I protest against a non-theistic Unitarianism in the interest of the very *agnostics* and *unchurched classes, themselves*, whom it hoped to reach by taking this position. My observation and experience convince me that it does not help us in reaching these classes, to give up our theistic or Christian ground. The more earnest and thoughtful agnostics—those who have any interest in our churches at all, or could be drawn to us on any condition—very few of them want us to remove our Christian basis.

＊　＊　＊

The question confronts us, not to be evaded, shall we, in the West, go on in the way the denomination has been going in the past—forward to help the world—to *lead* it, if we are true and noble enough, to a purer, higher, more practical, more vital Christianity—pressing on and up along that path which has the life and teachings of Jesus to light it, and God shining forever in its sky? or shall we turn aside to seek out some path in which neither Jesus, nor any teaching of Jesus, is anything more than incidental, and into whose sky God may come or not come, but at least is not the sun whose shining makes its day? . . .

Brethren of the West, this issue, however much we may shrink from it or regret it, is upon us; we cannot evade it; It is no time for indifference; too much is at stake.

At such a time, if ever, Unitarianism demands of us our best and truest service, of calm judgment, of broad and unfailing charity, of respect for others and their honest thought as we wish respect for ourselves and our thought, but, none the less, of clear thinking and of loyalty to the truth as God gives us to see the truth.

SOURCE: Jabez Sunderland, *The Issue in the West* (Chicago, 1886), 2–5, 10–15, 17–19, 29–30, 35–41, 44–45.

WILLIAM CHANNING GANNETT

"Things Commonly Believed Among Us"

1887

William Channing Gannett (1840–1923) was a Unitarian minister, a reformer favoring the rights both of women and of African Americans, a second-generation Transcendentalist, and the son of Ezra Stiles Gannett. He served congregations in Milwaukee, Wisconsin; East Lexington, Massachusetts; St. Paul, Minnesota; and Hinsdale, Illinois; as well as his longest-lasting pastorate, in Rochester, New York, from 1889 to 1908. Gannett worked in close affiliation with Jenkin Lloyd Jones and the Western Unitarian Conference and wrote many Sunday school lessons and hymns for use by the WUC. Gannett proposed his now-famous statement "Things Commonly Believed Among Us" at the Western Unitarian Conference gathering of 1887, in hopes that this statement could encompass the growing disparity between Christian-centered Unitarians and the "Unity men" (such as himself and Jones) who leaned toward a post-Christian Unitarianism. Echoes of his broad-mindedness can be seen in many of today's characterizations of contemporary Unitarian Universalism. Further Reading, William Henry Pease, "William Channing Gannett: A Social Biography," PhD thesis, University of Rochester, 1955.

—Emily Mace

Resolved, that while the Western Unitarian Conference has neither the wish nor the right to bind a single member by declarations concerning fellowship or doctrine, it yet thinks some practical good may be done by setting forth in simple words the things most commonly believed to-day among us,—the statement being always open to restatement and to be regarded only as the thought of the majority.

Therefore, speaking in the spirit and understanding above set forth, we delegates of the Western Unitarian churches in conference assembled at Chicago, May 19, 1887, declare our fellowship to be conditioned on no doctrinal tests, and welcome all who wish to join us to help establish truth and righteousness and love in the world.

* * *

In all matters of church government we are strict Congregationalists. We have no "creed" in the usual sense; that is, no articles of doctrinal belief which bind our churches and fix the conditions of our fellowship. Character has always been to us the supreme matter. We have doctrinal beliefs, and for the most part hold such beliefs in common; but above all "doctrines" we emphasize the principles of

450

Freedom, Fellowship, and Character in Religion. These principles make our all-sufficient test of fellowship. All names that divide "religion" are to us of little consequence compared with religion itself. Whoever loves Truth and lives the Good is, in a broad sense, of our religious fellowship; whoever loves the one or lives the other better than ourselves is our teacher, whatever church or age he may belong to. So our church is wide, our teachers many, and our holy writings large.

With a few exceptions we may be called Christian theists. . . . The general faith is hinted well in words which several of our churches have adopted for their covenant: "In the freedom of the truth and in the spirit of Jesus Christ, we unite for the worship of God and the service of man." It is hinted in such words as these: "Unitarianism is a religion of love to God and love to man." . . . But because we have no "creed" which we impose as test of fellowship, specific statements of belief abound among us,—always somewhat differing, always largely agreeing. One such we offer here.

We believe that to love the good and live the good is the supreme thing in religion;

We hold reason and conscience to be final authorities in matters of religious belief;

We honor the Bible and all inspiring scripture, old and new;

We revere Jesus and all holy souls that have taught men truth and righteousness and love, as prophets of religion;

We believe in the growing nobility of Man;

We trust the unfolding Universe as beautiful, beneficent, unchanging Order; to know this Order is truth; to obey it is right, and liberty, and stronger life;

We believe that good and evil invariably carry their own recompense, no good thing being failure and no evil thing success; that heaven and hell are states of being; that no evil can befall the good man in either life or death; that all things work together for the victory of Good;

We believe that *we* ought to join hands and work to *make* the good things better and the worst good, counting nothing good for self that is not good for all;

We believe that this self-forgetting, loyal life awakes in man the sense of union, here and now, with things eternal,—the sense of deathlessness; and this sense is to us an earnest of the life to come;

We worship One-in-All,—that Life whence suns and stars derive their orbits and the soul of man its Ought,—that Light which lighteth every man that cometh into the world, giving us power to become the sons of God, that Love with whom our souls commune. This One we name,—the Eternal God, our Father.

SOURCE: "Report of the Proceedings of the Thirty-third Annual Meeting of the Western Unitarian Conference," *Unity*, June 4, 1887, 200.

DRUDE KROG JANSON
A Saloonkeeper's Daughter
1887

Drude Krog Janson (1846–1934) emigrated from Norway to the United States in 1882, following her husband Kristofer, who was a Unitarian missionary to the Norwegian immigrant community in Minnesota. They were part of a liberal theological impulse throughout Scandinavia and the Scandinavian diaspora that led some of its most radical adherents to Unitarianism. (The same impulse led to the planting of Icelandic heritage congregations in both the United States and Canada.) In the United States, Janson was inspired by the women's rights activism of Lucy Stone—whom she heard speak at an American Women's Suffrage Association convention hosted by First Universalist Church of Minneapolis—and by Helen Campbell's study of working women, Prisoners of Poverty *(1887). Janson's novel about a saloonkeeper's daughter turned temperance lecturer and Unitarian minister anticipated the literary realism of Theodore Dreiser and offered a window into the ideals of the first generation of female ministers.*

—Dan McKanan

It had indeed been Astrid who had advertised a temperance lecture. During the past seven months she had worked intensely. Helene obtained books for her from the Athenaeum where she was a member. At five every morning Astrid would get up to read in them for a few hours before breakfast.

In those morning hours there was always such a pleasant quietness around her. Every thought came back so clearly and lodged in her mind as her own possession, and it was wonderful to feel her vision expand and her mind develop from day to day. She especially liked to study history. Nothing satisfied her so much as to follow the great intellectual movements as they spread through various countries. At the same time she was horrified to read of all the cruelty and terrible suffering that narrow-minded fanaticism and brutality and ignorance had brought to humanity. But there was also progress, and each generation was coming a little closer to the truth than the one before. Should one generation go under because of their sins and the sins of their parents, then some new movement would crest, full of spirit and life, to bring about suffering humanity's deliverance. Astrid enthusiastically followed the lives of great men and women who had been the means of improving the world.

Thus it was that the person of Jesus of Nazareth in all his human grandeur and beauty came to symbolize the new life for humanity, and his story filled her with intense enthusiasm. Never before had she been able to grasp his significance. He had always been so distant, so far removed. He was said to be God, and yet he was a human. She had previously paid no attention to him. But now in reading history independently she came to look at him as a human being, a persecuted and mocked human being, who dared to speak the truth and confront the powerful and mighty. With his fearless championship of truth and his love for the depressed and despised he regenerated the world and gave it a mission so large that even the best men and women were still stumbling over it. Yes, she loved him and fervently prayed to the spirit that is in all things for a tiny drop of his pure enthusiasm and for the courage to speak the truth. More and more frequently the idea came to her that she should become a minister like the one Bjørnson had spoken of. She would be a minister who took as her mission the defense of the oppressed and who taught her fellow beings that the main purpose in life was a noble life. But could she speak so others would be moved? Was her own enthusiasm pure enough and strong enough for her to influence others? Would those who heard her grow in their desire to live higher and nobler lives?

These were the questions that always faced her. And if she became quite certain of her mission, how would she ever be able to reach that goal? She talked with Helene about it—just as she talked about everything with her. Helene said she should just wait and keep on working as she was now doing. Once she became sure of herself a way would be opened up.

In the afternoons Astrid generally accompanied Helene on her house calls, and she often came into the most wretched part of Minneapolis, where squalor and humiliation were at home. She was deeply moved when she saw how often drunkenness was to blame for this misery. When they looked into a situation more closely, they often discovered that drunkenness lay at the bottom of the family's difficulty. To her it was dreadful to see how this vice was so ingrained in the Norwegian character. When she realized that her father was prospering on this misery and how she herself, even if against her will, had lived on it for a long time, then she felt the need to atone for her sin by helping the poor and forsaken wives and mothers, even though her own sin could never be fully expiated. She became convinced that she should speak publicly for temperance. There would be no break with her plan to enter the ministry. In fact, this might help her to reach it more easily. If she could bring about some actual blessing for someone by doing it, then she would not desire anything higher. From the moment she made her decision she used all the time she could spare to familiarize herself with the topic. And now she had announced her first lecture.

* * *

Astrid wanted to begin, but it was as if the power of speech had deserted her. This audience reminded her of one of the most terrible evenings in her life, the theater performance at Turner Hall. There were the same crude faces—indeed, worse—and here they were sitting and looking at her with malicious pleasure. She looked at the first row and saw Meyer, who was gloating as he sat staring at her. This time she was taken by surprise, and he had the delight of seeing her waver and involuntarily grab the lectern. A suspicion of a plot against her went through her, and the same fear that she had experienced that evening at Turner Hall returned to her. She could have screamed and run away. With a strong determination of will she pulled herself together, took a glass of water from the lectern, and drank. Her hands shook, but otherwise she looked quite calm. She straightened her back and looked proudly out over the audience. But when she opened her mouth to speak, Lundberg stood up. He spit across the floor and loudly cleared his throat. Astrid looked over at him. Then he said with a defiant face: "We Scandinavians have come here to say that we don't want this American practice of letting women preach forced on us. They can mind their own business, and we'll take care of ours."

Astrid glared at him. "Those who don't want to listen to me are free to leave," she said in a high voice. "I have rented this hall for the evening, so I think we'll turn to the topic we are gathered to talk about."

Lundberg sat down astonished. "These damned women," he mumbled, scratching himself behind his ears.

For a moment all became quite still, and Astrid began to speak. Fear had given her courage, and she forgot everything except that she was speaking for a cause that she loved. She impressed them with her calm, erect bearing. A power emanated from her that subdued the rowdy temperaments. Meyer began to fear that his plan would fail. Astrid had talked for a while, and the hall was quiet.

Then Meyer turned around and looked at Lundberg with a sneering smile. Lundberg saw it, and he broke out in a fury with a "Hey, there, boys!" and raised his whistle to his lips. With that the spell was broken. A hissing sound interrupted Astrid—first one, then one more. Soon it came from all sides accompanied by clapping of hands and tramping of feet. It was impossible for Astrid to get a word out.

* * *

Astrid did not say one word all the way home. She just squeezed Helene's arm firmly, and Helene felt her shaking. Finally, they were home. Helene breathed easier now that she had got her there. Astrid sank into the armchair, and Helene sat beside her, taking Astrid's head and laying it on her breast and tenderly stroking her hair without saying a word.

"Oh, no, it's no use for me," Astrid burst out in desperation. "I may just as well give everything up. The curse follows me."

"You don't mean what you're saying, Astrid. You know just as well as I do that you cannot and must not give up."

"Oh, yes, I know that, of course, but tell me what I should do. Wherever I turn, my past follows me, and that's the way it'll always be no matter what I attempt to do," she spoke bitterly, her voice still shaking with fear.

"I know, and here it will always be in your way," Helene answered calmly. "That's why I've been thinking that you should get away from here, Astrid."

Astrid raised her head suddenly and looked Helene in the eyes. "Oh, God, Helene, don't you think I have thought the same thing? But how? How? Can you tell me that?"

"Yes, I have a plan."

Astrid stared at her.

"I have often thought about it, but first I wanted you to have full confidence in yourself. This evening I think we both will agree that you are committed to going ahead and that you won't stop before you have reached your goal."

Astrid nodded.

Helene continued. "Actually, I'm happy about this evening since it forces us to make a decision. Tomorrow you and I will drive over to St. Paul to speak with the Reverend William Gannett, the Unitarian minister there. I know him, and I am certain that when I explain your position to him, he will be interested in helping you. I'll ask him to write to the president of the Unitarian university in Meadville, Pennsylvania, to see if he can find a scholarship for you at the school. Perhaps by working on the side at his house you can pay for your board and room. During the long summer vacations you may be able to earn enough to clothe yourself, and if that's not enough, then you know that I will help you as long as I have something. I'll get your travel money together myself. I have some savings, and I know of several who will give us a helping hand if I ask them. What do you think of that?"

Astrid had placed her elbows on the arms of her chair. She stared intently in Helen's face. Tears glittered in her eyes. "Tell me, Helene," she finally said gently, "what would I have done in this world without you?" She kissed Helene's hand, the hand that lived only to serve and help others.

The next day they went to St. Paul where they found the Reverend Gannett at home. He was a man with a pleasant face and two dark eyes. Most noticeable about him was his smile. It was melancholy, yet so mild and warm that it moved anyone who saw it. Helene told him as much of Astrid's history as she thought necessary to bring him to an understanding of her character and her needs and to see how necessary it was for her to go away.

He cast a critical glance at Astrid. "I don't doubt that I will be successful in getting Mr. Livermore interested in your case," he said in a friendly voice. "We don't have such an abundance of young enthusiastic and dynamic people that we can afford to let any go to waste." Again he smiled in the way that struck Astrid as so remarkable. How many endured agonies and battles of his soul it told of! But it also indicated an achieved peace and an infinite love for all human beings.

*   *   *

How happy Astrid was when they went back home. At last she was beginning to catch sight of land. She saw her future life following cleared paths where her thirst for clarity and enlightenment would be satisfied and guided by a goal that was great enough to take her through all difficulties. How she would work! With joy she felt her vibrant blood and her overflowing youth stream through her veins.

In the evening she stood in the middle of the bedroom floor. She had just taken off her dress when she happened to look at her arms. She saw that they were white and beautiful. A recollection came to her. She lifted up one arm and fondled it. How healthy and strong it was. She stroked it up and down several times before returning to Helene. "Oh, Helene, am I not fortunate? My body belongs to me, and no one else has a right to it. Just think! I am saved," she added slowly, kneeling down and laying her head in Helene's lap.

SOURCE: Drude Krog Janson, A *Saloonkeeper's Daughter*, trans. Gerald Thorson, ed. Orm Øverland (Baltimore: Johns Hopkins University Press, 2002), 139–145.

"Obedience to the Heavenly Vision"
1889

Mary Safford (1851–1927) was the catalyst for the Iowa Sisterhood, a net-work of female ministers who served Unitarian churches in the Midwest and beyond during the final decades of the nineteenth century. Working closely with her childhood friend and longtime companion Eleanor Gordon, Safford organized a literary society as a young adult and, at age twenty-seven, a Uni-tarian church in her hometown of Hamilton, Illinois. Ordained two years later, in 1880, she served churches in Humboldt, Algona, Sioux City, and Des Moines, Iowa, as well as Orlando, Florida. She also served as president of the Iowa Unitarian Association and edited its publication, Old & New. *She spoke tirelessly on behalf of women's suffrage and was much in demand as a guest preacher. This sermon was first delivered at the Western Unitarian Conference in Chicago in 1889 and repeated dozens of times thereafter. Fur-ther Reading: Cynthia Grant Tucker,* Prophetic Sisterhood: Liberal Women Ministers on the Frontier, 1880–1930 *(Boston: Beacon Press, 1990).*

—Dan McKanan

Among the great souls of the ages, the apostle Paul justly takes high marks. Because he united, in that rare combination, breadth of view with intensity of purpose, his plans were lofty in conception, bold in execution, and far reaching in their results. . . .

What was the secret of his power? . . . What was it I say which gave the world a man so broad in his thought, so inclusive in his sympathy yet so mature in his devotion? Let Paul himself make answer. "Wherefore, O King Agrippa, I was not disobedient unto the heavenly vision." In these words we find the key which unlocks the wealth of that great soul whose ardor culture did not quench, which made a world its debtor. When new light came it was welcomed and used. It matters little just how, and when, and where great truths dawn upon the soul; it matters more than words can tell whether these truths are welcomed and obeyed. And Paul was not disobedient unto the heavenly vision—We cannot tell just how this vision came to him. . . . Doubtless this vision came to him in a natural not miraculous way, was an inner experience not an external event, but it was nonetheless real. For God speaks to us as clearly in high thoughts and noble feelings as through the voiced commands in tones of thunder from the skies. What the eye of reason and conscience perceive surely is not less sacred than what the external eye beholds; hence whatever may have been the real nature of Paul's experience, that which most concerns us is the great fact that he was not disobedient unto the heavenly vision, that the truth revealed to him was wrought into his life, received his persistent ever loyal support.

For if such devotion ennobled the life of Paul not less will it exalt our lives. To us there has come a heavenly vision of eternal power and goodness which claims our obedience just as strongly as the truth made known to Paul demanded his unfaltering devotion. Aye, as the years of time speed on, as knowledge and wisdom increase and we see more clearly than our fathers saw, yet stronger and stronger grows our obligation to be true that we may not prove ungrateful for all we have received, for that heavenly vision which has slowly been prepared for us by the toil and struggle of the centuries. And so beautiful is the vision which gleams upon our sight as men and women of the liberal faith that we marvel that any are indifferent to its worth. For consider what it is as compared with what our fathers saw.

Gone is the frowning tyrant, the endless hell that cast a pall upon the days of our childhood, and instead we see a universe where law and love are one, where "nothing walks with aimless feet," where "not a worm is cloven in vain" but where all things slowly but surely and sublimely move toward "one far off divine event." In and through this majestic, orderly universe we find a Power divine, the mighty yet all loving one who guides the circling planets that go singing on their way yet stoops to "hold a human heart that it break not too far."

And this Eternal One who truly speaks in every law that plays upon our being comes near to us not only in the brave true life of Jesus but in every noble life. For we see man, not fallen from a high estate and utterly depraved but slowly climbing from better up to best, revealing more and more of the eternal love as he leaves behind him selfishness and low desires and reaches out the generous helping hand to those about him. We see him envisioned by laws which do not change, hence reaping always what he sows, saved from sin and the punishment of sin not by the merits of another but only through brave, persistent efforts to build up truth and love in his own being.

Hence we see as Paul saw that men ought everywhere to repent and turn to God doing works worthy of repentance. We see that it is not the naming of a name but the doing of the Father's will which gives entrance to that kingdom of truth and love, that real heaven of the soul which fadeth not away, that heaven which is joy and strength and peace. This is the heavenly vision our eyes behold today. Are we obedient to it? As individuals and as a church do we have that moral earnestness which Paul had, that intensive desire to share with others the great truths which gleam like stars upon our way? Thousands are still held in bondage by ignorance, by cruel views of God and man, by their own selfishness. Are we eager to give to them of the good we have received? Do we strive to show to them how beautiful it is to live when life is gladdened by a noble faith in God and man and duty? When is one sure that all things are rooted in unchanging love? We have organized this church, but are we doing all we have the power to do to help it grow, to make it a center of light and warmth in this community? A center from which there will constantly radiate the truth that liberates and lifts, the love that strengthens and consoles? Do we realize the obligation that rests upon us to carry forward our noble enterprise to larger and yet larger results?

Are we alive to the fact that as "eternal vigilance is the price of liberty" so eternal activity is the price of growth? That neither as individuals nor as a church can we make progress without effort and sacrifice? O, friends, if we would only be obedient to the heavenly vision that we enjoy today, would only proclaim most earnestly in words and deeds the glad gospel of eternal love, what might we not accomplish during the next few years!

I know men need food and clothing, but I know they also need the saving power of high thoughts and unselfish love, of that soul culture which give to life new meaning and glory. Surely it should be our joy to give what thus has power to bless. And the world is ready now to receive the truth which once it feared or scorned, if this truth is rightly presented, if it shines in the face and glows in the life as well as speaks on the tongue. For the leaven of liberal thought has been and still is working in thoughtful minds everywhere. Witness the giving up of the doctrine of endless punishment by thousands in orthodox churches and the growth of what our congregational friends are pleased to call the New Theology—a theology that is really the Unitarianism of fifty years ago.

We are entering upon a new era of religious thought. A greater reformation is now in progress than was that of the sixteenth century. Science and the Higher Biblical Criticism are fast making it impossible for rational human beings longer to hold views that once were deemed essential to salvation. The old creeds are rapidly being outgrown. But there is danger that in the strong reaction from many old time beliefs, men and women may lose sight of those saving truths, those eternal principles of morality, without which life is not worth the living. There is danger that in throwing aside the superstitions of the past, they may also lose that reverence and moral earnestness that are indispensable to real progress. Intellectual emancipation from error without moral education is not less dangerous than bigotry. The knowledge that increases our power to do good, if we are so inclined, also enables us to do more harm if we lack the moral training that would inspire us to use this knowledge worthily.

Hence the work of the liberal church today is to be obedient to its heavenly vision. Not only must we proclaim the saving truths we hold, we must also strive to build up these truths in our own lives and in the lives of others. As Paul endured perils by land and by sea, as he gave time and energy to the work of proclaiming at Damascus and Jerusalem and throughout all the coasts of Judea that men should turn to God and do works worthy of repentance, so ought we to endure and work and freely give of our best selves in striving to promote the gospel of character that has untold power to bless the world. We may not go as Paul went on missionary tours to faraway places, but here in Cherokee, we may increase our influence for good tenfold if we will but put forth our best efforts and earnestly use the means at our command.

But for the loyalty to truth, the heroic self-sacrifice, the unfaltering devotion of those who in loneliness and anguish of soul were true to their convictions in times past, you and I would not enjoy that religious liberty which is our priceless heritage. . . . We must realize our debt to the past, a debt that we cannot pay save by being brave and true and helpful in the present. And we must also think how much we owe to God who has given us reason, conscience, love, all the wonderful powers of being not to rust in us unused but to be employed for the helping of brothers and sisters. Surely in view of all we have received we are most ungrateful unless we are doing the very best we can to make some noble return for it. And if there are any here today who rejoice in the great truths of the liberal faith but are doing nothing to support this faith, let me urge you for your own sake as well as for the sake of others no longer to be disobedient unto the heavenly vision. If you have money to give, give it freely, give it gladly. If silver and gold you have none, give time, give thought, give work, give anything you have the power to give that will strengthen this church and help to make it a beacon light to storm tossed souls. If you can do nothing more than simply come to church, be sure to come each Sunday. Come not merely for your own sake but also for the sake of the noble cause that is strengthened by your presence and your interest. Stay not outside. Ask not, is it a fashionable church? Is it a popular church? Is it a wealthy church? Ask only, is it a church that proves the right to be by the grand truths it proclaims, the good work that it does, the noble lives it helps create. Heed no ignoble questionings about popularity, wealthy, or fashion, but obey your heavenly vision, be loyal to the truth you see, bravely stand by your convictions, and work for the human good. Then life will grow divine.

SOURCE: Mary Safford, "Obedience to the Heavenly Vision," Mary Safford Papers, State Historical Society of Iowa. As excerpted in Dorothy May Emerson, *Standing Before Us: Unitarian and Universalist Women and Social Reform 1776–1936* (Boston: Skinner House, 2000), 496–500.

Constitution and By-Laws of the First
Icelandic Unitarian Church of Winnipeg
1891

*Many religious liberals were among the Icelandic immigrants who settled in
Manitoba, Saskatchewan, Minnesota, and the Dakotas in the late nineteenth century. As these individuals separated from their inherited Luther-
anism, they created new congregations and societies. Stephan G. Stephansson
(1853–1927) established the Icelandic Cultural Society in 1888, drawing
inspiration from the Free Religious Association and the Ethical Culture
Society. Two years earlier, his friend Björn Pétursson (1826–1893) had made
an initial contact with the Unitarian Post Office Mission, an organization
established in 1881 to provide resources to potential Unitarians who lived far
from established congregations. He was referred to Jennie Elizabeth McCaine
(1838–1918), a charter member of Unity Church in Saint Paul, who persuaded
the American Unitarian Association to grant him a stipend as a missionary.
McCaine and Pétursson married in 1890, and in February 1891, they organized the First Icelandic Unitarian Society of Winnipeg. Further Reading:
V. Emil Gudmundson, The Icelandic Unitarian Connection: Beginnings
of Icelandic Unitarianism in North America, 1885–1900 (Winnipeg, MB:
Wheatfield Press, 1984).*

—Dan McKanan

The Main Beliefs Upon Which Unitarians Generally Agree

1. About God

Unitarians believe that there is only one God, changeless, which has existed for
eternity, who has created, sustained and governed all things by perfect laws which he
has himself established.

They believe that He is unprovable spirit but men best reach his nature if they
consider him as their all mild, almighty, all-wise, omnipotent, all-knowing heavenly
father. They believe that God is prepared to forgive every sinner who repents and
changes his ways; that his love is eternal and boundless, and the misery and wretchedness to which sin leads, according to God's laws, is only the discipline which leads
to improvement whenever the sinner so desires.

They believe that God is revealed only in his works in nature, in reason, in conscience of all men, but openly in those who have excelled in knowledge and have become leaders of mankind for the good.

2. About Jesus Christ

Unitarians believe that Jesus Christ was the Master Teacher and one of the purest of heart of men, who ever lived; that he taught us to know the path to God, and he himself trod that path with self-denial and love; and he is, for this reason, rightly called Our Savior and an example for all time.

3. About the Holy Spirit

Unitarians believe that the Holy Spirit is not a person, rather represents that spiritual power of God, which He operates through his creation, humanity, in a manner like the human spirit can have and has influence on another person.

4. About Man (Humanity)

Unitarians believe that man is created in God's image, i.e., God's undying spirit resides in us, and that we are rightly called God's children—sons and daughters. They believe that the human purpose is to return to the God from whence we came, and that [we] have the potential to reach this [purpose]and that everyone attains it sooner or later, through more or less experience and trials.

They believe that each sin has its own punishment, and every good work done with honesty has its own reward. They believe that man has free will to determine his own destiny and must always therefore bear responsibility for all his works.

5. About Eternal Life

They believe that the human spirit lives forever, since it is a part of the Spirit of God, and that after death it takes on eternal progress.

6. About the Resurrection

Unitarians believe that the human spirit has its own spiritual body after death, which leaves its earthly body.

7. About Heaven and Hell

Unitarians believe that Heaven represents the sun-rich state of the human soul after death while Hell is the undesirable state.

8. About Prayer

Unitarians believe that prayer uplifts the soul to God and is necessary for those who feel the need to seek.

9. About Church Practices

They consider baptism and communion to be authentic, beautiful, and actually meaningful church practices and for that reason useful although only to those who desire that they be practiced.

10. About the Bible

Unitarians believe that the Bible is the world's most important book for Christians because it explains the history, ethics and customs of those nations from which Jesus came; likewise because it relates words and works of Jesus of Nazareth and about how his disciples understood him though the stories are faulty and unreliable.

11. About the Devil

Unitarians do not believe that there is any personal devil; rather, the name of the devil represents evil in the world in all its aspects.

Since we, the undersigned, are convinced that the Christendom the Lutheran Church promotes is out of joint, archaic, and in some ways dangerous, we have determined to do what we can to establish a free Unitarian congregation among our fellow countrymen in Winnipeg, a Christian church built on that Unitarian foundation that is set forth in the 11 articles preceding, in the spirit of Jesus of Nazareth, and concerned with healthy rationalism and conscience.

SOURCE: Constitution and By-Laws of the First Icelandic Unitarian Church of Winnipeg, in V. Emil Gudmundson, *The Icelandic Unitarian Connection: Beginnings of Icelandic Unitarianism in North America, 1885–1900* (Winnipeg, MB: Wheatfield Press, 1984), 97–99.

MAGNÚS SKAPTASON

Sermon Delivered at Gimli
1891

*Just before the founding of the First Icelandic Unitarian Society of Winni-
peg, a Lutheran pastor serving multiple villages on the shores of Lake Winnipeg resigned his ministry to force a vote as to whether his congregations would
tolerate his preaching against eternal damnation. Most would, and their vote
to retain Magnús Skaptason as their minister led to the emergence of a network of congregations that formally organized as the Icelandic Conference of
Unitarian Churches in North America in 1901. It is noteworthy that Skaptason's "break-away" sermon, preached at several churches in the winter and
spring of 1891, emphasized theological positions more associated with Universalism than Unitarianism.*

—Dan McKanan

When I was a child (in age), I remember well what fright shot through me, when I
thought about the condition of the souls of the damned, and all the pains that they
were to endure throughout eternity. I thought about it during the day, I dreamt about
it at night, about all those endless pains, which had been described to me so dreadfully. When I matured . . . I began to doubt whether an all-good, all-merciful Father
was in reality so callous that he could not forgive his children, as earthly fathers
forgive their children—something I have seen and experienced personally. . . . The
doubt of earlier years has now become my fullest conviction, which is continually
strengthened as my idea of God has developed and matured. In addition, my belief
in Him has become firmer and built on a broader foundation which has also been
strengthened as I have seen his handiwork in the universe, and as I have acknowledged His rule in the small issues as in the large. His life is present in all existence;
His love abounds before me; His omnipotence and wisdom smile before me in every
straw, hide in every idea, and press through everything and everybody in all His
creation.

The punishment teaching is taught in the church. The preachers say it is the
Word of the Bible, and I know well that it seems to be found in many places of the
New Testament. . . .

Yes, the denominations (many sects) say it often about one another, that all go
there who have a different set of beliefs. "Sine ecclesia nulla salves," says the Catholic Church. . . . Everybody goes there who is not reborn by baptism of the Holy

Spirit, says the Augsburg Confession. . . . All other groups, all other denominations, go into the deep that boils in fire and brimstone. Thus most of the people in Asia, Africa, America, Australia, and Europe go there. In addition, if that is not sufficient, all those thousands of millions who lived on earth before Christ will go there. . . . The Augsburg Confession clearly condemns all the unbaptized to go there. The 400 million Buddhists will go there, as will the 200 million Moslems, the nearly 200 million Brahmins, the millions of dark-skinned people of the southern hemisphere. . . .

✻ ✻ ✻

That Christ could never have been able to teach eternal punishment, every one must admit, who believes or accepts the love of the Heavenly Father and the love of Jesus Christ. It seems to me to be impossible to believe otherwise. Where do we see such hatred in the life of Jesus Christ? Christ healed the sick, raised the dead to life, gave sight to the blind, bread to the hungry, consolation to the bereaved, strength to the sick, and hope to the downtrodden.

✻ ✻ ✻

But I certainly do not want to assuage or diminish punishment for committed sins. For as I am convinced that our living heavenly Father has never intended anyone to be tortured in eternal damnation, so am I convinced that He must punish us for even the smallest transgression. But the punishment is to be related to our betterment, for in that way we improve more and more; we come closer and closer to the light of our eternal, beneficent Father. Punishment is one of the Lord's plans in this world to lead souls to Himself, to peace, and to bliss.

SOURCE: Magnús Skaptason, "Sermon delivered at Gimli," in V. Emil Gudmundson, *The Icelandic Unitarian Connection: Beginnings of Icelandic Unitarianism in North America, 1885–1900* (Winnipeg, MB: Wheatfield Press, 1984), 103–114.

A Chorus of Faith

1893

Jenkin Lloyd Jones (1843–1918) was a Unitarian minister and peace activist.
He started his career as a missionary secretary for the Western Unitarian
Conference from 1875–1884, then served as minister to All Souls Church and
the Abraham Lincoln Centre in Chicago from 1884 until his death. Jones is
best remembered today as one of the individuals responsible for planning the
World's Parliament of Religions at the 1893 Columbian Exposition in Chi-
cago. Jones intended for the Parliament to reveal the essential unity of reli-
gious traditions and urged the inclusion of participants from non-Western
religious traditions. While the Parliament has been hailed by some as a key
moment in the history of religious pluralism, contemporary commentators
more often understood the Parliament as indicating the triumph of Chris-
tianity. In order to advance his progressive, cosmopolitan perspective, Jones
put together a collection of 160 excerpts from over one hundred speeches at the
Parliament, extracts that emphasized post-Christian perspectives. This selec-
tion is from Jones's introduction to the compilation. It emphasizes Jones's
beliefs concerning the Parliament and its role in proclaiming a "Universal
Religion" that perhaps transcended even liberal Christianity. Further Read-
ing: Thomas Graham, "Jenkin Lloyd Jones and the World's Parliament of
Religion of 1893," Collegium Proceedings 1, 1979; Richard Harlan Thomas,
"Jenkin Lloyd Jones: Lincoln's Soldier of Civil Righteousness," thesis, Rutgers
University, 1967.

—Emily Mace

This compilation is a book with a purpose. The compilers have no desire to conceal the fact, made obvious by the most casual examination, that those extracts have been taken that point to a much needed lesson. They have selected such passages as indicate the essential unity of all religious faiths at their best, the fundamental harmony in human nature made apparent by the noblest utterances of its representatives. They are aware that these selections may seem to prove too much. The reader will not forget that there were serious differences as well as profound harmonies, and that not all the speakers spoke up to these extracts. Still less is it to be expected that the speakers always lived up to these high standards.

* * *

If nothing else is left of the Parliament there will be left this sweet revelation of brotherhood. If ignorance and narrowness should still continue to blind the soul to the beauty of other faiths than its own, if the heart of Christendom should continue to yield no place for Confucius or Buddha, and their devotees still distrust or deny the spiritual loftiness of Jesus, yet those who attended the meetings of last September will send their hearts around the globe to find and to hold the individuals they there learned to respect and to love. The Parliament, if it has proved nothing else, has proved what a splendid thing human nature is to build a religious fellowship upon. Who cares for a creed which a prophet like Mozoomdar cannot sign? Who wants a church that has no room in it for a Pagan like Dharmapala? Who would insult the memory of Jesus by excluding from a so-called "Lord's table" those who served his brothers and sisters in the land of the cherry blossoms, the beautiful isles of the Pacific—those gentle teachers, Hirai, and his mild and cultivated associates? Having listened to the dignified Pung Quang Yu we can never again abuse the Chinese with as stupid a conscience. Having heard Bishop Arnett and Prince Massaquoi, it will be harder than ever to spell negro with two "g's." The Parliament demonstrated the essential piety of Terrence, when he said, "I deem nothing foreign that is human."

The second unity made perceptible at this Parliament was the unity of the prophecy, the harmony of the prophets. Thousands were made to feel by direct contact, thousands more will come to feel through the study of its triumphs, that the message of all the great teachers of religion is essentially the same. Jesus, Buddha, Confucius, Moses, Zoroaster, Sokrates and Mohammed taught, not so many different ways to God, but the same way, the only way, the way of service, the lonely way of truth-seeking, the homely way of loving and helping. Their followers invented other ways, of ritual and sacrament, of creed and confession, but in the final tests these short cuts of lesser minds all prove either supplementary or useless. The soul must travel the one highway, the way of character, the road of conduct, the path of morals. This alone brings the beatitudes of life.

Traveling this road we come to the third unity that bound together the parliament, made it a coherent and cohesive body: the unity of reverence, the sense of the mysterious in the infinite, the thought of God. There was but one faith pervading the Parliament except when some one began to number his divinities or to count the attributes of his deity, then disintegration was imminent. Perhaps the least fruitful day of the Parliament was the one set apart for the discussion of the divine nature. Let it be confessed that was rather a dry day. The Parliament was most triumphant when it took God for granted. The soul can be trusted on its Godward side if it is only developed on its manward side. Give the spirit its freedom and it will fast enough use its wings. Teach the mind to think and it will soon enough discover that it is "thinking God's thoughts after Him."

* * *

Christianity was thrown on the defensive on the floors of the Parliament. To borrow a World's Fair phrase, the so-called Pagans, "made the best exhibit." They were the most in demand. They enkindled the greatest enthusiasm. This is not wholly explained by the fact of novelty. Seventeen days would have exhausted the novelty of white and saffron robes had there not been, under these robes minds skilled to thought, spirits that probed through things local and transient to things universal and eternal. The Japanese won the American hearts in spite of their garb, their foreign tongue, and their so-called "heathen" antecedents. The representatives of the Orient triumphed over the audience by speaking unwelcome truths, telling them things they did not like to hear. These men triumphed because they left much of their baggage at home. The ecclesiasticism, the forms and the dogmas of these religions were not worth paying freight on from home, so they left them behind. They came as prophets and not as priests. They came to proclaim the universals, the things we hold in common. They came to show us that we held no monopoly upon the superlative things of the soul. The found us, unfortunately, in the midst of all our baggage, overlaid by our secondary things. Christianity was on the defensive only in so far as it tried to guard its peculiar, and what it may claim as exclusive prerogatives, when it tried to justify that which it ought to amend, and should be ashamed of. Christianity as the "only revealed religion," the "one true religion" set over against a "false religion" found itself in straightened circumstances at the Parliament. Its boast was denied in the most emphatic way such a denial could come. The claim was disproved by men who by their radiant faces, enkindled words and blameless lives, proved that they too, were inside of the Kingdom of God, partakers of his righteousness, though still outside the traditions and dogmas of Christianity. Christianity as one of the religious forces in the world, wrestling with error and struggling with crime, quickening hearts with love, nerving souls to do the right, has nothing to fear, but much, very much, to gain from this Parliament. It will grow strong by increasing its modesty; grow efficient by concentrating its forces and discovering its true enemies. Christianity as the gospel of love trying to reduce the hates of the world, as the gospel of light trying to reduce the ignorance of the world, as a progressive religion trying to appropriate the discoveries of science, the triumphs of commerce, and the mechanic arts, has received a magnificent impetus in this Parliament. So also have Buddhism as a religion of love, gentleness and service. And the same is true of Brahminism and all the others. These messengers from Japan, China, and India will go back with a larger conception of the work which awaits them. We may be sure they will put a more universal accent into their preaching, more progressive courage into their practice.

*   *   *

The Parliament will teach people that there is an Universal Religion. This must have its teachers and it will have its churches. This universal religion is not made of the shreds and tatters of other religions. It is not a patchwork of pieces cut out of other faiths, but it is founded on those things which all religions hold in common: the hunger of the heart for comradeship, the thirst of mind for truth, the passion of the soul for usefulness. In morality the voices of the prophets blend and the chorus is to become audible throughout the world. In ethics all the religions meet. Gentleness is everywhere and always a gospel. Character is always revelation. All writings that make for it are Scripture.

SOURCE: Jenkin Lloyd Jones, "Introduction," A Chorus of Faith: As Heard in the Parliament of Religions Held in Chicago (Chicago, 1893), 15–19, 21.

FANNIE BARRIER WILLIAMS

"What Can Religion Further Do to Advance the Condition of the American Negro?"

1893

Fannie Barrier Williams (1855–1944) was one of the most important leaders in Chicago's African-American community at the turn of the twentieth century and an ally of such social reformers as Jane Addams, Jenkin Lloyd Jones, Booker T. Washington, and W. E. B. DuBois. After Williams and her husband, S. Laing Williams, joined All Souls Church, she befriended Celia Parker Woolley, with whom she organized an integrated settlement house called the Frederick Douglass Center. Woolley, who was white, also nominated Williams for membership in the Chicago Woman's Club. After a vigorous public debate, she was voted in as the club's first African-American member. She was also the only African-American woman to speak at the 1893 Columbian Exposition in Chicago. Indeed, she spoke twice. This speech was given at the World's Parliament of Religions, held in conjunction with the Exposition. Further Reading: Wanda A. Hendricks, Fannie Barrier Williams: Crossing the Borders of Religion and Race (Urbana: University of Illinois Press, 2013).

—Dan McKanan

Believing, as we all do, that the saving power of religion pure and simple transcends all other forces that make for righteousness in human life, it is not too much to believe that when such a religion becomes a part of the breath and life, not only of the colored people, but of all the people in the country, there will be no place or time for the reign of prejudice and injustice. More of religion and less church may be accepted as a general answer to this question. In the first place, the churches have sent amongst us too many ministers who have had no sort of preparation and fitness for the work assigned them. With a due regard for the highly capable colored ministers of the country, I feel no hesitancy in saying that the advancement of our condition is more hindered by a large part of the ministry entrusted with the leadership than by any other single cause. No class of American citizens has had so little religion and so much vitiating nonsense preached to them as the colored people of this country. Only men of moral and mental force, of a patriotic regard for the relationship of the two races, can be of real service as ministers in the South. A man should have the qualifications of a teacher, the self-sacrificing spirit of a true missionary, and the enthusiasm of a reformer to do much good as a preacher among the negroes. There is needed less theology and more of human brotherhood, less declamation and more common sense and love for truth.

The home and social life of these people are in urgent need of the purifying power of religion. In nothing was slavery so savage and so relentless as in its attempted destruction of the family instinct of the negro race in America. Individuals not families, shelters not homes, herding not marriage, were the cardinal sins in that system of horrors. Religion should not utter itself only once or twice a week through a minister from a pulpit, but should open every cabin door and get immediate contact with those who have not yet learned to translate into terms of conduct the promptings of religion. There is needed in these new and budding homes of the race constructive morality. The colored people are eager to learn and know the lessons that make men and women morally strong and responsible. In pleading for some organized effort to improve the home life of these people, we are asking for nothing but what is recognized everywhere as the necessary protection to the homes of all civilized people.

There is still another and important need of religion in behalf of our advancement. In nothing do the American people so contradict the spirit of their institutions, the high sentiments of their civilization, and the maxims of their religion, as they do in practically denying to our colored men and women the full rights to life, liberty and the pursuit of happiness. The colored people have appealed to every source of power and authority for relief, but in vain. For the last twenty-five years we have gone to legislatures, to political parties, and even to churches for some cure for prejudice; but we have at last learned that help from these sources is merely palliative. It is a monstrous thing that nearly one-half of the so-called Evangelical churches of this country, those situated in the South, repudiate fellowship to every Christian man and woman who happens to be of African descent. The golden rule of fellowship taught in the Christian Bible becomes in practice the iron rule of race hatred. Can religion help the American people to be consistent and to live up to all they profess and believe in their government and religion? What we need is such a reinforcement of the gentle power of religion that all souls of whatever color shall be included within the blessed circle of its influence. It should be the province of religion to unite, and not to separate, men and women according to the superficial differences of race lines. The American negro in his environment needs the moral helpfulness of contact with men and women whose lives are larger, sweeter and stronger than his. The colored man has the right according to his worth to earn an honest living in every calling and branch of industry that makes ours the busiest of nations, but there is needed a more religious sense of justice that will permit him to exercise this right as freely as any other worthy citizen can do.

I believe that I correctly speak the feeling of the colored people in declaring our unyielding faith in the corrective influence of true religion. We believe that there is too much potency in the sentiment of human brotherhood, and in the still higher sentiment of the Fatherhood of God, to allow a whole race of hopeful men and women to remain long outside of the pale of that ever growing sympathetic interest of man in man.

SOURCE: Fannie Barrier Williams, "What Can Religion Further Do to Advance the Condition of the American Negro?" in John Henry Barrows, ed., *The World's Parliament of Religions* (Chicago, 1893), 2:1114–15.

CAROLINE BARTLETT CRANE

"What Women Can Do in Uniting the Culture and Religious Forces of Society"
1894

Caroline Bartlett (1858–1935) was a Unitarian minister, suffragist, reformer, and writer. She attended Carthage College and worked for a number of years after graduation as a journalist in several Midwestern cities. She studied the Unitarian ministry independently with William Channing Gannett and Oscar Clute, and in 1889, the Kalamazoo congregation ordained her as its minister, after which she moved the congregation to a new building and renamed it "People's Church." In 1896, she married Augustus Warren Crane. She served the congregation until 1898, and then focused on reform efforts in public health and sanitation. During her ministry, she became a noted speaker and writer about religious liberalism, as indicated by her participation in the organizing conference of the American Congress of Liberal Religious Societies in Chicago in 1894. This umbrella organization of liberal Unitarian, Universalist, Ethical Culture, Jewish, and independent religious liberals aimed to further the ecumenical and post-Christian spirit of the World's Parliament of Religions. The following excerpt comes from her address at the conference. Further Reading: Rickard O'Ryan, A Just Verdict: The Life of Caroline Bartlett Crane *(Kalamazoo: Western Michigan University Press, 1994).*

—Emily Mace

If I have indicated in a word some of the work which women are doing and shall do to unite the culture and moral forces of different classes and grades of society, surely enough has been said upon this subject when the great problem remains—namely, *the union of the culture and religious forces of the two co-ordinate halves of society, men and women.*

And be it understood, I make no special plea for woman. She may and does suffer from the divorce. But she is no longer asleep to her needs nor her defects. She is started on the road to progress at last, and she knows her goal. She, in touch with human service in the home, the school, the slum, the hospital, the world at large, leads a more interior life than you; she can evolve her soul's freedom and destiny alone, if she must. It will be imperfect, not roundly human, for the lack of you; but it will not be so imperfect as your expression of religion made without her help.

Because: she is the mother, not merely physical but spiritual, of humanity,—she mothers humanity, and what she sees in this child of hers, she keeps and ponders in her heart.

I would not boast. Indeed, I must admit whether I would or not, that men have thus far led the world in thought and action. Reasons can justly be assigned for this which do not imply woman's necessary and continued inferiority in influence here. But even were it true (which I will neither admit nor stop to argue) that men always will lead in thought and action, how does this touch our problem? In all the past of theology, men have been at the front, have lead the church *militant*, have conducted the great controversies, made the great schisms, formulated the creeds, hunted and impaled the heretics, set the standards and done the *preaching* of the world. Meanwhile, woman, thus relieved, has had some time to do the practicing. And let me ask, in passing, have you ever observed that where anyone names the qualities of the ideal church (which, under the present regime, we are so hopeless of reaching), they are precisely the qualities attributed to the ideal woman? Does not this suggest a hitherto unutilized means of bringing both nearer the ideal?

But now, what have the church and the world profited by this excessive division of function to which I have alluded? I will not speak of the moral effects, further than to affirm that this alienation of men and women along the higher lines of thought and life has been the chief producer of that pernicious double moral standard which has robbed manhood of one set of virtues and womanhood of another. Pass this by, but here we have, as the product of man's intellect, all the cruel and inhuman and separatist creeds, to combat and to disintegrate which, has been a great part of the life-work of all the liberal religious societies here assembled; to surmount which, is the gigantic task proposed by this Congress. "Salt," said the little boy, "is what makes potatoes taste bad when you don't put any on." Womanhood, I say, is what makes religion hard and inhuman when she hasn't any voice in it.

Calvinism is faultlessly logical. "Faultlessly logical"—what more would you? O, for a mighty rising of womanhood in that hour, to declare the forgotten wisdom of the ancients, that the true seat of the intellect is in the heart!

Do not misunderstand me. I repudiate that popular antithesis of man as a reasoning and woman as an emotional being. Both reason and emotion are *human* qualities, and the man or woman who is radically deficient in either, is not a well-rounded human being. If there be a sex difference, I say it is a difference of proportion and emphasis; and if it be (as I believe it is) characteristic of women that they are inclined to worship a throbbing ideal rather than a lifeless formula, by that token should they be respected and valued in a religious conference whose initial and central utterance is belief "in the great law and life of *love*." If I must choose between "Silas Marner" and "Dolly Winthrop," I will go with her who, out of obedience to that great law of life and love, says:

"Sometimes things come into my head when I'm leeching or poulticing, or such, as I could never think on when I'm sitting still. It comes into my head as Them above has got a deal tenderer heart nor what I've got, for I can't be any way better nor Them as made me. And all we've got to do is to trusten, Master Marner—to do the right thing as fur as we know, and to trusten. For if us as knows so little can see a bit o' good and rights, we may be sure there's a good and a rights bigger nor what we can know—I feel it i' my own insides as it must be so."

But why must we choose between two phases of human development that are by nature not mutually exclusive by mutually complementary? *This*, this is the solemn truth: that we never yet once have had, and that we never will have a *natural* religion, a religion of *humanity*, till the two co-ordinate elements of humanity mingle to create it. Men and women may separately struggle free from many of the errors of the past, but neither sex can ever rise above its innate incapacity to express in terms of itself the whole of humanity of which it is but half.

* * *

And this is the inevitable postscript appended to this "so long epistle which I have written with mine own hand." If it be time for the various branches of liberalism to quit outlining themselves severally against each other and against the background of Orthodoxy and to set at some united constructive work for the world, is it not time for men and women as human beings to do the same? What can women do thus to unite the culture and religious forces of society? They can refuse longer to talk of themselves and their achievements and possibilities (as I had determined to refuse in this case until I thought of a few things I would really like to say). They can resolutely labor to make mere sex distinctions as obsolete to the spirit and work of a congress like this as are the terms Unitarian, Universalist, Jew—all swallowed up and forgotten in the task set, the ideal striven for by the common humanity in us all when touched by the Divine brooding in all and over all.

Shall man execute this long delayed justice? or shall it be that woman must, at least, sadly assert her own discredited divine prerogative, take up that crown of *human*-hood, and crown herself?

SOURCE: Caroline Bartlett Crane, "What Women Can Do in Uniting the Culture and Religious Forces of Society," in *Proceedings of the First American Congress of Liberal Religious Societies* (Chicago, 1894), 19–21.

PHEBE HANAFORD

"Comments on Deuteronomy"

1895

Elizabeth Cady Stanton (1815–1902) was an abolitionist and a tireless agita-
tor for women's rights. As expressed during the Women's Rights Convention in
Seneca Falls, she believed a "perverted application of the Scriptures" played
an integral role in the oppression of women's rights. The Woman's Bible was
Stanton's response. Published in two volumes (1895 and 1898), the work con-
tains woman-centered commentaries on biblical passages. Phebe Hanaford
served on the revising (editorial) committee and was herself a contributor.
Hanaford believed that not all scriptural passages should be taken literally,
as many were degrading to women; rather, her scriptural interpretation was
that "Christ taught the equality of the sexes." Stanton believed that these
volumes would be her major contribution to women's rights, but they were
roundly rejected by woman suffragist organizations and most clergy alike,
proving too radical for their time. Further Reading: Kathi Kern, Mrs. Stan-
ton's Bible (Ithaca, NY: Cornell University Press, 2001).

—Patrice K. Curtis

In the early chapters of this book Moses' praises of Hebrew valor in marching into a land already occupied and utterly destroying men, women and children, seems much like the rejoicing of those who believe in exterminating the aboriginees in America. Evidently Moses believed in the survival of the fittest and that his own people were the fittest. He teaches the necessity of exclusiveness, that the hereditary traits of the people may not be lost by intermarriage. Though the Israelites, like the Puritans, had notable foremothers as well as forefathers, yet it was not the custom to mention them. Perhaps the word fathers meant both, as the word man in Scripture often includes woman. In the preface by Lord Bishop Ely, to what is popularly known as the Speaker's Bible, the remark is made that "whilst the Word of God is one, and does not change, it must touch at new points the changing phases of physical, philological and historical knowledge, and so the comments that suit one generation are felt by another to be obsolete." So, also, it is that with the higher education of women, their wider opportunities and the increasing sense of justice, many interpretations of the Bible are felt to be obsolete, hence the same reason exists for the Woman's Commentary, which is already popularly known as the Woman's Bible.

Deuteronomy is a name derived from the Greek and signifies that this is the second or duplicate law, because this, the last book of the Pentateuch, consists partly in a restatement of the law, as already given in other books. Deuteronomy contains also, besides special commands and advice not previously written, an account of the death of Moses. Johnson's Universal Cyclopedia states that "the authority of this book has been traditionally assigned to Moses, but, of course, the part relating to his death is not supposed to be written by himself, and indeed the last four chapters may have been added by another hand." DeWette declares that Moses could not have been the author. He not only points to the closing chapters as containing proof, but he refers to the anachronisms in earlier chapters, and insists that the general manner in which the Mosaic history is treated belongs to a period after the time of Moses.

* * *

This chapter of Deuteronomy in the solemnity and explicitness of its blessing and cursings must produce a deep impression on those who are desirous of pursuing a course which would promote personal and national prosperity. Reading chapter xix and remembering the history of the Jews from Moses to this day I reverently acknowledge the sure word of prophecy therein recorded. Chapter xxx also has high literary merit. Its euphony is in accordance with its solemn but encouraging warnings and promises. It touches the connection divinely ordained and eternally existing between life and goodness, death and sin, emphasizing the apostolic injunction, "cease to do evil, learn to do well." This chapter, giving the last directions of Moses and intimations of his departure from earth, is one of deep interest. How the Lord communicated to him that his end approached does not appear, but deeply impressed with the belief, he naturally called together Joshua and the Levites and gave his final charge. Whether fact or fiction this farewell is deeply interesting. . . .

Since I have proposed the elimination of some of the coarser portions of Deuteronomy, I wish to add the testimony of Stevens in his "Scripture Speculations," as to the general morality of this ancient code. "Barbarous as they were in many things, childish in more, their laws are as much in advance of them as of their contemporaries,—were even singular for humanity in that age, and not always equaled in ours. We forget that there were contemporary nations which justified stealing, authorized infanticide, legalized the murder of aged parents, associated lust with worship. None of these blots can be traced on the Jewish escutcheon. By preventing imprisonment for debt, Moses anticipated the latest discovery of modern philanthropy.

* * *

Even the mercy of Christianity was foreshadowed in his provision for the poor, who were never to cease out of the land; the prospered were to lend without interest, and never to harden their heart against a brother. The hovel of the poor was a sanctuary, and many a minute safeguard like the return of the debtor's garment at nightfall, to save him from suffering during the chilliness of the night, has waited to be brought to light by our more perfect knowledge of Jewish customs." But that the Scriptures, rightly interpreted, do not teach the equality of the sexes, I must be permitted to doubt. We who love the Old and New Testaments take "Truth for authority, and not authority for truth," as did our sainted Lucretia Mott, whose earnest appeals for liberty were often jewelled, as were Daniel Webster's most eloquent speeches, with some texts from the old Hebrew Bible.

SOURCE: Phebe Hanaford, "Comments on Deuteronomy," in *The Woman's Bible* (New York, 1895), 1:139–42.

"Creed and Conditions of Fellowship"
1899

When Universalists approved a loose profession of beliefs at Winchester, New Hampshire, in 1803, some participants worried that it would eventually harden into an overly restrictive creed. Indeed, the century that followed was marked by an ongoing debate about whether Universalist fellowship was limited by creedal boundaries. The General Conventions held in Chicago in 1897 and Boston in 1899 ended the debate with an amendment to the Constitution of the General Convention. The "Five Points" or "Boston Declaration" retained a central place for the Winchester Profession, but juxtaposed a modern summary of beliefs that echoed James Freeman Clarke's "Five Points of the New Theology," then popular among Unitarians. It also brought an end to heresy trials with a new version of the Liberty Clause that made it clear no one could be excluded for failure to profess a specific verbal formula. The five principles and the liberty clause (but not the restatement of the Winchester Profession) appeared on the masthead of the Leader *(the denominational paper) for decades thereafter. Further Reading: Russell E. Miller,* The Larger Hope: The Second Century of the Universalist Church in America, 1870– 1970 *(Boston: Unitarian Universalist Association, 1985), 65–93.*

—Dan McKanan

1. The Profession of Faith adopted by this body at its session at Winchester, N.H., A.D. 1803, is as follows:

Article I. We believe that the Holy Scriptures of the Old and New Testament contain a revelation of the character of God, and of the duty, interest and final destination of mankind.

Article II. We believe that there is one God, whose nature is Love, revealed in one Lord Jesus Christ, by one Holy Spirit of Grace, who will finally restore the whole family of mankind to holiness and happiness.

Article III. We believe that holiness and true happiness are inseparably connected, and that believers ought to be careful to maintain order and practice good works; for these things are good and profitable unto men.

2. The conditions of fellowship in this Convention shall be as follows:

I. The acceptance of the essential principles of the Universalist faith, to wit: The Universal Fatherhood of God; The spiritual authority and leadership of His Son Jesus Christ; The trustworthiness of the Bible as containing a revelation from God; The certainty of just retribution for sin; The final harmony of all souls with God. The Winchester Profession is commended as containing these principles, but neither this, nor any other precise form of words, is required as a condition of fellowship, provided always the principles as stated above be professed.

II. The acknowledgment of the authority of the General Convention and assent to its laws.

SOURCE: *Minutes of the Universalist General Convention: Biennial Session, Held in the City of Boston, Mass., 1899* (Providence, 1899), 47–48.

Bibliography of General Histories and Primary Source Collections

Ahlstrom, Sydney, and Jonathan S. Carey, eds. *An American Reformation: A Documentary History of Unitarian Christianity*. Middletown, CT: Wesleyan University Press, 1985.

Bressler, Ann Lee. *The Universalist Movement in America, 1770–1880*. New York: Oxford University Press, 2001.

Buehrens, John A. *Universalists and Unitarians in America: A People's History*. Boston: Skinner House, 2011.

Buehrens, John A., and Forrest Church. *A Chosen Faith: An Introduction to Unitarian Universalism*, rev. ed. Boston: Beacon Press, 1998.

Bumbaugh, David E. *Unitarian Universalism: A Narrative History*. Chicago: Meadville Lombard Press, 2000.

Cassara, Ernest. *Universalism in America: A Documentary History*. Boston: Beacon Press, 1971.

Emerson, Dorothy May. *Standing Before Us: Unitarian Universalist Women and Social Reform 1776–1936*. Boston: Skinner House, 2000.

Greenwood, Andrea, and Mark W. Harris. *An Introduction to the Unitarian and Universalist Traditions*. New York: Cambridge University Press, 2011.

Harris, Mark W. *The A to Z of Unitarian Universalism*. Lanham, MD: Scarecrow Press, 2009.

Myerson, Joel, ed. *Transcendentalism: A Reader*. New York: Oxford University Press, 2000.

Miller, Russell E. *The Larger Hope: The First Century of the Universalist Church in America 1770–1870*. Boston: Unitarian Universalist Association, 1979.

Miller, Russell E. *The Larger Hope: The Second Century of the Universalist Church in America 1870–1970*. Boston: Unitarian Universalist Association, 1985.

Morales, Peter, ed. *The Unitarian Universalist Pocket Guide*, 5th ed. Boston: Skinner House, 2012.

Parke, David B., ed. *The Epic of Unitarianism: Original Writings from the History of Liberal Religion*. Boston: Skinner House, 1985.

Parker, Kathy. *Sacred Service in Civic Space: Three Hundred Years of Community Ministry in Unitarian Universalism*. Chicago: Meadville Lombard Press, 2007.

Robinson, David. *The Unitarians and the Universalists*. Westport, CT: Greenwood Press, 1985.

Ross, Warren. *The Premise and the Promise: The Story of the Unitarian Universalist Association*. Boston: Skinner House, 2001.

Wilbur, Earl Morse. *A History of Unitarianism*. 2 vols. Cambridge, MA: Harvard University Press, 1945–1952.

Wright, Conrad, ed. *A Stream of Light: A Sesquicentennial History of American Unitarianism*. Boston: Unitarian Universalist Association, 1975.

Conrad, Wright, ed. *Three Prophets of Religious Liberalism: Channing, Emerson, Parker*. Boston: Beacon Press, 1961.

About the Contributors

BARRY ANDREWS is minister emeritus of the Unitarian Universalist Congregation at Shelter Rock in Manhasset, New York. He is the author or editor of *Emerson as Spiritual Guide*; *Thoreau as Spiritual Guide*; *A Dream Too Wild: Emerson Readings for Every Day of the Year*; and *The Spirit Leads: Margaret Fuller in Her Own Words*.

WAYNE ARNASON is a retired Unitarian Universalist minister. He has authored, co-authored, or edited several books, including *We Would Be One: A History of the Unitarian Universalist Youth Movements* and *Worship That Works*.

J.D. BOWERS is the author of *Joseph Priestley and English Unitarianism in America* and the director of the Honors College at the University of Missouri.

JOHN BUEHRENS was the sixth president of the Unitarian Universalist Association, serving from 1993 to 2001. He is the author of *Universalists and Unitarians in America: A People's History*, among other works.

PHYLLIS COLE is an emerita professor of English and Women's Studies at Penn State Brandywine, specializing in the history of women in the Transcendentalist movement. She is current president of the Margaret Fuller Society and co-editor of the essay collection *Toward a Female Genealogy of Transcendentalism*.

PATRICE K. CURTIS serves as parish minister for the Unitarian Universalists of Clearwater, Florida. She is a former presidential management intern and foreign affairs analyst for the Library of Congress.

DOROTHY MAY EMERSON is a semi-retired Unitarian Universalist parish and community minister. As founder of the Unitarian Universalist Women's Heritage Society, she developed and edited *Standing Before Us: Unitarian Universalist Women and Social Reform 1776–1936*. She received the Margaret Fuller Award for her work on Unitarian Universalist women and peace-making.

GAIL FORSYTH-VAIL is the adult programs director for the Unitarian Universalist Association. She served congregations for twenty-two years as a religious educator and is the co-author or editor of many faith development curricula and resources about Unitarian Universalist history, including *Missionaries, Builders, and Pathfinders*. She was the 2007 recipient of the Angus MacLean Award for Excellence in Religious Education.

GORDON GIBSON has served congregations in Massachusetts, Mississippi, and Indiana. He is the author of *Southern Witness: Unitarians and Universalists in the Civil Rights Era* and a co-founder of the Living Legacy Project. In 1984 he located Judith Sargent Murray's extensive personal papers, which were long believed to have been lost.

DEAN GRODZINS is a senior researcher at the Harvard Business School and a visiting scholar at the Massachusetts Historical Society. He is the former editor of *The Journal of Unitarian Universalist History*, former associate professor of history at Meadville Lombard Theological School, and the author of *American Heretic: Theodore Parker and Transcendentalism*.

AVERY (PETE) GUEST is an emeritus professor of sociology at the University of Washington. Since retirement, he has been writing a series of papers analyzing the social history of the Universalist denomination. His most recent paper describes the growth, or lack of growth, of the Unitarian and Universalist denominations in big cities in the early twentieth century.

MARK W. HARRIS has served as minister of the First Parish of Watertown, Unitarian Universalist, in Massachusetts, since 1996. He has taught Unitarian Universalist history and polity at Andover Newton Theological School and Harvard Divinity School. He is the author of *Elite: Uncovering Classism in Unitarian Universalist History*; *An Introduction to the Unitarian and Universalist Traditions* (with Andrea Greenwood); and the forthcoming *Historical Dictionary of Unitarian Universalism*, Second Edition.

LYNN GORDON HUGHES is the author of *Becoming Brownson: The Early Life of Orestes A. Brownson*. She has edited and published five books, including annotated editions of the *Autobiography of Adin Ballou* and *History of the Hopedale Community*, and written a children's book about life in the Hopedale Community. She is the owner and editor of the small press Blackstone Editions.

PETER HUGHES was the first editor of the *Dictionary of Unitarian and Universalist Biography* and has published articles on American Universalist history and on Reformation history in the *Journal of Unitarian Universalist History* and other periodicals. He is currently working on translations of the works of Servetus and other antitrinitarian writers. His most recent published book is *Declaratio*, a translation of the writings of Matteo Gribaldi.

MEGAN LLOYD JOINER is the senior minister at the Unitarian Society of New Haven in Hamden, Connecticut. She is a lifelong Unitarian Universalist.

DAVID JORGENSEN is a historian of early Christianity. His current research focuses on unity and diversity in the Christian movement in the second to fourth centuries.

He is a research associate at Colby College and teaches New Testament at Meadville Lombard Theological School. In 2016–17 he was a junior fellow at the Institute for Advanced Study at Central European University in Budapest, Hungary.

RICHARD KELLAWAY is minister emeritus of the First Unitarian Church in New Bedford, Massachusetts. He has been the associate director for United States Programs for the Unitarian Universalist Service Committee and the North American coordinator for the International Association for Religious Freedom. He recently published a biography of William J. Potter, a founder of the Free Religious Association.

LORI KENSCHAFT has taught at Boston and Harvard Universities and is the author of three books, including a biography of Lydia Maria Child. She is a member of the First Parish Unitarian Universalist of Arlington, Massachusetts, where she serves as clerk of the congregation and governing board, coordinator of the Mass Incarceration Working Group, and member of the Racial Justice Coordinating Committee.

NICOLE C. KIRK is a historian of American religion, material culture, and business in the late nineteenth and early twentieth centuries. Her research interests include how urbanization, technology, and commerce impacted American religion and constructions of race and class. Her forthcoming book with NYU Press is on John Wanamaker and his Philadelphia department store.

EMILY MACE served from 2011 to 2016 as the director of the Harvard Square Library, a digital library of Unitarian Universalist biographies, history, books, and media. You can find her online at emilyrmace.com.

NATALIE MALTER is a third-year master of divinity student at Harvard Divinity School and a candidate for Unitarian Universalist ministry. Her research interests include the history of the second wave feminist movement, women's ordination in Unitarian Universalism, and neo-paganism as an expression of twentieth-century feminist spirituality.

MARK D. MORRISON-REED is an affiliated faculty member at Meadville Lombard Theological School and coordinator of its Sankofa Archive. As a historian of the African-American presence in Unitarian Universalism, he is author/editor of nine books, most recently *The Selma Awakening* from Skinner House Books. He is a former president of the Canadian Unitarian Council.

SHERI PRUD'HOMME has served as minister of a number of Unitarian Universalist congregations in the Pacific Central District and has been a member of the adjunct faculty of Starr King School for the Ministry for over a decade. She has published an article in the *American Journal of Theology and Philosophy* and is working on a history of the First Unitarian Church of Oakland, California.

ERIK MARTINEZ RESLY serves as the lead organizer of The Sanctuaries, a racially and spiritually diverse arts community in Washington D.C. that works on the front lines of grassroots justice campaigns. He is a visual artist and ordained Unitarian Universalist minister.

MEG RICHARDSON teaches Unitarian Universalist history and polity at Starr King School for the Ministry, where she also directs the Unitarian Universalist certificate program. Her research interests in theology and church history include British Nonconformism in the nineteenth century and the life and work of Francis William Newman. Her fifth great-grandfather, a circuit-riding Universalist preacher, was mentioned in Joseph Priestley's memoir and letters.

SUSAN RITCHIE is the minister of the North Unitarian Universalist Congregation in Lewis Center, Ohio, and the director of the Unitarian Universalist House of Studies at the Methodist Theological School in Ohio. She is the author of *Children of the Same God: The Historical Relationship Between Unitarianism, Judaism, and Islam*.

CARL SCOVEL was ordained in 1957 and has served First Parish of Sudbury, Massachusetts, and King's Chapel in Boston. He has preached in one hundred thirty others. He has written for Unitarian Universalist periodicals and published a book with Charles Forman on King's Chapel's transition to Unitarianism.

MICHELLE WALSH teaches at the School of Social Work, Boston University. She is a licensed independent clinical social worker, an activist, and an ordained Unitarian Universalist community minister.

LYDIA WILLSKY-CIOLLO is assistant professor of Religious Studies at Fairfield University, specializing in American religious history. She has published in *The New England Quarterly, Nova Religio,* and *Spotlight on Teaching*. Her book, *American Unitarianism and the Protestant Dilemma: The Conundrum of Biblical Authority,* was published in 2015.

JEFF WILSON is an associate professor of Religious Studies and East Asian Studies at Renison University College, University of Waterloo. He is the author of *Mindful America: The Mutual Transformation of Buddhist Meditation and American Culture* and a frequent contributor to the *Journal of Unitarian Universalist History*.

SHARI WOODBURY is a parish minister serving Westside Unitarian Universalist Church in Fort Worth, Texas, where she resides with her family.

Index of Titles and Authors

Index of Genres and Themes

Gender and Sexuality

Theology

Unitarianism